The World Measurement Guide

The World Measurement Guide

Editorial information compiled by The Economist

© The Economist Newspaper Limited, England 1980

All rights reserved. No part of this publication may be reproduced or used in any form or by any means — graphic, electronic, or mechanical, including photocopying, recording, taping or information storage and retrieval systems — without permission of the publisher.

First published, as
'The Economist Guide to Weights & Measures'
in 1954
Second edition 1962

Third edition, revised and enlarged as
'The Economist Measurement Guide and Reckoner'
in 1975
Reprinted 1975

Fourth edition, revised as the
'The World Measurement Guide'
in 1980

ISBN 0 85058 045 5

Manufactured in England and
published by
The Economist Newspaper Limited
25 St James's Street
London
England SW1A 1HG

Printed in England by
Page Bros (Norwich) Limited
Norwich Norfolk

Bound by
Dorstel Press Limited
Harlow Essex

Introduction

In the period since the 1975 revision of this Guide, the United Kingdom has continued to change gradually to a metric system of measurements, but the transition time has lengthened from that set originally by the official plan. The need for information on the use of old and new systems will continue in the United Kingdom, as in the United States, for some time.

This new edition of the Guide updates the measurement information for changes occurring since 1975, and includes additional information on industrial measures as well as a new section which shows the measurement system for each country in the world having a system of units other than metric or imperial. This additional information replaces about two-thirds of the 'reckoner' pages and about one-half of the standard conversion tables; with the increasing availability of calculators since 1975, these are of less interest.

Additional information on industrial measurements includes a new table for converting 'barrels' of oil to tonnes. As with all measures of capacity, conversion to weight measurement produces a variable quantity depending on the density of the substance filling the container (for example, the 'bushel', a capacity unit, contains a widely varying weight according to the particular grain in the container). It is of use to note that, in the imperial system, 1 gallon of water weighs approximately 10 lb, and, in the metric system, 1 litre of water weighs approximately 1 kilogram; hence the conversions from gallon to litre, and from pound to kilogram, are about the same – although different by a factor of 10. That is:

  1 imperial gallon = 4.546 09 litres   = $4\frac{1}{2}$ litres (approx)
  10 pounds   = 4.535 923 7 kilograms = $4\frac{1}{2}$ kilograms (approx)

New industrial sections include light, optics and photography, health and music, and a new table of plant spacings is included in the agricultural section.

The new section on country systems other than metric or imperial includes some information on old systems not in current use. This is sometimes of help in countries which may retain old units or systems. The United Kingdom system is the main old system remaining from the spread of the use of Roman units throughout Europe, and from the even older systems of Sumeria (Iraq) where a mina unit was about 1 lb. Roman influence remains with the UK stone of 14 lb; this equals 2 cloves of 7 lb, a clove being 10 old Roman libras of about 0.7 lb each (the UK symbol for the pound weight remains as lb, originally from the Roman libra).

While the old system in the United Kingdom was consolidated in 1824 with the introduction of the imperial system, virtually all of Europe followed France by changing to the metric system in the 1800s; many did so by first linking their old units to new metric values (this procedure also being followed by China and Japan). In the country section the term 'ancient' means before 500 AD; 'medieval' is usually taken to mean from 500 to 1500 AD, but from the point of view of measurements, it is best used to mean, as here, 500 AD to 1800 AD: that is, up to the French revolution and introduction of the metric system. During this medieval period most of Europe had different systems (although mainly Roman based) with widely varying values for units.

The medieval United Kingdom, French, Netherlands and Spanish systems were the main ones to be spread throughout the world during early colonisation. The old English wine gallon still continues in use in the United States – which retained the old gallon, while the United Kingdom changed to the imperial gallon in 1824. The old Rhineland units of the Netherlands were in use until recently in South Africa, for example, the 'Cape foot'.

With the redefinition in 1976 of the UK gallon as 4.546 09 cubic decimetres, the UK capacity unit has gone back to the *form* of Queen Anne's time, for then (1706) the gallon was defined as 231 cubic inches; that is, the gallon depends on the unit of length, and not on the capacity containing a certain weight of water (both of which methods have been in use since ancient times for determining capacity units). The UK imperial gallon was to last about 150 years in its original form.

Use

Ease of use has been further improved by expansion of the index to include all units of other countries, previously shown separately. Summary tables for some conversions continue to be included throughout the book (mainly on pages 68–81); calculators can equally give an accurate conversion, but the tables give a quick check to show, for example, how many pounds there are in 10 kilograms, or how many millimetres in 10 inches. A detailed description of the use of those conversion tables follows.

Use of detailed conversion tables

From the summary tables for conversions on pages 64 to 67, which give the equivalent number for converting 1 unit, it is possible to determine the equivalent for 10, 100, 1 000, etc. units by moving the decimal point one place to the right for each 0. For example, 1 pound = 0.453 592 37 kilogram,
10 pounds = 4.535 923 7 kilograms,
1 000 (one thousand) pounds = 453.592 37 kilograms,
1 000 000 (one million) pounds = 453 592.37 kilograms.

In the same way, the equivalent conversion for 0.1, 0.01, 0.001, etc. can be obtained by moving the decimal point one place to the left for each decimal place in the unit to be converted; for example,
0.1 pound = 0.045 359 237 kilogram,
0.01 pound = 0.004 535 923 7 kilogram.

Further, since 1 000 kilograms equals 1 tonne (or megagram), then from
1 000 pounds = 453.592 37 kilograms the new conversion rate of
1 000 pounds = 0.453 592 37 tonne (megagram) and of
1 000 000 pounds = 453.592 37 tonnes (megagrams), can be obtained by moving the decimal point relating to kilograms three places to the left (also see page 15 for the relationship between metric multiples and submultiples).

Detailed conversions for some of the main units in use, usually up to the number of 100 or 1 000, are provided on pages 68 to 81. The tables are set out with, mainly, 10s at the side and single units at the top; so the first row, with 0 at the side, is the conversion for numbers from 0 to 9, and the second row for numbers from 10 to 19. That is, the number to be converted is the number at the side of a line, 10, added to the number at the top of a column. For example, to convert 11, it is necessary to find the '10' line and the '1' column, and the conversion of 11 is, as indicated below by the figures *4.990* (shown here in italics), the number in the position where line and column meet (example from page 77):

lb →	0	1	2
↓			
	kg	kg	kg
0	0.000	0.454	0.907
10	4.536	*4.990*	5.443
20	9.072	9.525	9.979

Conversions for some numbers other than those included in the tables can be obtained by adding together (or subtracting) the conversions for other numbers; for example, the conversion for 1 011 can be obtained from the table on page 77 by adding together the conversion for 1 000 and that for 11; this equals 453.592 kg plus 4.990 kg or 458.582 kg. However, the rounding is not always accurate for the last decimal place after making this calculation.

Notes

Definitions

Throughout the Guide, unless otherwise stated, the UK (imperial) system of weights and measures has been used, ounce refers to the avoirdupois ounce, US gallon refers to the US liquid gallon, and US hundredweight and US ton refer to the US short hundredweight and ton. The litre and its multiples as used throughout refer to the litre defined under the International System of Units (SI); this is emphasised in some cases by referring to the SI litre. The litre in the United Kingdom was defined as equal to the SI litre in 1976; before that the litre, as defined legally in the United Kingdom by the Weights and Measures Act 1963, was slightly different to the SI litre (also see pages 18 and 65).

Local measures may vary from district to district and only the most usual have been given; their use in many cases is being gradually replaced by units of the metric system. Many measures, such as bales, bushels and barrels are measures of capacity and therefore their weights are not necessarily constant.

The term 'weight' is used throughout, unless otherwise stated, to refer to the SI term 'mass' under the force of standard gravity in air; the term 'weight' does not appear in SI. A table showing variations of gravitational force over the earth is included on page 90.

Numbers

To distinguish decimals typographically, a point rather than a comma is used (the latter being usual on the European continent). Numbers are divided into thousands on either side of the decimal point by use of a space rather than a comma or point; however, in large tables such spaces are omitted for clarity, and the space is also sometimes omitted in untabulated four-digit numbers. For marking thousands to the left of the decimal point, it is usual to employ the comma in the United Kingdom and the point on the European continent.

Rounding is up or down to the nearest number; where the figure to be discarded is exactly midway, alternative methods of rounding are: to choose the even round value, to round alternately up and down, or to round at random up or down. In general, numbers in this Guide have been rounded to the nearest even number.

Conversion factors, as shown throughout this Guide, are usually given to 3 or more decimal places; however, when converting from a rounded number, the number as converted should usually be rounded back to the same number of significant figures as the original number. For example, where 500 miles (rounded to the nearest one hundred) is converted to kilometres, the resulting 804.672 kilometres should usually be rounded back to 800 kilometres.

Conversions made for trade purposes in the United Kingdom should have due regard to the Weights and Measures Acts 1963 and 1979 and related legislation and should be chosen so that rounding is in the customers' favour. For example, the pound is normally shown as rounded to the nearest number which is 454 grams; for UK trade purposes it is usually rounded down to 453 grams.

Names

Spelling as used throughout is that customary in the United Kingdom; however, the US spelling deka is used in place of deca. For the United States, main differences include liter for litre, meter for metre, sulfur for sulphur, etc. Country names have been abbreviated; further for Kampuchea see Cambodia and for Formosa see Taiwan. The following abbreviations have been used:

BS	British Standard
BSI	British Standards Institution
EEC	European Economic Community
FAO	Food and Agriculture Organisation of the United Nations
ICAO	International Civil Aviation Organisation
IMF	International Monetary Fund
ISO	International Organisation for Standardisation
UK	United Kingdom
UN	United Nations
US	United States

Acknowledgements

It is impossible to mention here all the sources which have been used in compiling this book, but all are gratefully acknowledged; British official statistics and other official information is reprinted by kind permission of HM Stationery Office.

Special acknowledgement is made to the following:

National statistical offices and embassies of various countries; National Bureau of Standards, US Department of Commerce; National Geographic Society; Commonwealth Secretariat; Food and Agriculture Organization of the United Nations; International Civil Aviation Organization; International Monetary Fund; International Organization for Standardization; International Union of Pure and Applied Chemistry; International Wool Secretariat; Organisation Internationale de Métrologie Légale; World Meteorological Organization; UK government departments and ministries; UK employers organisations and trade associations; UK Atomic Energy Authority; The Brewers' Society; British Broadcasting Corporation; British Gas Corporation; The British Petroleum Company Limited; British Standards Institution; British Steel Corporation; Central Statistical Office; The Chartered Institution of Building Services; Electrical Association for Women; The Electricity Council; Food & Wine from France (London); Forestry Commission; General Council of British Shipping; Institute of Geological Sciences; Institute of Petroleum; International Computers Limited; Iron and Steel Statistics Bureau; Kodak Limited; Medical Research Council; Meteorological Office; Metrication Board; Milk Marketing Board; National Physical Laboratory; National Water Council; Royal Astronomical Society; Royal Greenwich Observatory; Shell International Petroleum Company Limited; The Textile Institute; White Fish Authority.

Every care has been taken in the compilation of the information included, but responsibility for the accuracy thereof cannot be accepted.

Contents

Contents

Units with different equivalents

Barrel

a. United Kingdom (beer) = 36 UK gallons = 164 litres
b. United States: dry standard = 7 056 cubic inches = 116 litres
    petroleum = 42 US gallons = 159 litres
    standard cranberry = 5 826 cubic inches = 95.5 litres
    various (liquid) = 31 to 42 US gallons = 117 to 151 litres

Billion

a. United Kingdom, West Germany, Netherlands = a million million†
b. United States = a thousand million

Bushel

a. United Kingdom = 2 219.36 cubic inches = 36.37 litres
b. Old English, Winchester } = 2 150.42 cubic inches = 35.24 litres
   United States†† (struck‡)
c. United States (heaped‡‡) = 2 747.715 cubic inches = 45.03 litres

Centner or Zentner

a. United Kingdom = cental of 100 pounds = 45.36 kilograms
b. Commercial hundredweight in several European countries, generally 50 kilograms = 110.23 pounds
c. Metric centner of 100 kilograms = 220.46 pounds

Chain

a. United Kingdom: Gunter's } = 66 feet = 20.12 metres
    surveyors'
b. Engineers' = 100 feet = 30.48 metres

Foot

a. United Kingdom } = 12 inches = 0.304 8 metre
   United States customary
b. United States survey = 12.000 02 inches = 0.304 800 6 metre
c. Canada: Paris foot = 12.789 inches = 0.325 metre
d. Cape foot = 12.396 inches = 0.315 metre
e. Chinese foot (che or chih): old system = 14.1 inches = 0.358 metre
    new system = 13.123 inches = 0.333 33 metre

Gallon

a. United Kingdom = 277.42 cubic inches = 4.546 litres
b. Old English, Winchester, Wine } = 231 cubic inches = 3.785 litres
   United States, liquid
c. United States, dry = 268.802 5 cubic inches = 0.004 4 cubic metre

Gill

a. United Kingdom = 8.669 cubic inches = 142.1 millilitres
b. United States = 7.218 75 cubic inches = 118.3 millilitres

Hundredweight

a. United Kingdom } = 112 pounds = 50.8 kilograms
   United States, long
b. United States, short = 100 pounds = 45.4 kilograms

Link

a. United Kingdom: Gunter's } = 0.66 foot = 0.201 2 metre
    surveyors'
b. Engineers' = 1 foot = 0.304 8 metre

Mile

a. United Kingdom:
  imperial = 5 280 feet = 1.609 344 kilometres
  geographical ⎫
  nautical ⎬ = 6 080 feet = 1.853 184 kilometres
  sea ⎭ (in practice sometimes 6 000 feet = 1.828 8 kilometres)
b. United States = 5 280 feet = 1.609 344 kilometres
c. International nautical = 1 852 metres = 6 076.12 feet

Ounce

a. Dry: ounce = 437½ grains = 28.35 grams
    ounce troy = 480 grains = 31.10 grams
b. Liquid or fluid ounce:
i. United Kingdom = 1.734 cubic inches = 28.4 millilitres
   (20 fluid ounces = 1 pint)
ii. United States = 1.805 cubic inches = 29.6 millilitres
   (16 liquid ounces = 1 liquid pint)

Peck

a. United Kingdom = 554.839 cubic inches = 9.092 cubic decimetres (litres)
b. United States = 537.605 cubic inches = 8.810 cubic decimetres (litres)

Pint

a. United Kingdom = 34.677 4 cubic inches = 0.568 litre
b. United States:
i. dry = 33.600 312 5 cubic inches = 0.551 cubic decimetre (litre)
ii. liquid = 28.875 cubic inches = 0.473 litre

Pound

a. United Kingdom } avoirdupois pound = 0.454 kilogram
   United States
b. United States: troy pound = 0.373 kilogram = 0.823 pound (avoirdupois)
c. Spanish (libra) = 0.460 kilogram = 1.014 pounds (avoirdupois)
d. 'Amsterdam' = 0.494 kilogram = 1.089 pounds (avoirdupois)
e. Danish (pund) = 0.5 kilogram = 1.102 pounds (avoirdupois)
f. Française (livre) = 0.490 kilogram = 1.079 pounds (avoirdupois)

Quart

a. United Kingdom = 69.355 cubic inches = 1.137 litres
b. United States:
i. dry = 67.200 625 cubic inches = 1.101 cubic decimetres (litres)
ii. liquid = 57.75 cubic inches = 0.946 litre

Quarter

United Kingdom:
a. Capacity = 8 bushels = 64 gallons = 2.909 hectolitres = 0.290 9 cubic metre
b. Weight (mass) = 28 pounds = 12.701 kilograms
c. Cloth = 9 inches = 22.86 centimetres
d. Wines and spirits = 27½ to 30 gallons = 125 to 136 litres

Quintal

a. Hundredweight: United Kingdom = 112 pounds = 50.8 kilograms
    United States = 100 pounds = 45.4 kilograms
b. Metric quintal = 100 kilograms = 220.46 pounds
c. Spanish quintal = 46 kilograms = 101.4 pounds

Stone

United Kingdom:
a. Imperial = 14 pounds = 6.350 kilograms
b. Smithfield = 8 pounds = 3.629 kilograms

Ton

a. United Kingdom:
i. weight (mass) = 2 240 pounds = 1.016 tonnes
ii. shipping: register = 100 cubic feet = 2.832 cubic metres
b. United States:
i. short = 2 000 pounds = 0.907 tonnes
ii. long = 2 240 pounds = 1.016 tonnes
c. Metric ton (tonne) = 1 000 kilograms = 2 204.62 pounds
d. Spanish:
i. short (corta) = 2 000 libras = 0.920 2 tonne = 2 028.7 pounds
ii. long (larga) = 2 240 libras = 1.030 6 tonnes = 2 272.1 pounds

† The definition of one billion as a thousand million is becoming increasingly common in the United Kingdom and continental Europe. †† The most usual unit. ‡ Levelled off at the top. ‡‡ Used for apples.

Rough conversions

This table aims at providing rough conversions for some UK (imperial), US and metric (SI) measures. Metric units not generally recommended as SI units or for use with SI are marked with an asterisk (eg Calorie*). For more accurate conversions see pages 64–67.

Length

Width of thumb = 1 inch = 25 millimetres
1 inch   = $2\frac{1}{2}$ centimetres
2 inches = 5 centimetres

1 foot	= 30 centimetres	= $\frac{1}{3}$ metre
$3\frac{1}{4}$ feet	= 1 metre	
39 inches	= 1 metre	
11 yards	= 10 metres	
$\frac{5}{8}$ mile	= 1 kilometre	
5 miles	= 8 kilometres	
8 miles	= 7 nautical miles (international)	

Area

1 square inch	=	$6\frac{1}{2}$ square centimetres
2 square inches	=	13 square centimetres
$10\frac{3}{4}$ square feet	=	1 square metre
43 square feet	=	4 square metres
6 square yards	=	5 square metres
$2\frac{1}{2}$ acres	=	1 hectare
5 acres	=	2 hectares
250 acres	=	1 square kilometre
3 square miles	=	8 square kilometres

Volume and capacity

1 teaspoonful	=	5 millilitres
1 UK fluid ounce	=	28 millilitres
26 UK fluid ounces	=	25 US liquid ounces
3 cubic inches	=	49 cubic centimetres
	=	49 millilitres
$1\frac{3}{4}$ UK pints	=	1 litre
7 UK pints	=	4 litres
7 UK quarts	=	8 litres
5 UK pints	=	6 US liquid pints
19 US liquid pints	=	9 litres
1 UK gallon	=	$4\frac{1}{2}$ litres
2 UK gallons	=	9 litres
5 UK gallons	=	6 US gallons
1 US gallon	=	$3\frac{3}{4}$ litres
4 US gallons	=	15 litres
3 cubic feet	=	85 cubic decimetres
	=	85 litres
35 cubic feet	=	1 cubic metre
4 cubic yards	=	3 cubic metres
31 UK bushels	=	32 US bushels
$27\frac{1}{2}$ UK bushels	=	1 cubic metre
$28\frac{1}{3}$ US bushels	=	1 cubic metre
11 UK bushels	=	4 hectolitres
14 US bushels	=	5 hectolitres
1 US bushel (heaped)	=	$1\frac{1}{4}$ US bushels (struck)
1 US dry barrel	=	$3\frac{1}{2}$ US bushels
1 US cranberry barrel	=	$2\frac{3}{4}$ US bushels
1 barrel (petroleum)	=	42 US gallons = 35 UK gallons
1 barrel per day	=	50 tonnes per year

Yield

3 UK or US bushels per acre	=	2 quintals* per hectare
10 UK or US bushels per acre	=	9 hectolitres per hectare
1 UK hundredweight per acre	=	$1\frac{1}{4}$ quintals* per hectare
1 UK ton per acre	=	$2\frac{1}{2}$ tonnes per hectare
9 pounds per acre	=	10 kilograms per hectare

Weight (mass)

1 grain	=	65 milligrams
$15\frac{1}{2}$ grains	=	1 gram
11 ounces	=	10 ounces troy
1 ounce	=	28 grams
1 ounce troy	=	31 grams
1 pound	=	454 grams
35 ounces	=	1 kilogram
$2\frac{1}{4}$ pounds	=	1 kilogram
11 stones	=	70 kilograms
11 US hundredweights	=	5 quintals*
2 UK hundredweights	=	1 quintal*
2 205 pounds	=	1 tonne
11 US tons	=	10 tonnes
62 UK tons	=	63 tonnes
100 UK (long) tons	=	112 US (short) tons

Velocity (speed)

2 miles per hour	=	3 feet per second
9 miles per hour	=	4 metres per second
18 kilometres per hour	=	5 metres per second
11 kilometres per hour	=	10 feet per second
30 miles per hour	=	48 kilometres per hour
50 miles per hour	=	80 kilometres per hour
70 miles per hour	=	113 kilometres per hour

Fuel consumption

5 UK gallons per mile	=	14 litres per kilometre
20 miles per UK gallon	=	7 kilometres per litre
20 miles per UK gallon	=	14 litres per 100 kilometres
5 miles per US gallon	=	6 miles per UK gallon

Acceleration

Standard gravity	=	10 metres per second squared
	=	32 feet per second squared

Density and concentration

4 ounces per UK gallon	=	25 grams per litre
2 ounces per US gallon	=	15 grams per litre
1 pound per cubic foot	=	16 kilograms per cubic metre
$62\frac{1}{2}$ pounds per cubic foot	=	1 kilogram per litre
	=	density of 1

Force

$7\frac{1}{4}$ poundals	=	1 newton
1 pound-force	=	$4\frac{1}{2}$ newtons
9 pounds-force	=	40 newtons
1 kilogram-force	=	10 newtons

Pressure and stress

1 pound-force per square foot	=	48 pascals (newtons per square metre)
1 pound-force per square inch	=	7 kilopascals (kilonewtons per square metre)
1 bar	=	1 standard atmosphere
	=	$14\frac{1}{2}$ pounds-force per square inch
100 pounds-force per square inch	=	7 kilograms-force per square centimetre

Energy

18 British thermal units	=	19 kilojoules
4 British thermal units	=	1 kilocalorie*
1 kilocalorie* ('Calorie'*)	=	4 kilojoules

Power

4 UK horsepower	=	3 kilowatts
72 UK horsepower	=	73 metric horsepower*

10 lb
of water

The beginning of the Imperial Gallon
– and of the Imperial system

"And be it further enacted, That from and after the First Day of May One thousand eight hundred and twenty-five, the Standard Measure of Capacity, as well for Liquids as for dry Goods not measured by Heaped Measure, shall be the Gallon, containing Ten Pounds Avoirdupois Weight of distilled Water weighed in Air, at the Temperature of Sixty-two Degrees of Fahrenheit's Thermometer, the Barometer being at Thirty inches; and that a Measure shall be forthwith made of Brass, of such Contents as aforesaid, under the Directions of the Lord High Treasurer, or the Commissioners of His Majesty's Treasury of the United Kingdom, or any Three or more of them for the Time being; and such Brass Measure shall be and is hereby declared to be the Imperial Standard Gallon, and shall be and is hereby declared to be the Unit and only Standard Measure of Capacity . . .'

(An Act for ascertaining and establishing Uniformity of Weights and Measures, 17th June 1824)

Metric system

The system outlined here is the modern form of the metric system, referred to as the International System of Units (Système International d'Unités, or SI). The general form of this system was agreed in 1960, being designed to replace other forms of the metric system, such as the CGS system based on the centimetre, gram and second, and the MKS system based on the metre, kilogram and second.

Units or names not forming part of the main system of SI units, or recommended in that system for limited use, are marked in this section with an asterisk* (eg hectometre*).

Definitions and symbols of SI base and supplementary units are given on this page; definitions and symbols of derived and other units (some of which are shown in the chart below) are included on the following three pages.

Definitions of SI base units

Length: metre (m) = the length equal to 1 650 763.73 wavelengths in vacuum of the radiation corresponding to the transition between the levels $2p_{10}$ and $5d_5$ of the krypton-86 atom. That is, the SI unit is defined in terms of a number of wavelengths of a standard line of krypton-86; the number was chosen to define a metre of approximately the same length as the original metre which was about one forty-millionth of the circumference of the earth measured through the poles.

Proposals have been made to redefine the metre technically in terms of the unit of time and a specified value for the velocity of light in vacuum.

Mass: kilogram (kg) = the mass of the international prototype of the kilogram, which is in the custody of the Bureau International des Poids et Mesures (BIPM) at Sèvres, near Paris, France. This is a unit of mass and not of weight or force; it is approximately the same as the mass of one cubic decimetre (litre) of water at maximum density (4°C).

Time: second (s) = the duration of 9 192 631 770 periods of the radiation corresponding to the transition between the two hyperfine levels of the ground state of the caesium-133 atom. That is, the SI unit is defined in terms of the length of time for a certain frequency of vibration of a caesium-133 atom; the number of periods was chosen to define a second approximately the same as the 'ephemeris' second which is the fraction 1/86 400 of an average day for the tropical year 1900 of about $365\frac{1}{4}$ days.

Electric current: ampere (A) = that constant current which, if maintained in two straight parallel conductors of infinite length, of negligible circular cross-section, and placed 1 metre apart in vacuum, would produce between these conductors a force equal to 2×10^{-7} newton per metre of length.

Thermodynamic temperature: kelvin (K) = the fraction 1/273.16 of the thermodynamic temperature of the triple point of water. The triple point of water is the point where water, ice and water vapour are in equilibrium; it is 273.16 K.

Amount of substance: mole (mol) = the amount of substance of a system which contains as many elementary entities as there are atoms in 0.012 kilogram of carbon-12. The realisation of the mole is the determination of the Avogadro constant.
(Note: when the mole is used, the elementary entities must be specified and may be atoms, molecules, ions, electrons, other particles, or specified groups of such particles).

Luminous intensity: candela (cd) = the luminous intensity, in a given direction, of a source which emits monochromatic radiation with a frequency of 540×10^{12} hertz and which has a radiant intensity in that direction of 1/683 watt per steradian (revised definition from 1979).

Definitions of SI supplementary units

Plane angle: radian (rad) = the plane angle between two radii of a circle which cut off on the circumference an arc equal in length to the radius.

Solid angle: steradian (sr) = the solid angle which, having its vertex in the centre of a sphere, cuts off an area of the surface of the sphere equal to that of a square with sides of length equal to the radius of the sphere.

Outline of the main International System of Units (SI)

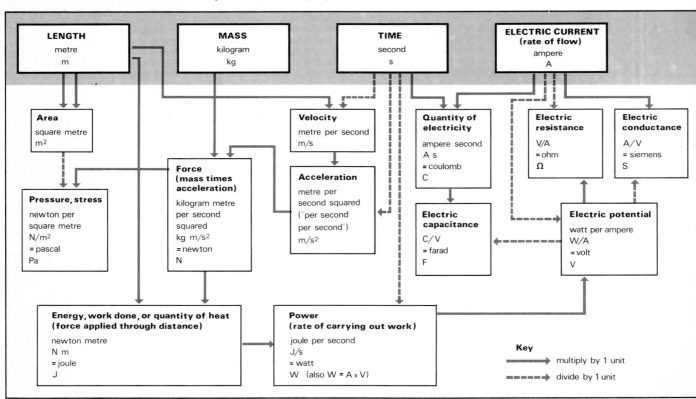

Metric system

Multiples and submultiples

The multiples and submultiples of the base and other units are shown below and on the following two pages for various types of measure; these are formed by applying established prefixes, which are the same whichever unit is used. Examples are: milligram (mg), millimetre (mm), kilowatt (kW), megawatt (MW).

Only one multiplying prefix is applied at one time to a given unit. Thus one thousandth of a milligram is not referred to as a millimilligram but as a microgram (µg). There are a few cases where, in attaching a prefix to the name of a unit, a contraction of the prefix name is made for convenience in pronunciation; for

example megohm, microhm and hectare. Unit names take a plural 's' when associated with numbers greater than 1, eg 1.5 metres; the names hertz, lux and siemens are, however, the same in the plural. Symbols are not altered in the plural form; eg 1.5 m.

The names and values of prefixes in use are given below; also indicated are the equivalent powers to base 10 of the multiplying factors which can be used to relate any multiple or submultiple to the main unit: for example 1 mm = 10^{-3} m and 1 MN = 10^6 N. The general use of prefixes representing 10 raised to a power which is a multiple of ±3 is recommended in SI; for example, millimetre (10^{-3} m), metre (m) and kilometre (10^3 m). Other prefixes, notably centi, deci, deka and hecto can be used where others are inconvenient. Myria, as a prefix symbol, is not an SI multiple, but is included for reference.

Prefix name	Prefix symbol	Factor by which the unit is multiplied		Description
atto	a	$10^{-18} =$	0.000 000 000 000 000 001	one UK trillionth; US quintillionth
femto	f	$10^{-15} =$	0.000 000 000 000 001	one UK billiardth, US quadrillionth
pico	p	$10^{-12} =$	0.000 000 000 001	one UK billionth; US trillionth
nano	n	$10^{-9} =$	0.000 000 001	one UK milliardth; US billionth
micro	µ	$10^{-6} =$	0.000 001	one millionth
milli	m	$10^{-3} =$	0.001	one thousandth
centi	c	$10^{-2} =$	0.01	one hundredth
deci	d	$10^{-1} =$	0.1	one tenth
deca (or deka)	da[a]	$10^1 =$	10	ten
hecto	h	$10^2 =$	100	one hundred
kilo	k	$10^3 =$	1 000	one thousand
myria*	my*	$10^4 =$	10 000	ten thousand
mega	M	$10^6 =$	1 000 000	one million
giga	G	$10^9 =$	1 000 000 000	one thousand million; UK milliard; US billion
tera	T	$10^{12} =$	1 000 000 000 000	one million million; UK billion[b], US trillion
peta	P	$10^{15} =$	1 000 000 000 000 000	one UK billiard; US quadrillion
exa	E	$10^{18} =$	1 000 000 000 000 000 000	one UK trillion; US quintillion

[a]Sometimes dk is used (eg in West Germany).　　[b]The definition of one billion as one thousand million is becoming increasingly common in the United Kingdom.

Length

1 000 picometres (pm)	= 1 nanometre (nm)
10 ångström (Å)*	= 1 nanometre
1 000 nanometres	= 1 micrometre (µm), also called 'micron' (µ)*
1 000 micrometres	= 1 millimetre (mm)
10 millimetres	= 1 centimetre (cm)
100 millimetres	= 1 decimetre (dm)
10 centimetres	= 1 decimetre
1 000 millimetres	= 1 metre
100 centimetres	= 1 metre
10 decimetres	= 1 metre
100 metres	= 1 hectometre (hm)*
1 000 metres	= 1 kilometre (km)
10 hectometres*	= 1 kilometre
1 000 kilometres	= 1 megametre (Mm)

nautical

1 852 metres	= 1 international nautical mile (n mile)

Area

100 square millimetres (mm²)	= 1 square centimetre (cm²)
100 square centimetres	= 1 square decimetre (dm²)
1 000 000 square millimetres	= 1 square metre (m²)
10 000 square centimetres	= 1 square metre
100 square decimetres	= 1 square metre
100 square metres	= 1 are (a)
10 ares	= 1 dekare or decare (daa)
10 000 square metres	= 1 square hectometre (hm²)*
	= 1 hectare (ha)
100 ares	= 1 hectare
10 dekares (or decares)	= 1 hectare
1 000 000 square metres	= 1 square kilometre (km²)
100 square hectometres*	= 1 square kilometre
100 hectares	= 1 square kilometre

Volume and capacity

1 000 cubic millimetres (mm³)	= 1 cubic centimetre (cm³ or cc*)
1 000 cubic centimetres	= 1 cubic decimetre (dm³)
1 000 cubic decimetres	= 1 cubic metre (m³)
1 000 cubic metres	= 1 cubic dekametre (dam³)*
1 000 cubic dekametres*	= 1 cubic hectometre (hm³)*
1 000 cubic hectometres*	= 1 cubic kilometre (km³)

The litre is defined for general use with SI units as follows:
litre (l or L) = 1 cubic decimetre (1964 definition which replaced the '1901' definition which was equal to 1.000 028 cubic decimetres). The 1901 definition of the litre continued in use in the United Kingdom until November 1, 1976, when it was replaced by the 1964 definition.
The symbol L for litre was added officially as an option to l in 1979.

1 microlitre (µl)	= 1 lambda*
1 000 microlitres	= 1 millilitre (ml)
1 millilitre	= 1 cubic centimetre
10 millilitres	= 1 centilitre (cl)
10 centilitres	= 1 decilitre (dl)
1 000 millilitres	= 1 litre (l or L)
100 centilitres	= 1 litre
100 litres	= 1 hectolitre (hl)
1 000 litres	= 1 kilolitre (kl)*
	= 1 cubic metre
10 hectolitres	= 1 cubic metre

Time

1 000 nanoseconds (ns)	= 1 microsecond (µs)
1 000 microseconds	= 1 millisecond (ms)
1 000 milliseconds	= 1 second
1 000 seconds	= 1 kilosecond (ks)

Metric system

Frequency

Definition: hertz (Hz) = the number of repetitions of a regular occurrence in 1 second.

1 000 hertz (Hz)	= 1 kilohertz (kHz)
1 000 kilohertz	= 1 megahertz (MHz)
1 000 megahertz	= 1 gigahertz (GHz)
1 000 gigahertz	= 1 terahertz (THz)
	= 1 fresnel*
1 000 terahertz	= 1 petahertz (PHz)
1 000 petahertz	= 1 exahertz (EHz)

Velocity

3.6 kilometres per hour (km/h)	= 1 metre per second (m/s)
3 600 kilometres per hour	= 1 kilometre per second (km/s)

nautical
1 international nautical mile per hour = 1 international knot (kn)

Acceleration

Definition: international standard gravity value (g_n) = 9.806 65 metres per second squared

1 galileo (Gal or gal*)*	= 1 centimetre per second squared (cm/s²)*
100 centimetres per second squared*	= 1 metre per second squared (m/s²)

Mass (weight)

The kilogram is the unit of mass in the International System; weight has a specialised meaning in metrology which is that the weight of a body is the product of its mass and the acceleration due to gravity. In SI units this would be a force (kg m/s²) which is measured in newtons. Where there is no ambiguity, it is common practice to use the term weight as meaning mass under the force of the earth's gravity, measured by comparing one body with another which is a standard of mass. Where there may be ambiguity, m (for mass) and f (for force) are sometimes added to the symbol: eg kgm (kilogram mass), kgf (kilogram force).

1 000 nanograms (ng)	= 1 microgram (µg or mcg*)[a]
1 000 micrograms	= 1 milligram (mg)
200 milligrams	= 1 metric carat (CM)[b]
1 000 milligrams	= 1 gram (g)
5 metric carats	= 1 gram
25 grams	= 1 mounce*[c]
100 grams	= 1 hectogram (hg)*
0.980 665 kilograms	= 1 glug*
1 000 000 milligrams	= 1 kilogram (kg)
1 000 grams	= 1 kilogram
9.806 65 kilograms	= 1 metric technical unit of mass[d]
100 kilograms	= 1 quintal (q)*
1 000 000 grams	= 1 megagram (Mg)
1 000 kilograms	= 1 megagram
10 quintals*	= 1 megagram
	= 1 tonne (t)
	= 1 metric ton
	= 1 millier*

[a] Or gamma (γ)*.   [b] CM is the UK abbreviation; abbreviations vary by country (eg, for West Germany it is Kt).   [c] Or metric ounce.   [d] Metric technical unit of mass = the mass that acquires an acceleration of 1 metre per second squared under the influence of a 1 kilogram force (also see under 'acceleration'). Also called the 'metric slug' or hyl and shown as kgm (kilogram mass).

Density and concentration

1 gram per cubic metre (g/m³)	= 1 milligram per cubic decimetre (mg/dm³)
1 000 milligrams per cubic decimetre	= 1 gram per cubic decimetre (g/dm³)
	= 1 gram per litre (g/l)
	= 1 kilogram per cubic metre (kg/m³)
1 000 kilograms per cubic metre	= 1 tonne per cubic metre (t/m³)
	= 1 kilogram per cubic decimetre (kg/dm³)
	= 1 kilogram per litre (kg/l)
	= 1 gram per cubic centimetre (g/cm³)
	= 1 gram per millilitre (g/ml)

Force

Definitions: newton (N) = that force which, applied to a mass of 1 kilogram, gives it an acceleration of 1 metre per second squared.

kilogram-force (kgf)*, also called kilopond (kp)* = that force which, applied to a mass of 1 kilogram, gives it the standard gravitational acceleration ('free fall') of 9.806 65 metres per second squared.

dyne (dyn)* = that force which, applied to a mass of 1 gram, gives it an acceleration of 1 centimetre per second squared = 10^{-5} N

10 micronewtons (µN)	= 1 dyne (dyn)*
1 000 micronewtons	= 1 millinewton (mN)
9.806 65 millinewtons	= 1 pond (p)*
10 millinewtons (mN)	= 1 centinewton (cN)
10 000 dynes*	= 1 crinal*
100 000 dynes*	= 1 newton
1 000 millinewtons (mN)	= 1 newton
9.806 65 newtons	= 1 kilogram-force (kgf)*
	= 1 kilopond (kp)*
1 000 newtons	= 1 kilonewton (kN)
	= 1 sthène or sten (sn)*
1 000 kilonewtons	= meganewton (MN)

Pressure and stress

Definition: pascal (Pa) = the pressure produced by a force of 1 newton applied, uniformly distributed, over an area of 1 square metre.

1 000 micropascals (µPa)	= 1 millipascal (mPa)
100 millipascals	= 1 dyne per square centimetre (dyn/cm²)*
	= 1 barye*
	= 1 microbar (µbar)
1 000 millipascals	= 1 pascal (Pa)
10 microbars	= 1 pascal
	= 1 newton per square metre (N/m²)
9.806 65 pascals	= 1 millimetre of water, conventional (mm H_2O)*
1 000 microbars	= 1 millibar (mbar or mb*)
100 pascals	= 1 millibar
	= 1 vac*
9.806 65 × 13.595 1 = 133.322 (approx.) pascals	= 1 millimetre of mercury, conventional (mm Hg)*
	= 1 torr (approx.)*
1 000 pascals	= 1 kilopascal (kPa)
10 millibars	= 1 kilopascal
	= 1 sthène per square metre (sn/m²)*
	= 1 pièze (pz)*
9 806.65 pascals	= 1 metre of water, conventional (m H_2O)*
98 065.5 pascals	= 1 technical atmosphere (at)*
	= 1 kilogram-force per square centimetre (kgf/cm²)*
	= 0.980 665 bar (bar or b*)
100 000 pascals	= 1 bar
1 000 millibars	= 1 bar
	= 1 hectopièze (hpz)
101 325 pascals	= 1 standard atmosphere (atm)*
760 torrs*	= 1 standard atmosphere*
	= 1.013 25 bars
1 000 000 pascals	= 1 megapascal (MPa)
1 000 kilopascals	= 1 megapascal
10 bars	= 1 megapascal
	= 1 newton per square millimetre (N/mm²)
100 bars	= 1 hectobar (hbar)
1 000 bars	= 1 kilobar (kbar)
1 000 megapascals	= 1 gigapascal (GPa)

Viscosity

Dynamic (or absolute)

1 centipoise (cP)	= 1 millipascal second (mPa s)
100 centipoises	= 1 poise (P)*
	= 1 dyne second per square centimetre (dyn s/cm²)*
	= 100 millipascal seconds
1 000 millipascal seconds	= 1 pascal second (Pa s)
	= 1 newton second per square metre (N s/m²)
	= 1 000 centipoises
	= 10 poises

Kinematic

1 centistokes (cSt)	= 1 square millimetre per second (mm²/s)
100 centistokes	= 1 stokes (St)*
	= 1 square centimetre per second (cm²/s)*
10 000 stokes*	= 1 square metre per second (m²/s)

Energy, work and quantity of heat

Definitions: joule (J) = the work done when the point of application of a force of 1 newton is displaced through a distance of 1 metre in the direction of the force.

erg* = 1 dyn acting through a distance of 1 centimetre = 10^{-7} J

10 000 ergs*	= 1 millijoule (mJ)
10 000 000 ergs*	= 1 joule
1 000 millijoules	= 1 joule
1 000 joules	= 1 kilojoule (kJ)
1 000 kilojoules	= 1 megajoule (MJ)
3.6 megajoules	= 1 kilowatt hour (kW h)
1 000 megajoules	= 1 gigajoule (GJ)
1 000 gigajoules	= 1 terajoule (TJ)

Power

Definitions: watt (W) = the power which in 1 second gives rise to energy of 1 joule.

metric horsepower (ch or CV or cv or PS or pk)* = the power which raises 75 kilograms against the force of gravity through a distance of 1 metre per second = 75 × 9.806 65 joules per second = 735.498 75 watts

1 000 microwatts (μw)	= 1 milliwatt (mW)
1 000 milliwatts	= 1 watt
1 000 watts	= 1 kilowatt (kW)
1 000 kilowatts	= 1 megawatt (MW)
1 000 000 kilowatts	= 1 gigawatt (GW)
1 000 megawatts	= 1 gigawatt
1 000 gigawatts	= 1 terawatt (TW)

Temperature

Definition: the unit 'degree Celsius' is equal to the unit 'kelvin'. The zero of the Celsius scale is the temperature of the ice point, which is 273.15 K (0.01 below the triple point of water); that is, degrees Celsius (°C) = K − 273.15.

Electricity and magnetism

1 000 picoamperes (pA)	= 1 nanoampere (nA)
1 000 nanoamperes	= 1 microampere (μA)
1 000 microamperes	= 1 milliampere (mA)
1 000 milliamperes	= 1 ampere
1 000 amperes	= 1 kiloampere (kA)

Definitions of other (derived) SI units:
coulomb (C) = the quantity of electricity carried in 1 second by a current of 1 ampere.

1 000 picocoulombs (pC)	= 1 nanocoulomb (nC)
1 000 nanocoulombs	= 1 microcoulomb (μC)
1 000 microcoulombs	= 1 millicoulomb (mC)
1 000 millicoulombs	= 1 coulomb
1 000 coulombs	= 1 kilocoulomb (kC)
1 000 kilocoulombs	= 1 megacoulomb (MC)

volt (V) = the difference of electric potential between two points of a conducting wire carrying a constant current of 1 ampere, when the power dissipated between these points is equal to 1 watt.

1 000 microvolts (μV)	= 1 millivolt (mV)
1 000 millivolts	= 1 volt
1 000 volts	= 1 kilovolt (kV)
1 000 kilovolts	= 1 megavolt (MV)

ohm (Ω) = the electric resistance between two points of a conductor when a constant potential difference of 1 volt, applied to these points, produces in the conductor a current of 1 ampere, the conductor not being the seat of any electromotive force.

1 000 microhm (μΩ)	= 1 milliohm (mΩ)
1 000 milliohm	= 1 ohm
1 000 ohms	= 1 kilohm (kΩ)
1 000 kilohms	= 1 megohm (MΩ)
1 000 megohms	= 1 gigohm (GΩ)

siemens (S) = 1 ampere per volt, being the unit of electric conductance; this unit has also been known as the reciprocal ohm (ohm^{-1}) or 'mho'.

1 000 microsiemens (μS)	= 1 millisiemens (mS)
1 000 millisiemens	= 1 siemens
1 000 siemens	= 1 kilosiemens (kS)

farad (F) = the capacitance of a capacitor between the plates of which there appears a difference of electric potential of 1 volt when it is charged by a quantity of electricity of 1 coulomb.

1 puff*	= 1 picofarad (pF)
1 000 000 picofarads	= 1 microfarad (μF)
1 000 000 microfarads	= 1 farad

weber (Wb) = the magnetic flux which, linking a circuit of 1 turn, would produce in it an electromotive force of 1 volt if it were reduced to zero at a uniform rate in 1 second.

henry (H) = the inductance of a closed circuit in which an electromotive force of 1 volt is produced when the electric current in the circuit varies uniformly at the rate of 1 ampere per second.

1 000 picohenrys (pH)	= 1 nanohenry (nH)
1 000 nanohenrys	= 1 microhenry (μH)
1 000 microhenrys	= 1 millihenry (mH)
1 000 millihenrys	= 1 henry

tesla (T) = the flux density in vacuum produced by a magnetic field of strength 1 ampere per metre; this is the unit of magnetic flux density and equals 1 weber per square metre.

1 000 nanoteslas (nT)	= 1 microtesla (μT)
1 000 microteslas	= 1 millitesla (mT)
1 000 milliteslas	= 1 tesla

Luminous flux

Definitions: lumen (lm) = the luminous flux emitted within unit solid angle of 1 steradian by a point source having a uniform luminous intensity of 1 candela.

lux (lx) = an illuminance of 1 lumen per square metre.

Radiation

Definition for radioactivity: becquerel (Bq) = 1 reciprocal second, being the unit of activity of a radionuclide. The activity is the number of radioactive disintegrations occurring per unit time in a given quantity of the radionuclide.

1 000 becquerels	= 1 kilobecquerel (kBq)
1 000 kilobecquerels	= 1 megabecquerel (MBq)
1 000 megabecquerels	= 1 gigabecquerel (GBq)

Definition for absorbed dose: gray (Gy) = 1 joule per kilogram, being the unit of absorbed dose in the field of ionising radiation. The absorbed dose is the mean energy imparted by ionising radiation to matter, per unit of mass of irradiated material, at the place of interest.

United Kingdom

Imperial (United Kingdom) system

The imperial system was established as such in 1824. The imperial gallon was defined as the only legal gallon, replacing the different ale and wine gallons. Although the troy pound was defined as the imperial standard under the 1824 Act, in 1855 the avoirdupois pound became the imperial standard. In 1878 the troy pound was abolished, although the troy ounce remained in use.

The imperial system was, until the late 1960s, the main system of measurement used in the British Commonwealth and South Africa; virtually every country using the imperial system began a change-over to the metric system beginning in the late 1960s and 1970s. In the United Kingdom the change is taking place gradually.

In the United Kingdom, the 'Weights and Measures Act 1963' established units of both the imperial and metric systems as 'United Kingdom primary standards', and the base units of the yard and pound were defined in terms of the metre and kilogram. The gallon was defined in terms of the cubic decimetre (litre) in 1976.

In the list below, units which are not officially authorised following the change to the metric system, or which are generally obsolescent are marked with an asterisk * (eg rod*). A substantial number of UK units were no longer officially authorised for UK use from September 1, 1980, including square inch, square mile, cubic foot, grain, stone, hundredweight, ton and horsepower. The deadline for decision on phasing out remaining imperial units, including the inch, foot, pint, gallon, ounce and pound, is officially planned as December 31, 1989.

Relationships are exact except where noted as approximate.

Length

Base unit definition: yard = 0.914 4 metre (replacing in 1963 the relationship: yard = approximately 0.914 397 metre)

1 000 000	micro-inches (μin)	= 1 inch (in)
1 000	milli-inches[a]	= 1 inch
4	inches	= 1 hand*[d]
7.92	inches	= 1 link (lk)*
12	inches	= 1 foot (ft)
3	feet	= 1 yard (yd)
25	links*	= 1 rod*
5.5	yards	= 1 rod*, pole* or perch*
100	links*	= 1 chain (ch)*[b, d]
66	feet	= 1 chain*[d]
22	yards	= 1 chain*[d]
4	rods*	= 1 chain*[d]
100	feet	= 1 engineers' chain*[c, d]
220	yards	= 1 furlong*[d]
10	chains*	= 1 furlong*[d]
5 280	feet	= 1 mile (mi)
1 760	yards	= 1 mile
80	chains*	= 1 mile
8	furlongs*	= 1 mile
3	miles	= 1 league*
nautical		
6	feet	= 1 fathom
100	fathoms (approx.)	= 1 cable length*[e]
6 080	feet	= 1 nautical mile*
		= the length of one minute of the meridian through Greenwich, that is 1/60th of the degree of latitude
6 087	feet	= 1 telegraph nautical mile*
10	cable lengths*	= 1 nautical mile*

[a] A milli-inch is sometimes called a mil' or a thou*.   [b] Also called a Gunter's or surveyor's chain.   [c] Also called Ramden's chain.   [d] In general, not lawful for UK trade from April 27, 1978.   [e] An alternative, less usual, value was 120 fathoms.

Area

Base unit definition: square yard = a superficial area equal to that of a square each side of which measures one yard.

1	circular mil	= area of a circle of diameter 0.001 inch (= π/4 × 0.000 001 square inch)
144	square inches*	= 1 square foot (ft²)
9	square feet*	= 1 square yard (yd²)
30.25	square yards	= 1 square rod*, pole* or perch*
484	square yards	= 1 square chain (ch²)*
1 210	square yards	= 1 rood*
4 840	square yards	= 1 acre (ac)
160	square rods*	= 1 acre
640	acres	= 1 square mile*

Volume

Base unit definition: cubic yard = a volume equal to that of a cube each edge of which measures one yard.

1 728	cubic inches*	= 1 cubic foot (ft³)*
46 656	cubic inches*	= 1 cubic yard (yd³)*
27	cubic feet*	= 1 cubic yard*
nautical		
100	cubic feet*	= 1 register ton (shipping)

Capacity

Base unit definition (1976): gallon = 4.546 09 cubic decimetres (exactly). This definition replaced the 1963 definition, which defined the gallon in terms of the weight (not mass) of water; that definition was that the gallon = the space occupied by 10 pounds weight of distilled water of density 0.998 859 gram per millilitre weighed in air of density 0.001 217 gram per millilitre against weights of density 8.136 grams per millilitre (using the 1901 definition of a litre which equals 1.000 028 cubic decimetre; this definition remained the legal definition in the United Kingdom until 1976, when it was established that 1 litre = 1 cubic decimetre exactly).
1 gallon (1963) = 1.000 000 41 gallon (1976)
1 gallon (1976) = 0.999 999 59 gallon (1963)

60	minims*	= 1 fluid drachm (fl drm)*
8	fluid drachms*	= 1 fluid ounce (fl oz)
5	fluid ounces	= 1 gill
20	fluid ounces	= 1 pint (pt)
4	gills	= 1 pint
40	fluid ounces	= 1 quart (qt)
2	pints	= 1 quart
160	fluid ounces	= 1 gallon (gal)
8	pints	= 1 gallon
4	quarts	= 1 gallon
2	gallons	= 1 peck*
4	pecks*	= 1 bushel (bu)*
8	gallons	= 1 bushel*
64	gallons	= 1 quarter (qr)*
8	bushels*	= 1 quarter*

Velocity

1 mile per hour (mph)	= 88 feet per minute (ft/min)
	= $1\frac{7}{15}$ feet per second (ft/s)

Weight (mass)

Definition: grain = 64.798 91 milligrams (the grain is the same whether avoirdupois, apothecaries' or troy weight).

Avoirdupois

Base unit definition: pound = 0.453 592 37 kilogram

437.5	grains (gr)*	= 1 ounce (oz)
16	drams (dr)*	= 1 ounce
7 000	grains*	= 1 pound (lb)
256	drams*	= 1 pound
16	ounces	= 1 pound
14	pounds	= 1 stone*
2	stones*	= 1 quarter (qr)*
9.806 65/0.3048 pounds = 32.174 (approx.) pounds		= 1 slug (technical unit of mass)
100	pounds	= 1 cental (ctl)*
112	pounds	= 1 hundredweight (cwt)*
4	quarters*	= 1 hundredweight*
35 840	ounces	= 1 ton*
2 240	pounds	= 1 ton*
20	hundredweights*	= 1 ton*

Imperial (United Kingdom) system

Apothecaries'

Note: apothecaries' units were officially discontinued for UK trade from 1971.

20 grains*	= 1 scruple*
24 grains*	= 1 pennyweight (dwt)*
60 grains*	= 1 drachm (drm)*
480 grains*	= 1 ounce (oz apoth)*
24 scruples*	= 1 ounce*
8 drachms*	= 1 ounce*
5 760 grains*	= 1 pound*
12 ounces*	= 1 pound*

Troy

(for weighing gold, silver, jewels, etc.; sometimes called 'fine' instead of 'troy').

480 grains*	= 1 ounce (oz tr)
24 grains*	= 1 pennyweight (dwt tr)*
20 pennyweights*	= 1 ounce
5 760 grains*	= 1 pound*
12 ounces	= 1 pound*

Force

Definitions: poundal = that force which applied to a mass of 1 pound, gives it an acceleration of 1 foot per second per second (per second squared).

pound force = that force which, applied to a mass of 1 pound, gives it the standard gravitational acceleration of 9.806 65 metres (approximately 32.174 048 feet) per second per second.

32.174 (approx.) poundals (pdl)* [a]	= 1 pound-force (lbf)* [a]
16 ounces-force (ozf)*	= 1 pound-force* [a]
2 240 pounds-force*	= 1 ton-force (tonf)* [a]

[a] In general, not authorised for UK use from September 1, 1980.

Work

Definition: horsepower = the power needed to raise 550 pounds through a height of one foot in one second (in general, the UK horsepower unit is not authorised for UK use from September 1, 1980).

550 foot pounds-force per second (ft lbf/s)* = 1 horsepower (hp)*

Quantity of heat

Definition: British thermal unit = 2.326 × 0.453 592 37 kilojoules or approximately 1.055 056 kilojoules (as defined internationally in 1956; the UK definition is 'the heat needed to raise the temperature of one pound of water through 1 degree Fahrenheit at or near 39.1 degrees Fahrenheit'). In general the British thermal unit is not authorised for UK use from September 1, 1980.

100 000 British thermal units (Btu)* = 1 therm

Heat flow

288 000 British thermal units per day (Btu/d)*	= 1 ton of refrigeration
12 000 British thermal units per hour (Btu/h)*	= 1 ton of refrigeration

Historical development of medieval measures

410–1215 AD

After the Roman occupation was ended, their measures were merged with those of the Angles, Saxons, Danes and Normans who occupied parts of Britain and brought their own measures with them.

The Saxon yard was established as a unit of length, and eventually fixed as a standard in iron in the 12th century. The grain was in use from the 8th century, and there were from 18 to 24 grains to the silver penny, varying by region and with time; generally there were 240 pennies to 1 pound.

In 1215 the Magna Carta established that there should be a single set of measures throughout the Kingdom; the London quarter was mentioned amongst other units.

1215–1351 AD

During this period, the main medieval system of measurements was codified by statute:

1266 (approximate; statute date uncertain)
The London system was defined by statute:

32 wheat corns	= 1 English penny (a sterling or d)
20 pennies	= 1 ounce
12 ounces	= 1 pound [a]
8 pounds	= 1 gallon of wine
8 gallons of wine	= 1 London bushel
8 London bushels	= 1 London quarter [b]

[a] Equal to 7 680 wheat grains; later also called the 'Tower' or 'moneyer's' pound.
[b] As mentioned in the Magna Carta.

1303 (approximate; statute date uncertain)
The 1266 London system was confirmed, and distinction made between a 'lesser' and a 'greater' pound (a range of special units was also defined):

12 pence	= 1 shilling
20 pence	= 1 ounce
12 ounces	= 1 'lesser' pound (= 20 shillings = 240 pence) [a]
15 ounces	= 1 'greater' pound (= 25 shillings = 300 pence) [b]
12½ pounds	= 1 London stone

[a] Equal to 5 400 (barley) grains; later to be replaced by the Troy pound.
[b] 'Commercial' or 'mercantile' pound, equal to 6 750 grains; later, modified to have 7 000 grains, and contain 16 ounces, to become the avoirdupois pound.

1324 (approximate; statute date uncertain)
Length and area units are codified:

3 barleycorns (round and dry)	= 1 inch
12 inches	= 1 foot
3 feet	= 1 yard (or ulnam)
5½ yards	= 1 perch
40 perches by 4 perches	= 1 acre (= 4 840 square yards)

1340 (14 Edward 3)
Established, for wool:

14 pounds (l)	= 1 stone
26 stones	= 1 sack (=364 pounds)

1351 (25 Edward 3)
Established as a general system (for which the term 'averdepois' was used in 1353):

14 pounds	= 1 stone
2 stones	= 1 quarter (= 28 pounds)
4 stones	= 1 half-hundredweight (= 56 pounds)
6½ stones	= 1 quarter-sack (= 91 pounds)
2 half-hundredweights	= 1 hundredweight (= 112 pounds)
26 stones	= 1 sack (= 364 pounds)

1351–1824 AD

The basic medieval system, as already established, was varied by some extensions and redefinitions; some main changes were:
1430 (9 Henry 6)

For cheese:	7 pounds (li)	= 1 clove
	32 cloves	= 1 wey (= 224 pounds)

1496 (12 Henry 7)
The Troy system became legal and the main system to use.
1526 (18 Henry 8)
The Troy system replaced the Tower system for weighing silver and gold.
1532 (24 Henry 8)
All meat was to be sold by Haberdepayes (averdupois) weight, replacing other 'mercantile' weights.
1558 (1 Elizabeth 1)
A set of standards was established for averdepois weight, retaining also the Troy weights (these being referred to as the 2 'ancient' weights).
1587 (30 Elizabeth 1)
The 1558 weights were redefined and clarified; the two pounds were confirmed for use, and the modern avoirdupois pound was established:

7 000 grains	= 1 pound (av)
112 pounds	= 1 hundredweight
2 240 pounds	= 1 ton

The furlong was increased from 625 feet to 660 feet; since the relationship of 8 furlongs to the mile was retained, the mile was increased from 5 000 feet to 5 280 feet.
1706 (5 Anne)
The wine gallon was defined as a cylinder with 7 inches diameter and 6 inches height, or a content of 231 cubic inches.
1824 (5 George 4)
The Imperial system was legally established.

Medieval system (summary)

Length[a]

			Equivalent in UK imperial units
		1 line	$\frac{1}{12}$ in
4	lines	= 1 barleycorn	$\frac{1}{3}$ in
9	lines	= 1 nail[b]	$\frac{3}{4}$ in
3	barleycorns	= 1 inch[c]	1 in
$2\frac{1}{4}$	inches	= 1 nail-of-a-yard[d]	$2\frac{1}{4}$ in
4	inches	= 1 hand[e]	4 in
$4\frac{1}{2}$	inches	= 1 finger	$4\frac{1}{2}$ in
9	inches	= 1 span	9 in
12	inches	= 1 foot	1 ft
$13\frac{1}{3}$	inches	= 1 long foot[f]	1.1 ft
$1\frac{1}{2}$	feet	= 1 cubit	18 in
3	feet	= 1 yard[g]	36 in
3	long feet	= 1 yard and hand[h]	40 in
20	nails-of-a-yard	= 1 ell[i]	45 in
5	feet	= 1 pace	5 ft
125	paces	= 1 furlong[j]	625 ft
8	furlongs	= 1 mile[j]	5 000 ft

surveyors' ('Gunter's') system (from about 1620)

		1 link	7.92 in
25	links	= 1 rod[k]	$16\frac{1}{2}$ ft
100	links	= 1 chain[l]	22 yd
10	chains	= 1 old rode[m]	220 yd

Area[a]

		1 sq rod or perch	$30\frac{1}{4}$ yd²
160	sq rod	= 1 acre[n]	4 840 yd²
10	acres	= 1 sq old rode	48 400 yd²
20	acres	= 1 yard[o]	20 acres
4	yards	= 1 hide[p]	80 acres
8	hides	= 1 knight's fee[q]	640 acres = 1 square mile

Capacity

wine measures[r]

			Equivalent in UK imperial units
231	cubic inches	= 1 wine gallon	0.83 gal
$31\frac{1}{2}$	wine gallons	= 1 wine barrel[s]	26.2 gal
2	wine barrels (63 wine gallons)	= 1 hogshead	52.5 gal
2	hogsheads (126 wine gallons)	= 1 pipe[t]	104.9 gal
2	pipes (252 wine gallons)	= 1 tun[u]	209.8 gal

ale measures[v]

282	cubic inches	= 1 ale gallon	1.02 gal
4	gallons	= 1 pin	4.07 gal
6	gallons	= 1 six	6.10 gal
2	pins (8 ale gallons)	= 1 firkin	8.13 gal
2	sixes (12 ale gallons)	= 1 anker	12.2 gal
2	firkins (16 ale gallons)	= 1 kilderkin[w]	16.3 gal
2	kilderkins (32 ale gallons)	= 1 barrel[x]	32.5 gal
2	barrels (64 ale gallons)	= 1 puncheon	65.1 gal
3	barrels (96 ale gallons)	= 1 butt	97.6 gal

corn measures[y]

$272\frac{1}{4}$	cubic inches	= 1 corn gallon	0.98 gal
8	corn gallons	= 1 corn bushel	7.85 gal
8	corn bushels (64 corn gallons)	= 1 quarter	63 gal

Weight

London system ('Tower' or 'moneyer's'; about 1303)[z]

			Equivalent in UK imperial units
32	wheat corns[aa]	= 1 English penny[bb]	$22\frac{1}{2}$ gr
12	pence	= 1 shilling	270 gr
20	pence	= 1 ounce	450 gr
6	ounces	= 1 half-pound	2 700 gr
8	ounces	= 1 mark*	3 600 gr
12	ounces	= 1 'lesser' pound[cc]	5 400 gr = 0.94 lb tr
15	ounces	= 1 'greater' pound[dd]	6 750 gr = 0.96 lb
16	ounces = 2 marks	= 1 dimark*[ee]	7 200 gr = 1.03 lb
8	pounds (greater)	= 1 gallon of wine	7.8 lb
$12\frac{1}{2}$	pounds (greater)	= 1 London stone	12.1 lb
8	gallons of wine	= 1 London bushel	62 lb
8	London bushels	= 1 London quarter	496 lb

*Not part of the main London system.

Averdepois system (1351)[ff]

			Equivalent in: UK imperial units
14	pounds	= 1 stone	$13\frac{1}{2}$ lb
2	stones (28 pounds)	= 1 quarter	27 lb
4	stones (56 pounds)	= 1 half-hundredweight	54 lb
$6\frac{1}{2}$	stones (91 pounds)	= 1 quarter-sack	$87\frac{3}{4}$ lb
8	stones (112 pounds)	= 1 hundredweight	108 lb
26	stones (364 pounds)	= 1 sack	351 lb

Troy system (1526)[gg]

		1 silver penny	12 gr
2	pennies	= 1 pennyweight	24 gr
20	pennyweights	= 1 ounce	480 gr
12	ounces	= 1 pound	5 760 gr (= 1 troy pound)
15	ounces	= 1 mercantile pound[hh]	7 200 gr

[a]The basic system was in general laid down in statute in the last half of the 13th century and early 14th century. As for other old measures, the actual sizes varied according to time and region. The old foot varied from 0.97 to 1.10 of the imperial foot, other units varying accordingly; area values varied markedly. [b]Approximate width of thumb-nail (about equal to the Roman digit). [c]Approximate width of thumb. [d]One-sixteenth of a yard (cloth unit), analogous to the nail as one-sixteenth of a foot. [e]As defined 1535 (27 Henry 8); also used as equal to 3 inches. [f]As introduced by Belgic tribes, and abolished in 1439. This was originally based on a Roman long foot, and remained as a Rhineland unit, and until recently as the Cape foot of South Africa. [g]Or gird or gyrd. [h]As introduced by Belgic tribes, and abolished 1439. [i]Or ulna or aulne; English unit of 'a yard and a quarter yard'. [j]Before 1588; the furlong was increased during the reign of Queen Elizabeth 1 to 660 ft (= 40 rods), the mile (old London mile of 5 000 ft) then becoming the 'statute' mile of 5 280 ft. [k]Surveyor's measure only; in the 16th century, 1 rod = 1 rood = 16 feet; also 1 rode = 660 ft. Rod equals perch or pole. [l]The breadth for the main definition of an acre. [m]The length for the main definition of an acre. [n]Area basically 4 rods or perches wide by 40 rods or perches long. [o]Or yard-land or virgate; varied from 14 to 30 acres. [p]Or hyde; household size area of a farm; varied from 60 to 120 acres. [q]Varied from 300 to 960 acres ($\frac{1}{2}$ to $1\frac{1}{2}$ square miles); the number of hides per knight's fee varied from 5 to 8, depending on the quality of the land. [r]Values for Queen Anne's wine gallon (1706); the value for Edward 3's gallon of the mid 1300s was 8 pounds of wine which would have been about 216 in³ (0.78 imperial gallon). [s]Or half-hogshead or quarter-cask. [t]Or cask. [u]Or 12 score and 12 wine gallons. [v]As established by Henry 8 in 1531. [w]Or rundlet. [x]Beer barrel is 36 gallons. [y]As defined end 15th century (Winchester corn gallon); about 1300 AD the corn gallon = 8 pounds of wheat = about 270 in³ (0.9 imperial gallon). The old London corn gallon was 268.8 in³, and London bushel 2 150.42 in³ (cylinder $18\frac{1}{2}$ in diameter and 8 in deep). [z]As mentioned in the Magna Carta (1215), and codified at about the end of the 13th century. [aa]Average of grains of wheat taken from the middle of the ear, and well dried. [bb]In early medieval times, the silver penny varied from 18 to $24\frac{1}{2}$ grains (barley grains which weigh about one-third more than wheat grains). [cc]London, Tower or moneyer's pound; later to be replaced by the Troy pound. [dd]Commercial, mercantile or merchant's pound; later to be replaced by the avoirdupois pound of 7 000 grains, with 16 ounces. [ee]The 'double mark' of Cologne and Hamburg, or merchant's pound of the Hanseatic League. [ff]Shown here based on the 'greater' pound of 6 750 grains; there were different commercial pounds in use, ranging up to 7 200 grains. [gg]At the date at which the Troy system replaced the Tower (London) system as the legal standard for money. [hh]Equal to 16 Tower ounces.

Miscellaneous old UK units

	Equivalent in UK imperial units
Barony of land (40 hides)	3 200 acres
Boll	140 pounds
Bolt of canvas	42 yards
Bovate	10–18 acres
Cask (cider)	110 gallons
Chopin (or Choppin)	$\frac{1}{2}$ pint
Faggot { wood	3 feet long, 2 feet around
Faggot { steel	120 pounds
Goad	$4\frac{1}{2}$ feet
Line { buttons	$\frac{1}{40}$ inch
Line { watches	$\frac{1}{12}$ inch
Perit	$\frac{1}{9\,600}$ grain
Pig (ballast)	56 pounds
Point, silversmith's	$\frac{1}{4\,000}$ inch
Tub (butter)	84 pounds
Yard of ale	1 to 3 pints

United States

Units of measurement used in the United States, referred to as US inch-pound ('customary') units, are in general the same as in the imperial system with exceptions noted on this page; these exceptions are mainly for measures of capacity, with minor differences for length and weight. Measures used in the United States which are not in the imperial system are also included here. Relationships are exact except where noted.

SI units are being used to an increasing extent.

Length

The United States yard is defined by reference to the SI metre, the relationship being, as in the imperial system, 1 yard = 0.914 4 metre (value from 1959). This yard and its associated foot are sometimes called the 'International' yard or foot.

The system is generally as for imperial except for Coast and Geodetic surveys which use the US survey foot (which was the value of the foot from 1893 until 1959).

1 US survey foot	= 1200/3937 m = approx. 1.000 002 ('international') ft

other units

10 milli-inches	= 1 calibre (caliber)
100 calibers	= 1 inch
40 lines	= 1 inch
6 inches	= 1 span
1 engineers' link	= 1 foot
30 inches	= 1 pace
33⅓ inches	= 1 vara (some states, especially Texas)

Imperial chain (22 yards) is called Gunter's or surveyors' chain

nautical

120 fathoms (approx.)	= 1 cable length
7.5 cable lengths (approx.)	= 1 mile
1 international nautical mile	= 1 852 metres = approx. 6 076.12 feet (as adopted 1954; before 1954: 1 US nautical mile = 6 080.2 feet)

Area

As for imperial system; additional units are:

100 square feet	= 1 square	1 square mile	= 1 section
177.1 acres	= 1 labor (Texas)	36 sections	= 1 township

Capacity

Measures of capacity differ, depending on whether the commodity being measured is dry or liquid; there are both dry and liquid pints, quarts and gallons.

Further, both the bushel (base unit of dry measure) and the gallon (base unit of liquid measure) differ from imperial measures because the United States retained old UK measures when the United Kingdom abolished these in 1824 as part of the change to the imperial system. The term Winchester is sometimes used for the United States bushel, gallon, or related measures.

The United States standard bushel (struck measure) contains 2 150.42 cubic inches (= approximately 1.24 cubic feet); this was originally a cylinder 18½ in diameter and 8 in deep. A heaped bushel varies; a usual measure is 2 747.715 cubic inches (= approximately 1.278 struck bushels).

The United States liquid gallon contains 231 cubic inches.

Dry measures

2 dry pints	= 1 dry quart
4 dry quarts	= 1 dry gallon
2 dry gallons	= 1 peck
8 dry gallons	= 1 bushel
4 pecks	= 1 bushel
36 bushels	= 1 chaldron
5 826 cubic inches	= 1 standard cranberry barrel
7 056 cubic inches	= 1 dry standard barrel (bbl)

relationship between capacity and volume

1 dry pint	= 33.600 312 5 cubic inches
1 dry quart	= 67.200 625 cubic inches
1 peck	= 537.605 cubic inches

relationship between US and UK measures

For each of these units the relationship between the US and UK measures, which is not exact, is as follows:
1 US dry pint, dry quart, dry gallon, peck or standard bushel
= 0.968 939 UK pint, quart, gallon, peck or bushel
1 UK pint, quart, gallon, peck or bushel
= 1.032 06 US dry pints, dry quarts, dry gallons, pecks or bushels

The barrel in the United States varies according to State and usage; there is no direct relationship with the United Kingdom, since there is no general UK definition of the barrel.

Liquid measures

60 minims	= 1 liquid (fluid) dram
8 liquid (fluid) drams	= 1 liquid (fluid) ounce
4 liquid (fluid) ounces	= 1 gill
16 liquid (fluid) ounces	= 1 liquid pint
4 gills	= 1 liquid pint
32 liquid (fluid) ounces	= 1 liquid quart
2 liquid pints	= 1 liquid quart
128 liquid (fluid) ounces	= 1 liquid gallon
32 gills	= 1 liquid gallon
8 liquid pints	= 1 liquid gallon
4 liquid quarts	= 1 liquid gallon
31 to 42 liquid gallons	= 1 barrel (liquid)
31.5 liquid gallons	= 1 barrel (some States)
	= 7 276.5 cubic inches
42 gallons	= 1 barrel (petroleum)
	= 9 702 cubic inches
2 barrels	= 1 hogshead (hhd)

relationship between capacity and volume

1 liquid (fluid) ounce	= 1.804 687 5 cubic inches
1 liquid gill	= 7.218 75 cubic inches
1 liquid pint	= 28.875 cubic inches
1 liquid quart	= 57.75 cubic inches

relationship between US and UK measures

The relationship between units in the US and UK systems are in general the same, but there are 4 liquid ounces to 1 gill in the US system compared with 5 fluid ounces to 1 gill in the United Kingdom; hence there are two groups of relationship for liquid measures compared with one for dry measures; one group is for units of the ounce and smaller sizes, and one for units larger than the ounce. These relationships, as shown below, are not exact:

up to liquid ounce:
1 US minim, liquid dram or liquid ounce
= 1.040 842 731 UK minims, fluid drachms, or fluid ounces
1 UK minim, fluid drachm or fluid ounce
= 0.960 759 94 US minim, liquid dram or liquid ounce
from up:
1 US gill, liquid pint, liquid quart or liquid gallon
= 0.832 674 185 UK gill, pint, quart or gallon
1 UK gill, pint, quart or gallon
= 1.200 949 926 US gills, liquid pints, liquid quarts or liquid gallons

Weight (mass)

The US avoirdupois pound is defined by reference to the kilogram, the exact relationship being, as for the United Kingdom, 1 pound = 0.453 592 37 kilogram. The avoirdupois ounce and the dram are also identical, but the stone and the quarter are not legal measures in the United States. The main US ton is the short ton of 2 000 lb and unless otherwise qualified it means this; the long or 'gross' ton of 2 240 lb is little used.

100 pounds	= 1 short hundredweight
32 000 ounces	= 1 short ton
2 000 pounds	= 1 short ton
20 short hundredweights	= 1 short ton

The troy pound is defined as 5 760 grains and is legal in the United States.

Force, pressure and stress

1 000 pounds-force (lbf) = 1 kip
1 000 pounds-force per square inch (lbf/in² or psi) = 1 kip per square inch (ksi)

Systems of measurement: other countries

In this section countries with systems or units other than those of the metric, United Kingdom and United States systems are listed by alphabetical order of country. Included also for some countries are systems and units which are no longer in use; these can be of help for historical work, or as a guide to values of units used in other countries which still use similar old units.

Some of the measures, especially ancient and old units, vary or varied by region or trade, in which case, as far as possible, the most usual values have been shown. Equivalents are given of units in the UK (imperial) and metric (SI) systems. It may be noted that all countries of the world (including those not using special units and so not included here) are using mainly the metric system or are planning to change to it—with the present exceptions of Brunei, Burma and South Yemen.

Afghanistan

Main system: metric

Other units (Kabul system):

Length

		UK units	Metric units
	1 gereh gazi sha	2.625 in	6.667 5 cm
	1 gazi jerib	29 in	73.66 cm
	1 gazi memar	32 in	81.28 cm
16 gereh gazi sha	= 1 gazi sha	42 in	1.066 8 m
3 gazi jerib	= 1 side of a beswasa	2.417 yd	2.210 m
60 gazi jerib	= 1 side of a jerib	48.34 yd	44.2 m

Area

		UK units	Metric units
	1 gazi jerib²	841 in²	0.542 6 m²
9 gazi jerib²	= 1 beswasa	5.84 yd²	4.884 m²
20 beswasa	= 1 beswa	116.8 yd²	97.68 m²
20 beswa	= 1 jerib	2 336.5 yd²	1 953.6 m²
40 jeribs	= 1 kulba	19.31 acre	7.814 ha

Weight

		UK units	Metric units
	1 nakhod	2.96 gr	191.8 mg
24 nakhod	= 1 misqal	71.04 gr	4.600 3 g
24 misqal	= 1 khord	3.894 oz	110.406 g
4 khord	= 1 pow	0.974 lb	441.625 g
4 pow	= 1 charak	3.894 lb	1.776 5 kg
4 charak	= 1 seer (Kabul)	15.58 lb	7.066 kg
5 seer	= 1 maund	77.9 lb	35.33 kg
16 maund	= 1 kharwar	1 246.2 lb	565.280 kg

Antigua

Main system: United Kingdom units

Other units in use:

Length

		UK units	Metric units
	1 node	4½ in	11.4 cm
2 nodes	= 1 sett	9 in	22.9 cm

Argentina

Main system: metric, compulsory from 1887 (SI metric from 1972)

Old units:

Length

		UK units	Metric units
	1 pulgada	0.948 in	2.41 cm
12 pulgadas	= 1 pié	0.948 ft	28.89 cm
3 piés	= 1 vara	34.12 in	86.67 cm
2 varas	= 1 braza	1.895 yd	1.733 m
75 brazas	= 1 cuadra	142.2 yd	130.0 m
3 000 brazas	= 1 legua	3.23 mi	5.20 km

Capacity: dry

		UK units	Metric units
	1 cuartilla	0.943 bu	34.3 l
4 cuartillas	= 1 fanega	3.77 bu	1.371 98 hl
7½ fanegas	= 1 tonelada	28.29 bu	1.029 m³
2 toneladas	= 1 lastre	56.59 bu	2.058 m³

Capacity: liquid

		UK units	Metric units
	1 octava	5.22 fl oz	148 ml
4 octavos	= 1 cuarta	1.045 pt	0.594 l
4 cuartas	= 1 frasco	0.522 gal	2.375 l
16 frascos	= 1 galon	8.36 gal	38 l
2 galons	= 1 barril	16.7 gal	76 l
1½ barrils	= 1 cuarter	25 gal	114 l
4 cuarters	= 1 pipa	100 gal	456 l

Weight

		UK units	Metric units
	1 grano	0.769 gr	0.05 g
36 granos	= 1 adarme	1.0128 dr	1.79 g
16 adarmes	= 1 onza	1.0128 oz	28.71 g
16 onzas	= 1 libra	1.0128 lb	459.4 g
25 libras	= 1 arroba	25.32 lb	11.48 kg
100 libras	= 1 quintal	101.28 lb	45.94 kg
20 quintals	= 1 tonelada	0.904 ton	0.919 t

Austria

Main system: metric, compulsory from 1871

Old units:

Lenght

		UK units	Metric units
12 zolls	1 zoll [a]	1.037 in	2.634 cm
6 fusz	= 1 fusz	1.037 ft	31.608 cm
4 000 klafter	= 1 klafter	1.037 fathom	1.896 m
	= 1 mile [b]	4.714 mi	7.586 km

Area

		UK units	Metric units
	1 joch [c]	1.422 acre	0.575 5 ha

Capacity

		UK units	Metric units
	1 seidel (beer) [c]	0.62 pt	0.353 6 l
	1 metze	13.5 gal	61.5 l

Volume

		UK units	Metric units
	1 ertragsfestmeter (efm) [c, d]	1.308 yd³	1 m³
	1 raummeter (rm) [c,e]	1.308 yd³	1 m³
	1 klafter ³	8.921 yd³	6.821 m³

Weight
old system

		UK units	Metric units
	1 ducat (Vienna)	53.873 gr	3.491 g
	1 loth [f]	9.52 oz	270.1 g
	1 marc	9.02 oz tr	280.6 g
2 marcs	= 1 pfund	1.237 lb	561 g

customs or zoll system (1871 law; metric linked)

		UK units	Metric units
	1 pfund [a]	1.102 lb	500 g
100 /funds	= 1 zentner	110.23 lb	50 kg
2 zentners	= 1 meterzentner [c]	220.46 lb	100 kg

[a] Or zollpfund.   [b] Postal.   [c] Still in use.   [d] For solid wood.   [e] For piled wood.
[f] Postal value: 257.2 g (9.07 oz).

Bahrain

Main system: metric, as conversion from UK system from 1978

Other units:

Length		Equivalent in: UK units	Metric units
	1 dhara	19 in	48.26 cm
Weight			
	1 grain	1 gr	64.8 mg
180 grains	= 1 tola	180 gr	11.66 g
38.89 tolas	= 1 ratl	1 lb	0.454 kg
4 ratls	= 1 ruba	4 lb	1.814 kg
14 rubas	= 1 maund	56 lb	25.40 kg
10 maunds	= 1 rafa	560 lb	254.01 kg

Bangladesh

Main system: UK units, with planned conversion to the metric system

Other units in use:

Length		Equivalent in: UK units	Metric units
	1 gira	2.25 in	5.715 cm
8 giras	= 1 hath	18 in	0.457 2 m
16 giras	= 1 gāz	1 yd	0.914 4 m
1 760 gāz	= 1 mile	1 mi	1.609 km
2 miles	= 1 crosh	2 mi	3.218 km
Area			
	1 katha	80⅔ yd²	67.4 m²
20 kathas	= 1 bigha	⅓ acre	0.135 ha
3 bighas	= 1 acre	1 acre	0.404 7 ha
Weight *general*			
	1 siki	45 gr	2.916 g
4 sikis	= 1 tola	180 gr	11.664 g
5 sikis	= 1 kanchha[a]	225 gr	14.580 g
5 tolas	= 1 chhatak (ch)	2.057 oz	58.319 g
4 chhataks	= 1 powa	0.514 lb	233.28 g
4 powas	= 1 seer[b] (sr)	2.057 lb	0.933 1 kg
5 seers	= 1 pushuri	10.29 lb	4.666 kg
40 seers	= 1 mon[c]	82.286 lb	37.324 kg
precious metals			
	1 dhan	0.468 75 gr	30.4 mg
4 dhans	= 1 rati	1.875 gr	121.5 mg
6 ratis	= 1 anna	11.25 gr	729.0 mg
8 ratis	= 1 masha	15 gr	972.0 mg
12 mashas	= 1 bhari[d]	180 gr	11.664 g
80 bharis	= 1 seer	2½ lb tr	0.933 1 kg

[a]Or powa chhatak. [b]Or sēr. [c]Or maund. [d]Or tóla.

Belgium

Main system: SI metric, first established as metric in 1816

Old units:

Length *medieval system*		Equivalent in: UK units	Metric units
	1 pouce	1.322 in	3.358 cm
10 pouces	= 1 pied	1.102 ft	33.58 cm
6 pieds	= 1 toise	1.102 fathom	2.015 m
1 000 toises	= 1 mille	1.252 mi	2.015 km
metric linked system			
	1 pouce	1.181 in	3 cm
10 pouces	= 1 pied	0.984 1 ft	30 cm
4 pieds	= 1 aune	1.312 yd	1.2 m

Capacity, dry[a]		Equivalent in: UK units	Metric units
	1 pot	1.320 qt	1½ l
10 pots	= 1 boisseau	0.412 bu	15 l
Capacity, liquid[a]			
	1 pot	0.880 pt	½ l
Weight[a]			
	1 livre	2.205 lb	1 kg

[a] Metric linked units

Belize

Main system: United Kingdom units; it is planned to introduce the metric system.

Other units in use (mainly in rural areas):

Area		Equivalent in: UK units	Metric units
	1 mecate[a]	0.129 acre	5.22 a
16 mecates	= 1 manzana	2.064 acre	0.835 ha
Capacity			
	1 quartia	2½ qt	2.841 l
2 quartias	= 1 almud	5 qt	5.683 l
3 almuds	= 1 benequen	15 qt	17.048 l
4 almuds	= 1 shushack	5 gal	22.73 l
12 almuds	= 1 cargo	15 gal	68.19 l
22 almuds	= 1 barrel	27½ gal	125.02 l
Weight			
	1 arroba[b]	25 lb	11.34 kg
4 arrobas	= 1 quintal	100 lb	45.36 kg
2 quintals	= 1 cargo[c]	200 lb	90.72 kg

[a]Or task. [b]Or block of chicle. [c]Or standard mule load.

Bolivia

Main system: metric, compulsory from 1893; also US units

Old units:

Length		Equivalent in: UK units	Metric units
	1 pulgada	0.947 in	2.406 cm
12 pulgadas	= 1 pie	0.947 ft	0.289 m
3 pies	= 1 vara	0.947 yd	0.866 m
Capacity			
	1 galon	0.74 gal	3.36 l
	1 arroba (dry)	6.70 gal	30.46 l
Weight			
	1 marco	0.507 lb	230 g
2 marcos	= 1 libra[a]	1.014 lb	460.0 g
25 libras	= 1 arroba	25.35 lb	11.50 kg
100 libras	= 1 quintal	101.4 lb	46.0 kg
2 quintals	= 1 fanega	202.8 lb	92 kg
10 fanegas	= 1 tonelada	0.905 ton	0.920 t

[a]Or arratel

Botswana

Main system: metric (SI), as conversion from UK system beginning 1969, generally complete from 1973.

Old units[a]:

		Equivalent in: UK units	Metric units
Length	1 Cape foot	1.033 ft	0.314 9 m
Area	1 morgen	2.116 54 acre	0.857 ha

[a] Discontinued from 1971.

Brazil

Main system: metric, compulsory from 1862

Old units:

		Equivalent in: UK units	Metric units
Length	1 palmo	8.75 in	22.22 cm
5 palmos	= 1 vara	3.645 ft	1.111 m
2 varas	= 1 braca	7.290 ft	2.222 m
Area	1 alqueiro: Sao Paulo	6 acres	2.43 ha
	1 alqueiro: Rio de Janeiro	12 acres	4.86 ha
Capacity	1 garrafa	1.171 pt	666 ml
48 garrafas	= 1 almud	7.028 gal	31.95 l
	1 alqueire	1 bushel	36.37 l
Weight	1 oitava	55.34 gr	3.586 mg
128 oitava	= 1 libra	1.012 lb	459 g
32 libras	= 1 arroba	32.385 lb	14.69 kg
4 arrobas	= 1 quintal	129.539 lb	58.75 kg
54 arrobas	= 1 tonelada	0.781 ton	0.793 t

Brunei

Main system: United Kingdom and metric systems

Other units in use:

		Equivalent in: UK units	Metric units
Length	1 ela	1 yd	0.914 4 m
Capacity	1 pau	$\frac{1}{2}$ pt	284 ml
4 paus	= 1 chupak	1 qt	1.137 l
4 chupaks	= 1 gantang[a]	1 gal	4.546 l
Weight	1 kupang[b]	0.583 gr	37.8 mg
10 kupangs[b]	= 1 chuchok[b, c]	5.833 3 gr	378 mg
10 chuchoks[b]	= 1 mas[b, d]	58$\frac{1}{3}$ gr	3.780 g
10 mas[b]	= 1 tahil	1$\frac{1}{3}$ oz	37.8 g
16 tahils	= 1 kati	1$\frac{1}{3}$ lb	0.605 kg
4 katis	= 1 gantang (paddy)	5$\frac{1}{3}$ lb	2.419 kg
6 katis	= 1 gantang (rice)	8 lb	3.629 kg
100 katis	= 1 pikul[e]	133$\frac{1}{3}$ lb	60.479 kg
300 katis	= 1 bhara	400 lb	181.437 kg
40 pikuls	= 1 koyan	5 333$\frac{1}{3}$ lb	2.419 t

[a] 1 gantang of rice weighs about 8 lb.　[b] For gold.　[c] Or hoon.　[d] Or chee.　[e] Or picul.

Bulgaria

Main system: metric

Other units in use:

		Equivalent in: UK units	Metric units
Capacity	1 oke	2.25 pt	1.28 l
	1 vedro	2.20 gal	10 l
2 vedros	= 1 krina	4.40 gal	20 l
Weight	1 untzia	1.058 oz	30 g
	1 oke	2.829 lb	1.282 kg
100 okes	= 1 tovar	282.85 lb	128.2 kg

Burma

Main system: United Kingdom units and, from 1920, metric units

Other units in use:

		Equivalent in: UK units	Metric units
Length	1 palgat	1 in	2.54 cm
18 palgats	= 1 taung[a]	18 in	45.72 cm
22 palgats	= 1 sandong	22 in	55.88 cm
4 taungs[d]	= 1 lan	6 ft	1.829 m
7 taungs[d]	= 1 tar[b]	10$\frac{1}{2}$ ft	3.200 m
20 tars	= 1 oke thapa	210 ft	64.008 m
7 000 sandongs	= 1 taing[c]	2.431 mi	3.912 km
11 200 taungs	= 1 kawtha	3.182 mi	5.121 km
80 oke thapas	= 1 kawtha	3.182 mi	5.121 km
4 kawthas	= 1 garwoke	12.727 mi	20.483 km
	1 yuzanar	47.121 mi	75.834 km
Capacity, dry	1 lame[e]	11$\frac{1}{4}$ fl oz	320 ml
2 lames	= 1 sale	1$\frac{1}{8}$ pt	639 ml
2 sales	= 1 khwet	1$\frac{1}{8}$ pt	1.279 l
2 khwets	= 1 pyi	2$\frac{1}{4}$ qt	2.557 l
2 pyis	= 1 sayut	4$\frac{1}{2}$ qt	5.114 l
2 sayuts	= 1 seik	1$\frac{1}{8}$ peck	10.229 l
2 seiks	= 1 khwe	2$\frac{1}{4}$ peck	20.457 l
2 khwes	= 1 thamardi tin[f]	1$\frac{1}{8}$ bu	40.915 l
3 thamardi tins	= 1 bag	3$\frac{3}{8}$ bu	1.227 hl
Capacity, liquid	1 lamany	$\frac{1}{2}$ pt	63 ml
2 lamanys	= 1 zalay	$\frac{9}{4}$ qt	126 ml
4 zalays	= 1 byee	$\frac{4}{9}$ qt	0.505 l
2 byees	= 1 zayoot	$\frac{8}{9}$ qt	1.010 l
2 zayoots	= 1 seik	1$\frac{7}{9}$ qt	2.020 l
2 seiks	= 1 kwai	$\frac{8}{9}$ gal	4.041 l
Weight	1 ywegale[g]	3$\frac{15}{16}$ gr	255 mg
2 ywegales	= 1 ywegyi	7$\frac{7}{8}$ gr	0.510 g
2 ywegyis	= 1 pai	15$\frac{3}{4}$ gr	1.021 g
2 pais	= 1 moo	31$\frac{1}{2}$ gr	2.041 g
2 moos	= 1 mat	0.144 oz	4.082 g
2 mats	= 1 ngamu	0.288 oz	8.165 g
2 ngamus	= 1 tical[h]	0.576 oz	16.33 g
12$\frac{1}{2}$ ticals	= 1 abucco	0.450 lb	204 g
33$\frac{1}{3}$ ticals	= 1 kati	1.2 lb	544 g
3 katis	= 1 viss[i]	3.6 lb	1.633 kg
	1 pyi[j]	4.688 lb	2.126 kg
100 viss	= 1 acheintaya	360 lb	163.29 kg
5 000 viss	= 1 kandy	18 000 lb	8.165 t

[a] Or taim or cubic or covid.　[b] Or dha or bamboo.　[c] Or dain.　[d] Also used with 4 sandongs = 1 lan = 7$\frac{1}{2}$ ft and 7 sandongs = 1 tar = 12$\frac{5}{6}$ ft.　[e] Or nozibu.　[f] Or teng or basket.　[g] Or ruay.　[h] Or tikal or kyat or baht; also used as 0.543 oz (15.39 g), other units varying accordingly.　[i] Or vis or peiktha; old value was 3.65 lb.　[j] For rice.

Cambodia

Main system: metric

Old units:

Length

		Equivalent in: UK units	Metric units
	1 annuk	0.059 milli-in	0.001 51 mm
12 annuks	= 1 pong chay	0.712 milli-in	0.018 1 mm
12 pong chays	= 1 khluon chay	8.54 milli-in	0.217 mm
12 khluon chays	= 1 krâp sran	0.103 in	2.604 mm
8 krâp srans	= 1 thneap	0.820 in	2.083 cm
12 thneaps	= 1 cham am	9.843 in	25 cm
2 cham ams	= 1 hat	19.685 in	50 cm
4 hats	= 1 phyéam	6.562 ft	2 m
20 phyéams	= 1 sen	131.2 ft	40 m
400 sens	= 1 yoch	9.942 mi	16 km

Volume

		Equivalent in: UK units	Metric units
	1 phlan[d]	3.531 ft³	0.1 m³
	1 kavan	5.368 ft³	0.152 m³

Capacity, dry

		Equivalent in: UK units	Metric units
	1 katang	1.65 gal	7½ l[b]
2 katang	= 1 tao	3.30 gal	15 l[b]
2 taos	= 1 thang	6.60 gal	30 l[b]

Weight

		Equivalent in: UK units	Metric units
	1 li[c]	0.579 gr	37.5 mg
10 lis	= 1 hun	5.787 gr	0.375 g
10 huns	= 1 chi	57.87 gr	3.75 g
10 chis	= 1 damleng[e]	1.323 oz	37.5 g
16 damlengs	= 1 néal[f]	1.323 lb	600 g
50 néals	= 1 chong	66.139 lb	30 kg
100 néals	= 1 hap[g]	1.181 cwt	60 kg

[a]Or chevron. [b]Also weight in number of kilograms for rice. [c]Or lin.
[d]Or chin. [e]Or taël. [f]Or livre. [g]Or picul.

Canada

Main system: SI metric, as conversion from United Kingdom units, beginning in general 1973 with 55% conversion implemented by early 1980, and completion planned for end 1981.

Old units:

Length
Quebec units

		Equivalent in: UK units	Metric units
	1 Paris foot[b, c]	12.789 in	0.324 84 m
18 Paris feet	= 1 perch[c]	19.18 ft	5.847 m
180 Paris feet	= 1 arpent[c]	191.8 ft	58.47 m

other

	1 vara	33⅓ in	0.847 m

Area
Quebec units

		Equivalent in: UK units	Metric units
	1 sq Paris foot	1.136 ft²	0.1055 m²
324 sq Paris feet	= 1 perch[c]	368.0 ft²	34.189 m²
100 perches	= 1 arpent[c]	0.845 acre	0.342 ha

other

	1 vara²	7.716 ft²	0.717 m²
1 000 vara²	= 1 labor	0.177 acre	716.8 m²
	1 caballeria	108 acres	43.7 ha
	1 section	1 mi²	2.590 km²

Capacity

	1 minot	1.07 bu	38.91 hl

Weight

	1 hundredweight[a, c]	100 lb	45.359 kg
20 hundredweights	= 1 ton	2 000 lb	0.907 18 t

[a]Or cental. [b]Pied. [c]Legal for use in trade.

Cape Verde

Main system: metric

Other units in use:

Length

		Equivalent in: UK units	Metric units
	1 pé	1 ft	0.304 8 m
	1 jarda	0.96 yd	0.88 m
2½ jardas	= 1 braça²	2.41 yd	2.2 m
2 braças	= 1 lança	4.81 yd	4.4 m
10 braças	= 1 linhada	24.1 yd	22 m

Area

		Equivalent in: UK units	Metric units
	1 vara	1.45 yd²	1.21 m²
	1 braça²	5.79 yd²	4.84 m²
4 braça²	= 1 lança²	23.15 yd²	19.36 m²
60 lança²	= 1 onça	0.287 acre	1 161.6 m²
112½ lança²	= 1 casel	0.538 acre	2 178 m²
4 onças	= 1 quarta	1.148 acre	0.464 64 ha
4 quartas	= 1 alqueres	4.593 acre	1.858 56 ha

Capacity, dry

		Equivalent in: UK units	Metric units
	1 quarta	2.287 gal	10.398 l
4 quartas	= 1 alqueire	1.144 bu	41.593 l
3 alqueires	= 1 barrica	3.431 bu	1.247 79 hl
20 barricas	= 1 moio	68.619 bu	24.955 8 hl

Capacity, liquid

		Equivalent in: UK units	Metric units
	1 garrafa	1.23 pt	0.7 l
1½ garrafas	= 1 folha	1.85 pt	1.05 l
2 garrafas	= 1 canada	1.23 qt	1.4 l
3½ garrafas	= 1 frasco	2.16 qt	2.45 l
1½ frascos	= 1 galão	3.26 qt	3.7 l

Weight

	1 libra[a]	1.012 lb	459 g
3 libras	= 1 pedra	3.036 lb	1.377 kg

[a]Or arratel.

Chile

Main system: metric from 1848 (SI metric from 1971)

Other units in use:

Length

		Equivalent in: UK units	Metric units
	1 linea	0.076 in	1.93 mm
	1 vara	32.91 in	83.59 cm
2 varas	= 1 braza	1.828 yd	1.672 m
75 brazas	= 1 cuadra	137.12 yd	125.39 m
36 cuadras	= 1 legua	2.805 mi	4.513 86 km

Area

	1 cuadra²	3.886 acre	1.572 ha

Volume

	1 pulgada maderera	1 440 in³	23.597 dm³

Capacity

	1 pinta	0.985 pt	0.56 l
	1 galón	3.995 qt	4.54 l
	1 almud (cereals)	7.109 qt	8.08 l
	1 arroba (North)	31.24 qt	35.5 l
	1 arroba (Centre)	35.2 qt	40 l
	1 fanega	2.67 bu	96.99 l

Weight

		Equivalent in: UK units	Metric units
	1 grano	1 gr	64.80 mg
	1 onza	1.014 oz	28.75 g
16 onzas	= 1 libra	1.014 lb	460 g
25 libras	= 1 arroba	25.35 lb	11.5 kg
4 arrobas	= 1 quintal	101.4 lb	46 kg

China

Main system: metric, compulsory from 1929.

Old units[a]:

Length
treaty system[b]

		Equivalent in: UK units	Metric units
	1 hao	0.001 41 in	35.814 μm
10 haos	= 1 li˘	0.014 1 in	0.358 1 mm
10 li's	= 1 fun[c]	0.141 in	3.581 4 mm
10 funs	= 1 ts'un[d]	1.41 in	3.581 4 cm
10 ts'uns	= 1 chih[e]	1.175 ft	35.814 cm
5 chihs	= 1 pu	5.875 ft	1.790 7 m
56 ts'uns	= 1 kung	6.58 ft	2.006 m
2 pus	= 1 zhang[f]	3.917 yd	3.581 4 m
10 zhangs	= 1 ying[g]	39.17 yd	35.814 m
18 yings	= 1 li˘	0.400 6 mi	0.645 km
250 lis˘	= 1 tu	100.142 mi	161.2 km

metric linked system[h]

	1 hao	0.001 31 in	$33\frac{1}{3}$ μm
10 haos	= 1 li˘	0.013 12 in	$\frac{1}{3}$ mm
10 li's	= 1 fun[c]	0.131 2 in	$3\frac{1}{3}$ mm
10 funs	= 1 ts'un[d]	1.312 3 in	$3\frac{1}{3}$ cm
10 ts'uns	= 1 chih[e]	1.093 6 ft	$\frac{1}{3}$ m
10 chihs	= 1 zhang[f]	3.645 yd	$3\frac{1}{3}$ m
10 zhangs	= 1 ying[g]	36.454 yd	$33\frac{1}{3}$ m
15 yins	= 1 li˘	546.8 yd	0.5 km

metric units

	1 wei mi	39.37 μin	1 μm
10 wei mis	= 1 hu mi	0.393 7 milli-in	10 μm
10 hu mis	= 1 si mi	3.937 milli-in	0.1 mm
10 si mis	= 1 hao mi	0.039 37 in	1 mm
10 hao mis	= 1 li' mi	0.393 7 in	1 cm
10 li' mis	= 1 fen mi	3.937 in	10 cm
10 fen mis	= 1 mi	1.094 yd	1 m
10 mis	= 1 shi' mi	10.936 yd	10 m
10 shi' mis	= 1 bei mi	109.4 yd	100 m
10 bei mis	= 1 gong li˘	0.621 mi	1 km

Area[i]
old system

	1 ching	121 ft²	11.241 m²
15 chings	= 1 chüo	1 815 ft²	168.62 m²
60 chings	= 1 mou[j]	$\frac{1}{6}$ acre	0.067 ha
10 mous	= 1 ch'ing[k]	$1\frac{2}{3}$ acre	0.674 ha

metric linked system[h]

	1 hao	0.797 yd²	$\frac{2}{3}$ m²
10 haos	= 1 li˘	7.973 yd²	$6\frac{2}{3}$ m²
10 li's	= 1 fen	79.733 yd²	$66\frac{2}{3}$ m²
10 fens	= 1 mu	0.164 7 acre	$6\frac{2}{3}$ a
100 mus	= 1 qing	16.474 acre	$6\frac{2}{3}$ ha

metric units

	1 gong li'[l]	1.196 yd²	1 m²
100 gong li's	= 1 gong mu	119.6 yd²	1 a
100 gong mus	= 1 gong qing	2.471 acre	1 ha
100 gong qings	= 1 fan gong li˘	247.1 acre	1 km²

Capacity[m]
old system

		Equivalent in: UK units	Metric units
	1 sho	0.364 4 fl oz	10.355 ml
10 shos	= 1 ko	0.182 2 pt	103.547 ml
10 kos	= 1 sheng	1.822 pt	1.035 l
10 shengs	= 1 tau	2.278 gal	10.354 71 l
5 taus	= 1 hu	11.39 gal	51.773 l
10 taus	= 1 tan	22.777 gal	1.035 5 hl

metric units[n]

	1 hao sheng (cuo)	16.894 minim	1 ml
10 hao shengs	= 1 li' sheng (shao)	0.352 fl oz	1 cl
10 li' shengs	= 1 fan sheng (he)	3.519 5 fl oz	10 cl
10 fan shengs	= 1 sheng (sheng)	1.759 8 pt	1 l
10 shengs	= 1 shi' sheng (dou[o])	2.199 7 gal	10 l
10 shi' shengs	= 1 bei sheng (dan)	2.749 6 bu	1 hl
10 bei shengs	= 1 gian sheng	27.496 bu	1 kl

Weight
treaty system[b]

	1 hu	0.000 58 gr	37.8 μg
10 hus	= 1 ssu[v]	0.005 8 gr	0.378 mg
10 ssus	= 1 hao	0.058 3 gr	3.78 mg
10 haos	= 1 li[p]	0.583 gr	37.799 mg
10 lis	= 1 fen[q]	$5\frac{5}{6}$ gr	377.99 mg
10 fens	= 1 ch'ien[r]	$58\frac{1}{3}$ gr	3.779 9 g
10 ch'iens	= 1 liang[s]	$1\frac{1}{3}$ oz	37.799 g
16 liangs	= 1 jin[t]	$1\frac{1}{3}$ lb	0.604 79 kg
100 jins	= 1 tan[u]	$133\frac{1}{3}$ lb	60.479 kg

metric linked system[h]

	1 ssu[v]	0.007 72 gr	0.5 mg
10 ssus	= 1 hao	0.077 16 gr	5 mg
10 haos	= 1 li[p]	0.771 6 gr	50 mg
10 li's	= 1 fen[q]	7.716 gr	0.5 g
10 fens	= 1 gián	0.176 4 oz	5 g
10 giáns	= 1 hang	1.764 oz	50 g
10 hangs	= 1 jin[t]	1.102 3 lb	0.5 kg
100 jin	= 1 tan[u]	110.23 lb	50 kg

metric units

	1 hao ke	0.015 43 gr	1 mg
10 hao ke's	= 1 li' ke'	0.154 32 gr	10 mg
10 li' ke's	= 1 fen ke'	1.543 2 gr	100 mg
10 fen ke's	= 1 ke'	15.432 gr	1 g
10 ke's	= 1 shi' ke'	0.352 74 oz	10 g
10 shi' ke's	= 1 bei ke'	3.527 4 oz	100 g
10 bei ke's	= 1 jin	2.204 6 lb	1 kg
100 jins	= 1 dan	220.46 lb	100 kg
10 dans	= 1 dun	0.984 2 ton	1 t

[a] Old spelling is used. [b] Standard 'treaty' or 'customs' values as agreed by treaty 1842–44 and 1858–60; identified sometimes by use of the term kung (official). Previous values varied by region; one common value was based on 1 chih = 1.05 ft (32 cm). [c] Or fen. [d] Or cun or Chinese inch. [e] Or ch'ih or cheh or che or Chinese foot; originally varied from 9 to 16 inches ($\frac{3}{4}$ to $1\frac{1}{3}$ ft). [f] Or chang. [g] Or yin. [h] Or 'market' system; established 1929 as a transitional system for use in the market, to accustom people to the use of the metric system. Units are identified by use of the term 'shih'; for example, shih chih is a market chih (equal to one-third of a metre). [i] General square measures are indicated by 'fan'; for example, 1 fan zhang = 1 zhang², 1 fan mi = 1 mi² = 1 m². [j] Or mu or man or mow or maw; values varied: Shanghai mou = 0.152 acre (0.061 ha), treaty mou = 0.190 acre (0.077 ha). Before 221 BC values varied from 0.03 ha to 0.12 ha. [k] Or king. [l] Equal to 1 fan mi (mi²). [m] General volume measures are indicated by 'li' fan'; for example, 1 li' fan mi = 1 mi³ = 1 m³. [n] Metric linked ('market') names with the same values are shown in brackets. [o] Or tou. [p] Or le or cash. [q] Or fên or fan or candareen or condorine. [r] Or tsein or mace. [s] Or léang or tael or tahil. [t] Or chin or kin or catty; old values included 1.316 lb (0.597 kg) and 1.579 lb (0.716 kg). [u] Or dan or picul or pecul. [v] Or si.

Colombia

Main system: metric, introduced from 1854; also some US units, including inch (pulgada), square foot (pie cuadrado), US gallon (galón) and petroleum barrel

Other units in use:

Length

		Equivalent in: UK units	Metric units
	1 pulgada	0.98 in	2.5 cm
8 pulgadas	= 1 cuarta	7.874 in	20 cm
4 cuartas	= 1 vara[a]	31.50 in	80 cm
4½ cuartas	= 1 yarda	35.43 in	90 cm
2 varas	= 1 braza	1.75 yd	1.6 m
100 varas	= 1 cuadra	87.49 yd	80 m
6 250 varas	= 1 legua	3.107 mi	5 km

Area

		Equivalent in: UK units	Metric units
	1 vara²	0.77 yd²	0.64 m²
1 cuadra²	= 1 fanegada	1.58 acre	0.64 ha

Capacity

		Equivalent in: UK units	Metric units
	1 azumbre	3.555 pt	2.02 l
	1 celemin	1.017 gal	4.625 l
12 celemines	= 1 fanega	12.21 gal	55.5 l

Weight

		Equivalent in: UK units	Metric units
	1 quilate	0.31 gr	20 mg
1 562½ quilates	= 1 onza	1.102 oz	31.25 g
16 onzas	= 1 libra	1.102 lb	500 g
25 libras	= 1 arroba	27.56 lb	12.5 kg
4 arrobas	= 1 quintal	110.2 lb	50 kg
1¼ quintals	= 1 saco de cafe	137.8 lb	62.5 kg
2 sacos	= 1 carga	275.6 lb	125 kg
8 cargas	= 1 tonelada	0.984 ton	1 t

[a] Or vara granadina.

Costa Rica

Main system: metric

Old units (those no longer in use are marked with an asterisk *):

Length

		Equivalent in: UK units	Metric units
	1 cuarta[a]	8.23 in	20.9 cm
	1 tercia*[b]	0.914 3 ft	27.87 cm
4 cuartas	= 1 vara*	0.914 3 yd	83.6 cm
3 tercias*	= 1 vara*	0.914 3 yd	83.6 cm
2 varas*	= 1 braza[c]	0.914 3 fathom	1.672 m
24 varas*	= 1 mecate*	21.94 yd	20.064 m

Area

		Equivalent in: UK units	Metric units
	1 vara²[d]	0.836 yd²	0.699 m²
1 250 vara²	= 1 solar*	1 044.84 yd²	873.62 m²
8 solars*	= 1 manzana[e]	1.727 acre	0.699 ha
64¾ manzanas	= 1 caballería*	111.82 acre	45.254 ha

Capacity

		Equivalent in: UK units	Metric units
	1 botella[f]	1.2 pt	67 cl
	1 cuartillo[g]	0.935 gal	4.25 l
4 cuartillos	= 1 cajuela[g]	3.74 gal	17 l
20 cajuelas	= 1 fanega (coffee)[h]	74.79 gal	340 l
24 cajuelas	= 1 fanega (other)[i]	89.75 gal	408 l

Weight

		Equivalent in: UK units	Metric units
	1 lata*	0.999 lb	453.1 g
	1 libra[j]	1.014 lb	460 g
2¼ libras	= 1 atado[k]	2.282 lb	1.035 kg
2 atados	= 1 tamuga[k]	4.564 lb	2.07 kg
25 libras	= 1 arroba[i]	25.35 lb	11.5 kg
4 arrobas	= 1 quintal[i]	101.4 lb	46 kg
125 libras (approx)	= 1 fardo de tabaco	127.0 lb	57.6 kg
	1 saco de café[l]	152.1 lb	69 kg
2 quintals	= 1 fanega*[m]	202.8 lb	92 kg
350 libras	= 1 carga*	354.9 lb	161 kg
1 800 libras	= 1 carga de papa*	1 825 lb	828 kg
2 000 libras	= 1 tonelada[n]	0.905 ton	0.920 t

[a] Only for wood. [b] Or pie. [c] Used by fishermen. [d] Is being replaced by the square metre. [e] Is being replaced by the hectare. [f] For milk only; is being replaced by the litre. Botella for wine and liquor varies between 70–75 cl (1.23–1.32 pt). [g] Is being replaced by the kilogram, except for fresh coffee berries. [h] For fresh coffee berries only. [i] For dry grains (eg maize), beans and fresh potatoes etc; is being replaced by the kilogram. [j] Mainly replaced by the kilogram. [k] Only for trading sugar cane juice that has been solidified by evaporation. [l] For exporting coffee beans. [m] Fanega de maize was 348.4 kg. [n] Is being replaced by the metric ton.

Cuba

Main system: metric, officially compulsory from 1858. Also used are units of UK and US systems, including inch (pulgada), foot (pie), pint, gallon, pound (libra) and ton (tonelada); and units of the original Spanish system (see Spain)

Other units in use (Cuban system):

Length

		Equivalent in: UK units	Metric units
	1 pulgada	0.927 in	2.356 cm
12 pulgadas	= 1 pie	0.927 ft	28.267 cm
3 pies	= 1 vara	0.927 yd	0.848 m
24 varas	= 1 cordel	22.26 yd	20.352 m
60 varas	= 1 side of a besana	55.64 yd	50.88 m
5 000 varas	= 1 legua	2.635 mi	4.24 km

Area

		Equivalent in: UK units	Metric units
	1 vara²	0.860 yd²	0.719 m²
576 vara²	= 1 cordel²	495.38 yd²	414.204 m²
6¼ cordel²	= 1 besana[a]	3 096.15 yd²	2 588.77 m²
18 cordel²	= 1 roza[b]	1.842 acre	0.746 ha
324 cordel²	= 1 caballería	33.162 acre	13.420 ha

Volume

		Equivalent in: UK units	Metric units
	1 taza	0.415 pt	236 ml
	1 botella	1.276 pt	725 ml
	1 cuartillo	1.513 pt	860 ml
3 botellas	= 1 frasco	3.827 pt	2.175 l
	1 pie de madera[c]	4.153 pt	2.360 l
	1 arroba (liquid)	3.550 gal	16.14 l
25 botellas	= 1 garrafón	3.987 gal	18.126 l
10 frascos	= 1 caneca	4.785 gal	21.751 l
	1 fanega (dry)	1.55 bu	0.563 hl
	1 pipa	104.9 gal	4.769 hl
	1 bocoy	145.7 gal	6.624 hl

Weight

		Equivalent in: UK units	Metric units
	1 onza	1.014 3 oz	28.756 g
16 onzas	= 1 libra	1.014 3 lb	460.093 g
25 libras	= 1 arroba	25.358 lb	11.502 kg
4 arrobas	= 1 quintal	101.43 lb	46.009 kg
20 quintals	= 1 tonelada	0.906 ton	0.920 2 t

agricultural

		Equivalent in: UK units	Metric units
	1 saco (coffee)	198.42 lb	90 kg
250 libras	= 1 saco (sugar)	253.58 lb	115.023 kg

[a] Or mesana. [b] Or rosa; also used as 10 000 vara² = 0.719 ha (1.78 acre). [c] Or de tabla de taller.

Cyprus

Main system: metric and UK systems, with gradual conversion to completely metric

Old units (some of which are still in use):

Length

		Equivalent in: UK units	Metric units
	1 roupi*	3 in	7.62 cm
8 roupis*	= 1 pic[e]	2 ft	0.609 6 m

Area

		Equivalent in: UK units	Metric units
	1 evlek	400 yd²	334.5 m²
4 evleks	= 1 donum[a]	1 600 yd²	1 337.8 m²

Capacity

		Equivalent in: UK units	Metric units
	1 oke	1.12 qt	1.273 l
2½ okes	= 1 Cyprus litre	2.8 qt	3.182 l
4 okes	= 1 kartos*	1.12 gal	5.092 l
8 okes (approx)	= 1 kouza*	2.25 gal	10.229 l
(225 okes	= 28 kouza*)		
28½ okes (approx)	= 1 kilé*	8 gal	36.369 l
(1 000 okes	= 35 kilé*)		
16 kouzas*	= 1 load*[b]	36 gal	163.659 l
4½ kilés*	= 1 load*[b]	36 gal	163.659 l

Weight

		Equivalent in: UK units	Metric units
	1 dram	1.792 dr	3.175 g
400 drams	= 1 oke[c]	2.8 lb	1.270 kg
720 drams	= 1 Cyprus litre*	5.04 lb	2.286 kg
44 okes	= 1 cantar*[d]	123.2 lb	55.883 kg
180 okes	= 1 Aleppo cantar[d, f]	504 lb	228.611 kg

*Not widely used. [a]Or scala. [b]Or gomari. [c]40 okes = 1 UK hundredweight (112 lb). [d]Or kantar. [e]Mainly used for textiles. [f]Used for carobs.

Czechoslovakia

Main system: metric, compulsory from 1876

Old units:

Length

	Equivalent in: UK units	Metric units
1 loket: Prague	1.946 ft	0.593 m
Moravia	1.949 ft	0.594 m
Silesia	1.900 ft	0.579 m
1 latro	1.048 fathom	1.917 m

Area

	Equivalent in: UK units	Metric units
1 mira[a]	2 294 yd²	1 918 m²

Volume [b]

	Equivalent in: UK units	Metric units
1 merice	15.5 gal	70.5 l

Weight

	Equivalent in: UK units	Metric units
1 custom quintal[c]	110.23 lb	50 kg

[a]Also called merice. [b]One cubic metre is called a plnometer. [c]For hops.

Denmark

Main system: metric, compulsory from 1910

Old units (some of which are still in use):

Length

		Equivalent in: UK units	Metric units
	1 point	0.007 15 in	0.181 63 mm
12 points	= 1 linie	0.085 81 in	2.179 54 mm
12 linies	= 1 tomme	1.029 70 in	2.615 446 cm
12 tommes	= 1 fod	1.029 70 ft	31.385 cm
2 fods	= 1 alen	0.686 47 yd	0.627 707 m
3 alens	= 1 favn	1.029 70 fathom	1.883 121 m
6 alens	= 1 rode	0.749 rod	3.766 m
2 000 rodes	= 1 mil	4.680 mi	7.532 km

Area

		Equivalent in: UK units	Metric units
	1 alen²	0.471 239 yd²	0.394 016 m²
	1 album	68.722 yd²	57.461 m²
3 albums	= 1 fjerdingkar	206.2 yd²	172.382 m²
4 fjerdingkars	= 1 skæpper	824.7 yd²	689.528 m²
14 000 alen²	= 1 tønde land	1.363 acre	0.551 623 ha
8 skæppers	= 1 tønde land (td ld)	1.363 acre	0.551 623 ha

Volume

		Equivalent in: UK units	Metric units
	1 pægle	0.425 pt	241.53 ml
4 pægles	= 1 pot	1.700 13 pt	0.966 120 l
2¼ pots	= 1 ottingkar	3.825 pt	2.173 77 l
2 ottingkars	= 1 fjerdingkar	0.956 3 gal	4.347 54 l
8 pots	= 1 viertel	1.700 13 gal	7.728 96 l
4 fjerdingkars	= 1 skæpper	3.825 gal	17.390 l
40 pots	= 1 ankre	8.501 gal	38.645 l
112 pots	= 1 tønde sild	2.975 bu	1.082 05 hl
120 pots	= 1 tjære tønde	3.188 bu	1.159 34 hl
136 pots	= 1 tønde øl[b]	28.90 gal	1.313 92 hl
8 skæppers	= 1 tønde korn (td)[a]	3.825 bu	1.391 21 hl
176 pots	= 1 kul tønde	4.675 bu	1.700 37 hl
24 ankres	= 1 fad øl	204.0 gal	9.275 hl
	1 fod³	1.092 ft³	30.916 dm³
72 fod³	= 1 favn brænde	2.911 4 yd³	2.225 94 m³

Weight
medieval system

		Equivalent in: UK units	Metric units
	1 ort	14.184 gr	919 mg
16 orts	= 1 lod	0.519 oz	14.706 g
2 lods	= 1 unser	1.037 oz	29.412 g
8 unsers	= 1 mark	0.519 lb	235.294 g
2 marks	= 1 pfund	1.037 lb	470.588 g

metric linked system

		Equivalent in: UK units	Metric units
	1 ort	7.716 gr	500 mg
10 orts	= 1 kvint	2.822 dr	5 g
100 kvints	= 1 pund	1.102 3 lb	500 g
16 punds	= 1 lispund	17.637 lb	8 kg
100 punds	= 1 centner[c]	110.231 lb	50 kg

[a]Dry tønde. [b]Liquid tønde. [c]Or zentner.

Dominica

Main system: UK units, converting to the metric system

Other unit in use:

Capacity

	Equivalent in: UK units	Metric units
1 barrel (for limes)	26 gal	1.182 hl

Dominican Republic

Main system; metric, from 1913; UK system is also used

Other units in use:

		Equivalent in: UK units	Metric units
Length			
	1 vara	32.91 in	0.836 m
	1 ona	1.299 yd	1.188 m
Area			
	1 tarea	752.1 yd²	628.8 m²
	1 caró[a]	3.194 acre	1.293 ha
1 200 tareas	= 1 caballería	186.5 acre	75.46 ha
Capacity			
	1 galón	0.713 gal	3.240 1 l
	1 fanega	1.526 bu	55.501 l
	1 pipa	126 gal	5 728 hl
Weight			
	1 onza	1 oz	28.35 g
16 onzas	= 1 libra	1 lb	453.6 g
25 libras	= 1 arroba	25 lb	11.34 kg
100 libras	= 1 quintal	100 lb	45.36 kg
	1 saco[b]	165.35 lb	75 kg

[a]Or carreau.   [b]Of coffee.

Ecuador

Main system: metric, compulsory from 1865 (SI metric from 1974)

Old units:

		Equivalent in: UK units	Metric units
Length			
	1 cuarto[a]	8.268 in	21 cm
4 cuartos	= 1 vara	0.919 yd	84 cm
100 varas	= 1 cuadra	91.9 yd	84 m
1 666⅔ varas	= 1 milla	0.87 mi	1.4 km
(10 000 varas	= 6 millas)		
	1 legua	3.107 mi	5 km
Area			
	1 cantero	527.4 yd²	441 m²
4 canteros	= 1 solar	0.436 acre	1 764 m²
4 solars	= 1 cuadra²	1.744 acre	0.705 6 ha
16 cuadra²	= 1 caballeria	27.90 acre	11.289 6 ha
Capacity			
	1 balde[b]	2.20 gal	10 l
Weight			
	1 libra	1.014 lb	460 g
12½ libras	= 1 botija	12.68 lb	5.75 kg
25 libras	= 1 arroba	25.35 lb	11.5 kg
28 libras	= 1 almud	28.40 lb	12.88 kg
50 libras	= 1 cuartilla	50.71 lb	23 kg
80 libras	= 1 tercio	81.13 lb	36.8 kg
100 libras	= 1 media[c]	101.4 lb	46 kg
4 cuartillas	= 1 fanega[d]	202.8 lb	92 kg

[a]Or palmo.   [b]Of milk.   [c]Or quintal.   [d]Or mula.

Egypt

Main system: metric, official from 1951

Old units:

		Equivalent in: UK units	Metric units
Length *ancient system*[a]			
	1 theb[b]	0.736 in	1.87 cm
4 thebs	= 1 choryos[c]	2.95 in	7·49 cm
12 thebs	= 1 schibr[d]	8.84 in	22.5 cm
24 thebs	= 1 cubit[e]	17.7 in	44.9 cm
28 thebs	= 1 royal cubit[f]	20.6 in	52.4 cm
100 royal cubits	= 1 khet	57.3 yd	52.4 m
Alexandria system[g]			
	1 theb	0.89 in	2.2 cm
4 thebs	= 1 choryos	3.5 in	9 cm
4 choryos	= 1 t'ser[h]	14.2 in	36 cm
6 choryos	= 1 Mekyas cubit[i]	21.3 in	54 cm
other old units[j]			
	1 qirat[k]	0.034 in	0.87 mm
6 qirat	= 1 habba shair	0.206 in	5.22 mm
1 000/9 habba shair	= 1 diraa: textiles	22.9 in	58 cm
	1 diraa: building[l]	29.5 in	75 cm
	1 kassaba[m]	11.6 ft	3.55 m
Area *ancient system*[a]			
	1 royal cubit²	0.329 yd²	0.275 m²
100 royal cubit²	= 1 cubit of land	32.9 yd²	27.5 m²
10 000 royal cubit²	= 1 set[n]	0.68 acre	0.275 ha
other old units[j]			
	1 diraa mémari²	6.055 ft²	0.5625 m²
	1 sahm	8.722 yd²	7.293 m²
24 sahms	= 1 kirat	209.34 yd²	175.035 m²
24 kirats	= 1 feddân[o]	1.038 acre	0.420 ha
Capacity *ancient system*[a]			
	1 henu	0.53 pt	300 ml
16 henus	= 1 hekat[p]	1.1 gal	4.8 l
20 hekat	= 1 khar[q]	2.62 bu	0.96 hl
30 hekat	= 1 royal cubit³	5.08 ft³	0.144 m³
Alexandria system[g]			
	1 log	0.86 pt	48.6 cl
12 logs	= 1 hin	1.28 gal	5.83 l
24 logs	= 1 sat	2.57 gal	11.7 l
4 sats	= 1 large artaba	10.3 gal	46.7 l
other old units			
	1 kadah[r]	3.63 pt	2.06 l
4 kadahs	= 1 rub[s]	1.815 gal	8.25 l
2 rubs	= 1 kilá[t]	3.63 gal	16.5 l
12 kilas	= 1 ardab[u]	5.44 bu	1.98 hl
8 ardabs	= 1 daribah	43.55 bu	15.84 hl
Weight *ancient system*[a]			
	1 kedet[v]	0.33 oz	9.4 g
10 kedets	= 1 deben	3.3 oz	94 g
10 debens	= 1 sep[w]	2.1 lb	0.94 kg
Alexandria system[g,x]			
	1 drachm	60 gr	3.89 g
2 drachms	= 1 didrachm	0.27 oz	7.78 g
2 didrachms	= 1 shekel[y]	0.55 oz	15.6 g
50 shekels	= 1 minah[w]	1.71 lb	778 g
60 minahs	= 1 talent	103 lb	46.7 kg

Egypt

Weight (cont)
other old units [j]

		Equivalent in: UK units	Metric units
	1 dirhem [z]	48.15 gr	3.12 g
144 dirhems	= 1 rottle [aa]	0.990 5 lb	0.449 kg
400 dirhems	= 1 oke [bb]	2.751 lb	1.248 kg
100 rottles	= 1 qantâr [cc]	99.05 lb	44.928 kg
200 okes	= 1 heml	4.913 cwt	249.6 kg

[a]As used about 3000 BC; approximate values. [b]Or digit. [c]Or abdah or palm. [d]Or terto or small span. [e]Natural or common or small cubit or remen; length of arm from elbow to extended finger tips. [f]Or sacred or building cubit; equal to 1 natural cubit plus 1 palm (choryos). Also shown as equal to $20\sqrt{2}$ digits (28.28 digits). [g]As settled under the Ptolemies about 300 BC. [h]Or foot. [i]As used for an ancient 'Nilometer' or meter for measuring the depth of the Nile. [j]Generally units from the medieval Arab system established about 700–900 AD; also see under Iraq concerning that system. [k]Or kirat. [l]Or diraa mémari. [m]Or cassaba or qasaba or qasab or gasab. [n]Or setat. [o]Or faddan. [p]Or hekt. [q]Or kor or sack. [r]Or keddah or kaledje or cadaa. [s]Or rob. [t]Or kilah or keila or kilé. [u]Or ardeb. [v]Or qedet or kite or kiti or kat. [w]Or mina. [x]For copper or brass; there was a lower value for silver, in general shown as one-half of the large values. [y]Or tetradrachm, or beqa for gold. [z]Or dirham; for trade. For silver, 45 gr (2.92 g). [aa]Or rotl or rotolo or ratel. [bb]Or oka or occa. [cc]Or qintar or cantar or cantaro or kantar or quintal; sometimes used as a UK linked value of 100 lb (45 kg) or metric value of 50 kg (110.2 lb).

El Salvador

Main system: metric, from 1886; also UK units

Other units in use:

		Equivalent in: UK units	Metric units
Length			
	1 pulgada	0·914 in	2.322 cm
12 pulgadas	= 1 pie	0·914 ft	27.86 cm
3 pies	= 1 vara	0.914 yd	0.836 m
2 varas	= 1 brazada	0.914 fathom	1.672 m
	1 legua	2.485 mi	4 km
Area			
	1 tarea	335–1 046 yd²	280–875 m²
	1 vara²	0.840 28 yd²	0.702 58 m²
100 vara²	= 1 cuadra	84.028 yd²	70.258 m²
10 000 vara²	= 1 manzana	1.736 acre	0.702 58 ha
64 manzanas	= 1 caballería	111.11 acre	44.965 ha
Volume			
	1 carretada	1.308 yd³	1 m³
3 carretadas	= 1 camionada	3.924 yd³	3 m³
Capacity			
	1 botella	1.320 pt	0.75 l
5 botellas	= 1 galón	0.825 gal	3.75 l
Weight			
	1 onza	1.014 oz	28.75 g
16 onzas	= 1 libra	1.014 lb	460 g
25 libras	= 1 arroba	25.35 lb	11.5 kg
100 libras	= 1 quintal	101.4 lb	46 kg
2 quintals	= 1 carga	202.8 lb	92 kg
18–30 libras	= 1 medio	18–30 lb	8.3–13.8 kg
24 medios	= 1 fanega	439–730 lb	199–331 kg
20 quintals	= 1 tonelada corta	0.905 ton	0.92 t
	1 carretada	1 short ton	0.907 t
3 carretadas	= 1 camionada	3 short tons	2.722 t

Ethiopia

Main system: metric, compulsory from 1963

Old units (some of which are still in use):

		Equivalent in: UK units	Metric units
Length			
	1 senzer [a]	9 in	22.86 cm
	1 kend: old	20 in	50.8 cm
	new	19.69 in	50 cm
Area			
	1 gasha [b]	100 acres	40 ha
Capacity			
	1 messe	1.3 qt	1.5 l
4 messe	= 1 cabaho	1.3 gal	6.0 l
	1 kunna [c]	0.968 gal	4.4 l
20 kunna	= 1 daula	2.422 bu	0.88 hl
Weight *old units*			
	1 derime [d]	40 gr	2.59 g
10 derimes	= 1 woket [e]	400 gr	25.9 g
12 derimes	= 1 mocha	1.097 oz	31.1 g
12 wokets	= 1 rotl [f]	0.686 lb	311 g
metric linked units			
	1 neter	0.992 lb	450 g
	1 kunna	11.02 lb	5 kg
	1 frasoulla [g]	37.48 lb	17 kg
20 kunnas	= 1 dawulla	220.5 lb	100 kg

[a]Or sinzer. [b]Or kalad: varied from 60–300 acres (24–120 ha), depending on the quality of the land. [c]Or kuna. [d]Or drachm. [e]Or wakea or ounce; also used as 28 g (0.988 oz). [f]Or rottolo or litre. [g]Or frasila or ferasla.

Fiji

Main system: UK units, converting to the metric system

Other unit in use:

		Equivalent in: UK units	Metric units
Weight			
	1 case (bananas)	72 lb	32.7 kg

Finland

Main system: metric, from 1886

Old units:

		Equivalent in: UK units	Metric units
Length			
	1 tum [a]	0.974 in	2.47 cm
12 tums	= 1 fot [b]	0.974 ft	29.69 cm
	1 peninkulma [c]	6.21 mi	10 km
Volume			
	1 famn [d]	141.3 ft³	4 m³
Capacity			
	1 kappe [e]: old	1.01 gal	4.58 l
	new	1.10 gal	5 l

[a]Or tumma. Old value; new value in use is 1 in (2.54 cm). [b]Or jalka. Old value; new value in use is 1 ft (30.48 cm). [c]Metric linked value. [d]Or syli; metric linked value. [e]Or kappa.

France

Main system: SI metric, compulsory as metric from 1794

Medieval system[a]:

Length		Equivalent in: UK units	Metric units
	1 point	0.007 4 in	0.188 mm
12 points	= 1 ligne[b]	0.088 8 in	2.256 mm
12 lignes	= 1 pouce[c]	1.066 in	2.707 cm
12 pouces	= 1 pied[d]	1.066 ft	0.324 84 m
6 322 points	= 1 aune	1.300 yd	1.188 m
5 pieds	= 1 brasse[e]	1.776 yd	1.624 m
6 pieds	= 1 toise	1.066 fathom	1.949 m
22 pieds	= 1 perche[f]	1.421 perch	7.146 m
2 000 toises	= 1 lieue de poste	2.422 mi	3.898 km

Area			
1 perche²	= 1 perche[g]	61.082 yd	51.072 m²
100 perches[g]	= 1 arpent	1.262 acre	0.510 72 ha

Capacity, dry			
	= 1 mesurette	1.788 fl oz	50.814 ml
16 mesurettes	= 1 litron	1.431 pt	0.813 l
16 litrons	= 1 boisseau[h]	2.861 gal	13.008 l
3 boisseaus	= 1 minot	1.07 bu	39.025 l
2 minots	= 1 mine	2.15 bu	78.05 l
2 mines	= 1 setier	4.29 bu	1.561 hl
3 setiers	= 1 quarteau	12.9 bu	4.683 hl
4 quarteaus	= 1 muid	51.5 bu	18.732 hl

Capacity, liquid			
	1 roquille	1.024 fl oz	29.10 ml
4 roquilles	= 1 posson[i]	4.097 fl oz	116.4 ml
4 possons	= 1 chopine[j]	0.819 pt	0.465 7 l
2 chopines	= 1 pinte[k]	1.639 pt	0.931 32 l
2 pintes	= 1 pot	3.278 pt	1.862 6 l
4 pots	= 1 velte[j]	1.639 gal	7.451 l

wine units[l]			
	1 velte	1.66 gal	7.540 l
15 veltes	= 1 feuillette	24.9 gal	1.131 hl
2 feuillettes	= 1 barrique	49.8 gal	2.262 hl
4 barriques	= 1 tonneau	199 gal	9.048 hl

Weight[m]			
	1 grain	0.820 gr	53.115 mg
24 grains	= 1 denier[n]	19.673 gr	1.275 g
3 deniers	= 1 gros[o]	59.018 gr	3.824 g
8 gros	= 1 once	1.079 oz	30.594 g
8 onces	= 1 marc	0.540 lb	244.8 g
12 onces	= 1 livre de Charlemagne[p]	0.809 lb	367.1 g
16 onces	= 1 livre[q]	1.079 lb	489.51 kg
100 livres	= 1 quintal	107.92 lb	48.951 kg

In general, the system which applied before 1794 and the introduction of the metric system. Values varied in different regions of France, and those shown are generally those for Paris. The French medieval system in general began with measures introduced by Charlemagne (768–814 AD); in particular he introduced the 'pied de roi' and the 'livre esterlin' which was based on the Arab yusdroman.   [b]Paris line.   [c]Paris inch.   [d]Paris foot or pied de roi.   [e]Marine.   [f]Or verge; also in use as equal to 18 pieds.   [g]Perche squared (carrée).   [h]Or bushel; metric linked boisseau (at 1812) was 12½ l.   [i]Or poisson.   [j]Or setier (name used for both chopine and velte).   [k]Legal Paris value; a value of 0.951 21 l was often used.   [l]Bordeaux values.   [m]As settled in general 1350 and used until 1789; other weight systems were also in use.   [n]Or scruple.   [o]Or drachme.   [p]Or livre esterlin; as established by Charlemagne. Livre poids-de-marc or poids de Paris; metric livre became ½ kilogram (1.102 lb).

Gambia

Main system: UK units and metric system

Other unit in use:

Weight		Equivalent in: UK units	Metric units
	1 load (cocoa)	60 lb	27.2 kg

Germany, West

Main system: metric, compulsory from 1872

Old units:[a]

Length[b]		Equivalent in: UK units	Metric units
	1 strich	0.0412 in	1.046 mm
25 strichs	= 1 zoll[c]	1.03 in	26.15 mm
12 zolls	= 1 fuss	1.03 ft	31.39 cm
25½ zolls	= 1 stab[d]	2.19 ft	66.69 cm
12 fuss	= 1 rute	0.749 rod	3.766 m

Area			
	1 morgen[b]	0.631 acre	0.255 ha

Capacity, dry[b]			
	1 maess[e]	1.511 pt	0.859 l
4 maess	= 1 metze	0.756 gal	3.435 l
4 metzes	= 1 viertel	3.022 gal	13.74 l
4 viertels	= 1 scheffel[f]	1.511 bu	54.96 l
12 scheffels	= 1 malter	18.13 bu	6.595 hl
2 malters	= 1 winspel	36.3 bu	13.19 hl
6 malters	= 1 last	108.8 bu	39.57 hl

Capacity, liquid[b]			
	1 ort[g]	0.378 pt	215 ml
2 orts	= 1 schoppen[h]	0.756 pt	429 ml
2 schoppens	= 1 maess[e]	1.511 pt	0.859 l
2 maess	= 1 kanne[i]	3.022 pt	1.718 l
40 maess	= 1 ancre[i]	7.556 gal	34.35 l
2 ancres	= 1 eimer[k]	15.11 gal	68.70 l
2 eimers	= 1 ohm	30.2 gal	1.374 hl
3 eimers	= 1 oxhoft[l]	45.3 gal	2.061 hl
6 ohms	= 1 fuder	181 gal	8.244 hl

Weight old system[b]			
	1 lot[m]	0.516 oz	14.62 g
2 lots	= 1 unzen	1.031 oz	29.23 g
8 unzens	= 1 marc	0.516 lb	233.8 g
16 unzens	= 1 pfund	1.031 lb	467.7 g

metric linked system[n]			
	1 lot[m]	0.353 oz	10 g
50 lots	= 1 pfund[o]	1.102 lb	500 g
100 pfunds	= 1 zentner	110.231 lb	50 kg
2 zentners	= 1 doppelzentner	220.46 lb	100 kg

herring units			
	1 kantje	163.1 lb	74 kg
	1 barrel	220.46 lb	100 kg

[a]Values varied by region.   [b]Value(s) for Prussia, in general as established 1816.   [c]Also used to mean the UK inch.   [d]Or aune.   [e]Or mass or maass or pot or quartier or small maess or small pot.   [f]Or bushel.   [g]Or paele or pegel.   [h]Or noessel or quart or quartel or viertel or planken or seidel: metric linked schoppen was 0.5 l (0.88 pt).   [i]Or large maess or large pot.   [j]Or anker.   [k]Or aime or aimer. Values varied markedly; often there were 40, 60, 64 or 72 maess per eimer (here shown as 80).   [l]Or barrique or hogshead.   [m]Or loth.   [n]As established by the German Zollverein (Customs Union) in 1854.   [o]Or zollpfund or zollverein pound.

Ghana

Main system: metric, as conversion in 1974 from the UK system

Other unit in use:

Weight		Equivalent in:	
		UK units	Metric units
1 load (cocoa): old		60 lb	27.2 kg
new		66.1 lb	30 kg

Greece

Main system: metric, compulsory from 1959

Old units:

Length
ancient system[a]

		Equivalent in:	
		UK units	Metric units
	1 daktylos[b]	0.758 in	1.92 cm
2 daktylos	= 1 kondylos[c]	1.52 in	3.85 cm
2 kondylos	= 1 palaiste[d]	3.03 in	7.70 cm
2 palaistes	= 1 hemipodion[e]	6.06 in	15.4 cm
1¼ hemipodions	= 1 lichar[f]	7.58 in	19.2 cm
1½ hemipodions	= 1 spithame[g]	9.09 in	23.1 cm
16 daktylos	= 1 poush[h]	1.010 ft	30.8 cm
2 hemipodions	= 1 poush[h]	1.010 ft	30.8 cm
2¼ hemipodions	= 1 pygme[i]	1.137 ft	34.6 cm
2½ hemipodions	= 1 pygon[j]	1.263 ft	38.5 cm
3 hemipodions	= 1 pechus[k]	1.516 ft	46.2 cm
1½ pous	= 1 pechus[k]	1.516 ft	46.2 cm
2½ pous	= 1 hema[l]	2.526 ft	0.770 m
6 pous	= 1 orguia[m]	6.063 ft	1.848 m
10 pous	= 1 arkana	10.10 ft	3.08 m
10 orguias	= 1 amma	60.63 ft	18.5 m
10 arkansas	= 1 plethron[n]	101.0 ft	30.8 m
600 pous	= 1 stadion[o]	606 ft	185 m
4 stadions	= 1 hippicon[p]	808 yds	739 m
30 stadions	= 1 parasang[q]	3.445 mi	5.544 km
2 parasangs	= 1 schoinos[r]	6.890 mi	11.09 km

metric linked units (masonry)

	1 pic[s]	2.461 ft	75 cm
2 pics	= 1 pecheus	4.921 ft	1.5 m

Area
ancient system[a]

1 plethron²	= 1 stremma[t]	10 211 ft²	949 m²

metric linked units

	1 pic²	6.055 ft²	0.562 5 m²
	1 royal stremma	10 764 ft²	1 000 m²

Capacity
ancient system[a]

	1 cochliarion	0.17 fl oz	4.9 ml
10 cochliarions	= 1 kyathos[u]	0.9 pt	49 ml
1½ kyathos	= 1 oxybaphon[v]	0.13 pt	73 ml
2 oxybaphons	= 1 hemikotylion[w]	0.26 pt	146 ml
2 hemikotylions	= 1 kotyle[x]	0.51 pt	292 ml
2 kotyles	= 1 xeste[y]	1.028 pt	584 ml
6 xestes	= 1 konge[z]	6.17 pt	3.51 l
6 konges	= 1 amphora[aa]	4.63 gal	21.0 l
50 xestes	= 1 metretes[bb]	6.43 gal	29.2 l
1⅓ metretes	= 1 medimnos	1.07 bu	39.0 l

other old units

	1 koilon	7.30 gal	33.2 l
	1 kilo[cc]	1.04 bu	37.7 l

Weight
ancient system[a]

		Equivalent in:	
		UK units	Metric units
	1 sitarion	1.04 gr	68 mg
1½ sitarions	= 1 calc[dd]	1.56 gr	101 mg
8 calcs	= 1 obol[ee]	12.5 gr	0.81 g
2 obols	= 1 gramma	25.0 gr	1.62 g
3 grammas	= 1 drachma[ff]	75.0 gr	4.86 g
2 drachmas	= 1 didrachm[gg]	150 gr	9.72 g
4 drachmas	= 1 tetradrachm	300 gr	19.4 g
100 drachmas	= 1 mna[hh]	1.072 lb	486 g
60 mnas	= 1 talanton[ii]	64.3 lb	29.2 kg

other old units

	1 dram	1.78 gr	115.3 mg
	1 Venetian litre[jj]	1.058 lb	480 g
	1 oka[kk]	2.83 lb	1.28 kg
44 okas	= 1 kantar[ll]	124.2 lb	56.32 kg

UK and metric linked units

	1 drachma[mm]	½ oz	14.175 g
32 drachmas	= 1 Ionian litre	1 lb	454 g
	1 tonos	1.48 ton	1½ t

[a]System of about 500 BC; values varied from state to state. One possible consistent set of values is shown here. [b]Fingerbreadth; UK linked value for one daktylos or palamé is 1 inch. [c]Middle knuckle. [d]Or paleste or doron or palm. [e]Half-foot. [f]Span of thumb and index finger. [g]Span of all fingers. [h]Greek foot; values varied from about 0.97 ft (30 cm) to 1.15 ft (35 cm), other units varying accordingly. Olympic foot is generally shown as 1.051 ft (32.05 cm). [i]Short cubit; elbow to start of the fingers. [j]Short cubit; elbow to end of knuckles of closed fist. [k]Normal cubit; elbow to end of fingertips. [l]Pace or step. [m]Or dynia or fathom; stretch of both arms. [n]The Moreas plethron was 116.9 ft (35.64 m). [o]Or stade; length of the Olympian stadion or athletic track for the short foot-race. [p]Length of a horse racing course. [q]Day's journey (Persian origin). [r]Varied from 1 to 4 parasangs. [s]Or pik or pike or picki or dira mimari. Royal pic is 1 metre (39.37 in). [t]The ancient stremma varied from 880–1 270 m²; the Moreas stremma was 1 270 m² (13 672 ft²). [u]Gourd. [v]Saucer. [w]Half-cup. [x]Or cotyle; cup. [y]Sixth part. [z]Or conge. [aa]Or chu or chou; water or wine jar. [bb]Or metreta; also used as 1½ or 2 times the amphora. [cc]Or quilo or kilé; metric linked kilo is 1 hectolitre. [dd]Or chalque. [ee]Iron spit. [ff]Handful. [gg]Or stater or shekel. [hh]Or mina; before 594 BC the mna was equal to 72 drachmas. In the metric linked system the mna was 1½ kg. [ii]Or talent (balance); shown here as the weight of water contained by a metretes. [jj]For raisins; values also used were 1.052 lb (477 g) and 0.992 lb (450 g). [kk]Or oke. [ll]Or cantar or stater or quintal; also used as 123.2 lb (55.88 kg). [mm]Or drachme.

Guatemala

Main system: metric

Other units in use:

Length

		Equivalent in:	
		UK units	Metric units
	1 pulgada	0.914 in	2.322 cm
9 pulgadas	= 1 cuarta	8.23 in	20.90 cm
12 pulgadas	= 1 pie[a]	10.97 in	27.86 cm
3 pies	= 1 vara	0.914 yd	0.836 m
24 varas	= 1 mecate[b]	21.94 yd	20.06 m
6 666⅔ varas	= 1 legua	3.463 mi	5.573 km
(20 000 varas	= 3 leguas)		

Area

	1 vara²	7.52 ft²	0.70 m²
10 000 vara²	= 1 manzana	1.73 acre	0.70 ha
64 manzanas	= 1 caballería	110.5 acre	44.72 ha

Capacity

	1 botella	1.14 pt	65 cl
	1 cuartillo	2.04 pt	1.16 l
	1 cajuela	3.65 gal	16.60 l
48 cuartillos	= 1 fanega	1.526 bu	0.555 hl

Guatemala

Weight

		Equivalent in: UK units	Metric units
	1 onza	1.014 oz	28.75 g
16 onzas	= 1 libra	1.014 lb	460.0 g
25 libras	= 1 arroba	25.35 lb	11.5 kg
100 libras	= 1 quintal	101.4 lb	46.0 kg
20 quintals	= 1 tonelada	0.905 ton	0.920 t

[a]Or tercia.   [b]Or task.

Guyana

Main system: UK units, changing to the metric system with planned completion by end 1982

Old unit:

Area

	Equivalent in: UK units	Metric units
1 Rhynland acre	1.052 acre	0.426 ha

Haiti

Main system: metric, from 1921

Other units in use:

Length

		Equivalent in: UK units	Metric units
	1 ligne	0.088 8 in	2.256 mm
12 lignes	= 1 pouce	1.066 in	2.707 cm
12 pouces	= 1 pied	1.066 ft	0.324 8 m
44 pouces	= 1 aune	1.302 yd	1.191 m
	1 aune (textiles)	1.53 yd	1.40 m

Area

	Equivalent in: UK units	Metric units
1 carreau de terre	3.193 acre	1.292 ha

Volume

	Equivalent in: UK units	Metric units
1 barrique	49.493 gal	2.25 hl

Weight

	Equivalent in: UK units	Metric units
1 livre française	1.079 lb	0.489 kg
1 sac (coffee)	132.3 lb	60 kg

Honduras

Main system: metric, from 1912; also UK and US units

Other units in use:

Length

		Equivalent in: UK units	Metric units
	1 punto	0.006 34 in	0.161 07 mm
12 puntos	= 1 linea	0.076 10 in	1.932 9 mm
12 lineas	= 1 pulgada	0.913 17 in	2.319 4 cm
12 pulgadas	= 1 pie	0.913 17 ft	27.833 cm
3 pies	= 1 vara	0.913 17 yd	0.835 m
5 000 varas	= 1 legua	2.594 mi	4.175 km

Area

		Equivalent in: UK units	Metric units
	1 vara²	0.833 874 yd²	0.697 225 m²
10 000 vara²	= 1 manzana	1.722 880 acres	0.697 225 ha
64½ (approx) manzanas	= 1 caballeria[a]	111.266 acres	45.027 914 ha

Capacity, dry

		Equivalent in: UK units	Metric units
	1 medida	5.054 pt	2.872 l
	1 arroba	3.65 gal	16.6 l
16 medidas	= 1 medio	10.108 gal	45.95 l
24 medios	= 1 fanega	30.323 bu	11.028 hl

Capacity, liquid

		Equivalent in: UK units	Metric units
	1 onza	1.014 fl oz	2.88 cl
24 onzas	= 1 botella	1.216 pt	69.12 cl
5 botellas	= 1 galón	0.760 gal	3.456 l

Weight

		Equivalent in: UK units	Metric units
	1 onza	1.014 oz	28.76 g
16 onzas	= 1 libra	1.014 lb	460 g
3⅛ libras	= 1 mancuerna	3.169 lb	1.437 5 kg
25 libras	= 1 arroba	25.35 lb	11.5 kg
100 libras	= 1 quintal [b]	101.4 lb	46 kg
	1 saco [c]	152.1 lb	69 kg

maize (corn) units

		Equivalent in: UK units	Metric units
	1 mano	2½ lb	1.134 kg
40 manos	= 1 red	100 lb	45.359 kg

[a]More exactly 64.581 611 manzanas.   [b]Or fardo of tobacco.   [c]Of coffee.

Hongkong

Main system: UK system, with gradual conversion to the metric system

Other units in use (old Chinese system)[l]:

Length

		Equivalent in: UK units	Metric units
	1 fan[a]	0.146 25 in	3.714 75 mm
10 fans	= 1 tsün [b]	1.462 5 in	37.147 5 mm
10 tsüns	= 1 chek [c]	1.218 75 ft	0.371 475 m
24 tsüns	= 1 ma [d]	0.975 yd	0.891 54 m
10 cheks	= 1 cheung	4.062 5 yd	3.714 75 m
150 cheungs	= 1 lei [e]	0.346 236 mi	0.557 21 km

Area

		Equivalent in: UK units	Metric units
	1 dau chung	806.7 yd²	674.5 m²
	1 mow	1 008 yd²	842.8 m²

Capacity

		Equivalent in: UK units	Metric units
	1 hop	3.519 5 fl oz	10 cl
10 hops	= 1 sing	1.759 8 pt	1 l
10 sings	= 1 dau	2.199 7 gal	10 l
10 daus	= 1 seh	21.997 gal	1 hl

Weight

		Equivalent in: UK units	Metric units
	1 fan[f]	5.833 33 gr	0.377 99 g
10 fans	= 1 tsin [g]	0.133 33 oz	3.779 9 g
10 tsins	= 1 leung [h]	1⅓ oz	37.799 g
16 leungs[k]	= 1 kan [i]	1⅓ lb	0.604 79 kg
100 kans	= 1 tam [j]	133⅓ lb	60.479 kg

gold

		Equivalent in: UK units	Metric units
	1 tael	1.203 37 oz tr	37.429 0 g

[a]Or fun.   [b]Or ts'un (Chinese inch).   [c]Or cheh (Chinese foot); the value can vary down to 0.958 ft (0.292 m) according to trade.   [d]Chinese yard; for the retail sale of cloth.   [e]Chinese mile; may vary up to 0.42 mi (0.68 km).   [f]Or fun or hoon or candareen.   [g]Or chin or mace.   [h]Or tael or tahil.   [i]Or gun or catty or cate or kati.   [j]Or darm or picul.   [k]Values may vary; in particular for fish 12 or 14 leungs may be taken as equal to 1 kan.   [l]Values vary according to trade and place; old Chinese units are gradually being replaced by metric.

Hungary

Main system: metric (SI from 1980), compulsory from 1876

Old units:

Length		Equivalent in: UK units	Metric units
	1 zögöl [d]	1.037 fathom	1.896 m
	1 marok	4.148 mi	6.676 km
	1 meile [a]	5.191 mi	8.354 km

Area			
	1 négyszögöl [c]	4.301 56 yd²	3.596 65 m²
1 000 négyszögöls	= 1 small Hungarian yoke	0.888 75 acres	0.359 665 ha
1 200 négyszögöls	= 1 Hungarian yoke	1.066 50 acres	0.431 598 ha
1 600 négyszögöls	= 1 cadastral yoke [b]	1.422 acres	0.575 464 ha

Capacity			
	1 ako	11.94 gal	0.543 hl

Weight			
	1 mázsa [e]	220.5 lb	100 kg
10 mázsas	= 1 tonna	0.984 ton	1 t
10 tonnas	≐ 1 vagon	9.842 ton	10 t

[a] Or marfold. [b] Katasztrális hold. [c] Square fathom. [d] Fathom. [e] Quintal.

Iceland

Main system: metric, from 1907 (compulsory from 1909)

Other units:

Length		Equivalent in: UK units	Metric units
	1 tomma [a]: old	1.030 in	2.61 cm
	new	1 in	2.54 cm
	1 sjomila	1.15 mi	1.855 km

Area			
	1 engjateigur	0.788 acre	0.319 ha

Volume			
	1 teningsfet	1.091 ft³	0.030 9 m³

Capacity			
	1 síldar tunna [b]	26.0–26.4 gal	1.18–1.20 hl
	1 síldar mál	33 gal	1.5 hl

[a] Or thumlungur. [b] Herring barrel.

India

Main system: metric, from 1956 (compulsory from 1967)

Old units (no longer in use):

Length [a]		Equivalent in: UK units	Metric units
	1 ungul [b]	0.75 in	1.905 cm
24 unguls	= 1 taim [c]	18 in	45.72 cm
2 taims	= 1 gaz [d]	1 yd	91.44 cm
2 gaz	= 1 danda [e]	2 yd	1.828 8 m
3 gaz	= 1 lath	3 yd	2.743 2 m
60 gaz	= 1 jarib	60 yd	54.864 m
2 000 gaz	= 1 koss [f]	1.136 mi	1.828 8 km

Area [a]			
	1 taim²	0.25 yd²	0.209 m²
6 400 taim²	= 1 bigha [g]	0.331 acre	0.134 ha
4 bighas	= 1 cawnie [h]	1.322 acre	0.535 ha

Capacity [i]		Equivalent in: UK units	Metric units
	1 puddee [j]	2.703 pt	1.536 2 l
8 puddees	= 1 mercal [k]	2.703 gal	12.29 l

Weight [l]			
	1 punk [m]	0.141 gr	9.11 mg
4 punks	= 1 dhan	0.562 gr	36.4 mg
4 dhans	= 1 ruttee [n]	2.25 gr	146 mg
8 ruttees	= 1 masha [o]	18 gr	1.166 g
10 mashas	= 1 tola	180 gr	11.664 g
	1 tank [p]	200 gr	12.960 g
5 tolas	= 1 chittack [q]	2.057 oz	58.319 g
4 chittacks	= 1 pa	0.514 lb	233.28 g
72 tanks	= 1 seer [r]	2.057 lb	0.933 1 kg
16 chittacks	= 1 seer [r]	2.057 lb	0.933 1 kg
2 seers	= 1 adowly	4.114 lb	1.866 kg
5 seers	= 1 passeree [s]	10.285 lb	4.665 kg
40 seers	= 1 maund [t]	82.286 lb	37.324 kg
20 maunds	= 1 candy [u]	0.734 69 ton	0.746 48 t

[a] Calcutta values; values varied markedly by region. [b] Or unglee or angula or anguli. [c] Or hath or hat'h or haut or hasta or moolum or kovid or cubit; for Madras the value varied from 18 to 21 in (45–54 cm). [d] Or guz; the value varied from 14 in to about 50 in (35–130 cm). Other values included Bombay 27 in (69 cm), Madras 33 in (84 cm). [e] Or dhanu or bow. [f] Or coss or kor. [g] Originally the area ploughed by a pair of oxen in 1 day. [h] Or cawney. [i] Grain units; Madras values. [j] UK linked value was 100 in³ (1.64 l). [k] Or marcal. [l] UK linked 'railway' or 'government' weights established 1833. [m] Or punkho. [n] Or retti. [o] Or mas. [p] Or tang; for pearls, 1 tank equalled 50 gr (3.24 g). [q] Or chittak or chattauck. [r] Other values included: Madras 0.617 lb (280 g), Bombay 0.72 lb (327 g). [s] Or dhurree or vis or viss or visham; UK linked passeree was also 10 lb (4.5 kg) and visham 3 lb (1.36 kg). [t] Other values included: Madras 25 lb (11.3 kg), Bombay 28 lb (12.7 kg). [u] Other values included: Madras 500 lb (227 kg), Bombay 560 lb (254 kg).

Indonesia

Main system: metric, from 1923

Other units in use:

Length		Equivalent in: UK units	Metric units
	1 el [a]	2.26 ft	0.687 8 m
	1 roede [b, c]	4.12 yd [d]	3.767 4 m
400 roedes	= 1 Java paal [k]	0.936 mi	1.507 km

Area			
	1 roede²	16.975 yd²	14.193 m²
500 roede²	= 1 bahu [e]	1.754 acre	0.709 65 ha
2 bahus	= 1 djung	3.507 acre	1.419 3 ha
2 djungs	= 1 panchar	7.01 acre	2.839 ha

Capacity			
	1 gantang	1.887 gal	8.576 6 l

Weight old Amsterdam measures			
	1 lood	0.544 5 oz	15.44 g
2 loods	= 1 ons	1.089 oz	30.88 g
16 ons	= 1 pond	1.089 lb	494.1 g

old Asian measures			
	1 catty [j]	1.361 6 lb	617.613 g
100 cattys	= 1 picol [g]	136.16 lb	61.761 kg
27 picols	= 1 koyang [h]	1.641 ton	1.668 t

precious metals			
	1 wang	0.725 dwt tr	1.127 g
3 wangs	= 1 tali	2.174 dwt tr	3.381 g
2 talis	= 1 suku	4.348 dwt tr	6.761 g
4 sukus	= 1 real	0.869 5 oz tr	27.045 g
2 reals	= 1 thail	1.739 oz tr	54.09 g

Indonesia

Weight (cont)
opium

		Equivalent in: UK units	Metric units
	1 timbang[i]	5.957 gr	386.01 mg
10 timbangs	= 1 tji	59.57 gr	3.860 1 g
10 tjis	= 1 thail	1.362 oz	38.601 g

other (trade) measures

		UK units	Metric units
	1 briquette	1.10 lb	0.50 kg
	1 litre[f]	1.76 lb	0.80 kg
	1 sack (cement)	88 lb or 110 lb	40 kg or 50 kg
	1 bale	397 lb	180 kg

[a]Amsterdam measure. [b]Rijnlandse. [c]Or tjengkal. [d]Sometimes used as 4.02 yd or 4 yd. [e]Or bouw or bau. [f]Rice. [g]Or picul. [h]For Jakarta; for Semarang: 28 picols, for Surabaja: 30 picols. [i]Or mata or hoon. [j]Or katti. [k]Or pal; for Sumatra 1.151 mi (1.852 km).

Iran

Main system: metric, compulsory from 1933

Old units:

Length

		Equivalent in: UK units	Metric units
	1 bahar	1.28 in	3.25 cm
2 bahars	= 1 gireh[a]	2.56 in	6.50 cm
2 girehs	= 1 ourob	5.12 in	13 cm
2 ourobs	= 1 charac[b]	0.853 ft	26 cm
4 characs	= 1 zar[b, c]	1.14 yd	1.04 m
6 000 zars	= 1 farsang[b, d]	3.88 mi	6.24 km

Area

		UK units	Metric units
	1 zar²	1.294 yd²	1.081 6 m²
1 000 zar²	= 1 jerib	0.267 acre	0.108 2 ha

Capacity, dry

		UK units	Metric units
	1 sextario	0.579 pt	329 ml
4 sextarios	= 1 chemica[e]	2.32 pt	1.32 l
2 chemicas	= 1 capicha[f]	4.63 pt	2.63 l
22 sextarios	= 1 sabbitha	1.59 gal	7.24 l
25 sextarios	= 1 collothum[g]	1.81 gal	8.23 l
30 chemicas	= 1 legana	1.09 bu	39.5 l
50 chemicas	= 1 artaba	1.81 bu	65.9 l

Capacity, liquid [h]

		UK units	Metric units
	1 chemica[e]	2.32 pt	1.32 l
2 chemicas	= 1 capicha	4.63 pt	2.63 l
6¼ chemicas	= 1 collothum	1.81 gal	8.23 l
	1 menor	2.76 gal	12.55 l

Weight [i]

		UK units	Metric units
	1 una	0.188 gr	12.21 mg
4 unas	= 1 gandom[j]	0.754 gr	48.83 mg
	1 abbas[k]	2.894 gr	187.5 mg
4 gandoms	= 1 nokhod[l]	3.014 gr	195 mg
4 nokhods	= 1 dung[m]	12.06 gr	781 mg
6 dungs	= 1 miskal[b, n]	72.34 gr	4.687 5 g
2 miskals	= 1 dirhem	0.331 oz	9.375 g
8 dirhems	= 1 seer[b, o]	2.646 oz	75 g
1¼ seers	= 1 pinar	3.307 oz	93.75 g
1 000 abbas	= 1 danar	6.614 oz	187.5 g
2 pinars	= 1 danar	6.614 oz	187.5 g
2 danars	= 1 abbassi	0.827 lb	375 g
1¼ abbassis	= 1 rottel[p]	1.033 lb	468.75 g
10 seers	= 1 tcharak[b, q]	1.653 lb	0.75 kg
2 tcharaks	= 1 saddirham[r]	3.307 lb	1.5 kg
4 tcharaks	= 1 man[b, s]	6.614 lb	3 kg
2 mans	= 1 man-i-shah	13.23 lb	6 kg
2 man-i-shahs	= 1 rey[t]	26.46 lb	12 kg
100 mans	= 1 kharvar[b, u]	661.4 lb	300 kg

[a]Or gareh; metric gireh is equal to 10 cm. [b]In common use. [c]Or zer or zaz or gaz or guz or arish or arshin; metric zar is equal to 1 metre. [d]Or farsakh-song or parasang or persakh. [e]Or chenica. [f]Or capiche. [g]Or collothun. [h]As a metric linked unit, 1 paimaneh is 1 litre. [i]Metric linked values. [j]Or gandum. [k]Or abas; for weighing pearls. [l]Or nakhod or carat. [m]Or dong. [n]Or miscal. [o]Or sihr. [p]Or rotl. [q]Metric linked value; a frequently used value is 0.742 2 kg, other units varying accordingly. [r]Or nim-man. [s]Or batman or man-i-Tabriz. [t]Or man-i-rey. [u]Or karwar or kharwar.

Iraq

Main system: metric

Old units:

Length
ancient Sumerian system [a]

		Equivalent in: UK units	Metric units
	1 sossus	0.065 in	1.65 mm
10 sossus	= 1 shusi[ff]	0.65 in	1.65 cm
20 sossus	= 1 digit	1.3 in	3.3 cm
3 digits	= 1 handbreadth[b]	3.9 in	9.9 cm
5 handbreadths	= 1 small kus[c]	19.4 in	49.4 cm
2 small kus	= 1 large kus[c]	1.08 yd	99 cm
12 large kus	= 1 gar	13 yd	11.9 m
60 gars	= 1 ush[d]	778 yd	711 m
30 ush	= 1 kasbu[e]	13.3 mi	21.3 km

medieval Arab system [f]

		UK units	Metric units
	1 chabba[g]	0.13 in	3.3 mm
6 chabbas	= 1 assbaa[h]	0.778 in	1.97 cm
4 assbaas	= 1 cabda[i]	3.11 in	7.9 cm
4 cabdas	= 1 foot	1.037 ft	31.6 cm
24 assbaas	= 1 deraga cabda	18.7 in	47.4 cm
27 assbaas	= 1 deraga (Al-Mamoun)[j]	21 in	53.3 cm
32 assbaas	= 1 deraga akhdam[k]	25 in	63 cm
4 deraga cabdas	= 1 kathouah	6.2 ft	1.9 m
2 kathouahs	= 1 cassaba	12.4 ft	3.8 m
1 500 cassabas	= 1 parasang	3.53 mi	5.69 km
8 parasangs	= 1 marhala	28.3 mi	45.5 km

other old units

		UK units	Metric units
	1 dhiraa[l]: Aleppo	27.0 in	68.5 cm
	1 dhiraa[l]: Mosul	27.6 in	70 cm
	1 dhiraa[l]: Baghdad	29.3 in	74.5 cm

Area
ancient Sumerian system [a]

		UK units	Metric units
	1 she	2.2 in²	14 cm²
180 shes	= 1 gin	2.7 ft²	0.25 m²
60 gins	= 1 sar[m]	18 yd²	15 m²
1 800 sars	= 1 gan[n]	6.7 acre	2.7 ha

medieval Arab system [f]

		UK units	Metric units
	1 cassaba²	17.18 yd²	14.4 m²
400 cassaba²	= 1 feddan	1.42 acre	0.575 ha

metric linked units

		UK units	Metric units
	1 olc	119.6 yd²	100 m²
25 olcs	= 1 mishara[o]	0.618 acre	0.25 ha
20 misharas	= 1 faddan	12.355 acre	5 ha

Capacity
ancient Sumerian system [a]

		UK units	Metric units
1 handbreadth³	= 1 sila[p]	58.8 in³	0.963 l
5 silas	= 1 gin	1.06 gal	4.82 l
60 gins	= 1 gur[gg]	63.6 gal	2.89 hl

UK linked unit

		UK units	Metric units
	1 teneka[q]	4 gal	18.184 l

Weight
ancient Sumerian system [a]

		UK units	Metric units
	1 se[r]	0.69 gr	45 mg
120 ses	= 1 light shekel	0.188 oz	5.34 g
1½ light shekels	= 1 shekel[s]	0.283 oz	8.02 g
60 shekels	= 1 light mina	1.06 lb	481 g
2 light minas	= 1 great mina	2.12 lb	0.962 kg
60 light minas	= 1 talent	64 lb	29 kg

Iraq

Weight (cont)
medieval Arab system [f]

		Equivalent in: UK units	Metric units
	1 kambeh[t]	0.752 gr	48.75 mg
	1 hebbeh[u]	1.003 gr	65 mg
4 kambehs	= 1 kirat[v]	3.01 gr	195 mg
3 hebbehs	= 1 kirat[v]	3.01 gr	195 mg
16 kirats	= 1 dirhem[w]	48.15 gr	3.12 g
96 kambehs	= 1 mitkal	72.22 gr	4.68 g
12 dirhems	= 1 wukiyeh[x]	1.321 oz	37.4 g
10 wukiyehs	= 1 yusdroman[y]	0.825 lb	374 g
12 wukiyehs	= 1 rottle	0.990 5 lb	449 g
2 rottles	= 1 minah	1.981 lb	0.899 kg
400 dirhems	= 1 oke[z]	2.751 lb	1.248 kg
100 rottles	= 1 qantar[aa]	99·05 lb	44.928 kg
125 rottles	= 1 kikkar[hh]	123.8 lb	56.16 kg
200 okes	= 1 heml	550.3 lb	249.6 kg

other old units: Baghdad weight

	1 okiya [bb]	2.30 lb	1.041 7 kg
4 okiyas	= 1 hogga[cc]	9.186 lb	4.167 kg
6 hoggas	= 1 mann	55.12 lb	25 kg
4 manns	= 1 wazna[dd]	220.5 lb	100 kg
	1 kintar	604.7 lb	274.3 kg
20 waznas	= 1 tughar	1.968 ton	2 t

other old units: Basra weight

	1 okiya[bb]	7.071 lb	3.207 5 kg
20 okiyas	= 1 mann (coffee)	141.4 lb	64.150 kg
24 okiyas	= 1 mann (hillana)	169.7 lb	76.980 kg
32 okiyas	= 1 wazna[dd]	226.3 lb	102.640 kg
20 waznas	= 1 tughar	2.020 ton	2.052 8 t

other old units: Mosul weight

	1 okiya[bb]	4.526 oz	128.3 g
12 okiyas	= 1 small hogga[cc]	2.394 lb	1.539 6 kg
16 okiyas	= 1 big hogga[cc]	4.526 lb	2.052 8 kg
8 small hoggas	= 1 small mann		
6½ big hoggas	= 1 wazna[ee]	29.417 lb	13.343 kg
20 waznas	= 1 tughar	588.33 lb	266.864 kg

other old units: Istanbul weight

	1 dirham	0.113 oz	3.207 5 g
100 dirhams	= 1 okiya[bb]	0.707 lb	320.75 g
4 okiyas	= 1 hogga[cc]	2.83 lb	1.283 kg

[a]System of about 2500 BC (also, in general, later Babylonian system). Values and relationships varied; approximate values are shown. [b]Or palm. [c]Or ammatu (Babylonian cubit). [d]Or stadion. [e]Or parasang. [f]System which developed with the Arab Empire which had its beginning in the Hejira year of 622 AD; this Empire spread from Arabia (which now includes Iraq and Saudi Arabia and other states of the Arabian peninsula) to Syria, Egypt and across North Africa to Spain. During the period up to about 900 AD the system influenced European units, particularly in use of the barley grain and carat; Charlemagne (768–814) based his livre esterlin on the yusdroman (Arab pound). Values shown here are approximate. [g]Barley grain. [h]Digit. [i]Palm. [j]Or 'black' cubit. [k]Cubit of Omar. [l]Or diraa or ziraa or dhra or deraga. [m]Garden. [n]Field. [o]Or meshara or dönüm. [p]Babylonian: qa or ka; volume which holds 1 great mina of water. [q]Or safiha or tin. [r]Or she (Babylonian: seum); wheat grain. [s]For measuring silver; daric for gold. [t]Or kamha; wheat grain. [u]Or chabba; barley grain. [v]Or carat. [w]Or dirham or derhem or drachme. [x]Or onckie or ounce. [y]Or Arab pound. [z]Or oka or occa. [aa]Or qintar or cantar or cantaro·or kantar or quintal. [bb]Or oqiya. [cc]Or hukka. [dd]Or wazma. [ee]Or big mann. [ff]Babylonian: ubanu. [gg]Babylonian: kurru. [hh]Also used as 722 lb (327.5 kg).

Ireland

Main system: metric, as a gradual conversion from the UK system

Old units:

Length

		Equivalent in: UK units	Metric units
7 yards	= 1 perch or pole	7 yd	6.400 8 m

Area		Equivalent in: UK units	Metric units
49 yard²	= 1 perch²	49 yd²	40.97 m²
	1 Cunningham acre	1.291 4 acre	0.522 6 ha
160 perch²	= 1 Irish acre	1.619 8 acre	0.655 5 ha

Israel

Main system: metric, established in 1928

Old units:

Length
ancient Hebrew system [a]

		Equivalent in: UK units	Metric units
	1 ezba[b]	0.76 in	1.94 cm
4 ezbas (ezba'ot)	= 1 tefah[c]	3.1 in	7.8 cm
3 tefahs (tefahim)	= 1 zeret[d]	9.2 in	23 cm
6 tefahs (tefahim)	= 1 amma[e]	18.4 in	47 cm
7 tefahs (tefahim)	= 1 sacred amma[f]	21.4 in	54 cm

Area
ancient Hebrew system [a]

	1 amma²	= 1 garmida	0.35 yd²	0.30 m²
2 500 amma²	= 1 beit-se'a	885 yd²	740 m²
7 500 amma²	= 1 beit-zemed	0.55 acre	0.22 ha

other

1 metric dunam[g]	1 196 yd²	1 000 m²

Capacity, dry
ancient Hebrew system [a]

	1 log	0.93 pt	53 cl
4 logs (lugim)	= 1 qav[h]	3.7 pt	2.1 l
	1 omer[i]	6.7 pt	3.8 l
3 qavs (qabim[j])	= 1 hin	1.4 gal	6.3 l
2 hins (hinim)	= 1 se'a[k]	2.8 gal	12.7 l
10 omers (omarim)	= 1 efa[l]	1.04 bu	38 l
3 se'as (se'im)	= 1 efa[l]	1.04 bu	38 l
5 efas (efot)	= 1 letekh[m]	5.2 bu	1.9 hl
2 letekhs (letakhim)	= 1 homer	10.4 bu	3.8 hl

Capacity, liquid
ancient Hebrew system [a]

	1 log	0.93 pt	53 cl
4 logs (lugim)	= 1 qav[h]	3.7 pt	2.1 l
3 qavs (qabim)	= 1 hin	1.4 gal	6.3 l
6 hins (hinim)	= 1 bat[n]	8.4 gal	38 l
10 bats (battim)	= 1 kor[o]	84 gal	3.8 hl

Weight
ancient Hebrew system [a]

	1 gera[p]	9.8 gr	633 mg
5 geras (gerot)	= 1 rova[q]	49 gr	3.2 g
2 rovas (reva'im)	= 1 beka[r]	98 gr	6.3 g
2 bekas (beka'im)	= 1 shekel[s]	0.45 oz	12.7 g
2 shekels (shekalim)	= 1 sacred shekel	0.89 oz	25.3 g
50 shekels (shekalim)	= 1 gold mane[t]	1.40 lb	633 g
60 shekels (shekalim)	= 1 sacred mane[t]	1.68 lb	760 g
60 gold manes (manim)	= 1 talent[u]	84 lb	38 kg

other old units (no longer in use)

1 rotl: north Israel	5.29 lb	2.40 kg
1 rotl: south Israel	6.35 lb	2.88 kg

[a]Estimated values vary considerably; one possible consistent set of values is shown here. [b]Or etzba; fingerbreadth. [c]Or tophah; handbreadth. [d]Or zereth; span. [e]Or ammah or cubit. [f]Cubit and handbreadth. [g]Or dunum or dönüm. [h]Or kab or cab. [i]Or oner or gomor or homer. [j]Or qabin. [k]Or se'ah or sat or saton. [l]Or éfa or ephah. [m]Or letek. [n]Or bath. [o]Or cor or chomor. [p]Or gerah or obol. [q]Or rebah. [r]Or bekah. [s]Common shekel; also used as containing 12 geras (instead of 20). [t]Or mina or minah or manhe or maneh; also used as containing 40 and 80 shekels. [u]Or kikkar or kiccar or kikkor; shown here as the weight of water contained by a bat (bath).

Italy

Main system: metric, compulsory from 1861 (SI from 1978)

Old units:

Length
ancient Roman system [a]

		Equivalent in: UK units	Metric units
	1 digitus [b]	0.727 in	1.85 cm
1⅓ digitus	= 1 uncia [c]	0.970 in	2.46 cm
4 digitus	= 1 palma [d]	2.91 in	7.39 cm
16 digitus	= 1 pes [e]	0.970 ft	29.56 cm
12 uncias	= 1 pes [e]	0.970 ft	29.56 cm
20 digitus	= 1 palmipes [f]	1.212 ft	36.95 cm
1½ pes	= 1 cubitus [g]	1.455 ft	44.34 cm
2½ pes	= 1 gradus [h]	2.425 ft	0.739 m
5 pes	= 1 passus [i]	4.85 ft	1.478 m
10 pes	= 1 decempeda [j]	9.70 ft	2.956 m
625 pes	= 1 stadium	606 ft	185 m
8 stadiums	= 1 mile passum [k]	0.918 mi	1.478 km
4 mile passum	= 1 schoenus	3.674 mi	5.912 km

Area
ancient Roman system [a]

		Equivalent in: UK units	Metric units
	1 pes²	0.941 ft²	0.087 m²
100 pes²	= 1 scrupulus [l]	10.45 yd²	8.74 m²
36 scrupulus	= 1 clima [m]	376 yd²	315 m²
4 climas	= 1 actus [n]	1 505 yd²	1 258 m²
2 actus	= 1 jugerum [o]	0.622 acre	0.252 ha
2 jugerums	= 1 heredium [p]	1.244 acre	0.503 ha
100 herediums	= 1 centuria [q]	124.4 acre	50.33 ha
4 centurias	= 1 saltus [r]	0.777 mi²	2.013 km²

Capacity
ancient Roman system [a]
general

		Equivalent in: UK units	Metric units
	1 ligula	0.02 pt	11.2 ml
4 ligulas	= 1 cyathus [s]	0.08 pt	45 ml
1½ cyathus	= 1 acetabulum [t]	0.12 pt	67 ml
2 acetabulums	= 1 quartarius [u]	0.24 pt	135 ml
2 quartarius	= 1 hemina [v]	0.47 pt	269 ml
2 heminas	= 1 sextarius [w]	0.95 pt	0.538 l

dry

8 sextarius	= 1 semodius [x]	7.6 pt	4.30 l
2 semodius	= 1 modius [y]	0.95 peck	8.61 l

liquid

6 sextarius	= 1 congius	5.68 pt	3.23 l
4 congius	= 1 urna [z]	2.84 gal	12.9 l
2 urnas	= 1 amphora [aa]	5.68 gal	25.8 l
20 amphoras	= 1 culleus [bb]	114 gal	5.17 hl

other old units
dry

	1 starello	0.506 bu	18.4 l
1⅓ starellos	= 1 stajo	0.675 bu	24.53 l
2 starellos	= 1 quartarella	1.012 bu	36.80 l
2 quartarellas	= 1 quarto	2.024 bu	0.736 hl
2 quartos	= 1 rubbiatella	4.05 bu	1.472 hl
2 rubbiatellas	= 1 rubbio	8.10 bu	2.944 hl

liquid

	1 quartuccio	0.201 pt	114 ml
4 quartuccios	= 1 foglietta	0.802 pt	456 ml
4 fogliettas	= 1 boccale	3.208 pt	1.823 l
	1 caffiso (Sicily)	4.7 gal	21.2 l
32 boccales	= 1 barile	12.83 gal	58.34 l
16 bariles	= 1 botte	205.3 gal	9.33 hl

Weight
ancient Roman system [a]

		Equivalent in: UK units	Metric units
	1 siliqua [cc]	2.88 gr	187 mg
3 siliquas	= 1 obolus [dd]	8.6 gr	0.560 g
2 obolus	= 1 scrupulus [ee]	17.3 gr	1.12 g
3 scrupulus	= 1 drachma [ff]	51.9 gr	3.36 g
2 drachmas	= 1 sicilicus [gg]	0.237 oz	6.72 g
2 sicilicus	= 1 semuncia	0.474 oz	13.4 g
2 semuncias	= 1 uncia [hh]	0.948 oz	26.9 g
3 uncias	= 1 quadrans	2.84 oz	80.6 g
12 uncias	= 1 libra [ii]	0.711 lb	323 g
80 libras	= 1 talentum [jj]	56.89 lb	25.8 kg

other old units

	1 grano	0.757 gr	49.05 mg
24 granos	= 1 denaro [kk]	18.17 gr	1.18 g

[a]System from about 300 BC to 400 AD. [b]Approximate width of finger; under metric linked units 1 dito is 1 cm. [c]One-twelfth of a foot. [d]Approximate width of a hand. [e]Approximate length of a foot. Values varied, other values included 0.978 ft (29.8 cm); there was also a long foot of 1.037 ft (31.6 cm). [f]Foot and palm. [g]Or cubit or ulna (later, ell); approximate length from elbow to end of fingers. [h]Step. [i]Approximate length of pace (full cycle of two steps or 'double step'). [j]Or pertica; rod or pole. [k]Or miliarum or milliare or miglio (1 000 paces). [l]Or scruple. [m]Or clime. [n]Cattle drive. [o]Or juger or Roman acre. [p]Hereditary estate; later the French arpent. [q]100 divisions. [r]Woodland. [s]Ladle. [t]Cup-shaped vessel. [u]One-quarter. [v]One-half. [w]One-sixth. [x]One-half measure. [y]Measure. [z]Urn. [aa]Or quadrantal (jar); equal to pes³, and containing 80 libras of water in the revised system shown here. [bb]Leather sack. [cc]Pod. [dd]Metal spit. [ee]Scruple. [ff]Handful. [gg]Also used as containing 4 scruples rather than 6. [hh]Ounce. [ii]Or libbra. Values in the ancient system varied over time from 0.67–0.75 lb (300–340 g); before 200 BC there were 100 drachmas to the libra compared with the 96 drachmas to the libra shown here. In the 19th century, before changing to the metric system, values varied in Italy by region; some values were: Genoa 0.699 lb (317 g), Naples 0.707 lb (321 g), Rome 0.748 lb (339 g), Florence and Leghorn 0.749 lb (340 g). The metric linked libbra was 1 kilogram. [jj]Greek unit; shown as the weight of water contained by one amphora. [kk]Metric linked denaro was 1 gram.

Japan

Main system: metric, from 1921

Old units [a]:

Length

		Equivalent in: UK units	Metric units
	1 mō	0.001 193 in	0.030 303 mm
10 mō	= 1 rin	0.011 93 in	0.303 03 mm
10 rin	= 1 bu	0.119 3 in	3.030 3 mm
10 bu	= 1 sun [b]	1.193 03 in	3.030 3 cm
10 sun	= 1 shaku [c]	0.994 2 ft	0.303 03 m
5 shaku	= 1 hiro	1.657 yd	1.515 15 m
6 shaku	= 1 ken	1.988 yd	1.818 18 m
10 shaku	= 1 jō	3.314 yd	3.030 3 m
360 shaku	= 1 chô	119.3 yd	109.09 m
12 960 shaku	= 1 ri [d]	2.440 mi	3.927 27 km

kujira shaku system

	1 bu	0.148 8 in	3.78 mm
10 bu	= 1 sun	1.488 in	3.78 cm
10 sun	= 1 shaku	1.240 ft	37.8 cm
10 shaku	= 1 jo	4.134 yd	3.78 m

Area

	1 shaku	0.355 8 ft²	0.033 058 m²
10 shaku	= 1 gō	3.558 ft²	0.330 58 m²
10 gō	= 1 tsubo [e]	3.954 yd²	3.305 8 m²
30 tsubo	= 1 sê	118.61 yd²	99.174 m²
10 sê	= 1 tan	0.245 acre	991.74 m²
10 tan	= 1 cho	2.451 acre	0.991 74 ha

Japan

		Equivalent in: UK units	Metric units
Volume			
	1 sai[f]	0.983 ft³	27.826 dm³
10 sai	= 1 koku	0.363 96 yd³	0.278 26 m³
216 sai	= 1 ryutsubo	7.861 yd³	6.010 m³
Capacity			
	1 shaku	0.634 9 fl oz	18.039 ml
10 shaku	= 1 gô	6.349 fl oz	18.039 cl
10 gô	= 1 shō	3.174 pt	1.803 9 l
10 shō	= 1 to	3.968 gal	18.039 07 l
10 to	= 1 koku	39.680 gal	1.803 9 hl
Weight			
	1 mō	0.057 87 gr	3.75 mg
10 mō	= 1 rin	0.578 7 gr	37.5 mg
10 rin	= 1 fun	5.787 gr	375 mg
10 fun	= 1 momme[g]	0.132 3 oz	3.75 g
4 momme	= 1 nijo	0.529 oz	15 g
10 momme	= 1 tael	1.323 oz	37.5 g
10 tael	= 1 hyaku-me[h]	13.228 oz	375 g
160 momme	= 1 kin	1.323 lb	600 g
1 000 momme	= 1 kwan[i]	8.267 lb	3.75 kg
100 kin	= 1 picul	132.28 lb	60 kg

[a]As established 1891 in the form of metric linked values, and in use until 1966.
[b]For cloth 1.49 in (3.788 cm).   [c]10/33 metre; before 1891 12.5/33 metre
= 0.378 8 m (1.243 ft).   [d]As a marine measure, equals 1 international nautical
mile.   [e]Or bu; equal to 1 ken².   [f]Shaku³.   [g]Or mommé or manne or me.   [h]Or
hiyaka-me.   [i]Or kan or kwamme.

Jersey

Main system: UK units, changing gradually to the metric system

Other units:

		Equivalent in: UK units	Metric units
Length			
	1 pied de perche[a]	11 in	279 mm
	1 aune[b, c]	4 ft	1.22 m
24 pied de perche	= 1 perche[a]	22 ft	6.7 m
Area[a]			
	1 pied de perche²	121 in²	780.6 cm²
576 pied de perche²	= 1 perche²	484 ft²	44.97 m²
Capacity[b, d]			
	1 pot	3.476 pt	1.975 l
10 pots	= 1 cabot	4.344 gal	19.75 l

[a]Still in use for land sales.   [b]No longer in use.   [c]Or ella.   [d]Another old
capacity unit was the siextonny (or sixtonnier), which contained about 7 lb of
potatoes.

Main system: metric, compulsory from 1953

Old units:

		Equivalent in: UK units	Metric units
Length			
	1 dra: textiles	26.8 in	68 cm
	1 dra: building	29.8 in	75.8 cm
Area			
	1 dunum[a]	0.247 acre	0.1 ha
Capacity			
	1 saa: oil[b]	1.32 gal	6 l
	1 mid: oil[c]	3.96 gal	18 l

		Equivalent in: UK units	Metric units
Weight			
	1 dirham	49.462 gr	3.205 l g
66⅔ dirhams[d]	= 1 oquia[e]: Shami	7.537 oz	213.67 g
75 dirhams	= 1 oquia[e]: Nabulsi	8.479 oz	240.38 g
400 dirhams	= 1 okka	2.826 lb	1.282 kg
2 okkas	= 1 rotl: Shami	5.653 lb	2.564 kg
100 rotls	= 1 kantar: Shami	565.3 lb	256.41 kg
225 okkas	= 1 kantar: Nabulsi	635.9 lb	288.46 kg

[a]Or dönüm.   [b]Balka district.   [c]Agloun and Kerak districts.   [d]200/3.   [e]Or
okia.

Jugoslavia

Main system: metric, from 1876

Other units in use:

		Equivalent in: UK units	Metric units
Length			
	1 hvat	2.073 yd	1.896 m
Area			
	1 hvat²	4.301 yd²	3.597 m²
	1 dunum	1 196 yd²	1 000 m²
1 600 hvat²	= 1 katastarsko jutro	1.422 acre	0.575 5 ha
2 000 hvat²	= 1 lanac	1.777 acre	0.719 2 ha
Weight			
	1 vagon[a]	9.842 ton	10 t

[a]Or wagon.

Korea, North

Main system: metric

Other units in use:

		Equivalent in: UK units	Metric units
Length			
	1 ri	429.492 yd	392.727 m
Area			
	1 pyong[a]	3.953 7 yd²	3.305 8 m²
3 000 pyongs	= 1 jungbo	2.450 6 acre	0.991 74 ha

[a]Equal to (400/121) m².

Korea, South

Main system: metric

Other units in use:

		Equivalent in: UK units	Metric units
Length			
	1 mo	0.001 193 in	0.030 303 mm
10 mos	= 1 ri	0.011 93 in	0.303 03 mm
10 ris	= 1 pun	0.119 3 in	3.030 3 mm
10 puns	= 1 chi	1.193 03 in	3.030 3 cm
10 chis	= 1 chok[a]	0.994 2 ft	0.303 03 m
6 choks	= 1 kan[b]	1.988 yd	1.818 18 m
60 kans	= 1 chung	119.3 yd	109.09 m
36 chungs	= 1 li	2.440 mi	3.927 27 km

Korea, South

Area

		Equivalent in: UK units	Metric units
	1 jak	0.355 8 ft²	0.033 058 m²
	1 chok²	0.988 ft²	0.091 827 m²
10 jaks	= 1 hop	3.558 ft²	0.330 58 m²
3.6 chok²	= 1 hop	3.558 ft²	0.330 58 m²
10 hops	= 1 pyong[c]	3.954 yd²	3.305 8 m²
30 pyongs	= 1 myo	118.61 yd²	99.174 m²
10 myos	= 1 tan	1 186.1 yd²	991.74 m²
10 tans	= 1 chungbo	2.451 acre	0.991 74 ha

Volume

1 kan³	= 1 ippyong [d]	7.861 yd³	6.010 5 m³

timber units

1 chi² × 12 chok	= 1 jae	0.117 9 ft³	3.339 dm³
72 chok³	= 1 pyong	2.620 yd³	2.003 5 m³

Capacity

	1 jak	0.634 9 fl oz	18.039 ml
10 jaks	= 1 hop	6.349 fl oz	18.039 cl
10 hops	= 1 dai	3.174 pt	1.803 9 l
5 dai	= 1 small mal	1.984 gal	9.019 5 l
10 dai	= 1 big mal	3.968 gal	18.039 l
100 dai	= 1 suk	39.680 gal	1.803 9 hl

Weight

	1 don [e]	0.132 3 oz	3.75 g
10 dons	= 1 yang	1.323 oz	37.5 g
16 yangs	= 1 keun[f]	1.323 lb	600 g
100 yangs	= 1 kwan	8.267 lb	3.75 kg

[a]10/33 metre.   [b]Or ken.   [c]Tile measure.   [d]Also pyong for gravel.   [e]Or donchung.   [f]Or kon or catty.

Kuwait

Main system: metric, from 1962

Other unit in use:

		Equivalent in: UK units	Metric units
Weight			
	1 maund	56 lb	25.4 kg

Laos

Main system: metric

Other units in use:

		Equivalent in: UK units	Metric units
Length			
	1 kabiet	0.164 in	4.167 mm
4 kabiets	= 1 niou	0.656 in	1⅔ cm
6 nious	= 1 kam	3.937 in	10 cm
2 kams	= 1 khup[a]	7.874 in	20 cm
2 khups	= 1 sok [b]	1.312 ft	40 cm
5 soks	= 1 va[c]	2.187 yd	2 m
20 vas	= 1 sénh	43.74 yd	40 m
500 vas	= 1 lackilo	0.621 mi	1 km
Area			
1 va²	= 1 talangva	4.784 yd²	4 m²
100 talangvas	= 1 ngane	478.4 yd²	400 m²
4 nganes	= 1 rai	0.395 acre	0.16 ha

Capacity

		Equivalent in: UK units	Metric units
	1 phaï mû	2.2 pt	1.25 l
2 phaï mû	= 1 kob	4.4 pt	2.5 l
2 kobs	= 1 khanan	1.1 gal	5 l
4 khanans	= 1 kalong [d]	4.4 gal	20 l
10 kalongs	= 1 thang[e]	44 gal	200 l

Weight
general

	1 li	0.579 gr	37.5 mg
10 lis	= 1 houn	5.787 gr	375 mg
25 lis	= 1 kâ	14.47 gr	937.5 mg
2 kâs	= 1 fuang	28.94 gr	1.875 g
2 fuangs	= 1 salung [f]	57.87 gr	3.75 g
4 salungs	= 1 bath[g]	0.529 oz	15 g
8 baths	= 1 hoi	4.233 oz	120 g
10 hois	= 1 xang [h]	2.646 lb	1.2 kg
10 xangs	= 1 mune[i]	26.455 lb	12 kg
5 munes	= 1 picul [j]	132.28 lb	60 kg
2 piculs	= 1 sène	264.55 lb	120 kg
10 sènes	= 1 lane	1.181 ton	1.2 t

opium

10 houns	= 1 bak	57.87 gr	3.75 g
10 baks	= 1 bia[k]	1.206 oz tr	37.5 g
10 bias	= 1 pong	12.06 oz tr	375 g

[a]Or khub.   [b]Also sometimes used as 50 cm.   [c]Or va-yiet.   [d]Or bok.   [e]Also sometimes used as 40 litres.   [f]Or bak.   [g]Or bat.   [h]Or sang or phan.   [i]Or mun.   [j]Or hab.   [k]Or hong.

Lebanon

Main system: metric, compulsory from 1935; also some UK units

Other units in use:

		Equivalent in: UK units	Metric units
Length			
textiles			
	1 kirat	1.115 in	2.833 cm
24 kirats	= 1 drah [a]	26.772 in	68 cm
agriculture and construction			
	1 kirat	1.243 in	3.158 cm
24 kirats	= 1 drah [a]	29.843 in	75.8 cm
Area			
	1 qassabeh	28.48 yd²	23.814 m²
	1 marasseh	59.80 yd²	50 m²
1 600 drah² (land)	= 1 denum[b]	0.227 acre	919.302 m²
4 000–6 000 drah²	= 1 kadne[c]	0.57–0.85 acre	0.23–0.34 ha
Weight			
	1 derham[d]	49.46 gr	3.205 g
66⅔ derhams	= 1 okiya[e]	0.471 0 lb	213.665 g
6 okiyas	= 1 oke[f]	2.826 3 lb	1.281 99 kg
2 okes	= 1 rottolo[g]	5.652 6 lb	2.563 97 kg
100 rottolos	= 1 kantar	565.26 lb	256.397 kg
agriculture			
	1 med[d] (wheat)	40–44 lb	18–20 kg
	1 qilli[h] (olive oil)	73.513 lb	33.345 kg
	1 tablé (cereals)	33.069 lb	15 kg
10 tablés	= 1 chinbul[i] (cereals)	330.69 lb	150 kg

[a]Or zirah or pic or piq.   [b]Or dunum or dönüm; cadastral (or metric) denum equals 1 000 m².   [c]Or kadneh or cadné; one day's work by a pair of oxen.   [d]Or mudd or dirham or dirhem.   [e]Or once.   [f]Or okka or ocque.   [g]Or rotol or rottol; in the mountains 1 rottolo is 2.935 g for oil and 3.206 g for soap.   [h]Or kollé.   [i]Or chombol.

Libya

Main system: metric

Other units in use:

Length
textiles

		Equivalent in: UK units	Metric units
	1 palmo	9.84 in	25 cm
	1 dra Arbi	1.61 ft	49 cm
	1 handaza (or pik)	2.23 ft	68 cm
	1 gana	1.7 yd	1.6 m

land

	1 draa milki	1.64 ft	50 cm
2 draa milkis	= 1 passo	1.09 yd	1 m
35 passos	= 1 habl	38.3 yd	35 m

Area

	1 gadula	14.65 yd²	12.25 m²
	1 dönüm	1 099 yd²	919 m²
100 gadulas	= 1 jabia	1 465 yd²	1 225 m²
	1 keila	0.79 acre	0.32 ha
3 keilas	= 1 sāa	2.37 acre	0.96 ha

Capacity, dry

	1 misura	4.36 gal	19.8 l
	1 teman	5.90 gal	26.8 l
	1 kilé	0.99 bu	36 l
	1 sāa	3.27 bu	1.188 hl

cereals

	1 marta	4.56 gal	20.75 l
14 martas	= 1 ueba	7.99 bu	2.905 hl

Capacity, liquid

	1 gurraf	4.06 pt	2.307 l
6⅛ gurrafs	= 1 jarra	3.11 gal	14.13 l

Weight
general

	1 dirham [a]	0.113 oz	3.205 g
10 dirhams	= 1 ukia [b]	1.131 oz	32.05 g
16 ukies[c]	= 1 ratl[c]	1.131 lb	512.8 g
40 ukias	= 1 oke[d]	2.826 lb	1.282 kg
40 okes	= 1 kantar (Tripolitania)	113.1 lb	51.28 kg
50 okes	= 1 kantar (Cyrenaica)	141.3 lb	64.10 kg

gold, silver and silk

	1 charruba	2.958 gr	191.7 mg
16 charrubas	= 1 dirham[a]	0.098 6 oz tr	3.067 2 g
24 charrubas	= 1 metkal[e]	0.147 9 oz tr	4.600 8 g
10 dirhams	= 1 ukia	0.986 1 oz tr	30.672 g

[a]Or dramma. [b]Or ukie for ostrich feathers and spinning wools. [c]For ostrich feathers and spinning wools. [d]Or oka. [e]For gold.

Luxembourg

Main system: metric, compulsory from 1820

Old unit:

Area

	Equivalent in: UK units	Metric units
1 food² (used in hide processing)	3.28 ft²	0.304 8 m²

Macao

Main system: metric

Other units in use:

Length
old Portuguese system

		Equivalent in: UK units	Metric units
	1 polegada	1.083 in	2.75 cm
8 polegadas	= 1 palmo	8.661 in	22 cm
12 polegadas	= 1 pé	1.083 ft	0.33 m
2 pés	= 1 côvado	2.165 ft	0.66 m
3⅓ pés	= 1 vara	1.203 yd	1.10 m
6 pés	= 1 toesa	1.083 fathom	1.98 m
2 varas	= 1 braça	2.406 yd	2.20 m

old Chinese system

	1 li	0.014 8 in	0.376 mm
10 lis	= 1 condorim	0.148 in	3.76 mm
10 condorims	= 1 ponto	1.480 in	3.76 cm
10 pontos	= 1 côvado[a]	1.234 ft	0.376 m

Area[b]
old Chinese system

	1 ponto	1.967 in²	12.69 cm²
100 pontos	= 1 côvado	1.366 ft²	0.126 9 m²
25 côvados	= 1 pu	3.79 yd²	3.172 5 m²
4 pus	= 1 cheong	15.18 yd²	12.69 m²
6 cheongs	= 1 fan	91.06 yd²	76.14 m²
10 fans	= 1 maz[c]	910.6 yd²	761.4 m²

Volume
old Chinese system

	1 hap	3.629 fl oz	103.1 ml
10 haps	= 1 chupa	1.814 pt	1.031 l
10 chupas	= 1 ganta	2.267 9 gal	10.31 l
10 gantas	= 1 seak	22.679 gal	103.1 l

Weight
old Portuguese system

	1 grão	0.756 gr	49 mg
	1 oitava	0.126 5 gr	3.59 g
8 oitavas	= 1 onça	1.012 oz	28.69 g
16 onças	= 1 arrátel[d]	1.012 lb	459 g
32 arrátels	= 1 arroba	32.38 lb	14.688 kg
4 arrobas	= 1 quintal	129.5 lb	58.752 kg

old Chinese system

	1 li	0.583 gr	37.799 mg
10 lis	= 1 condorim	5.833 gr	377.99 mg
10 condorims	= 1 maz	0.133 33 oz	3.779 9 g
10 mazes	= 1 tael	1⅓ oz	37.799 g
16 taels	= 1 cate	1⅓ lb	604.79 g
100 cates	= 1 pico	133⅓ lb	60.479 kg

[a]Varies from 0.356–0.376 m. [b]In the old Portuguese system quadrada or quadrado means 'squared'. [c]Or mau. [d]The German pound (arrátel alemão) has a value of 502.18 grams.

Malaysia

Main system: metric, as a gradual conversion from the UK system

Other units in use:

Length

		Equivalent in: UK units	Metric units
	1 chum	1.475 in	3.746 5 cm
	1 jengkal	9 in	22.86 cm
10 chums	= 1 check	14.75 in	37.465 cm
2 jengkals	= 1 hesta	1½ ft	45.72 cm
2 hestas	= 1 ela	1 yd	0.914 4 m
2 elas	= 1 depa	1 fathom	1.828 8 m
10 checks	= 1 cheung	4.097 yd	3.746 m

Malaysia

		Equivalent in: UK units	Metric units
Area			
	1 depa²	36 ft²	3.345 m²
4 depa²	= 1 jemba	144 ft²	13.378 m²
16⅔ jembas	= 1 lelong	2 400 ft²	222.97 m²
100 jembas	= 1 penjuru	14 400 ft²	1 337.8 m²
	1 relong	0.71 acre	0.287 ha
24 lelongs	= 1 orlong	1.322 acre	0.535 ha
Volume *Sarawak*			
	1 panchang	108 ft³	3.058 m³
Capacity, dry			
	1 lang	1 pt	56.826 cl
6 400 langs	= 1 koyan	100 bu	36.369 hl
Capacity, liquid			
	1 pau	½ pt	284.1 ml
4 paus	= 1 chupak	1 qt	1.137 l
4 chupaks	= 1 gantang	1 gal	4.546 l
10 gantangs	= 1 para[a]	10 gal	45.46 l
	1 tun	252 gal	11.456 hl
80 paras	= 1 koyan	800 gal	36.369 hl
Weight *general*			
	1 hoon	5⅚ gr	378 mg
10 hoons	= 1 chee	58⅓ gr	3.78 g
16 hoons	= 1 mace[d]	93⅓ gr	6.047 9 g
10 chees	= 1 tahil	1⅓ oz	37.8 g
16 tahils	= 1 kati[b]	1⅓ lb	604.8 g
135 maces	= 1 chapah[d]	1.8 lb	0.816 kg
4 katis	= 1 gantang	5⅓ lb	2.419 kg
50 chapahs	= 1 para[d]	90 lb	40.823 kg
100 katis	= 1 pikul[c]	133⅓ lb	60.479 kg
25 gantangs	= 1 pikul[c]	133⅓ lb	60.479 kg
3 pikuls	= 1 bhara	400 lb	181.4 kg
40 pikuls	= 1 koyan	5 333⅓ lb	2.419 t
precious metals			
	1 saga	4⅓ gr	280.8 mg
12 sagas	= 1 mayam	52 gr	3.370 g
16 mayams	= 1 bongkal	1.733 oz tr	53.913 g
12 bongkal	= 1 kati	20.8 oz tr	646.95 g

[a]Bandu in Sabah and Sarawak.   [b]Or catty.   [c]Or picul.   [d]Sabah.

Malta

Main system: metric, from 1921; also UK system, with gradual conversion to a completely metric system

Other units in use:

		Equivalent in: UK units	Metric units
Length			
	1 pulzier	0.859 in	21.83 mm
12 pulziers	= 1 xiber[a]	10.312 in	26.19 cm
8 xibers	= 1 qasba[b]	2.292 yd	2.095 m
Area			
	1 kejla	22.41 yd²	18.735 m²
10 kejlas	= 1 siegh	224.1 yd²	187.354 m²
6 sieghs	= 1 tomna	0.278 acre	0.112 ha
16 tomnas	= 1 modd	4.444 acre	1.798 ha
Capacity, dry *cereals*			
	1 tomnas	4 gal	18.184 l
16 tomnas	= 1 modd[c]	8 bu	2.909 hl
25 modds	= 1 tumoli	200 bu	72.737 hl

		Equivalent in: UK units	Metric units
Capacity, liquid *oil and milk*			
	1 terz	11¼ fl oz	32.0 cl
2 terz	= 1 nofs	1.125 pt	63.9 cl
2 nofs	= 1 kartocc	1.125 qt	1.279 l
4 kartoccs	= 1 kwarta	1.125 gal	5.114 l
4 kwartas	= 1 caffiso	4½ gal	20.46 l
beer, wine and spirits			
	1 pinta	1 gill	142 ml
2 pintas	= 1 terz	½ pt	284 ml
2 terz	= 1 nofs	1 pt	568 ml
2 nofs	= 1 kartocc	1 qt	1.136 l
4¾ kartoccs	= 1 kwarta	1.187 5 gal	5.398 l
2 kwartas	= 1 garra	2.375 gal	10.797 l
4 garras	= 1 barmil[d]	9½ gal	43.188 l
Weight			
	1 uqija	0.933 oz	26.460 g
17⅟₇ uqijas	= 1 libra	1 lb	453.6 g
30 uqijas	= 1 rotolo[e]	1¾ lb	0.794 kg
5 rotolos	= 1 wizna	8¾ lb	3.969 kg
20 wiznas	= 1 cantar[f]	175 lb	79.379 kg
2.8 cantars	= 1 salm	490 lb	222.3 kg

[a]Or palmi.   [b]Or canna.   [c]Or salma tumoli.   [d]Or barril.   [e]Or ratal.   [f]Or cantaro or qantar.

Mauritius

Main system: metric, from 1878

Other units in use:

		Equivalent in: UK units	Metric units
Length			
	1 ligne	0.088 8 in	2.255 83 mm
12 lignes	= 1 pouce	1.066 in	2.707 cm
12 pouces	= 1 pied	1.066 ft	0.324 84 m
44 pouces	= 1 aune[a]	1.303 yd	1.191 m
6 pieds	= 1 toise[b]	1.066 fathom	1.949 m
10 pieds	= 1 gaulette[c]	3.552 yd	3.248 4 m
20 pieds	= 1 perche	1.292 perch	6.496 8 m
	1 lieue	2.485 mi	4 km
Area			
	1 perche²	50.481 yd²	42.208 m²
100 perche²	= 1 arpent	1.043 acre	0.422 ha
Volume			
	1 pied³	1.210 ft³	0.034 28 m³
80 pied³	= 1 corde[d]	96.84 ft³	2.742 m³
Capacity			
	1 pinte, reputed	⅔ pt	37.86 cl
	1 chopine	0.703 9 pt	40 cl
2 pintes, reputed	= 1 quart[e], reputed	26⅔ fl oz	75.77 cl
2 chopines	= 1 bouteille	1.408 pt	80 cl
	1 pinte, colonial	1.639 pt	0.931 3 l
8 pintes, colonial	= 1 velte	1.639 gal	7.450 5 l
	1 tierçon	42.01 gal	1.91 hl
	1 barrique	49.98 gal	2.272 hl
Weight *old French units*			
	1 grain	0.819 7 gr	53.115 mg
72 grains	= 1 gros	59.02 gr	3.824 g
8 gros	= 1 once	1.079 oz	30.594 g
16 onces	= 1 livre[f]	1.079 lb	0.489 51 kg
other			
	1 livre	1.102 lb	0.5 kg

[a]For textiles.   [b]For masonry.   [c]For land.   [d]For fuel wood.   [e]Or quart de bouteille.   [f]Livre poids-de-marc.

Mexico

Main system: metric, compulsory from 1862

Old units:

Length

		Equivalent in: UK units	Metric units
	1 linea	0.076 4 in	1.940 mm
12 lineas	= 1 pulgada	0.916 in	2.327 8 cm
12 pulgadas	= 1 pie	10.997 in	27.933 3 cm
3 pies	= 1 vara	0.916 4 yd	0.838 00 m
5 000 varas	= 1 legua	2.604 mi	4.190 km

Area

		Equivalent in: UK units	Metric units
	1 fanega[a]	8.812 acre	3.566 3 ha
12 fanegas	= 1 caballería	105.75 acre	42.795 3 ha
	1 sitio de ganado mayor	6.778 mi²	17.556 1 km²

Capacity, dry

		Equivalent in: UK units	Metric units
	1 cuartillo	3.329 pt	1.891 98 l
4 cuartillos	= 1 almud	1.665 gal	7.567 9 l
	1 cuarterón	5.5 gal	25 l
12 almuds	= 1 fanega	2.497 bu	0.908 149 hl
2 fanegas	= 1 carga	4.994 bu	1.816 298 hl

Capacity, liquid

		Equivalent in: UK units	Metric units
	1 cuartillo	0.803 pt	0.456 264 l
	1 cuartillo (oil)	0.891 pt	0.506 162 l
	1 frasco	4.164 pt	2.366 l
18 cuartillos	= 1 jarra	1.807 gal	8.212 752 l
	1 barril	16.72 gal	76 l

Weight

		Equivalent in: UK units	Metric units
	1 adarme	27.745 gr	1.797 837 g
2 adarmes	= 1 ochava	55.490 gr	3.595 675 g
16 adarmes	= 1 onza[b]	1.014 67 oz	28.765 396 g
16 onzas	= 1 libra	1.014 67 lb	460.246 34 g
25 libras	= 1 arroba	25.367 lb	11.506 158 kg
4 arrobas	= 1 quintal	101.467 lb	46.024 634 kg
160 libras	= 1 tercio	162.35 lb	73.639 kg
3 quintals	= 1 carga[c]	304.4 lb	138.074 kg

[a]Fanega de sembradura de maiz.   [b]Or marco.   [c]In metric linked from the carga is 140 kg (308.6 lb).

Mongolia

Main system: metric

Other units in use:

Length

		Equivalent in: UK units	Metric units
	1 li	0.012 6 in	0.32 mm
10 lis	= 1 pun	0.126 in	3.2 mm
10 puns	= 1 imagu	1.260 in	3.2 cm
10 imagus	= 1 tokhoi[a]	1.049 9 ft	32 cm
5 tokhois	= 1 aldan	1.749 8 yd	1.6 m
2 aldans	= 1 khos aldan[b]	3.499 6 yd	3.2 m
36 aldans	= 1 khubi	62.992 yd	57.6 m
10 khubis	= 1 gatsar	629.92 yd	576 m

Area

		Equivalent in: UK units	Metric units
	1 aldan²	3.062 yd²	2.56 m²
360 aldan²	= 1 ure	0.227 7 acre	921.6 m²
100 ures	= 1 gubiar	22.773 acre	9.216 ha

Capacity

		Equivalent in: UK units	Metric units
	1 shin	1.143 8 pt	65 cl
10 shins	= 1 sulga[c]	1.429 8 gal	6.5 l
10 sulgas	= 1 dan	14.298 gal	65 l

Weight

		Equivalent in: UK units	Metric units
	1 khou	0.057 9 gr	3.75 mg
10 khous	= 1 li	0.578 7 gr	37.5 mg
10 lis	= 1 pun	5.787 gr	375 mg
10 puns	= 1 tsin	57.87 gr	3.75 g
10 tsins	= 1 lan	1.323 oz	37.5 g
16 lans	= 1 dzhin	1.323 lb	600 g

[a]Or chi.   [b]Or chang.   [c]Or du.

Morocco

Main system: metric

Other units in use:

Length

		Equivalent in: UK units	Metric units
	1 tomini	2.75 in	6.985 cm
8 tominis	= 1 drah[d]	22 in	0.558 8 m

Area

		Equivalent in: UK units	Metric units
	1 tamna	269.1 yd²	225 m²
2 tamnas	= 1 courd[a]	538.2 yd²	450 m²
2 courds	= 1 aftari[b]	1 076.4 yd²	900 m²
	1 khedem	1 196.0 yd²	0.1 ha
2 aftaris	= 1 âbraa[c]	2 152.8 yd²	0.18 ha
2 âbraas	= 1 tarialte	0.889 6 acre	0.36 ha
5 khedems	= 1 gouffa	1.236 acre	0.5 ha

Capacity

		Equivalent in: UK units	Metric units
	1 tomini	1.283 gal	5.83 l
	1 kard	2.199 7 gal	10 l
	1 kula[e]	5.290 gal	24.047 l
4 kards	= 1 kharrouba	8.799 gal	40 l
8 tominis	= 1 mudd	1.283 bu	46.7 l
	1 fanega	1.540 bu	0.56 hl

Weight

old system

		Equivalent in: UK units	Metric units
	1 rotal	1.13 lb	513 g
100 rotals	= 1 kantar[g]	113 lb	51.26 kg

metric linked system

		Equivalent in: UK units	Metric units
	1 oukeia	4.409 oz	125 g
2 oukeias	= 1 rabâa	8.818 oz	250 g
2 rabâas	= 1 rotal[f]	1.102 lb	500 g
200 rotals	= 1 kantar[g]	220.46 lb	100 kg

[a]Or moud or rabia or tarabiit.   [b]Or saa or tmen.   [c]Or izenbi or sdal.   [d]Or kala; metric drah is 0.5 m (19.69 in).   [e]For oil.   [f]Or rtel.   [g]Or cantar or quintal.

Nepal

Main system: domestic and Indian, with gradual conversion to the metric system beginning 1968

Domestic system:

Length

		Equivalent in: UK units	Metric units
	1 bitta	9 in	22.86 cm
2 bittas	= 1 haat[a]	18 in	45.72 cm
2 haats	= 1 guz[a]	1 yd	0.914 4 m
	1 kosh	2 mi	3.219 km

Nepal

Area

mountains

		UK units	Metric units
	1 matomana	0.951 yd²	0.795 m²
8 matomanas	= 1 matopathi	7.605 yd²	6.359 m²
20 matopathis	= 1 matomuri	152.1 yd²	127.18 m²
4 matomuris	= 1 ropani [b]	608.4 yd²	508.72 m²

plain

	1 dhur	20.25 yd²	16.929 m²
20 dhurs	= 1 kattha	404.9 yd²	338.57 m²
20 katthas	= 1 bigha	1.673 acre	0.677 141 ha

Capacity

	1 mana [c]	1 pt	56.83 cl
8 manas	= 1 pathi	1 gal	4.546 l

Weight

	1 pao	6.86 oz	194.4 g
4.8 paos	= 1 seer [d]	2.057 lb	0.933 1 kg
2.5 seers	= 1 dharni	5.142 lb	2.332 8 kg
16 dharnis	= 1 maund	82.28 lb	37.324 2 kg

[a]For textiles. [b]Kathmandu valley. [c]For cereals. [d]Seer (terai); seer (hills) is 0.797 8 kg (1.759 lb).

Netherlands

Main system: metric, compulsory from 1820

Old units:

Length

old Amsterdam units

		UK units	Metric units
	1 duim	1.013 in	2.574 cm
11 duims	= 1 voet [a]	11.147 in	28.313 cm
	1 ell	2.257 ft	0.687 8 m

old Rhineland (Rijnlandse) units

	1 duim.	1.031 in	2.618 cm
12 duims	= 1 voet [a]	1.031 ft	31.417 cm
12 voets	= 1 roe [b]	0.750 rod	3.770 m

UK linked unit

	1 vadem	2 yd	1.829 m

metric linked units

	1 streep	0.039 37 in	1 mm
10 streeps	= 1 duim	0.393 7 in	1 cm
10 duims	= 1 palm	3.937 in	10 cm
10 palms	= 1 ell	1.094 yd	1 m
10 ells	= 1 roe [b]	1.988 rod	10 m

Area

old Rhineland (Rijnlandse) units

1 roe²	= 1 roede	16.999 yd²	14.213 m²
100 roedes	= 1 hout	1 699.9 yd²	1 421.3 m²
3 houts	= 1 Rhineland acre	1.054 acre	0.426 4 ha
2 Rhineland acres	= 1 morgen	2.107 acre	0.852 8 ha

metric linked units

100 roe²	= 1 roe² [c] = 1 bunder [d]	119.6 yd²	100 m²
		2.471 acre	1 ha

Capacity

old Amsterdam units

	1 mutsje	0.267 pt	15.2 cl
8 mutsjes	= 1 mengel	2.134 pt	1.212 l
2 mengels	= 1 stoop	0.533 gal	2.425 l
16 stoops	= 1 ancre	8.53 gal	38.8 l
6 ancres	= 1 okshoofd [e]	51.21 gal	2.328 hl
340 mengels	= 1 pijp [f]	90.68 gal	4.122 5 hl

metric linked units

		UK units	Metric units
10 maatjes	1 maatje = 1 kan [g]	0.176 pt 1.760 pt	10 cl 1 l
5 kans	= 1 spint	1.099 8 gal	5 l
6 kans	= 1 stoop	1.319 8 gal	6 l
10 kans	= 1 schepel	2.199 7 gal	10 l
10 schepels	= 1 mud [h]	21.997 gal	1 hl
10 muds	= 1 wise [i]	219.97 gal	10 hl
30 muds	= 1 last	659.9 gal	30 hl

wine units

	1 boot [j]	116.58 gal	5.3 hl
	1 pijp [f]	118.78 gal	5.4 hl
	1 halbstück [k]	131.98 gal	6 hl

Weight

old Amsterdam units

	1 grein	0.99 gr	0.064 g
60 greins	= 1 drachma	59.6 gr	3.86 g
4 drachmas	= 1 lood [l]	0.545 oz	15.4 g
2 loods	= 1 ons	1.089 oz	30.9 g
8 ons	= 1 mark	0.545 lb	247 g
2 marks	= 1 pond	1.089 lb	494.1 g

metric linked units

	1 korrel	1.543 gr	100 mg
10 korrels	= 1 wichtje	15.432 gr	1 g
100 wichtjes	= 1 ons	3.527 oz	100 g
5 ons	= 1 pond	1.102 lb	500 g
20 ponds	= 1 lood	22.046 lb	10 kg
200 loods	= 1 last	1.968 ton	2 t

[a]Or foot. [b]Or roede. [c]Or vierkante roede. [d]Or mud or mudde. [e]Or barrel. [f]Or pipe; for port wine. [g]As liquid measure; kop for dry measure. [h]Or vat or zak. [i]Or fuder for Rhine wine. [j]Or butt; for sherry. [k]For Rhine wine. [l]Or loot.

Netherlands Antilles

Main system: metric

Other units in use:

Weight

		UK units	Metric units
	1 pintji	0.827 lb	0.375 kg
2 pintjis	= 1 cana	1.65 lb	0.75 kg

Nicaragua

Main system: metric, from 1893

Other units in use:

Length

		UK units	Metric units
	1 pulgada	0.919 in	$2\frac{1}{3}$ cm
9 pulgadas	= 1 cuarta	8.27 in	21 cm
12 pulgadas	= 1 tercia	0.919 ft	28 cm
4 cuartas	= 1 vara	0.919 yd	0.84 m
24 varas	= 1 mecate	22.05 yd	20.16 m
2 200 varas	= 1 milla	1.148 mi	1.848 km

Area

	1 vara²	7.595 ft²	0.705 6 m²
10 000 vara²	= 1 manzana	1.744 acre	0.705 6 ha
64 manzanas	= 1 caballería	111.59 acre	45.158 ha

Capacity

	1 cuarta	5.866 fl oz	$16\frac{2}{3}$ cl
4 cuartas	= 1 botella	1.173 pt	$\frac{2}{3}$ l
25 botellas	= 1 cajuela	3.666 gal	$16\frac{2}{3}$ l

43

Nicaragua

Weight

		Equivalent in: UK units	Metric units
	1 onza	1.014 oz	28.75 g
16 onzas	= 1 libra[a]	1.014 lb	460 g
25 libras	= 1 arroba	25.353 lb	11.5 kg
	1 caja	35.27 lb	16 kg
4 arrobas	= 1 quintal[c]	101.4 lb	46 kg
150 libras	= 1 saco[b]	152.1 lb	69 kg
2 quintals	= 1 carga	202.8 lb	92 kg
3½ quintals	= 1 fanega	354.9 lb	161 kg
20 quintals	= 1 tonelada	0.905 ton	0.92 t

[a]Also used as 460.24 g, other units varying accordingly. [b]For coffee. [c]For sugar, 1 quintal = 100 lb (45.4 kg).

Nigeria

Main system: metric, as conversion from the UK system, in general complete from 1977

Other units in use:

		Equivalent in: UK units	Metric units
Capacity, dry			
	1 mudu[a]	2½ lb	1.13 kg
2 mudus	= 1 tiya[a]	5 lb	2.27 kg
Weight			
	1 load (cocoa)	60 lb	27.2 kg

[a]Values vary according to region.

Norway

Main system: metric from 1875 (compulsory from 1882)

Old units (no longer in use):

		Equivalent in: UK units	Metric units
Length			
	1 fot	1.029 ft	0.313 7 m
6 fots	= 1 favn	1.029 fathom	1.882 m
6 000 favns	= 1 mil[a]	7.018 mi	11.295 km
Volume			
	1 favn[b]	84.755 ft³	2.4 m³
Capacity			
	1 pot	1.698 pt	0.965 l
18 pots	= 1 skjeppe	3.821 gal	17.37 l
8 skjeppes	= 1 korn-tönde[c]	30.569 gal	1.390 hl
	1 korn-topmaal	35.195 gal	1.6 hl
Weight			
	1 quenten	60 gr	3.89 g
4 quentens	= 1 loth	0.549 oz	15.6 g
2 loths	= 1 ounce	1.098 oz	31.1 g
8 ounces	= 1 mark	0.549 lb	249 g
2 marks	= 1 pund[d]	1.098 lb	498.1 g
16 punds	= 1 lispond	17.57 lb	7.969 kg
100 punds	= 1 centner	109.81 lb	49.81 kg
20 lisponds	= 1 shippond[e]	351.4 lb	159.4 kg

[a]Metric linked mil was 10 km. [b]For fuelwood. [c]Metric linked korn-tönde was 1.4 hl. [d]Metric linked pund was 500 g. [e]Approximately equal to 1 English sack of wool (364 lb).

Oman

Main system: metric, as official conversion from the domestic system from November 15, 1974

Old units:

		Equivalent in: UK units	Metric units
Length[a]			
	1 rajabah[b]	1.18 in	3 cm
6 rajabahs	= 1 fatar[c]	7.09 in	18 cm
8 rajabahs	= 1 shibr[d]	9.45 in	24 cm
	1 dhara	18 in	45.7 cm
6 shibrs	= 1 ba'a[e]	1.57 yd	1.44 m
20 000 shibrs	= 1 farsakh	3.0 mi	4.8 km
Weight			
general			
	1 Maria Theresa thaler	0.989 58 oz	28.05 g
6 Maria Theresa thalers	= 1 kiya	5.937 5 oz	168.3 g
24 kiyas	= 1 Muscat maund	8.906 lb	4.040 kg
10 Muscat maunds	= 1 farasalah	89.06 lb	40.4 kg
200 Muscat maunds	= 1 bahár	0.795 ton	0.808 t
cereals[a]			
	1 pali	0.6 lb	280 g
40 palis	= 1 ferrah	25 lb	11.3 kg
20 ferrahs	= 1 khandi	500 lb	227 kg

[a]Relationships and values varied markedly. [b]First joint of finger to tip. [c]Span from first finger to thumb. [d]Span of hand. [e]Span of outstretched arms.

Pakistan

Main system: metric system, as gradual conversion from the UK system

Other units in use:

		Equivalent in: UK units	Metric units
Length			
	1 unglie	¾ in	1.905 cm
3 unglies	= 1 girah	2¼ in	5.715 cm
8 girahs	= 1 hath[a]	18 in	0.457 2 m
16 girahs	= 1 gaz[b]	1 yd	0.914 4 m
2 gaz	= 1 danda	2 yd	1.828 8 m
22 gaz	= 1 jareeb[c]	1 ch	20.117 m
1 000 dandas	= 1 coss	1.136 mi	1.828 8 km
88 unglies	= 1 karam	5½ ft	1.676 4 m
Area			
	1 karam²	3.361 yd²	2.810 m²
	1 anna	20⅙ yd²	16.862 m²
9 karam²	= 1 marla	30.25 yd²	25.293 m²
6 annas	= 1 guntha	121 yd²	101.17 m²
4 gunthas	= 1 jareeb²	484 yd²	404.69 m²
20 marlas	= 1 kanal	605 yd²	505.86 m²
4 jareeb²	= 1 kanee	1 936 yd²	1 618.7 m²
4 kanals	= 1 bigha	0.5 acre	0.202 34 ha
10 jareeb²	= 1 ghumaon[d]	1 acre	0.405 ha
2 bighas	= 1 ghumaon[d]	1 acre	0.405 ha
25 ghumaons	= 1 moraba[e]	25 acre	10.117 ha
Weight[f]			
	1 khashkha	0.029 3 gr	1.898 mg
8 khashkhas	= 1 chawal	0.234 4 gr	15.187 mg
8 chawals	= 1 ruttee	1.875 gr	121.5 mg
8 ruttees	= 1 masha	15 gr	0.972 g
12 mashas	= 1 tola	180 gr	11.664 g
5 tolas	= 1 chattak	2.057 oz	58.319 g
4 chattaks	= 1 pao	0.514 lb	233.28 g
4 paos	= 1 seer	2.057 lb	0.933 1 kg
40 seers	= 1 maund	82.286 lb	37.324 kg

[a]Or cubit. [b]Or yard. [c]Or chain. [d]Or acre. [e]Or marabba. [f]Standard 1939 weights.

Panama

Main system: metric system, as gradual conversion from the UK system

Other units in use:

Capacity		Equivalent in: UK units	Metric units
	1 botella	1.332 pt	75.7 cl
	1 azumbre	3.555 pt	2.02 l
	1 celemin	1.017 gal	4.625 l

Paraguay

Main system: metric, from 1901

Other units in use:

Length		Equivalent in: UK units	Metric units
	1 linea	0.079 in	2.006 mm
12 lineas	= 1 pulgada	0.947 7 in	2.406 cm
12 pulgadas	= 1 pie	0.947 7 ft	28.89 cm
3 pies	= 1 vara	2.843 ft	86.66 cm
	1 cuerda[a]	76.42 yd	69.88 m
100 varas	= 1 cuadra	94.77 yd	86.66 m
50 cuadras	= 1 legua	2.692 mi	4.333 km
Area			
100 vara²	1 vara²	8.08 ft²	0.751 m²
	= 1 liño	89.8 yd²	75.1 m²
Capacity, dry			
	1 almude	5.28 gal	24 l
12 almudes	= 1 fanega	7.92 bu	2.88 hl
Capacity, liquid			
	1 cuarta	1.33 pt	75.73 cl
4 cuartas	= 1 frasco	5.33 pt	3.029 l
32 frascos	= 1 barril	21.32 gal	96.93 l
6 barrils	= 1 pipa	127.9 gal	5.816 hl
Weight			
	1 onza	1.012 oz	28.688 g
16 onzas	= 1 libra	1.012 lb	459.0 g
25 libras	= 1 arroba	25.298 lb	11.475 kg
4 arrobas	= 1 quintal	101.2 lb	45.9 kg
20 quintals	= 1 tonelada	0.904 ton	0.918 t

[a]Or cordel.

Peru

Main system: metric, from 1869

Other units in use:

Length		Equivalent in: UK units	Metric units
	1 vara	33 in	83.82 cm
	1 legua	3.452 mi	5.556 km
Area			
	1 topo: Cuzco	0.67 acre	0.272 ha
	1 topo: general	0.86 acre	0.349 ha
	1 topo: Puno	1.14 acre	0.461 ha
	1 fanegada[a]	1.60 acre	0.646 ha
50 fanegadas	= 1 yugada	79.8 acre	32.3 ha
Capacity			
	1 arroba (wine)	3.54 gal	16.1 l
	1 fanega	1.53 bu	55.5 l
Weight			
	1 adarme	27.7 gr	1.797 g
16 adarmes	= 1 onza	1.014 oz	28.75 g
16 onzas	= 1 libra	1.014 lb	460 g
25 libras	= 1 arroba	25.35 lb	11.5 kg
4 arrobas	= 1 quintal	101.41 lb	46 kg
	1 saco (coffee)	152.12 lb	69 kg
20 quintals	= 1 tonelada	0.905 ton	0.92 t

[a]Variable.

Philippines

Main system: metric, compulsory from January 1, 1975

Old units:

Length		Equivalent in: UK units	Metric units
	1 vara[a]	0.927 yd	84.75 cm
Area			
	1 cuerda	0.971 acre	0.393 ha
Capacity			
	1 chupa	13.2 fl oz	37.5 cl
8 chupas	= 1 ganta	5.28 pt	3 l
16 gantas	= 1 tinaja	10.56 gal	48 l
25 gantas	= 1 cavan[b]	16.5 gal	75 l
Weight[c] *old Asian system*			
	1 tael	1.394 oz	39.531 g
16 taels	= 1 catty	1.394 lb	632.5 g
100 cattys	= 1 picul[d]	139.44 lb	63.25 kg
2 piculs	= 1 bale (fibres)	278.9 lb	126.5 kg
old Spanish system			
	1 libra	1.014 lb	460 g
25 libras	= 1 arroba	25.353 lb	11.5 kg
4 arrobas	= 1 quintal[e]	101.41 lb	46 kg
agriculture			
	1 kaing[f]	42–46 lb	19–21 kg
	1 cavan: paddy rice	97 lb	44 kg
	1 cavan: milled rice	123 lb	56 kg
3 kaings	= 1 US standard box	126–139 lb	57–63 kg

[a]Also used as 83.6 cm (0.914 yd). [b]Or caban or sack; the cavan is also used to mean 23½ gantas (70½ litres) for milled rice (weighing 50 kilograms). [c]In the metric system 1 metric carat is a kilates. [d]For sugar. [e]For tobacco; net weight (gross weight = 50 kg). [f]Or basket.

Poland

Main system: metric

Old units (no longer in use):

Length[a]		Equivalent in: UK units	Metric units
	1 calow	0.945 in	2.40 cm
12 calows	= 1 stopa	0.945 ft	28.8 cm
2 stopas	= 1 lokiec	1.890 ft	57.6 cm

Capacity
old system, liquid [b]

		UK units	Metric units
	1 kwarti [c]	1.67 pt	0.948 l
4 kwartis	= 1 garniec	0.834 gal	3.793 l
36 garniecs	= 1 beczka	30.0 gal	136.54 l
2 beczkas	= 1 stangiew	60.1 gal	273.08 l

metric linked system

	1 kwarti	1.76 pt	1 l
4 kwartis	= 1 garniec	0.880 gal	4 l
25 garniecs	= 1 beczka	22.0 gal	100 l
2 beczkas	= 1 stangiew	44.0 gal	200 l

Weight

	1 funt: old[b]	0.894 lb	405.5 g
	new[d]	1.102 lb	500 g

[a] As established 1819; previously, the stopa (foot) was 29.777 cm, other units varying accordingly. [b] Before 1819. [c] Dry kwarti was 0.919 l, other units varying accordingly. [d] Metric linked, from 1819.

Portugal

Main system: metric, compulsory from 1872

Old units:

Length		Equivalent in: UK units	Metric units
	1 grao	0.18 in	4.58 mm
6 graos	= 1 polegada	1.083 in	27.5 mm
8 polegadas	= 1 palmo	8.66 in	22 cm
12 polegadas	= 1 pé	1.083 ft	33 cm
3 palmos	= 1 côvado	2.165 ft	66 cm
5 palmos	= 1 vara	1.203 yd	1.10 m
2 varas	= 1 braça	2.406 yd	2.20 m
	1 estadio	281.3 yd	257.3 m
8 estadios	= 1 milha	1.279 mi	2.058 km
5 000 varas	= 1 lan: land	3.4 mi	5.50 km
5 555 varas	= 1 lan: sea	3.8 mi	6.11 km

Capacity, dry [a]

	1 oitavo	3.04 pt	1.73 l
2 oitavos	= 1 quarto	0.76 gal	3.460 l
4 quartos	= 1 alqueire	3.04 gal	13.841 l
4 alqueires	= 1 fanega	1.522 bu	55.364 l

Capacity, liquid [b]

	1 quartilho	0.606 pt	0.345 l
2 quartilhos	= 1 meias-canada	1.21 pt	0.689 l
2 meias-canadas	= 1 canada	2.43 pt	1.38 l
6 canadas	= 1 alqueire [c]	1.819 gal	8.27 l
2 alqueires	= 1 almude	3.64 gal	16.54 l
13 almudes	= 1 barrique	47.3 gal	215 l
2 barriques	= 1 pipa[d]	94.6 gal	430 l
2 pipas	= 1 tonelada[e]	189 gal	860 l

Weight
old system

		Equivalent in: UK units	Metric units
	1 onça	1.012 oz	28.688 g
8 onças	= 1 marco	0.506 lb	229.5 g
16 onças	= 1 arratel [f]	1.012 lb	459 g
32 arratels	= 1 arroba	32.382 lb	14.688 kg
4 arrobas	= 1 quintal	129.526 lb	58.752 kg
54 arrobas	= 1 tonelada[e]	0.781 ton	0.793 t

metric linked system

	1 onça	1.033 oz	29.30 g
16 onças	= 1 arratel [f]	1.033 lb	468.75 g
32 arratels	= 1 arroba	33.07 lb	15 kg
4 arrobas	= 1 quintal	132.28 lb	60 kg

[a] Usual values; for Continental Portugal 1 alqueire varied from 13 to 18 l, for Madeira from 10 to 14 l, and for Azores from 10 to 16 l, other units varying accordingly. [b] Lisbon old system. [c] Or cantaro or pot. [d] Metric linked pipa is 500 l. [e] Or tonnelada or tonneau or tonel. [f] Or libra or pound.

Puerto Rico

Main system: US system

Other units in use:

Area		Equivalent in: UK units	Metric units
	1 parcela	1 175.2 yd²	982.6 m²
4 parcelas	= 1 cuerda	0.971 acre	0.393 ha

Weight

	1 libra	1.016 lb	461 g

Rumania

Main system: metric, compulsory from 1884

Old unit:

Length		Equivalent in: UK units	Metric units
	1 halibin	27.6 in	70.1 cm

Main system: UK and metric systems, with gradual conversion to a completely metric system

Other units in use:

Weight		Equivalent in: UK units	Metric units
	1 case: bananas	56 lb	25.401 kg
	1 case: taro	72 lb	32.659 kg

Sao Tome & Principe

Main system: metric

Other unit in use:

Length		Equivalent in: UK units	Metric units
	1 vara	5.29 yd	4.84 m

Saudi Arabia

Main system: metric, compulsory from 1964

Old units[a]:

Length

		Equivalent in: UK units	Metric units
1 busa		1 in	2.54 cm
5½ busas	= 1 baa	5½ in	13.97 cm
6 busas	= 1 fitr	6 in	15.24 cm
7 busas	= 1 shibr	7 in	17.78 cm
3 fitrs	= 1 dira[b]	18 in	45.7 cm
25 busas	= 1 gudge	25 in	63.5 cm
1½ diras	= 1 hindaza[c]	27 in	68.6 cm

Area

		Equivalent in: UK units	Metric units
1 feddan		1.038 acre	0.42 ha

Capacity

		Equivalent in: UK units	Metric units
1 köddi[d]		1.089 gal	4.95 l
40 köddis	= 1 ardeb	5.444 bu	1.98 hl

Weight

		Equivalent in: UK units	Metric units
1 rotl[e]		1.020 lb	462.5 g
2 rotls	= 1 mahud	2.039 lb	0.925 kg
	1 oke	2.751 lb	1.248 kg
	1 wazna	3.5 lb	1.588 kg
	1 faunt	3.9 lb	1.769 kg
	1 kela	7.1 lb	3.221 kg
	1 ruba	20.6 lb	9.344 kg
	1 maund	82.28 lb	37.32 kg
	1 kantar	113.2 lb	51.35 kg
	1 tomande[f]	187.17 lb	84.90 kg
	1 behar[g]	439.45 lb	199.3 kg

[a] In general units based on the medieval Arab system established about 800—900 AD; also see under Iraq concerning that system. [b] Or ovido or covido (cubit); values varied from 17.6 to 19 (44.7 to 48.3 cm). [c] Or great ovido (great cubit); values varied from 26.4 to 28.5 in (67.1 to 72.4 cm). [d] Also used as 7.58 l (1.67 gal). [e] Or rottle or rattel; also used as 0.990 5 lb (449.3 g) or UK linked as 1 lb (453.6 g). [f] For rice. [g] Or bahar; also used in UK linked form as 450 lb (204.1 kg).

Main system: officially metric, from 1876; the UK system has also been in use but conversion to a fully metric system is planned

Other units (some of which are still in use):

Length

		Equivalent in: UK units	Metric units
1 ligne*		0.088 8 in	2.256 mm
12 lignes*	= 1 pouce*	1.066 in	2.707 cm
12 pouces*	= 1 pied*	1.066 ft	0.324 84 m
44 pouces*	= 1 aune[a]	1.303 yd	1.191 077 m
45 pouces*	= 1 ell[b]	4 ft	1.219 m
6 pieds*	= 1 toise*[c]	1.066 fathom	1.949 m
6 pieds*	= 1 brasse*[d]	1.066 fathom	1.949 m
10 pieds*	= 1 gaulette*	10.657 ft	3.248 4 m
20 pieds*	= 1 perche[e]	21.315 ft	6.496 8 m

Area

		Equivalent in: UK units	Metric units
10 000 pied²	= 1 arpent[e]	1.043 acre	0.422 08 ha

Volume

		Equivalent in: UK units	Metric units
1 corde		158 ft³	4.47 m³

Capacity

		Equivalent in: UK units	Metric units
	1 chopine[f]	0.598 pt	34 cl
2 chopines	= 1 bouteille[g]	1.197 pt	68 cl
	1 pinte*	1.639 pt	0.931 3 l
8 pintes*	= 1 velte*	1.639 gal	7.450 5 l
	1 toque*	4.839 gal	22 l
30 veltes*	1 barrique[h]	35.979 gal	1.636 hl
	= 1 cash*	49.17 gal	2.235 hl
	1 muid*	7.374 bu	2.682 hl

Weight

		Equivalent in: UK units	Metric units
	1 grain*	0.820 gr	53.115 mg
72 grains*	= 1 gros*	59.02 gr	3.824 g
8 gros*	= 1 once*	1.079 oz	30.594 g
2 onces*	= 1 huitième*[i]	2.158 oz	61.188 g
4 huitièmes*	= 1 demi-livre*[i]	0.540 lb	244.75 g
16 onces*	= 1 livre*[j]	1.079 lb	489.51 g

* No longer in use.
[a] For textiles. [b] For textiles; old ell was 3¾ ft. [c] For masonry (old measure); modern toise is a volume measure equal to 40 ft³. [d] Modern brasse is taken as equal to 1 fathom. [e] For land. [f] Also can be 40 cl. [g] Also can be 80 cl. [h] For beer. [i] For sugar. [j] The livre (pound) is generally used to mean ½ kg (1.102 lb).

Sierra Leone

Main system: metric, as conversion from the UK system

Other units in use:

Area

		Equivalent in: UK units	Metric units
1 town lot		3 750 ft²	348.39 m²

Capacity

		Equivalent in: UK units	Metric units
	1 cup	0.586 pt	33.3 cl
30 cups	= 1 kettle	2.197 gal	9.99 l
4 kettles	= 1 bushel	1.1 bu	40 l
2 bushels	= 1 bag	2.2 bu	80 l

Weight

		Equivalent in: UK units	Metric units
1 load (cocoa)		60 lb	27.2 kg

Singapore

Main system: metric, as conversion from the UK system

Old units (some of which are still in use):

Length

		Equivalent in: UK units	Metric units
	1 chhun[a,b]	1.475 in	3.746 5 cm
	1 jengkal	9 in	22.86 cm
10 chhuns	= 1 chhek[a,c]	14.75 in	37.465 cm
2 jengkals	= 1 hesta	18 in	45.72 cm
2 hestas	= 1 ela	1 yd	0.914 4 m
2 elas	= 1 depa	2 yd	1.828 8 m
10 checks	= 1 cheung	4.097 yd	3.746 5 m

Area

		Equivalent in: UK units	Metric units
	1 depa²	4 yd²	3.345 m²
4 depa²	= 1 jemba	16 yd²	13.378 m²
	1 lelong	2 400 ft²	222.97 m²
100 jembas	= 1 penjuru	0.331 acre	0.134 ha
	1 relong	0.709 acre	0.287 ha
24 lelongs	= 1 orlong	1.322 acre	0.535 ha

Singapore

Capacity

		UK units	Metric units
	1 pau	0.5 pt	284.1 ml
4 paus	= 1 chupak[a]	1 qt	1.137 l
4 chupaks	= 1 gantang[a]	1 gal	4.546 l
10 gantangs	= 1 para[d, f]	10 gal	45.461 l
63 gantangs	= 1 hogshead[d]	63 gal	2.864 hl
2 hogsheads[d]	= 1 pipe[d]	126 gal	5.728 hl
2 pipes[d]	= 1 tun[d]	252 gal	11.456 hl
80 paras[d]	= 1 koyan[d]	800 gal	36.369 hl

Weight
general

		UK units	Metric units
	1 tahil[a]	1⅓ oz	37.799 g
16 tahils	= 1 kati[a]	1⅓ lb	604.79 g
100 katis	= 1 pikul[a]	133⅓ lb	60.479 kg
3 pikuls	= 1 bhara[e]	400 lb	181.4 kg
40 pikuls	= 1 koyan	2.381 ton	2.419 t

precious metals: old units

		UK units	Metric units
	1 saga	4⅓ gr	280.8 mg
12 sagas	= 1 mayam	52 gr	3.370 g
16 mayams	= 1 bongkal	1.733 oz tr	53.913 g
12 bongkals	= 1 kati	20.8 oz tr	646.95 g

precious metals and medecine[a]

		UK units	Metric units
	1 lea	0.532 gr	34.447 mg
10 leas	= 1 fern	5.316 gr	0.344 47 g
10 ferns	= 1 chien	0.121 51 oz	3.444 74 g
10 chiens	= 1 tael	1.215 1 oz	34.447 4 g

[a] Still in use.   [b] Or chum.   [c] Or check.   [d] Liquid measure.   [e] Or bara.
[f] Or bandu.

Somalia

Main system: metric; also UK system, with gradual conversion to completely metric

Other units in use:

Length

		UK units	Metric units
	1 cubito	22 in	55.88 cm
7 cubitos	= 1 top	4.3 yd	3.91 m

Area

	UK units	Metric units
1 dareb	0.618 acre	0.25 ha
1 darat	1.977 acre	0.80 ha

Capacity, dry

		UK units	Metric units
	1 chela	2.392 pt	1.359 l
15 chelas	= 1 tabla	4.484 gal	20.385 l
8 tablas	= 1 gizla	35.87 gal	1.631 hl

Capacity, liquid

	UK units	Metric units
1 caba	0.797 pt	453 ml
1 tanica	3.96 gal	18 l

Weight

		UK units	Metric units
	1 okia	0.988 oz	28 g
16 okias	= 1 rottolo	0.988 lb	448 g
	1 sus	3.25 lb	1.475 kg
36 rottolos	= 1 frasla[a]	35.56 lb	16.128 kg
10 fraslas	= 1 gizla	355.56 lb	161.28 kg

[a] Or farsalah.

South Africa

Main system: SI metric, as conversion from the UK system from 1974

Old units (no longer in use):

Length

		UK units	Metric units
	1 Cape inch	1.033 in	2.624 cm
12 Cape inches	= 1 Cape foot	1.033 ft	0.314 86 m
12 Cape feet	= 1 Cape rood	12.396 ft	3.778 3 m

Area

		UK units	Metric units
	1 Cape rood²	17.073 yd²	14.276 m²
600 Cape rood²	= 1 morgen	2.117 acre	0.856 53 ha

Capacity

	UK units	Metric units
1 kanne[a]	2.618 pt	1.488 l
1 gantang	2.024 gal	9.201 l
1 anker	7.5 gal	34.10 l
1 balli	10.119 gal	46 l
1 muid[b]	3 bu	1.091 hl

[a] Or kanna.   [b] Or mud.

Soviet Union

Main system: metric, from 1927 (SI metric from 1963)

Old units:

Length[a]

		UK units	Metric units
	1 liniya	0.1 in	2.54 mm
10 liniyas	= 1 duim	1 in	2.54 cm
17½ liniyas	= 1 verchok[b]	1¾ in	4.445 cm
8 verchoks	= 1 fuss	14 in	35.6 cm
2 fuss	= 1 archine[c]	28 in	71.12 cm
3 archines	= 1 sajon[d]	7 ft	2.134 m
1 500 archines	= 1 verst[e]	0.662 9 mi	1.067 km

Area[a]

		UK units	Metric units
	1 sajon²	49 ft²	4.552 m²
2 400 sajon²	= 1 dessetine[f]	2.700 acre	1.093 ha

Capacity, dry

		UK units	Metric units
	1 čast	0.192 pt	109.3 ml
30 časts	= 1 garnetz	0.721 gal	3.279 8 l
8 garnetz	= 1 chetverik	5.772 gal	26.24 l
8 chetveriks	= 1 chetvert	46.17 gal	2.099 hl

Capacity, liquid

		UK units	Metric units
	1 charka	0.216 pt	123 ml
5 charkas	= 1 boutylka (vodka)	1.082 pt	61.5 cl
6¼ charkas	= 1 boutylka (wine)	1.353 pt	76.9 cl
10 charkas	= 1 schtoff[g]	2.164 pt	1.23 l
10 schtoffs	= 1 vedro	2.705 gal	12.299 l
36 vedros	= 1 pipe	97.40 gal	4.428 hl
40 vedros	= 1 bočka	108.2 gal	4.920 hl

Weight

		UK units	Metric units
	1 doli[h]	0.685 735 gr	44.435 mg
12/5 dolis	= 1 grain	0.960 gr	62.2 mg
96 dolis	= 1 zolotnik	65.831 gr	4.266 g
3 zolotniks	= 1 lolti[i]	0.451 oz	12.80 g
8 zolotniks	= 1 lana	1.204 oz	34.13 g
96 zolotniks	= 1 funt[j]	0.902 82 lb	409.5 g
40 funts	= 1 pood[k]	36.113 lb	16.380 kg
10 poods	= 1 berkovec[l]	361.13 lb	163.80 kg
30 poods	= 1 packen	0.484 ton	0.491 4 t

[a] As linked to the UK system in 1833; the old Russian system was about 1% larger with the fuss equal to 14.14 in, and other units varying accordingly.
[b] Or versock.   [c] Or arshin.   [d] Or sagene or sazhene (1 fathom); also used as 6 ft.
[e] Or versta.   [f] Or desätine.   [g] Or krus'ka.   [h] Or dolia.   [i] Or loth.   [j] Or founte.
[k] Or poud.   [l] Or berkovets or berkowitz.

Spain

Main system: metric, compulsory from 1859

Old units (some of which are still in use)[a]:

Length

		Equivalent in: UK units	Metric units
	1 linea	0.0762 in	1.935 mm
12 lineas	= 1 pulgada	0.914 in	2.322 cm
9 pulgadas	= 1 palmo	8.227 in	20.90 cm
12 pulgadas	= 1 pie	0.91416 ft	27.864 cm
3 pies	= 1 vara	0.914 yd	0.8359 m
2 varas	= 1 braza	0.914 fathom	1.672 m
2 brazas	= 1 estado	3.657 yd	3.344 m
75 brazas	= 1 cuadra	137.1 yd	125.4 m
3333⅓ brazas	= 1 legua[b]	3.463 mi	5.573 km
(10 000 brazas	= 3 leguas)		

Area

		Equivalent in: UK units	Metric units
	1 estado²	13.374 yd²	11.182 m²
576 estado²	= 1 fanegada[c]	1.592 acre	0.6426 ha

Capacity, dry

		Equivalent in: UK units	Metric units
	1 racione	0.509 pt	0.289 l
4 raciones	= 1 cuartillo	1.017 qt	1.156 l
4 cuartillos	= 1 celemín[d]	1.017 gal	4.625 l
12 celemínes	= 1 fanega[e]	1.526 bu	55.501 l
12 fanegas	= 1 cahiz	18.31 bu	6.66 hl

Capacity, liquid

		Equivalent in: UK units	Metric units
	1 octavillo	0.443 pt	0.252 l
2 octavillos	= 1 cuartillo	0.887 pt	0.504 l
4 cuartillos	= 1 azumbre	3.548 pt	2.016 l
8 azumbres	= 1 arroba[f]	3.548 gal	16.128 l
27 arrobas	= 1 pipe[g]	95.8 gal	4.355 hl
30 arrobas	= 1 bota[g]	106.4 gal	4.838 hl

Weight

		Equivalent in: UK units	Metric units
	1 grano	0.770 gr	49.9 mg
12 granos	= 1 tomín	9.245 gr	599.1 mg
3 tomíns	= 1 adarme	27.74 gr	1.797 g
8 tomíns	= 1 castellano	73.96 gr	4.793 g
16 adarmes	= 1 onza	1.0143 oz	28.756 g
8 onzas	= 1 marco	0.5072 lb	230.045 g
16 onzas	= 1 libra[h]	1.0143 lb	460.093 g
25 libras	= 1 arroba	25.36 lb	11.502 kg
4 arrobas	= 1 quintal[i]	101.43 lb	46.009 kg
2000 libras	= 1 tonelada, corto	0.906 ton	0.9202 t
2240 libras	= 1 tonelada, grande	1.014 ton	1.0306 t

[a] In general Castilian values; values vary by region. [b] Values have varied considerably, 1 legua being 5000 varas in medieval times. [c] Or marco real or fanega; the land necessary to plant 1 fanega of wheat. Value established 1801. [d] Or almude. [e] One liquid fanega equals 13.3 gal (60.6 l). [f] Or cántara. Values varied for wine and oil and by area; one arroba of oil equalled 12.563 l (2.763 gal). [g] For wine. [h] Castilian or Catalonian; in some areas there were 12, 17 or 20 onzas to 1 libra. [i] Castilian; one quintal, Catalonia equalled 41.6 kg (91.7 lb).

Sri Lanka

Main system: metric, as gradual conversion from the UK system beginning in 1974 and in general completed by 1980

Old units:

Area

		Equivalent in: UK units	Metric units
	1 square[a]	100 yd²	83.613 m²

Capacity, dry
old units

		Equivalent in: UK units	Metric units
	1 measure	1.87 pt	1.06 l
24 measures	= 1 parah	5.62 gal	25.5 l
8 parahs	= 1 anóman[b]	5.62 bu	2.04 hl

UK linked units

		Equivalent in: UK units	Metric units
	1 measure	1 qt	1.137 l
32 measures	= 1 bushel	1 bu	36.369 l

Capacity, liquid
old units

		Equivalent in: UK units	Metric units
	1 seer	1.87 pt	1.06 l
24 seers	= 1 parah	5.62 gal	25.5 l

UK linked unit

		Equivalent in: UK units	Metric units
	1 bottle	1⅓ pt	75.7 cl

Weight[c]

		Equivalent in: UK units	Metric units
	1 candy: general	500 lb	226.8 kg
	1 candy: copra	560 lb	254.012 kg

[a] In use in the building trade. [b] Or ammonam or amomam. [c] UK linked units.

Sudan

Main system: metric

Other units in use:

Length

		Equivalent in: UK units	Metric units
	1 linia	0.125 in	3.175 mm
8 linias	= 1 busa	1 in	2.54 cm
12 busas	= 1 qadam	1 ft	0.3048 m
	1 Sudan diraa	1.9 ft	0.58 m
	1 rageil[a]	0.916 fathom	1.676 m
4 diraas	= 1 ud[b]	2.54 yd	2.32 m

Area

		Equivalent in: UK units	Metric units
	1 makhammus[c]	0.798 acre	0.32289 ha
	1 feddan	1.04 acre	0.42 ha
	1 kordofan mukhamas[c]	1.796 acre	0.72662 ha
	1 qadaa	5.446 acre	2.204 ha

Capacity, dry

		Equivalent in: UK units	Metric units
	1 qadah[d]	3.629 pt	2.06251 l
2 qadahs	= 1 malwa	7.259 pt	4.125 l
2 malwas	= 1 ruba	1.815 gal	8.25 l
2 rubas	= 1 keila	3.629 gal	16.5 l
12 keilas	= 1 ardeb[e]	5.444 bu	1.98 hl

Weight
general

		Equivalent in: UK units	Metric units
	1 kirat	3.009 gr	195 mg
16 kirats	= 1 dirham	48.149 gr	3.12 g
12 dirhams	= 1 okia[f]	1.321 oz	37.44 g
12 okias	= 1 rotl	0.9905 lb	449.28 g
100 rotls	= 1 kantar	99.05 lb	44.928 kg
315 rotls	= 1 large kantar	312.01 lb	141.523 kg

gold

		Equivalent in: UK units	Metric units
	1 habba	1.543 gr	100 mg
320 habbas	= 1 wagia dahabia	1.029 oz tr	32 g

Bedouin units

		Equivalent in: UK units	Metric units
	1 hemla	165.08 lb	74.88 kg
4⅙ hemlas	= 1 hembl	687.84 lb	312 kg

[a] For depth of wells only. [b] For agricultural land on Nile banks. [c] For agriculture only. [d] Or kadah. [e] Standard ardeb is 1.95 hl (5.362 bu). [f] Or wagia.

Surinam

Main system: metric

Other units in use[a]:

		Equivalent in: UK units	Metric units
Length			
1 el		2.257 ft	0.687 8 m
Area			
1 Rhineland acre		1.054 acre	0.426 4 ha
Weight			
1 ons		3.527 oz	100 g
5 ons	= 1 pond	1.102 lb	500 g

[a]Former Netherlands measures.

Sweden

Main system: metric, compulsory from 1878

Old units:

		Equivalent in: UK units	Metric units
Length			
	1 tum[a]	1.169 in	2.969 cm
10 tums	= 1 fot	0.974 ft	0.296 9 m
2 fots	= 1 alen	1.948 ft	0.593 8 m
6 fots	= 1 favn[b]	0.974 fathom	1.781 5 m
10 fots	= 1 stöng	3.247 yd	2.969 2 m
10 stöngs	= 1 ref	32.471 yd	29.692 m
360 refs	= 1 mil[c]	6.642 mi	10.689 km
Area			
	1 kannland	52.721 yd²	44.08 m²
3½ kannlands	= 1 kappland	184.525 yd²	154.29 m²
16 kapplands	= 1 spanland	0.61 acre	0.247 ha
2 spanlands	= 1 tunnland	1.22 acre	0.494 ha
Volume			
	1 fot³	0.924 ft³	26.172 l
6 fot³	= 1 ahm	5.545 ft³	1.570 hl
Capacity			
	1 jumfru	1.438 fl oz	40.9 ml
64 jumfrus	= 1 kanne[d]	4.602 pt	2.615 l
64 kannes	= 1 tonne	4.602 bu	1.674 hl
Weight			
	1 ort	0.150 oz	4.251 5 g
50 orts	= 1 mark	7.498 oz	212.6 g
100 orts	= 1 skal-pund[e]	0.937 lb	425.15 g
100 skal-punds	= 1 centner	93.730 lb	42.515 kg
	1 ships-pund	374.8 lb	170 kg
	1 ships-last	2.411 ton	2.45 t

[a]Or zoll; originally there were 12 tums to 1 fot.   [b]Or famn.   [c]Or meile; new mil is standardised at 10 km (6.214 mi).   [d]Or kanna.   [e]Or skaal-pund; metric linked pund is 500 g (1.102 lb).

Switzerland

Main system: metric, compulsory from 1877

Old units[a]:

		Equivalent in: UK units	Metric units
Length			
	1 trait[b]	0.011 8 in	0.3 mm
10 traits	= 1 ligne[c]	0.118 in	3 mm
10 lignes	= 1 pouce[d]	1.181 in	3 cm
10 pouces	= 1 pied[e]	0.984 3 ft	30 cm
2 pieds	= 1 demi-aune[f]	1.968 5 ft	60 cm
2 demi-aunes	= 1 aune	3.937 ft	1.2 m
6 pieds	= 1 toise[g]	0.984 3 fathom	1.8 m
10 pieds	= 1 perche[h]	3.281 yd	3 m
1 600 perches	= 1 lieue[i]	2.983 mi	4.8 km
Area			
	1 perche²	10.764 yd²	9 m²
400 perche²	= 1 arpent[j]	0.890 acre	0.36 ha
6 400 arpents	= 1 lieue²	8.896 mi²	23.04 km²
Capacity, dry			
	1 emine[k]	2.640 pt	1.5 l
10 emines	= 1 quarteron[l]	3.300 gal	15 l
10 quarterons	= 1 sac[m]	4.124 bu	1.5 hl
Capacity, liquid			
	1 pot[n]	2.640 pt	1.5 l
25 pots	= 1 setier[o]	8.249 gal	37.5 l
100 pots	= 1 muid[p]	32.995 gal	1.5 hl
Weight			
	1 grain	1.005 gr	65.104 mg
20 grains	= 1 scruple	20.09 gr	1.302 g
3 scruples	= 1 drachme[q]	0.138 oz	3.906 g
4 drachmes	= 1 loth[r]	0.551 oz	15.625 g
2 loths	= 1 once[s]	1.102 oz	31.25 g
12 onces	= 1 livre de pharmacie	12.06 oz apoth	375 g
16 onces	= 1 livre[t]	1.102 lb	500 g
100 livres	= 1 quintal[u]	100.2 lb	50 kg

[a]Metric linked; in use between 1836 and 1877. Before 1836 measures varied according to town or region.   [b]Or strich.   [c]Or linie.   [d]Or zoll.   [e]Or fuss.
[f]Or brache or elle.   [g]Or klafter.   [h]Or rute.   [i]Lieue itinéraire or stunde.
[j]Or juchart.   [k]Or immi.   [l]Or viertel or boisseau.   [m]Or malter.   [n]Or maass.
[o]Or brente or viertelsaum.   [p]Or saum.   [q]Or viertellot.   [r]Or lot.   [s]Or unze.
[t]Or pfund.   [u]Or zentner.

Syria

Main system: metric, compulsory from 1935

Other units in use[a]:

		Equivalent in: UK units	Metric units
Length			
	1 dra[b,c]: Aleppo & Homs	26.8 in	68 cm
	Damascas	27.6 in	70 cm
	1 dra maghmari[d]	29.8 in	75.8 cm
Area			
	1 dra maghmari²	0.688 yd²	0.575 m²
	1 kassabé	28.48 yd²	23.814 m²
1 600 dra maghmari²	= 1 dönüm[e]: Aleppo & Homs[f]	1 099.5 yd²	919.3 m²
	1 feddan: Aleppo	0.57–0.85 ac	0.23–0.34 ha
Capacity			
	1 teminye	2.12 qt	2.41 l
	1 rebée	1.04 gal	4.75 l
	1 saagh	2.14 gal	9.73 l
	1 garava	3.19 gal	14.5 l
	1 mudd: Chakba	5.72 gal	26 l
	Soueida[g]	6.05 gal	27.5 l

Syria

Weight
Damascus

		Equivalent in: UK units	Metric units
	1 dirham	49.461 gr	3.205 g
66⅔ dirhams	= 1 okia	7.537 oz	213.7 g
6 okias	= 1 oke	2.826 lb	1.282 kg
2 okes	= 1 rottol [h]	5.65 lb	2.565 kg
100 rottols	= 1 kantar [i]	565.5 lb	256.5 kg

Aleppo & Homs

	1 dirham	49.461 gr	3.205 g
100 dirhams	= 1 okia	11.31 oz	320.5 g
10 okias	= 1 rottol [h]	7.066 lb	3.205 kg
100 rottols	= 1 kantar [i]	706.6 lb	320.5 kg

[a] Values vary markedly by region. [b] Or dhira or pic or pik. [c] For textiles.
[d] For land. [e] Or tartous. [f] For Latakia and Mohazafat 957 yd² (800 m²); for
Damascus 1 099.1 yd² (919 m²). [g] And Salkhad. [h] Or rottle. Other values are:
for Soueida 5.5 lb (2.5 kg); for Salkhad 5.64 lb (2.556 kg); for Chakba 5.88 lb
(2.666 kg). [i] Or cantar or cantaro.

Taiwan

Main system: metric, compulsory from 1954

Old units and metric names:

Length
Metric units

		Equivalent in: UK units	Metric units
	1 kung li′	0.039 37 in	1 mm
10 kung li′s	= 1 kung fun	0.393 7 in	1 cm
10 kung funs	= 1 kung t′sun	3.937 in	10 cm
10 kung t′suns	= 1 kung ch′ih	1.093 6 yd	1 m
10 kung ch′ihs	= 1 kung chang	10.936 yd	10 m
10 kung changs	= 1 kung yin	109.36 yd	100 m
10 kung yins	= 1 kung li″	0.621 4 mi	1 km

Area
old units (no longer in use)

	1 bin	3.954 yd²	3.306 m²
	1 chia or ko	2.397 acre	0.969 9 ha

metric units

	1 bing-fang kung ch′ih	1.196 yd²	1 m²
100 bing-fang kung ch′ihs	= 1 kung mou	119.6 yd²	1 a
100 kung mous	= 1 kung ch′ing	2.471 acre	1 ha

Capacity
metric units

	1 kung ts′o	16.894 minim	1 ml
10 kung ts′os	= 1 kung so	0.352 fl oz	1 cl
10 kung sos	= 1 kung ho	3.519 5 fl oz	10 cl
10 kung hos	= 1 kung sheng	1.759 8 pt	1 l
10 kung shengs	= 1 kung tou	2.199 7 gal	10 l
10 kung tous	= 1 kung tan	2.749 6 bu	1 hl
10 kung tans	= 1 kung ping	27.496 bu	1 kl

Weight
old unit (no longer in use)

	1 tai or catty	1.323 lb	600 g

metric units

	1 kung szu	0.015 43 gr	1 mg
10 kung szus	= 1 kung hao	0.154 32 gr	10 mg
10 kung haos	= 1 kung chu	1.543 2 gr	100 mg
10 kung chus	= 1 kung k′o	15.432 gr	1 g
10 kung k′os	= 1 kung ch′ien	0.352 74 oz	10 g
10 kung ch′iens	= 1 kung liang	3.527 4 oz	100 g
10 kung liangs	= 1 kung chin	2.204 6 lb	1 kg
10 kung chins	= 1 kung heng	22.046 lb	10 kg
10 kung hengs	= 1 kung tan	220.46 lb	100 kg
10 kung tans	= 1 kung tun	0.984 2 ton	1 t

Tanzania

Main system: metric (SI), as conversion from the UK system beginning in 1967

Old units:

Length

		Equivalent in: UK units	Metric units
	1 mkono	18 in	45.72 cm
2 mkonos	= 1 wari	1 yd	0.914 4 m

Capacity

	1 robo kibaba	0.440 pt	0.25 l
2 robo kibabas	= 1 musu kibaba	0.880 pt	0.50 l
2 musu kibabas	= 1 kibaba	1.760 pt	1 l
4 kibabas	= 1 pishi	0.880 gal	4 l

Weight

	1 ratili	1 lb	453.6 g
478 wakiahs	= 1 maund [a]	2.95 lb	1.338 kg
6 ratilis	= 1 kaila [a]	6 lb	2.722 kg
36 ratilis	= 1 frasila [b, d]	36 lb	16.33 kg
10 frasilas	= 1 girla [a, c]	360 lb	163.3 kg

[a] Zanzibar. [b] Or frazila or frasla or farsalah. [c] Or gisla. [d] Also used in
Zanzibar as 35 lb (15.88 kg).

Thailand

Main system: metric, introduced in 1923 and compulsory from 1947

Old units [a]:

Length

		Equivalent in: UK units	Metric units
	1 niu	0.820 in	2.083 cm
12 nius	= 1 khup [b]	0.820 ft	25 cm
2 khups	= 1 sok [c]	1.640 ft	50 cm
4 soks	= 1 wa [d]	2.187 yd	2 m
20 was	= 1 sen	43.74 yd	40 m
400 sens	= 1 yote	9.942 mi	16 km

Area

	1 wa²	4.784 yd²	4 m²
100 wa²	= 1 ngan	478.4 yd²	400 m²
4 ngans	= 1 rai [e]	0.395 acre	0.16 ha

Capacity

	1 thanan [f]	1.760 pt	1 l
20 thanans	= 1 sat [g]	4.40 gal	20 l
50 sats	= 1 ban	220 gal	10 hl
2 bans	= 1 kwien	440 gal	20 hl

Weight

	1 fuang	28.94 gr	1.875 g
2 fuangs	= 1 salung [h]	57.87 gr	3.75 g
4 salungs	= 1 baht [i]	0.529 oz	15 g
4 bahts	= 1 tamlung [j]	2.116 oz	60 g
10 tamlungs	= 1 catty	1.323 lb	600 g
2 cattys	= 1 chang	2.646 lb	1.2 kg
100 cattys	= 1 picul [k]	132.28 lb	60 kg
20 piculs	= 1 koyan	1.181 ton	1.2 t

[a] Metric linked, as standardised in 1923 (previously had varied by district).
[b] Or keup or kup. [c] Or sauk or sawk. [d] Or wah or va. [e] Or sen². [f] Or tanan
or fanan. [g] Or thang. [h] Or solung. [i] Or tical or kyat. [j] Or tael. [k] Or hal or
hap or taam.

Trinidad & Tobago

Main system: UK system, with gradual conversion to the metric system

Other unit in use:

Weight		Equivalent in: UK units	Metric units
	1 fanega (for cocoa beans)	110 lb	49.9 kg

Tunisia

Main system: metric

Other units sometimes in use:

Length		Equivalent in: UK units	Metric units
	1 pik Arbi [a]	1.618 ft	49.3 cm
	1 pik Turki [b]	2.117 ft	64.5 cm
	1 pik Andoulsi [c]	2.128 ft	64.9 cm

Capacity [d]			
	1 sa' [e]	$\frac{2}{3}$ gal	3.031 l
12 sa's	= 1 wiba [f]	1 bu	36.369 l
16 wibas	= 1 kfiz [g]	16 bu	5.819 hl

Weight			
	1 metical [h]	60.7 gr	3.936 g
8 meticals	= 1 uzan	1.1107 oz	31.487 g
16 uzans	= 1 rottel [i]	1.1107 lb	503.8 g
100 rottels	= 1 cantar	111.07 lb	50.38 kg

[a] For linen. [b] For silk. [c] For wool. [d] For cereals. UK linked units; previously 1 wiba was 0.908 bu (33.03 l), other units varying accordingly. [e] Or saha or saw or zah. [f] Or weba or quiba. [g] Or cafiso. [h] Or termini. [i] Or rottolo; number of uzans per rottel has varied from 16 to 42.

Turkey

Main system: metric, from 1931

Old units:

Length old units		Equivalent in: UK units	Metric units
	1 endazeh [a]	25.6 in	65 cm
	1 arshin [b]: çarsi [c]	26.8 in	68 cm
	1 arshin [b]: mimar [d]	29.8 in	75.8 cm
7 500 arshin (mimar)	= 1 fershı kadım	3.532 mi	5.685 km
metric linked units			
	1 khat .	0.394 in	1 cm
10 khats	= 1 parmak	3.937 in	10 cm
10 parmaks	= 1 arshin	1.094 yd	1 m
1 000 arshins	= 1 mil [e]	0.621 mi	1 km
10 mils	= 1 pharoagh [f]	6.214 mi	10 km
3 pharoaghs	= 1 konak	18.6 mi	30 km

Area old units		Equivalent in: UK units	Metric units
	1 evlek	0.172 yd²	0.144 m²
4 evleks	= 1 arshin (mimar)²	0.687 yd²	0.575 m²
	1 koltuk	1.770 yd²	1.480 m²
1 600 arshin (mimar)²	= 1 dönüm [g]	0.227 acre	919.3 m²
3 600 arshin (mimar)²	= 1 girib [h]	0.511 acre	0.207 ha
metric linked units			
	1 girib [h]	2.471 acre	1 ha
25 giribs	= 1 dönüm [g]	61.78 acre	25 ha

Capacity Istanbul system		Equivalent in: UK units	Metric units
	1 zarf	0.51 gal	2.3 l
2 zarfs	= 1 kutu	1.0 gal	4.6 l
2 kutus	= 1 şinik	2.0 gal	9.2 l
2 şiniks	= 1 ölçek	4.1 gal	18.5 l
2 ölçeks	= 1 kileh [i]	8.1 gal	37 l
Anatolian system			
	1 gödük [i]	5.6 gal	25.2 l
	1 hak	7.4 gal	33.7 l
2 gödüks	= 1 ölçek	11.1 gal	50.5 l
3 haks	= 1 kileh [i]	22.2 gal	101 l
2 ölçeks	= 1 kileh [i]	22.2 gal	101 l
other old units			
	1 oke	1.28 pt	72.7 cl
	1 rottol	2.8 pt	1.6 l
	1 alma [k]	1.15 gal	5.24 l
1 arshin (mimar)³	= 1 ambar	0.569 yd³	0.435 m³
metric linked unit			
1 parmak³	= 1 sultchek	1.76 pt	1 l

Weight old system		Equivalent in: UK units	Metric units
	1 habbe	0.012 gr	0.783 mg
	1 zevre	0.032 gr	2.09 mg
4 habbes	= 1 kıtmir	0.048 gr	3.13 mg
3 zevres	= 1 nakır	0.097 gr	6.26 mg
2 kıtmırs	= 1 nakır	0.097 gr	6.26 mg
2 nakirs	= 1 fitil	0.193 gr	12.5 mg
4 fitils	= 1 buğday [l]	0.773 gr	50.1 mg
4 buğdays	= 1 krat [m]	3.09 gr	200 mg
2 krats	= 1 çekirdek	6.19 gr	401 mg
2 çekirdeks	= 1 denk	12.37 gr	0.802 g
4 denks	= 1 drachma [n]	0.113 oz	3.207 g
1½ drachmas	= 1 miskal [o]	0.170 oz	4.811 g
50 drachmas	= 1 tuht	0.354 lb	160.4 g
176 drachmas	= 1 ludra	1.245 lb	0.564 kg
400 drachmas	= 1 oke [p]	2.828 lb	1.283 kg
2 okes	= 1 rottol	5.657 lb	2.566 kg
3 rottols	= 1 batman	16.97 lb	7.698 kg
112 tuhts	= 1 kental	39.60 lb	17.96 kg
100 ludras	= 1 kantar	124.45 lb	56.45 kg
44 okes	= 1 kantar	124.45 lb	56.45 kg
4 kantars	= 1 tcheki [q]	497.8 lb	225.8 kg
metric linked units			
	1 drachma [n]	0.353 oz	10 g
100 drachmas	= 1 oke [p]	2.205 lb	1 kg
10 okes	= 1 batman	22.05 lb	10 kg
10 batmans	= 1 kantar [r]	220.46 lb	100 kg

[a] Or lesser pic or pik. [b] Or greater pic or pik or archin. [c] For textiles. [d] For land and construction. [e] Or mill. [f] Journey of 2 hours. [g] Or deunum. [h] Or djerib. [i] Or kilesi. [j] Or ruplaği. [k] Or almude or meter. [l] Or kamha or grain. [m] Or kerât. [n] Or dirhem or dram. [o] Or mitkal. [p] Or okka or ock. [q] Value of new tcheki is 249.99 kg (551.1 lb). [r] Or quintal.

Uruguay

Main system: metric, from 1862

Other units in use:

Length

		Equivalent in: UK units	Metric units
100 varas	1 vara	0.939 yd	0.859 m
60 cuadras	= 1 cuadra	93.941 yd	85.9 m
	= 1 legua	3.203 mi	5.154 km

Area

		Equivalent in: UK units	Metric units
2 700 cuadra²	1 cuadra²	1.823 acre	0.738 ha
	= 1 suerte	4 923 acre	1 992 ha

Capacity

		Equivalent in: UK units	Metric units
2 fanegas	1 fanega	3.774 bu	1.373 hl
	= 1 double fanega	7.549 bu	2.745 hl

Weight
old units

		Equivalent in: UK units	Metric units
	1 libra	1.013 lb	459.4 g
25 libras	= 1 arroba	25.320 lb	11.485 kg
4 arrobas	= 1 quintal	101.28 lb	45.940 kg

metric linked units

		Equivalent in: UK units	Metric units
	1 arroba	22.046 lb	10 kg
10 arrobas	= 1 fanega	220.46 lb	100 kg

Venezuela

Main system: metric from 1875 (compulsory from 1914)

Other units in use:

Length

	Equivalent in: UK units	Metric units
1 vara	33 in	0.838 m
1 cabulla	87.5 yd	80 m
1 legua	3.458 mi	5.565 km

Area

	Equivalent in: UK units	Metric units
1 vara[a]	1.029 yd²	0.860 m²
1 plaza[b,c]	12–24 yd²	10–20 m²
1 tarea[b]	60–996 yd²	50–833 m²
1 cuartilla	120–2 990 yd²	100–2 500 m²
1 almud	478–30 617 yd²	400–25 600 m²
1 area[a]	664 yd²	555 m²
1 medida[c,d]	747 yd²	625 m²
1 fanegada	1.1–9.9 acre	0.45–4 ha
1 medio[e]	1.24 acre	0.5 ha
1 tablón	1.48–2.47 acre	0.6–1.0 ha
1 cuadro: East	1.58–2.47 acre	0.64–1.0 ha
1 cuadro: West	1.58–4.45 acre	0.64–1.8 ha
1 carga	2.471 acre	1 ha
1 legua	3 954–6 178 acre	1 600–2 500 ha

Capacity, dry

	Equivalent in: UK units	Metric units
1 lata[f]	1¼–4 gal	7–17 l
1 cajon[f]	5½–12 gal	25–55 l
1 huacal[f]	6–15 gal	28–70 l
1 canasto[f]	6–30 gal	28–140 l
1 ceston[f]	15 gal	70 l
1 fanega	3.23 bu	1.17 hl

Capacity, liquid

	Equivalent in: UK units	Metric units
1 arroba	3.55 gal	16.136 l
1 barril[f]	15–22 gal	70–100 l

Weight

		Equivalent in: UK units	Metric units
	1 vara[g]	0.551 lb	250 g
	1 libra	1.016 lb	460.9 g
	1 paquete[h]	2.6–4.4 lb	1.2–2 kg
	1 cuartilla	4.4–22 lb	2–10 kg
	1 mancuerna	4.4–33 lb	2–15 kg
	1 litro	5.5 lb	2.5 kg
	1 botijuela[i]	11.0 lb	5 kg
	1 madeja	11–33 lb	5–15 kg
	1 palito	20–40 lb	9–18 kg
	1 almud	20–110 lb	9–50 kg
	1 cuenta	22–110 lb	10–50 kg
25 libras	= 1 arroba	25.403 lb	11.522 kg
	1 caja	40–139 lb	18–63 kg
	1 bulto	40–176 lb	18–80 kg
	1 cabulla	44 lb	20 kg
	1 saco	44–132 lb	20–60 kg
	1 carga	49–761 lb	22–345 kg
	1 tercio	88 lb	40 kg
4 arrobas	= 1 quintal	101.6 lb	46.09 kg
	1 fanega	101–882 lb	46–400 kg
	1 paca	110 lb	50 kg
	1 mara	110–441 lb	50–200 kg
	1 cuadro	132 lb	60 kg
	1 mil	882 lb	400 kg
	1 punto	1 323 lb	600 kg

[a]Aragua.　[b] For agriculture.　[c] Sucre.　[d] Or litro.　[e] Portuguesa.
[f]Approximate value; original value in terms of weight.　[g] Or bojote or manojo.
[h]Or paquette.　[i] Or el cotejo.

Vietnam

Main system: metric

Old units:

Length

		Equivalent in: UK units	Metric units
	1 vi	1.575 μ in	40 nm
10 vis	= 1 hôt	15.75 μ in	0.4 μm
10 hôts	= 1 ti	157·5 μ in	4 μm
10 tis	= 1 hào	1.575 milli-in	0.04 mm
10 hàos	= 1 ly	15.75 milli-in	0.4 mm
10 lys	= 1 phân	0.157 in	4 mm
10 phâns	= 1 tâc	1.575 in	4 cm
10 tâcs	= 1 thuốc[a]	1.312 ft	0.4 m
5 thuốcs	= 1 ngũ	2.187 yd	2 m
2 ngũs	= 1 truờng	4.374 yd	4 m

Area

		Equivalent in: UK units	Metric units
	1 gang[b]	0.431 ft²	0.04 m²
4 gangs	= 1 ghê'[c]	1.722 ft²	0.16 m²
6 gangs	= 1 phân	2.583 ft²	0.24 m²
10 phâns	= 1 tâc[d]	2.870 yd²	2.4 m²
25 ghês	= 1 than	4.784 yd²	4 m²
10 tâcs	= 1 thuốc[a]	28.70 yd²	24 m²
9 thans	= 1 miếng	43.06 yd²	36 m²
10 miếngs	= 1 sào[e]	430.6 yd²	360 m²
10 sàos	= 1 mẫu	0.890 acre	0.36 ha

Volume
general

		Equivalent in: UK units	Metric units
1 thuốc³	= 1 lai	2.26 ft³	0.064 m³
1 ngũ² × 1 thuốc	= 1 lé	2.09 yd³	1.6 m³
10 lés	= 1 hôc	20.9 yd³	16 m³

soil measures

		Equivalent in: UK units	Metric units
1 lai	= 1 ô	2.26 ft³	0.064 m³
1 lé	= 1 than	2.09 yd³	1.6 m³
9 thans	= 1 miếng	18.834 yd³	14.4 m³
10 miếngs	= 1 sào	188.34 yd³	144 m³
10 sàos	= 1 mẫu	1 883.4 yd³	1 440 m³

Vietnam

		Equivalent in: UK units	Metric units
Capacity, cereals			
	1 túc	0.056 minim	0.003 3 ml
6 túcs	= 1 quê	0.338 minim	0.02 ml
10 quês	= 1 toât	3.379 minim	0.2 ml
10 toâts	= 1 sao	33.787 minim	2 ml
10 saos	= 1 thuốc	0.704 fl oz	2 cl
5 thuốcs	= 1 lé	3.520 fl oz	10 cl
2 lés	= 1 cắp	7.039 fl oz	20 cl
5 lés	= 1 bât	0.880 pt	50 cl
2 bâts	= 1 dấuᶠ	1.76 pt	1 l
2 dấus	= 1 thăng	3.52 pt	2 l
10 thăngs	= 1 thùng	4.4 gal	20 l
15 thăngs	= 1 phuong	6.6 gal	30 l
2 phuongs	= 1 hôc	13.2 gal	60 l
Weight			
	1 vi	0.000 058 gr	0.003 778 mg
10 vis	= 1 hôt	0.000 583 gr	0.037 78 mg
10 hôts	= 1 ti	0.005 83 gr	0.377 8 mg
10 tis	= 1 hào	0.058 3 gr	3.778 mg
10 hàos	= 1 ly	0.583 gr	37.78 mg
10 lys	= 1 phân	5.833 gr	377.8 mg
10 phâns	= 1 đồngᵍ	0.133 oz	3.778 g
10 đồngs	= 1 langʰ	1.333 oz	37.783 g
16 langs	= 1 cân	1.333 lb	604.5 g
10 câns	= 1 yến	13.33 lb	6.045 kg
10 yếns	= 1 ta	133.3 lb	60.453 kg

ᵃOr xích. ᵇOr ly. ᶜOr khẩu or ô. ᵈOr thốn. ᵉOr cao. ᵗOr uyên for rice.
ᵍOr tiền. ʰOr tael.

Yemen, North

Main system: metric, in general from 1975

Old units:

		Equivalent in: UK units	Metric units
Length			
	1 dra	2.198 ft	0.670 m
Capacity			
	1 nafer	1.10 pt	0.625 l
64 nafers	= 1 kada	8.8 gal	40 l
80 nafers	= 1 thoum	11 gal	50 l
Weight			
	1 rotle: sugar ᵃ	1.235 lb	560 g
	1 rotle: meat ᵇ	1.482 lb	672 g
	1 rotle: liquid ᶜ	1.715 lb	778 g
	1 okka	1.874 lb	0.850 kg
	1 frasla	24.74 lb	11.22 kg
	1 kada: barley, local	51.4 lb	23.3 kg
	1 kada: sorghum red	59.3 lb	26.9 kg
	1 kada: barley, foreign	59.5 lb	27.0 kg
	1 kada: maizeᵈ	64.3 lb	29.2 kg
	1 kada: sorghum yellow	68.3 lb	31.0 kg
	1 kada: wheatᵉ	71.0 lb	32.2 kg
	1 kada: beans	73.2 lb	33.2 kg
6.4 kadas	= 1 nafer	f	f
8 kadas	= 1 thoum	f	f

ᵃAlso for tea and coffee. ᵇAlso for vegetables and fruit. ᶜFor milk, oil etc.
ᵈAlso for lentils and broad beans. ᵉAlso for fenugreek and green beans.
ᶠValues vary according to the value of the kada shown above.

Yemen, South

Main system: UK system

Other units in use:

		Equivalent in: UK units	Metric unit
Length			
	1 dira	18 in	45.7 cm
2 diras	= 1 war ᵃ	1 yd	0.914 4 m
3.6 diras	= 1 qama	5.4 ft	1.65 m
Area			
	1 faddanᵇ	1 acre	0.405 ha
Capacity			
	1 keilaᶜ	1 bu	36 l
Weight			
	1 tia	18 gr	1.166 g
10 tias	= 1 tola	180 gr	11.664 g
	1 ratl	1 lb	453.6 g
80 tolas	= 1 seer	2.057 lb	0.933 kg
2½ ratls	= 1 qasa	2½ lb	1.134 kg
	1 thamin	5¼ lb	2.381 kg
	1 frasilaᵈ,ᶠ	28 lb	12.7 kg
40 seers	= 1 maund	82.286 lb	37.32 kg
	1 qadah	200 lb	90.72 kg
24 frasilas	= 1 kandiᵉ,ᶠ	672 lb	304.8 kg

ᵃOr yarda. ᵇOr dhumd. ᶜHolds about 50 lb (23 kg) of grain; values vary from
region to region. ᵈOr local maund. ᵉOr candy. ᶠValues vary.

Zaire

Main system: metric, from 1910

Other unit in use:

		Equivalent in: UK units	Metric units
Weight			
	1 sac (coffee)	132.28 lb	60 kg

Zambia

Main system: metric from 1971, as conversion from the UK system

Other unit in use:

		Equivalent in: UK units	Metric unit
Capacity			
	1 debbie (paraffin)	4 gal	18.184 l

Other countries units summary

This table lists alphabetically some of the most important units, other than metric, imperial or United States, used, or recently used, in countries other than the United Kingdom or United States. Some of these measures vary from district to district in which case, as far as possible, the most representative have been chosen. Since most countries have changed, or are changing, to the metric system, the use of these measures varies from country to country; any country for which a measure is not in general use or is generally obsolescent is marked with an asterisk *. In general, special names for standard metric units are not included here. For China, the official system is metric, with Chinese names assigned to units; in this section the term 'old' refers to units established as 'treaty' or 'customs' units and 'new' to the metric linked equivalents established in 1929 (sometimes referred to as 'market' units).

Unit	Country	Equivalent in: UK units	Metric units
Abbas	Iran	2.894 grains	187.5 milligrams
Abbassi	Iran	0.827 pound	375 grams
Adarme	Mexico / Peru	27.7 grains	1.798 grams
Aftari or Saa	Morocco	1 076.4 sq. yards	900 sq. metres
Alen	Denmark	0.686 5 yard	0.627 7 metre
Almud or Almude	Chile	7.109 quarts	8.08 litres
	Ecuador	28.4 pounds	12.88 kilograms
	Mexico	1.665 gallons	7.568 litres
	Paraguay	5.28 gallons	24 litres
	Portugal	3.64 gallons	16.5 litres
Alqueire	Portugal	1.82 gallons	8.27 litres
Anker	South Africa*	7½ gallons	34.096 litres
Anna	Pakistan	20.17 sq. yards	16.86 sq. metres
Archin or Archine: see Dhara			
Ardab or Ardeb	Egypt / Saudi Arabia* / Sudan	5.444 bushels	1.98 hectolitres
Area	Venezuela	664 sq. yards	555 sq. metres
Arpent	Canada: Quebec: length	191.8 feet	58.47 metres
	area	0.845 acre	0.342 hectare
	Mauritius / Seychelles	1.043 acres	0.422 hectare
Arrátel see Libra			
Arroba or Cántara	Bolivia	25.35 pounds	11.5 kilograms
	Brazil	32.4 pounds	14.7 kilograms
	Chile	25.35 pounds	11.5 kilograms
	Colombia	27.56 pounds	12.5 kilograms
	Cuba	25.36 pounds	11.502 kilograms
	Dominican Rep.	25 pounds	11.34 kilograms
	Ecuador	25.35 pounds	11.5 kilograms
	Macao	32.38 pounds	14.688 kilograms
	Mexico	25.37 pounds	11.51 kilograms
	Paraguay	25.298 pounds	11.475 kilograms
	Peru: capacity	3.54 gallons	16.1 litres
	weight	25.35 pounds	11.5 kilograms
	Philippines	25.35 pounds	11.5 kilograms
	Portugal	33.07 pounds	15 kilograms
	Spain: capacity	3.548 gallons	16.128 litres
	weight	25.36 pounds	11.502 kilograms
	Uruguay	25.32 pounds	11.485 kilograms
	Venezuela	25.40 pounds	11.52 kilograms
Arshin: see Dhara			
Artaba	Iran	1.81 bushels	65.9 litres
Aune (textiles)	Haiti	1.53 yards	1.4 metres
	Mauritius / Seychelles*	1.303 yards	1.19 metres
Azumbre	Colombia / Panama	3.555 pints	2.02 litres
	Spain	3.548 pints	2.016 litres
Baa	Saudi Arabia	5.5 inches	13.97 centimetres
Bag	Burma	27 gallons	1.227 hectolitres
Bahar or Behar	Iran	1.28 inches	3.25 centimetres
	Saudi Arabia	450 pounds	204.115 kilograms
Baht, Bat, Bath, Kyat or Tical	Burma	0.576 ounce	16.33 grams
	Laos / Thailand	0.529 ounce	15 grams

Unit	Country	Equivalent in: UK units	Metric units
Bahu, Bau or Bouw	Indonesia	1.753 6 acres	0.709 65 hectare
Bak: see Salung			
Balli	South Africa*	10.119 gallons	46 litres
Ban	Thailand	220 gallons	10 hectolitres
Bandu: see Para			
Barril, Barmil or Barrique	Malta: beer, wine and spirits	9.5 gallons	43.188 litres
	Mauritius	49.98 gallons	2.272 hectolitres
	Mexico	16.72 gallons	76 litres
	Paraguay	21.32 gallons	96.93 litres
Bat: see Baht			
Bath: see Baht			
Bau: see Bahu			
Behar: see Bahar			
Besana	Cuba	3 096.1 sq. yards	2 588.77 sq. metres
Bhara	Brunei / Malaysia	400 pounds	181.4 kilograms
Bigha	India* / Pakistan	0.331 acre / 0.5 acre	0.134 hectare / 0.202 hectare
Bin	Taiwan*	3.954 sq. yards	3.306 sq. metres
Bocoy	Cuba*	145.7 gal	6.624 hectolitres
Bongkal	Malaysia	1.733 ounces troy	53.9 grams
Boot	Netherlands	116.6 gallons	530 litres
Botella	Cuba	1.276 pints	0.725 litre
	Nicaragua	1.173 pints	0.667 litre
	Panama	1.332 pints	0.757 litre
Botija	Ecuador	12.68 pounds	5.75 kilograms
Botijuela	Venezuela	11 pounds	5 kilograms
Bouw: see Bahu			
Bow: see Danda			
Braça, Brasse, Braza or Brazada	Argentina*	1.895 yards	1.733 metres
	Chile*	1.828 yards	1.672 metres
	Colombia	1.750 yards	1.60 metres
	El Salvador	1.828 yards	1.672 metres
	Macao	2.41 yards	2.2 metres
	Seychelles	1.066 fathom	1.949 metres
Bu	Japan*	0.119 3 inch	3.030 millimetres
Bu (area): see Tsubo			
Caba	Somalia	0.797 pint	0.453 litre
Cabaho	Ethiopia	1.3 gallons	6.0 litres
Caballería	Costa Rica	111.82 acres	45.254 hectares
	Cuba	33.16 acres	13.42 hectares
	Ecuador	27.9 acres	11.29 hectares
	El Salvador	111.11 acres	44.965 hectares
	Mexico	105.75 acres	42.795 hectares
	Nicaragua	111.59 acres	45.158 hectares
Cabulla	Venezuela	44 pounds	20 kilograms
Cadné or Kadne	Lebanon*	0.57–0.85 acre	0.23–0.34 hectare
Caffiso	Malta	4.5 gallons	20.457 litres
Caja	Nicaragua	35.27 pounds	16 kilograms
	Venezuela	40–139 pounds	18–63 kilograms
Cajuela	Costa Rica	3.74 gallons	17 litres
	Guatemala	3.65 gallons	16.60 litres
	Nicaragua	3.67 gallons	16.67 litres
Candareen: see Hoon			
Candy or Kandy	Burma	18 000 pounds	8.165 tonnes
	India: Bombay*	560 pounds	254 kilograms
	Madras*	500 pounds	226.8 kilograms
Caneca	Cuba*	4.785 gallons	21.751 litres
Canna: see Qasba			
Cantar: see Kantar			
Cántara: see Arroba			
Cantero	Ecuador	527 sq. yards	441 sq. metres
Capicha	Iran	4.63 pints	2.63 litres
Carga	Colombia	275.6 pounds	125 kilograms
	Costa Rica	354.9 pounds	161 kilograms
	Nicaragua	202.8 pounds	92 kilograms
	Mexico: capacity	4.994 bushels	181.63 litres
	weight	304.4 pounds	138.1 kilograms
Carreau de terre	Haiti	3.193 acres	1.292 hectares
Cash	Seychelles*	49.17 gallons	2.235 hectolitres

Unit	Country	Equivalent in: UK units	Metric units
Cate, Catty, Chin, Gun, Jin, Kan, Kati, Katti, Keun or Kinn	Brunei	1.333 pounds	0.605 kilogram
	China: old*		
	new*	1.102 pounds	0.5 kilogram
	Hongkong	1.333 pounds	0.605 kilogram
	Indonesia	1.362 pounds	0.618 kilogram
	Japan*	1.323 pounds	0.6 kilogram
	Korea, South		
	Malaysia	1.333 pounds	0.605 kilogram
	Singapore		
	Thailand	1.323 pounds	0.6 kilogram
Cavan	Philippines	16.5 gallons	75 litres
Celemín	Colombia		
	Panama	1.02 gallons	4.625 litres
	Spain*		
Centner: see Zentner			
Chang or Zhang	China: new*	3.645 yards	3.333 metres
	Thailand	2.65 pounds	1.2 kilograms
Charac	Iran	0.853 foot	26 centimetres
Charak	Afghanistan	3.894 pounds	1.766 kilograms
Charruba	Libya	2.958 grains	191.7 milligrams
Chattack, Chhatak or Chittack	Bangladesh		
	India*	2.057 ounces	58.32 grams
	Pakistan		
Chawal	Pakistan	0.234 grain	15.19 milligrams
Che, Check, Cheh, Chek, Chhek or Chih	China: old*	14.1 inches	0.358 14 metre
	new*	13.123 inches	0.333 3 metre
	Hongkong	14.625 inches	0.371 475 metre
	Malaysia		
	Singapore	14.75 inches	0.374 6 metre
Chela	Somalia	1.196 quarts	1.359 litres
Chemica	Iran	1.16 quarts	1.32 litres
Cheong	Macao	15.18 sq. yards	12.69 sq. metres
Cheung	Hongkong	4.063 yards	3.715 metres
	Malaysia		
	Singapore*	4.097 yards	3.746 metres
Chhatak: see Chattak			
Chhek: see Che			
Chhun or Chum	Malaysia		
	Singapore	1.475 inches	37.465 millimetres
Chi, Chin or Tsin	Cambodia	0.132 ounce	3.75 grams
	Hongkong	0.133 ounce	3.78 grams
	Mongolia	0.132 ounce	3.75 grams
Chia or Ko	Taiwan*	2.396 7 acres	0.969 9 hectare
Chih: see Che			
Chin: see Cate			
Chittack: see Chattak			
Cho, Chô, Chungbo or Jungbo	Japan: length*	119.303 yards	109.09 metres
	area*		
	Korea, North	2.451 acres	0.991 7 hectare
	Korea, South		
Chok	Korea, South	11.930 inches	0.303 0 metre
Chong	Cambodia*	66.139 pounds	30 kilograms
Chum: see Chhun			
Chung	Korea, South	357.906 feet	109.09 metres
Chungbo: see Cho			
Chupa	Philippines	0.66 pint	375 millilitres
Collothum	Iran	1.81 gallons	8.23 litres
Condorim	Macao: length	0.148 inch	3.76 millimetres
	weight	5.833 grains	377.99 milligrams
Corde	Mauritius	96.84 cu. feet	2.742 cu. metres
	Seychelles*	158 cu. feet	4.47 cu. metres
Cordel or Cuerda	Cuba	22.26 yards	20.352 metres
	Paraguay	76.42 yards	69.88 metres
Coss or Koss or Kor	India*		
	Pakistan	2000 yards	1.828 8 kilometres
Courd, Moud, Rabia or Tarabiit	Morocco	538.2 sq. yards	450 sq. metres
Côvado	Macao	26 inches	66 centimetres
Cuadra	Argentina*	142 yards	130.0 metres
	Chile*	137.12 yards	125.39 metres
	Colombia	87.5 yards	80 metres
	Ecuador	91.9 yards	84 metres
	Paraguay	94.77 yards	86.66 metres
	Uruguay	94 yards	85.9 metres

Unit	Country	Equivalent in: UK units	Metric units
Cuadro	Venezuela	132.3 pounds	60 kilograms
Cuarta or Cuarto (length)	Colombia*	7.9 inches	20 centimetres
	Costa Rica	8.228 inches	20.9 centimetres
	Ecuador		
	Nicaragua	8.3 inches	21 centimetres
Cuarta (capacity)	Nicaragua	5.87 fl. ounces	167 millilitres
	Paraguay	1.33 pint	0.757 litre
Cuarterón	Mexico	5.5 gallons	25 litres
Cuartilla	Ecuador	50.7 pounds	23 kilograms
Cuartillo (liquid)	Costa Rica	3.74 quarts	4.25 litres
	Cuba	1.513 pints	0.86 litre
	Guatemala	1.02 quarts	1.16 litres
	Mexico	0.80 pint	0.456 litre
	Spain	0.887 pint	0.504 litre
Cubit, Cubito, Hat, Hath, Hesta Taim, or Taung	Burma	1.5 feet	0.457 2 metre
	Cambodia	1.64 feet	0.5 metre
	India*		
	Malaysia		
	Pakistan	1.5 feet	0.457 2 metre
	Singapore		
	Somalia	22 inches	0.558 8 metre
Cuerda: see Cordel			
Cun: see Ts'un			
Cyprus litre: see litre			
Dai	Korea, South	1.587 quarts	1.804 litres
Dain: see Taing			
Damleng: see Liang			
Dan: see Picul			
Danda, Dhanu or Bow	India*		
	Pakistan	2 yards	1.828 8 metres
Danar	Iran	6.614 ounces	187.5 grams
Darat	Somalia	1.977 acres	0.80 hectare
Dareb	Somalia	0.62 acre	0.25 hectare
Dariba	Egypt	43.55 bushels	15.84 hectolitres
Darm: see Picul			
Dau chung	Hongkong	806.7 sq. yards	674.5 sq. metres
Dawulla	Ethiopia	220.46 pounds	100 kilograms
Demi-livre	Seychelles*	0.54 pound	244.75 grams
Denum: see Dunam			
Depa	Malaysia		
	Singapore*	2 yards	1.828 8 metres
Derhem: see Dirham			
Deunam: see Dunam			
Dhanu: see Danda			
Dhara, Dhira, Dhiraa, Dhra, Dira, Diraa, Dra, Drah, Drahi, Archin, Archine, Arshin, Pic or Pik	Bahrain	19 inches	48.26 centimetres
	Cyprus	24 inches	60.96 centimetres
	Greece:		
	royal pic	39.37 inches	1 metre
	mason's pic*	29.53 inches	75 centimetres
	Iraq: Aleppo*	27.0 inches	68.5 centimetres
	Baghdad*	29.3 inches	74.5 centimetres
	Mosul*	27.6 inches	70 centimetres
	Jordan:		
	building*	29.8 inches	75.8 centimetres
	textiles*	26.8 inches	68 centimetres
	Lebanon:		
	land*	29.8 inches	75.8 centimetres
	textiles*	26.8 inches	68 centimetres
	Morocco	22 inches	55.88 centimetres
	Saudi Arabia*	18 inches	45.7 centimetres
	Soviet Union	28 inches	71.12 centimetres
	Sudan	22.8 inches	58 centimetres
	Syria (textiles):		
	Aleppo	26.8 inches	68 centimetres
	Damascus	27.6 inches	70 centimetres
	Turkey: carsi	26.8 inches	68 centimetres
	mimar	29.8 inches	75.8 centimetres
Dhumd: see Faddan			

Unit	Country	Equivalent in: UK units	Metric units
Dirham, Derhem, Dirhem, Dram, Dramma or Drachma	Cyprus	49.0 grains	3.175 grams
	Egypt	48.1 grains	3.12 grams
	Iran	0.331 ounce	9.375 grams
	Iraq*	49.5 grains	3.207 5 grams
	Jordan* Lebanon* Libya	49.46 grains	3.205 grams
	Sudan	48.1 grains	3.12 grams
	Syria	49.46 grains	3.205 grams
	Turkey*	49.5 grains	3.207 5 grams
Djung	Indonesia	3.507 acres	1.419 hectares
Don	Korea, South	57.9 grains	3.75 grams
Dönüm, see Dunam			
Doppelzentner	Germany, West	220.462 pounds	100 kilograms
Dou	China: new*	2.2 gallons	10 litres
Dra, Drah or Drahi: see Dhara			
Dra arbi	Libya	19.3 inches	49 centimetres
Drachma: see Dirham			
Dra maghrari	Syria	29.8 inches	75.8 centimetres
Dram or Dramma: see Dirham			
Dun: see Picul			
Dunam, Denum, Deunum, Dönüm, Dulum, Dunum, Scala or Tartous	Cyprus Israel Jordan Jugoslavia Lebanon*	1 600 sq. yards	1 337.8 sq. metres
		1 196 sq. yards	1 000 sq. metres
	Libya Syria Turkey*	1 099 sq. yards	919 sq. metres
Dung	Iran	12.06 grains	781 milligrams
El, Ell or Ela	Indonesia	27.08 inches	0.687 8 metre
	Malaysia	1 yard	0.914 4 metre
	Seychelles: old*	3.75 feet	1.143 metres
	new	4 feet	1.219 metres
El cotejo	Venezuela	11 pounds	5 kilograms
Endazeh	Turkey*	25.6 inches	65 centimetres
Evlek	Cyprus	400 sq. yards	334.5 sq. metres
Faddan, Feddân or Dhumd	Egypt	1.04 acres	0.42 hectare
	Iraq (metric)	12.36 acres	5 hectares
	Saudi Arabia* Sudan	1.04 acres	0.42 hectare
	Yemen, South	1 acre	0.405 hectare
Fan	Hongkong	0.146 inch	3.715 millimetres
	Macao	91.06 sq. yards	76.14 sq. metres
Fan (weight): see Hoon			
Fanega, Marco real or Mula	Argentina	3.77 bushels	1.372 hectolitres
	Bolivia	203 pounds	92 kilograms
	Chile*	2.67 bushels	96.99 litres
	Colombia Dominican Rep.	1.53 bushels	55.5 litres
	Ecuador	202.8 pounds	92 kilograms
	Honduras	30.323 bushels	11.028 hectolitres
	Mexico	2.497 bushels	90.815 litres
	Nicaragua	354.9 pounds	161 kilograms
	Paraguay	7.919 bushels	2.88 hectolitres
	Spain	1.53 bushels	55.5 litres
	Trinidad & Tob.	110 pounds	49.9 kilograms
	Uruguay	220.462 pounds	100 kilograms
Fanegada	Colombia	1.58 acres	0.64 hectare
	Peru	1.596 acres	0.65 hectare
	Spain	1.592 acres	0.64 hectare
Farsang	Iran	3.88 miles	6.24 kilometres
Faunt	Saudi Arabia*	3.9 pounds	1.769 kilograms
Favn or Famn	Denmark	1.029 7 fathoms	1.883 metres
	Sweden*	0.974 fathom	1.781 metres
Feddân: see Faddan			
Foot	Canada: Quebec (Paris foot)	12.789 inches	0.325 metre
	South Africa (Cape foot)*	1.033 feet	0.315 metre

Unit	Country	Equivalent in: UK units	Metric units
Frasala, Frasila or Frasoulla	Ethiopia	37.48 pounds	17 kilograms
	Somalia	35.56 pounds	16.128 kilograms
	Tanzania	36 pounds	16.33 kilograms
	Yemen, South	28 pounds	12.7 kilograms
Frasco	Argentina	2.088 quarts	2.375 litres
	Cuba	1.914 quarts	2.175 litres
	Paraguay	2.665 quarts	3.029 litres
Fuang	Laos Thailand	28.94 grains	1.875 grams
Fuder	Germany, West	181 gallons	8.244 hectolitres
	Netherlands	220 gallons	10 hectolitres
Fun: See Hoon			
Gadula	Libya	14.65 sq. yards	12.25 sq. metres
Galón	Chile*	3.995 quarts	4.54 litres
	El Salvador	3.3 quarts	3.75 litres
Gana	Libya	1.7 yards	1.6 metres
Gandom	Iran	0.754 grain	48.83 milligrams
Ganta or Gantang	Indonesia Malaysia:	1.887 gallons	8.577 litres
	capacity	1 gallon	4.546 litres
	weight	5.33 pounds	2.419 kilograms
	Philippines	0.66 gallon	3 litres
Garava	Syria	3.19 gallons	14.5 litres
Garra	Malta	2.375 gallons	10.797 litres
Garrafón	Cuba*	3.987 gallons	18.126 litres
Gasha	Ethiopia	100 acres	40 hectares
Gaulette	Mauritius Seychelles*	3.552 yards	3.248 metres
Gián	China: new*	77.2 grains	5 grams
Girah	Pakistan	2.25 inches	5.715 centimetres
Gireh	Iran	2.56 inches	6.50 centimetres
Gizla	Somalia:		
	capacity	35.87 gallons	163.08 litres
	weight	355.6 pounds	161.28 kilograms
Gô	Japan*	6.35 fl. ounces	180.39 millilitres
Gō	Japan*	3.558 sq. feet	0.330 6 sq. metre
Gomari or Load	Cyprus	36 gallons	163.659 litres
Gouffa	Morocco	1.24 acres	0.50 hectare
Grain	Mauritius Seychelles*	0.820 grain	53.1 milligrams
Gros	Mauritius Seychelles	59.0 grains	3.824 grams
Gudge, Gaz, Guz, Ver or Zar	India: Bengal*	36 inches	0.914 4 metre
	Bombay*	27 inches	0.685 8 metre
	Madras*	33 inches	0.838 2 metre
	Iran	1.14 yards	1.04 metres
	Pakistan	36 inches	0.914 4 metre
Gun: see Cate			
Hab: see Picul			
Habba	Sudan	1.543 grains	100 milligrams
Habba shair	Egypt	0.206 inch	5.22 millimetres
Habl	Libya	38.3 yards	35.0 metres
Hal: see Picul			
Halbstück	Netherlands	132 gallons	600 litres
Halibin	Rumania	27.6 inches	0.701 metre
Haml: see Hembl			
Handaza	Libya	26.8 inches	0.681 metre
Hang: see Liang			
Hao	China: new: length*	1.3 milli-inches	33.3 micrometres
	weight*	0.077 2 grain	5 milligrams
Hap: see Picul			
Hat: see Cubit			
Hath: see Cubit			
He'	China: new*	3.519 5 fl. ounces	100 millilitres
Hembl or Haml	Sudan	687.841 pounds	312 kilograms
Heml	Egypt	550.274 pounds	249.6 kilograms
Hemla	Sudan	165.082 pounds	74.88 kilograms
Hesta: see Cubit			
Hiro	Japan*	1.657 yards	1.515 metres
Hogga	Iraq: Baghdad*	9.186 6 pounds	4.167 kilograms
Hogshead	Singapore	63 gallons	286.4 litres
Hoi	Laos	4.23 ounces	120 grams

Unit	Country	Equivalent in: UK units	Metric units
Hoon, Houn, Hun, Fan, Fun or Candareen	Cambodia	5.787 grains	0.375 gram
	Hongkong	5.833 grains	0.378 gram
	Japan* / Laos	5.787 grains	0.375 gram
Hop	Korea, South: area	3.558 sq. feet	0.330 6 sq. metre
	capacity	6.349 fl. ounces	180.4 millilitres
Houn: see Hoon			
Huitieme	Seychelles*	2.158 ounces	61.188 grams
Hun: see Hoon			
Hvat	Jugoslavia	2.073 yards	1.896 metres
Hyaku-me	Japan*	13.228 ounces	375 grams
Ippyong	Korea, South	7.86 cu. yards	6.01 cu. metres
Jabia	Libya	1 465 sq. yards	1 225 sq. metres
Jae (timber)	Korea, South	0.118 cu. foot	3.339 cu. decimetres
Jak	Korea, South: area	0.356 sq. foot	0.033 sq. metre
	capacity	0.635 fl. ounce	18.039 millilitres
Jarra	Libya	3.11 gallons	14.13 litres
	Mexico	1.81 gallons	8.212 8 litres
Jemba	Malaysia	144 sq. feet	13.378 sq. metres
Jengkal	Malaysia / Singapore	9 inches	22.86 centimetres
Jerib	Afghanistan	2 336.5 sq. yards	0.195 36 hectare
	Iran	1 293.6 sq. yards	0.108 17 hectare
Jerib, side of	Afghanistan	48.3 yards	44.2 metres
Jin: see Cate			
Jō	Japan*	3.314 yards	3.030 3 metres
Jumfru	Sweden*	0.072 pint	40.9 millilitres
Jungbo: see Cho			
Jutro, katastarsko	Jugoslavia	1.422 acres	0.576 hectare
Kâ	Laos	14.5 grains	937.5 milligrams
Kabiet	Laos	0.164 inch	4.167 millimetres
Kadah or Qadah	Egypt / Sudan	3.63 pints	2.06 litres
Kadne: see Cadné			
Kala: see Drah			
Kalong	Laos	4.4 gallons	20 litres
Kam	Laos	3.937 inches	10 centimetres
Kan: see Ken			
Kanal	Pakistan	605 sq. yards	505.86 sq. metres
Kanchha	Bangladesh	225 grains	14.580 grams
Kandy: see Candy			
Kanee	Pakistan	1 936 sq. yards	0.161 9 hectare
Kanne	South Africa*	1.309 quarts	1.49 litres
Kantar, Kintar, Cantar, Qantar or Quantar	Cyprus	123.2 pounds	55.883 kilograms
	Egypt: general	99.049 pounds	44.928 kilograms
	metric	110.2 pounds	50 kilograms
	Greece*	124.164 pounds	56.32 kilograms
	Lebanon*	565.3 pounds	256.4 kilograms
	Libya: Cyrenaica	141.3 pounds	64.10 kilograms
	Tripolitania	113.1 pounds	51.28 kilograms
	Malta	175 pounds	79.38 kilograms
	Morocco	220.5 pounds	100 kilograms
	Sudan: small	99.049 pounds	44.928 kilograms
	large	312 pounds	141.5 kilograms
	Syria: Aleppo	706.6 pounds	320.5 kilograms
	Damascus	565.5 pounds	256.5 kilograms
	Turkey*	124.5 pounds	56.45 kilograms
Kantje	Germany, West	163.14 pounds	74 kilograms
Karam	Pakistan	5.5 feet	1.676 metres
Kard	Morocco	2.2 gallons	10 litres
Kartocc	Malta: beer, wine and spirits	1 quart	1.136 5 litres
	oil and milk	1.125 quarts	1.279 litres
Kartos	Cyprus	4.5 quarts	5.09 litres
Kassabe	Syria	28.48 sq. yards	23.814 sq. metres
Kati: see Cate			
Kavan	Cambodia	5.368 cubic feet	0.152 cubic metre
Kawtha	Burma	3.182 miles	5.121 kilometres
Keila or Kila	Egypt	3.63 gallons	16.5 litres
	Libya	0.79 acre	0.32 hectare
	Sudan	3.63 gallons	16.5 litres
Kejla	Malta	22.407 sq. yards	18.735 sq. metres
Kela	Saudi Arabia*	7.1 pounds	3.220 5 kilograms
Ken or Kan	Japan* / Korea, South	5.965 feet	1.818 metres
Kend	Ethiopia: new	1.64 feet	0.5 metre
Keun: see Cate			
Khanan	Laos	1.1 gallon	5 litres
Kharrouba	Morocco	8.799 gallons	40 litres
Kharvar or Kharwar	Iran	661.4 pounds	300 kilograms
	Afghanistan	1 246.2 pounds	565.28 kilograms
Khashkha	Pakistan	0.029 grain	1.898 milligrams
Khedem	Morocco	1 196 sq. yards	0.10 hectare
Khluon chay	Cambodia	8.54 milli-inches	0.217 millimetre
Khord	Afghanistan	3.89 ounces	110.406 grams
Khup	Laos	7.87 inches	20 centimetres
	Thailand	9.84 inches	25 centimetres
Kila: see Keila			
Kilé, Kileh or Kilesi	Cyprus	8 gallons	36.37 litres
	Libya	7.92 gallons	36 litres
	Turkey*	8.14 gallons	37 litres
Kin: see Cate			
Kintar: see Kantar			
Kirat	Lebanon: agriculture	1.24 inches	3.16 centimetres
	textiles	1.12 inches	2.83 centimetres
	Sudan	3.009 grains	195 milligrams
Ko: see Chia			
Kob	Laos	4.4 pint	2.5 litre
Koku	Japan*	39.680 gallons	1.804 hectolitres
Kollé or Qilli	Lebanon	73.51 pounds	33.345 kilograms
Kor: see Coss			
Kordofan	Sudan	1.796 acres	0.726 6 hectare
Koss: see Coss			
Kouza	Cyprus	2.25 gallons	10.229 litres
Koyan	Brunei	5 333.3 pounds	2 419 kilograms
	Malaysia: capacity	800 gallons	36.37 hectolitres
	weight	5 333.3 pounds	2 419 kilograms
	Singapore: capacity	800 gallons	36.37 hectolitres
	weight	5 333.3 pounds	2 419 kilograms
Krâp sran	Cambodia	0.102 5 inch	2.604 millimetres
Kunna	Ethiopia: capacity	0.968 gallon	4.4 litres
	weight	11.02 pounds	5 kilograms
Kwan	Japan* / Korea, South	8.27 pounds	3.75 kilograms
Kwarta	Malta: beer, wine and spirits	1.187 gallons	5.398 litres
	oil and milk	1.125 gallons	5.114 litres
Kwe	Burma	4.5 gallons	20.46 litres
Kwien	Thailand	440 gallons	20 hectolitres
Kyat: see Baht			
Lackilo	Laos	0.621 mile	1 kilometre
Lan	Burma	6 feet	1.829 metres
	Mongolia	1.323 ounces	37.5 grams
Lan: also see Legua			
Lanac	Jugoslavia	1.777 acres	0.719 hectare
Lane	Laos	1.181 tons	1.2 tonnes
Last	Netherlands	660 gallons	30 hectolitres
Lata	Costa Rica	0.999 pound	453.1 grams
Legana	Iran	1.09 bushels	39.5 litres

Unit	Country	Equivalent in: UK units	Metric units
	Chile*	2.805 miles	4.514 kilometres
	Cuba	2.63 miles	4.24 kilometres
	Ecuador	3.107 miles	5 kilometres
	El Salvador	2.485 miles	4 kilometres
Legua,	Guatemala	3.463 miles	5.573 kilometres
League,	Mauritius	2.485 miles	4 kilometres
Lan or	Mexico	2.604 miles	4.190 kilometres
Lieue	Paraguay	2.69 miles	4.33 kilometres
	Peru	3.452 miles	5.56 kilometres
	Portugal	3.4 miles	5.50 kilometres
	Spain	3.463 miles	5.573 kilometres
	Uruguay	3.2 miles	5.15 kilometres
Lei: see Li˘			
Lelong	Malaysia / Singapore	2 400 sq. feet	222.97 sq. metres
Leung: see Liang			
Li´ or Li	China: new*	0.013 1 inch	0.333 millimetre
(length)	Macao	0.014 8 inch	0.376 millimetre
	Mongolia	0.012 6 inch	0.32 millimetre
	Cambodia	0.579 grain	37.5 milligrams
Li˘ or Lin	China: new*	0.772 grain	50 milligrams
(weight)	Laos	0.579 grain	37.5 milligrams
	Macao	0.583 grain	37.8 milligrams
	China: old*	705 yards	645 metres
Li˘ or Lei	new*	546.8 yards	500 metres
	Hongkong	609.375 yards	557.213 metres
	Korea, South	2.44 miles	3.927 kilometres
Liang,	Brunei	1.333 ounces	37.8 grams
Damleng,	Cambodia	1.323 ounces	37.5 grams
Hang,	China: old*	1.333 ounces	37.8 grams
Leung,	new*	1.764 ounces	50 grams
Taël, or	Hongkong	1.333 ounces	37.8 grams
Tahil	Macao		
	Argentina		
	Bolivia	1.012 8 pounds	459.4 grams
	Chile*	1.014 1 pounds	460 grams
	Colombia*	1.102 3 pounds	500 grams
	Costa Rica	1.014 1 pounds	460 grams
	Cuba	1.014 3 pounds	460.09 grams
	Dominican Rep.	1 pound	453.6 grams
	Ecuador		
Libra	El Salvador	1.014 1 pounds	460 grams
or Arrátel	Guatemala		
	Honduras	1.014 pounds	460 grams
	Macao	1.012 pounds	459 grams
	Mexico	1.015 pounds	460.2 grams
	Paraguay	1.012 pounds	459 grams
	Peru	1.014 1 pounds	460 grams
	Philippines	1.014 1 pounds	460 grams
	Spain	1.014 3 pounds	460.09 grams
	Venezuela	1.016 pounds	460.9 grams
Lieue: see Legua			
	Haiti		
Ligne	Mauritius	0.088 8 inch	2.256 millimetres
	Seychelles*		
	Chile*		
Linea	Honduras	0.076 1 inch	1.93 millimetres
	Mexico	0.076 4 inch	1.94 millimetres
	Paraguay	0.079 inch	2.006 millimetres
Linia	Sudan	0.125 inch	3.175 millimetres
Liño	Paraguay	89.8 sq. yards	75 sq. metres
	Cyprus:		
	capacity	2.8 quarts	3.182 litres
	weight	5.04 pounds	2.286 kilograms
Litre	Greece*:		
	Ionian	1 pound	453.6 grams
	Venetian	1.058 pounds	480 grams
	Haiti: française		
	Mauritius:	1.079 pounds	489.5 grams
Livre	colonial		
	general	1.102 pounds	500 grams
	Seychelles	1.079 pounds	489.5 grams
Load: see Gomari			
Lood	Indonesia	238.3 grains	15.44 grams
	Netherlands	22.046 pounds	10 kilograms

Unit	Country	Equivalent in: UK units	Metric units
Maatje	Netherlands	0.176 pint	0.1 litre
Mace	Malaysia	93.3 grains	6.048 grams
Madeja	Venezuela	11–33 pounds	5–15 kilograms
Makhammus	Sudan	0.798 acre	0.323 hectare
	Korea, South:		
Mal	small	1.984 gallons	9.019 5 litres
	large	3.968 gallons	18.039 litres
Malwa	Sudan	3.629 quarts	4.125 litres
Mancuerna	Honduras	3.17 pounds	1.437 5 kilograms
	Venezuela	4.4–33 pounds	2–15 kilograms
Mann	Iraq: Baghdad*	55.12 pounds	25 kilograms
	Belize	2.064 acres	0.835 hectare
Manzana	Costa Rica	1.727 acres	0.698 9 hectare
	Guatemala	1.73 acres	0.70 hectare
	Nicaragua	1.744 acres	0.705 6 hectare
Mara	Venezuela	110–441 pounds	50–200 kilograms
Marabba	Pakistan	25 acres	10.117 hectares
Marasseh	Lebanon	59.80 sq. yards	50 sq. metres
Marco real: see Fanega			
Marfold: see Mil			
Marla	Pakistan	30.25 sq. yards	25.293 sq. metres
Marta	Libya	0.571 bushel	0.207 5 hectolitre
Masha	Bangladesh / Pakistan	15 grains	972 milligrams
Mau or Maz	Macao: area	910.6 sq. yards	761.4 sq. metres
	weight	0.133 ounce	3.78 grams
	Bahrain	56 pounds	25.4 kilograms
	Bangladesh	82.286 pounds	37.32 kilograms
	India: Bombay*	28 pounds	12.7 kilograms
Maund	Madras*	25 pounds	11.3 kilograms
or Mon	standard*	82.286 pounds	37.32 kilograms
	Oman: Muscat	8.9 pounds	4.04 kilograms
	Pakistan	82.286 pounds	37.32 kilograms
	Yemen, South		
Mayam	Malaysia	52 grains	3.37 grams
Maz: see Mau			
Mecate	Costa Rica	21.942 yards	20.064 metres
orTask	Guatemala		
	Nicaragua	22.05 yards	20.16 metres
Media: see Quintal			
Medida	Honduras	2.527 quarts	2.872 litres
	Venezuela	747 sq. yards	625 sq. metres
Medio	El Salvador	18–30 pounds	8.3–13.8 kilograms
	Honduras	1.263 bushels	45.95 litres
	Venezuela	1.24 acres	0.50 hectare
Meile: see Mil			
Menor	Iran	2.76 gallons	12.55 litres
Messe	Ethiopia	1.3 quarts	1.5 litres
Metkal: see Miskal			
Metze	Austria	13.53 gallons	61.5 litres
Mid	Jordan*	3.96 gallons	18 litres
	Denmark	4.680 5 miles	7.532 5 kilometres
Mil, Meile	Hungary	5.19 miles	8.35 kilometres
or Marfold	Sweden: new*	6.214 miles	10 kilometres
	Venezuela	882 pounds	400 kilograms
Milla	Ecuador	0.87 mile	1.4 kilometres
Minot	Canada	1.07 bushels	38.91 hectolitres
Mishara	Iraq*	0.62 acre	0.25 hectare
Miskal,	Afghanistan	71.04 grains	4.600 grams
Miscal,	Iran*	72.34 grains	4.687 5 grams
Misqal or	Libya: gold	71.0 grains	4.601 grams
Metkal			
Misura	Libya	0.544 bushel	0.198 hectolitre
Mkono	Tanzania	18 inches	45.72 centimetres
Mō	Japan*: weight	0.058 grain	3.75 milligrams
	length	1.193 milli-inches	30.303 micrometres
	Korea, South		
Mocha	Ethiopia	1.097 ounces	31.1 grams
Modd	Malta	4.444 acres	1.798 hectares
Momme	Japan*	0.132 ounce	3.75 grams
Mon: see Maund			
Moraba	Pakistan	25 acres	10.117 hectares
Morgen	South Africa*	2.117 acres	0.856 5 hectare
Moud: see Courd			

Unit	Country	Equivalent in: UK units	Metric units
Mud or Muid	Netherlands	2.75 bushels	1 hectolitre
	Seychelles*	7.374 bushels	2.682 hectolitres
	South Africa*	3 bushels	1.09 hectolitres
Mudd	Syria: Chakba	5.72 gallons	26 litres
	Soueida	6.05 gallons	27.5 litres
Mula: see Fanega			
Mune or Mun	Laos	26.46 pounds	12 kilograms
Musu kibaba	Tanzania	0.44 quart	0.50 litre
Myo	Korea, South	118.61 sq. yards	99.174 sq. metres
Nakhod	Afghanistan	2.96 grains	191.8 milligrams
or Nokhod	Iran	3.01 grains	195 milligrams
Néal	Cambodia	1.323 pounds	600 grams
Neter	Ethiopia	0.99 pound	450 grams
Ngamu	Burma	0.288 ounce	8.165 grams
Ngan	Laos	} 478.4 sq. yards	400 sq. metres
or Ngane	Thailand		
Nijo	Japan*	0.529 ounce	15 grams
Niu or Niou	Laos	0.656 inch	1.667 centimetres
	Thailand	0.82 inch	2.083 centimetres
Nokhod: see Nakhod			
Ochava	Macao	55.3 grains	3.59 grams
or Oitava	Mexico	55.5 grains	3.60 grams
Ock, Oka, Oke or Okka	Cyprus: capacity	1.12 quarts	1.273 litres
	weight	2.8 pounds	1.270 kilograms
	Greece*	2.83 pounds	1.28 kilograms
	Jordan*	} 2.826 pounds	1.282 kilograms
	Lebanon*		
	Libya		
	Saudi Arabia*	2.751 pounds	1.248 kilograms
	Syria	2.826 pounds	1.282 kilograms
	Turkey*	2.828 pounds	1.283 kilograms
Oke thapa	Burma	210 feet	64.008 metres
Okia, Okiya, Once, Oqiya, Oquia, Ukia, Wagia, Wakea or Woket	Ethiopia	0.914 ounce	25.9 grams
	Iraq: Baghdad*	2.30 pounds	1.042 kilograms
	Mosul*	4.526 ounces	128.3 grams
	Jordan: Nabulsi*	8.479 ounces	240.4 grams
	Shami*	} 7.537 ounces	213.7 grams
	Lebanon		
	Libya	1.131 ounces	32.05 grams
	Somalia	0.99 ounce	28 grams
	Sudan	1.32 ounces	37.44 grams
	Syria: Aleppo	11.31 ounces	320.5 grams
	Damascus	7.54 ounces	213.7 grams
Okshoofd	Netherlands	51.2 gallons	232.8 litres
Olc	Iraq*	119.6 sq. yards	100 sq. metres
Ona	Dominican Rep.	1.299 yards	1.188 metres
Onca or Onza = 1/16 of a libra or arrátel			
Once or Oqiya or Oquia: see Okia			
Ons	Indonesia	1.089 ounces	30.88 grams
Orlong	Malaysia	1.32 acres	0.535 hectare
Oukeia	Morocco	4.41 ounces	125 grams
Ouroub	Iran	5.12 inches	13 centimetres
Paal or Pal	Indonesia: Java	0.936 mile	1.507 kilometres
	Sumatra	1.151 miles	1.852 kilometres
Paca	Venezuela	110 pounds	50 kilograms
Palito	Venezuela	20–40 pounds	9–18 kilograms
Palmi, Palmo or Xiber	Libya	9.84 inches	25 centimetres
	Macao	8.66 inches	22 centimetres
	Malta	10.312 inches	26.19 centimetres
	Spain	8.227 inches	20.9 centimetres
Panchang	Malaysia*	108 cu. feet	3.06 cu. metres
Pao or Powa	Bangladesh	} 3 600 grains	233.276 grams
	Pakistan		
Paquete	Venezuela	2.6–4.4 pounds	1.2–2.0 kilograms
Para or Bandu	Malaysia	} 10 gallons	45.46 litres
	Singapore		
Passo	Libya	1.09 yards	1 metre
Pau	Brunei	} 0.5 pint	284 millilitres
	Malaysia		
	Singapore		

Unit	Country	Equivalent in: UK units	Metric units
Pé	Macao	13 inches	33 centimetres
Pecul: see Picul			
Peninkulma	Finland*	6.21 miles	10 kilometres
Penjuru	Malaysia	} 0.331 acre	0.133 78 hectare
	Singapore		
Perch or Perche	Canada: Quebec length	1.162 perches	5.847 metres
	area	368.0 sq. feet	34.19 sq. metres
	Mauritius Seychelles	} 1.292 perches	6.497 metres
Pfund: see Pund			
Phai mû	Laos	2.2 pints	1.25 litres
Phyéam	Cambodia*	6.562 feet	2 metres
Pic: see Dhara			
Picul, Pikul, Pecul, Pico, Picol, Hab, Hal, Hap, Ta, Taam, Tam, Tan, Dan, Dun or Darm	Brunei	133.33 pounds	60.479 kilograms
	Cambodia	132.28 pounds	60 kilograms
	China: old*	133.33 pounds	60.479 kilograms
	new*	110.23 pounds	50 kilograms
	Hongkong	133.33 pounds	60.479 kilograms
	Indonesia	136.16 pounds	61.761 kilograms
	Japan*	} 132.28 pounds	60 kilograms
	Laos		
	Macao	} 133.33 pounds	60.479 kilograms
	Malaysia		
	Philippines	139.44 pounds	63.249 kilograms
	Singapore	133.33 pounds	60.479 kilograms
	Thailand	132.28 pounds	60 kilograms
	Vietnam	133.28 pounds	60.453 kilograms
Pie, Pié, Pied, or Tercia	Costa Rica	0.914 foot	0.279 metre
	Cuba	0.927 foot	0.282 7 metre
	Guatemala	0.914 foot	0.279 metre
	Haiti Mauritius	} 1.066 feet	0.324 8 metre
	Mexico	0.916 foot	0.279 metre
	Nicaragua	0.919 foot	0.28 metre
	Paraguay	0.948 foot	0.289 metre
	Seychelles	1.066 feet	0.324 8 metre
	Spain	0.914 foot	0.279 metre
Pijp	Netherlands	118.8 gallons	5.40 hectolitres
Pik: see Dhara			
Pinar	Iran	3.307 ounces	93.75 grams
Pinta	Chile*	0.985 pint	0.56 litre
Pinte	Mauritius and Seychelles: colonial	1.639 pints	931.3 millilitres
	reputed	0.666 2 pint	378.6 millilitres
Pipa or Pipe	Argentina	100.3 gallons	4.56 hectolitres
	Cuba*	104.9 gallons	4.769 hectolitres
	Dominican Rep.	126 gallons	5.728 hectolitres
	Paraguay	127.9 gallons	5.816 hectolitres
	Singapore	126 gallons	5.728 hectolitres
Pishi	Tanzania	0.88 gallon	4 litres
Plaza	Venezuela	12–24 sq. yards	10–20 sq. metres
Polegada	Macao	1.08 inches	27.5 millimetres
Pond	Indonesia	1.089 pounds	494.1 grams
	Netherlands	1.102 pounds	500 grams
Ponto	Macao	1.480 inches	3.76 centimetres
Pood or Poud	Soviet Union	36.113 pounds	16.38 kilograms
Pouce	Haiti Mauritius Seychelles*	} 1.066 inches	27.07 millimetres
Pow	Afghanistan	0.974 pound	441.625 grams
Powa: see Pao			
Pu	Macao	3.79 sq. yards	3.172 5 sq. metres
Pulgada	Colombia	0.98 inch	25 millimetres
	Cuba	0.927 inch	23.6 millimetres
	Honduras	0.913 inch	23.2 millimetres
	Mexico	0.916 inch	23.3 millimetres
	Nicaragua	0.919 inch	23.3 millimetres
	Paraguay	0.948 inch	24.1 millimetres
	Spain*	0.914 inch	23.2 millimetres
Pulgada maderera	Chile	1 440 cu. inches	23.597 cu. decimetres
Pulzier	Malta	0.859 inch	21.83 millimetres
Pun	Korea, South	0.119 inch	3.03 millimetres

Unit	Country	Equivalent in: UK units	Metric units
Pund or Pfund	Denmark / Germany, West	1.102 pounds	0.5 kilogram
Punto	Honduras	0.006 34 inch	0.161 millimetre
Pushuri	Venezuela	1 323 pounds	600 kilograms
	Bangladesh	10.286 pounds	4.666 kilograms
Pyi	Burma: capacity	2.25 quarts	2.557 litres
	weight	4.69 pounds	2.126 kilograms
Pyong	Korea, South	3.954 sq. yards	3.306 sq. metres
Qadaa	Sudan	5.45 acres	2.204 hectares
Qadah: see Kadah			
Qantar or Quantar: see Kantar			
Qasba or Canna	Malta	2.292 yards	2.095 metres
Qilli: see Kollé			
Qing	China: new*	16.473 7 acres	6.667 hectares
Quilate	Colombia	0.309 grain	20 milligrams
	Argentina	101.28 pounds	45.94 grams
	Belize	100 pounds	45.36 grams
	Bolivia / Chile*	101.41 pounds	46 kilograms
	Colombia	110.23 pounds	50 kilograms
	Costa Rica	101.41 pounds	46 kilograms
	Cuba	101.43 pounds	46.009 kilograms
	Czechoslovakia	110.23 pounds	50 kilograms
	Dominican Rep.	100 pounds	45.36 kilograms
Quintal or Media	Ecuador / Guatemala / Honduras	101.41 pounds	46 kilograms
	Macao	129.53 pounds	58.752 kilograms
	Mexico	101.5 pounds	46.02 kilograms
	Paraguay	101.2 pounds	45.9 kilograms
	Peru / Phillipines	101.41 pounds	46 kilograms
	Portugal	132.28 pounds	60 kilograms
	Spain	101.43 pounds	46.009 kilograms
	Venezuela	101.6 pounds	46.09 kilograms
Rabâa	Morocco	8.82 ounces	250 grams
Rabia: see Court			
Rageil	Sudan	1.833 yards	1.676 metres
Rai	Laos / Thailand	0.395 acre	0.16 hectare
Ratal, Ratel, Ratili, Ratl, Rattel, Rotal, Rotl, Rotol, Rotolo, Rottel, Rottle, Rottol or Rottolo	Egypt	0.990 5 pound	0.449 kilogram
	Iran	1.033 pounds	0.469 kilogram
	Jordan* / Lebanon*	5.653 pounds	2.564 kilograms
	Libya	1.13 pounds	0.513 kilograms
	Malta	1.75 pounds	0.794 kilogram
	Morocco: new	1.012 pounds	500 grams
	Saudia Arabia*	1.02 pound	0.462 kilogram
	Somalia	0.988 pound	0.448 kilogram
	Sudan	0.990 5 pound	0.449 kilogram
	Syria	5.655 pounds	2.565 kilograms
	Tanzania	1 pound	0.454 kilogram
Real	Indonesia	417 grains	27.045 grams
Rebée	Syria	1.04 gallons	4.75 litres
Relong	Malaysia / Singapore*	0.71 acre	0.287 hectare
Rey	Iran	26.46 pounds	12 kilograms
Ri	Japan*	2.44 miles	3.927 kilometres
	Korea, South	0.011 93 inch	0.303 millimetre
Rin	Japan: length	0.011 93 inch	0.303 millimetre
	weight	0.579 grain	37.5 milligrams
Robo kibaba	Tanzania	0.22 quart	0.25 litre
Roe / Roede	Netherlands: / Rhineland	0.75 rod / 16.999 sq. yards	3.770 metres / 14.213 sq. metres
Rotal, Rotl, Rotol, Rotolo, Rottel, Rottle, Rottol or Rottolo: see Ratal			
Roupi	Cyprus	3 inches	7.62 centimetres
Rtel: see Ratal			
Ruba	Saudi Arabia* / Sudan	20.6 pounds / 1.815 gallons	9.344 kilograms / 8.25 litres
Rute	Germany, West	0.749 rod	3.766 metres
Ruttee	Pakistan	1.875 grains	121.5 milligrams

Unit	Country	Equivalent in: UK units	Metric units
Saa: see Aftari			
Sâa	Libya: area / capacity	2.37 acres / 3.27 bushels	0.96 hectare / 1.188 hectolitres
Saagh	Syria	2.14 gallons	9.73 litres
Sabbitha	Iran	1.59 gallons	7.24 litres
Sac or Saco	Colombia / Haiti	137.8 pounds / 132.3 pounds	62.5 kilograms / 60 kilograms
Saddirham	Iran	3.307 pounds	1.5 kilograms
Saga	Malaysia	4.333 grains	281 milligrams
Sai	Japan	0.983 cu. feet	27.826 cu decimetres
Sale	Burma	1.125 pints	0.639 litre
Salung or Bak	Laos / Thailand	57.87 grains	3.75 grams
Sandong	Burma	22 inches	55.88 centimetres
Sat: see Thang			
Sauk or Sawk: see Sok			
Sayut	Burma	4.50 quarts	5.114 litres
Scala: see Dunam			
Schepel	Netherlands	2.2 gallons	10 litres
Sê	Japan*	118.61 sq. yards	99.174 sq. metres
Seer or Sihr	Afghanistan	15.58 pounds	7.066 kilograms
	Bangladesh / India*	2.057 pounds	0.933 kilogram
	Iran	2.646 ounces	75 grams
	Pakistan / Yemen, South	2.057 pounds	0.933 kilogram
Seik	Burma: dry / liquid	1.125 pecks / 1.78 quarts	10.229 litres / 2.020 litres
Sen or Sénh	Cambodia / Laos / Thailand	43.74 yards	40 metres
Sène	Laos	264.6 pounds	120 kilograms
Sextario	Iran	0.579 pint	329 millilitres
Shaku	Japan: length* / capacity*	11.93 inches / 0.635 fl. ounce	0.303 metre / 18.039 millilitres
Shao	China: new*	0.352 fl. ounce	10 millilitres
Shibr	Saudi Arabia*	7 inches	17.78 centimetres
Shō	Japan*	0.397 gallon	1.803 9 litres
Shushack	Belize	5 gallons	22.73 litres
Si or Ssu	China: new*	0.007 716 grain	0.5 milligram
Siegh	Malta	224.07 sq. yards	187.354 sq. metres
Sihr: see Seer			
Siki	Bangladesh	45 grains	2.92 grams
Sok, Sauk or Sawk	Laos / Thailand	15.748 inches / 19.685 inches	40 centimetres / 50 centimetres
Solar	Costa Rica / Ecuador	1 044.8 sq. yards / 2 109.7 sq. yards	873.6 sq. metres / 1764 sq. metres
Spint	Netherlands	1.1 gallons	5 litres
Square	Sri Lanka	100 sq. yards	83.61 sq. metres
Ssu: see Si			
Stoop	Netherlands	1.32 gallons	6 litres
Stremma	Greece: royal / old (Moreas)*	0.247 1 acre / 0.313 8 acre	1 000 sq. metres / 1 270 sq. metres
Suerte	Uruguay	4 923 acres	19.92 sq. kilometres
Suk	Korea, South	39.680 gallons	1.804 hectolitres
Suku	Indonesia	104.3 grains	6.761 grams
Sun	Japan*	1.193 inches	3.030 3 centimetres
Sus	Somalia	3.25 pounds	1.475 kilograms
Ta or Taam: see Picul			
Tabla	Somalia	4.484 gallons	20.385 litres
Tablon	Venezuela	1.48–2.47 acres	0.6–1.0 hectare
Taël: see Liang			
Tahil: see Liang			
Taim: see Cubit			
Taing or Dain	Burma	2.43 miles	3.91 kilometres
Talangva	Laos	4.783 9 sq. yards	4 sq. metres
Tali	Indonesia	52.2 grains	3.381 grams
Tam: see Picul			
Tamna	Morocco	269.1 sq. yards	225 sq. metres
Tamuga	Costa Rica	4.564 pounds	2.070 kilograms
Tan	Japan* / Korea, South	1 186.1 sq. yards	991.74 sq. metres
Tan (China): see picul			

Unit	Country	Equivalent in: UK units	Metric units
Tanica or Teneka	Iraq*	4 gallons	18.184 litres
	Somalia	3.96 gallons	18 litres
Tarabiit see Courd			
Tarea	Dominican Rep.	752.1 sq. yards	628.8 sq. metres
	Venezuela	60–996 sq. yards	50–833 sq. metres
Tarialte	Morocco	0.89 acre	0.36 hectare
Tartous: see Dunam			
Task: see Mecate			
Taung: see Cubit			
Taza	Cuba	0.415 pint	236 millilitres
Tcharak	Iran	1.653 pounds	0.75 grams
Teman	Libya	5.90 gallons	26.82 litres
Teminye	Syria	2.12 quarts	2.41 litres
Teningsfet	Iceland	1.091 cu. feet	0.030 9 cu. metre
Tercia: see Pie			
Tercio	Ecuador	81.1 pounds	36.8 kilograms
	Mexico	162.3 pounds	73.64 kilograms
	Venezuela	88 pounds	40 kilograms
Terz	Malta: beer, wine and spirits	10 fl. ounces	284.1 millilitres
	oil and milk	11.25 fl. ounces	319.6 millilitres
Thail	Indonesia: opium	595.7 grains	38.601 grams
	diamonds	834.7 grains	54.09 grams
Thang or Sat	Laos	44 gallons	200 litres
	Thailand	4.40 gallons	20 litres
Thneap	Cambodia	0.820 inch	2.083 centimetres
Tical: see Baht			
Tierçon	Mauritius	42.01 gallons	1.91 hectolitres
Tji	Indonesia	59.57 grains	3.860 grams
To	Japan*	3.97 gallons	18.039 litres
Toesa	Macao	2.17 yards	1.98 metres
Toise	Mauritius / Seychelles	1.066 fathoms	1.949 metres
Tola	Bangladesh / India* / Bangladesh Pakistan	180 grains	11.664 grams
Tomme	Denmark	1.029 7 inches	2.615 4 centimetres
Tomna	Malta: area	0.277 8 acre	0.112 4 hectare
	volume	4 gallons	18.184 litres
Tønde land	Denmark	1.363 acres	0.552 hectare
Tonelada, Tonnelada, Tonneau or Tonel	Argentina: capacity*	28.29 bushels	1.029 cu. metres
	weight*	0.904 ton	0.919 tonne
	Bolivia	0.905 ton	0.920 tonne
	Colombia	0.984 ton	1 tonne
	Cuba: short Spanish	0.906 ton	0.920 2 tonne
	long Spanish	1.014 tons	1.030 6 tonnes
	Costa Rica El Salvador Guatemala Nicaragua	0.905 ton	0.920 tonne
	Paraguay	0.904 ton	0.918 tonne
	Peru	0.905 ton	0.920 tonne
	Portugal: capacity	189 gallons	860 litres
	weight	0.781 ton	0.793 tonne
	Spain: short	0.906 ton	0.920 2 tonne
	long	1.014 tons	1.030 6 tonnes
Top	Somalia	4.3 yards	3.91 metres
Topo	Peru: Cuzco	0.67 acre	0.272 hectare
	general	0.86 acre	0.349 hectare
	Puno	1.14 acres	0.461 hectare
Toque	Seychelles*	4.839 gallons	22 litres
Tsin: see Chi			
Tsubo or Bu	Japan*	3.95 sq. yards	3.31 sq. metres
Ts'un or Cun	China: old*	1.41 inches	3.58 centimetres
	new*	1.312 inches	3.33 centimetres
	Hongkong	1.46 inches	3.714 75 centimetres
Tughar	Iraq: Baghdad*	1.968 tons	2 tonnes
	Basra*	2.020 tons	2.053 tonnes
	Mosul*	588.3 pounds	266.864 kilograms
Tumoli	Malta	200 bushels	72.74 hectolitres
Tun	Malaysia / Singapore	252 gallons	11.456 hectolitres
Ud	Sudan	2.54 yards	2.32 metres
Ueba	Libya	7.99 bushels	2.905 hectolitres
Ukia: see Okia			
Una	Iran	0.188 grain	12.21 milligrams
Unglie or Ungul	India* / Pakistan	0.75 inch	1.905 centimetres
Uqija	Malta	0.933 ounce	26.5 grams
Va, Wa or Wah	Laos / Thailand	2.187 yards	2 metres
Vadem	Netherlands	2 yards	1.83 metres
Vagon	Jugoslavia	9.842 tons	10 tonnes
Vara	Argentina*	34.1 inches	86.7 centimetres
	Chile*	32.9 inches	83.6 centimetres
	Colombia	31.5 inches	80 centimetres
	Costa Rica	32.9 inches	83.6 centimetres
	Cuba	33.4 inches	84.8 centimetres
	Dominican Rep.	32.9 inches	83.6 centimetres
	Ecuador	33.1 inches	84 centimetres
	El Salvador Guatemala	32.9 inches	83.6 centimetres
	Honduras	32.9 inches	83.5 centimetres
	Macao	43.3 inches	1.10 metres
	Mexico	33 inches	83.8 centimetres
	Nicaragua	33.1 inches	84 centimetres
	Paraguay	34.1 inches	86.7 centimetres
	Peru	33 inches	83.8 centimetres
	Spain*	32.9 inches	83.6 centimetres
	Uruguay	33.8 inches	85.9 centimetres
	Venezuela: length	33 inches	83.8 centimetres
	weight	0.551 pound	250 grams
Velte	Mauritius / Seychelles	1.639 gallons	7.450 5 litres
Ver: see Gudge			
Verst or Versta	Soviet Union	0.662 9 mile	1.067 kilometres
Viss	Burma	3.6 pounds	1.633 kilograms
Voet	Netherlands: Amsterdam	0.929 foot	28.3 centimetres
	Rhineland	1.031 feet	31.4 centimetres
Wa or Wah: see Va			
Wagia or Wakea: see Okia			
Wang	Indonesia	17.39 grains	1.127 grams
Wazna	Iraq: Baghdad*	220.46 pounds	100 kilograms
	Basra*	226.28 pounds	102.64 kilograms
	Mosul*	29.417 pounds	13.343 kilograms
	Saudi Arabia*	3.5 pounds	1.588 kilograms
Wise	Netherlands	219.969 gallons	1 000 litres
Wizna	Malta	8.75 pounds	3.969 kilograms
Woket: see Okia			
Xang	Laos	2.646 pounds	1.2 kilograms
Xiber: see Palmi			
Yarda	Colombia	0.984 yard	0.9 metre
Ying	China: new*	36.45 yards	33.33 metres
Yoch or Yote	Cambodia / Thailand	9.94 miles	16 kilometres
Yuzanar	Burma	47.121 miles	75.834 kilometres
Zar: see Gudge			
Zentner or Centner	Denmark / Germany, West	110.23 pounds	50 kilograms
Zhang: see Chang			
Zoll	Germant, West	1.03 inches	2.62 centimetres

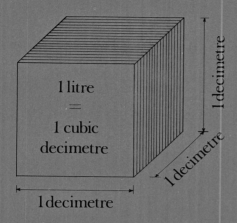

1 litre
=
1 cubic
decimetre

1 decimetre

1 decimetre

1 decimetre

The end of the Imperial gallon

- now defined in terms of the metric system

'For the definitions of ''Gallon'' and ''Litre'' in Part IV of
Schedule 1 to the said Act of 1963 there shall be substituted
the following definitions:

''GALLON'' = 4.546 09 cubic decimetres''.
''LITRE''   = a cubic decimetre''.'

(Weights and Measures, The Units of Measurement
Regulations 1976, 1976 No. 1674)

Conversions: summary

Exact values are shown in bold type in this conversions summary; other values are generally shown to six significant figures.

Numbers are shown in full: where the short-hand notation using numbers equal to or larger than one and under 10 associated with powers of 10 is preferred, these can be obtained as follows: a positive power as suffix to the ten indicates the number of digits to the left of the decimal point less one, and a negative power the number of noughts between the decimal point and the first real number, plus one. For example, 304.8 mm = 3.048×10^2 mm and 0.003 048 mm = 3.048×10^{-3} mm (also see page 15 regarding multiples and sub-multiples). Non-metric units are UK (imperial) unless otherwise stated. In this section no distinction is made between UK or metric units which are no longer authorised and those which remain authorised; see pages 14–19 for further information. More detailed conversions for main units are given in the tables on pages 68–83 with a description of the use of those tables on page 5.

	Multiply number of	by	to obtain equivalent number of
Length	Milli-inches (mils or 'thou')	**25.4**	micrometres (µm)
	Inches (in)	**25.4**	millimetres (mm)
		2.54	centimetres (cm)
		0.025 4	metres (m)
	Hands	**101.6**	millimetres
	Links (lk)	**0.201 168**	metres
	Feet (ft)	**304.8**	millimetres
		30.48	centimetres
		0.304 8	metres
	US survey feet	0.304 801	
	Yards (yd)	**0.914 4**	
	Fathoms	**1.828 8**	
	Rods	**5.029 2**	
	Chains (ch)	**20.116 8**	
	Engineers' chains	**30.48**	metres
	Furlongs	**201.168**	
	Miles, statute (mi)	**1 609.344**	
	Miles, international nautical	**1 852**	
	Miles, UK nautical	**1 853.184**	
	Miles, telegraph nautical	**1 855.317 6**	
	Chains	**0.020 116 8**	
	Engineers' chains	**0.030 48**	
	Furlongs	**0.201 168**	
	Miles, statute	**1.609 344**	kilometres (km)
	Miles, international nautical	**1.852**	
	Miles, UK nautical	**1.853 184**	
	Miles, telegraph nautical	**1.855 317 6**	
	Miles, statute	0.868 976	miles, international nautical

Multiply number of	by	to obtain equivalent number of
Micrometres	0.039 370 1	milli-inches
Millimetres	0.039 370 1	inches
Centimetres	0.393 701	inches
	0.049 709 7	links
	0.032 808 4	feet
	0.032 808 3	US survey feet
Metres	39.370 1	inches
	4.970 97	links
	3.280 84	feet
	3.280 83	US survey feet
	1.093 61	yards
	0.546 807	fathoms
	0.198 839	rods
	0.049 709 7	chains
	0.004 970 97	furlongs
Kilometres	49.709 7	chains
	32.808 4	engineers' chains
	4.970 97	furlongs
	0.621 371	miles, statute
	0.539 957	miles, international nautical
	0.539 612	miles, UK nautical
	0.538 991	miles, telegraph nautical
Miles, international nautical	1.150 78	miles, statute

	Multiply number of	by	to obtain equivalent number of
Area	Circular mils	506.707	square micrometres (µm²)
	Square inches (in²)	**645.16**	square millimetres (mm²)
		6.451 6	square centimetres (cm²)
	Square feet (ft²)	**929.030 4**	square centimetres
		0.092 903 04	square metres
	Square yards (yd²)	**0.836 127 36**	square metres (m²)
		0.008 361 273 6	ares (a)
	Square chains (ch²)	**404.685 642 24**	square metres
		4.046 856 422 4	ares
		0.404 685 642 24	dekares (daa)
	Roods	**1 011.714 105 6**	square metres
		10.117 141 056	ares
		1.011 714 105 6	dekares
		0.101 171 410 56	hectares (ha)
	Acres	**4 046.856 422 4**	square metres
		40.468 564 224	ares
		0.404 685 642 24	hectares
	Square miles (mi²)	**258.998 811 033 6**	hectares
		2.589 988 110 336	sq. kilometres (km²)
	US townships	**93.239 571 972 096**	square kilometres

Multiply number of	by	to obtain equivalent number of
Square micrometres	0.001 973 53	circular mils
Square millimetres	0.001 550 00	square inches
Square centimetres	0.155 000	square inches
	0.001 076 39	square feet
Square metres	10.763 9	square feet
	1.195 99	square yards
	0.002 471 05	square chains
Ares	119.599	square yards
	0.247 105	square chains
	0.098 842 2	roods
	0.024 710 5	acres
Dekares	2.471 05	square chains
	0.988 422	roods
	0.247 105	acres
Hectares	9.884 22	roods
	2.471 05	acres
	0.003 861 02	square miles
Square kilometres	247.105	acres
	0.386 102	square miles
	0.010 725 1	US townships

Volume and capacity

Left columns

Multiply number of	by	to obtain equivalent number of
Cubic inches (in³)	0.576 744	UK fluid ounces (UK fl oz)
	0.554 113	US liquid ounces (US liq oz)
	0.028 837 20	UK pints (UK pt)
	0.003 604 65	UK gallons (UK gal)
Cubic inches	16.387 064	cubic centimetres (cm³) also SI millilitres (ml)
UK fluid ounces	28.413 062 5	
US liquid ounces	29.573 5	
US liquid pints (US liq pt)	473.176 473	
UK pints	568.261 25	
US liquid quarts (US liq qt)	946.352 946	
UK quarts (UK qt)	1 136.522 5	
US liquid gallons (US liq gal)	3 785.411 784	
UK gallons	4 546.09	
Cubic inches	0.016 387 064	cubic decimetres (dm³) also SI litres (l or L)
US liquid pints	0.473 176 473	
UK pints	0.568 261 25	
US liquid quarts	0.946 352 946	
Litres (1901 definition)	1.000 028	
UK quarts	1.136 522 5	
US liquid gallons	3.785 411 784	
UK gallons	4.546 09	
UK gallons (1963 definition)	4.546 091 88	
Cubic feet (ft³)	28.316 846 592	
Cubic feet	7.480 52	US liquid gallons
	6.228 84	UK gallons
	0.803 564	US bushels (US bu)
	0.778 604	UK bushels (UK bu)
UK gallons	0.045 460 9	SI hectolitres (hl)
US bushels	0.352 391	
UK bushels	0.363 687 2	
US liquid gallons	0.003 785 411 784	cubic metres (m³) also kilolitres kl
US dry gallons	0.004 404 88	
UK gallons	0.004 546 09	
Cubic feet	0.028 316 846 592	
US bushels	0.035 239 1	
UK bushels	0.036 368 72	
Barrels, bulk (36 UK gallons)	0.163 659 24	
Barrels, petroleum (42 US gallons)	0.158 987 294 928	
Cubic yards (yd³)	0.764 554 857 984	

Right columns

Multiply number of	by	to obtain equivalent number of
Cubic centimetres also SI millilitres (ml)	0.061 023 7	cubic inches
	0.035 195 1	UK fluid ounces
	0.033 814 0	US liquid ounces
	0.002 113 38	US liquid pints
	0.001 759 75	UK pints
	0.001 056 69	US liquid quarts
	0.000 879 877	UK quarts
	0.000 264 172	US liquid gallons
	0.000 219 969	UK gallons
UK fluid ounces	1.733 87	cubic inches
UK pints	34.677 4	
UK quarts	69.354 9	
UK gallons	277.419	
Cubic decimetres also SI litres	61.023 7	cubic inches
	35.195 1	UK fluid ounces
	33.814 0	US liquid ounces
	2.113 38	US liquid pints
	1.759 75	UK pints
	1.056 69	US liquid quarts
	0.999 972	litres (1901 definition)
	1.056 69	US liquid quarts
	0.879 877	UK quarts
	0.264 172	US liquid gallons
	0.219 969	UK gallons
	0.035 314 7	cubic feet
US liquid gallons	0.133 681	cubic feet
UK gallons	0.160 544	
US bushels	1.244 46	
UK bushels	1.284 35	
SI hectolitres	26.417 2	US liquid gallons
	21.996 9	UK gallons
	2.837 76	US bushels
	2.749 62	UK bushels
Cubic metres	264.172	US liquid gallons
	227.021	US dry gallons
	219.969	UK gallons
	35.314 7	cubic feet
	28.377 6	US bushels
	27.496 2	UK bushels
	6.110 26	barrels, bulk (36 UK gallons)
	6.289 81	barrels, petroleum (42 US gallons)
	1.307 95	cubic yards

Weight (mass)

Left columns

Multiply number of	by	to obtain equivalent number of
Grains (gr)	64.798 91	milligrams (mg)
	0.323 994 55	metric carats
	0.064 798 91	grams (g)
Scruples	1.295 978 2	grams
Pennyweights (dwt)	1.555 173 84	
Drams (dr)	1.771 85	
Drachms (drm)	3.887 934 6	
Ounces (oz)	28.349 523 125	
Ounces troy (oz tr)	31.103 476 8	
Ounces	0.911 458	ounces troy
Ounces troy	155.517 384	metric carats
Ounces	0.028 349 523 125	kilograms (kg)
Pounds (lb)	0.453 592 37	
Stones	6.350 293 18	
US (short) hundredweights (US cwt)	45.359 237	
UK (long) hundredweights (UK cwt)	50.802 345 44	
US (short) tons	907.184 74	
UK (long) tons	1 016.046 908 8	
Slugs	14.593 9	kilograms
	1.488 16	hyls (metric slugs)

Right columns

Multiply number of	by	to obtain equivalent number of
Milligrams	0.015 432 4	grains
Metric carats	3.086 47	
Grams	15.432 4	
Metric carats	0.006 430 15	ounces troy
Grams	0.771 618	scruples
	0.643 015	pennyweights
	0.564 383	drams
	0.257 206	drachms
	0.035 274 0	ounces
	0.032 150 7	ounces troy
Ounces troy	1.097 14	ounces
Kilograms	35.274 0	ounces
	32.150 7	ounces troy
	2.204 62	pounds
	0.157 473	stones
	0.022 046 2	US (short) hundredweights
	0.019 684 1	UK (long) hundredweights
	0.001 102 31	US (short) tons
	0.000 984 207	UK (long) tons
Hyls (metric slugs)	9.806 65	kilograms
	0.671 969	slugs

	Multiply number of	by	to obtain equivalent number of	Multiply number of	by	to obtain equivalent number of
Weight (mass) cont	US (short) hundred-weights	**0.453 592 37**	} metric quintals (q)	Metric quintals	2.204 62	US (short) hundred-weights
	UK (long) hundred-weights	**0.508 023 454 4**			1.968 41	UK (long) hundred-weights
	Pounds	**0.000 453 592 37**	} megagrams (Mg) =tonnes(t)	Megagrams = tonnes	2 204.62	pounds
	JS (short) tons	**0.907 184 74**			1.102 31	US (short) tons
	JK (long) tons	**1.016 046 908 8**			0.984 207	UK (long) tons
Velocity	Inches per minute (in/min)	0.423 333	} millimetres per second (mm/s)	Millimetre per second	2.362 20	inches per minute
	Feet per minute (ft/min)	**5.08**			0.196 850	feet per minute
	Miles per hour (mph)	**1.609 344**	kilometres per hour (km/h)	Kilometres per hour	0.621 371	} miles per hour
		0.447 04	metres per second (m/s)	Metres per second	2.236 94	
	International knots	1.150 78	miles per hour	Kilometres per hour	0.539 957	} international knots
		0.999 361	UK knots	Miles per hour	0.868 976	
		0.514 444	metres per second	UK knots	1.000 64	
				Metres per second	1.943 84	
Fuel consumption	Miles per UK gallon	0.354 006	} kilometres per SI litre (km/l)	Kilometre per SI litre	2.824 81	miles per UK gallon
	Miles per US gallon	0.425 144			2.352 15	miles per US gallon
	UK gallons per mile	282.481	} SI litres per 100 kilometres (l/100 km)	SI litres per 100 kilometres	0.003 540 06	UK gallons per mile
	US gallons per mile	235.215			0.004 251 44	US gallons per mile
Weight (mass) per unit length or area	UK (long) tons per mile (UK ton/mile)	0.631 342	} tonnes per kilometre (t/km) also kilograms per metre kg/m)	Tonnes per kilometre also Kilograms per metre	1.583 93	UK (long) tons per mile
	Pounds per foot (lb/ft)	1.488 16			0.671 969	pounds per foot
	Pounds per square inch (lb/in²)	70.307 0	grams per sq. centimetre (g/cm²)	Grams per sq. centimetre	0.014 223 3	pounds per square inch
	Pounds per acre (lb/acre)	1.120 85	kilograms per hectare (kg/ha)	Kilograms per hectare	0.892 179	pounds per acre
Density and concentration	Ounces per UK gallon (oz/UK gal)	6.236 02	kilograms per cubic metre (kg/m³) also grams per SI SI litre (g/l)	Kilograms per cubic metre also Grams per SI litre	0.160 359	ounces per UK gallon
	Ounces per US liquid gallon (oz/US liq gal)	7.489 15			0.133 526	ounces per US liquid gallon
	Pounds per cubic foot (lb/ft³)	16.018 5			0.062 428 0	pounds per cubic foot
Force	Poundals (pdl)	0.138 255	} newtons (N)	Newtons	7.233 01	poundals
	Ounces-force (ozf)	0.278 014			3.596 94	ounces-force
	Pounds-force (lbf)	4.448 22			0.224 809	pounds-force
	Newtons	0.101 972	} kilograms-force (kgf) or kiloponds (kp)	Kilograms-force or Kiloponds	**9.806 65**	newtons
	Pounds-force	**0.453 592 37**			2.204 62	pounds-force
	US (short) tons-force (US tonf)	8.896 44	} kilonewtons (kN)	Kilonewtons	0.112 404	US (short) tons-force
	UK (long) tons-force (UK tonf)	9.964 02			0.100 361	UK (long) tons-force
Torque (moment of force)	Poundals foot (pdl ft)	0.042 140 1	} newton metres (N m)	Newton metres	23.730 4	poundals foot
	Pounds-force foot (lbf ft)	1.355 82			0.737 562	pounds-force foot
Pressure and stress	Poundals per sq. foot (pdl/ft²)	1.488 16	pascals (Pa) also newtons per square metre (N/m²)	Pascals also Newtons per square metre	0.671 969	poundals per sq. foot
	Pounds-force per sq. foot (lbf/ft²)	47.880 3			0.020 885 4	pounds-force per square foot
	Pounds-force per sq. foot	0.478 803	} millibars (mbar)	Millibars	2.088 54	pounds-force per sq. foot
	Inches of water (in H₂O)	**2.490 889 1**			0.401 463	inches of water
	Inches of mercury (in Hg)	33.863 9			0.029 530 0	inches of mercury
	Pounds-force per sq. inch (lbf/in²)	68.947 6			0.014 503 8	pounds-force per sq. inch
	Pounds-force per sq. inch	6.894 76	kilopascals (kPa) also kilonewtons per sq. metre (kN/m²)	Kilopascals also Kilonewtons per square metre	0.145 038	pounds-force per sq. inch

	Multiply number of	by	to obtain equivalent number of	Multiply number of	by	to obtain equivalent number of
Pressure and stress cont.	Pounds-force per sq. inch	0.070 307 0	kilograms-force per sq. centimetre (kgf/cm²)	Kilograms-force per square centimetre	14.223 3	pounds-force per sq. inch
	Pounds-force per sq. inch	0.068 947 6	bars (bar)	Bars	14.503 8	pounds-force per sq. inch
	UK tons-force per sq. foot (UK tonf/ft²)	1.072 52			0.932 385	UK tons-force per sq. foot
	Pounds-force per sq. inch	0.006 894 76	megapascals (MPa) *also* newtons per sq. millimetre (N/mm²)	Megapascals *also* Newtons per square millimetre	145.038	pounds-force per sq. inch
	UK tons-force per sq. foot	0.107 252			9.323 85	UK tons-force per sq. foot
	UK tons-force per sq. inch (UK tonf/in²)	15.444 3			0.064 749 0	UK tons-force per sq. inch
	Pounds-force per sq. inch	0.000 703 07	kilograms-force per sq. millimetre (kgf/mm²)	Kilograms-force per square millimetre	1 422.33	pounds-force per sq. inch
	UK tons-force per sq. inch	1.574 88			0.634 971	UK tons-force per sq. inch
	UK tons-force per sq. foot	0.010 725 2	hectobars (hbar)	Hectobars	93.238 5	UK tons-force per sq. foot
	UK tons-force per sq. inch	1.544 43			0.647 490	UK tons-force per sq. inch
Energy, work, quantity of heat	Foot poundals (ft pdl)	0.042 140 1	joules (J)	Joules	23.730 4	foot poundals
	Foot pounds-force (ft lbf)	1.355 82			0.737 562	foot pounds-force
	Calories, thermochemical or defined (cal$_{th}$)	4.184			0.239 006	calories, thermochemical or defined
	Calories, 15°C (cal$_{15}$)	4.185 5			0.238 920	calories, 15°C
	Calories, international table (cal$_{IT}$)	4.186 8			0.238 846	calories, international table
	Kilograms-force metre (kgf/m)	9.806 65			0.101 972	kilograms-force metre
	British thermal units (Btu)	1.055 06	Kilojoules (kJ)	Kilojoules	0.947 817	British thermal units
	Watt hours (W h)	3.6			0.277 778	watt hours
	Kilocalories, international table (kcal$_{IT}$)	4.186 8			0.238 846	kilocalories, international table
	UK horsepower hours (hph)	0.745 700	kilowatt hours (kW h)	Kilowatt hours	1.341 02	UK horsepower hours
	UK horsepower hours	2.684 52	megajoules (MJ)	Megajoules	0.372 506	UK horsepower hours
	Kilowatt hours	3.6			0.277 778	kilowatt hours
	Thermies, international table (th$_{IT}$)	4.186 8			0.238 846	thermies, international table
	Therms	105.506			0.009 478 17	therms
Power	Foot pounds-force per second (ft lbf/s)	1.355 82	watts (W)	Watts	0.737 562	foot pounds-force per second
	Metric horsepower (ch or PS)	735.499			0.001 359 62	metric horsepower
	UK horsepower (hp)	745.700			0.001 341 02	UK horsepower
	Metric horsepower	0.735 499	kilowatts (kW)	Metric horsepower	0.986 320	UK horsepower
	UK horsepower	0.745 700		Kilowatts	1.359 62	metric horsepower
	UK horsepower	1.013 87	metric horsepower		1.341 02	UK horsepower
Heat flow rate	British thermal units per hour (Btu/h)	0.293 071	watts	Watts	3.412 14	British thermal units per hour
	Kilocalories, international table, per hour (kcal$_{IT}$/h)	1.163			0.859 845	kilocalories, international table, per hour
	Tons of refrigeration (12 000 Btu/h)	3 516.85			0.000 284 345	tons of refrigeration
Heat energy content	British thermal units per pound (Btu/lb)	2.326	joules per gram (J/g) *also* kilojoules per kilogram (kJ/kg)	Joules per gram *also* kilojoules per kilogram	0.429 923	British thermal units per pound
	Kilocalories, international table, per kilogram (kcal$_{IT}$/kg)	4.186 8			0.238 846	kilocalories, international table, per kilogram
Light	Foot-lamberts	3.426 26	candelas per sq. metre (cd/m²)	Candelas per sq. metre	0.291 864	foot-lamberts
	Candelas per square foot (cd/ft²)	10.763 9			0.092 903 0	candelas per square foot
	Lumens per square foot (lm/ft²) *also* foot-candles	10.763 9	lux (lx) *also* lumens per sq. metre (lm/m²)	Lux	0.092 903 0	lumens per square foot *also* foot-candles
Plane angle	Degrees (°)	0.017 453 3	radians (rad)	Radians	57.295 8	degrees
	Grades (g) or gons	0.015 708 0			63.662 0	grades or gons

Conversions: length

Use of the table: the number of inches to be converted, which is made up by the number of inches at the head of a column and the fraction at the side of a line, is converted to the number in the position where line and column meet. For example, 1 1/64 in = 1 in + 1/64 in = 25.797 mm

Inches and fractions of an inch to Millimetres   1 in = 25.4 mm

in →	0	1	2	3	4	5	6	7	8	9	10	11	← in
↓	mm	mm	mm	mm	mm	mm	mm	mm	mm	mm	mm	mm	↓
0	0.000	25.400	50.800	76.200	101.600	127.000	152.400	177.800	203.200	228.600	254.000	279.400	0
1/64	0.397	25.797	51.197	76.597	101.997	127.397	152.797	178.197	203.597	228.997	254.397	279.797	1/64
1/32	0.794	26.194	51.594	76.994	102.394	127.794	153.194	178.594	203.994	229.394	254.794	280.194	1/32
3/64	1.191	26.591	51.991	77.391	102.791	128.191	153.591	178.991	204.391	229.791	255.191	280.591	3/64
1/16	1.588	26.988	52.388	77.788	103.188	128.588	153.988	179.388	204.788	230.188	255.588	280.988	1/16
5/64	1.984	27.384	52.784	78.184	103.584	128.984	154.384	179.784	205.184	230.584	255.984	281.384	5/64
3/32	2.381	27.781	53.181	78.581	103.981	129.381	154.781	180.181	205.581	230.981	256.381	281.781	3/32
7/64	2.778	28.178	53.578	78.978	104.378	129.778	155.178	180.578	205.978	231.378	256.778	282.178	7/64
1/8	3.175	28.575	53.975	79.375	104.775	130.175	155.575	180.975	206.375	231.775	257.175	282.575	1/8
9/64	3.572	28.972	54.372	79.772	105.172	130.572	155.972	181.372	206.772	232.172	257.572	282.972	9/64
5/32	3.969	29.369	54.769	80.169	105.569	130.969	156.369	181.769	207.169	232.569	257.969	283.369	5/32
11/64	4.366	29.766	55.166	80.566	105.966	131.366	156.766	182.166	207.566	232.966	258.366	283.766	11/64
3/16	4.762	30.162	55.562	80.962	106.362	131.762	157.162	182.562	207.962	233.362	258.762	284.162	3/16
13/64	5.159	30.559	55.959	81.359	106.759	132.159	157.559	182.959	208.359	233.759	259.159	284.559	13/64
7/32	5.556	30.956	56.356	81.756	107.156	132.556	157.956	183.356	208.756	234.156	259.556	284.956	7/32
15/64	5.953	31.353	56.753	82.153	107.553	132.953	158.353	183.753	209.153	234.553	259.953	285.353	15/64
1/4	6.350	31.750	57.150	82.550	107.950	133.350	158.750	184.150	209.550	234.950	260.350	285.750	1/4
17/64	6.747	32.147	57.547	82.947	108.347	133.747	159.147	184.547	209.947	235.347	260.747	286.147	17/64
9/32	7.144	32.544	57.944	83.344	108.744	134.144	159.544	184.944	210.344	235.744	261.144	286.544	9/32
19/64	7.541	32.941	58.341	83.741	109.141	134.541	159.941	185.341	210.741	236.141	261.541	286.941	19/64
5/16	7.938	33.338	58.738	84.138	109.538	134.938	160.338	185.738	211.138	236.538	261.938	287.338	5/16
21/64	8.334	33.734	59.134	84.534	109.934	135.334	160.734	186.134	211.534	236.934	262.334	287.734	21/64
11/32	8.731	34.131	59.531	84.931	110.331	135.731	161.131	186.531	211.931	237.331	262.731	288.131	11/32
23/64	9.128	34.528	59.928	85.328	110.728	136.128	161.528	186.928	212.328	237.728	263.128	288.528	23/64
3/8	9.525	34.925	60.325	85.725	111.125	136.525	161.925	187.325	212.725	238.125	263.525	288.925	3/8
25/64	9.922	35.322	60.722	86.122	111.522	136.922	162.322	187.722	213.122	238.522	263.922	289.322	25/64
13/32	10.319	35.719	61.119	86.519	111.919	137.319	162.719	188.119	213.519	238.919	264.319	289.719	13/32
27/64	10.716	36.116	61.516	86.916	112.316	137.716	163.116	188.516	213.916	239.316	264.716	290.116	27/64
7/16	11.112	36.512	61.912	87.312	112.712	138.112	163.512	188.912	214.312	239.712	265.112	290.512	7/16
29/64	11.509	36.909	62.309	87.709	113.109	138.509	163.909	189.309	214.709	240.109	265.509	290.909	29/64
15/32	11.906	37.306	62.706	88.106	113.506	138.906	164.306	189.706	215.106	240.506	265.906	291.306	15/32
31/64	12.303	37.703	63.103	88.503	113.903	139.303	164.703	190.103	215.503	240.903	266.303	291.703	31/64
1/2	12.700	38.100	63.500	88.900	114.300	139.700	165.100	190.500	215.900	241.300	266.700	292.100	1/2
33/64	13.097	38.497	63.897	89.297	114.697	140.097	165.497	190.897	216.297	241.697	267.097	292.497	33/64
17/32	13.494	38.894	64.294	89.694	115.094	140.494	165.894	191.294	216.694	242.094	267.494	292.894	17/32
35/64	13.891	39.291	64.691	90.091	115.491	140.891	166.291	191.691	217.091	242.491	267.891	293.291	35/64
9/16	14.288	39.688	65.088	90.488	115.888	141.288	166.688	192.088	217.488	242.888	268.288	293.688	9/16
37/64	14.684	40.084	65.484	90.884	116.284	141.684	167.084	192.484	217.884	243.284	268.684	294.084	37/64
19/32	15.081	40.481	65.881	91.281	116.681	142.081	167.481	192.881	218.281	243.681	269.081	294.481	19/32
39/64	15.478	40.878	66.278	91.678	117.078	142.478	167.878	193.278	218.678	244.078	269.478	294.878	39/64
5/8	15.875	41.275	66.675	92.075	117.475	142.875	168.275	193.675	219.075	244.475	269.875	295.275	5/8
41/64	16.272	41.672	67.072	92.472	117.872	143.272	168.672	194.072	219.472	244.872	270.272	295.672	41/64
21/32	16.669	42.069	67.469	92.869	118.269	143.669	169.069	194.469	219.869	245.269	270.669	296.069	21/32
43/64	17.066	42.466	67.866	93.266	118.666	144.066	169.466	194.866	220.266	245.666	271.066	296.466	43/64
11/16	17.462	42.862	68.262	93.662	119.062	144.462	169.862	195.262	220.662	246.062	271.462	296.862	11/16
45/64	17.859	43.259	68.659	94.059	119.459	144.859	170.259	195.659	221.059	246.459	271.859	297.259	45/64
23/32	18.256	43.656	69.056	94.456	119.856	145.256	170.656	196.056	221.456	246.856	272.256	297.656	23/32
47/64	18.653	44.053	69.453	94.853	120.253	145.653	171.053	196.453	221.853	247.253	272.653	298.053	47/64
3/4	19.050	44.450	69.850	95.250	120.650	146.050	171.450	196.850	222.250	247.650	273.050	298.450	3/4
49/64	19.447	44.847	70.247	95.647	121.047	146.447	171.847	197.247	222.647	248.047	273.447	298.847	49/64
25/32	19.844	45.244	70.644	96.044	121.444	146.844	172.244	197.644	223.044	248.444	273.844	299.244	25/32
51/64	20.241	45.641	71.041	96.441	121.841	147.241	172.641	198.041	223.441	248.841	274.241	299.641	51/64
13/16	20.638	46.038	71.438	96.838	122.238	147.638	173.038	198.438	223.838	249.238	274.638	300.038	13/16
53/64	21.034	46.434	71.834	97.234	122.634	148.034	173.434	198.834	224.234	249.634	275.034	300.434	53/64
27/32	21.431	46.831	72.231	97.631	123.031	148.431	173.831	199.231	224.631	250.031	275.431	300.831	27/32
55/64	21.828	47.228	72.628	98.028	123.428	148.828	174.228	199.628	225.028	250.428	275.828	301.228	55/64
7/8	22.225	47.625	73.025	98.425	123.825	149.225	174.625	200.025	225.425	250.825	276.225	301.625	7/8
57/64	22.622	48.022	73.422	98.822	124.222	149.622	175.022	200.422	225.822	251.222	276.622	302.022	57/64
29/32	23.019	48.419	73.819	99.219	124.619	150.019	175.419	200.819	226.219	251.619	277.019	302.419	29/32
59/64	23.416	48.816	74.216	99.616	125.016	150.416	175.816	201.216	226.616	252.016	277.416	302.816	59/64
15/16	23.812	49.212	74.612	100.012	125.412	150.812	176.212	201.612	227.012	252.412	277.812	303.212	15/16
61/64	24.209	49.609	75.009	100.409	125.809	151.209	176.609	202.009	227.409	252.809	278.209	303.609	61/64
31/32	24.606	50.006	75.406	100.806	126.206	151.606	177.006	202.406	227.806	253.206	278.606	304.006	31/32
63/64	25.003	50.403	75.803	101.203	126.603	152.003	177.403	202.803	228.203	253.603	279.003	304.403	63/64

Use of the tables: the number to be converted, which is made up by adding
the unit at the side of a line to the unit at the head of a column,
is converted to the number in the position where line and column meet.
For example, 11 miles = 10 miles + 1 mile = 17.703 km

Miles to Kilometres   1 mile = 1.609 344 km

miles →	0	1	2	3	4	5	6	7	8	9	← miles
↓	km	km	km	km	km	km	km	km	km	km	↓
0	0.000	1.609	3.219	4.828	6.437	8.047	9.656	11.265	12.875	14.484	0
10	16.093	17.703	19.312	20.921	22.531	24.140	25.750	27.359	28.968	30.578	10
20	32.187	33.796	35.406	37.015	38.624	40.234	41.843	43.452	45.062	46.671	20
30	48.280	49.890	51.499	53.108	54.718	56.327	57.936	59.546	61.155	62.764	30
40	64.374	65.983	67.592	69.202	70.811	72.420	74.030	75.639	77.249	78.858	40
50	80.467	82.077	83.686	85.295	86.905	88.514	90.123	91.733	93.342	94.951	50
60	96.561	98.170	99.779	101.389	102.998	104.607	106.217	107.826	109.435	111.045	60
70	112.654	114.263	115.873	117.482	119.091	120.701	122.310	123.919	125.529	127.138	70
80	128.748	130.357	131.966	133.576	135.185	136.794	138.404	140.013	141.622	143.232	80
90	144.841	146.450	148.060	149.669	151.278	152.888	154.497	156.106	157.716	159.325	90
100	160.934										100

miles →	0	10	20	30	40	50	60	70	80	90	← miles
↓	km	km	km	km	km	km	km	km	km	km	↓
0	0.000	16.093	32.187	48.280	64.374	80.467	96.561	112.654	128.748	144.841	0
100	160.934	177.028	193.121	209.215	225.308	241.402	257.495	273.588	289.682	305.775	100
200	321.869	337.962	354.056	370.149	386.243	402.336	418.429	434.523	450.616	466.710	200
300	482.803	498.897	514.990	531.084	547.177	563.270	579.364	595.457	611.551	627.644	300
400	643.738	659.831	675.924	692.018	708.111	724.205	740.298	756.392	772.485	788.579	400
500	804.672	820.765	836.859	852.952	869.046	885.139	901.233	917.326	933.420	949.513	500
600	965.606	981.700	997.793	1013.887	1029.980	1046.074	1062.167	1078.260	1094.354	1110.447	600
700	1126.541	1142.634	1158.728	1174.821	1190.915	1207.008	1223.101	1239.195	1255.288	1271.382	700
800	1287.475	1303.569	1319.662	1335.756	1351.849	1367.942	1384.036	1400.129	1416.223	1432.316	800
900	1448.410	1464.503	1480.596	1496.690	1512.783	1528.877	1544.970	1561.064	1577.157	1593.251	900
1000	1609.344										1000

Kilometres to Miles   1 km = 0.621 371 mile

km →	0	1	2	3	4	5	6	7	8	9	← km
↓	miles	miles	miles	miles	miles	miles	miles	miles	miles	miles	↓
0	0.000	0.621	1.243	1.864	2.485	3.107	3.728	4.350	4.971	5.592	0
10	6.214	6.835	7.456	8.078	8.699	9.321	9.942	10.563	11.185	11.806	10
20	12.427	13.049	13.670	14.292	14.913	15.534	16.156	16.777	17.398	18.020	20
30	18.641	19.263	19.884	20.505	21.127	21.748	22.369	22.991	23.612	24.233	30
40	24.855	25.476	26.098	26.719	27.340	27.962	28.583	29.204	29.826	30.447	40
50	31.069	31.690	32.311	32.933	33.554	34.175	34.797	35.418	36.040	36.661	50
60	37.282	37.904	38.525	39.146	39.768	40.389	41.010	41.632	42.253	42.875	60
70	43.496	44.117	44.739	45.360	45.981	46.603	47.224	47.846	48.467	49.088	70
80	49.710	50.331	50.952	51.574	52.195	52.817	53.438	54.059	54.681	55.302	80
90	55.923	56.545	57.166	57.788	58.409	59.030	59.652	60.273	60.894	61.516	90
100	62.137										100

km →	0	10	20	30	40	50	60	70	80	90	← km
↓	miles	miles	miles	miles	miles	miles	miles	miles	miles	miles	↓
0	0.000	6.214	12.427	18.641	24.855	31.069	37.282	43.496	49.710	55.923	0
100	62.137	68.351	74.565	80.778	86.992	93.206	99.419	105.633	111.847	118.061	100
200	124.274	130.488	136.702	142.915	149.129	155.343	161.557	167.770	173.984	180.198	200
300	186.411	192.625	198.839	205.052	211.266	217.480	223.694	229.907	236.121	242.335	300
400	248.548	254.762	260.976	267.190	273.403	279.617	285.831	292.044	298.258	304.472	400
500	310.686	316.899	323.113	329.327	335.540	341.754	347.968	354.182	360.395	366.609	500
600	372.823	379.036	385.250	391.464	397.678	403.891	410.105	416.319	422.532	428.746	600
700	434.960	441.174	447.387	453.601	459.815	466.028	472.242	478.456	484.670	490.883	700
800	497.097	503.311	509.524	515.738	521.952	528.166	534.379	540.593	546.807	553.020	800
900	559.234	565.448	571.661	577.875	584.089	590.303	596.516	602.730	608.944	615.157	900
1000	621.371										1000

Conversions: area

Use of the tables: the number to be converted, which is made up by addi…
the unit at the side of a line to the unit at the head of a column,
is converted to the number in the position where line and column meet.
For example, 11 in² = 10 in² + 1 in² = 70.968 cm²

Square inches to Square centimetres   1 in² = 6.451 6 cm²

in² →	0	1	2	3	4	5	6	7	8	9
↓	cm²	cm²	cm²	cm²	cm²	cm²	cm²	cm²	cm²	cm²
0	0.000	6.452	12.903	19.355	25.806	32.258	38.710	45.161	51.613	58.064
10	64.516	70.968	77.419	83.871	90.322	96.774	103.226	109.677	116.129	122.580
20	129.032	135.484	141.935	148.387	154.838	161.290	167.742	174.193	180.645	187.096
30	193.548	200.000	206.451	212.903	219.354	225.806	232.258	238.709	245.161	251.612
40	258.064	264.516	270.967	277.419	283.870	290.322	296.774	303.225	309.677	316.128
50	322.580	329.032	335.483	341.935	348.386	354.838	361.290	367.741	374.193	380.644
60	387.096	393.548	399.999	406.451	412.902	419.354	425.806	432.257	438.709	445.160
70	451.612	458.064	464.515	470.967	477.418	483.870	490.322	496.773	503.225	509.676
80	516.128	522.580	529.031	535.483	541.934	548.386	554.838	561.289	567.741	574.192
90	580.644	587.096	593.547	599.999	606.450	612.902	619.354	625.805	632.257	638.708
100	645.160									

in² →	0	10	20	30	40	50	60	70	80	90
↓	cm²	cm²	cm²	cm²	cm²	cm²	cm²	cm²	cm²	cm²
0	0.000	64.516	129.032	193.548	258.064	322.580	387.096	451.612	516.128	580.644
100	645.160	709.676	774.192	838.708	903.224	967.740	1032.256	1096.772	1161.288	1225.804
200	1290.320	1354.836	1419.352	1483.868	1548.384	1612.900	1677.416	1741.932	1806.448	1870.964
300	1935.480	1999.996	2064.512	2129.028	2193.544	2258.060	2322.576	2387.092	2451.608	2516.124
400	2580.640	2645.156	2709.672	2774.188	2838.704	2903.220	2967.736	3032.252	3096.768	3161.284
500	3225.800	3290.316	3354.832	3419.348	3483.864	3548.380	3612.896	3677.412	3741.928	3806.444
600	3870.960	3935.476	3999.992	4064.508	4129.024	4193.540	4258.056	4322.572	4387.088	4451.604
700	4516.120	4580.636	4645.152	4709.668	4774.184	4838.700	4903.216	4967.732	5032.248	5096.764
800	5161.280	5225.796	5290.312	5354.828	5419.344	5483.860	5548.376	5612.892	5677.408	5741.924
900	5806.440	5870.956	5935.472	5999.988	6064.504	6129.020	6193.536	6258.052	6322.568	6387.084
1000	6451.600									

Square centimetres to Square inches   1 cm² = 0.155 000 in²

cm² →	0	1	2	3	4	5	6	7	8	9
↓	in²	in²	in²	in²	in²	in²	in²	in²	in²	in²
0	0.000	0.155	0.310	0.465	0.620	0.775	0.930	1.085	1.240	1.395
10	1.550	1.705	1.860	2.015	2.170	2.325	2.480	2.635	2.790	2.945
20	3.100	3.255	3.410	3.565	3.720	3.875	4.030	4.185	4.340	4.495
30	4.650	4.805	4.960	5.115	5.270	5.425	5.580	5.735	5.890	6.045
40	6.200	6.355	6.510	6.665	6.820	6.975	7.130	7.285	7.440	7.595
50	7.750	7.905	8.060	8.215	8.370	8.525	8.680	8.835	8.990	9.145
60	9.300	9.455	9.610	9.765	9.920	10.075	10.230	10.385	10.540	10.695
70	10.850	11.005	11.160	11.315	11.470	11.625	11.780	11.935	12.090	12.245
80	12.400	12.555	12.710	12.865	13.020	13.175	13.330	13.485	13.640	13.795
90	13.950	14.105	14.260	14.415	14.570	14.725	14.880	15.035	15.190	15.345
100	15.500									

cm² →	0	10	20	30	40	50	60	70	80	90
↓	in²	in²	in²	in²	in²	in²	in²	in²	in²	in²
0	0.000	1.550	3.100	4.650	6.200	7.750	9.300	10.850	12.400	13.950
100	15.500	17.050	18.600	20.150	21.700	23.250	24.800	26.350	27.900	29.450
200	31.000	32.550	34.100	35.650	37.200	38.750	40.300	41.850	43.400	44.950
300	46.500	48.050	49.600	51.150	52.700	54.250	55.800	57.350	58.900	60.450
400	62.000	63.550	65.100	66.650	68.200	69.750	71.300	72.850	74.400	75.950
500	77.500	79.050	80.600	82.150	83.700	85.250	86.800	88.350	89.900	91.450
600	93.000	94.550	96.100	97.650	99.200	100.750	102.300	103.850	105.400	106.950
700	108.500	110.050	111.600	113.150	114.700	116.250	117.800	119.350	120.900	122.450
800	124.000	125.550	127.100	128.650	130.200	131.750	133.300	134.850	136.400	137.950
900	139.500	141.050	142.600	144.150	145.700	147.250	148.800	150.350	151.900	153.450
1000	155.000									

Use of the tables: the number to be converted, which is made up by adding the unit at the side of a line to the unit at the head of a column, is converted to the number in the position where line and column meet.
For example, 11 acres = 10 acres + 1 acre = 4.452 ha

Acres to Hectares   1 acre = 0.404 686 ha

acres →	0	1	2	3	4	5	6	7	8	9	← acres
↓	ha	ha	ha	ha	ha	ha	ha	ha	ha	ha	↓
0	0.000	0.405	0.809	1.214	1.619	2.023	2.428	2.833	3.237	3.642	0
10	4.047	4.452	4.856	5.261	5.666	6.070	6.475	6.880	7.284	7.689	10
20	8.094	8.498	8.903	9.308	9.712	10.117	10.522	10.927	11.331	11.736	20
30	12.141	12.545	12.950	13.355	13.759	14.164	14.569	14.973	15.378	15.783	30
40	16.187	16.592	16.997	17.401	17.806	18.211	18.616	19.020	19.425	19.830	40
50	20.234	20.639	21.044	21.448	21.853	22.258	22.662	23.067	23.472	23.876	50
60	24.281	24.686	25.091	25.495	25.900	26.305	26.709	27.114	27.519	27.923	60
70	28.328	28.733	29.137	29.542	29.947	30.351	30.756	31.161	31.565	31.970	70
80	32.375	32.780	33.184	33.589	33.994	34.398	34.803	35.208	35.612	36.017	80
90	36.422	36.826	37.231	37.636	38.040	38.445	38.850	39.255	39.659	40.064	90
100	40.469										100

acres →	0	10	20	30	40	50	60	70	80	90	← acres
↓	ha	ha	ha	ha	ha	ha	ha	ha	ha	ha	↓
0	0.000	4.047	8.094	12.141	16.187	20.234	24.281	28.328	32.375	36.422	0
100	40.469	44.515	48.562	52.609	56.656	60.703	64.750	68.797	72.843	76.890	100
200	80.937	84.984	89.031	93.078	97.125	101.171	105.218	109.265	113.312	117.359	200
300	121.406	125.453	129.499	133.546	137.593	141.640	145.687	149.734	153.781	157.827	300
400	161.874	165.921	169.968	174.015	178.062	182.109	186.155	190.202	194.249	198.296	400
500	202.343	206.390	210.437	214.483	218.530	222.577	226.624	230.671	234.718	238.765	500
600	242.811	246.858	250.905	254.952	258.999	263.046	267.093	271.139	275.186	279.233	600
700	283.280	287.327	291.374	295.421	299.467	303.514	307.561	311.608	315.655	319.702	700
800	323.749	327.795	331.842	335.889	339.936	343.983	348.030	352.077	356.123	360.170	800
900	364.217	368.264	372.311	376.358	380.405	384.451	388.498	392.545	396.592	400.639	900
1000	404.686										1000

Hectares to Acres   1 ha = 2.471 054 acres

ha →	0	1	2	3	4	5	6	7	8	9	← ha
↓	acres	acres	acres	acres	acres	acres	acres	acres	acres	acres	↓
0	0.000	2.471	4.942	7.413	9.884	12.355	14.826	17.297	19.768	22.239	0
10	24.711	27.182	29.653	32.124	34.595	37.066	39.537	42.008	44.479	46.950	10
20	49.421	51.892	54.363	56.834	59.305	61.776	64.247	66.718	69.190	71.661	20
30	74.132	76.603	79.074	81.545	84.016	86.487	88.958	91.429	93.900	96.371	30
40	98.842	101.313	103.784	106.255	108.726	111.197	113.668	116.140	118.611	121.082	40
50	123.553	126.024	128.495	130.966	133.437	135.908	138.379	140.850	143.321	145.792	50
60	148.263	150.734	153.205	155.676	158.147	160.618	163.090	165.561	168.032	170.503	60
70	172.974	175.445	177.916	180.387	182.858	185.329	187.800	190.271	192.742	195.213	70
80	197.684	200.155	202.626	205.097	207.569	210.040	212.511	214.982	217.453	219.924	80
90	222.395	224.866	227.337	229.808	232.279	234.750	237.221	239.692	242.163	244.634	90
100	247.105										100

ha →	0	10	20	30	40	50	60	70	80	90	← ha
↓	acres	acres	acres	acres	acres	acres	acres	acres	acres	acres	↓
0	0.000	24.711	49.421	74.132	98.842	123.553	148.263	172.974	197.684	222.395	0
100	247.105	271.816	296.526	321.237	345.948	370.658	395.369	420.079	444.790	469.500	100
200	494.211	518.921	543.632	568.342	593.053	617.763	642.474	667.185	691.895	716.606	200
300	741.316	766.027	790.737	815.448	840.158	864.869	889.579	914.290	939.000	963.711	300
400	988.422	1013.132	1037.843	1062.553	1087.264	1111.974	1136.685	1161.395	1186.106	1210.816	400
500	1235.527	1260.237	1284.948	1309.659	1334.369	1359.080	1383.790	1408.501	1433.211	1457.922	500
600	1482.632	1507.343	1532.053	1556.764	1581.474	1606.185	1630.896	1655.606	1680.317	1705.027	600
700	1729.738	1754.448	1779.159	1803.869	1828.580	1853.290	1878.001	1902.711	1927.422	1952.133	700
800	1976.843	2001.554	2026.264	2050.975	2075.685	2100.396	2125.106	2149.817	2174.527	2199.238	800
900	2223.948	2248.659	2273.370	2298.080	2322.791	2347.501	2372.212	2396.922	2421.633	2446.343	900
1000	2471.054										1000

71

Use of the tables: the number to be converted, which is made up by adding the unit at the side of a line to the unit at the head of a column, is converted to the number in the position where line and column meet. For example, 11 mile² = 10 mile² + 1 mile² = 28.490 km²

Square miles to Square kilometres 1 mile² = 2.589 988 km²

mile² →	0	1	2	3	4	5	6	7	8	9	← mile²
↓	km²	km²	km²	km²	km²	km²	km²	km²	km²	km²	↓
0	0.000	2.590	5.180	7.770	10.360	12.950	15.540	18.130	20.720	23.310	0
10	25.900	28.490	31.080	33.670	36.260	38.850	41.440	44.030	46.620	49.210	10
20	51.800	54.390	56.980	59.570	62.160	64.750	67.340	69.930	72.520	75.110	20
30	77.700	80.290	82.880	85.470	88.060	90.650	93.240	95.830	98.420	101.010	30
40	103.600	106.190	108.780	111.369	113.959	116.549	119.139	121.729	124.319	126.909	40
50	129.499	132.089	134.679	137.269	139.859	142.449	145.039	147.629	150.219	152.809	50
60	155.399	157.989	160.579	163.169	165.759	168.349	170.939	173.529	176.119	178.709	60
70	181.299	183.889	186.479	189.069	191.659	194.249	196.839	199.429	202.019	204.609	70
80	207.199	209.789	212.379	214.969	217.559	220.149	222.739	225.329	227.919	230.509	80
90	233.099	235.689	238.279	240.869	243.459	246.049	248.639	251.229	253.819	256.409	90
100	258.999										100

mile² →	0	10	20	30	40	50	60	70	80	90	← mile²
↓	km²	km²	km²	km²	km²	km²	km²	km²	km²	km²	↓
0	0.000	25.900	51.800	77.700	103.600	129.499	155.399	181.299	207.199	233.099	0
100	258.999	284.899	310.799	336.698	362.598	388.498	414.398	440.298	466.198	492.098	100
200	517.998	543.898	569.797	595.697	621.597	647.497	673.397	699.297	725.197	751.097	200
300	776.996	802.896	828.796	854.696	880.596	906.496	932.396	958.296	984.195	1010.095	300
400	1035.995	1061.895	1087.795	1113.695	1139.595	1165.495	1191.395	1217.294	1243.194	1269.094	400
500	1294.994	1320.894	1346.794	1372.694	1398.594	1424.493	1450.393	1476.293	1502.193	1528.093	500
600	1553.993	1579.893	1605.793	1631.693	1657.592	1683.492	1709.392	1735.292	1761.192	1787.092	600
700	1812.992	1838.892	1864.791	1890.691	1916.591	1942.491	1968.391	1994.291	2020.191	2046.091	700
800	2071.990	2097.890	2123.790	2149.690	2175.590	2201.490	2227.390	2253.290	2279.190	2305.089	800
900	2330.989	2356.889	2382.789	2408.689	2434.589	2460.489	2486.389	2512.288	2538.188	2564.088	900
1000	2589.988										1000

Square kilometres to Square miles 1 km² = 0.386 102 mile²

km² →	0	1	2	3	4	5	6	7	8	9	← km²
↓	mile²	mile²	mile²	mile²	mile²	mile²	mile²	mile²	mile²	mile²	↓
0	0.000	0.386	0.772	1.158	1.544	1.931	2.317	2.703	3.089	3.475	0
10	3.861	4.247	4.633	5.019	5.405	5.792	6.178	6.564	6.950	7.336	10
20	7.722	8.108	8.494	8.880	9.266	9.653	10.039	10.425	10.811	11.197	20
30	11.583	11.969	12.355	12.741	13.127	13.514	13.900	14.286	14.672	15.058	30
40	15.444	15.830	16.216	16.602	16.988	17.375	17.761	18.147	18.533	18.919	40
50	19.305	19.691	20.077	20.463	20.850	21.236	21.622	22.008	22.394	22.780	50
60	23.166	23.552	23.938	24.324	24.711	25.097	25.483	25.869	26.255	26.641	60
70	27.027	27.413	27.799	28.185	28.572	28.958	29.344	29.730	30.116	30.502	70
80	30.888	31.274	31.660	32.046	32.433	32.819	33.205	33.591	33.977	34.363	80
90	34.749	35.135	35.521	35.908	36.294	36.680	37.066	37.452	37.838	38.224	90
100	38.610										100

km² →	0	10	20	30	40	50	60	70	80	90	← km²
↓	mile²	mile²	mile²	mile²	mile²	mile²	mile²	mile²	mile²	mile²	↓
0	0.000	3.861	7.722	11.583	15.444	19.305	23.166	27.027	30.888	34.749	0
100	38.610	42.471	46.332	50.193	54.054	57.915	61.776	65.637	69.498	73.359	100
200	77.220	81.081	84.942	88.803	92.665	96.526	100.387	104.248	108.109	111.970	200
300	115.831	119.692	123.553	127.414	131.275	135.136	138.997	142.858	146.719	150.580	300
400	154.441	158.302	162.163	166.024	169.885	173.746	177.607	181.468	185.329	189.190	400
500	193.051	196.912	200.773	204.634	208.495	212.356	216.217	220.078	223.939	227.800	500
600	231.661	235.522	239.383	243.244	247.105	250.966	254.827	258.688	262.549	266.410	600
700	270.272	274.133	277.994	281.855	285.716	289.577	293.438	297.299	301.160	305.021	700
800	308.882	312.743	316.604	320.465	324.326	328.187	332.048	335.909	339.770	343.631	800
900	347.492	351.353	355.214	359.075	362.936	366.797	370.658	374.519	378.380	382.241	900
1000	386.102										1000

Use of the tables: the number to be converted, which is made up by adding
the unit at the side of a line to the unit at the head of a column,
is converted to the number in the position where line and column meet.
For example, 11 in³ = 10 in³ + 1 in³ = 180.258 cm³

Cubic inches to Cubic centimetres   1 in³ = 16.387 064 cm³

in³ →	0	1	2	3	4	5	6	7	8	9	← in³
↓	cm³	cm³	cm³	cm³	cm³	cm³	cm³	cm³	cm³	cm³	↓
0	0.000	16.387	32.774	49.161	65.548	81.935	98.322	114.709	131.097	147.484	0
10	163.871	180.258	196.645	213.032	229.419	245.806	262.193	278.580	294.967	311.354	10
20	327.741	344.128	360.515	376.902	393.290	409.677	426.064	442.451	458.838	475.225	20
30	491.612	507.999	524.386	540.773	557.160	573.547	589.934	606.321	622.708	639.095	30
40	655.483	671.870	688.257	704.644	721.031	737.418	753.805	770.192	786.579	802.966	40
50	819.353	835.740	852.127	868.514	884.901	901.289	917.676	934.063	950.450	966.837	50
60	983.224	999.611	1015.998	1032.385	1048.772	1065.159	1081.546	1097.933	1114.320	1130.707	60
70	1147.094	1163.482	1179.869	1196.256	1212.643	1229.030	1245.417	1261.804	1278.191	1294.578	70
80	1310.965	1327.352	1343.739	1360.126	1376.513	1392.900	1409.288	1425.675	1442.062	1458.449	80
90	1474.836	1491.223	1507.610	1523.997	1540.384	1556.771	1573.158	1589.545	1605.932	1622.319	90
100	1638.706										100

in³ →	0	10	20	30	40	50	60	70	80	90	← in³
↓	cm³	cm³	cm³	cm³	cm³	cm³	cm³	cm³	cm³	cm³	↓
0	0.000	163.871	327.741	491.612	655.483	819.353	983.224	1147.094	1310.965	1474.836	0
100	1638.706	1802.577	1966.448	2130.318	2294.189	2458.060	2621.930	2785.801	2949.672	3113.542	100
200	3277.413	3441.283	3605.154	3769.025	3932.895	4096.766	4260.637	4424.507	4588.378	4752.249	200
300	4916.119	5079.990	5243.860	5407.731	5571.602	5735.472	5899.343	6063.214	6227.084	6390.955	300
400	6554.826	6718.696	6882.567	7046.438	7210.308	7374.179	7538.049	7701.920	7865.791	8029.661	400
500	8193.532	8357.403	8521.273	8685.144	8849.015	9012.885	9176.756	9340.626	9504.497	9668.368	500
600	9832.238	9996.109	10159.980	10323.850	10487.721	10651.592	10815.462	10979.333	11143.204	11307.074	600
700	11470.945	11634.815	11798.686	11962.557	12126.427	12290.298	12454.169	12618.039	12781.910	12945.781	700
800	13109.651	13273.522	13437.392	13601.263	13765.134	13929.004	14092.875	14256.746	14420.616	14584.487	800
900	14748.358	14912.228	15076.099	15239.970	15403.840	15567.711	15731.581	15895.452	16059.323	16223.193	900
1000	16387.064										1000

Cubic centimetres to Cubic inches   1 cm³ = 0.061 024 in³

cm³ →	0	1	2	3	4	5	6	7	8	9	← cm³
↓	in³	in³	in³	in³	in³	in³	in³	in³	in³	in³	↓
0	0.000	0.061	0.122	0.183	0.244	0.305	0.366	0.427	0.488	0.549	0
10	0.610	0.671	0.732	0.793	0.854	0.915	0.976	1.037	1.098	1.159	10
20	1.220	1.281	1.343	1.404	1.465	1.526	1.587	1.648	1.709	1.770	20
30	1.831	1.892	1.953	2.014	2.075	2.136	2.197	2.258	2.319	2.380	30
40	2.441	2.502	2.563	2.624	2.685	2.746	2.807	2.868	2.929	2.990	40
50	3.051	3.112	3.173	3.234	3.295	3.356	3.417	3.478	3.539	3.600	50
60	3.661	3.722	3.783	3.844	3.906	3.967	4.028	4.089	4.150	4.211	60
70	4.272	4.333	4.394	4.455	4.516	4.577	4.638	4.699	4.760	4.821	70
80	4.882	4.943	5.004	5.065	5.126	5.187	5.248	5.309	5.370	5.431	80
90	5.492	5.553	5.614	5.675	5.736	5.797	5.858	5.919	5.980	6.041	90
100	6.102										100

cm³ →	0	10	20	30	40	50	60	70	80	90	← cm³
↓	in³	in³	in³	in³	in³	in³	in³	in³	in³	in³	↓
0	0.000	0.610	1.220	1.831	2.441	3.051	3.661	4.272	4.882	5.492	0
100	6.102	6.713	7.323	7.933	8.543	9.154	9.764	10.374	10.984	11.595	100
200	12.205	12.815	13.425	14.035	14.646	15.256	15.866	16.476	17.087	17.697	200
300	18.307	18.917	19.528	20.138	20.748	21.358	21.969	22.579	23.189	23.799	300
400	24.409	25.020	25.630	26.240	26.850	27.461	28.071	28.681	29.291	29.902	400
500	30.512	31.122	31.732	32.343	32.953	33.563	34.173	34.784	35.394	36.004	500
600	36.614	37.224	37.835	38.445	39.055	39.665	40.276	40.886	41.496	42.106	600
700	42.717	43.327	43.937	44.547	45.158	45.768	46.378	46.988	47.599	48.209	700
800	48.819	49.429	50.039	50.650	51.260	51.870	52.480	53.091	53.701	54.311	800
900	54.921	55.532	56.142	56.752	57.362	57.973	58.583	59.193	59.803	60.414	900
1000	61.024										1000

Use of the tables: the number to be converted, which is made up by adding the unit at the side of a line to the unit at the head of a column, is converted to the number in the position where line and column meet. For example, 11 UK gal = 10 UK gal + 1 UK gal = 13.210 US gal

UK gallons to US gallons   1 UK gal = 1.200 950 US gal

UK gal →	0	1	2	3	4	5	6	7	8	9	← UK gal
↓	US gal	US gal	US gal	US gal	US gal	US gal	US gal	US gal	US gal	US gal	↓
0	0.000	1.201	2.402	3.603	4.804	6.005	7.206	8.407	9.608	10.809	0
10	12.009	13.210	14.411	15.612	16.813	18.014	19.215	20.416	21.617	22.818	10
20	24.019	25.220	26.421	27.622	28.823	30.024	31.225	32.426	33.627	34.828	20
30	36.028	37.229	38.430	39.631	40.832	42.033	43.234	44.435	45.636	46.837	30
40	48.038	49.239	50.440	51.641	52.842	54.043	55.244	56.445	57.646	58.847	40
50	60.047	61.248	62.449	63.650	64.851	66.052	67.253	68.454	69.655	70.856	50
60	72.057	73.258	74.459	75.660	76.861	78.062	79.263	80.464	81.665	82.866	60
70	84.066	85.267	86.468	87.669	88.870	90.071	91.272	92.473	93.674	94.875	70
80	96.076	97.277	98.478	99.679	100.880	102.081	103.282	104.483	105.684	106.885	80
90	108.085	109.286	110.487	111.688	112.889	114.090	115.291	116.492	117.693	118.894	90
100	120.095										100

US gallons to UK gallons   1 US gal = 0.832 674 UK gal

US gal →	0	1	2	3	4	5	6	7	8	9	← US gal
↓	UK gal	UK gal	UK gal	UK gal	UK gal	UK gal	UK gal	UK gal	UK gal	UK gal	↓
0	0.000	0.833	1.665	2.498	3.331	4.163	4.996	5.829	6.661	7.494	0
10	8.327	9.159	9.992	10.825	11.657	12.490	13.323	14.155	14.988	15.821	10
20	16.653	17.486	18.319	19.152	19.984	20.817	21.650	22.482	23.315	24.148	20
30	24.980	25.813	26.646	27.478	28.311	29.144	29.976	30.809	31.642	32.474	30
40	33.307	34.140	34.972	35.805	36.638	37.470	38.303	39.136	39.968	40.801	40
50	41.634	42.466	43.299	44.132	44.964	45.797	46.630	47.462	48.295	49.128	50
60	49.960	50.793	51.626	52.458	53.291	54.124	54.956	55.789	56.622	57.455	60
70	58.287	59.120	59.953	60.785	61.618	62.451	63.283	64.116	64.949	65.781	70
80	66.614	67.447	68.279	69.112	69.945	70.777	71.610	72.443	73.275	74.108	80
90	74.941	75.773	76.606	77.439	78.271	79.104	79.937	80.769	81.602	82.435	90
100	83.267										100

UK bushels to US bushels   1 UK bu = 1.032 057 US bu

UK bu →	0	1	2	3	4	5	6	7	8	9	← UK bu
↓	US bu	US bu	US bu	US bu	US bu	US bu	US bu	US bu	US bu	US bu	↓
0	0.000	1.032	2.064	3.096	4.128	5.160	6.192	7.224	8.256	9.289	0
10	10.321	11.353	12.385	13.417	14.449	15.481	16.513	17.545	18.577	19.609	10
20	20.641	21.673	22.705	23.737	24.769	25.801	26.833	27.866	28.898	29.930	20
30	30.962	31.994	33.026	34.058	35.090	36.122	37.154	38.186	39.218	40.250	30
40	41.282	42.314	43.346	44.378	45.410	46.443	47.475	48.507	49.539	50.571	40
50	51.603	52.635	53.667	54.699	55.731	56.763	57.795	58.827	59.859	60.891	50
60	61.923	62.955	63.988	65.020	66.052	67.084	68.116	69.148	70.180	71.212	60
70	72.244	73.276	74.308	75.340	76.372	77.404	78.436	79.468	80.500	81.532	70
80	82.565	83.597	84.629	85.661	86.693	87.725	88.757	89.789	90.821	91.853	80
90	92.885	93.917	94.949	95.981	97.013	98.045	99.077	100.110	101.142	102.174	90
100	103.206										100

US bushels to UK bushels   1 US bu = 0.968 939 UK bu

US bu →	0	1	2	3	4	5	6	7	8	9	← US bu
↓	UK bu	UK bu	UK bu	UK bu	UK bu	UK bu	UK bu	UK bu	UK bu	UK bu	↓
0	0.000	0.969	1.938	2.907	3.876	4.845	5.814	6.783	7.752	8.720	0
10	9.689	10.658	11.627	12.596	13.565	14.534	15.503	16.472	17.441	18.410	10
20	19.379	20.348	21.317	22.286	23.255	24.223	25.192	26.161	27.130	28.099	20
30	29.068	30.037	31.006	31.975	32.944	33.913	34.882	35.851	36.820	37.789	30
40	38.758	39.726	40.695	41.664	42.633	43.602	44.571	45.540	46.509	47.478	40
50	48.447	49.416	50.385	51.354	52.323	53.292	54.261	55.230	56.198	57.167	50
60	58.136	59.105	60.074	61.043	62.012	62.981	63.950	64.919	65.888	66.857	60
70	67.826	68.795	69.764	70.733	71.701	72.670	73.639	74.608	75.577	76.546	70
80	77.515	78.484	79.453	80.422	81.391	82.360	83.329	84.298	85.267	86.236	80
90	87.205	88.173	89.142	90.111	91.080	92.049	93.018	93.987	94.956	95.925	90
100	96.894										100

Use of the tables: the number to be converted, which is made up by adding the unit at the side of a line to the unit at the head of a column, is converted to the number in the position where line and column meet.
For example, 11 UK bu = 10 UK bu + 1 UK bu = 4.001 hl

UK bushels to SI hectolitres   1 UK bu = 0.363 687 hl

UK bu →	0	1	2	3	4	5	6	7	8	9	← UK bu
	hl	hl	hl	hl	hl	hl	hl	hl	hl	hl	
0	0.000	0.364	0.727	1.091	1.455	1.818	2.182	2.546	2.909	3.273	0
10	3.637	4.001	4.364	4.728	5.092	5.455	5.819	6.183	6.546	6.910	10
20	7.274	7.637	8.001	8.365	8.728	9.092	9.456	9.820	10.183	10.547	20
30	10.911	11.274	11.638	12.002	12.365	12.729	13.093	13.456	13.820	14.184	30
40	14.547	14.911	15.275	15.639	16.002	16.366	16.730	17.093	17.457	17.821	40
50	18.184	18.548	18.912	19.275	19.639	20.003	20.366	20.730	21.094	21.458	50
60	21.821	22.185	22.549	22.912	23.276	23.640	24.003	24.367	24.731	25.094	60
70	25.458	25.822	26.185	26.549	26.913	27.277	27.640	28.004	28.368	28.731	70
80	29.095	29.459	29.822	30.186	30.550	30.913	31.277	31.641	32.004	32.368	80
90	32.732	33.096	33.459	33.823	34.187	34.550	34.914	35.278	35.641	36.005	90
100	36.369										100

SI hectolitres to UK bushels   1 hl = 2.749 616 UK bu

hl →	0	1	2	3	4	5	6	7	8	9	← hl
	UK bu	UK bu	UK bu	UK bu	UK bu	UK bu	UK bu	UK bu	UK bu	UK bu	
0	0.000	2.750	5.499	8.249	10.998	13.748	16.498	19.247	21.997	24.747	0
10	27.496	30.246	32.995	35.745	38.495	41.244	43.994	46.743	49.493	52.243	10
20	54.992	57.742	60.492	63.241	65.991	68.740	71.490	74.240	76.989	79.739	20
30	82.488	85.238	87.988	90.737	93.487	96.237	98.986	101.736	104.485	107.235	30
40	109.985	112.734	115.484	118.233	120.983	123.733	126.482	129.232	131.982	134.731	40
50	137.481	140.230	142.980	145.730	148.479	151.229	153.978	156.728	159.478	162.227	50
60	164.977	167.727	170.476	173.226	175.975	178.725	181.475	184.224	186.974	189.723	60
70	192.473	195.223	197.972	200.722	203.472	206.221	208.971	211.720	214.470	217.220	70
80	219.969	222.719	225.468	228.218	230.968	233.717	236.467	239.217	241.966	244.716	80
90	247.465	250.215	252.965	255.714	258.464	261.213	263.963	266.713	269.462	272.212	90
100	274.962										100

US bushels to SI hectolitres   1 US bu = 0.352 391 hl

US bu →	0	1	2	3	4	5	6	7	8	9	← US bu
	hl	hl	hl	hl	hl	hl	hl	hl	hl	hl	
0	0.000	0.352	0.705	1.057	1.410	1.762	2.114	2.467	2.819	3.172	0
10	3.524	3.876	4.229	4.581	4.933	5.286	5.638	5.991	6.343	6.695	10
20	7.048	7.400	7.753	8.105	8.457	8.810	9.162	9.515	9.867	10.219	20
30	10.572	10.924	11.277	11.629	11.981	12.334	12.686	13.038	13.391	13.743	30
40	14.096	14.448	14.800	15.153	15.505	15.858	16.210	16.562	16.915	17.267	40
50	17.620	17.972	18.324	18.677	19.029	19.381	19.734	20.086	20.439	20.791	50
60	21.143	21.496	21.848	22.201	22.553	22.905	23.258	23.610	23.963	24.315	60
70	24.667	25.020	25.372	25.725	26.077	26.429	26.782	27.134	27.486	27.839	70
80	28.191	28.544	28.896	29.248	29.601	29.953	30.306	30.658	31.010	31.363	80
90	31.715	32.068	32.420	32.772	33.125	33.477	33.830	34.182	34.534	34.887	90
100	35.239										100

SI hectolitres to US bushels   1 hl = 2.837 759 US bu

hl →	0	1	2	3	4	5	6	7	8	9	← hl
	US bu	US bu	US bu	US bu	US bu	US bu	US bu	US bu	US bu	US bu	
0	0.000	2.838	5.676	8.513	11.351	14.189	17.027	19.864	22.702	25.540	0
10	28.378	31.215	34.053	36.891	39.729	42.566	45.404	48.242	51.080	53.917	10
20	56.755	59.593	62.431	65.268	68.106	70.944	73.782	76.620	79.457	82.295	20
30	85.133	87.971	90.808	93.646	96.484	99.322	102.159	104.997	107.835	110.673	30
40	113.510	116.348	119.186	122.024	124.861	127.699	130.537	133.375	136.212	139.050	40
50	141.888	144.726	147.563	150.401	153.239	156.077	158.915	161.752	164.590	167.428	50
60	170.266	173.103	175.941	178.779	181.617	184.454	187.292	190.130	192.968	195.805	60
70	198.643	201.481	204.319	207.156	209.994	212.832	215.670	218.507	221.345	224.183	70
80	227.021	229.859	232.696	235.534	238.372	241.210	244.047	246.885	249.723	252.561	80
90	255.398	258.236	261.074	263.912	266.749	269.587	272.425	275.263	278.100	280.938	90
100	283.776										100

Conversions: weight (mass)

Grains to Grams   1 gr = 0.064 799 g

gr →	0	1	2	3	4	5	6	7	8	9	← gr
	g	g	g	g	g	g	g	g	g	g	
0	0.000	0.065	0.130	0.194	0.259	0.324	0.389	0.454	0.518	0.583	0
10	0.648	0.713	0.778	0.842	0.907	0.972	1.037	1.102	1.166	1.231	10
20	1.296	1.361	1.426	1.490	1.555	1.620	1.685	1.750	1.814	1.879	20
30	1.944	2.009	2.074	2.138	2.203	2.268	2.333	2.398	2.462	2.527	30
40	2.592	2.657	2.722	2.786	2.851	2.916	2.981	3.046	3.110	3.175	40
50	3.240	3.305	3.370	3.434	3.499	3.564	3.629	3.694	3.758	3.823	50
60	3.888	3.953	4.018	4.082	4.147	4.212	4.277	4.342	4.406	4.471	60
70	4.536	4.601	4.666	4.730	4.795	4.860	4.925	4.990	5.054	5.119	70
80	5.184	5.249	5.314	5.378	5.443	5.508	5.573	5.638	5.702	5.767	80
90	5.832	5.897	5.961	6.026	6.091	6.156	6.221	6.285	6.350	6.415	90
100	6.480										100

Grams to Grains   1 g = 15.432 358 gr

g →	0	1	2	3	4	5	6	7	8	9	← g
	gr	gr	gr	gr	gr	gr	gr	gr	gr	gr	
0	0.000	15.432	30.865	46.297	61.729	77.162	92.594	108.027	123.459	138.891	0
10	154.324	169.756	185.188	200.621	216.053	231.485	246.918	262.350	277.782	293.215	10
20	308.647	324.080	339.512	354.944	370.377	385.809	401.241	416.674	432.106	447.538	20
30	462.971	478.403	493.835	509.268	524.700	540.133	555.565	570.997	586.430	601.862	30
40	617.294	632.727	648.159	663.591	679.024	694.456	709.888	725.321	740.753	756.186	40
50	771.618	787.050	802.483	817.915	833.347	848.780	864.212	879.644	895.077	910.509	50
60	925.942	941.374	956.806	972.239	987.671	1003.103	1018.536	1033.968	1049.400	1064.833	60
70	1080.265	1095.697	1111.130	1126.562	1141.995	1157.427	1172.859	1188.292	1203.724	1219.156	70
80	1234.589	1250.021	1265.453	1280.886	1296.318	1311.750	1327.183	1342.615	1358.048	1373.480	80
90	1388.912	1404.345	1419.777	1435.209	1450.642	1466.074	1481.506	1496.939	1512.371	1527.803	90
100	1543.236										100

Ounces (avoirdupois) to Grams   1 oz = 28.349 523 g

oz →	0	1	2	3	4	5	6	7	8	9	← oz
	g	g	g	g	g	g	g	g	g	g	
0	0.000	28.350	56.699	85.049	113.398	141.748	170.097	198.447	226.796	255.146	0
10	283.495	311.845	340.194	368.544	396.893	425.243	453.592	481.942	510.291	538.641	10
20	566.990	595.340	623.690	652.039	680.389	708.738	737.088	765.437	793.787	822.136	20
30	850.486	878.835	907.185	935.534	963.884	992.233	1020.583	1048.932	1077.282	1105.631	30
40	1133.981	1162.330	1190.680	1219.029	1247.379	1275.729	1304.078	1332.428	1360.777	1389.127	40
50	1417.476	1445.826	1474.175	1502.525	1530.874	1559.224	1587.573	1615.923	1644.272	1672.622	50
60	1700.971	1729.321	1757.670	1786.020	1814.369	1842.719	1871.069	1899.418	1927.768	1956.117	60
70	1984.467	2012.816	2041.166	2069.515	2097.865	2126.214	2154.564	2182.913	2211.263	2239.612	70
80	2267.962	2296.311	2324.661	2353.010	2381.360	2409.709	2438.059	2466.409	2494.758	2523.108	80
90	2551.457	2579.807	2608.156	2636.506	2664.855	2693.205	2721.554	2749.904	2778.253	2806.603	90
100	2834.952										100

Grams to Ounces (avoirdupois)   1 g = 0.035 274 oz

g →	0	1	2	3	4	5	6	7	8	9	← g
	oz	oz	oz	oz	oz	oz	oz	oz	oz	oz	
0	0.000	0.035	0.071	0.106	0.141	0.176	0.212	0.247	0.282	0.317	0
10	0.353	0.388	0.423	0.459	0.494	0.529	0.564	0.600	0.635	0.670	10
20	0.705	0.741	0.776	0.811	0.847	0.882	0.917	0.952	0.988	1.023	20
30	1.058	1.093	1.129	1.164	1.199	1.235	1.270	1.305	1.340	1.376	30
40	1.411	1.446	1.482	1.517	1.552	1.587	1.623	1.658	1.693	1.728	40
50	1.764	1.799	1.834	1.870	1.905	1.940	1.975	2.011	2.046	2.081	50
60	2.116	2.152	2.187	2.222	2.258	2.293	2.328	2.363	2.399	2.434	60
70	2.469	2.504	2.540	2.575	2.610	2.646	2.681	2.716	2.751	2.787	70
80	2.822	2.857	2.892	2.928	2.963	2.998	3.034	3.069	3.104	3.139	80
90	3.175	3.210	3.245	3.280	3.316	3.351	3.386	3.422	3.457	3.492	90
100	3.527										100

se of the tables: the number to be converted, which is made up by adding
e unit at the side of a line to the unit at the head of a column,
 converted to the number in the position where line and column meet.
or example, 11 lb = 10 lb + 1 lb = 4.990 kg

ounds to Kilograms   1 lb = 0.453 592 kg

ote. This table can also be used for the 'force' conversion of pounds-force to kilograms-force (kiloponds).

lb →	0	1	2	3	4	5	6	7	8	9	← lb
↓	kg	kg	kg	kg	kg	kg	kg	kg	kg	kg	↓
0	0.000	0.454	0.907	1.361	1.814	2.268	2.722	3.175	3.629	4.082	0
10	4.536	4.990	5.443	5.897	6.350	6.804	7.257	7.711	8.165	8.618	10
20	9.072	9.525	9.979	10.433	10.886	11.340	11.793	12.247	12.701	13.154	20
30	13.608	14.061	14.515	14.969	15.422	15.876	16.329	16.783	17.237	17.690	30
40	18.144	18.597	19.051	19.504	19.958	20.412	20.865	21.319	21.772	22.226	40
50	22.680	23.133	23.587	24.040	24.494	24.948	25.401	25.855	26.308	26.762	50
60	27.216	27.669	28.123	28.576	29.030	29.484	29.937	30.391	30.844	31.298	60
70	31.751	32.205	32.659	33.112	33.566	34.019	34.473	34.927	35.380	35.834	70
80	36.287	36.741	37.195	37.648	38.102	38.555	39.009	39.463	39.916	40.370	80
90	40.823	41.277	41.730	42.184	42.638	43.091	43.545	43.998	44.452	44.906	90
100	45.359										100

lb →	0	10	20	30	40	50	60	70	80	90	← lb
↓	kg	kg	kg	kg	kg	kg	kg	kg	kg	kg	↓
0	0.000	4.536	9.072	13.608	18.144	22.680	27.216	31.751	36.287	40.823	0
100	45.359	49.895	54.431	58.967	63.503	68.039	72.575	77.111	81.647	86.183	100
200	90.718	95.254	99.790	104.326	108.862	113.398	117.934	122.470	127.006	131.542	200
300	136.078	140.614	145.150	149.685	154.221	158.757	163.293	167.829	172.365	176.901	300
400	181.437	185.973	190.509	195.045	199.581	204.117	208.652	213.188	217.724	222.260	400
500	226.796	231.332	235.868	240.404	244.940	249.476	254.012	258.548	263.084	267.619	500
600	272.155	276.691	281.227	285.763	290.299	294.835	299.371	303.907	308.443	312.979	600
700	317.515	322.051	326.587	331.122	335.658	340.194	344.730	349.266	353.802	358.338	700
800	362.874	367.410	371.946	376.482	381.018	385.554	390.089	394.625	399.161	403.697	800
900	408.233	412.769	417.305	421.841	426.377	430.913	435.449	439.985	444.521	449.056	900
000	453.592										1000

Kilograms to Pounds   1 kg = 2.204 623 lb

ote. This table can also be used for the 'force' conversion of kilograms-force (kiloponds) to pounds-force

kg →	0	1	2	3	4	5	6	7	8	9	← kg
↓	lb	lb	lb	lb	lb	lb	lb	lb	lb	lb	↓
0	0.000	2.205	4.409	6.614	8.818	11.023	13.228	15.432	17.637	19.842	0
10	22.046	24.251	26.455	28.660	30.865	33.069	35.274	37.479	39.683	41.888	10
20	44.092	46.297	48.502	50.706	52.911	55.116	57.320	59.525	61.729	63.934	20
30	66.139	68.343	70.548	72.753	74.957	77.162	79.366	81.571	83.776	85.980	30
40	88.185	90.390	92.594	94.799	97.003	99.208	101.413	103.617	105.822	108.027	40
50	110.231	112.436	114.640	116.845	119.050	121.254	123.459	125.663	127.868	130.073	50
60	132.277	134.482	136.687	138.891	141.096	143.300	145.505	147.710	149.914	152.119	60
70	154.324	156.528	158.733	160.937	163.142	165.347	167.551	169.756	171.961	174.165	70
80	176.370	178.574	180.779	182.984	185.188	187.393	189.598	191.802	194.007	196.211	80
90	198.416	200.621	202.825	205.030	207.235	209.439	211.644	213.848	216.053	218.258	90
100	220.462										100

kg →	0	10	20	30	40	50	60	70	80	90	← kg
↓	lb	lb	lb	lb	lb	lb	lb	lb	lb	lb	↓
0	0.000	22.046	44.092	66.139	88.185	110.231	132.277	154.324	176.370	198.416	0
100	220.462	242.508	264.555	286.601	308.647	330.693	352.740	374.786	396.832	418.878	100
200	440.925	462.971	485.017	507.063	529.109	551.156	573.202	595.248	617.294	639.341	200
300	661.387	683.433	705.479	727.525	749.572	771.618	793.664	815.710	837.757	859.803	300
400	881.849	903.895	925.942	947.988	970.034	992.080	1014.126	1036.173	1058.219	1080.265	400
500	1102.311	1124.358	1146.404	1168.450	1190.496	1212.542	1234.589	1256.635	1278.681	1300.727	500
600	1322.774	1344.820	1366.866	1388.912	1410.958	1433.005	1455.051	1477.097	1499.143	1521.190	600
700	1543.236	1565.282	1587.328	1609.375	1631.421	1653.467	1675.513	1697.559	1719.606	1741.652	700
800	1763.698	1785.744	1807.791	1829.837	1851.883	1873.929	1895.975	1918.022	1940.068	1962.114	800
900	1984.160	2006.207	2028.253	2050.299	2072.345	2094.391	2116.438	2138.484	2160.530	2182.576	900
000	2204.623										1000

Conversions: pressure and stress

Use of the tables: the number to be converted, which is made up by adding the unit at the side of a line to the unit at the head of a column, is converted to the number in the position where line and column meet. For example, 11 lbf/in² = 10 lbf/in² + 1 lbf/in² = 0.773 kgf/cm²

Pounds-force ('pounds') per square inch to Kilograms-force per square centimetre   1 lbf/in² = 0.070 307 kgf/cm²

lbf/in² →	0	1	2	3	4	5	6	7	8	9	← lbf/in²
↓	kgf/cm²	kgf/cm²	kgf/cm²	kgf/cm²	kgf/cm²	kgf/cm²	kgf/cm²	kgf/cm²	kgf/cm²	kgf/cm²	
0	0.000	0.070	0.141	0.211	0.281	0.352	0.422	0.492	0.562	0.633	
10	0.703	0.773	0.844	0.914	0.984	1.055	1.125	1.195	1.266	1.336	1
20	1.406	1.476	1.547	1.617	1.687	1.758	1.828	1.898	1.969	2.039	2
30	2.109	2.180	2.250	2.320	2.390	2.461	2.531	2.601	2.672	2.742	3
40	2.812	2.883	2.953	3.023	3.094	3.164	3.234	3.304	3.375	3.445	4
50	3.515	3.586	3.656	3.726	3.797	3.867	3.937	4.007	4.078	4.148	5
60	4.218	4.289	4.359	4.429	4.500	4.570	4.640	4.711	4.781	4.851	6
70	4.921	4.992	5.062	5.132	5.203	5.273	5.343	5.414	5.484	5.554	7
80	5.625	5.695	5.765	5.835	5.906	5.976	6.046	6.117	6.187	6.257	8
90	6.328	6.398	6.468	6.539	6.609	6.679	6.749	6.820	6.890	6.960	9
100	7.031										10

Kilograms-force per square centimetre to Pounds-force ('pounds') per square inch   1 kgf/cm² = 14.223 343 lbf/in²

kgf/cm² →	0	1	2	3	4	5	6	7	8	9	← kgf/cm²
↓	lbf/in²	lbf/in²	lbf/in²	lbf/in²	lbf/in²	lbf/in²	lbf/in²	lbf/in²	lbf/in²	lbf/in²	
0	0.000	14.223	28.447	42.670	56.893	71.117	85.340	99.563	113.787	128.010	
10	142.233	156.457	170.680	184.903	199.127	213.350	227.573	241.797	256.020	270.244	1
20	284.467	298.690	312.914	327.137	341.360	355.584	369.807	384.030	398.254	412.477	2
30	426.700	440.924	455.147	469.370	483.594	497.817	512.040	526.264	540.487	554.710	3
40	568.934	583.157	597.380	611.604	625.827	640.050	654.274	668.497	682.720	696.944	4
50	711.167	725.391	739.614	753.837	768.061	782.284	796.507	810.731	824.954	839.177	5
60	853.401	867.624	881.847	896.071	910.294	924.517	938.741	952.964	967.187	981.411	6
70	995.634	1009.857	1024.081	1038.304	1052.527	1066.751	1080.974	1095.197	1109.421	1123.644	7
80	1137.867	1152.091	1166.314	1180.537	1194.761	1208.984	1223.208	1237.431	1251.654	1265.878	8
90	1280.101	1294.324	1308.548	1322.771	1336.994	1351.218	1365.441	1379.664	1393.888	1408.111	9
100	1422.334										10

Pounds-force ('pounds') per square inch to Newtons per square millimetre   1 lbf/in² = 0.006 895 N/mm²

lbf/in² →	0	100	200	300	400	500	600	700	800	900	← lbf/in²
↓	N/mm²	N/mm²	N/mm²	N/mm²	N/mm²	N/mm²	N/mm²	N/mm²	N/mm²	N/mm²	
0	0.000	0.689	1.379	2.068	2.758	3.447	4.137	4.826	5.516	6.205	
1000	6.895	7.584	8.274	8.963	9.653	10.342	11.032	11.721	12.411	13.100	100
2000	13.790	14.479	15.168	15.858	16.547	17.237	17.926	18.616	19.305	19.995	200
3000	20.684	21.374	22.063	22.753	23.442	24.132	24.821	25.511	26.200	26.890	300
4000	27.579	28.269	28.958	29.647	30.337	31.026	31.716	32.405	33.095	33.784	400
5000	34.474	35.163	35.853	36.542	37.232	37.921	38.611	39.300	39.990	40.679	500
6000	41.369	42.058	42.747	43.437	44.126	44.816	45.505	46.195	46.884	47.574	600
7000	48.263	48.953	49.642	50.332	51.021	51.711	52.400	53.090	53.779	54.469	700
8000	55.158	55.848	56.537	57.226	57.916	58.605	59.295	59.984	60.674	61.363	800
9000	62.053	62.742	63.432	64.121	64.811	65.500	66.190	66.879	67.569	68.258	900
10000	68.948										1000

Newtons per square millimetre to Pounds-force ('pounds') per square inch   1 N/mm² = 145.037 738 lbf/in²

N/mm² →	0	1	2	3	4	5	6	7	8	9	← N/mm²
↓	lbf/in²	lbf/in²	lbf/in²	lbf/in²	lbf/in²	lbf/in²	lbf/in²	lbf/in²	lbf/in²	lbf/in²	
0	0.000	145.038	290.075	435.113	580.151	725.189	870.226	1015.264	1160.302	1305.340	
10	1450.377	1595.415	1740.453	1885.491	2030.528	2175.566	2320.604	2465.642	2610.679	2755.717	1
20	2900.755	3045.792	3190.830	3335.868	3480.906	3625.943	3770.981	3916.019	4061.057	4206.094	2
30	4351.132	4496.170	4641.208	4786.245	4931.283	5076.321	5221.359	5366.396	5511.434	5656.472	3
40	5801.510	5946.547	6091.585	6236.623	6381.660	6526.698	6671.736	6816.774	6961.811	7106.849	4
50	7251.887	7396.925	7541.962	7687.000	7832.038	7977.076	8122.113	8267.151	8412.189	8557.227	5
60	8702.264	8847.302	8992.340	9137.377	9282.415	9427.453	9572.491	9717.528	9862.566	10007.604	6
70	10152.642	10297.679	10442.717	10587.755	10732.793	10877.830	11022.868	11167.906	11312.944	11457.981	7
80	11603.019	11748.057	11893.094	12038.132	12183.170	12328.208	12473.245	12618.283	12763.321	12908.359	8
90	13053.396	13198.434	13343.472	13488.510	13633.547	13778.585	13923.623	14068.661	14213.698	14358.736	9
100	14503.774										10

Use of the tables: the number to be converted, which is made up by adding the unit at the side of a line to the unit at the head of a column, is converted to the number in the position where line and column meet. For example, 11 lbf/in² = 10 lbf/in² + 1 lbf/in² = 0.758 bar

Pounds-force ('pounds') per square inch to Bars   1 lbf/in² = 0.068 948 bar

lbf/in² →	0	1	2	3	4	5	6	7	8	9	← lbf/in²
↓	bar	bar	bar	bar	bar	bar	bar	bar	bar	bar	↓
0	0.000	0.069	0.138	0.207	0.276	0.345	0.414	0.483	0.552	0.621	0
10	0.689	0.758	0.827	0.896	0.965	1.034	1.103	1.172	1.241	1.310	10
20	1.379	1.448	1.517	1.586	1.655	1.724	1.793	1.862	1.931	1.999	20
30	2.068	2.137	2.206	2.275	2.344	2.413	2.482	2.551	2.620	2.689	30
40	2.758	2.827	2.896	2.965	3.034	3.103	3.172	3.241	3.309	3.378	40
50	3.447	3.516	3.585	3.654	3.723	3.792	3.861	3.930	3.999	4.068	50
60	4.137	4.206	4.275	4.344	4.413	4.482	4.551	4.619	4.688	4.757	60
70	4.826	4.895	4.964	5.033	5.102	5.171	5.240	5.309	5.378	5.447	70
80	5.516	5.585	5.654	5.723	5.792	5.861	5.929	5.998	6.067	6.136	80
90	6.205	6.274	6.343	6.412	6.481	6.550	6.619	6.688	6.757	6.826	90
00	6.895										100

Bars to Pounds-force ('pounds') per square inch   1 bar = 14.503 774 lbf/in²

bar →	0.0	0.1	0.2	0.3	0.4	0.5	0.6	0.7	0.8	0.9	← bar
↓	lbf/in²	lbf/in²	lbf/in²	lbf/in²	lbf/in²	lbf/in²	lbf/in²	lbf/in²	lbf/in²	lbf/in²	↓
0	0.000	1.450	2.901	4.351	5.802	7.252	8.702	10.153	11.603	13.053	0
1	14.504	15.954	17.405	18.855	20.305	21.756	23.206	24.656	26.107	27.557	1
2	29.008	30.458	31.908	33.359	34.809	36.259	37.710	39.160	40.611	42.061	2
3	43.511	44.962	46.412	47.862	49.313	50.763	52.214	53.664	55.114	56.565	3
4	58.015	59.465	60.916	62.366	63.817	65.267	66.717	68.168	69.618	71.068	4
5	72.519	73.969	75.420	76.870	78.320	79.771	81.221	82.672	84.122	85.572	5
6	87.023	88.473	89.923	91.374	92.824	94.275	95.725	97.175	98.626	100.076	6
7	101.526	102.977	104.427	105.878	107.328	108.778	110.229	111.679	113.129	114.580	7
8	116.030	117.481	118.931	120.381	121.832	123.282	124.732	126.183	127.633	129.084	8
9	130.534	131.984	133.435	134.885	136.335	137.786	139.236	140.687	142.137	143.587	9
10	145.038										10

Pounds-force ('pounds') per square inch to Kilopascals   1 lbf/in² = 6.894 757 kPa

lbf/in² →	0	1	2	3	4	5	6	7	8	9	← lbf/in²
↓	kPa	kPa	kPa	kPa	kPa	kPa	kPa	kPa	kPa	kPa	↓
0	0.000	6.895	13.790	20.684	27.579	34.474	41.369	48.263	55.158	62.053	0
10	68.948	75.842	82.737	89.632	96.527	103.421	110.316	117.211	124.106	131.000	10
20	137.895	144.790	151.685	158.579	165.474	172.369	179.264	186.158	193.053	199.948	20
30	206.843	213.737	220.632	227.527	234.422	241.317	248.211	255.106	262.001	268.896	30
40	275.790	282.685	289.580	296.475	303.369	310.264	317.159	324.054	330.948	337.843	40
50	344.738	351.633	358.527	365.422	372.317	379.212	386.106	393.001	399.896	406.791	50
60	413.685	420.580	427.475	434.370	441.264	448.159	455.054	461.949	468.843	475.738	60
70	482.633	489.528	496.423	503.317	510.212	517.107	524.002	530.896	537.791	544.686	70
80	551.581	558.475	565.370	572.265	579.160	586.054	592.949	599.844	606.739	613.633	80
90	620.528	627.423	634.318	641.212	648.107	655.002	661.897	668.791	675.686	682.581	90
00	689.476										100

Kilopascals to Pounds-force ('pounds') per square inch   1 kPa = 0.145 038 lbf/in²

kPa →	0	1	2	3	4	5	6	7	8	9	← kPa
↓	lbf/in²	lbf/in²	lbf/in²	lbf/in²	lbf/in²	lbf/in²	lbf/in²	lbf/in²	lbf/in²	lbf/in²	↓
0	0.000	0.145	0.290	0.435	0.580	0.725	0.870	1.015	1.160	1.305	0
10	1.450	1.595	1.740	1.885	2.031	2.176	2.321	2.466	2.611	2.756	10
20	2.901	3.046	3.191	3.336	3.481	3.626	3.771	3.916	4.061	4.206	20
30	4.351	4.496	4.641	4.786	4.931	5.076	5.221	5.366	5.511	5.656	30
40	5.802	5.947	6.092	6.237	6.382	6.527	6.672	6.817	6.962	7.107	40
50	7.252	7.397	7.542	7.687	7.832	7.977	8.122	8.267	8.412	8.557	50
60	8.702	8.847	8.992	9.137	9.282	9.427	9.572	9.718	9.863	10.008	60
70	10.153	10.298	10.443	10.588	10.733	10.878	11.023	11.168	11.313	11.458	70
80	11.603	11.748	11.893	12.038	12.183	12.328	12.473	12.618	12.763	12.908	80
90	13.053	13.198	13.343	13.489	13.634	13.779	13.924	14.069	14.214	14.359	90
00	14.504										100

Use of the tables: the number to be converted, which is made up by adding
the unit at the side of a line to the unit at the head of a column,
is converted to the number in the position where line and column meet.
For example, 11 tonf/in² = 10 tonf/in² + 1 tonf/in² = 169.887 N/mm²

UK tons-force ('tons') per square inch to Newtons per square millimetre   1 tonf/in² = 15.444 256 N/mm²

tonf/in² →	0	1	2	3	4	5	6	7	8	9 ← tonf/in	
↓	N/mm²	N/mm²	N/mm²	N/mm²	N/mm²	N/mm²	N/mm²	N/mm²	N/mm²	N/mm²	
0	0.000	15.444	30.889	46.333	61.777	77.221	92.666	108.110	123.554	138.998	
10	154.443	169.887	185.331	200.775	216.220	231.664	247.108	262.552	277.997	293.441	1
20	308.885	324.329	339.774	355.218	370.662	386.106	401.551	416.995	432.439	447.883	2
30	463.328	478.772	494.216	509.660	525.105	540.549	555.993	571.437	586.882	602.326	3
40	617.770	633.215	648.659	664.103	679.547	694.992	710.436	725.880	741.324	756.769	4
50	772.213	787.657	803.101	818.546	833.990	849.434	864.878	880.323	895.767	911.211	5
60	926.655	942.100	957.544	972.988	988.432	1003.877	1019.321	1034.765	1050.209	1065.654	6
70	1081.098	1096.542	1111.986	1127.431	1142.875	1158.319	1173.763	1189.208	1204.652	1220.096	7
80	1235.541	1250.985	1266.429	1281.873	1297.318	1312.762	1328.206	1343.650	1359.095	1374.539	8
90	1389.983	1405.427	1420.872	1436.316	1451.760	1467.204	1482.649	1498.093	1513.537	1528.981	9
100	1544.426										10

Newtons per square millimetre to UK tons-force ('tons') per square inch   1 N/mm² = 0.064 749 tonf/in²

N/mm² →	0	1	2	3	4	5	6	7	8	9 ← N/mm	
↓	tonf/in²	tonf/in²	tonf/in²	tonf/in²	tonf/in²	tonf/in²	tonf/in²	tonf/in²	tonf/in²	tonf/in²	
0	0.000	0.065	0.129	0.194	0.259	0.324	0.388	0.453	0.518	0.583	
10	0.647	0.712	0.777	0.842	0.906	0.971	1.036	1.101	1.165	1.230	1
20	1.295	1.360	1.424	1.489	1.554	1.619	1.683	1.748	1.813	1.878	2
30	1.942	2.007	2.072	2.137	2.201	2.266	2.331	2.396	2.460	2.525	3
40	2.590	2.655	2.719	2.784	2.849	2.914	2.978	3.043	3.108	3.173	4
50	3.237	3.302	3.367	3.432	3.496	3.561	3.626	3.691	3.755	3.820	5
60	3.885	3.950	4.014	4.079	4.144	4.209	4.273	4.338	4.403	4.468	6
70	4.532	4.597	4.662	4.727	4.791	4.856	4.921	4.986	5.050	5.115	7
80	5.180	5.245	5.309	5.374	5.439	5.504	5.568	5.633	5.698	5.763	8
90	5.827	5.892	5.957	6.022	6.086	6.151	6.216	6.281	6.345	6.410	9
100	6.475										10

UK tons-force ('tons') per square foot to Bars   1 tonf/ft² = 1.072 518 bar

tonf/ft² →	0	1	2	3	4	5	6	7	8	9 ← tonf/ft	
↓	bar	bar	bar	bar	bar	bar	bar	bar	bar	bar	
0	0.000	1.073	2.145	3.218	4.290	5.363	6.435	7.508	8.580	9.653	
10	10.725	11.798	12.870	13.943	15.015	16.088	17.160	18.233	19.305	20.378	1
20	21.450	22.523	23.595	24.668	25.740	26.813	27.885	28.958	30.030	31.103	2
30	32.176	33.248	34.321	35.393	36.466	37.538	38.611	39.683	40.756	41.828	3
40	42.901	43.973	45.046	46.118	47.191	48.263	49.336	50.408	51.481	52.553	4
50	53.626	54.698	55.771	56.843	57.916	58.988	60.061	61.134	62.206	63.279	5
60	64.351	65.424	66.496	67.569	68.641	69.714	70.786	71.859	72.931	74.004	6
70	75.076	76.149	77.221	78.294	79.366	80.439	81.511	82.584	83.656	84.729	7
80	85.801	86.874	87.946	89.019	90.091	91.164	92.237	93.309	94.382	95.454	8
90	96.527	97.599	98.672	99.744	100.817	101.889	102.962	104.034	105.107	106.179	9
100	107.252										10

Bars to UK tons-force ('tons') per square foot   1 bar = 0.932 385 tonf/ft²

bar →	0	1	2	3	4	5	6	7	8	9 ← ba	
↓	tonf/ft²	tonf/ft²	tonf/ft²	tonf/ft²	tonf/ft²	tonf/ft²	tonf/ft²	tonf/ft²	tonf/ft²	tonf/ft²	
0	0.000	0.932	1.865	2.797	3.730	4.662	5.594	6.527	7.459	8.391	
10	9.324	10.256	11.189	12.121	13.053	13.986	14.918	15.851	16.783	17.715	1
20	18.648	19.580	20.512	21.445	22.377	23.310	24.242	25.174	26.107	27.039	2
30	27.972	28.904	29.836	30.769	31.701	32.633	33.566	34.498	35.431	36.363	3
40	37.295	38.228	39.160	40.093	41.025	41.957	42.890	43.822	44.755	45.687	4
50	46.619	47.552	48.484	49.416	50.349	51.281	52.214	53.146	54.078	55.011	5
60	55.943	56.876	57.808	58.740	59.673	60.605	61.537	62.470	63.402	64.335	6
70	65.267	66.199	67.132	68.064	68.997	69.929	70.861	71.794	72.726	73.658	7
80	74.591	75.523	76.456	77.388	78.320	79.253	80.185	81.118	82.050	82.982	8
90	83.915	84.847	85.779	86.712	87.644	88.577	89.509	90.441	91.374	92.306	9
100	93.239										10

Use of the tables: the number to be converted, which is made up by adding the unit at the side of a line to the unit at the head of a column, is converted to the number in the position where line and column meet.
For example, 11 ft lbf = 10 ft lbf + 1 ft lbf = 14.914 J

Conversions: energy, work and heat

Foot pounds-force to Joules — 1 ft lbf = 1.355 818 J

ft lbf →	0	1	2	3	4	5	6	7	8	9	← ft lbf
↓	J	J	J	J	J	J	J	J	J	J	↓
0	0.000	1.356	2.712	4.067	5.423	6.779	8.135	9.491	10.847	12.202	0
10	13.558	14.914	16.270	17.626	18.981	20.337	21.693	23.049	24.405	25.761	10
20	27.116	28.472	29.828	31.184	32.540	33.895	35.251	36.607	37.963	39.319	20
30	40.675	42.030	43.386	44.742	46.098	47.454	48.809	50.165	51.521	52.877	30
40	54.233	55.589	56.944	58.300	59.656	61.012	62.368	63.723	65.079	66.435	40
50	67.791	69.147	70.503	71.858	73.214	74.570	75.926	77.282	78.637	79.993	50
60	81.349	82.705	84.061	85.417	86.772	88.128	89.484	90.840	92.196	93.551	60
70	94.907	96.263	97.619	98.975	100.331	101.686	103.042	104.398	105.754	107.110	70
80	108.465	109.821	111.177	112.533	113.889	115.245	116.600	117.956	119.312	120.668	80
90	122.024	123.379	124.735	126.091	127.447	128.803	130.159	131.514	132.870	134.226	90
100	135.582										100

Joules to Foot pounds-force — 1 J = 0.737 562 ft lbf

J →	0	1	2	3	4	5	6	7	8	9	← J
↓	ft lbf	ft lbf	ft lbf	ft lbf	ft lbf	ft lbf	ft lbf	ft lbf	ft lbf	ft lbf	↓
0	0.000	0.738	1.475	2.213	2.950	3.688	4.425	5.163	5.900	6.638	0
10	7.376	8.113	8.851	9.588	10.326	11.063	11.801	12.539	13.276	14.014	10
20	14.751	15.489	16.226	16.964	17.701	18.439	19.177	19.914	20.652	21.389	20
30	22.127	22.864	23.602	24.340	25.077	25.815	26.552	27.290	28.027	28.765	30
40	29.502	30.240	30.978	31.715	32.453	33.190	33.928	34.665	35.403	36.141	40
50	36.878	37.616	38.353	39.091	39.828	40.566	41.303	42.041	42.779	43.516	50
60	44.254	44.991	45.729	46.466	47.204	47.942	48.679	49.417	50.154	50.892	60
70	51.629	52.367	53.104	53.842	54.580	55.317	56.055	56.792	57.530	58.267	70
80	59.005	59.743	60.480	61.218	61.955	62.693	63.430	64.168	64.905	65.643	80
90	66.381	67.118	67.856	68.593	69.331	70.068	70.806	71.544	72.281	73.019	90
100	73.756										100

British thermal units to Kilojoules — 1 Btu = 1.055 056 kJ

Btu →	0	1	2	3	4	5	6	7	8	9	← Btu
↓	kJ	kJ	kJ	kJ	kJ	kJ	kJ	kJ	kJ	kJ	↓
0	0.000	1.055	2.110	3.165	4.220	5.275	6.330	7.385	8.440	9.496	0
10	10.551	11.606	12.661	13.716	14.771	15.826	16.881	17.936	18.991	20.046	10
20	21.101	22.156	23.211	24.266	25.321	26.376	27.431	28.487	29.542	30.597	20
30	31.652	32.707	33.762	34.817	35.872	36.927	37.982	39.037	40.092	41.147	30
40	42.202	43.257	44.312	45.367	46.422	47.478	48.533	49.588	50.643	51.698	40
50	52.753	53.808	54.863	55.918	56.973	58.028	59.083	60.138	61.193	62.248	50
60	63.303	64.358	65.413	66.469	67.524	68.579	69.634	70.689	71.744	72.799	60
70	73.854	74.909	75.964	77.019	78.074	79.129	80.184	81.239	82.294	83.349	70
80	84.404	85.460	86.515	87.570	88.625	89.680	90.735	91.790	92.845	93.900	80
90	94.955	96.010	97.065	98.120	99.175	100.230	101.285	102.340	103.395	104.451	90
100	105.506										100

Kilojoules to British thermal units — 1 kJ = 0.947 817 Btu

kJ →	0	1	2	3	4	5	6	7	8	9	← kJ
↓	Btu	Btu	Btu	Btu	Btu	Btu	Btu	Btu	Btu	Btu	↓
0	0.000	0.948	1.896	2.843	3.791	4.739	5.687	6.635	7.583	8.530	0
10	9.478	10.426	11.374	12.322	13.269	14.217	15.165	16.113	17.061	18.009	10
20	18.956	19.904	20.852	21.800	22.748	23.695	24.643	25.591	26.539	27.487	20
30	28.435	29.382	30.330	31.278	32.226	33.174	34.121	35.069	36.017	36.965	30
40	37.913	38.861	39.808	40.756	41.704	42.652	43.600	44.547	45.495	46.443	40
50	47.391	48.339	49.286	50.234	51.182	52.130	53.078	54.026	54.973	55.921	50
60	56.869	57.817	58.765	59.712	60.660	61.608	62.556	63.504	64.452	65.399	60
70	66.347	67.295	68.243	69.191	70.138	71.086	72.034	72.982	73.930	74.878	70
80	75.825	76.773	77.721	78.669	79.617	80.564	81.512	82.460	83.408	84.356	80
90	85.304	86.251	87.199	88.147	89.095	90.043	90.990	91.938	92.886	93.834	90
100	94.782										100

Conversions: temperature

Use of the table: corresponding degrees on the Fahrenheit and Celsius scales are shown, where, for example, 32 °F = 0 °C and 212 °F = 100 °C.
The degree Celsius has been converted to the degree Fahrenheit by multiplying by 9, dividing by 5 and adding 32. The degree Fahrenheit has been converted to the degree Celsius by subtracting 32 multiplying by 5 and dividing by 9.

Fahrenheit and Celsius (centigrade)

°F	°C	°F	°C	°F	°C	°F	°C	°F	°C	°F	°C
-459.67	-273.15	0	-17.8	20	-6.7	40	4.4	60	15.6	80	26.7
-450	-267.8	0.5	-17.5	20.3	-6.5	40.1	4.5	60.5	15.8	80.5	26.9
-418	-250	1	-17.2	20.5	-6.4	40.5	4.7	60.8	16	80.6	27
-400	-240	1.4	-17	21	-6.1	41	5	61	16.1	81	27.2
-350	-212.2	1.5	-16.9	21.2	-6	41.5	5.3	61.5	16.4	81.5	27.5
-328	-200	2	-16.7	21.5	-5.8	41.9	5.5	61.7	16.5	82	27.8
-300	-184.4	2.3	-16.5	22	-5.6	42	5.6	62	16.7	82.4	28
-250	-156.7	2.5	-16.4	22.1	-5.5	42.5	5.8	62.5	16.9	82.5	28.1
-238	-150	3	-16.1	22.5	-5.3	42.8	6	62.6	17	83	28.3
-200	-128.9	3.2	-16	23	-5	43	6.1	63	17.2	83.3	28.5
-150	-101.1	3.5	-15.8	23.5	-4.7	43.5	6.4	63.5	17.5	83.5	28.6
-148	-100	4	-15.6	23.9	-4.5	43.7	6.5	64	17.8	84	28.9
-140	-95.6	4.1	-15.5	24	-4.4	44	6.7	64.4	18	84.2	29
-130	-90	4.5	-15.3	24.5	-4.2	44.5	6.9	64.5	18.1	84.5	29.2
-120	-84.4	5	-15	24.8	-4	44.6	7	65	18.3	85	29.4
-112	-80	5.5	-14.7	25	-3.9	45	7.2	65.3	18.5	85.1	29.5
-110	-78.9	5.9	-14.5	25.5	-3.6	45.5	7.5	65.5	18.6	85.5	29.7
-100	-73.3	6	-14.4	25.7	-3.5	46	7.8	66	18.9	86	30
-95	-70.6	6.5	-14.2	26	-3.3	46.4	8	66.2	19	86.5	30.3
-94	-70	6.8	-14	26.5	-3.1	46.5	8.1	66.5	19.2	86.9	30.5
-90	-67.8	7	-13.9	26.6	-3	47	8.3	67	19.4	87	30.6
-85	-65	7.5	-13.6	27	-2.8	47.3	8.5	67.1	19.5	87.5	30.8
-80	-62.2	7.7	-13.5	27.5	-2.5	47.5	8.6	67.5	19.7	87.8	31
-76	-60	8	-13.3	28	-2.2	48	8.9	68	20	88	31.1
-75	-59.4	8.5	-13.1	28.4	-2	48.2	9	68.5	20.3	88.5	31.4
-70	-56.7	8.6	-13	28.5	-1.9	48.5	9.2	68.9	20.5	88.7	31.5
-67	-55	9	-12.8	29	-1.7	49	9.4	69	20.6	89	31.7
-65	-53.9	9.5	-12.5	29.3	-1.5	49.1	9.5	69.5	20.8	89.5	31.9
-60	-51.1	10	-12.2	29.5	-1.4	49.5	9.7	69.8	21	89.6	32
-58	-50	10.4	-12	30	-1.1	50	10	70	21.1	90	32.2
-55	-48.3	10.5	-11.9	30.2	-1	50.5	10.3	70.5	21.4	90.5	32.5
-50	-45.6	11	-11.7	30.5	-0.8	50.9	10.5	70.7	21.5	91	32.8
-49	-45	11.3	-11.5	31	-0.6	51	10.6	71	21.7	91.4	33
-45	-42.8	11.5	-11.4	31.1	-0.5	51.5	10.8	71.5	21.9	91.5	33.1
-40	-40	12	-11.1	31.5	-0.3	51.8	11	71.6	22	92	33.3
-35	-37.2	12.2	-11	32	0	52	11.1	72	22.2	92.3	33.5
-31	-35	12.5	-10.8	32.5	0.3	52.5	11.4	72.5	22.5	92.5	33.6
-30	-34.4	13	-10.6	32.9	0.5	52.7	11.5	73	22.8	93	33.9
-25	-31.7	13.1	-10.5	33	0.6	53	11.7	73.4	23	93.2	34
-22	-30	13.5	-10.3	33.5	0.8	53.5	11.9	73.5	23.1	93.5	34.2
-20	-28.9	14	-10	33.8	1	53.6	12	74	23.3	94	34.4
-15	-26.1	14.5	-9.7	34	1.1	54	12.2	74.3	23.5	94.1	34.5
-13	-25	14.9	-9.5	34.5	1.4	54.5	12.5	74.5	23.6	94.5	34.7
-10	-23.3	15	-9.4	34.7	1.5	55	12.8	75	23.9	95	35
-9.4	-23	15.5	-9.2	35	1.7	55.4	13	75.2	24	95.5	35.3
-9	-22.8	15.8	-9	35.5	1.9	55.5	13.1	75.5	24.2	95.9	35.5
-8	-22.2	16	-8.9	35.6	2	56	13.3	76	24.4	96	35.6
-7.6	-22	16.5	-8.6	36	2.2	56.3	13.5	76.1	24.5	96.5	35.8
-7	-21.7	16.7	-8.5	36.5	2.5	56.5	13.6	76.5	24.7	96.8	36
-6	-21.1	17	-8.3	37	2.8	57	13.9	77	25	97	36.1
-5.8	-21	17.5	-8.1	37.4	3	57.2	14	77.5	25.3	97.5	36.4
-5	-20.6	17.6	-8	37.5	3.1	57.5	14.2	77.9	25.5	97.7	36.5
-4	-20	18	-7.8	38	3.3	58	14.4	78	25.6	98	36.7
-3	-19.4	18.5	-7.5	38.3	3.5	58.1	14.5	78.5	25.8	98.5	36.9
-2.2	-19	19	-7.2	38.5	3.6	58.5	14.7	78.8	26	98.6	37
-2	-18.9	19.4	-7	39	3.9	59	15	79	26.1	99	37.2
-1	-18.3	19.5	-6.9	39.2	4	59.5	15.3	79.5	26.4	99.5	37.5
-0.4	-18			39.5	4.2	59.9	15.5	79.7	26.5		

Use of the table: corresponding degrees on the Fahrenheit and Celsius scales are shown, where, for example, 32 °F = 0 °C, and 212 °F = 100 °C.
The degree Celsius has been converted to the degree Fahrenheit by multiplying by 9, dividing by 5 and adding 32. The degree Fahrenheit has been converted to the degree Celsius by subtracting 32, multiplying by 5 and dividing by 9.

°F	°C	°F	°C	°F	°C	°F	°C	°F	°C	°F	°C
100	37.8	120	48.9	140	60	160	71.1	200	93.3	240	115.6
100.4	38	120.2	49	140.5	60.3	161	71.7	201	93.9	245	118.3
100.5	38.1	120.5	49.2	140.9	60.5	161.6	72	201.2	94	248	120
101	38.3	121	49.4	141	60.6	162	72.2	202	94.4	250	121.1
101.3	38.5	121.1	49.5	141.5	60.8	163	72.8	203	95	255	123.9
101.5	38.6	121.5	49.7	141.8	61	163.4	73	204	95.6	257	125
102	38.9	122	50	142	61.1	164	73.3	204.8	96	260	126.7
102.2	39	122.5	50.3	142.5	61.4	165	73.9	205	96.1	265	129.4
102.5	39.2	122.9	50.5	142.7	61.5	165.2	74	206	96.7	266	130
103	39.4	123	50.6	143	61.7	166	74.4	206.6	97	270	132.2
103.1	39.5	123.5	50.8	143.5	61.9	167	75	207	97.2	275	135
103.5	39.7	123.8	51	143.6	62	168	75.6	208	97.8	280	137.8
104	40	124	51.1	144	62.2	168.8	76	208.4	98	284	140
104.5	40.3	124.5	51.4	144.5	62.5	169	76.1	209	98.3	285	140.6
104.9	40.5	124.7	51.5	145	62.8	170	76.7	210	98.9	290	143.3
105	40.6	125	51.7	145.4	63	170.6	77	210.2	99	293	145
105.5	40.8	125.5	51.9	145.5	63.1	171	77.2	211	99.4	295	146.1
105.8	41	125.6	52	146	63.3	172	77.8	212	100	300	148.9
106	41.1	126	52.2	146.3	63.5	172.4	78	213	100.6	302	150
106.5	41.4	126.5	52.5	146.5	63.6	173	78.3	213.8	101	305	151.7
106.7	41.5	127	52.8	147	63.9	174	78.9	214	101.1	310	154.4
107	41.7	127.4	53	147.2	64	174.2	79	215	101.7	311	155
107.5	41.9	127.5	53.1	147.5	64.2	175	79.4	215.6	102	315	157.2
107.6	42	128	53.3	148	64.4	176	80	216	102.2	320	160
108	42.2	128.3	53.5	148.1	64.5	177	80.6	217	102.8	325	162.8
108.5	42.5	128.5	53.6	148.5	64.7	177.8	81	217.4	103	329	165
109	42.8	129	53.9	149	65	178	81.1	218	103.3	330	165.6
109.4	43	129.2	54	149.5	65.3	179	81.7	219	103.9	335	168.3
109.5	43.1	129.5	54.2	149.9	65.5	179.6	82	219.2	104	338	170
110	43.3	130	54.4	150	65.6	180	82.2	220	104.4	340	171.1
110.3	43.5	130.1	54.5	150.5	65.8	181	82.8	221	105	345	173.9
110.5	43.6	130.5	54.7	150.8	66	181.4	83	222	105.6	347	175
111	43.9	131	55	151	66.1	182	83.3	222.8	106	350	176.7
111.2	44	131.5	55.3	151.5	66.4	183	83.9	223	106.1	355	179.4
111.5	44.2	131.9	55.5	151.7	66.5	183.2	84	224	106.7	356	180
112	44.4	132	55.6	152	66.7	184	84.4	224.6	107	360	182.2
112.1	44.5	132.5	55.8	152.5	66.9	185	85	225	107.2	365	185
112.5	44.7	132.8	56	152.6	67	186	85.6	226	107.8	370	187.8
113	45	133	56.1	153	67.2	186.8	86	226.4	108	374	190
113.5	45.3	133.5	56.4	153.5	67.5	187	86.1	227	108.3	375	190.6
113.9	45.5	133.7	56.5	154	67.8	188	86.7	228	108.9	380	193.3
114	45.6	134	56.7	154.4	68	188.6	87	228.2	109	383	195
114.5	45.8	134.5	56.9	154.5	68.1	189	87.2	229	109.4	385	196.1
114.8	46	134.6	57	155	68.3	190	87.8	230	110	390	198.9
115	46.1	135	57.2	155.3	68.5	190.4	88	231	110.6	392	200
115.5	46.4	135.5	57.5	155.5	68.6	191	88.3	231.8	111	395	201.7
115.7	46.5	136	57.8	156	68.9	192	88.9	232	111.1	400	204.4
116	46.7	136.4	58	156.2	69	192.2	89	233	111.7	450	232.2
116.5	46.9	136.5	58.1	156.5	69.2	193	89.4	233.6	112	482	250
116.6	47	137	58.3	157	69.4	194	90	234	112.2	500	260
117	47.2	137.3	58.5	157.1	69.5	195	90.6	235	112.8	572	300
117.5	47.5	137.5	58.6	157.5	69.7	195.8	91	235.4	113	600	315.6
118	47.8	138	58.9	158	70	196	91.1	236	113.3	700	371.1
118.4	48	138.2	59	158.5	70.3	197	91.7	237	113.9	752	400
118.5	48.1	138.5	59.2	158.9	70.5	197.6	92	237.2	114	932	500
119	48.3	139	59.4	159	70.6	198	92.2	238	114.4	1000	537.8
119.3	48.5	139.1	59.5	159.5	70.8	199	92.8	239	115	1832	1000
119.5	48.6	139.5	59.7	159.8	71	199.4	93			2000	1093.3

Fractions to Decimals

Fraction	Decimal equivalent	Fraction	Decimal equivalent
1/2	0.5	1/37	0.027 027
1/3	0.333 333	1/38	0.026 316
1/4	0.25	1/39	0.025 641
1/5	0.2	1/40	0.025
1/6	0.166 667	1/41	0.024 390
1/7	0.142 857	1/42	0.023 810
1/8	0.125	1/43	0.023 256
1/9	0.111 111	1/44	0.022 727
1/10	0.1	1/45	0.022 222
1/11	0.090 909	1/46	0.021 739
1/12	0.083 333	1/47	0.021 277
1/13	0.076 923	1/48	0.020 833
1/14	0.071 429	1/49	0.020 408
1/15	0.066 667	1/50	0.02
1/16	0.062 5	1/51	0.019 608
1/17	0.058 824	1/52	0.019 231
1/18	0.055 556	1/53	0.018 868
1/19	0.052 632	1/54	0.018 519
1/20	0.05	1/55	0.018 182
1/21	0.047 619	1/56	0.017 857
1/22	0.045 455	1/57	0.017 544
1/23	0.043 478	1/58	0.017 241
1/24	0.041 667	1/59	0.016 949
1/25	0.04	1/60	0.016 667
1/26	0.038 462	1/61	0.016 393
1/27	0.037 037	1/62	0.016 129
1/28	0.035 714	1/63	0.015 873
1/29	0.034 483	1/64	0.015 625
1/30	0.033 333	1/65	0.015 385
1/31	0.032 258	1/66	0.015 152
1/32	0.031 25	1/67	0.014 925
1/33	0.030 303	1/68	0.014 706
1/34	0.029 412	1/69	0.014 493
1/35	0.028 571	1/70	0.014 286
1/36	0.027 778		

Fractions 3rds	6ths	12ths	24ths	Decimal equivalent
			1	0.041 667
		1	2	0.083 333
			3	0.125
	1	2	4	0.166 667
			5	0.208 333
		3	6	0.25
			7	0.291 667
1	2	4	8	0.333 333
			9	0.375
		5	10	0.416 667
			11	0.458 333
	3	6	12	0.5
			13	0.541 667
		7	14	0.583 333
			15	0.625
2	4	8	16	0.666 667
			17	0.708 333
		9	18	0.75
			19	0.791 667
	5	10	20	0.833 333
			21	0.875
		11	22	0.916 667
			23	0.958 333
3	6	12	24	1

Fractions 1/2's	1/4's	8ths	16ths	32nds	64ths	Decimal equivalent (all figures are exact)
					1	0.015 625
				1	2	0.031 25
					3	0.046 875
			1	2	4	0.062 5
					5	0.078 125
				3	6	0.093 75
					7	0.109 375
		1	2	4	8	0.125
					9	0.140 625
				5	10	0.156 25
					11	0.171 875
			3	6	12	0.187 5
					13	0.203 125
				7	14	0.218 75
					15	0.234 375
	1	2	4	8	16	0.25
					17	0.265 625
				9	18	0.281 25
					19	0.296 875
			5	10	20	0.312 5
					21	0.328 125
				11	22	0.343 75
					23	0.359 375
		3	6	12	24	0.375
					25	0.390 625
				13	26	0.406 25
					27	0.421 875
			7	14	28	0.437 5
					29	0.453 125
				15	30	0.468 75
					31	0.484 375
1	2	4	8	16	32	0.5
					33	0.515 625
				17	34	0.531 25
					35	0.546 875
			9	18	36	0.562 5
					37	0.578 125
				19	38	0.593 75
					39	0.609 375
	5		10	20	40	0.625
					41	0.640 625
				21	42	0.656 25
					43	0.671 875
			11	22	44	0.687 5
					45	0.703 125
				23	46	0.718 75
					47	0.734 375
	3	6	12	24	48	0.75
					49	0.765 625
				25	50	0.781 25
					51	0.796 875
			13	26	52	0.812 5
					53	0.828 125
				27	54	0.843 75
					55	0.859 375
		7	14	28	56	0.875
					57	0.890 625
				29	58	0.906 25
					59	0.921 875
			15	30	60	0.937 5
					61	0.953 125
				31	62	0.968 75
					63	0.984 375
2	4	8	16	32	64	1

Special measurements

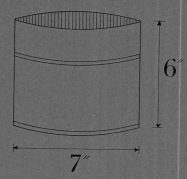

6″

7″

Queen Anne's Wine Gallon

- introduced to clarify duties payable, and now the United States liquid gallon

'And to the End the Contents of the Wine Gallon, whereby the Duties hereby granted are to be levied, may be ascertained and known to all her Majesty's subjects, and that all Disputes and Controversies touching the Wine Measures, according to which any Customs, Subsidies, or other Duties, are, from and after the first Day of May one thousand seven hundred and seven, to be paid or payable to her Majesty, her Heirs or Successors, may be settled, Be it further enacted and declared by the Authority aforesaid That any round Vessel (commonly called a Cylinder) having an even Bottom, and being seven Inches Diameter throughout, and six Inches deep from the Top of the Inside to the Bottom, or any Vessel containing two hundred thirty-one cubical Inches, and no more, shall be deemed and taken to be a lawful Wine Gallon; and it is hereby declared, That two hundred fifty-two Gallons, consisting each of two hundred thirty-one cubical Inches, shall be deemed a Ton of Wine, and that one hundred twenty-six such Gallons shall be deemed a Butt or Pipe of Wine, and that sixty-three such Gallons shall be deemed an Hogshead of Wine.'

(An Act for continuing several Subsidies, Impositions, and Duties, and for making Provisions therein mentioned to raise Money by Way of Loan for the Service of the War, and other her Majesty's necessary and important Occasions, and for ascertaining the Wine Measure, A.D. 1706, Chapter 27)

Note: in fact, the cylinder specified contains approximately 230.907 cubic inches, using the accurate value of π; 231 cubic inches is a rounded value using π equal to $3\frac{1}{7}$ (3.142 857 . . .) in place of 3.141 592 . . .

Space and time

Space

Measures

Newton's law of gravity: $F = -G \, m_1 m_2 / r^2$
where F is the force exerted by the masses m_1 and m_2 at a distance apart of r,
and G = gravitational constant = $6.672\,0 \times 10^{-11}$ Nm^2/kg^2
Astronomical unit (AU) = mean sun to earth distance
= 149.597 87 million kilometres (1.495 978 7 $\times 10^{11}$ m)
= approximately 92.956 million miles
The above is the international value.
Parsec (pc or psc*) = the distance at which 1 astronomical unit (AU) subtends
an angle of 1 second of arc
= 206 265 AU
= approximately 3.085 68 $\times 10^{13}$ km = approximately 1.917 $\times 10^{13}$ miles

Light-year (ly) = approximate distance travelled by light in 1 year
= 9.460 53 $\times 10^{12}$ km = 5.878 $\times 10^{12}$ miles
Light-second = 2.997 9 $\times 10^5$ km or about 300 000 km (186 286 mi)
Light-minute = 1.798 8 $\times 10^7$ km or about 18 000 000 km (11 177 000 mi)
Light-hour = 1.079 3 $\times 10^9$ km or about 1 079 million km (671 million mi)

The universe

The limit of the observable universe is about 1.2 $\times 10^{23}$ km
(1.2 $\times 10^{10}$ light-years). The mass of the observable universe is about 10^{23} solar
masses or 10^{50} tonnes.

The furthest quasars are about 1.2 $\times 10^{23}$ km away (about 12 000 mn light-
years) at about the edge of the observable universe.
The nearest star to the earth, other than the sun, is Proxima Centauri which is
4.3 light-years away (4 $\times 10^{13}$ km).

The solar system

	Distance from the sun			Radius (equatorial)			Mass				Gravity	
	in AU	in million miles	in million kilometres	relative to earth (=1)	miles ('000)	km ('000)	relative to earth (=1)	UK tons (× 10²¹ or US billion trillion)	kilograms (× 10²⁴ or US trillion trillion)		relative to earth (=1)	in metres per second squared
Sun	0	0	0	109	432	696	333 000	1 960 000	1 990 000		28	274
Mercury	0.387	36	58	0.38	1.5	2.4	0.056	0.33	0.33		0.38	3.7
Venus	0.723	67	108	0.95	3.8	6.1	0.81	4.80	4.87		0.92	9.0
Earth	1	93[b]	150[b]	1	4.0	6.4	1	5.88	5.98		1	9.8
Moon	1	93	150	0.27	1.1	1.7	0.012	0.071	0.073		0.16	1.6
Mars	1.523	142	228	0.53	2.1	3.4	0.107	0.63	0.64		0.38	3.7
Jupiter	5.203	483	778	11.2	44.4	71.3	318	1 870	1 900		2.69	26.4
Saturn	9.539	887	1 427	9.42	37.5	60.1	95.1	559	568		1.16	11.4
Uranus	19.18	1 780	2 870	3.84	15.3	24.5	14.5	85.5	86.9		0.94	9.2
Neptune	30.06	2 795	4 497	3.93	15.6	25.1	17.2	101	103		1.2	11.8
Pluto	39.44	3 670	5 900	0.2[a]	0.8[a]	1.2[a]	0.17[a]	1[a]	1[a]		0.43[a]	4.2[a]

[a] Approximate.   [b] Or 8.3 light-minutes. Average distance; for the earth the perihelion distance (at the point nearest to the sun) is 147.1 $\times 10^6$ km = 91.4 $\times 10^6$ mi = 8.
light-minutes, and the aphelion distance (at the point farthest from the sun) is 153.1 $\times 10^6$ km = 95.1 $\times 10^6$ mi = 8.5 light-minutes.

Solar energy
The photon energy from the sun's radiation is mainly in the wavelength range
300–2 700 nanometres (3–27 $\times 10^{-7}$ m) or 1 $\times 10^{15}$ to 1 $\times 10^{14}$ hertz; that is,
the visible light range and just into the infrared range (also see page 128).
Energy given out by the sun's radiation is equal to about 1 400 watts per square
metre of cross section through which the rays pass; this is called the 'solar
constant' = 1 400 W/m^2 = 1.4 kW/m^2.

Earth satellites

Moon

Average distance of the moon from the earth is
384 000 kilometres = 239 000 miles = 1.28 light-seconds.
At the mean perigee (nearest point) the distance is 363 300 km = 225 700 mi,
and at the mean apogee (farthest point) the distance is
405 500 km = 252 000 mi.

Man-made satellites

Above about 1 500 km (1 000 mi) a satellite is generally free of air drag. Above
about 36 000–40 000 km the gravitational effects of the sun and moon become
relatively more important.
A satellite at a height of about 35 860 km (22 280 mi) travels around the earth at
about the period of the earth's rotation (23 hours 56 minutes), and so hovers
over one place on earth (given a suitable orbit). The path of the orbit is about
265 000 km (165 000 mi). Communications satellites are usually at about this
height.

Some examples of orbit ranges for man-made satellites are
(showing perigee – shortest orbital distance from the earth, and apogee –
greatest orbital distance from the earth):

	perigee (km)	apogee (km)
reconnaissance	135	330
	166	319
	628	632
weather	677	904
	818	848
	1 092	1 104
navigation	895	1 149
	980	1 011
communications	35 051	36 525
	35 785	35 789
	35 800	35 800

Some International Telecommunications Union definitions concerning satelli
are:
Satellite: a body which revolves around another body of preponderant mass a
which has a motion primarily and permanently determined by the force of
attraction of that other body.
Geosynchronous satellite: an earth satellite whose period of revolution is equ
to the period of rotation of the earth about its axis.
Geostationary satellite: a geosynchronous satellite whose circular and direct
orbit lies in the plane of the earth's equator and which thus remains fixed relati
to the earth; by extension, a satellite which remains approximately fixed relati
to the earth.
Deep space: space at distances from the earth approximately equal to, or
greater than, the distance between the earth and the moon.

The earth

Radius:

	kilometres	miles
at equator	6 378	3 963
average	6 371	3 959
at poles	6 357	3 950

Circumference: approximately 40 million metres = 40 000 kilometres
= 25 000 miles

Length of 1 degree of latitude or longitude (1/360 of circumference):

	kilometres	miles	nautical miles (international)
Latitude			
at 0° latitude (equator)	110.57	68.70	59.70
at 45° latitude	111.13	69.05	60.01
at 90° latitude (poles)	111.70	69.41	60.31
Longitude			
at latitude of:			
0	111.32	69.17	60.11
5	110.90	68.91	59.88
10	109.64	68.13	59.20
15	107.55	66.83	58.07
20	104.65	65.03	56.51
25	100.95	62.73	54.51
30	96.49	59.60	52.10
35	91.29	56.72	49.29
40	85.40	53.06	46.11
45	78.85	48.99	42.58
50	71.70	44.55	38.71
55	64.00	39.77	34.56
60	55.80	34.67	30.13
65	47.18	29.31	25.47
70	38.19	23.73	20.62
75	28.90	17.96	15.61
80	19.39	12.05	10.47
85	9.74	6.05	5.26
90	0.00	0.00	0.00

Velocities

Average speed in orbit around the sun = 29.78 km/s = 18.5 mile/s = 66 600 miles per hour
Escape speed at surface = 11.2 km/s = 7.0 mile/s = 25 200 miles per hour
Rotational speed at equator = 0.465 km/s = 0.29 mile/s
= 1 670 km per hour = 1 040 miles per hour

Structure

Volume of earth = 1.08×10^{21} m³ = 1.42×10^{21} yd³
Density of earth = 5 520 kg/m³ = relative density of 5.5

Greatest height: Mt Everest = 8 848 m = 29 028 ft
Greatest depth: Marianas trench = 11 030 m = 35 960 ft

Earthquake measurement

Richter scale

The Richter scale defines the magnitude of an earthquake in terms of the energy released; this has usually been measured by means of a seismometer which determines the amplitude of the seismic waves resulting from an earthquake. The Richter scale was first formulated in 1935 and there have been subsequent revisions; the main types are:
Local magnitude scale (M_L)
Surface-wave magnitude scale (M_S)
Body-wave magnitude scale (M_b)
Of these, the surface-wave scale has been the most generally used.

One estimate of the energy equivalents of the Richter scale, showing also the equivalent in terms of explosions, is as follows:

Scale	Joules [a]	Explosion equivalent TNT terms [b]	Nuclear weapon terms [c]
0 [d]	7.9×10^2	175 mg	
1	6.0×10^4	13 g	
2	4.0×10^6	0.89 kg	
3	2.4×10^8	53 kg	
4	1.3×10^{10}	3 tons	
5 [e]	6.3×10^{11}	140 tons	
6 [f]	2.7×10^{13}	6 kilotons	$\frac{1}{3}$ atomic bomb
7	1.1×10^{15}	240 kilotons	12 atomic bombs
8	3.7×10^{16}	$8\frac{1}{4}$ megatons	$\frac{1}{3}$ hydrogen bomb
9	1.1×10^{18}	250 megatons	13 hydrogen bombs
10	3.2×10^{19}	7 000 megatons	350 hydrogen bombs

[a] Using the approximate relationship $\log_{10}(J \times 10^7) = 9.9 + 1.9M - 0.024M^2$ where M is the scale number and J is the energy in joules. Other formulae used to give the energy relationship are: $\log_{10}(J \times 10^7) = 1.5 M + 11.8$ and $\log_{10}(J \times 10^7) = 2.4 M - 1.2$. [b] Using the standard that 1 kg of TNT produces 4.5×10^6 J. [c] Also see page 173 (weapons); one atomic bomb is equivalent to 6.3 on the Richter scale, and one hydrogen bomb to 8.2. [d] Approximately equivalent to the shock caused by an average man jumping from a table; negative values on the Richter scale are possible (for energy less than 7.9×10^2 J). [e] Potentially damaging to structures. [f] Potentially capable of general destruction; widespread damage is usually caused above magnitude 6.5.

Some examples of earthquake magnitudes are as follows:

	Richter scale (surface-wave or M_S scale) [a]
Scotland, Boxing Day 1979	4.5
San Francisco, Jan 1980	5.5
Greece, June 1978	6.5
Japan, June 1978	7.5
San Francisco, 1906	8.3
Chile, 1960	8.3
Alaska, 1964	8.4
Colombia, 1906	8.6
Krakatoa, 1883	9.9 (estimate)

[a] Another magnitude scale, the seismic moment scale (M_o) has been introduced in the late 1970s. This measures directly the energy of an earthquake in terms of the area of the fault, the average displacement on the fault, and the shear strength of the faulted rock. With this new scale, the Chile 1960 earthquake is rated 9.5, the Alaska 1964 earthquake is rated 9.2, and the Colombia 1906 earthquake is rated 8.8.

The frequency of occurrence of large earthquakes throughout the world is approximately as follows:

Richter scale	Number of earthquakes per year
6.0–6.9	266
7.0–7.9	18
8.0–8.9	$1\frac{1}{2}$

Mercalli scale

The effect of any earthquake depends not only on its magnitude as measured by the Richter scale, but also on the nearness of the epicentre to centres of population and on other factors such as the depth of the epicentre. The Mercalli scale and its modifications measure earthquakes in terms of the effect they have at any particular point. The following is the intensity Mercalli scale (MSK 1964 modification):

Scale	Effect (abbreviated description)
I	Not noticeable
II	Scarcely noticeable
III	Partially observed only
IV	Widely observed, rattles windows and doors
V	Sleeping people awakened
VI	Frightening
VII	Damage to buildings
VIII	Some panic and destruction of buildings
IX	General panic and general damage to buildings
X	General destruction of buildings
XI	Catastrophe – severe damage and distortion of ground
XII	Landscape changes, and virtually all structures are destroyed

The earth

Wind speed

Beaufort scale

The Beaufort scale is related to wind speed by the formula $v = kN^{1\frac{1}{2}}$
where v = average wind speed
      N = Beaufort number
      k = 1.87 for miles per hour, 3.0 for kilometres per hour, and 0.83 for
           metres per second

General scale

Force	Description	Conditions (abbreviated):		Equivalent speed at 10 metres height		
		on land	at sea	knots	miles per hour	metres per second
0	Calm	Smoke rises vertically	Sea like a mirror	less than 1	less than 1	0.0–0.2
1	Light air	Smoke drifts	Ripples	1–3	1–3	0.3–1.5
2	Light breeze	Leaves rustle	Small wavelets	4–6	4–7	1.7–3.3
3	Gentle breeze	Wind extends light flag	Large wavelets, crests break	7–10	8–12	3.4–5.4
4	Moderate breeze	Raises paper and dust	Small waves, some white horses	11–16	13–18	5.5–7.9
5	Fresh breeze	Small trees in leaf sway	Moderate waves, many white horses	17–21	19–24	8.0–10.7
6	Strong breeze	Large branches in motion	Large waves form, some spray	22–27	25–31	10.8–13.8
7	Near gale	Whole trees in motion	Sea heaps up, white foam streaks	28–33	32–38	13.9–17.1
8	Gale	Breaks twigs off trees	Moderately high waves, well-marked foam streaks	34–40	39–46	17.2–20.7
9	Strong gale	Slight structural damage	High waves, crests start to tumble over	41–47	47–54	20.8–24.4
10	Storm	Trees uprooted, considerable structural damage	Very high waves, white sea tumbles	48–55	55–63	24.5–28.4
11	Violent storm	Very rarely experienced, widespread damage	Exceptionally high waves, edges of wave crests blown to froth	56–63	64–72	28.5–32.6
12	Hurricane	—	Sea completely white with driving spray	64 & over	73 & over	32.7–over

Revised scale: as used in the climatological summaries of the WMO (World Meteorological Organisation) Historical Sea Surface Temperature Data Project

Force	Metres per second: interval	mean	Force	Metres per second: interval	mean	Force	Metres per second: interval	mean	Force	Metres per second: interval	mean
0	0–1.3	0.8	4	6.7–8.9	7.8	8	16.5–19.2	17.8	12	30.1 and over	32.2
1	1.4–2.7	2.0	5	9.0–11.3	10.2	9	19.3–22.4	20.8			
2	2.8–4.5	3.6	6	11.4–13.8	12.6	10	22.5–26.0	24.2			
3	4.6–6.6	5.6	7	13.9–16.4	15.1	11	26.1–30.0	28.0			

Wave height

The approximate height of average waves for different strengths of wind is shown in the following table, which indicates for each wind strength the average wave height and the likely maximum wave height:

Beaufort scale force	Height of waves Feet average	maximum	Metres average	maximum
0	0	0	0	0
1	$\frac{1}{4}$	$\frac{1}{4}$	0.1	0.1
2	$\frac{1}{2}$	1	0.2	0.3
3	2	3	0.6	1
4	$3\frac{1}{2}$	5	1	$1\frac{1}{2}$
5	6	$8\frac{1}{2}$	2	$2\frac{1}{2}$
6	$9\frac{1}{2}$	13	3	4
7	$13\frac{1}{2}$	19	4	$5\frac{1}{2}$
8	18	25	$5\frac{1}{2}$	$7\frac{1}{2}$
9	23	32	7	10
10	29	41	9	$12\frac{1}{2}$
11	37	52	$11\frac{1}{2}$	16
12	over 45 [a]		over 14 [a]	

[a] For the North Sea, wave heights can reach 55–100 ft (17–30 m); in general, the maximum height is reached once in 50 years (100 feet is a '50 year wave')

Atmosphere

The normal composition of clean, dry atmospheric air at sea level is shown below:

Constituent gas	Content, % by volume
Nitrogen (N_2)	78.084
Oxygen (O_2)	20.947 6
Argon (Ar)	0.934
Carbon dioxide (CO_2)	0.033
Neon (Ne)	0.001 818
Helium (He)	0.000 524
Krypton (Kr)	0.000 114
Xenon (Xe)	0.000 008 7
Hydrogen (H_2)	0.000 05
Methane (CH_4)	0.000 2
Nitrous oxide (N_2O)	0.000 05
Ozone (O_3)	Summer: 0 to 0.000 007
	Winter: 0 to 0.000 002
Sulphur dioxide (SO_2)	0 to 0.000 1
Nitrogen dioxide (NO_2)	0 to 0.000 002
Ammonia (NH_3)	0 to trace
Carbon monoxide (CO)	0 to trace
Iodine (I_2)	0 to 0.000 001

The earth

Some of the sea-level values of the ICAO Standard Atmosphere are:

	Metric	UK (imperial) equivalent
Temperature	288.15 K = 15°C	518.67°R = 59 °F
Pressure	1 013.25 millibars	2 116.2 lbf/ft²
Gravitational acceleration	9.806 65 m/s²	32.174 ft/s²
Density	1.225 0 kg/m³	0.076 474 lb/ft³
Viscosity:		
dynamic	$1.789\,4 \times 10^{-5}$ kg m^{-1} s^{-1}	$1.202\,4 \times 10^{-5}$ lb ft^{-1} s^{-1}
kinematic	$1.460\,7 \times 10^{-5}$ m²/s	$1.572\,3 \times 10^{-4}$ ft²/s
Particle speed	458.94 m/s	1 505.7 ft/s
Speed of sound	340.294 m/s	1 116.45 ft/s

Upper levels of atmosphere. The troposphere is the layer of air extending upwards about 10–12 km ($6\frac{1}{2}$–$7\frac{1}{2}$ mi), in which temperature gradually falls with height. The stratosphere is the layer above the troposphere and in that layer the temperature remains constant. The tropopause is the interface between the troposphere and stratosphere; its height is about 10–12 km and temperature about 210 K (−60°C).

Air density

The following tables show the variation in air density with varying air pressure and temperature, and with varying altitude.

Density (kg/m³) for different pressures and temperatures (in typical laboratory air with 50% humidity)

Air pressure (kPa = 10 mb)	Air temperature (°C)		
	10 kg/m³	20 kg/m³	30 kg/m³
95	1.167	1.124	1.083
96	1.179	1.136	1.094
97	1.191	1.148	1.106
98	1.203	1.160	1.117
99	1.216	1.172	1.129
100	1.228	1.184	1.140
101	1.240	1.196	1.152
102	1.253	1.207	1.163
103	1.265	1.219	1.175
104	1.277	1.231	1.186
105	1.290	1.243	1.198

Density (kg/m³) and pressure (kPa = 10 mb) for varying altitude (for a standard atmosphere)

Altitude	Pressure (kPa)	Density (kg/m³)
metres		
−250	104.3	1.255
−100	102.5	1.237
−50	101.9	1.231
0 (sea level)	101.3	1.225
50	100.7	1.219
100	100.1	1.213
250	98.4	1.196
500	95.5	1.167
750 ($\frac{3}{4}$ km)	92.6	1.139
kilometres		
1	89.9	1.112
$2\frac{1}{2}$	74.7	0.957
5	54.0	0.736
$7\frac{1}{2}$	38.3	0.557
10	26.5	0.414
20	5.5	0.089
30	1.2	0.018
40	0.3	0.004
50	0.1	0.001

Temperature

Temperature intervals: kelvin (K) = degree Celsius (°C) or centigrade
degree Rankine (°R) = degree Fahrenheit (°F)
Temperature scales: the thermodynamic scales of kelvin and Rankine are fixed such that the zero on the scale is the theoretical zero of temperature (absolute zero); this is the level at which any gas would theoretically be reduced to zero volume − since gases at constant pressure lose approximately 1/273 of their volume at 0 °C for each fall of 1 °C in their temperature.
Where K, °C, °R, °F refer to temperatures on their scales:

°C = K − 273.15	K = °C + 273.15
°F = °R − 459.67	°R = °F + 459.67
°C = $\frac{5}{9}$(°F − 32)	°F = $\frac{9}{5}$°C + 32
K = $\frac{5}{9}$°R	°R = $\frac{9}{5}$K

Some notable temperatures:

	°C	°F	K	°R
Theoretical zero	−273.15	−459.67	0	0
Space	−270	−454	3	5
Ice point of water	0	32	273.15	491.67
Triple point of water	0.01	32.02	273.16	491.69
Atmosphere:				
FAO reference	10	50	283.15	509.67
ICAO	15	59	288.15	518.67
Fine summer day (UK)	20	68	293.15	527.67
Blood heat, man	37	98.6	310.15	558.27
Boiling point of water	100	212	373.15	671.67
White heat (approx.)	1 300	2 370	1 570	2 830

Standard temperature and pressure (stp) is 0°C and 1.013 25 bar.

Curie point (or Curie temperature) = the temperature at which ferromagnetic material loses its magnetism (becomes paramagnetic); this varies according to the mixture of metals.

Degree days

A degree day usually means a period of 24 hours during which the outside temperature is one degree below an accepted base. In the United Kingdom the base outside temperature is 15.5 °C (60 °F approx); this is considered consistent with an inside temperature of 18.3 °C (65 °F) − comfortable for normal domestic purposes − the difference being made up by other heat sources such as people, lights, cooking appliances etc. In New York the base used is 69 °F (20.6 °C).
Hence, for the United Kingdom one degree day equals a 24 hour period during which the outside temperature is at an average of 14.5 °C compared with the base of 15.5 °C. Official figures are published for the United Kingdom for different regions on a monthly basis. For example, for December 1979, the number of degree days was 292 for South East England − or an average of 9.4 degrees below the base per day (the month being 31 days). This is equivalent to a temperature of about 6 °C, compared with a usual average daily temperature for December of about 5°C.

Surface area

	square kilometres (million)	square miles (million)		square kilometres (million)	square miles (million)
The earth	510.07	196.94	*Main land areas*		
of which: water	361.64	139.63	Asia	44.03	17.00
land	148.43	57.31	Africa	30.26	11.68
Main seas			America: north	24.19	9.34
Pacific	166.24	64.19	south	17.82	6.88
Atlantic	86.56	33.42	Antarctica	13.21	5.10
Indian	73.43	28.35	Europe	10.40	4.02
Arctic	9.49	3.66	Australia	7.69	2.97

The earth

Gravity variation

The internationally agreed standard value for gravity on earth (g_n), 9.806 65 metres per second per second, is the acceleration of a freely falling body on to the rotating earth; it is the value which approximates to that applying at 45° latitude. Actual gravity values vary according to latitude, altitude, etc. For Greenwich the approximate value is 9.811 88 m/s² (local gravity or g_L). Variations need to be allowed for where accuracy is required; for example, for barometers or 'weighing' machines (which measure the effect of gravitational force on mass).

The following table gives a standard set of variations by latitude and altitude (height above sea level); actual gravities will vary according to local geological conditions, so this table is approximate.

Latitude (degrees)	Altitude (metres)					
	0	500	1000	10000	20000	30000
	m/s²	m/s²	m/s²	m/s²	m/s²	m/s²
0	9.7805	9.7789	9.7774	9.7496	9.7188	9.6879
5	9.7809	9.7793	9.7778	9.7500	9.7192	9.6883
10	9.7820	9.7805	9.7790	9.7512	9.7203	9.6895
15	9.7840	9.7824	9.7809	9.7531	9.7222	9.6914
20	9.7865	9.7850	9.7835	9.7557	9.7248	9.6940
25	9.7897	9.7882	9.7866	9.7589	9.7280	9.6971
30	9.7934	9.7919	9.7903	9.7626	9.7317	9.7008
35	9.7975	9.7960	9.7944	9.7666	9.7358	9.7049
40	9.8018	9.8003	9.7987	9.7709	9.7401	9.7092
41	9.8027	9.8011	9.7996	9.7718	9.7410	9.7101
42	9.8036	9.8020	9.8005	9.7727	9.7419	9.7110
43	9.8045	9.8029	9.8014	9.7736	9.7428	9.7119
44	9.8054	9.8038	9.8023	9.7745	9.7437	9.7128
45	9.8063	9.8047	9.8032	9.7754	9.7446	9.7137
46	9.8072	9.8056	9.8041	9.7763	9.7455	9.7146
47	9.8081	9.8066	9.8050	9.7772	9.7464	9.7155
48	9.8090	9.8075	9.8059	9.7781	9.7473	9.7164
49	9.8099	9.8083	9.8068	9.7790	9.7482	9.7173
50	9.8108	9.8092	9.8077	9.7799	9.7491	9.7182
51	9.8117	9.8101	9.8086	9.7808	9.7499	9.7191
52	9.8125	9.8110	9.8095	9.7817	9.7508	9.7200
53	9.8134	9.8119	9.8103	9.7826	9.7517	9.7208
54	9.8143	9.8127	9.8112	9.7834	9.7526	9.7217
55	9.8151	9.8136	9.8120	9.7843	9.7534	9.7226
60	9.8192	9.8177	9.8161	9.7884	9.7575	9.7266
65	9.8230	9.8214	9.8199	9.7921	9.7613	9.7304
70	9.8262	9.8246	9.8231	9.7953	9.7644	9.7336
75	9.8287	9.8272	9.8257	9.7979	9.7670	9.7362
80	9.8307	9.8291	9.8276	9.7998	9.7689	9.7381
85	9.8318	9.8303	9.8287	9.8010	9.7701	9.7392
90	9.8322	9.8307	9.8291	9.8013	9.7705	9.7396

The % correction for divergence from standard gravity is then as follows:

Latitude (degrees)	Altitude (metres)					
	0	500	1000	10000	20000	30000
	%	%	%	%	%	%
0	−0.27	−0.28	−0.30	−0.58	−0.90	−1.21
5	−0.26	−0.28	−0.29	−0.58	−0.89	−1.21
10	−0.25	−0.27	−0.28	−0.57	−0.88	−1.19
15	−0.23	−0.25	−0.26	−0.55	−0.86	−1.18
20	−0.21	−0.22	−0.24	−0.52	−0.83	−1.15
25	−0.17	−0.19	−0.20	−0.49	−0.80	−1.12
30	−0.13	−0.15	−0.17	−0.45	−0.76	−1.08
35	−0.09	−0.11	−0.12	−0.41	−0.72	−1.04
40	−0.05	−0.07	−0.08	−0.36	−0.68	−0.99
41	−0.04	−0.06	−0.07	−0.36	−0.67	−0.98
42	−0.03	−0.05	−0.06	−0.35	−0.66	−0.98
43	−0.02	−0.04	−0.05	−0.34	−0.65	−0.97
44	−0.01	−0.03	−0.04	−0.33	−0.64	−0.96
45	0.00	−0.02	−0.04	−0.32	−0.63	−0.95
46	0.01	−0.01	−0.03	−0.31	−0.62	−0.94
47	0.01	0.00	−0.02	−0.30	−0.61	−0.93
48	0.02	0.01	−0.01	−0.29	−0.61	−0.92
49	0.03	0.02	0.00	−0.28	−0.60	−0.91
50	0.04	0.03	0.01	−0.27	−0.59	−0.90
51	0.05	0.04	0.02	−0.26	−0.58	−0.89
52	0.06	0.04	0.03	−0.25	−0.57	−0.88
53	0.07	0.05	0.04	−0.25	−0.56	−0.88
54	0.08	0.06	0.05	−0.24	−0.55	−0.87
55	0.09	0.07	0.06	−0.23	−0.54	−0.86
60	0.13	0.11	0.10	−0.19	−0.50	−0.82
65	0.17	0.15	0.13	−0.15	−0.46	−0.78
70	0.20	0.18	0.17	−0.12	−0.43	−0.75
75	0.23	0.21	0.19	−0.09	−0.40	−0.72
80	0.24	0.23	0.21	−0.07	−0.38	−0.70
85	0.26	0.24	0.23	−0.06	−0.37	−0.69
90	0.26	0.24	0.23	−0.05	−0.37	−0.68

Time

Universe and earth

The following is a broad outline of the main ages of the universe and the earth

Era, period and epoch	Years ago (year at beginning; all times are approximate)		Characteristics
Origin of the universe (estimates vary markedly)	20 000 000 000 to 10 000 000 000	$(2 \times 10^{10}$ or 20 000 million) $(1 \times 10^{10}$ or 10 000 million)	
Origin of the sun	5 000 000 000	$(5 \times 10^{9}$ or 5 000 million)	
Origin of the earth	4 600 000 000	$(4.6 \times 10^{9}$ or 4 600 million)	
Pre-Cambrian Eozoic	3 500 000 000	(3.5×10^{9})	First signs of fossilised microbes
Archaeozoic	2 500 000 000	(2.5×10^{9})	First signs of sponges and seaweeds
Proterozoic	1 500 000 000	(1.5×10^{9})	
Palaeozoic Cambrian	600 000 000	(6×10^{8})	First appearance of abundant fossils
Ordovician	500 000 000	(5×10^{8})	Vertebrates emerge
Silurian or Gothlandian	440 000 000	(4.4×10^{8})	Fishes emerge
Devonian	400 000 000	(4×10^{8})	Primitive plants emerge
Carboniferous	350 000 000	(3.5×10^{8})	Amphibians emerge
Permian	270 000 000	(2.7×10^{8})	Reptiles emerge
Mesozoic Triassic	225 000 000	(2.25×10^{8})	Seed plants emerge
Jurassic	180 000 000	(1.8×10^{8})	Age of dinosaurs
Cretaceous	135 000 000	(1.35×10^{8})	Flowering plants emerge; dinosaurs extinct at end of this period
Cenozoic Tertiary: Eocene	70 000 000	(7×10^{7})	Mammals emerge
Oligocene	40 000 000	(4×10^{7})	
Miocene	25 000 000	(2.5×10^{7})	
Pliocene	11 000 000	(1.1×10^{7})	
Quaternary: Pleistocene or Glacial	3 000 000	(3×10^{6})	Ice age; stone age man emerges
Holocene or Recent	10 000	(1×10^{4})	Modern man emerges

Time scales

Several time scales are in use which are distinct but for many purposes interchangeable; following are descriptions of the main time scales.

Universal time

Universal time (UT) is a time scale based on the rotation of the earth about its axis, and is directly related to the alternation of day and night. 1200 UT is mean noon on the Greenwich meridian. Time scales for civil use must not drift in the long term relative to UT. The universal time calculated directly from immediately observed sidereal time (based on the rotation of the earth) is denoted by UT0. For more precise work, UT0 is adjusted for observed polar motion and denoted by UT1; UT1 corrected for extrapolated seasonal variation in the rate of rotation of the earth is denoted by UT2.

UT is now known to be very slightly irregular and unpredictable, so that other time scales described below are normally used in very precise work, unless rotation of the earth is a factor – as for example in work by surveyors and astronomers.

The terms UT and universal time are sometimes used to mean UTC (for which see below).

Atomic time

Atomic time (TA) is any time scale formed by counting from some initial instant in SI seconds (that is, atomic seconds, as defined on page 14, which have been the definition of the second since 1967). International atomic time (TAI) is the atomic time scale that was recognized by the Conférence Générale des Poids et Mesures in 1971. It is formed by the Bureau International de l'Heure on the basis of atomic clock data contributed by establishments in many countries, and its unit is the SI second at sea level.

Coordinated universal time

Coordinated universal time (UTC) is the time scale that is made available by radio signals. It was introduced in its present form on January 1, 1972 and was designed to make both UT1 and TAI accessible with appropriate accuracy. UTC differs from TAI by a whole number of exact seconds and never differs from UT1 by more than 0.9 seconds. The relationship with UT1 is maintained by inserting or deleting a 'leap-second' in the UTC scale as the last second of a calendar month if astonomical observations show that one is needed. The decision to introduce a leap-second is taken by the Bureau Internationale de l'Heure and is announced at least eight weeks in advance.

The Conférence Générale des Poids et Mesures in 1975 recognised and recommended the use of UTC as the basis of national civil time scales.

Greenwich mean time

Greenwich mean time (GMT) was the original basis for UT; it now usually means UTC. GMT has been the basis of legal time in Great Britain since 1880; before 1925, 0000 GMT meant Greenwich noon, and since then 0000 GMT has meant Greenwich midnight.

Ephemeris time

Ephemeris time (ET) is a time scale determined from astronomical observations of the orbital motions of the earth, moon and planets in the solar system. Between 1960 and 1967 the second was defined in terms of ephemeris time, which is more uniform than UT1, but less precise and less accessible than TA. The ephemeris second was defined as the fraction 1/31 556 925.974 7 of the tropical year for 1900, January 0 at 12 h ET. It is equal to 1/86 400 part of a day of that tropical year, which is defined as equal to 365.242 198 78 days, decreasing at the rate of 0.000 006 14 days per century (about 400 million years ago there were about 400 days to the year). A tropical year is the time between two consecutive passages in the same direction of the sun through the earth's equatorial plane. ET is not in general use.

Time

Time units

10 nanoseconds	= 1 shake
1 000 nanoseconds	= 1 microsecond
1 000 microseconds	= 1 millisecond
864 milliseconds (10^{-5} day)	= 1 blink
1 000 milliseconds	= 1 second
60 seconds	= 1 minute (min)
3 600 seconds	= 1 hour (h)
60 minutes	= 1 hour
86 400 seconds	= 1 day (d)
1 440 minutes	= 1 day
24 hours	= 1 day
604 800 seconds	= 1 week
10 080 minutes	= 1 week
168 hours	= 1 week
7 days	= 1 week
28 days	= 1 lunar month
28–31 days	= 1 calendar month[a]
31 556 925 seconds (approx)	= 1 year
365 days	= 1 standard year
366 days	= 1 leap year
12 calendar months	= 1 calendar year
10 years	= 1 decade
25 years	= 1 generation
100 years	= 1 century
1 000 years	= 1 millennium
1 000 000 years	= 1 cron or aeon

[a]For calendar months in the Gregorian system, April, June, September and November have 30 days; all other months except February have 31 days. February has 28 days except in leap years, when it has 29.
For Christian years AD, a year is a leap year in the Gregorian calendar if its year number is divisible by 4 unless it is also divisible by 100 (ie, ends in 00); then it is only a leap year if divisible by 400.

Hourly time systems

24-hour	12-hour	Marine watches (bells)	24-hour	12-hour	Marine watches (bells)
	am			pm	
		Middle			Afternoon
0030	12.30	1	1230	12.30	1
0100	1.00	2	1300	1.00	2
0130	1.30	3	1330	1.30	3
0200	2.00	4	1400	2.00	4
0230	2.30	5	1430	2.30	5
0300	3.00	6	1500	3.00	6
0330	3.30	7	1530	3.30	7
0400	4.00	8	1600	4.00	8
		Morning			First dog
0430	4.30	1	1630	4.30	1
0500	5.00	2	1700	5.00	2
0530	5.30	3	1730	5.30	3
0600	6.00	4	1800	6.00	4
0630	6.30	5			Second dog
0700	7.00	6	1830	6.30	1
0730	7.30	7	1900	7.00	2
0800	8.00	8	1930	7.30	3
		Forenoon	2000	8.00	8
0830	8.30	1			First
0900	9.00	2	2030	8.30	1
0930	9.30	3	2100	9.00	2
1000	10.00	4	2130	9.30	3
1030	10.30	5	2200	10.00	4
1100	11.00	6	2230	10.30	5
1130	11.30	7	2300	11.00	6
1200	12.00	8	2330	11.30	7
	(noon)		2400	12.00	8
			= 0000	(midnight)	

Calendars

Roman, Julian and Gregorian calendars

The Roman calendar is usually taken as dating from 753 BC in terms of the Gregorian calendar, that being the date of the founding of Rome.
The Julian calendar system was established by Julius Caesar in the Roman year 707 (46 BC), the main feature being the insertion of an extra day every four years, to allow for the fact that every year has about $365\frac{1}{4}$ days, and not 365 days.

The Christian era numbering system was established about 525 AD (Roman year 1278). In this system the era begins with 1 AD, the preceding year being 1 BC; there is no year 0 in the chronological reckoning, so the first century (100 years) ended with December 31, 100 AD. According to this system, the century ends with the end of the year ending in 00, and not with the year ending in 99, so that the end of the 20th century would be December 31, 2000, and not December 31, 1999. That is the position for the Christian calendar; in general, common usage takes the position that the century ends with, for the above example, December 31, 1999, and that January 1, 2000 starts a new century – in the same way that common usage considers that the decade of the eighties started with January 1, 1980. For astronomical purposes, the common sense view is taken, with the year before 1 AD being the year 0, and the year before that the year −1. Hence the year 1 BC = 0, 2 BC = −1, 2001 BC = −2000, etc.

Gregorian calendar

The mean Julian calendar year was established as $365\frac{1}{4}$ days, whereas in fact the year is slightly less; using $365\frac{1}{4}$ days leads to an excess number of days amounting to about 3 days every 400 years. In 1582 Pope Gregory corrected this by establishing his calendar in which leap years occur in centurial years only where they are divisible by 400, instead of in every centurial year which was the position under the Julian calendar. Hence, leap years occur in the Gregorian calendar in 1600 and 2000, but not in 1700, 1800 and 1900, which were leap years under the Julian calendar. The reform consisted in changing October 5, 1582 to be October 15, 1582, that is by losing 10 days. The British government changed to the Gregorian calendar in 1752, changing September 3, 1752 to be September 14, 1752, a loss of 11 days (there having been an extra day lost after 1582 in the year 1700, which was a leap year for the Julian calendar but not for the Gregorian).
For changing from the Julian to the Gregorian calendar, 11 days should be added to the date from September 3, 1752 up to February 28, 1800; 12 days up to February 28, 1900, and 13 days up to February 28, 2100 (2000 being a leap year in both systems).

Julian period

The Julian period lasts 7980 years, being the common multiple of the 28 year solar cycle, 19 year lunar cycle, and 15 year cycle of indiction (a Roman accounting year). The Julian epoch began when all three cycles began together; this was established as BC 4713, January 1, being day 0, and the count of days from Greenwich noon on that day ($0^d 12^h$) is known as a Julian day number (JD).

Following are some Julian Day numbers (day commencing at Greenwich noon)

Julian period	Julian calendar	Julian Day number (January 1)	Gregorian calendar	Julian Day number (January 1)
1	4713 BC	0		
2713	2001 BC	99 0558		
4613	101 BC	168 4533		
4713	1 BC	172 1058		
4714	1 AD	172 1424		
4813	100 AD	175 1058		
6213	1500 AD	226 8933	1500 AD	226 8924
6613	1900 AD	241 5033	1900 AD	241 5021
6693	1980 AD	244 4253	1980 AD	244 4240
6713	2000 AD	245 1558	2000 AD	245 1545

Time

Approximate equivalents of years according to different calendars
(years beginning in 1980)

Christian	Iranian (Moslem solar)	Indian (Saka)	Ethiopian	Hebrew (origin varies)	Moslem (lunar)
1980	1359	1902	1973	5741	1401

Calendars used in various countries

Figures in brackets denote the number of days in that month

Gregorian	Iranian[b]	Indian[c]	Ethiopian[d]	Hebrew[e]	Moslem[a]
January					
February					
March	Favardin (31)	Chaitra (30)			
April	Ordibehesht (31)	Vaisakha (31)			
May	Khordad (31)	Jyaistha (31)			
June	Tir (31)	Asadha (31)			
July	Mordad (31)	Sravana (31)			
August	Sharivar (31)	Bhadra (31)			
September	Mehr (30)	Asvina (30)	Maskerem (30)	Tishri (30)	
October	Aban (30)	Kartika (30)	Tikimit (30)	Cheshvan[f] (29 or 30)	
November	Azar (30)	Agrahayana (30)	Hidar (30)	Kislev (29 or 30)	Muharram (30)
December	Dey (30)	Pausa (30)	Tahsas (30)	Tevet (30)	Saphar (29)
(January)	Bahman (30)	Magha (30)	Tir (30)	Shevat (30)	Rabia I (30)
(February)	Esfand (28 or 29)	Phalguna (30)	Yekatit (30)	Adar (29)	Rabia II (29)
(March)			Megabit (30)	Nissan (30)	Gamada I (30)
(April)			Miazia (30)	Iyyar (29)	Gamada II (29)
(May)			Guenbot (30)	Sivan (30)	Rajab (30)
(June)			Sene (30)	Tammuz (29)	Shaaban (29)
(July)			Hamle (30)	Av (30)	Ramadan (30)
(August)			Nahassie (30 + 5 or 6[g])	Ellul (29)	Shawwal (29)
(September)					Dhulkaada (30)
(October)					Dhulheggia (29 or 30)

In 1980 the Moslem (Hejira) lunar year begins November 9th, but this varies from year to year, being 10 or 11 days earlier each year in terms of the Gregorian. In each 30 years 19 years have 354 days (are 'common') and 11 have 355 days (are 'intercalary').
Months begin about the 21st of the corresponding Gregorian month.
Months begin about the 22nd of the corresponding Gregorian month.
Months begin on the 11th of the corresponding Gregorian month.
The date of the New Year varies, but normally falls in the second half of September in the Gregorian calendar; the general calendar position is maintained by adding, in some years, an extra period of 11 days, Adar Sheni, following the month of Adar.
Called Marcheshvan before 5740.   gPagume.

Standard times

Since the earth makes one complete revolution in 24 hours, 1 hour corresponds to a longitude of 360/24 = 15 degrees, and ½ hour to 7½ degrees.
Under the system of zone time, zones are established within which national standards are in general the same, and differ from other zones by ½ hour or 1 hour; ideal time zones are centred on meridians at multiples of 15° east or west of Greenwich. Since the apparent motion of the sun is from east to west, time in zones east of Greenwich is ahead of (a later time than) Greenwich Mean Time (GMT) and in zones west of Greenwich it is behind (an earlier time than) GMT. At longitude 180° E or W of Greenwich there is a time difference of 1 day on either side of the line. An international date line is established defining the day to which countries near the line adhere; the date line does not keep to the 180° line exactly but varies to include, for example, Tonga, which then has a time 13 hours ahead of GMT. See page 115 for a map showing the date line, and also a broad guide to longitudes. In the following list countries and areas are shown with standard times fast (+) or slow (−) in hours on GMT. In the list the hour is marked with an asterisk (*) where summer time is generally kept (usually one hour in advance of standard time).

+4½	Afghanistan
+1*	Albania
MT*	Algeria
+5½	Andaman Islands
+1	Andorra
+1	Angola
−4	Antigua
−3	Argentina
GMT	Ascension Island
	Australia
+10*	a. Victoria, New South Wales, Tasmania, Queensland
+9½*	b. South Australia*
+9½	c. Northern Territory
+8	d. Western Australia
+1*	Austria
−1*	Azores
−5*	Bahamas
+3	Bahrain
+1*	Balearic Islands
+6	Bangladesh
−4	Barbados
+1*	Belgium
−6	Belize
+1	Benin
−4*	Bermuda
+5½	Bhutan
−4	Bolivia
+2	Botswana

Time

	Brazil
−3	a. East, including all coast and Brasilia
−4	b. West
−5	c. Territory of Acre
+5	British Indian Ocean Territory
+8	Brunei
+2*	Bulgaria
+6½	Burma
+2	Burundi
+7	Cambodia
+1	Cameroon
	Canada
	The adoption of Daylight Saving Time is at the discretion of individual states and cities.
−3½*	a. Newfoundland
−4*	b. Atlantic Zone: Labrador, New Brunswick, Nova Scotia, Prince Edward Is., Quebec (East of Pte des Monts)
−5*	c. Eastern Zone: North-West Territory (East), Ottawa, Ontario, Quebec (West of Pte des Monts)
−6*	d. Central Zone: Manitoba, North-West Territory (Central), Saskatchewan (East)
−7*	e. Mountain Zone: Alberta, North-West Territory (Mountain), Saskatchewan (West)
−8*	f. Pacific Zone: British Columbia
−8*	g. Yukon Territory
GMT*	Canary Islands
−1	Cape Verde
−5	Cayman Islands
+1	Central African Republic
+1	Chad
GMT*	Channel Islands
−4*	Chile
+8	China
+7	Christmas Island
+6½	Cocos-Keeling Islands
−5	Colombia
+3	Comoros
+1	Congo
−10	Cook Islands
−6	Costa Rica
−5*	Cuba
+3	Cyprus: North
+2*	Cyprus: South
+1*	Czechoslovakia
+1*	Denmark
+3	Djibouti
−4	Dominica
−4	Dominican Republic
−5	Ecuador
+2	Egypt
−6	El Salvador
+1	Equatorial Guinea
+3	Ethiopia
	Falkland Islands
−4	a. General
−4*	b. Port Stanley
GMT	Faroes
+12	Fiji
+2	Finland
+1*	France
+1	Gabon
GMT	Gambia
+1*	Germany, East
+1*	Germany, West
GMT	Ghana
+1	Gibraltar
+2*	Greece

	Greenland
−1*	a. Scoresby Sound
−3*	b. Angmagssalik, West Coast except Thule
−4	c. Thule area
−4	Grenada
−4	Guadeloupe
+10	Guam
−6	Guatemala
−3	Guiana, French
GMT	Guinea
GMT	Guinea—Bissau
−3	Guyana
−5	Haiti
−6	Honduras
+8*	Hongkong
+1*	Hungary
GMT	Iceland
+5½	India
	Indonesia
+7	a. Western Zone: Java, Sumatra, Bali, Bangka, Billiton, Madura
+8	b. Central Zone: Kalimantan, Sulawesi, Flores, Soembawa, Soemba, Timor, Lombok
+9	c. Eastern Zone: Molucca Islands, Tanimbar, Kai, Aroe, West Irian
+3½*	Iran
+3	Iraq
GMT*	Ireland
+2	Israel
+1*	Italy
GMT	Ivory Coast
−5*	Jamaica
+9	Japan
+2	Jordan
+1	Jugoslavia
+3	Kenya
	Kiribati
+11½	a. Ocean Island
+12	b. Gilbert Islands
−11	c. Phoenix Islands
−10	d. Line Islands
+9	Korea, North
+9	Korea, South
+3	Kuwait
+7	Laos
+2	Lebanon
+2	Lesotho
GMT	Liberia
+2	Libya
+1	Liechtenstein
+1*	Luxembourg
+8	Macao
+3	Madagascar
GMT	Madeira
+2	Malawi
	Malaysia
+7½	a. Peninsular
+8	b. Sabah, Sarawak
+5	Maldives
GMT	Mali
+1*	Malta
−4	Martinique
GMT	Mauritania
+4	Mauritius
	Mexico
−6	a. Mexico City
−7	b. Baja California Sur, States of Sonara, Sinaloa and Nayarit
−8*	c. Baja California Norte
−11	Midway Islands
+1*	Monaco
+8	Mongolia
−4	Montserrat

ime

GMT	Morocco
+2	Mozambique
+11½	Nauru
+5⅔	Nepal
+1*	Netherlands
−4	Netherlands Antilles
+11	New Caledonia
+12*	New Zealand
−6	Nicaragua
+1	Niger
+1	Nigeria
−11	Niue
+11½	Norfolk Island
+1*	Norway
+4	Oman
	Pacific Islands, US
+10	a. Northern Marianas and western Caroline Islands
+11	b. Truk Island
+12	c. Eastern Caroline Islands and Marshall Islands
+5	Pakistan
−5	Panama
+10	Papua New Guinea
−4*	Paraguay
−5	Peru
+8	Philippines
−9	Pitcairn
+1*	Poland
−10	Polynesia, French
GMT*	Portugal
−4	Puerto Rico
+3	Qatar
+4	Reunion
+2*	Rumania
+2	Rwanda
−4	St Christopher
GMT	St Helena
−4	St Lucia
−3	St Pierre and Miquelon
−4	St Vincent
−11	Samoa, American
−11	Samoa, Western
+1*	San Marino
GMT	Sao Tome & Principe
+3	Saudi Arabia
GMT	Senegal
+4	Seychelles
GMT	Sierra Leone
+7½	Singapore
+11	Solomon Islands
+3	Somalia
+2	South Africa
+2	South-West Africa
	Soviet Union
	Chief towns
+3	a. Kiev, Leningrad, Moscow, Odessa
+4	b. Archangel, Volgograd, Tiflis
+5	c. Ashkhabad, Sverdlovsk
+6	d. Alma-Ata, Karaganda, Omsk
+7	e. Novosibirsk, Krasnoyarsk
+8	f. Irkutsk
+9	g. Yakutsk
+10	h. Khabarovsk, Vladivostok
+11	i. Magadan, Yuzhno-Sakhalinsk (Sakhalin Island)
+12	j. Petropavlovsk-Kamchatskiy
+13	k. Anadyr
+1*	Spain
+5½	Sri Lanka
+2	Sudan
−3½	Surinam
+2	Swaziland

+1*	Sweden
+1	Switzerland
+2	Syria
+8	Taiwan
+3	Tanzania
+7	Thailand
+8	Timor, East
GMT	Togo
+13	Tonga
−4	Trinidad and Tobago
+1	Tunisia
+3	Turkey
−5	Turks and Caicos Islands
+12	Tuvalu
+3	Uganda
+4	United Arab Emirates
GMT*	United Kingdom
	United States of America
−5*	a. Eastern Zone (Indiana does not keep summer time): Connecticut, Delaware, District of Colombia (Washington), Indiana, Florida, Georgia, Maine, Maryland, Massachusetts, Michigan, New Hampshire, New Jersey, New York, North Carolina, Ohio, Pennsylvania, Rhode Island, South Carolina, Vermont, Virginia, West Virginia
−6*	b. Central Zone: Albama, Arkansas, Illinois, Iowa, Kansas, Kentucky, Louisiana, Minnesota, Mississippi, Missouri, Nebraska, North Dakota, Oklahoma, South Dakota, Tennessee, Texas, Wisconsin
−7*	c. Mountain Zone (Arizona does not keep summer time): Arizona, Colorado, Idaho, Montana, New Mexico, Utah, Wyoming
−8*	d. Pacific Zone: California, Nevada, Oregon, Washington State
	e. Alaska:
−8*	Ketchikan to Skagway
−9*	Skagway to 141° West long.
−10*	141° West long. to 162° West long.
−11*	162° West long. to Westernmost point
−10	f. Hawaii
GMT	Upper Volta
−3*	Uruguay
+11	Vanuatu
+1*	Vatican
−4	Venezuela
+7	Vietnam
−4	Virgin Islands, British
−4	Virgin Islands, US
+12	Wallis and Futuna Islands
+3	Yemen, North
+3	Yemen, South
	Zaire
+1	a. Kinshasa, Mbandaka
+2	b. Orientale, Kivu, Katanga, Kasai
+2	Zambia
+2	Zimbabwe

In this section conversions from imperial to metric measures are shown as **exact** equivalents. In the process of change to the metric system most countries adopt the nearest equivalent in metric terms for the same basic unit; for example, a 100 lb unit = 45.359 kg, which may become a 45 kg or 50 kg unit in a metric system.

There is a continuous process of gradual change to the metric system, and many capacity units shown here with weight equivalents in rounded imperial units are changing to rounded metric units.

Special units shown here are usually capacity measures, for which the weight contained varies according to the density of the product concerned; eg, hectolitre.

Extraction rates and equivalent rates shown in this section are in general averages and vary from year to year.

Plant spacing

Square or rectangular spacing

The number of seeds or plants required for planting in different spacings are shown in the following tables in terms of both hectares and acres. For usual 'square' or 'rectangular' spacing, with even spacing within rows and between rows, the number of seeds or plants is the number per row multiplied by the number of rows. Here, the number is shown to one decimal place for the number of rows (assuming an area in the form of a square); this applies only where there is more than 1 hectare or acre involved. If only 1 hectare or acre is to be planted, then only the actual whole number of rows should be used. For example, with spacing at 1.5 m intervals and rows at 1.5 m intervals there are 66.7 rows for a hectare in the shape of a square, giving 4 444 plants per hectare. For only 1 hectare, it would only be possible to use 66 rows and space 66 plants per row, so that the actual number would be 66 × 66 = 4 356.

Planting densities for different spacing between plants in a row, and between rows

Plants per hectare; spacing between plants and rows in centimetres

Number of rows per hectare	Spacing of rows cm →	Spacing within rows											
		10	12	14	16	18	20	25	30	35	40	45	5
1000.0	10	1000000	833333	714286	625000	555556	500000	400000	333333	285714	250000	222222	20000
833.3	12	833333	694444	595238	520833	462963	416667	333333	277778	238095	208333	185185	16666
714.3	14	714286	595238	510204	446429	396825	357143	285714	238095	204082	178571	158730	14285
625.0	16	625000	520833	446429	390625	347222	312500	250000	208333	178571	156250	138889	12500
555.6	18	555556	462963	396825	347222	308642	277778	222222	185185	158730	138889	123457	11111
500.0	20	500000	416667	357143	312500	277778	250000	200000	166667	142857	125000	111111	10000
400.0	25	400000	333333	285714	250000	222222	200000	160000	133333	114286	100000	88889	8000
333.3	30	333333	277778	238095	208333	185185	166667	133333	111111	95238	83333	74074	6666
285.7	35	285714	238095	204082	178571	158730	142857	114286	95238	81633	71429	63492	5714
250.0	40	250000	208333	178571	156250	138889	125000	100000	83333	71429	62500	55556	5000
222.2	45	222222	185185	158730	138889	123457	111111	88889	74074	63492	55556	49383	4444
200.0	50	200000	166667	142857	125000	111111	100000	80000	66667	57143	50000	44444	4000

Number of rows per hectare	Spacing of rows m →	Spacing within rows												
		0.5	0.6	0.7	0.8	0.9	1.0	1.1	1.2	1.3	1.4	1.5	5.0	10.0
200.0	0.5	40000	33333	28571	25000	22222	20000	18182	16667	15385	14286	13333	4000	2000
166.7	0.6	33333	27778	23810	20833	18519	16667	15152	13889	12821	11905	11111	3333	166
142.9	0.7	28571	23810	20408	17857	15873	14286	12987	11905	10989	10204	9524	2857	142
125.0	0.8	25000	20833	17857	15625	13889	12500	11364	10417	9615	8929	8333	2500	125
111.1	0.9	22222	18519	15873	13889	12346	11111	10101	9259	8547	7937	7407	2222	111
100.0	1.0	20000	16667	14286	12500	11111	10000	9091	8333	7692	7143	6667	2000	100
90.9	1.1	18182	15152	12987	11364	10101	9091	8264	7576	6993	6494	6061	1818	90
83.3	1.2	16667	13889	11905	10417	9259	8333	7576	6944	6410	5952	5556	1667	83
76.9	1.3	15385	12821	10989	9615	8547	7692	6993	6410	5917	5495	5128	1538	76
71.4	1.4	14286	11905	10204	8929	7937	7143	6494	5952	5495	5102	4762	1429	71
66.7	1.5	13333	11111	9524	8333	7407	6667	6061	5556	5128	4762	4444	1333	66
50.0	2.0	10000	8333	7143	6250	5556	5000	4545	4167	3846	3571	3333	1000	50
40.0	2.5	8000	6667	5714	5000	4444	4000	3636	3333	3077	2857	2667	800	40
33.3	3.0	6667	5556	4762	4167	3704	3333	3030	2778	2564	2381	2222	667	33
28.6	3.5	5714	4762	4082	3571	3175	2857	2597	2381	2198	2041	1905	571	28
25.0	4.0	5000	4167	3571	3125	2778	2500	2273	2083	1923	1786	1667	500	25
22.2	4.5	4444	3704	3175	2778	2469	2222	2020	1852	1709	1587	1481	444	22
20.0	5.0	4000	3333	2857	2500	2222	2000	1818	1667	1538	1429	1333	400	20
16.7	6.0	3333	2778	2381	2083	1852	1667	1515	1389	1282	1190	1111	333	16
14.3	7.0	2857	2381	2041	1786	1587	1429	1299	1190	1099	1020	952	286	14
12.5	8.0	2500	2083	1786	1562	1389	1250	1136	1042	962	893	833	250	12
11.1	9.0	2222	1852	1587	1389	1235	1111	1010	926	855	794	741	222	11
10.0	10.0	2000	1667	1429	1250	1111	1000	909	833	769	714	667	200	10

Plant spacing

Plants per acre; spacing between plants and rows in inches

Number of rows per acre	Spacing of rows (in →)	4	5	6	7	8	9	10	11	12	15	18	21	24
26.1	4	392040	313632	261360	224023	196020	174240	156816	142560	130680	104544	87120	74674	65340
00.9	5	313632	250906	209088	179218	156816	139392	125453	114048	104544	83635	69696	59739	52272
17.4	6	261360	209088	174240	149349	130680	116160	104544	95040	87120	69696	58080	49783	43560
57.8	7	224023	179218	149349	128013	112011	99566	89609	81463	74674	59739	49783	42671	37337
13.1	8	196020	156816	130680	112011	98010	87120	78408	71280	65340	52272	43560	37337	32670
78.3	9	174240	139392	116160	99566	87120	77440	69696	63360	58080	46464	38720	33189	29040
50.5	10	156816	125453	104544	89609	78408	69696	62726	57024	52272	41818	34848	29870	26136
27.7	11	142560	114048	95040	81463	71280	63360	57024	51840	47520	38016	31680	27154	23760
08.7	12	130680	104544	87120	74674	65340	58080	52272	47520	43560	34848	29040	24891	21780
67.0	15	104544	83635	69696	59739	52272	46464	41818	38016	34848	27878	23232	19913	17424
39.1	18	87120	69696	58080	49783	43560	38720	34848	31680	29040	23232	19360	16594	14520
19.3	21	74674	59739	49783	42671	37337	33189	29870	27154	24891	19913	16594	14224	12446
04.4	24	65340	52272	43560	37337	32670	29040	26136	23760	21780	17424	14520	12446	10890

Plants per acre; spacing between plants and rows in feet

Number of rows per acre	Spacing of rows (ft →)	1	2	3	4	5	6	7	8	9	10	15	20	25	30	35	40
08.7	1	43560	21780	14520	10890	8712	7260	6223	5445	4840	4356	2904	2178	1742	1452	1245	1089
04.4	2	21780	10890	7260	5445	4356	3630	3111	2723	2420	2178	1452	1089	871	726	622	545
69.6	3	14520	7260	4840	3630	2904	2420	2074	1815	1613	1452	968	726	581	484	415	363
52.2	4	10890	5445	3630	2723	2178	1815	1556	1361	1210	1089	726	545	436	363	311	272
41.7	5	8712	4356	2904	2178	1742	1452	1245	1089	968	871	581	436	348	290	249	218
34.8	6	7260	3630	2420	1815	1452	1210	1037	908	807	726	484	363	290	242	207	182
29.8	7	6223	3111	2074	1556	1245	1037	889	778	691	622	415	311	249	207	178	156
26.1	8	5445	2723	1815	1361	1089	908	778	681	605	545	363	272	218	182	156	136
23.2	9	4840	2420	1613	1210	968	807	691	605	538	484	323	242	194	161	138	121
20.9	10	4356	2178	1452	1089	871	726	622	545	484	436	290	218	174	145	124	109
13.9	15	2904	1452	968	726	581	484	415	363	323	290	194	145	116	97	83	73
10.4	20	2178	1089	726	545	436	363	311	272	242	218	145	109	87	73	62	54
8.3	25	1742	871	581	436	348	290	249	218	194	174	116	87	70	58	50	44
7.0	30	1452	726	484	363	290	242	207	182	161	145	97	73	58	48	41	36
6.0	35	1245	622	415	311	249	207	178	156	138	124	83	62	50	41	36	31
5.2	40	1089	545	363	272	218	182	156	136	121	109	73	54	44	36	31	27

Equilateral triangle spacing

Where each plant is placed at the corner of an equilateral triangle more plants can be used per hectare or acre. The number of plants with this method is shown in the following tables

The number of plants for the same area is in general increased with equilateral spacing by about 15%; this derives from $\frac{1}{2}$ tan 60° (each angle of an equilateral triangle being 60°) or 0.866, this being the distance between rows where the spacing is a unit of 1.0: that is, an increase in the ratio of 1.0/0.866 or 1.155 or 15.5% (there is, however, 1 fewer plant per row every second row, which is allowed for here).

Plants per hectare; spacing between plants and rows in metres

Number of rows per hectare[a]	Distance between rows[b] (metres)	Distance between plants in a row[c] (metres)	Number of plants per hectare
154.7	0.087	0.1	1 154 123
577.4	0.173	0.2	288 386
384.9	0.260	0.3	128 108
288.7	0.346	0.4	72 024
230.9	0.433	0.5	46 073
192.5	0.520	0.6	31 979
165.0	0.606	0.7	23 483
144.3	0.693	0.8	17 970
128.3	0.779	0.9	14 191
115.5	0.866	1.0	11 489
23.1	4.330	5.0	450
11.5	8.660	10.0	110

Plants per acre; spacing between plants and rows in feet

Number of rows per acre[a]	Distance between rows[b] (feet)	Distance between plants in a row[c] (feet)	Number of plants per acre
241.0	0.866 (10.4 in)	1	50 178
120.5	1.732 (20.8 in)	2	12 514
80.3	2.598	3	5 549
60.2	3.464	4	3 114
48.2	4.330	5	1 988
40.2	5.196	6	1 377
34.4	6.062	7	1 009
30.1	6.928	8	771
26.8	7.794	9	608
24.1	8.660	10	491
16.1	12.990	15	216
12.0	17.321	20	120
8.0	25.981	30	52
6.0	34.641	40	28

[a]Assuming a square area. [b]In which plants are spaced out to form equilateral triangles. [c]Also distance between plants as spaced in rows.

The same qualification as mentioned on the facing page applies: where there is not an exact number of rows, then for a single hectare or acre the number of plants will be less — as, for example, with spacing at 1.0 m, there are 115.5 rows for a square hectare, which would be only 115 actual rows for a single hectare.

Cereals, other than rice

Breadgrains are usually defined as wheat and rye.

Foddergrains are defined as barley, oats, maize, sorghum and millet.

Corn is often used locally to describe the main cereal crop of the district (eg, in England it may refer to wheat; in Scotland and Ireland to oats). Under UK Corn Acts, corn was first defined as wheat, barley, and oats, and now means wheat, barley, oats, rye and maize (British corn means any such produce of the United Kingdom, Channel Islands or Isle of Man). Throughout the United States, Canada and South America corn specifically refers to maize.

Yield: for wheat, one-half of crop is grain and one-half straw; for rye, one-third is grain and two-thirds straw.

United Kingdom measures

The agriculture industry in the United Kingdom in general officially changed to the use of the metric system from 1976/77.

Old dry measures

2 pints	= 1 quart	2 bushels	= 1 strike
2 quarts	= 1 pottle	4 bushels	= 1 coomb (or coom)
2 pottles	= 1 gallon	8 bushels	= 1 quarter
2 gallons	= 1 peck	4 quarters	= 1 chaldron
4 pecks	= 1 bushel	5 quarters	= 1 load (or wey or weigh)
8 gallons	= 1 bushel	2 loads	= 1 last

Barrel
Wheat = 280 lb = 127.006 kg   Oats = 196 lb = 88.904 kg
Barley = 224 lb = 101.605 kg

Bushel
Wheat = 60 lb = 27.216 kg   Oats = 39 lb = 17.690 kg
Barley = 50 lb = 22.680 kg   Maize = 56 lb = 25.401 kg
Rye = 56 lb = 25.401 kg

Firlot
Wheat = 60 lb = 27.216 kg   Oats = 57 lb = 25.855 kg
Barley = 73 lb = 33.112 kg

Hobbet
Wheat = 168 lb = 76.204 kg   Barley = 147 lb = 66.678 kg

Kemple
Straw = 440 lb = 199.581 kg

Load
Hay and straw = 36 trusses

Quarter (malting industry)
Barley = 448 lb = 203.209 kg   Malt = 336 lb = 152.407 kg

Truss
Hay: old (Sept 1 – June 1)   = 56 lb = 25.401 kg
    new (June 2 – Aug 31)   = 60 lb = 27.216 kg
Straw   = 36 lb = 16.329 kg

Windle
Wheat = 220 lb = 99.790 kg

Measures in other countries

Ardab or Ardeb: Egypt
Wheat = 330.693 lb = 150 kg   Maize = 308.647 lb = 140 kg
Barley = 264.555 lb = 120 kg   Sorghum = 308.647 lb = 140 kg
Millet = 308.647 lb = 140 kg
Sudan
Wheat = 357.149 lb = 162 kg   Maize = 332.898 lb = 151 kg
Barley = 317.466 lb = 144 kg   Sorghum = 321.875 lb = 146 kg
Rye = 357.149 lb = 162 kg

Bag or muid: Zambia
Barley and oats (uncrushed) = 154.32 lb = 70 kg
Wheat, rye and maize   = 198.4 lb = 90 kg
Zimbabwe and South Africa
Wheat, rye, maize, millet and sorghum = 200 lb = 90.718 kg
Barley and oats   = 150 lb = 68.039 kg

Basket: Burma
Wheat = 72 lb = 32.659 kg   Rice, paddy = 46 lb = 20.865 kg

Bolsa: Uruguay
Wheat = 145–157 lb = 66–71 kg   Barley = 110 lb = 50 kg

Bushel
International corn bushel = 60 lb = 27.216 kg
United States
Wheat = 60 lb = 27.216 kg   Corn = 56 lb = 25.401 kg
Barley = 48 lb = 21.772 kg   Millet = 50 lb = 22.680 kg
Rye = 56 lb = 25.401 kg   Sorghum = 56 lb = 25.401 kg
Oats = 32 lb = 14.515 kg
Canada
Wheat, barley, rye, corn: as for the United States
Oats = 34 lb = 15.422 kg   Mixed grains = 45 lb = 20.412 kg
Australia
Wheat = 60 lb = 27.216 kg   Maize = 56 lb = 25.401 kg
Barley = 50 lb = 22.680 kg   Millet = 60 lb = 27.216 kg
Rye = 60 lb = 27.216 kg   Sorghum = 60 lb = 27.216 kg
Oats = 40 lb = 18.144 kg
New Zealand
Wheat, barley, oats, maize: as for Australia
Rye = 56 lb = 25.401 kg   Millet = 35 lb = 15.876 kg

Chombol: Lebanon
Wheat = 330.693 lb = 150 kg

Fanega: Costa Rica
Maize = 768 lb = 348.36 kg
Ecuador
Wheat and barley = 249.122 lb = 113 kg
Morocco
Wheat = 97.003 lb = 44 kg
Spain
Wheat and rye = 95.328 lb = 43.240 kg   Oats = 55.116 lb = 25 kg
Barley = 73.194 lb = 33.200 kg   Maize = 88.185 lb = 40 kg

Hectolitre: Finland
Wheat = 174.165 lb = 79 kg   Rye = 158.733 lb = 72 kg
Barley = 143.300 lb = 65 kg   Oats = 110.231 lb = 50 kg
Morocco
Wheat = 169.756 lb = 77 kg
Netherlands
Wheat = 165.347 lb = 75 kg   Rye = 154.324 lb = 70 kg
Barley = 143.300 lb = 65 kg   Oats = 110.231 lb = 50 kg
Norway
Wheat = 169.756 lb = 77 kg   Rye = 158.733 lb = 72 kg
Barley = 143.300 lb = 65 kg   Oats = 112.436 lb = 51 kg

Kilá: Egypt
Wheat = 27.558 lb = 12.5 kg

Kilé or Kileh: Cyprus
Wheat = 58.8 lb = 26.671 kg   Rye = 60 lb = 27.216 kg
Turkey
Wheat = 66 lb = 30 kg   Rye = 62 lb = 28 kg
Barley = 57 lb = 26 kg   Oats = 53 lb = 24 kg

Koku: Japan
Wheat = 302.584 lb = 137.25 kg   Rye = 311.954 lb = 141.5 kg
Barley: Oats = 173.615 lb = 78.75 kg
common = 239.754 lb = 108.75 kg   Maize = 289.358 lb = 131.25 kg
naked = 305.892 lb = 138.75 kg

Korn tonde (or tonde korn): Denmark
Wheat = 237 lb = 107.5 kg   Oats = 154.324 lb = 70 kg

Last: Netherlands
Wheat = 4 960.4 lb = 2 250 kg   Rye = 4 629.7 lb = 2 100 kg
Barley = 4 299.0 lb = 1 950 kg   Oats = 3 306.9 lb = 1 500 kg

Modd: Malta
Wheat = 490 lb = 222.260 kg

Mudd or Med: Lebanon
Wheat = 40–44 lb = 18–20 kg

Suk: Korea, South
Wheat = 304.238 lb = 138 kg   Rye = 273.373 lb = 124 kg
Barley (common) = 218.258 lb = 99 kg   Oats = 171.961 lb = 78 kg

ereals, other than rice

Wheat flour

xtraction rate, general:
00 units of grain   = 72 units of flour

Measures
 arrel:
 nited Kingdom & United States   = 196 lb = 88.904 kg

 ther UK measures:
 allon   = 7 lb = 3.175 kg   Boll or bag   = 140 lb = 63.503 kg
 eck   = 14 lb = 6.350 kg   Load or pack = 240 lb = 108.862 kg
 ushel = 56 lb = 25.401 kg   Sack   = 280 lb = 127.006 kg

Some special conversions for agriculture

In the tables below detailed conversions are given for the weight of the UK or US wheat bushel (of 60 pounds), or international corn bushel (of 60 pounds), relating this to tonnes. These can be used for any bushel containing 60 pounds. On the following two pages detailed conversions are given for agricultural yields. The tables for conversion between US (short) hundredweights per acre and quintals per hectare (bottom half of the following page) can also be used for conversions between pounds per acre and kilograms per hectare. The tables on pages 100 and 101 for conversions using quintals per hectare can also be used as follows: for conversions from tonnes per hectare, by moving the decimal point in the table one place to the right, and for conversions from kilograms per hectare by moving the decimal point two places to the left; conversions to tonnes per hectare can be obtained by moving the decimal point one place to the left, and to kilograms per hectare by moving the decimal point two places to the right. See pages 74 and 75 for conversions between the capacity measures of UK bushels, US bushels and hectolitres. Also, for capacity measurement:
1 UK bushel per acre = 0.898 691 hectolitre per hectare
1 hectolitre per hectare = 1.112 730 UK bushels per acre

UK or US bushels (of 60 pounds) to Tonnes   1 bu = 0.027 216 t

bu →	0	10	20	30	40	50	60	70	80	90	←	bu
↓	t	t	t	t	t	t	t	t	t	t		↓
0	0.00	0.27	0.54	0.82	1.09	1.36	1.63	1.91	2.18	2.45		0
100	2.72	2.99	3.27	3.54	3.81	4.08	4.35	4.63	4.90	5.17		100
200	5.44	5.72	5.99	6.26	6.53	6.80	7.08	7.35	7.62	7.89		200
300	8.16	8.44	8.71	8.98	9.25	9.53	9.80	10.07	10.34	10.61		300
400	10.89	11.16	11.43	11.70	11.97	12.25	12.52	12.79	13.06	13.34		400
500	13.61	13.88	14.15	14.42	14.70	14.97	15.24	15.51	15.79	16.06		500
600	16.33	16.60	16.87	17.15	17.42	17.69	17.96	18.23	18.51	18.78		600
700	19.05	19.32	19.60	19.87	20.14	20.41	20.68	20.96	21.23	21.50		700
800	21.77	22.04	22.32	22.59	22.86	23.13	23.41	23.68	23.95	24.22		800
900	24.49	24.77	25.04	25.31	25.58	25.85	26.13	26.40	26.67	26.94		900
1000	27.22											1000

bu →	0	100	200	300	400	500	600	700	800	900	←	bu
↓	t	t	t	t	t	t	t	t	t	t		↓
0	0.00	2.72	5.44	8.16	10.89	13.61	16.33	19.05	21.77	24.49		0
1000	27.22	29.94	32.66	35.38	38.10	40.82	43.54	46.27	48.99	51.71		1000
2000	54.43	57.15	59.87	62.60	65.32	68.04	70.76	73.48	76.20	78.93		2000
3000	81.65	84.37	87.09	89.81	92.53	95.25	97.98	100.70	103.42	106.14		3000
4000	108.86	111.58	114.31	117.03	119.75	122.47	125.19	127.91	130.63	133.36		4000
5000	136.08	138.80	141.52	144.24	146.96	149.69	152.41	155.13	157.85	160.57		5000
6000	163.29	166.01	168.74	171.46	174.18	176.90	179.62	182.34	185.07	187.79		6000
7000	190.51	193.23	195.95	198.67	201.40	204.12	206.84	209.56	212.28	215.00		7000
8000	217.72	220.45	223.17	225.89	228.61	231.33	234.05	236.78	239.50	242.22		8000
9000	244.94	247.66	250.38	253.10	255.83	258.55	261.27	263.99	266.71	269.43		9000
10000	272.16											10000

Tonnes to UK or US bushels (of 60 pounds)   1 t = 36.743 710 bu

t →	0	1	2	3	4	5	6	7	8	9	←	t
↓	bu	bu	bu	bu	bu	bu	bu	bu	bu	bu		↓
0	0.00	36.74	73.49	110.23	146.97	183.72	220.46	257.21	293.95	330.69		0
10	367.44	404.18	440.92	477.67	514.41	551.16	587.90	624.64	661.39	698.13		10
20	734.87	771.62	808.36	845.11	881.85	918.59	955.34	992.08	1028.82	1065.57		20
30	1102.31	1139.06	1175.80	1212.54	1249.29	1286.03	1322.77	1359.52	1396.26	1433.00		30
40	1469.75	1506.49	1543.24	1579.98	1616.72	1653.47	1690.21	1726.95	1763.70	1800.44		40
50	1837.19	1873.93	1910.67	1947.42	1984.16	2020.90	2057.65	2094.39	2131.14	2167.88		50
60	2204.62	2241.37	2278.11	2314.85	2351.60	2388.34	2425.08	2461.83	2498.57	2535.32		60
70	2572.06	2608.80	2645.55	2682.29	2719.03	2755.78	2792.52	2829.27	2866.01	2902.75		70
80	2939.50	2976.24	3012.98	3049.73	3086.47	3123.22	3159.96	3196.70	3233.45	3270.19		80
90	3306.93	3343.68	3380.42	3417.17	3453.91	3490.65	3527.40	3564.14	3600.88	3637.63		90
00	3674.37											100

UK or US bushels (of 60 pounds) per acre to Quintals (100 kilograms) per hectare   1 bu/acre = 0.672 511 q/ha

bu/acre→	0	1	2	3	4	5	6	7	8	9	←bu/acre
↓	q/ha	q/ha	q/ha	q/ha	q/ha	q/ha	q/ha	q/ha	q/ha	q/ha	↓
0	0.000	0.673	1.345	2.018	2.690	3.363	4.035	4.708	5.380	6.053	0
10	6.725	7.398	8.070	8.743	9.415	10.088	10.760	11.433	12.105	12.778	10
20	13.450	14.123	14.795	15.468	16.140	16.813	17.485	18.158	18.830	19.503	20
30	20.175	20.848	21.520	22.193	22.865	23.538	24.210	24.883	25.555	26.228	30
40	26.900	27.573	28.245	28.918	29.590	30.263	30.935	31.608	32.281	32.953	40
50	33.626	34.298	34.971	35.643	36.316	36.988	37.661	38.333	39.006	39.678	50
60	40.351	41.023	41.696	42.368	43.041	43.713	44.386	45.058	45.731	46.403	60
70	47.076	47.748	48.421	49.093	49.766	50.438	51.111	51.783	52.456	53.128	70
80	53.801	54.473	55.146	55.818	56.491	57.163	57.836	58.508	59.181	59.853	80
90	60.526	61.198	61.871	62.543	63.216	63.889	64.561	65.234	65.906	66.579	90
100	67.251										100

Quintals (100 kilograms) per hectare to UK or US bushels (of 60 pounds) per acre   1 q/ha = 1.486 965 bu/acre

q/ha→	0	1	2	3	4	5	6	7	8	9	←q/ha
↓	bu/acre	bu/acre	bu/acre	bu/acre	bu/acre	bu/acre	bu/acre	bu/acre	bu/acre	bu/acre	↓
0	0.000	1.487	2.974	4.461	5.948	7.435	8.922	10.409	11.896	13.383	0
10	14.870	16.357	17.844	19.331	20.818	22.304	23.791	25.278	26.765	28.252	10
20	29.739	31.226	32.713	34.200	35.687	37.174	38.661	40.148	41.635	43.122	20
30	44.609	46.096	47.583	49.070	50.557	52.044	53.531	55.018	56.505	57.992	30
40	59.479	60.966	62.453	63.940	65.426	66.913	68.400	69.887	71.374	72.861	40
50	74.348	75.835	77.322	78.809	80.296	81.783	83.270	84.757	86.244	87.731	50
60	89.218	90.705	92.192	93.679	95.166	96.653	98.140	99.627	101.114	102.601	60
70	104.088	105.575	107.061	108.548	110.035	111.522	113.009	114.496	115.983	117.470	70
80	118.957	120.444	121.931	123.418	124.905	126.392	127.879	129.366	130.853	132.340	80
90	133.827	135.314	136.801	138.288	139.775	141.262	142.749	144.236	145.723	147.210	90
100	148.697										100

US (short) hundredweights per acre to Quintals (100 kilograms) per hectare   1 US cwt/acre = 1.120 851 q/ha

US cwt/acre →	0	1	2	3	4	5	6	7	8	9←US cwt/acre
↓	q/ha	q/ha	q/ha	q/ha	q/ha	q/ha	q/ha	q/ha	q/ha	q/ha	↓
0	0.000	1.121	2.242	3.363	4.483	5.604	6.725	7.846	8.967	10.088	0
10	11.209	12.329	13.450	14.571	15.692	16.813	17.934	19.054	20.175	21.296	10
20	22.417	23.538	24.659	25.780	26.900	28.021	29.142	30.263	31.384	32.505	20
30	33.626	34.746	35.867	36.988	38.109	39.230	40.351	41.471	42.592	43.713	30
40	44.834	45.955	47.076	48.197	49.317	50.438	51.559	52.680	53.801	54.922	40
50	56.043	57.163	58.284	59.405	60.526	61.647	62.768	63.889	65.009	66.130	50
60	67.251	68.372	69.493	70.614	71.734	72.855	73.976	75.097	76.218	77.339	60
70	78.460	79.580	80.701	81.822	82.943	84.064	85.185	86.306	87.426	88.547	70
80	89.668	90.789	91.910	93.031	94.151	95.272	96.393	97.514	98.635	99.756	80
90	100.877	101.997	103.118	104.239	105.360	106.481	107.602	108.723	109.843	110.964	90
100	112.085										100

Quintals (100 kilograms) per hectare to US (short) hundredweights per acre   1 q/ha = 0.892 179 US cwt/acre

q/ha→	0	1	2	3	4	5	6	7	8	9	←q/ha
↓	US cwt/acre	US cwt/acre	US cwt/acre	US cwt/acre	US cwt/acre	US cwt/acre	US cwt/acre	US cwt/acre	US cwt/acre	US cwt/acre	↓
0	0.000	0.892	1.784	2.677	3.569	4.461	5.353	6.245	7.137	8.030	0
10	8.922	9.814	10.706	11.598	12.491	13.383	14.275	15.167	16.059	16.951	10
20	17.844	18.736	19.628	20.520	21.412	22.304	23.197	24.089	24.981	25.873	20
30	26.765	27.658	28.550	29.442	30.334	31.226	32.118	33.011	33.903	34.795	30
40	35.687	36.579	37.472	38.364	39.256	40.148	41.040	41.932	42.825	43.717	40
50	44.609	45.501	46.393	47.285	48.178	49.070	49.962	50.854	51.746	52.639	50
60	53.531	54.423	55.315	56.207	57.099	57.992	58.884	59.776	60.668	61.560	60
70	62.453	63.345	64.237	65.129	66.021	66.913	67.806	68.698	69.590	70.482	70
80	71.374	72.267	73.159	74.051	74.943	75.835	76.727	77.620	78.512	79.404	80
90	80.296	81.188	82.080	82.973	83.865	84.757	85.649	86.541	87.434	88.326	90
100	89.218										100

UK (long) hundredweights per acre to Quintals (100 kilograms) per hectare   1 UK cwt/acre = 1.255 353 q/ha

UK cwt/acre →	0	1	2	3	4	5	6	7	8	9 ← UK cwt/acre	
↓	q/ha	q/ha	q/ha	q/ha	q/ha	q/ha	q/ha	q/ha	q/ha	q/ha	↓
0	0.000	1.255	2.511	3.766	5.021	6.277	7.532	8.787	10.043	11.298	0
10	12.554	13.809	15.064	16.320	17.575	18.830	20.086	21.341	22.596	23.852	10
20	25.107	26.362	27.618	28.873	30.128	31.384	32.639	33.895	35.150	36.405	20
30	37.661	38.916	40.171	41.427	42.682	43.937	45.193	46.448	47.703	48.959	30
40	50.214	51.469	52.725	53.980	55.236	56.491	57.746	59.002	60.257	61.512	40
50	62.768	64.023	65.278	66.534	67.789	69.044	70.300	71.555	72.810	74.066	50
60	75.321	76.577	77.832	79.087	80.343	81.598	82.853	84.109	85.364	86.619	60
70	87.875	89.130	90.385	91.641	92.896	94.151	95.407	96.662	97.918	99.173	70
80	100.428	101.684	102.939	104.194	105.450	106.705	107.960	109.216	110.471	111.726	80
90	112.982	114.237	115.493	116.748	118.003	119.259	120.514	121.769	123.025	124.280	90
100	125.535										100

Quintals (100 kilograms) per hectare to UK (long) hundredweights per acre   1 q/ha = 0.796 589 UK cwt/acre

q/ha →	0	1	2	3	4	5	6	7	8	9 ← q/ha	
↓	UK cwt/acre	UK cwt/acre	UK cwt/acre	UK cwt/acre	UK cwt/acre	UK cwt/acre	UK cwt/acre	UK cwt/acre	UK cwt/acre	UK cwt/acre	↓
0	0.000	0.797	1.593	2.390	3.186	3.983	4.780	5.576	6.373	7.169	0
10	7.966	8.762	9.559	10.356	11.152	11.949	12.745	13.542	14.339	15.135	10
20	15.932	16.728	17.525	18.322	19.118	19.915	20.711	21.508	22.304	23.101	20
30	23.898	24.694	25.491	26.287	27.084	27.881	28.677	29.474	30.270	31.067	30
40	31.864	32.660	33.457	34.253	35.050	35.846	36.643	37.440	38.236	39.033	40
50	39.829	40.626	41.423	42.219	43.016	43.812	44.609	45.406	46.202	46.999	50
60	47.795	48.592	49.388	50.185	50.982	51.778	52.575	53.371	54.168	54.965	60
70	55.761	56.558	57.354	58.151	58.948	59.744	60.541	61.337	62.134	62.930	70
80	63.727	64.524	65.320	66.117	66.913	67.710	68.507	69.303	70.100	70.896	80
90	71.693	72.490	73.286	74.083	74.879	75.676	76.472	77.269	78.066	78.862	90
100	79.659										100

UK (long) tons per acre to Quintals (100 kilograms) per hectare   1 UK ton/acre = 25.107 066 q/ha

UK ton/acre →	0	0.5	1.0	1.5	2.0	2.5	3.0	3.5	4.0	4.5 ← UK ton/acre	
↓	q/ha	q/ha	q/ha	q/ha	q/ha	q/ha	q/ha	q/ha	q/ha	q/ha	↓
0	0.000	12.554	25.107	37.661	50.214	62.768	75.321	87.875	100.428	112.982	0
5	125.535	138.089	150.642	163.196	175.749	188.303	200.857	213.410	225.964	238.517	5
10	251.071	263.624	276.178	288.731	301.285	313.838	326.392	338.945	351.499	364.052	10
15	376.606	389.160	401.713	414.267	426.820	439.374	451.927	464.481	477.034	489.588	15
20	502.141	514.695	527.248	539.802	552.355	564.909	577.463	590.016	602.570	615.123	20
25	627.677	640.230	652.784	665.337	677.891	690.444	702.998	715.551	728.105	740.658	25
30	753.212	765.766	778.319	790.873	803.426	815.980	828.533	841.087	853.640	866.194	30
35	878.747	891.301	903.854	916.408	928.961	941.515	954.069	966.622	979.176	991.729	35
40	1004.283	1016.836	1029.390	1041.943	1054.497	1067.050	1079.604	1092.157	1104.711	1117.264	40
45	1129.818	1142.371	1154.925	1167.479	1180.032	1192.586	1205.139	1217.693	1230.246	1242.800	45
50	1255.353	1267.907	1280.460	1293.014	1305.567	1318.121	1330.674	1343.228	1355.782	1368.335	50

Quintals (100 kilograms) per hectare to UK (long) tons per acre   1 q/ha = 0.039 829 UK ton/acre

q/ha →	0	10	20	30	40	50	60	70	80	90 ← q/ha	
↓	UK ton/acre	UK ton/acre	UK ton/acre	UK ton/acre	UK ton/acre	UK ton/acre	UK ton/acre	UK ton/acre	UK ton/acre	UK ton/acre	↓
0	0.000	0.398	0.797	1.195	1.593	1.991	2.390	2.788	3.186	3.585	0
100	3.983	4.381	4.780	5.178	5.576	5.974	6.373	6.771	7.169	7.568	100
200	7.966	8.364	8.762	9.161	9.559	9.957	10.356	10.754	11.152	11.551	200
300	11.949	12.347	12.745	13.144	13.542	13.940	14.339	14.737	15.135	15.533	300
400	15.932	16.330	16.728	17.127	17.525	17.923	18.322	18.720	19.118	19.516	400
500	19.915	20.313	20.711	21.110	21.508	21.906	22.304	22.703	23.101	23.499	500
600	23.898	24.296	24.694	25.093	25.491	25.889	26.287	26.686	27.084	27.482	600
700	27.881	28.279	28.677	29.075	29.474	29.872	30.270	30.669	31.067	31.465	700
800	31.864	32.262	32.660	33.058	33.457	33.855	34.253	34.652	35.050	35.448	800
900	35.846	36.245	36.643	37.041	37.440	37.838	38.236	38.635	39.033	39.431	900
1000	39.829										1000

Rice

When harvested rice is known as paddy, rough, raw or unhusked. After the husk has been removed it is called brown or cargo rice. This is then put through a milling process and the result is milled, cleaned or white rice.

Measures: paddy

Ardab or Ardeb

Egypt	=	264.555 lb =	120 kg

Bag or Sack

Brazil	=	110.2 lb	=	50 kg
Ghana	=	168 lb	=	76.204 kg
Malawi	=	160 lb	=	72.575 kg
South Africa	=	150 lb	=	68.039 kg
Surinam	=	154.324 lb	=	70 kg
Taiwan	=	260.145 lb	=	118 kg
Zambia	=	149.914 lb	=	68 kg

Bandu

Malaysia: Sabah	=	53⅓ lb	=	24.192 kg

Basket

Burma	=	46 lb	=	20.865 kg

Bushel

Australia	=	42 lb	=	19.051 kg
Sri Lanka	=	46 lb	=	20.865 kg
United States	=	45 lb	=	20.412 kg

Cavan

Philippines	=	97.003 lb =	44 kg

Dariba

Egypt	=	2 083.368 lb =	945 kg

Gantang

Brunei and Malaysia	=	5⅓ lb	=	2.42 kg

Katang

Cambodia	=	13.228 lb =	6 kg

Koku

Japan	=	223.218 lb =	101.25 kg

Kwien

Thailand	=	2 226.667 lb =	1 010 kg

Suk

Korea, South	=	220.462 lb =	100 kg

Thang

Cambodia	=	52.911 lb =	24 kg

Tao

Cambodia	=	26.455 lb =	12 kg

Measures: milled

Bag or Sack

Egypt	=	220.462 lb =	100 kg
Ghana	=	240 lb	=	108.862 kg
Malawi	=	200 lb	=	90.718 kg
South Africa	=	160 lb	=	72.575 kg
Surinam	=	220.462 lb =	100 kg
Taiwan	=	220.462 lb =	100 kg

Basket

Burma	=	75 lb	=	34.019 kg

Bushel

Sri Lanka	=	64 lb	=	29.03 kg

Catty

Taiwan	=	1.323 lb =	0.60 kg

Cavan

Philippines	=	123.459 lb =	56 kg

Chupak

Brunei	=	2 lb	=	0.9 kg

Gantang

Brunei and Malaysia	=	8 lb	=	3.629 kg

Katang

Cambodia	=	16.535 lb =	7.5 kg

Koku

Japan	=	322.426 lb =	146.25 kg

Kwien

Thailand	= 3 042.379 lb =	1 380 kg

Pocket

Swaziland	=	100 lb	=	45.359 kg
Zambia	=	99.208 lb =	45 kg

Suk

Korea, South	=	317.466 lb =	144 kg

Thang

Cambodia	=	66.139 lb =	30 kg

Tao

Cambodia	=	33.069 lb =	15 kg

Extraction rates

Units of milled rice per 100 units of paddy

FAO: general	65	Malaysia (Peninsular)	63
India and Pakistan	67	United States	66
Japan	70		

Units of brown rice per 100 units of paddy

Japan	80	United States	82
Korea, South	76		

Units of milled rice per 100 units of brown

Japan	90	United States	81

Sugar

Measures

Bag or Sack

Brazil		= 132.277 lb	=	60 kg
Colombia		= 110.231 lb	=	50 kg
Cuba =	250 Spanish libras	= 253.6 lb	=	115.0 kg
	or 325 Spanish libras	= 329.6 lb	=	149.5 kg
Dominican Republic		= 250–260 lb		113–118 kg
Philippines		= 140 lb		63.503 kg
Taiwan		= 220.462 lb	=	100 kg
Thailand		= 220.462 lb	=	100 kg

Extraction rates

Units of refined sugar per 100 units of raw sugar:

UN	= 90
FAO	= 92
Australia	= 96.5
Canada	= 93
Jamaica	= 92.3
Mexico	= 94.3
United Kingdom	= 95
United States	= 93.46

Units of raw sugar per 100 units of:
a. sugar beet

France	= 14.09
United Kingdom	= 14.30

b. sugar cane

Australia	= 15.30
Jamaica	= 10.60
Mexico	= 11.00
Philippines	= 12.00

Vegetables

United Kingdom measures

Beans:	barrel	= 280 lb	= 127.006 kg
	bushel box	= 30 lb	= 13.608 kg
Cabbages:	half bag	= 36–40 lb	= 16.3–18.1 kg
	mat	= 56–60 lb	= 25.4–27.2 kg
Carrots:	half bag	= 56 lb	= 25.401 kg
Onions:	case	= 120 lb	= 54.431 kg
Peas:	half bag	= 40 lb	= 18.144 kg
	bushel box	= 30–36 lb	= 13.6–16.3 kg
Potatoes:	bag	= 112 lb	= 50.802 kg
	barrel	= 200 lb	= 90.718 kg
	bushel	= 60 lb	= 27.216 kg
	cubic foot	= about 42 lb	about 19 kg
	sack (metric)	= 55.116 lb	= 25 kg

Other measures

Broad beans: Ardab or Ardeb
| Egypt: whole | = 341.716 lb | = 155 kg |
| split | = 317.466 lb | = 144 kg |

Chick-peas: Ardab or Ardeb
Egypt = 330.693 lb = 150 kg
Hectolitre
Portugal = 169.756 lb = 77 kg

Dry beans: Bushel
Canada and United States = 60 lb = 27.216 kg
Hectolitre
Portugal = 167.551 lb = 76 kg
Suk
Korea, South = 317.466 lb = 144 kg

Dry peas: Ardab or Ardeb
Egypt = 352.740 lb = 160 kg
Bushel
Canada and United States = 60 lb = 27.216 kg

Lentils: Ardab or Ardeb
| Egypt: whole | = 352.740 lb | = 160 kg |
| split | = 326.284 lb | = 148 kg |

Potatoes: Bushel
Canada and United States = 60 lb = 27.216 kg

Extraction rates

Peas: United Kingdom: 100 units fresh makes 69 units canned
Tomatoes: United States: 100 units farm makes 64 units canned

Fruit

United Kingdom measures

Apples:	barrel	= 120 lb	= 54.431 kg
	bushel or case	= 40 lb	= 18.144 kg
Cherries:	sieve	= 48 lb	= 21.772 kg
Pears:	bushel	= 48 lb	= 21.772 kg
Plums:	sieve	= 56 lb	= 25.401 kg

Other measures

Apples: Box
United States = 43 lb = 19.504 kg
Bushel
Australia = 42 lb = 19.051 kg
Canada = 45 lb = 20.412 kg
New Zealand = 40 lb = 18.144 kg
United States = 48 lb = 21.772 kg
Number
Brazil: 100 apples = 22 lb = 10 kg

Apricots: Bushel
Australia = 48 lb = 21.772 kg
New Zealand = 42 lb = 19.051 kg
Lug
United States = 24–25 lb = 10.9–11.3 kg

Bananas: Bunch or stem
Belize = 50 lb = 22.680 kg
Brazil = 22–26 lb = 10–12 kg
Colombia = 55 lb = 25 kg
Costa Rica = 80 lb = 36.287 kg
Dominican Republic = 50 lb = 22.680 kg
Ecuador = 72.8 lb = 33 kg
Fiji = 36 lb = 16.329 kg
Guatemala = 71 lb = 32.205 kg
Mexico = 44.1 lb = 20 kg
Nicaragua = 35 lb = 15.876 kg
Panama = 79.4 lb = 36 kg
Paraguay = 37.5 lb = 17 kg
Venezuela = 37.5 lb = 17 kg
Bushel
Australia = 56 lb = 25.401 kg
Case
Fiji = 72 lb = 32.659 kg
Number
Puerto Rico: 100 bananas = 33 lb = 15 kg

Cherries: Bushel
Australia = 48 lb = 21.772 kg
Canada = 50 lb = 22.680 kg
New Zealand = 42 lb = 19.051 kg
Lug
United States = 18–20 lb = 8.2–9.1 kg

Cranberries: Carton
United States = 24 lb = 10.886 kg

Grapefruit: Box
United States:
California Desert Valleys
and Arizona = 64 lb = 29.030 kg
California, other = 67 lb = 30.391 kg
Florida = 85 lb = 38.555 kg
Texas = 80 lb = 36.287 kg
} 1 carton = ½ box
Bushel
Australia = 42 lb = 19.051 kg
Case
Australia = 42 lb = 19.051 kg
Jamaica = 75 lb = 34.019 kg
Number
Surinam: 100 grapefruit = 110.2 lb = 50 kg
Turkey: 100 grapefruit = 55.1 lb = 25 kg

Grapes: Lug
United States: California = 22–23 lb = 10.0–10.4 kg

Lemons: Box
United States = 76 lb = 34.473 kg
Bushel
Australia = 48 lb = 21.772 kg
Case
Israel (exports) = 33–35 lb = 15–16 kg
Number
Cyprus: 100 lemons = 27.6 lb = 12.5 kg

Oranges: Box or case
Israel = 33–46 lb = 15–21 kg
Jamaica = 80 lb = 36.287 kg
Trinidad and Tobago = 80 lb = 36.287 kg
United States: California, Arizona = 76 lb = 34.473 kg
Florida, Texas = 90 lb = 40.823 kg
Bushel
Australia = 48 lb = 21.772 kg
Number
Brazil: 100 oranges = 44 lb = 20 kg

Peaches: Bushel
Australia = 45 lb = 20.412 kg
United States = 48 lb = 21.772 kg

Fruit

Pears: Bushel
Australia = 45 lb = 20.412 kg
Canada = 50 lb = 22.680 kg

Carton
United States = 36–48 lb = 16.3–21.8 kg
Number
Brazil: 100 pears = 30.865 lb = 14 kg

Pineapples: Bushel
Australia = 42 lb = 19.051 kg
Number
Brazil: 100 pineapples (hawaii) = 507.1 lb = 230 kg

Plums: Bushel
Australia = 58 lb = 26.308 kg
New Zealand = 42 lb = 19.051 kg

Carton or lug
United States = 28 lb = 12.7 kg

Extraction rates: United States

Pounds fresh to give 1 pound dried:

Apples	8	Peaches: freestone	$6\frac{1}{2}$	Pears	$6\frac{1}{2}$	
Apricots	6	clingstone	$7\frac{1}{2}$	Prunes	2.9–3.1	

Alcoholic beverages

Beverages containing alcohol are produced by a process of fermentation which turns sugar from cereals, grapes, etc., into alcohol and carbon dioxide.

Beer

Beer is obtained from malted grain, usually barley. The malting process involves soaking the grain in water after which it is allowed to germinate and is dried in a malt kin. The malted grain is then milled (gently crushed) at the brewery and mashed with hot water to produce an aqueous extract (wort) which contains sugars resulting from the enzymic breakdown of the starch in the malt. The malt is then boiled with hops to impart the hop flavour and bitterness. In many countries and many beers brewing sugars are also added and these are dissolved at this stage. The sugars in the wort are converted to alcohol and CO_2 during fermentation by yeast and the resulting product, after the yeast has completed its task and settled out, is beer.
Ale and lagers are brewed in the same basic way, although lagers are in general produced more slowly and at lower temperatures. The yeast used for lager brewing is usually of the bottom fermenting kind; that is, it tends to sink to the bottom of the vessel during fermentation unlike ale yeast which usually rises to the surface. After fermentation all beer has to be matured and is then packaged.

Barley is the main cereal used in Europe; in Germany there is a law, the Reinheitsgebot, which prevents the use of anything but barley malt for brewing beer. In France, up to 30% of other malts, rice, sugar, etc. can be used. In Japan, saké is made from rice, and has an alcoholic content of about 12–16% by volume.

Measures

United Kingdom

Legal measures of the United Kingdom for the retail of beer or cider other than in a container are: $\frac{1}{3}$ pint, $\frac{1}{2}$ pint or a multiple of $\frac{1}{2}$ pint.
General trade measures for bottles and cans following metrication are:

Nip bottle	=	180 ml =	6.34 fl oz = 0.317 pt (formerly 0.25 pt)
Small bottle/can	=	275 ml =	9.68 fl oz = 0.484 pt (formerly 0.5 pt)
Large can	=	440 ml =	15.5 fl oz = 0.775 pt
Large bottle	=	550 ml =	19.4 fl oz = 0.97 pt (formerly 1 pt)
Flagon	=	1 130 ml =	39.8 fl oz = 1.99 pt (formerly 2 pt, or 1 quart)

Old English units:

Quarter-anker	= $2\frac{1}{2}$ gallons	= 3 US gallons	= 11.4 litres
Pin	= $4\frac{1}{2}$ gallons	= 5.4 US gallons	= 20.5 litres
Half-anker	= 5 gallons	= 6 US gallons	= 22.7 litres
Six	= 6 gallons	= 7.2 US gallons	= 27.3 litres
Firkin = 2 pins	= 9 gallons	= 10.8 US gallons	= 41 litres
Anker	= 10 gallons	= 12 US gallons	= 45 litres
Kilderkin, half-barrel or rundlet = 2 firkins	= 18 gallons	= 22 US gallons	= 82 litres
Half-hogshead	= 27 gallons	= 32 US gallons	= 123 litres
Barrel = 2 kilderkins	= 36 gallons	= 43 US gallons	= 164 litres
Tierce	= 42 gallons	= 50 US gallons	= 191 litres
Hogshead[a] = $1\frac{1}{2}$ barrels	= 54 gallons	= 65 US gallons	= 245 litres
Puncheon = 2 barrels	= 72 gallons	= 86 US gallons	= 327 litres
Butt or pipe = 2 hogsheads	= 108 gallons	= 130 US gallons	= 491 litres
Tun = 2 butts or pipes	= 216 gallons	= 259 US gallons	= 982 litres

[a]Old measure; sometimes a new hogshead of ale = puncheon = 72 gallons.

United States

Barrel =	31 US gallons		
	= 0.717 UK barrels	= 25.8 UK gallons	= 117 litres
Tun =	252 US gallons	= 210 UK gallons	= 954 litres

Canada

Barrel =	25 UK gallons		
	= 0.694 UK barrels	= 30 US gallons	= 114 litres

Strength

Specific gravity (relative density)

Alcohol content is measured for excise purposes in the United Kingdom in terms of specific gravity (or relative density = the ratio between the weight of a certain volume of a substance and the weight of the same volume of water, the temperature being specified), described usually as degrees – compared to 1 000 degrees for pure water.

During the process of fermentation, specific gravity falls; starting from the specific gravity of the wort (original gravity or OG), every fall of 1 degree is equivalent to an increase of alcoholic content by volume of approximately 0.102 or one tenth percentage.

For example, a beer with original gravity of 1 055° would have a 4% alcohol content if it had fermented to a specific gravity of 1 015°, and $4\frac{1}{2}$% if it had reached 1010°.

Gravity is sometimes expressed in terms of the excess of specific gravity over the water standard of 1 000; hence in the example mentioned, a 55 excess gravity has dropped to 15 (27% of the original) or 10 (18% of the original). A good drop (or 'attenuation') is a drop to about $\frac{1}{4}$ or $\frac{1}{5}$ of the original excess gravity, and a poor attenuation to about $\frac{1}{3}$. Where present gravity is not known, a rough approximation is that present gravity = $\frac{1}{4}$ original gravity.

The average original gravity of home-produced beer in the United Kingdom is shown in the following table:

Year ended March 31	Average gravity in degrees	Year ended March 31	Average gravity in degrees
1914	1052.80	1964	1037.41
1920	1039.41	1965	1037.43
1925	1042.97	1966	1037.41
1930	1042.90	1967	1037.26
1935	1041.06	1968	1037.15
1940	1040.62	1969	1036.93
1945	1034.54	1970	1036.78
1950	1033.71	1971	1036.65
1955	1036.91	1972	1036.68
1956	1037.04	1973	1036.79
1957	1037.20	1974	1037.05
1958	1037.29	1975	1037.18
1959	1037.35	1976	1037.35
1960	1037.06	1977	1037.26
1961	1037.25	1978	1037.28
1962	1037.46	1979	1037.41
1963	1037.53		

There is no direct relationship between type of beer and original gravity, but in general, brown ales have original gravity well into the 1040s, stouts up to about 1050 or more, and pale ales up to 1060; strong ale usually refers to beers with original gravity of 1060 or more.

For UK excise purposes a bulk barrel of 36 imperial gallons is used, whatever the gravity, and duty is charged on the worts, that is, the liquid produced from the mash before fermentation has begun. A deduction of 6% is made to allow for wastage before the beer is ready for consumption. A standard barrel is used for comparative purposes; this is 36 gallons at an original gravity of 1055°, or the equivalent quantity at that standard. Hence

$$\text{standard barrels} = \text{bulk barrels} \times \frac{\text{excess gravity}}{55}$$

Brewers' pound

This is an alternative measure of excess specific gravity. It is the number of pounds by which a barrel of beer, measured at 60°F, exceeds 360 pounds (the approximate weight of a bulk barrel of water).

Hence excess gravity is equal to brewers' pounds divided by 360 and multiplied by 1 000; also

specific gravity = 1 000 + excess gravity
    = 1 000 + (brewers' pounds/0.36)

and brewers' pounds = (specific gravity − 1 000) × 0.36

lcoholic beverages

Vines and spirits

Vines

he alcohol content of wine is obtained from grapes by fermentation of freshly ressed grape juice; EEC 'wine' is by regulation to be obtained only from grapes. Vine is about 70% of the weight of crushed grapes. The sugar content of a grape aries between about 12% and 27% by weight. The grapes are broken and rushed to form must (unfermented grape juice); yeast which has settled on the kins of grapes before gathering (or added where necessary) produces ermentation, and as alcohol is formed it releases the red colour in the skins where the grapes are coloured (and also from the pulp in Teinturier grapes, as his is also coloured).

lassification of wines
he general EEC grading of wines is as follows:
QPRD (Vins de qualité produits dans des régions déterminées): quality wines roduced in defined areas.
ns de table: other wines produced in the EEC. These can be branded wines or ines within the region of production named (that is, Vins de Pays in France)
ins importés: wines not produced in the EEC.

he best known gradings within VQPRD are as follows:

rance
AOC, AC or AOC (Appellation d'Origine Contrôlée): top quality wines subject strict laws of origin and content. Main areas are in Alsace, Bordeaux, urgundy, Champagne, Loire, Rhône valley, etc.; limitations include those on uantity (in terms of hectolitres per hectare), sugar content of must (in terms of rams per litre) and strength (in terms of percentage strength of alcohol by olume). The following are examples of the maximum yield for AC (AOC) wines hectolitres per hectare:

oire Valley		*Burgundy*	
ouraine	45	Côte de Nuits	35
hinon	40	Côte de Beaune	35
aumur: still white	45	Mâcon	50
sparkling	60	Mâcon Villages	45
red	40	Beaujolais	50
njou: white	45	Beaujolais (the growths)	40
rosé	45	*Côtes du Rhône*	
red	40	Hermitage	40
luscadet	40	Château Grillet	32
ordeaux		Châteauneuf du Pape	35
lédoc	45	Côtes du Rhône	50
largaux	40	*South East*	
auternes	25	Fitou	40
ntre-deux-mers	50	Corbières	50
ordeaux	50	*Corsica*	
		Vin de Corse: Coteaux d'Ajaccio	45
		Vin de Corse: Patrimonio	45

DQS (Vins délimités de qualité supérieure): limitations include those of region, ype of vine, methods of growing the vine and making the wine, maximum yield, lcohol content and taste.

Vest Germany
ualitätswein: limitations are on region, type of grape, and alcoholic content (a inimum alcoholic content of $8\frac{1}{2}$%), and taste.
ualitätswein mit Prädikat, with similar limitations as for Qualitätswein, plus a inimum alcoholic content of 9% obtained from the original sugar content with o additional sugar.

pirits

he alcohol content of spirits is obtained by distillation from wines or other quids containing alcohol. Alcohol boils at 78°C (173°F) so that, on the pplication of heat, it distils before water which boils at 100°C (212°F). The riginal liquid may be wine, fruit or fermented cereal mash.

Vhisky
lain types are:
cotland: malt whisky made from malted barley, and grain whisky made from arley and matured for at least 3 years; most commercial brands are blends of bout 40% malt and 60% grain. 1 ton of barley is estimated to produce pproximately 105 proof gallons of whisky (60 gallons of pure alcohol).

United States: bourbon whisky is made from at least 51% corn (maize), distilled at not more than 160° US proof; and aged for not less than 4 years.
Corn whisky is made from a mash of at least 80% corn.
Rye whisky is made from at least 51% rye.

Measures: retail

United Kingdom
Usual measures in the United Kingdom for retail supply, other than in a container, of whisky or other spirits are: $\frac{1}{6}$, $\frac{1}{5}$, $\frac{1}{4}$ or $\frac{1}{3}$ gill, giving approximately 32, 26, 21 or 16 singles per bottle respectively; the smaller singles are more usual in the South, and the larger in the North and Scotland. Usually 1 tot = $\frac{1}{4}$ gill = 35.5 ml.
1 bottle of wine or spirits usually contained $26\frac{2}{3}$ fluid ounces = 27.8 US liquid ounces = 75.8 centilitres; this is sometimes referred to as a 'reputed' or 'spirit' quart. With the change to the metric system, this size has been replaced by a 75 cl bottle (26.4 fluid ounces or 0.99 of a reputed quart bottle).
A 1 litre bottle size (35 fluid ounces) is occasionally used for wines imported from the European continent in bottle, and is being used increasingly with the change to the metric system.

Reputed quart bottle =
$26\frac{2}{3}$ fluid ounces = $5\frac{1}{3}$ gills = $1\frac{1}{3}$ pints = $\frac{1}{6}$ gallon = 75.8 centilitres
Noggin =
5 fluid ounces = 1 gill = $\frac{1}{4}$ pint = $\frac{1}{32}$ gallon = 142 millilitres
Miniature =
2 fluid ounces = $\frac{2}{5}$ gill = $\frac{1}{10}$ pint = $\frac{1}{80}$ gallon = 57 millilitres
Case: usually 1 dozen bottles.
Tappit hen: mainly used in Scotland, it has no fixed capacity but may hold from 3 to a dozen bottles; most usual capacity is 6 bottles = 1 gallon; of port usually equals 3 bottles.
Demijohn: a wicker-covered glass jar which may hold anything from 2 to 12 gallons.
Mineral water

Baby	= 4–5 fluid ounces	= 114–142 millilitres
Split	= 6–7 fluid ounces	= 170–200 millilitres
Large	= $8\frac{1}{2}$–$9\frac{1}{2}$ fluid ounces	= 241–270 millilitres

Sizes for carafes of wine in the United Kingdom were fixed from 1977 at: 25 cl, 50 cl, 75 cl or 1 litre; or 10 fl oz ($\frac{1}{2}$ pint) or 20 fl oz (1 pint).

France
A 1 litre bottle is a standard size.
1 bottle of wine has the following specified capacity:

Champagne	80 centilitres (1.06 reputed quarts)
Anjou, Bordeaux, Burgundy	75 centilitres (0.99 reputed quart)
Alsace	72 centilitres (0.95 reputed quart)

A bottle size of 70 centilitres (0.92 reputed quart) is sometimes used.
Half-bottles are generally one-half of the above capacity.
Special sizes are:
Pot beaujolais = 45 centilitres (0.59 reputed quart)
Fillette angevine (Anjou) = 35 centilitres (0.46 reputed quart)

West Germany
1 bottle of wine has the following capacity:
Moselle and Rhine 70 centilitres (0.92 reputed quart)

Sizes for champagne larger than 1 bottle:

Magnum	= 2 bottles	Methuselah[b]	= 8 bottles
Double-magnum	= 4 bottles	Salmanazar	= 12 bottles
Jéroboam[a]	= 4 bottles	Balthazar	= 16 bottles
Réhoboam	= 6 bottles	Nebuchadnezzar	= 20 bottles

[a]In Burgundy a jéroboam is 4 bottles and in Bordeaux 5 or 6 bottles.
[b]Impériale in Bordeaux and Tappinger for hock.
In the United Kingdom a jéroboam is usually 6 bottles and a réhoboam 8 bottles.
Wine is not usually matured in sizes above magnum.

Measures: wholesale

The following measures are approximate:

Aum or Ohm			
Rhenish (Alsatian, Hock and Moselle)	= 33 UK gallons	= 40 US gallons	= 150 litres
Barrique			
Anjou, Touraine	= 51 UK gallons	= 61 US gallons	= 232 litres
Bordeaux	= 49 UK gallons	= 59 US gallons	= 225 litres
Burgundy, Nantes	= 50 UK gallons	= 60 US gallons	= 228 litres

Alcoholic beverages

Butt or Bota

Sherry	= 110 UK gallons	= 132 US gallons	= 500 litres
Whisky	= 108 UK gallons	= 130 US gallons	= 491 litres

Feuillette
Burgundy:

Saône et Loire and Côte d'Or	= 25 UK gallons	= 30 US gallons	= 114 litres
Yonne (Chablis)	= 29 UK gallons	= 35 US gallons	= 132 litres

Hogshead

Australia South Africa	= 65 UK gallons	= 78 US gallons	= 295 litres
Brandy	= 60 UK gallons	= 72 US gallons	= 273 litres
Claret	= 46–49 UK gallons	= 55–59 US gallons	= 209–225 litres
Madeira Marsala	= 46 UK gallons	= 55 US gallons	= 209 litres
Port	= 58 UK gallons	= 70 US gallons	= 264 litres
Sherry	= 55 UK gallons	= 66 US gallons	= 250 litres
Whisky	= 56 UK gallons	= 67 US gallons	= 255 litres

Leaguer

South Africa	= 127 UK gallons	= 153 US gallons	= 577 litres

Muid

Aisne	= 57 UK gallons	= 68 US gallons	= 260 litres
Hérault	= 151 UK gallons	= 181 US gallons	= 685 litres
Montpellier	= 134 UK gallons	= 161 US gallons	= 608 litres

Octave

Sherry	= 13¾ UK gallons	= 16½ US gallons	= 62½ litres
Whisky	= 14 UK gallons	= 17 US gallons	= 64 litres

Pièce

Burgundy: Côte d'Or	= 50 UK gallons	= 60 US gallons	= 228 litres
Mâcon	= 47½ UK gallons	= 57 US gallons	= 216 litres
Beaujolais	= 47 UK gallons	= 56½ US gallons	= 214 litres

Pipe

Lisbon	= 117 UK gallons	= 141 US gallons	= 530 litres
Madeira	= 92 UK gallons	= 110 US gallons	= 418 litres
Marsala	= 93 UK gallons	= 112 US gallons	= 423 litres
Port or Tarragona	= 115–117 UK gal	= 138–141 US gal	= 522–535 litres
Teneriffe	= 100 UK gallons	= 120 US gallons	= 455 litres

Puncheon

Brandy	= 112–120 UK gal	= 135–144 US gal	= 509–546 litres
Rum	= 90–110 UK gal	= 108–132 US gal	= 409–500 litres
Whisky	= 95–120 UK gal	= 114–144 US gal	= 432–546 litres

Quarter

Brandy	= 30 UK gallons	= 36 US gallons	= 136 litres
Port	= 29 UK gallons	= 35 US gallons	= 132 litres
Sherry	= 27½ UK gallons	= 33 US gallons	= 125 litres
Whisky	= 28 UK gallons	= 34 US gallons	= 127 litres

Queue

Burgundy	= 100 UK gallons	= 120 US gallons	= 456 litres
Champagne	= 47½ UK gallons	= 57 US gallons	= 216 litres

Stück

Hock	= 264 UK gallons	= 317 US gallons	= 1 200 litres

Tierçon

Languedoc	= 50 UK gallons	= 60 US gallons	= 228 litres

Tonneau

Bordeaux	= 198 UK gallons	= 238 US gallons	= 900 litres

Usual general relationships are:

2 octaves	= 1 quarter		2 feuilletes	= 1 pièce
2 quarters	= 1 hogshead		2 pièces	= 1 queue
2 hogsheads	= 1 butt, pipe or puncheon		3 tierçon	= 1 muid
2 pipes	= 1 tonne, tonneau or tun		4 barriques	= 1 tonneau

Strength

The process of fermentation in wine stops when the original sugar content is used up in producing alcohol (when the wine is 'brut' or totally dry), or when the alcohol level is raised to about 15%, after which level the process of fermentation is in general terminated naturally, leaving some sugar content.

For some sweet wines (such as Sauternes) the original sugar content is so high that a good level of sugar remains after a 15% alcohol level has been achieved, but usually a level of only 10–12% alcohol content is achieved.

When there is not enough sugar in the juice, sugar is sometimes added to help increase the alcoholic content (this is called 'chaptalisation'). Fortified wines, such as port and sherry, including also 'vins doux naturels' in France, have had brandy or pure alcohol added to arrest fermentation before all sugar has been used up, and to increase alcoholic content (such wines are usually called 'dessert' wines in the United States).

Must contains about 70–85% water, the remainder being mainly carbohydrates. Alcohol is about 48% of the weight of sugar fermented.

The detailed relationship between sugar content of must and subsequent alcohol content (without adding sugar) is approximately as shown in the following table (at 15°C); the 'excess gravity' shown is the number of grams by which 1 litre of the must is heavier than 1 litre of distilled water (also called 'must-weight'). Excess gravity for zero sugar content is taken in this table as 11; values for this measure can vary.

Sugar content	Excess gravity	Alcohol content	Sugar content	Excess gravity	Alcohol content
grams per litre	grams	% by volume	grams per litre	grams	% by volume
0	11	0.0	150	68	8.8
18	18	1.1	160	71	9.4
50	30	3.0	170	75	10.0
60	34	3.5	180	79	10.6
70	37	4.1	190	83	11.2
80	41	4.7	200	87	11.8
90	45	5.3	210	90	12.4
100	49	5.9	220	94	13.0
110	52	6.5	230	98	13.6
120	56	7.1	240	101	14.2
130	60	7.7	250	105	14.7
140	64	8.3	255	107	15.0

For general conversions between weight and volume, the FAO takes the specific gravity (relative density) of wine as 1 000 (excess gravity = 0), so that, as with water, 1 litre weighs 1 kilogram, 1 hectolitre weighs 1 quintal, and 1 kilolitre weighs 1 tonne.

United Kingdom measures

Official UK measures for alcohol changed from old UK measures to metric measures with effect from January 1, 1980. Litres and hectolitres replaced the gallon, the Celsius temperature scale replaced the Fahrenheit, and the Sikes proof system for ascertaining the alcoholic strength of spirits and other liquids was replaced by a system of measurement by reference to percentages of alcohol by volume, as established by the Organisation Internationale de Métrologie Légale (OIML) and laid down in EEC regulations for use in the EEC. Following are the official definitions of alcoholic strength:
'alcoholic strength by volume' means the ratio of the volume of alcohol present in a mixture of water and ethanol at 20°C to the total volume of the mixture at the same temperature expressed as parts of alcohol per 100 parts of the mixture (with symbol: % vol);
'alcoholic strength by mass' means the ratio of the mass of alcohol present in a mixture of water and ethanol to the total mass of the mixture expressed as parts of alcohol per 100 parts of the mixture (with symbol: % mas).

For mixtures of alcohol (ethyl alcohol or ethanol) and water, the table on the facing page gives the relationship between density (kg/m³ in air at 20 °C) and strength by volume (at 20 °C) and by mass. These are the official UK relationships; for the purpose of estimating duty, figures beyond the first decimal place are disregarded whatever their value: eg, 46.37% vol is taken as 46.3% vol.

The new system replaced the former Sikes system which had been in use in the United Kingdom since 1816. This defined proof spirit as a mixture of ethyl alcohol and water which has a weight in air equal to twelve-thirteenths (approximately 0.923 08) of an equal volume of distilled water at 51°/51°F (10.56°/10.56°C). Proof spirit contained 49.2% alcohol by weight; the percentage of alcohol in proof spirit by volume varied at different temperatures, due to the differing coefficients of expansion of alcohol and water. At 60°F (15.56 °C) it was 57.10% and at 20°C (68°F) 57.15%. The temperatures used for UK excise purposes were 60°/60°F. Alcohol content was expressed in terms of percentages (or 'degrees') of proof spirit.

Alcoholic beverages

Measurement of alcoholic strength by density

Density in air at 20 °C kg/m³	Alcoholic strength (% of ethanol) by volume at 20 °C (% vol)	by mass (% mas)	Density in air at 20 °C kg/m³	Alcoholic strength (% of ethanol) by volume at 20 °C (% vol)	by mass (% mas)	Density in air at 20 °C kg/m³	Alcoholic strength (% of ethanol) by volume at 20 °C (% vol)	by mass (% mas)	Density in air at 20°C kg/m³	Alcoholic strength (% of ethanol) by volume at 20 °C (% vol)	by mass (% mas)
997.15	0.00	0.00	959	31.70	26.06	909	59.57	51.66	849	83.23	77.27
997.1	0.03	0.03	958.5	32.08	26.39	908	60.02	52.11	848	83.57	77.68
997	0.10	0.08	958	32.46	26.71	907	60.47	52.56	847	83.91	78.09
996	0.76	0.60	957.5	32.84	27.04	906	60.91	53.00	846	84.25	78.50
995	1.44	1.14	957	33.21	27.36	905	61.36	53.45	845	84.59	78.91
994	2.13	1.69	956.5	33.58	27.68	904	61.80	53.89	844	84.93	79.32
993	2.83	2.24	956	33.95	27.99	903	62.24	54.33	843	85.26	79.72
992	3.54	2.81	955.5	34.31	28.31	902	62.67	54.77	842	85.59	80.13
991	4.26	3.39	955	34.67	28.62	901	63.11	55.21	841	85.92	80.53
990	5.00	3.98	954.5	35.02	28.93	900	63.54	55.65	840	86.25	80.93
989	5.75	4.59	954	35.37	29.23	899	63.97	56.09	839	86.58	81.34
988	6.52	5.20	953.5	35.72	29.54	898	64.40	56.53	838	86.90	81.74
987	7.30	5.83	953	36.07	29.84	897	64.82	56.97	837	87.22	82.14
986	8.09	6.47	952.5	36.14	30.14	896	65.25	57.41	836	87.54	82.54
985	8.90	7.12	952	36.75	30.43	895	65.67	57.84	835	87.86	82.94
984	9.72	7.78	951.5	37.09	30.73	894	66.09	58.28	834	88.18	83.34
983	10.55	8.46	951	37.42	31.02	893	66.51	58.71	833	88.49	83.74
982	11.40	9.15	950.5	37.75	31.31	892	66.93	59.15	832	88.81	84.13
981	12.26	9.85	950	38.08	31.60	891	67.34	59.58	831	89.12	84.53
980	13.14	10.57	949.5	38.40	31.89	890	67.76	60.01	830	89.42	84.92
979	14.03	11.30	949	38.73	32.17	889	68.17	60.45	829	89.73	85.31
978.5	14.47	11.66	948	39.36	32.74	888	68.58	60.88	828	90.03	85.71
978	14.93	12.03	947	39.99	33.29	887	68.99	61.31	827	90.33	86.10
977.5	15.38	12.40	946	40.61	33.84	886	69.39	61.74	826	90.63	86.49
977	15.84	12.78	945	41.22	34.39	885	69.80	62.17	825	90.93	86.87
976.5	16.29	13.15	944	41.82	34.93	884	70.20	62.60	824	91.22	87.26
976	16.75	13.53	943	42.41	35.46	883	70.60	63.03	823	91.51	87.65
975.5	17.21	13.91	942	43.00	35.99	882	71.00	63.45	822	91.80	88.03
975	17.68	14.29	941	43.58	36.51	881	71.40	63.88	821	92.09	88.41
974.5	18.14	14.68	940	44.15	37.02	880	71.79	64.31	820	92.37	88.79
974	18.61	15.06	939	44.71	37.54	879	72.19	64.74	819	92.66	89.17
973.5	19.07	15.45	938	45.27	38.05	878	72.58	65.16	818	92.94	89.55
973	19.54	15.83	937	45.82	38.55	877	72.97	65.59	817	93.21	89.93
972.5	20.00	16.22	936	46.37	39.05	876	73.36	66.01	816	93.49	90.30
972	20.47	16.60	935	46.91	39.55	875	73.74	66.43	815	93.76	90.68
971.5	20.93	16.99	934	47.44	40.04	874	74.13	66.86	814	94.03	91.05
971	21.40	17.37	933	47.97	40.53	873	74.51	67.28	813	94.29	91.42
970.5	21.86	17.76	932	48.49	41.02	872	74.89	67.70	812	94.56	91.79
970	22.32	18.14	931	49.01	41.50	871	75.28	68.13	811	94.82	92.15
969.5	22.78	18.52	930	49.53	41.99	870	75.65	68.55	810	95.08	92.52
969	23.24	18.90	929	50.04	42.46	869	76.03	68.97	809	95.33	92.88
968.5	23.69	19.28	928	50.55	42.94	868	76.41	69.39	808	95.59	93.24
968	24.14	19.66	927	51.05	43.42	867	76.78	69.81	807	95.84	93.60
967.5	24.59	20.04	926	51.55	43.89	866	77.15	70.23	806	96.08	93.96
967	25.04	20.41	925	52.05	44.36	865	77.52	70.65	805	96.33	94.32
966.5	25.48	20.79	924	52.54	44.83	864	77.89	71.06	804	96.57	94.67
966	25.92	21.16	923	53.03	45.29	863	78.26	71.48	803	96.81	95.02
965.5	26.36	21.52	922	53.51	45.76	862	78.62	71.90	802	97.05	95.37
965	26.79	21.89	921	54.00	46.22	861	78.99	72.32	801	97.28	95.72
964.5	27.22	22.25	920	54.48	46.68	860	79.35	72.73	800	97.51	96.07
964	27.65	22.61	919	54.95	47.14	859	79.71	73.15	799	97.74	96.41
963.5	28.07	22.97	918	55.43	47.60	858	80.07	73.56	798	97.96	96.75
963	28.49	23.32	917	55.90	48.05	857	80.43	73.98	797	98.18	97.09
962.5	28.90	23.67	916	56.37	48.51	856	80.78	74.39	796	98.40	97.43
962	29.31	24.02	915	56.83	48.96	855	81.14	74.80	795	98.61	97.77
961.5	29.72	24.37	914	57.29	49.42	854	81.49	75.22	794	98.83	98.10
961	30.12	24.71	913	57.76	49.87	853	81.84	75.63	793	99.04	98.43
960.5	30.52	25.05	912	58.21	50.32	852	82.19	76.04	792	99.24	98.76
960	30.92	25.39	911	58.67	50.77	851	82.54	76.45	791	99.44	99.09
959.5	31.31	25.73	910	59.12	51.22	850	82.89	76.86	790	99.64	99.41
									788.16	100.00	100.00

Alcoholic beverages

Other measures of strength

Tralles (used in some European countries) = a scale at 60°F, expressed as percentages of alcohol by volume.
US proof spirit = a scale by volume at 60°F, where 100% alcohol is 200 per cent proof spirit, and percentage of proof spirit is throughout double the actual percentage of alcohol by volume, so that 50% alcohol, for example, is 100 per cent proof spirit. Hence US proof spirit = Tralles × 2. US proof is sometimes expressed, as for Sikes, in terms of percentages above or below 100 degrees proof – which is 50% by volume in US terms.
Gay-Lussac (°GL; used in France and Belgium) = a scale in degrees at 15°C (59°F), expressed as percentages of alcohol by volume. Hence Gay-Lussac is approximately the same as Tralles, but based on 59°F instead of 60°F.
A detailed table showing the relationship between Sikes and some other systems of measuring alcohol content is given on the facing page; it may be noted that there is only a very small difference at the level of accuracy shown between Gay-Lussac and the percentage by volume at 20°C. Tralles measure is the same as Gay-Lussac in the table, except for strengths marked *, which are 0.1 higher for Tralles.
The following table shows the approximate strengths of some alcoholic drinks as consumed in the United Kingdom, as measured in the old UK (Sikes) proof system and the new system of alcohol content by volume.

	Proof spirit (Sikes) %	Alcohol content % by volume (% vol)
Whisky Gin Rum	70	40
Vodka	65.5 or 80	37½ or 46
Sherry Port Madeira	26–38½	15–22
Bordeaux:		
Sauternes	24	14
Other white	19–23	11–13
Red	17–20	10–11½
Burgundy:		
White	18–24	10¼–14
Red	17–24	10–14
Champagne	22–23	12½–13

Beer: by gravity

original	present		
1060	1015	9.8	5.6
1050	1012	8.2	4.7
1040	1010	6.6	3.8
1030	1007	5.0	2.9

In the United Kingdom wine is classified for duty purposes, as from January 1, 1976, on a three-strength structure determined by the percentage of alcohol by volume at 20°C: lower (15% and under), middle (over 15% and up to 18%) and higher (over 18% and up to 22%); over 22% duty is charged on each 1% or part of 1%. This structure replaced the previous two-strength structure, classified as light or heavy and using the Sikes proof strengths in the classification; the old light classification was 27° proof or under (under about 15.5% vol) for British and Commonwealth wines and 25° proof or under (under about 14.4% vol) for other wines. Hence the new 'lower' wine classification corresponds roughly to the old 'light' classification.

Cocoa

The word 'cocoa' is an English corruption of 'cacao'. There are very approximately 400 cocoa beans to the pound (900 per kilogram).

Measures

The unit most generally used is the bag or sack of 60 kg (132.277 lb).
Other measures

Arroba: Brazil	= 15 kg (33 lb)
Bag: Ghana, Nigeria	= 62.5 kg (138 lb)
Cameroon, Ivory Coast	= 65 kg (143 lb)
Load: Ghana	= 30 kg (66 lb)

Extraction rates

100 units of beans give: 80 units cocoa liquor or paste, or
40 units cocoa butter
and 40 units cocoa cake and powder

Coffee

Measures

Most official statistics refer to green coffee. The international trade bag of 60 kg (132.277 lb) is the most important unit.
El Salvador uses a bag of 69 kg (152.12 lb)

1 metric quintal	= 1⅔ bags (of 60 kg)
1 tonne	= 16⅔ bags (of 60 kg)

Extraction rates

The fruit of the coffee tree is called a cherry. Inside each cherry, covered by pulp, are normally two beans or berries each enclosed in a skin called parchment.
It takes about 5 lb of cherries to make 1 lb of green commercial coffee. Roasting from green into regular coffee causes a further reduction by 16%. Roasting from green to soluble coffee causes a reduction from 3 units of green coffee to 1 unit of soluble. Details of extraction rates are:

Fresh coffee berries yield	20% clean green coffee
Parchment coffee yields	83.3% clean green coffee
Dry cherries yield	50% clean green coffee
1 unit green coffee yields	0.84 units roasted regular coffee
1 unit green coffee yields	0.333 units roasted soluble coffee

Tea

There are two main types of tea, produced from the same plant: green tea is unfermented, while black tea undergoes full fermentation. There are other types, including oolong tea, which is partially fermented.

Measures

Bangladesh:	package	= 104 lb	= 47.174 kg
India:	chest	= 100–128 lb	= 45–58 kg
Japan:	kin	= 1.323 lb	= 0.6 kg

Tobacco

Green weight basis (or farm sales weight or wet weight) represents the weight at which tobacco is sold by the grower after curing, and is about 20% of the weight before curing.
On purchase from the grower, the tobacco is dried and in consequence, for flue-cured tobacco, the dry weight of leaf is about 90% of the green weight.
After curing and drying (and usually a certain amount of stemming and stripping) the tobacco has to be stored for about 3 years to mature. Flue-cured tobacco loses about 11.3%, and air-cured about 13.6% of sales weight.
Before the tobacco undergoes final manufacture it has to be thoroughly stemmed or stripped (having the mid-rib of the leaf removed). The dry weight after stemming forms 70–80% of the dry weight of the unstemmed leaf.

1000 average sized cigarettes contain approximately 1 kilogram (2.205 pounds) of tobacco; 100 contain 100 grams or 3.5 ounces. 1 000 cigarillos or cigars contain approximately 1.1 to 8.4 kilograms (2.5 to 18.6 pounds) of tobacco depending on size. An average rate for 1000 cigars is 4½ kilograms (10 pounds)

Measures

Costa Rica:	Fardo		= 127 lb	= 57.6 kg
Honduras:	Fardo		= 101.4 lb	= 46 kg
United States				
Bale:	cigar leaf		= 150–175 lb	= 68–79 kg
Case:	cigar leaf		= 250–365 lb	= 113–166 kg
Hogshead:	Maryland		= 775 lb	= 351.534 kg
	flue-cured		= 950 lb	= 430.913 kg
	Burley		= 975 lb	= 442.253 kg
	dark air-cured		= 1150 lb	= 521.631 kg
	Virginia fire-cured		= 1350 lb	= 612.350 kg
	Kentucky and Tennessee fire-cured		= 1 500 lb	= 680.389 kg
Venezuela:	Paca		= 110.231 lb	= 50 kg
	Vara		= 0.55 lb	= 0.25 kg

Rubber

Natural rubber is obtained as latex from the rubber tree; it is defined for trade purposes as the dry content weight of latex, excluding balata, gutta-percha, and all rubber-allied gums, as the latter generally go into different uses from those which are usual for natural rubber.

Dry content weight is 60% of actual latex weight.

Measure: Malaysia
bale of block rubber = 75 lb = 34 kg

Alcoholic beverages

Sikes and other systems of measurement of alcoholic strength

United Kingdom (Sikes) percentage of proof spirit	Density in air at 20°C kg/m³	Alcoholic strength (% of ethanol) by volume at 20°C (% vol)	by mass (% mas)	United States percentage of US proof spirit	Gay-Lussac degrees	United Kingdom (Sikes) percentage of proof spirit	Density in air at 20°C kg/m³	Alcoholic strength (% of ethanol) by volume at 20°C (% vol)	by mass (% mas)	United States percentage of US proof spirit	Gay-Lussac degrees
0	997.1	0.0	0.0	0.0	0.0	60	955.5	34.3	28.3	68.5	34.3
1	996.3	0.6	0.5	1.1	0.6	61	954.7	34.9	28.8	69.6	34.9
2	995.5	1.1	0.9	2.3	1.1*	62	953.8	35.5	29.3	70.7	35.4
3	994.6	1.7	1.4	3.4	1.7	63	953.1	36.0	29.8	71.9	36.0
4	993.8	2.3	1.8	4.6	2.3	64	952.2	36.6	30.3	73.0	36.6
5	992.9	2.9	2.3	5.7	2.9	65	951.3	37.2	30.8	74.2	37.1
6	992.2	3.4	2.7	6.8	3.4	66	950.4	37.8	31.4	75.3	37.7
7	991.3	4.0	3.2	8.0	4.0	67	949.6	38.3	31.8	76.4	38.3
8	990.5	4.6	3.7	9.1	4.6	68	948.8	38.9	32.3	77.6	38.9
9	989.8	5.2	4.1	10.3	5.2	69	947.8	39.5	32.8	78.7	39.4
10	988.9	5.8	4.6	11.4	5.7	70	947.0	40.0	33.3	79.9	40.0
11	988.3	6.3	5.0	12.5	6.3	71	946.0	40.6	33.8	81.0	40.6
12	987.5	6.9	5.5	13.7	6.9	72	945.1	41.2	34.3	82.1	41.1
13	986.7	7.5	6.0	14.8	7.4	73	944.0	41.8	34.9	83.3	41.7
14	986.1	8.1	6.4	16.0	8.0	74	943.2	42.3	35.4	84.4	42.3
15	985.4	8.6	6.9	17.1	8.6	75	942.2	42.9	35.9	85.6	42.9
16	984.6	9.2	7.4	18.3	9.2	76	941.1	43.5	36.4	86.7	43.4
17	983.9	9.8	7.8	19.4	9.7	77	940.2	44.0	36.9	87.8	44.0
18	983.3	10.3	8.3	20.5	10.3	78	939.2	44.6	37.4	89.0	44.6
19	982.6	10.9	8.7	21.7	10.9	79	938.1	45.2	38.0	90.1	45.1
20	982.0	11.4	9.2	22.8	11.5	80	937.1	45.8	38.5	91.3	45.7
21	981.3	12.0	9.7	24.0	12.0	81	936.1	46.3	39.0	92.4	46.3
22	980.6	12.6	10.1	25.1	12.6	82	935.0	46.9	39.5	93.6	46.8
23	979.9	13.2	10.6	26.2	13.2	83	933.9	47.5	40.1	94.7	47.4
24	979.4	13.7	11.1	27.4	13.7*	84	932.9	48.0	40.6	95.8	48.0
25	978.7	14.3	11.5	28.5	14.3	85	931.8	48.6	41.1	97.0	48.5
26	978.0	14.9	12.0	29.7	14.9	86	930.8	49.1	41.6	98.1	49.1
27	977.4	15.5	12.5	30.8	15.5	87	929.7	49.7	42.1	99.3	49.7
28	976.8	16.0	12.9	31.9	16.0	88	928.5	50.3	42.7	100.4	50.2*
29	976.2	16.6	13.4	33.1	16.6	89	927.5	50.8	43.2	101.5	50.8
30	975.5	17.2	13.9	34.2	17.2	90	926.3	51.4	43.7	102.7	51.4
31	975.0	17.7	14.3	35.4	17.8	91	925.2	52.0	44.3	103.8	52.0
32	974.3	18.3	14.8	36.5	18.3	92	924.1	52.5	44.8	105.0	52.5
33	973.7	18.9	15.3	37.6	18.9	93	922.8	53.1	45.4	106.1	53.1
34	973.1	19.4	15.7	38.8	19.5	94	921.6	53.7	45.9	107.2	53.7
35	972.4	20.1	16.3	39.9	20.1	95	920.3	54.3	46.5	108.4	54.2*
36	971.8	20.6	16.8	41.1	20.6	96	919.2	54.8	47.0	109.5	54.8
37	971.2	21.2	17.2	42.2	21.2	97	918.0	55.4	47.6	110.7	55.4
38	970.6	21.8	17.7	43.4	21.7*	98	916.7	56.0	48.2	111.8	56.0
39	970.0	22.3	18.1	44.5	22.3	99	915.6	56.5	48.6	112.9	56.5
40	969.4	22.9	18.6	45.6	22.9	100	914.4	57.1	49.2	114.1	57.1
41	968.7	23.5	19.1	46.8	23.5	101	913.1	57.7	49.8	115.2	57.7
42	968.1	24.1	19.6	47.9	24.0	102	912.0	58.2	50.3	116.4	58.2
43	967.5	24.6	20.0	49.1	24.6	103	910.7	58.8	50.9	117.5	58.8
44	966.8	25.2	20.6	50.2	25.2	104	909.4	59.4	51.5	118.7	59.4
45	966.1	25.8	21.1	51.3	25.7*	105	908.1	60.0	52.1	119.8	60.0
46	965.6	26.3	21.5	52.5	26.3	110	901.8	62.8	54.9	125.5	62.8
47	964.9	26.9	22.0	53.6	26.9	115	894.9	65.7	57.9	131.2	65.6
48	964.2	27.5	22.5	54.8	27.5	120	888.2	68.5	60.8	136.9	68.5
49	963.6	28.0	22.9	55.9	28.0	125	881.0	71.4	63.9	142.6	71.3
50	962.9	28.6	23.4	57.0	28.6	130	873.8	74.2	66.9	148.3	74.2
51	962.1	29.2	23.9	58.2	29.1	135	866.2	77.1	70.1	154.0	77.0
52	961.5	29.7	24.4	59.3	29.7	140	858.5	79.9	73.3	159.7	79.9
53	960.8	30.3	24.9	60.5	30.3	145	850.5	82.7	76.7	165.4	82.7
54	960.0	30.9	25.4	61.6	30.9	150	842.3	85.5	80.0	171.1	85.6
55	959.2	31.5	25.9	62.7	31.5	155	833.3	88.4	83.6	176.8	88.4
56	958.6	32.0	26.3	63.9	32.0	160	824.1	91.2	87.2	182.5	91.3
57	957.8	32.6	26.8	65.0	32.6	165	813.8	94.1	91.1	188.2	94.1
58	957.0	33.2	27.4	66.2	33.2	170	802.6	96.9	95.2	194.0	96.9
59	956.3	33.7	27.8	67.3	33.7	175.3	788.2	100.0	100.0	200.0	100.0

Vegetable oilseeds and oil

Measures

Coconuts: number
FAO conversion rate: 1 000 nuts = 1 tonne

Copra
Candy: Sri Lanka = 560 lb = 254.012 kg

Cottonseed
Ardab or Ardeb: Egypt   = 264.555 lb = 120 kg
Bushel: United States (average) = 32 lb   = 14.515 kg

Groundnuts (peanuts), unshelled
Ardab or Ardeb: Egypt   = 165.35 lb = 75 kg
Bushel: United States: Virginia = 17 lb   = 7.711 kg
Runners = 21 lb   = 9.525 kg
Spanish = 25 lb   = 11.340 kg

Linseed
Ardab or Ardeb: Egypt   = 268.964 lb = 122 kg
Bushel: Australia, Canada
and United States = 56 lb   = 25.401 kg

Rapeseed
Bushel: United States = 50 & 60 lb = 22.7 & 27.2 kg
Koku: Japan = 264.555 lb = 120 kg

Sesame seed
Ardab or Ardeb: Egypt = 264.555 lb = 120 kg
Bushel: Sri Lanka = 50 lb   = 22.680 kg
United States = 46 lb   = 20.865 kg
Koku: Japan = 251.327 lb = 114 kg

Soyabeans
Bushel: Canada & United States = 60 lb   = 27.216 kg
Koku: Japan = 284.396 lb = 129 kg
Suk: Korea, South = 297.624 lb = 135 kg

Oilseed extraction rate
Groundnuts: 100 units unshelled = 60–70 units shelled

Oils: volume to weight
Average rates for the United States are:

	1 litre weighs		1 US gallon weighs	
	lb	kg[a]	lb	kg
Castor oil	2.1	0.96	8.0	3.6
Cottonseed oil	2.0	0.92	7.7	3.5
Groundnut oil	2.0	0.92	7.7	3.5
Linseed oil	2.0	0.92	7.7	3.5
Olive oil	2.0	0.91	7.6	3.5
Palm oil	2.0	0.92	7.7	3.5
Soyabean oil	2.0	0.92	7.7	3.5

[a]Figures in this column are approximately the same as relative density.

Oils: extraction rates

Extraction rates for oilseeds can vary greatly. The percentage rates given below are average rates:

Average oil equivalent of 100 units of oilseed

Castor seed	45	Linseed	34	Rapeseed	35
Copra	64	Mustard seed	23	Safflower seed	30
Cottonseed	16	Niger seed	35	Sesame seed	45
Groundnuts:		Oiticica seed	45	Soyabeans	17
shelled	45	Olives	15	Sunflower seed	35
unshelled	32	Palm kernels	47	Tung nuts	16
Hempseed	24	Perilla seed	37	Others	30
Kapok seed	18	Poppy seed	41		

Textile fibres: seed, bast, etc.

Cotton

Unginned, raw or seed cotton is cotton straight from the plant. After it has been processed the seeds are separated from the lint (seed hairs) by a gin, and the fibre which is produced is called ginned cotton or cotton lint.

In addition to cotton lint, the cotton plant produces cotton linters, which are short white lengths of fuzz, almost pure cellulose, which clings to the cotton seed and is extracted and used separately from the cotton lint.

To convert unginned cotton to ginned or lint the overall conversion factor generally used is one-third. An average conversion in the United States is 1 lb ginned = 3.26 lb unginned, including trash; the rate varies widely.

Staple length of cotton is usually about $\frac{5}{8}$–2 in (approximately 15–50 mm) and can be classified according to the length of the filaments as follows:

Short staple	= less than $\frac{7}{8}$ in	= less than 22.2 mm
Medium staple	= $\frac{7}{8}$–$1\frac{1}{8}$ in	= 22.2–28.6 mm
Long staple	= $1\frac{1}{8}$–$1\frac{5}{16}$ in	= 28.6–33.3 mm
Extra-long staple	= more than $1\frac{5}{16}$ in	= more than 33.3 mm

Longer staple types produce the finest cottons. Sea Island cotton has a staple length over 2 in (50 mm).

Cotton fibre has a diameter of about 10–20 micrometres ('microns'), and a relative density of about 1.5. Cellulose content is 88–96%.

Measures

Running bale is an actual bale, that is a bale of any weight. A standard bale is 500 lb gross (226.8 kg) or 478 lb net = 216.8 kg
The degree of compression for a cotton bale is usually 12–32 lb/ft³ (192–153 kg/m³); a universal density bale has a density of at least 28 lb/ft³ (448.5 kg/m³).

United States
Bale: gross (including sack) = 500 lb = 226.796 kg
net = 480 lb = 217.724 kg

Brazil
Bale = 396.8 lb = 180 kg

Egypt
Bale = 730 lb = 331.122 kg

India, Bangladesh and Pakistan
Bale = 392 lb   = 177.808 kg
Candy = 784 lb   = 355.616 kg

Venezuela
Paca (bale) = 110–441 lb = 50–200 kg

Other

Jute: after harvesting, the fibre is removed from the stalk by retting (soaking until the fibre becomes free); dry fibre yield from green weight of plant is 5–7%.

Measures
Bangladesh: bale = 400 lb   = 181.437 kg
Brazil: bale = 440.9 lb = 200 kg
India: bale = 396.8 lb = 180 kg

Kenaf (or mesta): this fibre is similar to jute but of lower quality; finest qualities of kenaf are equivalent to medium quality jute, while average qualities are used in a mixture with jute.

Flax: after harvesting, flax is retted to remove the fibre from the stalks and the resultant straw is then dried and scutched (beaten to remove bark, etc. from fibres). The yield of scutched flax is 5–15% of straw weight or 2–5% of green weight; short broken fibres are referred to as tow. Flaxseed('linseed') is the source of linseed oil; other flax varieties are used for linen fibre.

United Kingdom: bale = 448 lb   = 203.209 kg

Textile fibres: seed, bast, etc.

Hemp: this term is used to describe a range of fibres, usually classified as soft or hard.
soft fibres: consist of two main types, true hemp and sunn (or Indian hemp).
hard fibres: the chief types are sisal, manila (or abaca) and henequén; other varieties include Mauritius hemp, phormium (or New Zealand flax or hemp) and maguey.

Measures

United Kingdom: stone	= 32 lb	= 14.515 kg
Mexico: paca or bale (average) of henequen	= 405.7 lb	= 184 kg
New Zealand: bale of phormium	= 400 lb	= 181.437 kg
Philippines: bale of manila	= 278 lb	= 126 kg

Coir: the source of the fibre is coconut husks; it is removed after allowing the fruit to 'ret'. 1 000 coconuts provide about 300 lb (130 kg) of mattress fibre and 300 lb (136 kg) of better quality bristle fibre.

Livestock products: textiles

Wool

Greasy: raw wool shorn from the sheep's back; from 30–65% of the weight consists of dirt and other impurities. Average weight of fleece per sheep 10–11 lb (4½–5 kg).

Rough washed wool: is wool which has been washed on the sheep before clipping; it has a pure wool content of about 80%.

Scoured: is wool that has been clipped and then washed, and has a pure wool content of around 90%. Weight of scoured wool is roughly 60% of weight of greasy wool.

Slipe, pulled or skin wool: is wool off dead sheep skins which have been rough washed; the pure wool content is about 80%.

Actual weight: is used in trade returns and includes all forms (greasy, scoured, cleaned and pulled) with no regard to the clean content.

Cleaned content: is a statistical term and represents the weight of the wool if it could be completely clean and free from moisture. Average world conversion factor from 'greasy' to 'clean' basis is 0.58.

Measures

United Kingdom (old units)

Clove	=	7 lb	= 3.175 kg
Stone	=	14 lb	= 6.350 kg
Stone (Scotland)	=	24 lb	= 10.886 kg
Score	=	20 lb	= 9.072 kg
Tod	=	28 lb	= 12.701 kg
Wey	=	182 lb	= 82.554 kg
Pack	=	240 lb	= 108.862 kg
Sack = 2 weys	=	364 lb	= 165.108 kg
Last = 12 sacks	=	4 368 lb	= 1 981.291 kg

Other

Argentina:	bale (average)	= 925 lb	= 420 kg
Australia:	bale – greasy	= 348 lb	= 158 kg
	scoured	= 256 lb	= 116 kg
New Zealand:	bale – gross	= 335 lb	= 152 kg
	washed	= 300 lb	= 136 kg

Quality

There are three main quality groups for wool generally used, the top two quality groups being for apparel; the following division is based on Bradford quality counts:

Merino wool	60s and up	(23 'microns' and finer)
Crossbred wool	46s to 58s	(36 to 25 'microns')
Carpet wool	up to 44s	(38 'microns' and coarser)

Bradford quality groups are based on the fineness of wool; the 100s level was originally determined as the level for the finest wool that could be spun (see also 'textiles'). The table below shows some approximate relationships for different types of wool classification. There is no general international standard classification, but fibre diameter measurement in terms of 'microns' (micrometres) is used to an increasing extent. The comparisons shown here have been adapted from information supplied by the Commonwealth Secretariat and the International Wool Secretariat.

Quality classification of wool

United Kingdom Bradford quality groups	Fibre diameter in micrometres ('microns')	United States Boston quality groups	France	Germany	Argentina
Merino					
70–64s	19–21	64s	105	AA–A	Fine supra
64s	21	64–60s	Prime merino	A	Merina
64–60s	21–23	60s	Prime croisée	A–B	Merina prima
60s	23	60–58s	Prime croisée I	B	Prima
Crossbred:					
fine					
60–58s	23–25	58s fine	Croisée I	B–CI	Prima–Cruza I
58s fine	25	58–56s	Croisée I–II	CI	Cruza (fina) I
58–56s	25–28	56s	Croisée II	CI–CII	Cruza (fina) I–II
56s fine	28	56–50s	Croisée II–III	CII	Cruza (fina) II
medium					
56–52s	28–31	50s fine	Croisée III	CII–DI	Cruza (mediana) II–III
52s	31	50–48s	Croisée III–IV	DI	Cruza (mediana) III
50–48s	33–34	48–46s	Croisée IV	DI–DII	Cruza (mediana) III–IV
coarse					
50–48s	33–34	48–46s	Croisée IV–V	DII	Cruza (gruesa) IV
48–46s	34–36	46–44s	Croisée V	DII–E	Cruza (gruesa) V
46s	36	44s	Croisée V–VI	E	Cruza (gruesa) VI

Livestock products: textiles

Clean yields of wool

The following estimates, made by the Commonwealth Secretariat, give the clean yield conversion factors for the chief types of wool entering international trade. These factors are average estimates and are necessarily approximate.

Country of origin	Overall clip			Exports		
	1950–51	1970–71	1975–76	1950–51	1970–71	1975–76
Australia: Merino (greasy)	$56\frac{1}{2}$	$55\frac{1}{2}$	$59\frac{1}{2}$	58	57	61
Crossbred (greasy)	$60\frac{1}{2}$	$59\frac{1}{2}$	$62\frac{1}{2}$	62	61	64
Scoured	90	93	93	90	93	93
New Zealand: Merino (greasy)	$54\frac{1}{2}$	64	64	$56\frac{1}{2}$	66	66
Crossbred (greasy)	67	73	73	69	75	73
Scoured	90	95	95	90	95	95
Slipe	81	82	82	81	82	82
South Africa: Merino (greasy)	$49\frac{1}{2}$	$52\frac{1}{2}$[d]	$52\frac{1}{2}$[d]	51	$54\frac{1}{2}$[d]	$54\frac{1}{2}$[d]
Lesotho and Transkei	$40\frac{1}{2}$	$36\frac{1}{2}$[d]	$36\frac{1}{2}$[d]	—	38[d]	38[d]
Karakul, crossbred, etc. (greasy)	57	$48\frac{1}{2}$[d]	$48\frac{1}{2}$[d]	—	50[d]	50[d]
Scoured	91	92[d]	92[d]	91	92[d]	92[d]
Argentina: Merino (greasy)	42	50[d]	50[d]	42	50[d]	50[d]
Crossbred (greasy)	66	61[d]	61[d]	66	62[d]	62[d]
Scoured	95	$94\frac{1}{2}$[d]	$94\frac{1}{2}$[d]	95	$94\frac{1}{2}$[d]	$94\frac{1}{2}$[d]
Slipe	81	$80\frac{1}{2}$[d]	$80\frac{1}{2}$	81	$80\frac{1}{2}$[d]	$80\frac{1}{2}$[d]
Uruguay: Merino (greasy)	49[a]	56[d]	56[d]	49[a]	57[d]	57[d]
Crossbred (greasy)	65	69[d]	69[d]	65	70[d]	70[d]
Chile: Crossbred (greasy)	58	$53\frac{1}{2}$	$53\frac{1}{2}$	60	59	57
United Kingdom: Fleece (greasy)	65	66	66	65	—	—
Fleece (washed)	77	$76\frac{1}{2}$	$76\frac{1}{2}$	77	—	—
Skin	75	75	75	75	75[b]	75[b]
Scoured	95	95	95	95	95[c]	95[c]

[a] Refers only to fine merino (64s and up).   [b] Wool pulled from imported skins and subsequently exported.   [c] Imported wool scoured in the UK then exported.   [d] 1968–69; best estimate for later years.

Other textile fibres

Silk: the silk worm produces a continuous filament of two threads stuck together, which is woven into a cocoon. There may be up to 4 000 yards or metres of silk in a cocoon, but only about 600–900 yards or metres can be reeled off into the continuous filament known as 'nett silk'. The tough outer husk and the soft inner portions can be combed and spun into 'spun silk', consisting of fibres. Raw silk equivalent = 25% of actual weight of cocoons.
Reeled silk = 17% of actual weight of coccoons.

Mohair: comes from the Angora goat. The staple length is 4–10 inches (100–250 mm); the Bradford quality grouping is 28s to 50s. Clean yield is about 80% greasy weight.

Cashmere: comes from the Cashmere goat. The undercoat hairs are $1\frac{1}{2}$–$3\frac{1}{2}$ inches (38–90 mm) in length and very soft; the outercoat is 2–5 inches (50–130 mm) and is much coarser. Each animal yields about 4 oz (100 g) of fibre a year.

Camel: the undercoat hairs are 1–5 inches (25–130 mm) long; the coarse overcoat is 5–12 inches (130–300 mm) long; a camel yields about 5–10 lb (2–$4\frac{1}{2}$ kg) of hair a year.

Llama: staple length is 10–12 inches (250–300 mm) and the hair is coarse.

Alpaca: staple length is 6–12 inches (150–300 mm) and the quality is finer than llama.

Angora: comes from the Angora rabbit. The hairs can be up to 5 inches (130 mm) long, averaging $2\frac{1}{2}$ inches (about 60 mm) and one rabbit will yield about $\frac{1}{2}$–2 lb ($\frac{1}{4}$–1 kg) of hair a year.

Hides and skins

Measures

United Kingdom
The UK hides and skins industry converted to the metric system from 1971.
Old units:
10 skins   = 1 dicker
20 dickers = 1 last

Argentina
Pesada of dry hides	= 35 libras = 35.45 lb = 16.1 kg
Pesada of salted hides	= 60 libras = 60.77 lb = 27.6 kg
Pesada of washed sheepskins	= 30 libras = 30.38 lb = 13.8 kg

Luxembourg (old unit)
Food^2 = 3.28 ft^2 = 0.304 8 m^2

Average weight per piece (wet-salted)

Cattle hides: developed countries = 55 lb = 25 kg
developing countries
(including calfskins) = 26 lb = 12 kg
Soviet Union   = 33 lb = 15 kg
Calfskins   = 11 lb = 5 kg
Sheepskins =   4 lb = 2 kg
Goatskins   = $3\frac{7}{8}$ lb = $1\frac{3}{4}$ kg

Livestock products: textiles

Conversion rates

- unit weight of dry hides is about 2.5 units of wet-salted hides.
- unit of sole leather = 1.4 units of cattlehide, wet-salted
- square foot (929 cm²) of light cattle and calf leather (average thickness) = 1 lb (0.5 kg) of cattlehide/calfskin, wet-salted
- square foot (929 cm²) of light goat and sheep leather (average thickness) = $\frac{1}{3}$ lb (0.15 kg) of sheep/goatskin, dry.
- pair of boots or shoes = 0.6 ft² (560 cm²) of sole leather
    + 1.5 ft² (1 390 cm²) of upper leather
    + 1 ft² (929 cm²) of sheep/goat skin

Livestock products: food

Milk and milk products

Milk

United Kingdom
- litre = 2.27 lb = 1.030 kg
- gallon = 10.32 lb = 4.68 kg
- million gallons = 4 600 tons = 4 681 tonnes

United States
- US gallon = 8.6 lb = 3.9 kg

The weight of a litre or gallon of milk varies according to the density, which is determined by the fat content. For the United Kingdom, 1 litre of milk with butterfat content of 3.7% weighs 1.029 69 kg, 1.029 69 being the density. The average fat content of milk in the United Kingdom is 3.8%. The UN uses a relative density of 1.031 for milk.

Conversion rates

United Kingdom

	Litres of milk for 1 tonne of product		
	England & Wales	Scotland	Northern Ireland
Milk	971	971	971
Condensed milk: full cream	2 595	2 595	2 550
skimmed	2 953	2 953	2 953
Milk powder: full cream	8 054	8 054	8 054
skimmed	10 755	10 740	10 850
whey	16 644	16 644	16 644
Cream with fat content of:			
2%	3 130	3 130	3 130
8%	4 740	4 740	4 740
23%	6 055	6 055	6 055
35%	9 355	9 355	9 355
48%	12 960	12 960	12 960
55%	14 910	14 910	14 910
Butter			
Cornish: summer	22 281	—	—
winter	20 671	—	—
Non-Cornish: summer	22 854	23 267	22 911
winter	21 865	21 653	21 468
Cheese			
Cheddar/Dunlop	10 291		10 291
Cheshire	9 620		
Lancashire	9 620		
Derby	9 843	summer 10 108	9 620
Double Gloucester	10 067	winter 9 931	
Leicester	10 067		
Caerphilly	9 038		
Wensleydale	9 396		
Stilton	8 949		
	Litres of skimmed milk		
Casein			
edible	36 690	36 690	36 690
industrial: May–Nov	36 690	36 690	36 690
Dec–Apr	39 820	39 820	39 820

United States
Units of milk (average) required for 1 unit of each product:

Butter	21.7	Cream, sweetened	10.8
Cheese, cheddar	8.7	Dry milk, whole	7.2
Condensed milk, whole	2.3	Evaporated milk, whole	2.135

Measures

Butter
United Kingdom (old units)

Roll	= 24 oz	= 680 g	Tub	= 84 lb	= 38.102 kg
Firkin	= 56 lb	= 25.401 kg	Barrel	= 224 lb	= 101.605 kg

United States
Box = 64 lb = 29.03 kg

Cheese
United Kingdom (old units)

Clove	= 8 lb	= 3.629 kg	
Stone	= 16 lb	= 7.257 kg	
Stone (Scotland)	= 24 lb	= 10.886 kg	
Suffolk wey	= 32 cloves	= 256 lb	= 116.120 kg
Essex wey	= 42 cloves	= 336 lb	= 152.407 kg

Eggs

EEC egg grades

Applying to class A (fresh eggs) and class B (second quality or preserved eggs)

1	70 g or over	3	60–65 g	5	50–55 g	7	under 45 g
2	65–70 g	4	55–60 g	6	45–50 g		

United Kingdom

Measures
- 1 great or long hundred = 120 eggs = 10 dozen eggs
- 1 case or box = 360 eggs = 3 long hundreds

Grades (old units; replaced by EEC grades from January 1, 1978)
- A large egg = not less than $2\frac{3}{16}$ oz = 62.0 g
- A standard egg = $2\frac{3}{16}$–$1\frac{7}{8}$ oz = 62.0–53.2 g
- A medium egg = $1\frac{7}{8}$–$1\frac{5}{8}$ oz = 53.2–46.1 g
- A small egg = $1\frac{5}{8}$–$1\frac{1}{2}$ oz = 46.1–42.5 g

Weight
- 1 standard egg = 2 oz = 56.7 grams
- 1 UK (long) ton = 17 400 standard eggs
- 1 tonne = 17 100 standard eggs

Conversion rates
Of a 60 g egg, about 8 g is shell, 15 g is yolk and 37 g is white
100 units of shell eggs make 80 units of frozen eggs
100 units of shell eggs makes 24 units of dried eggs

United States

1 case = 30 dozen eggs = 360 eggs = 47 lb = 21.319 kg
1 average egg = 2.09 oz = 59 g
100 units of eggs make 26 units of dried whole eggs

World

Numbers and weight (as used by the FAO)

	Eggs per tonne	Grams per egg		Eggs per tonne	Grams per egg
Africa			*Asia*		
Ethiopia	25 000	40	Cyprus & Israel	17 600	57
Kenya, Malawi,			Turkey	18 800	53
South Africa,			Other	20 000	50
Zambia and			*Europe, western*		
Zimbabwe	17 600	57	Denmark	16 667	60
Other	20 000	50	Other	17 600	57
America, north			*Europe, eastern*		
Greenland	16 667	60	Bulgaria	17 840	56
Other	17 600	57	Soviet Union		
America, south	17 600	57	and other	18 000	55
			Oceania	17 600	57

Livestock products: food

Livestock and meat

Livestock units

Totals of livestock are sometimes computed in terms of livestock units, the average live or carcass weight of animals.
Average relationships for live weight as used by the FAO are:

From 1 unit of ↓	to →	Camels	Buffalo, horses or mules	Cattle or asses	Pigs	Sheep or goats
Camels	=	1	1.1	1.4	5.5	11
Buffalo, horses or mules	=	0.9	1	1.25	5.0	10
Cattle or asses	=	0.7	0.8	1	4.0	8
Pigs	=	0.2	0.2	0.25	1	2
Sheep or goats	=	0.1	0.1	0.125	0.5	1

Meat

Live weight: weight of animal on the hoof.
Carcass, dead or slaughter weight: weight of carcass when killed, that is, live weight less the weight of hide, feet, head, blood, offals, etc.

United Kingdom measures (old units)

Beef: firkin = 100 lb = 45.359 kg   tierce = 304 lb = 137.892
      barrel = 200 lb = 90.718 kg

Pork: firkin = 100 lb = 45.359 kg   tierce = 320 lb = 145.15 kg

For pigs, 1 score deadweight = 20 lb = 9.072 kg.

Smithfield stone = 8 lb = 3.63 kg. This measure is legally obsolete but it is unofficially used. It is the approximate dressed carcass weight yielded by a live weight of 1 imperial stone of 14 pounds – that is, a yield of about 57%.

Live weight to carcass weight

100 units live weight becomes the following units of carcass weight (approx):

	Beef & veal	Pork	Mutton & lamb	Horse meat	Poultry
Africa	52	70	50	52	70
America, North	57	60	50	51	89
America, South	55	67	48	64	75
Asia: Middle East	48	74	49	na	70
other	50	58	57	48	75
Europe	53	73	48	51	72
Oceania	55	70	49	50	75
World average	55	66	51	51	82

Fish

Main fishing terms, as used by the FAO, are:
Gross removal (total live weight of fish caught or killed)
less pre-catch losses (including losses through gear lost)
= Gross catch (total live weight of fish caught)
less discarded catch (undersized or undesirable fish discarded)
= Retained catch (total live weight of fish retained)
less net utilisation and other (consumption by crew, bait, dumped, etc)
= Nominal catch (live weight equivalent of landings)
less losses due to dressing etc (dumped heads, etc)
= Landings (net weight of gutted, filleted, etc fish products as landed)
'Catch' usually means nominal catch; the term catch is more suitable for use in the case of whales and seals, where original data is in terms of numbers. The term production is more suitable than nominal catch for primary production of seaweeds, guano, seabirds eggs, pearls, shells, sponges, etc.

Measures

(old UK units unless otherwise specified)

Bag: for shellfish (cockles and mussels in shell), usually 1 cwt = 8 stones = 112 lb = 51 kg.
Can vary from 7 to 10 stones = 98–140 lb = 45–65 kg approximately.

Barrel: the legal size for Scottish barrels was discontinued in 1963; usually,
1 herring barrel = 26⅔ gallons = 121 litres = 1.21 hectolitres
½ herring barrel = 13⅓ gallons = 61 litres.
1 hectolitre = 0.83 barrel.
Contents of a barrel numbered about 700 to 1 100 fish for Scotch cured herring, and weighed, for pickle-salted herrings, about 320 lb = 145 kg of which some 262 lb = 120 kg is fish, the rest being pickle.
A continental barrel holds about 100 kg (220 lb).
For Iceland, a herring barrel (slldartunna) equals 118–120 litres (approx. 26½ UK gallons).
For whale oil, a barrel weighs 375 lb or 170 kg (= 0.17 tonne).

Basket: contents of a basket of herring weigh approximately 44 kg (7 stones).
Formerly 1 basket = ¼ cran = 9⅜ gallons = 42.6 litres.

Box: for white fish, contents of a box weigh 40 kg in North Shields and Eyemouth; formerly a box weighed usually from 5 to 10 stones (30 to 60 kg). For kippers, a box, usually 1 stone (6⅓ kg), contains about 24 pairs of average kippers.
Formerly, for herring, 1 box was usually one-quarter or one-sixth of a cran; also one-third or one-fifth. Norway box was one-half cran.

Bushel: used in Britain before 1978; for sprats, weighed about 56 lb (25½ kg).

Cran: herring in Britain are usually sold by weight: a normal size box is 25 kg, the catch being sold in units of 100 kg; box sizes of 40 kg and 50 kg are also used. Before 1975, herring not sold by weight in Britain were usually sold by the cran, a measure of volume; the cran was officially not lawful for trade from Sept. 1, 1980.
1 cran = 37½ gallons = 6.02 cubic feet = 170.5 litres = 1.705 hectolitres.
1 hectolitre = 0.59 cran.
Contents of a cran varied from 700 to 2 500 according to season and ground, and weighed about 25–30 stones (160–190 kg).

Draft: equalled 21 lb (9½ kg) of eels.

Kantje (keg): German herring measure of 74 kg (163 lb).

Kit: following metrication, the kit usually means 63½ kilograms; formerly
1 kit = 10 stones = 140 pounds = 63½ kilograms.
16 kits = 1 UK ton. The kit varied from 60 lb (about 4¼ stones) to 12 stones.

Last: equals 100 long hundreds.

Long hundred: equals 132 fresh herrings or 120 mackerel.

Margarine: equals 66 lb (30 kg) fresh herrings. or 14 lb (6⅓ kg) kippers.

Peck: for shrimps, weighs about 10 to 14 pounds (4½–6⅓ kg).

Síldarmál: Icelandic herring measure of 150 litres (33 UK gallons).

Tub: equals 3 pecks, or 6 gallons (27 litres).

Warp: equals 4 herrings or mackerel.

Wash: equals 4 gallons (18 litres) of oysters.

Densities and stowage rates

The following are average rates:

	Density: lb/ft³	kg/m³	Stowage rate: ft³/ton	m³/tonne
Whole fresh herring in bulk	58.2	930	38.5	1.1
Whole fresh mackerel in bulk	50.0	800	45	1.3
Whole fresh sprats in bulk	53.2	850	42	1.2
Whole fresh capelin in bulk	62.5	1 000	36	1.0
Whole fresh cod in bulk gutted	57.5	920	39	1.1
Crushed block ice	40	640	56	1.6

Marine rope

With conversion to the metric system, circumference in inches is replaced by diameter in millimetres:
approximately, circumference in inches × 8 = diameter in millimetres.

Trawl warps: standard coil lengths are: 200m, 400m, 600m, 800m. Trawl marks are at 50m (approximately 25 fathoms) and 20m (approximately 10 fathoms) for inshore fishing.

ish

Conversions

The United Nations uses a multiplying factor of 0.66 to convert quantities from a wet salted to a dried salted basis.

The FAO uses a wide range of conversion factors for converting between landings (of fish in various stages) and nominal catch (live weight of the fish). Examples of conversion factors are:

Atlantic cod (fresh, chilled, iced)
Multiplying factors to convert from landings to live weight equivalent

Gutted, tail on:

	head on	head off	Fillets, skin on:	
Poland (Baltic Sea)	1.17	1.68	Poland (Baltic Sea)	2.56
Belgium	1.18	1.64		
Canada	1.20	1.38		
Denmark	1.18	1.60		
England & Wales	1.20	1.50		
Greenland	1.22	1.52		

The following are some UK multiplying factors for converting from landed weight of whole fish to weight of fish product; whole fish are taken as landed gutted with heads on, except for the following which are normally landed whole ungutted: herring, sprat, mackerel, pilchard, redfish, salmon and dogfish.

Product	Multiplying factor	Product	Multiplying factor
Wet fillets with skin:		Smoked fish:	
cod	0.47	kipper	0.65–0.70
haddock: large	0.47	red herring	0.60–0.80
hake	0.55		
plaice	0.52	Edible portion in general:	
redfish	0.35	salmon	0.64
white fish in general	0.47	sea trout	0.63
herring in general	0.53	brown trout	0.68
		lobster	0.44
Wet steaks:		Norway lobster	0.20–0.27
salmon	0.60–0.65	prawn	0.40
halibut	0.70–0.75	oyster	0.11–0.17
		mussel	0.08–0.20

Classification

A 3-alpha identifier system is used by the FAO for identifying fish; some main codes are as follows:

ALK	Alaska Pollack	NEP	Norway lobster (nephrops)
COD	Atlantic cod	PIL	European pilchard (sardine)
HAD	Haddock	PLE	European plaice
HER	Atlantic herring	POK	Saithe (pollock)
JAP	Japanese pilchard (sardine)	RED	Atlantic redfishes
LEM	Lemon sole	SCA	Sea scallop
MAC	Atlantic mackerel	SKJ	Skipjack tuna
MUS	Blue mussel	SPR	Sprat

Major fishing areas for statistical purposes

The chart below outlines the main fishing areas as used by the FAO; the key to the numbers in the chart is as follows:

Inland waters

01	Africa
02	America, North and Central
03	America, South
04	Asia
05	Europe
06	Oceania
07	Soviet Union
08	Antarctica

Marine areas

Atlantic ocean and adjacent seas

18	Arctic sea
21	Atlantic, Northwest
27	Atlantic, Northeast
31	Atlantic, Western Central
34	Atlantic, Eastern Central
37	Mediterranean and Black Sea
41	Atlantic, Southwest
47	Atlantic, Southeast
48	Atlantic, Antarctic

Indian ocean and adjacent seas

51	Indian ocean, Western
57	Indian ocean, Eastern
58	Indian ocean, Antarctic

Pacific ocean and adjacent seas

61	Pacific, Northwest
67	Pacific, Northeast
71	Pacific, Western Central
77	Pacific, Eastern Central
81	Pacific, Southwest
87	Pacific, Southeast
88	Pacific, Antarctic

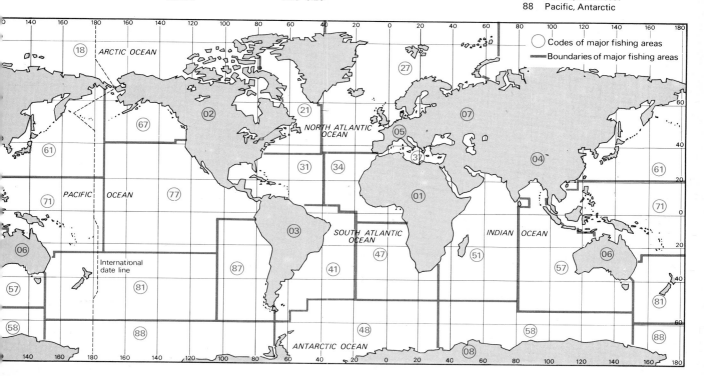

Timber

Definitions

Coniferous (softwoods): all woods derived from trees classified botanically as gymnosperms; e.g. pine, spruce, larch, etc. The term 'softwood' is used in some countries to include woods which are physically soft, even though some of them may be taken from broadleaved trees.

Non-coniferous (hardwoods): all woods derived from trees classified botanically as angiosperms; e.g. oak, beech, maple, ebony. Most of this group are physically hard. However, this category also includes broadleaved species such as the poplar which are physically soft and in some countries are grouped as softwoods.

Measures

Piled measures are for stacked wood, with air between different pieces of wood. Board foot, foot board measure (fbm), board measure, or super foot = a unit of lumber measuring one foot long, one foot wide and one inch thick or its equivalent = 1/12 cubic foot.

Cord foot	= 16 cubic feet
Cunit	= 100 cubic feet
Cord	= 128 piled cubic feet = 8 cord feet
Fathom	= 216 piled cubic feet
Hoppus foot	= cylinder 1 foot long, with circumference (girth) of 4 feet (quarter-girth of 1 foot)
Load	= 40 cubic feet of roundwood
	= 50 cubic feet of sawnwood (= 1 ton of 50 cubic feet)
Stack	= 180 cubic feet of roundwood

Standard: St Petersburg (Petrograd) = 165 piled cubic feet
Göteborg = 180 piled cubic feet
English = 270 piled cubic feet

Stère (st) = Raummeter (Rm) = Festmeter (Fm) = wisse = 1 piled cubic metre

Detailed conversions between board feet and cubic metres are provided below, and between hoppus feet and cubic metres on the facing page.

Volume conversions

Solid

From	to	Cubic metres	Cubic feet	Hoppus feet	1000 board feet	Standards (Petrograd)
		multiply by				
Cubic metres		1	35.3	27.7	0.424	0.214
Cubic feet		0.028 3	1	0.785	0.012	0.006 06
Hoppus feet		0.036 1	1.273	1	0.0153	0.007 72
1000 board feet		2.36	83.3	65.4	1	0.505
Standards (Petrograd)		4.67	165	129.6	1.98	1
Loads: roundwood		1.13	40	31.4	0.48	0.242
sawnwood		1.42	50	39.27	0.6	0.303
Cords[a]		3.62	128	100.53	1.54	0.776
Fathoms[a]		6.12	216	169.65	2.59	1.309

[a]For conversion from piled to true solid volume also apply the percentages indicated by the table below in the range 65% to 75%; for example a fathom of pitprops, converting from piled to solid volume without bark is, in terms of hoppus feet, 70% of 169.65 = 119 hoppus feet (in practice usually taken as 120 hoppus feet).

Recovery (saleable timber)

This is normally taken as 60% of the underbark volume but it is extremely variable depending upon the end use of the timber and size of material being sawn; the smaller the dimensions the lower the recovery rate on average. It may be as high as 75% for some uses. Hence conversion to roundwood equivalent is obtained by multiplying by 1·67 or 1.33. Solid volume without bark is normally taken as 65%, 70% or 75% of the piled overall measurement for roundwood, depending on the type of timber; some rough conversions are:

Pulpwood: coniferous	= 75%	Fuelwood: coniferous	= 70%
general	= 72%	broadleaved	= 65%
Pitprops: general	= 70%	general	= 65%

Board feet to Cubic metres   1 bd ft = 0.002 360 m³

bd ft →	0	100	200	300	400	500	600	700	800	900	←	bd ft
↓	m³	m³	m³	m³	m³	m³	m³	m³	m³	m³		
0	0.000	0.236	0.472	0.708	0.944	1.180	1.416	1.652	1.888	2.124		0
1000	2.360	2.596	2.832	3.068	3.304	3.540	3.776	4.012	4.248	4.484		1000
2000	4.719	4.955	5.191	5.427	5.663	5.899	6.135	6.371	6.607	6.843		2000
3000	7.079	7.315	7.551	7.787	8.023	8.259	8.495	8.731	8.967	9.203		3000
4000	9.439	9.675	9.911	10.147	10.383	10.619	10.855	11.091	11.327	11.563		4000
5000	11.799	12.035	12.271	12.507	12.743	12.979	13.215	13.451	13.686	13.922		5000
6000	14.158	14.394	14.630	14.866	15.102	15.338	15.574	15.810	16.046	16.282		6000
7000	16.518	16.754	16.990	17.226	17.462	17.698	17.934	18.170	18.406	18.642		7000
8000	18.878	19.114	19.350	19.586	19.822	20·058	20.294	20.530	20.766	21.002		8000
9000	21.238	21.474	21.710	21.946	22.182	22.418	22.653	22.889	23.125	23.361		9000
10000	23.597											10000

Cubic metres to Board feet   1 m³ = 423.776 001 bd ft

m³ →	0	1	2	3	4	5	6	7	8	9	←	m³
↓	bd ft	bd ft	bd ft	bd ft	bd ft	bd ft	bd ft	bd ft	bd ft	bd ft		
0	0.000	423.776	847.552	1271.328	1695.104	2118.880	2542.656	2966.432	3390.208	3813.984		0
10	4237.760	4661.536	5085.312	5509.088	5932.864	6356.640	6780.416	7204.192	7627.968	8051.744		10
20	8475.520	8899.296	9323.072	9746.848	10170.624	10594.400	11018.176	11441.952	11865.728	12289.504		20
30	12713.280	13137.056	13560.832	13984.608	14408.384	14832.160	15255.936	15679.712	16103.488	16527.264		30
40	16951.040	17374.816	17798.592	18222.368	18646.144	19069.920	19493.696	19917.472	20341.248	20765.024		40
50	21188.800	21612.576	22036.352	22460.128	22883.904	23307.680	23731.456	24155.232	24579.008	25002.784		50
60	25426.560	25850.336	26274.112	26697.888	27121.664	27545.440	27969.216	28392.992	28816.768	29240.544		60
70	29664.320	30088.096	30511.872	30935.648	31359.424	31783.200	32206.976	32630.752	33054.528	33478.304		70
80	33902.080	34325.856	34749.632	35173.408	35597.184	36020.960	36444.736	36868.512	37292.288	37716.064		80
90	38139.840	38563.616	38987.392	39411.168	39834.944	40258.720	40682.496	41106.272	41530.048	41953.824		90
100	42377.600											100

Timber

Hoppus feet to Cubic metres   1 h ft = 0.036 054 m³

h ft →	0	1	2	3	4	5	6	7	8	9	← h ft
↓	m³	m³	m³	m³	m³	m³	m³	m³	m³	m³	↓
0	0.00000	0.03605	0.07211	0.10816	0.14422	0.18027	0.21632	0.25238	0.28843	0.32449	0
10	0.36054	0.39660	0.43265	0.46870	0.50476	0.54081	0.57687	0.61292	0.64897	0.68503	10
20	0.72108	0.75714	0.79319	0.82924	0.86530	0.90135	0.93741	0.97346	1.00952	1.04557	20
30	1.08162	1.11768	1.15373	1.18979	1.22584	1.26189	1.29795	1.33400	1.37006	1.40611	30
40	1.44217	1.47822	1.51427	1.55033	1.58638	1.62244	1.65849	1.69454	1.73060	1.76665	40
50	1.80271	1.83876	1.87481	1.91087	1.94692	1.98298	2.01903	2.05509	2.09114	2.12719	50
60	2.16325	2.19930	2.23536	2.27141	2.30746	2.34352	2.37957	2.41563	2.45168	2.48773	60
70	2.52379	2.55984	2.59590	2.63195	2.66801	2.70406	2.74011	2.77617	2.81222	2.84828	70
80	2.88433	2.92038	2.95644	2.99249	3.02855	3.06460	3.10066	3.13671	3.17276	3.20882	80
90	3.24487	3.28093	3.31698	3.35303	3.38909	3.42514	3.46120	3.49725	3.53330	3.56936	90
100	3.60541										100

Cubic metres to Hoppus feet   1 m³ = 27.736 074 h ft

m³ →	0	1	2	3	4	5	6	7	8	9	← m³
↓	h ft	h ft	h ft	h ft	h ft	h ft	h ft	h ft	h ft	h ft	↓
0	0.000	27.736	55.472	83.208	110.944	138.680	166.416	194.153	221.889	249.625	0
10	277.361	305.097	332.833	360.569	388.305	416.041	443.777	471.513	499.249	526.985	10
20	554.721	582.458	610.194	637.930	665.666	693.402	721.138	748.874	776.610	804.346	20
30	832.082	859.818	887.554	915.290	943.027	970.763	998.499	1026.235	1053.971	1081.707	30
40	1109.443	1137.179	1164.915	1192.651	1220.387	1248.123	1275.859	1303.595	1331.332	1359.068	40
50	1386.804	1414.540	1442.276	1470.012	1497.748	1525.484	1553.220	1580.956	1608.692	1636.428	50
60	1664.164	1691.901	1719.637	1747.373	1775.109	1802.845	1830.581	1858.317	1886.053	1913.789	60
70	1941.525	1969.261	1996.997	2024.733	2052.470	2080.206	2107.942	2135.678	2163.414	2191.150	70
80	2218.886	2246.622	2274.358	2302.094	2329.830	2357.566	2385.302	2413.038	2440.775	2468.511	80
90	2496.247	2523.983	2551.719	2579.455	2607.191	2634.927	2662.663	2690.399	2718.135	2745.871	90
100	2773.607										100

Densities

The average weight at shipment of different types of wood given below are those used by the FAO:

		Pounds per cubic foot	Kilograms per cubic metre	Tonnes per cubic metre (relative density)
Saw logs:	coniferous	44	700	0.7
	broadleaved	46–50	730–800	0.73–0.8
Pulpwood:	coniferous	41	650	0.65
	broadleaved	47	750	0.75
	general	42	675	0.675
Pitprops:	coniferous	44	700	0.7
	broadleaved	50	800	0.8
	general	45	725	0.725
Other industrial wood:				
	coniferous	44	700	0.7
	broadleaved	50	800	0.8
	general	47	750	0.75
Fuelwood:	coniferous	39	625	0.625
	broadleaved	47	750	0.75
	general	45	725	0.725
Sawnwood:	coniferous	34	550	0.55
	broadleaved	44	700	0.7
Sleepers		49	780	0.78
Plywood		41	650	0.65
Veneer sheets		47	750	0.75

The weight (mass) of timber can be obtained from the volume table on page 119 by multiplying the number of cubic metres by the value of kilograms or tonnes per cubic metre shown above. For cut timber, weight (mass) can be obtained for various sizes by using the steel tables on pages 155 and 156, in conjunction with a multiplier to allow for different densities; some calculated multipliers are given on page 153.

Bark

The following table gives some estimates of the percentage amount of bark on roundwood (adapted from tables of the UK Forestry Commission).

Under bark top diameter in millimetres	Bark as percentage (approximate) of underbark volume (percentages applying for lengths from 2–8 metres)				
	Norway spruce	Sitka spruce	Douglas fir	Scots pine	European larch
100	10	13½	16½	16½	25
150	10	11	14	14	22
200	9½	10	13	14	20½
250	9	9	13	15½	20
300	8½	8½	13½	17½	20½
350	8	8	13½	19½	21
400	7½	7½	14	21½	21½
500	6½	7	14½	23½	22½
600	6	7	15	25	23½
700	6	6½	15	26	24½
800	6	6½	15½	27	25

Note. The above percentages are for converting from underbark volume to overbark volume, by adding the percentages specified to underbark volume. The percentages to be subtracted from overbark volume to obtain underbark volume can be obtained by using the percentage 'reversals' table on page 222; that table can be used for converting any percentages from one type into the other. For example, the percentage reversal of 10 is 9.1; so, for Norway spruce with a top-diameter underbark of 100–150 mm, the percentage to be subtracted from overbark volume to obtain underbark volume is 9.1% or approximately 9%.

Top-diameter refers to the end of timber with the smallest diameter; the other measure normally used is mid-diameter which is approximately equal to the average diameter for any length of timber.

117

Timber

Detailed tables are provided below for converting between diameter and circumference. The facing page provides a summary table giving volume from mid-diameter (which table can be used generally to convert any form of cylinder from the diameter to volume).

The standard detailed tables for converting radius (one-half diameter) to area, given on pages 196–199, can also be used for obtaining volume from mid-diameter outside the range of diameter shown in this section. Volume is then length multiplied by area of a cross-section (circle), area of the circle having been obtained from radius in those tables.

Girth (circumference) to Diameter   1 unit girth is equivalent to 0.318 (1/π) unit diameter

Girth →	0	1	2	3	4	5	6	7	8	9	← Girth
0	0.000	0.318	0.637	0.955	1.273	1.592	1.910	2.228	2.546	2.865	0
10	3.183	3.501	3.820	4.138	4.456	4.775	5.093	5.411	5.730	6.048	10
20	6.366	6.685	7.003	7.321	7.639	7.958	8.276	8.594	8.913	9.231	20
30	9.549	9.868	10.186	10.504	10.823	11.141	11.459	11.777	12.096	12.414	30
40	12.732	13.051	13.369	13.687	14.006	14.324	14.642	14.961	15.279	15.597	40
50	15.915	16.234	16.552	16.870	17.189	17.507	17.825	18.144	18.462	18.780	50
60	19.099	19.417	19.735	20.054	20.372	20.690	21.008	21.327	21.645	21.963	60
70	22.282	22.600	22.918	23.237	23.555	23.873	24.192	24.510	24.828	25.146	70
80	25.465	25.783	26.101	26.420	26.738	27.056	27.375	27.693	28.011	28.330	80
90	28.648	28.966	29.285	29.603	29.921	30.239	30.558	30.876	31.194	31.513	90
100	31.831	32.149	32.468	32.786	33.104	33.423	33.741	34.059	34.377	34.696	100
110	35.014	35.332	35.651	35.969	36.287	36.606	36.924	37.242	37.561	37.879	110
120	38.197	38.515	38.834	39.152	39.470	39.789	40.107	40.425	40.744	41.062	120
130	41.380	41.699	42.017	42.335	42.654	42.972	43.290	43.608	43.927	44.245	130
140	44.563	44.882	45.200	45.518	45.837	46.155	46.473	46.792	47.110	47.428	140
150	47.746	48.065	48.383	48.701	49.020	49.338	49.656	49.975	50.293	50.611	150
160	50.930	51.248	51.566	51.885	52.203	52.521	52.839	53.158	53.476	53.794	160
170	54.113	54.431	54.749	55.068	55.386	55.704	56.023	56.341	56.659	56.977	170
180	57.296	57.614	57.932	58.251	58.569	58.887	59.206	59.524	59.842	60.161	180
190	60.479	60.797	61.115	61.434	61.752	62.070	62.389	62.707	63.025	63.344	190
200	63.662	63.980	64.299	64.617	64.935	65.254	65.572	65.890	66.208	66.527	200
210	66.845	67.163	67.482	67.800	68.118	68.437	68.755	69.073	69.392	69.710	210
220	70.028	70.346	70.665	70.983	71.301	71.620	71.938	72.256	72.575	72.893	220
230	73.211	73.530	73.848	74.166	74.485	74.803	75.121	75.439	75.758	76.076	230
240	76.394	76.713	77.031	77.349	77.668	77.986	78.304	78.623	78.941	79.259	240

Diameter to Girth (circumference)   1 unit diameter is equivalent to 3.142 (π) units girth

Diameter →	0	1	2	3	4	5	6	7	8	9	← Diameter
0	0.000	3.142	6.283	9.425	12.566	15.708	18.850	21.991	25.133	28.274	0
10	31.416	34.558	37.699	40.841	43.982	47.124	50.265	53.407	56.549	59.690	10
20	62.832	65.973	69.115	72.257	75.398	78.540	81.681	84.823	87.965	91.106	20
30	94.248	97.389	100.531	103.673	106.814	109.956	113.097	116.239	119.381	122.522	30
40	125.664	128.805	131.947	135.088	138.230	141.372	144.513	147.655	150.796	153.938	40
50	157.080	160.221	163.363	166.504	169.646	172.788	175.929	179.071	182.212	185.354	50
60	188.496	191.637	194.779	197.920	201.062	204.204	207.345	210.487	213.628	216.770	60
70	219.911	223.053	226.195	229.336	232.478	235.619	238.761	241.903	245.044	248.186	70
80	251.327	254.469	257.611	260.752	263.894	267.035	270.177	273.319	276.460	279.602	80
90	282.743	285.885	289.027	292.168	295.310	298.451	301.593	304.734	307.876	311.018	90
100	314.159	317.301	320.442	323.584	326.726	329.867	333.009	336.150	339.292	342.434	100
110	345.575	348.717	351.858	355.000	358.142	361.283	364.425	367.566	370.708	373.850	110
120	376.991	380.133	383.274	386.416	389.557	392.699	395.841	398.982	402.124	405.265	120
130	408.407	411.549	414.690	417.832	420.973	424.115	427.257	430.398	433.540	436.681	130
140	439.823	442.965	446.106	449.248	452.389	455.531	458.673	461.814	464.956	468.097	140
150	471.239	474.380	477.522	480.664	483.805	486.947	490.088	493.230	496.372	499.513	150
160	502.655	505.796	508.938	512.080	515.221	518.363	521.504	524.646	527.788	530.929	160
170	534.071	537.212	540.354	543.496	546.637	549.779	552.920	556.062	559.203	562.345	170
180	565.487	568.628	571.770	574.911	578.053	581.195	584.336	587.478	590.619	593.761	180
190	596.903	600.044	603.186	606.327	609.469	612.611	615.752	618.894	622.035	625.177	190
200	628.319	631.460	634.602	637.743	640.885	644.026	647.168	650.310	653.451	656.593	200
210	659.734	662.876	666.018	669.159	672.301	675.442	678.584	681.726	684.867	688.009	210
220	691.150	694.292	697.434	700.575	703.717	706.858	710.000	713.142	716.283	719.425	220
230	722.566	725.708	728.849	731.991	735.133	738.274	741.416	744.557	747.699	750.841	230
240	753.982	757.124	760.265	763.407	766.549	769.690	772.832	775.973	779.115	782.257	240

Timber

Diameter, mid, in millimetres, by length in metres, to Volume in cubic metres

Example: a sawlog 2.0 metres long, with mid-diameter 160 mm, has a volume of 0.040 cubic metre.
Note. For diameter in centimetres delete the last zero from the number of millimetres.

Length in metres →	1.0	1.5	2.0	2.5	3.0	3.5	4.0	4.5	5.0	6.0	7.0	8.0	9.0	10.0	Length ← in metres
Mid diameter in millimetres ↓	m³	m³	m³	m³	m³	m³	m³	m³	m³	m³	m³	m³	m³	m³	Mid diameter in millimetres ↓
70	0.004	0.006	0.008	0.010	0.012	0.013	0.015	0.017	0.019	0.023	0.027	0.031	0.035	0.038	70
80	0.005	0.008	0.010	0.013	0.015	0.018	0.020	0.023	0.025	0.030	0.035	0.040	0.045	0.050	80
90	0.006	0.010	0.013	0.016	0.019	0.022	0.025	0.029	0.032	0.038	0.045	0.051	0.057	0.064	90
100	0.008	0.012	0.016	0.020	0.024	0.027	0.031	0.035	0.039	0.047	0.055	0.063	0.071	0.079	100
110	0.010	0.014	0.019	0.024	0.029	0.033	0.038	0.043	0.048	0.057	0.067	0.076	0.086	0.095	110
120	0.011	0.017	0.023	0.028	0.034	0.040	0.045	0.051	0.057	0.068	0.079	0.090	0.102	0.113	120
130	0.013	0.020	0.027	0.033	0.040	0.046	0.053	0.060	0.066	0.080	0.093	0.106	0.119	0.133	130
140	0.015	0.023	0.031	0.038	0.046	0.054	0.062	0.069	0.077	0.092	0.108	0.123	0.139	0.154	140
150	0.018	0.027	0.035	0.044	0.053	0.062	0.071	0.080	0.088	0.106	0.124	0.141	0.159	0.177	150
160	0.020	0.030	0.040	0.050	0.060	0.070	0.080	0.090	0.101	0.121	0.141	0.161	0.181	0.201	160
170	0.023	0.034	0.045	0.057	0.068	0.079	0.091	0.102	0.113	0.136	0.159	0.182	0.204	0.227	170
180	0.025	0.038	0.051	0.064	0.076	0.089	0.102	0.115	0.127	0.153	0.178	0.204	0.229	0.254	180
190	0.028	0.043	0.057	0.071	0.085	0.099	0.113	0.128	0.142	0.170	0.198	0.227	0.255	0.284	190
200	0.031	0.047	0.063	0.079	0.094	0.110	0.126	0.141	0.157	0.188	0.220	0.251	0.283	0.314	200
210	0.035	0.052	0.069	0.087	0.104	0.121	0.139	0.156	0.173	0.208	0.242	0.277	0.312	0.346	210
220	0.038	0.057	0.076	0.095	0.114	0.133	0.152	0.171	0.190	0.228	0.266	0.304	0.342	0.380	220
230	0.042	0.062	0.083	0.104	0.125	0.145	0.166	0.187	0.208	0.249	0.291	0.332	0.374	0.415	230
240	0.045	0.068	0.090	0.113	0.136	0.158	0.181	0.204	0.226	0.271	0.317	0.362	0.407	0.452	240
250	0.049	0.074	0.098	0.123	0.147	0.172	0.196	0.221	0.245	0.295	0.344	0.393	0.442	0.491	250
260	0.053	0.080	0.106	0.133	0.159	0.186	0.212	0.239	0.265	0.319	0.372	0.425	0.478	0.531	260
270	0.057	0.086	0.115	0.143	0.172	0.200	0.229	0.258	0.286	0.344	0.401	0.458	0.515	0.573	270
280	0.062	0.092	0.123	0.154	0.185	0.216	0.246	0.277	0.308	0.369	0.431	0.493	0.554	0.616	280
290	0.066	0.099	0.132	0.165	0.198	0.231	0.264	0.297	0.330	0.396	0.462	0.528	0.594	0.661	290
300	0.071	0.106	0.141	0.177	0.212	0.247	0.283	0.318	0.353	0.424	0.495	0.565	0.636	0.707	300
310	0.075	0.113	0.151	0.189	0.226	0.264	0.302	0.340	0.377	0.453	0.528	0.604	0.679	0.755	310
320	0.080	0.121	0.161	0.201	0.241	0.281	0.322	0.362	0.402	0.483	0.563	0.643	0.724	0.804	320
330	0.086	0.128	0.171	0.214	0.257	0.299	0.342	0.385	0.428	0.513	0.599	0.684	0.770	0.855	330
340	0.091	0.136	0.182	0.227	0.272	0.318	0.363	0.409	0.454	0.545	0.636	0.726	0.817	0.908	340
350	0.096	0.144	0.192	0.241	0.289	0.337	0.385	0.433	0.481	0.577	0.673	0.770	0.866	0.962	350
360	0.102	0.153	0.204	0.254	0.305	0.356	0.407	0.458	0.509	0.611	0.713	0.814	0.916	1.018	360
370	0.108	0.161	0.215	0.269	0.323	0.376	0.430	0.484	0.538	0.645	0.753	0.860	0.968	1.075	370
380	0.113	0.170	0.227	0.284	0.340	0.397	0.454	0.510	0.567	0.680	0.794	0.907	1.021	1.134	380
390	0.119	0.179	0.239	0.299	0.358	0.418	0.478	0.538	0.597	0.717	0.836	0.956	1.075	1.195	390
400	0.126	0.188	0.251	0.314	0.377	0.440	0.503	0.565	0.628	0.754	0.880	1.005	1.131	1.257	400
410	0.132	0.198	0.264	0.330	0.396	0.462	0.528	0.594	0.660	0.792	0.924	1.056	1.188	1.320	410
420	0.139	0.208	0.277	0.346	0.416	0.485	0.554	0.623	0.693	0.831	0.970	1.108	1.247	1.385	420
430	0.145	0.218	0.290	0.363	0.436	0.508	0.581	0.653	0.726	0.871	1.017	1.162	1.307	1.452	430
440	0.152	0.228	0.304	0.380	0.456	0.532	0.608	0.684	0.760	0.912	1.064	1.216	1.368	1.521	440
450	0.159	0.239	0.318	0.398	0.477	0.557	0.636	0.716	0.795	0.954	1.113	1.272	1.431	1.590	450
460	0.166	0.249	0.332	0.415	0.499	0.582	0.665	0.748	0.831	0.997	1.163	1.330	1.496	1.662	460
470	0.173	0.260	0.347	0.434	0.520	0.607	0.694	0.781	0.867	1.041	1.214	1.388	1.561	1.735	470
480	0.181	0.271	0.362	0.452	0.543	0.633	0.724	0.814	0.905	1.086	1.267	1.448	1.629	1.810	480
490	0.189	0.283	0.377	0.471	0.566	0.660	0.754	0.849	0.943	1.131	1.320	1.509	1.697	1.886	490
500	0.196	0.295	0.393	0.491	0.589	0.687	0.785	0.884	0.982	1.178	1.374	1.571	1.767	1.963	500
600	0.283	0.424	0.565	0.707	0.848	0.990	1.131	1.272	1.414	1.696	1.979	2.262	2.545	2.827	600
700	0.385	0.577	0.770	0.962	1.155	1.347	1.539	1.732	1.924	2.309	2.694	3.079	3.464	3.848	700
800	0.503	0.754	1.005	1.257	1.508	1.759	2.011	2.262	2.513	3.016	3.519	4.021	4.524	5.027	800
900	0.636	0.954	1.272	1.590	1.909	2.227	2.545	2.863	3.181	3.817	4.453	5.089	5.726	6.362	900
1000	0.785	1.178	1.571	1.963	2.356	2.749	3.142	3.534	3.927	4.712	5.498	6.283	7.069	7.854	1000
1100	0.950	1.425	1.901	2.376	2.851	3.326	3.801	4.276	4.752	5.702	6.652	7.603	8.553	9.503	1100
1200	1.131	1.696	2.262	2.827	3.393	3.958	4.524	5.089	5.655	6.786	7.917	9.048	10.179	11.310	1200
1300	1.327	1.991	2.655	3.318	3.982	4.646	5.309	5.973	6.637	7.964	9.291	10.619	11.946	13.273	1300
1400	1.539	2.309	3.079	3.848	4.618	5.388	6.158	6.927	7.697	9.236	10.776	12.315	13.854	15.394	1400
1500	1.767	2.651	3.534	4.418	5.301	6.185	7.069	7.952	8.836	10.603	12.370	14.137	15.904	17.671	1500
1600	2.011	3.016	4.021	5.027	6.032	7.037	8.042	9.048	10.053	12.064	14.074	16.085	18.096	20.106	1600

Industry

Chemicals

Fundamental data

An atom consists of elementary particles; its diameter is approximately 1–5 Å (100–500 picometres). Components of an atom are:

The nucleus containing protons or neutrons (that is nucleons, the term used to cover either protons or neutrons).
Proton = a positively charged particle with a positive electrical charge of $1.602\,189 \times 10^{-19}$ coulomb and a mass at rest of approximately $1.672\,649 \times 10^{-27}$ kg ($1\,836.152 \times$ mass of an electron).

Neutron = an electrically neutral particle with a mass, at approximately $1.674\,954 \times 10^{-27}$ kg, about equal to that of a proton.

A cloud of electrons
Electron = a negatively charged particle with a negative electrical charge of $1.602\,189 \times 10^{-19}$ coulomb and a mass at rest of $9.109\,534 \times 10^{-31}$ kg.
The number of electrons is equal to the number of protons, since the complete atom is electrically neutral.
Electrons are generally envisaged as circulating in orbits or levels with different energy values. If an electron moves (or is moved) from one level to another, then the frequency of the radiation emitted is:
v = difference in energy values/h,
where h is the Planck constant (also see page 150).
Radiation having a single fixed frequency is called a 'line'; transitions between different levels for different elements yield radiations with different frequencies (also see page 14 concerning the definition of the metre, page 128 for the general range of frequencies, and page 150 for radiation).

The number of atoms in 12 grams of carbon-12 (in a mole of substance) = $6.022\,045 \times 10^{23}$ (Avogadro constant).

Half life = the time taken for the activity of a radioactive substance to decay to half its original value by radioactive disintegration; that is for half of the atoms present to disintegrate. It is necessary to measure in terms of the half life rather than the whole life, since the latter is infinite – activity is never quite zero. The half life for uranium-238 is 4.47×10^9 years, for uranium-235 it is 7.04×10^8 years; for radium-226 it is 1 600 years; for lead 26.8 minutes.

Also see atomic energy section (pages 140–141)

The elements

An element is the smallest substance which can be isolated by chemical analysis, and the chemical properties are determined by the number of electrons (equal to the number of protons).

The atomic number of an element is the number of protons in the nucleus, and the atomic mass number is the number of nucleons (protons + neutrons) in the nucleus. Atomic weight or mass is approximately the mass number multiplied by the mass of a nucleon.

Isotopes of an element have the same chemical properties (same number of protons and therefore same atomic number) but different numbers of neutrons (different mass numbers) and so different atomic weights; for example, the main isotopes of uranium (atomic number 92) have mass numbers 235 and 238 (143 and 146 neutrons). Isotopes are usually written symbolically in the form uranium-235, U-235, $^{235}_{92}U$ or ^{235}U.
The carbon isotope containing 6 protons and 6 neutrons in its nucleus, $^{12}_{6}C$, is the base of the SI unit for substance. The atomic weights of other elements are defined with reference to carbon-12 (see following table). The mass of this carbon isotope is defined as equal to 12u exactly, where u = unified atomic mass unit = $1.660\,566 \times 10^{-27}$ kg (approximately). This unit is also abbreviated as amu, and was formerly called a Dalton (generally then valued at $1.660\,33 \times 10^{-27}$ kg).

Transuranic elements are artificial elements, for example plutonium, with an atomic number higher than the 92 of uranium, which is the heaviest element in terms of atomic weight occurring naturally.

A nuclide is an atomic species of a single atomic number and a single mass number.

Atomic weights

The following table of atomic weights is included with acknowledgement to the International Union of Pure and Applied Chemistry. It refers to atomic weights as agreed in 1977. The values shown apply to elements as they exist naturally on earth and to certain artificial elements.

When the weights are used with due regard to the footnotes they are considered reliable to ± 1 in the last digit or ± 3 if that digit is marked with an asterisk *.

Values in parentheses are used for certain radioactive elements whose atomic weights cannot be quoted precisely without knowledge of origin; the value given is the atomic mass number of the isotope of that element of longest known half life.

Table of atomic weights

Scaled to the relative atomic weight (mass) of carbon-12, symbol $A_r(^{12}C) = 12$

Name	Symbol	Atomic number	Atomic weight, A_r (E)
Actinium	Ac	89	227.0278[d]
Aluminium	Al	13	26.98154
Americium	Am	95	(243)
Antimony (Stibium)	Sb	51	121.75*
Argon	Ar	18	39.948*[a, b]
Arsenic	As	33	74.9216
Astatine	At	85	(210)
Barium	Ba	56	137.33[b]
Berkelium	Bk	97	(247)
Beryllium	Be	4	9.01218
Bismuth	Bi	83	208.9804
Boron	B	5	10.81[a, c]
Bromine	Br	35	79.904
Cadmium	Cd	48	112.41[b]
Caesium	Cs	55	132.9054
Calcium	Ca	20	40.08[b]
Californium	Cf	98	(251)
Carbon	C	6	12.011[a]
Cerium	Ce	58	140.12[b]
Chlorine	Cl	17	35.453
Chromium	Cr	24	51.996
Cobalt	Co	27	58.9332
Copper	Cu	29	63.546*[a]
Curium	Cm	96	(247)
Dysprosium	Dy	66	162.50*
Einsteinium	Es	99	(252)
Erbium	Er	68	167.26*
Europium	Eu	63	151.96[b]
Fermium	Fm	100	(257)
Fluorine	F	9	18.998403
Francium	Fr	87	(223)
Gadolinium	Gd	64	157.25*[b]
Gallium	Ga	31	69.72
Germanium	Ge	32	72.59*
Gold	Au	79	196.9665
Hafnium	Hf	72	178.49*
Helium	He	2	4.00260[b]
Holmium	Ho	67	164.9304
Hydrogen	H	1	1.0079[a]
Indium	In	49	114.82[b]
Iodine	I	53	126.9045
Iridium	Ir	77	192.22*
Iron	Fe	26	55.847*
Krypton	Kr	36	83.80[b, c]
Lanthanum	La	57	138.9055*[b]
Lawrencium	Lr	103	(260)
Lead	Pb	82	207.2 [a, b]
Lithium	Li	3	6.941*[a, b, c]
Lutetium	Lu	71	174.967
Magnesium	Mg	12	24.305[b]
Manganese	Mn	25	54.9380
Mendelevium	Md	101	(258)
Mercury	Hg	80	200.59*
Molybdenum	Mo	42	95.94
Neodymium	Nd	60	144.24*[b]
Neon	Ne	10	20.179*[c]

Chemicals

Name	Symbol	Atomic number	Atomic weight, $A_r(E)$
Neptunium	Np	93	237.0482[d]
Nickel	Ni	28	58.70
Niobium	Nb	41	92.9064
Nitrogen	N	7	14.0067
Nobelium	No	102	(259)
Osmium	Os	76	190.2[b]
Oxygen	O	8	15.9994[*,a]
Palladium	Pd	46	106.4[b]
Phosphorus	P	15	30.97376
Platinum	Pt	78	195.09[*]
Plutonium	Pu	94	(244)
Polonium	Po	84	(209)
Potassium (Kalium)	K	19	39.0983[*]
Praseodymium	Pr	59	140.9077
Promethium	Pm	61	(145)
Protactinium	Pa	91	231.0359[d]
Radium	Ra	88	226.0254[b, d]
Radon	Rn	86	(222)
Rhenium	Re	75	186.207
Rhodium	Rh	45	102.9055
Rubidium	Rb	37	85.4678[*,b]
Ruthenium	Ru	44	101.07[*,b]
Samarium	Sm	62	150.4[b]
Scandium	Sc	21	44.9559
Selenium	Se	34	78.96[*]
Silicon	Si	14	28.0855[*]
Silver	Ag	47	107.868[b]
Sodium (Natrium)	Na	11	22.98977
Strontium	Sr	38	87.62[b]
Sulphur	S	16	32.06[a]
Tantalum	Ta	73	180.9479[*]
Technetium	Tc	43	(98)
Tellurium	Te	52	127.60[*,b]
Terbium	Tb	65	158.9254
Thallium	Tl	81	204.37[*]
Thorium	Th	90	232.0381[b, d]
Thulium	Tm	69	168.9342
Tin	Sn	50	118.69[*]
Titanium	Ti	22	47.90[*]
Tungsten		see Wolfram	
Unnilhexium[e]	Unh[e]	106	(263)
Unnilpentium[e]	Unp[e]	105	(262)
Unnilquadium[e]	Unq[e]	104	(261)
Uranium	U	92	238.029[b, c]
Vanadium	V	23	50.9415[*]
Wolfram	W	74	183.85[*]
Xenon	Xe	54	131.30[b, c]
Ytterbium	Yb	70	173.04[*]
Yttrium	Y	39	88.9059
Zinc	Zn	30	65.38
Zirconium	Zr	40	91.22[b]

[a]Element for which known variations in isotopic composition in normal terrestrial material prevent a more precise atomic weight being given; $A_r(E)$ values should be applicable to any 'normal' material.
[b]Element for which geological specimens are known in which the element has an anomalous isotopic composition, such that the difference between the atomic weight of the element in such specimens and that given in the table may exceed considerably the implied uncertainty.
[c]Element for which substantial variations in A_r from the value given can occur in commercially available material because of inadvertent or undisclosed change of isotopic composition.
[d]Element for which the value of A_r is that of the radioisotope of longest half-life.
[e]Name and symbol not finalised.

Melting and boiling points

Melting and boiling points for various substances are shown below, with temperatures in degrees celsius (centigrade) and kelvin.

	Melting point °C	K	Boiling point °C	K
Aluminium	660.46[b]	933.61[b]	2 056	2 329
Antimony	630.755[b]	903.905[b]	1 380	1 650
Barium	850	1 120	1 140	1 410
Boron	2 300	2 570	2 550	2 820
Cadmium	321.108[b]	594.258[b]	767	1 040
Calcium	810	1 080	1 200	1 470
Carbon	3 500	3 800	4 200	4 500
Chlorine	−102	172	−35	239
Cobalt	1 495[b]	1 768[b]	2 900	3 200
Copper	1 084.88[b]	1 358.03[b]	2 300	2 600
Fluorine	−223	50	−187	86
Gold	1 064.43[b]	1 337.58[b]	2 600	2 900
Helium	−272	1	−269	4
Hydrogen	−259	14	−252.753[a]	20.397[a]
Iron	1 535	1 808	3 000	3 300
Krypton	−169	104	−152	121
Lead	327.502[b]	600.652[b]	1 620	1 890
Magnesium	651	924	1 110	1 380
Manganese	1 260	1 530	1 900	2 200
Mercury	−38.836[b]	234.314[b]	356.66[a]	629.81[a]
Molybdenum	2 623[a]	2 896[a]	3 700	4 000
Neon	−249	24	−246	27
Nickel	1 455[b]	1 728[b]	2 900	3 200
Nitric acid	−42	231	86	359
Nitrogen	−210	63	−195.806[a]	77.344[a]
Oxygen	−218	55	−183	90
Phosphorus	44	317	280	553
Platinum	1 769[b]	2 042[b]	4 300	4 600
Potassium	62	335	760	1 030
Radium	960	1 230	1 140	1 410
Silver	961.93[b]	1 235.08[b]	1 950	2 220
Sodium	97	371	880	1 150
Sulphur	120	393	445	718
Sulphuric acid	10	284	340	610
Tin	231.9681[b]	505.1181[b]	2 260	2 530
Tungsten	3 422[a]	3 695[a]	5 900	6 200
Uranium	1 133	1 406	3 500	3 800
Vanadium	1 710	1 980	3 000	3 300
Water	0	273.15	100	373.15
Zinc	419.58[b]	692.73[b]	907	1 180

[a]Temperature established in connection with the International Practical Temperature Scale (IPTS).   [b]IPTS freezing point at standard atmosphere.

Relative density

The relationship between mass and volume is indicated by the density of a substance, measured usually in kilograms per cubic metre (kg/m³) or kilograms per litre (kg/l). Relative density (RD), the internationally recognised term for specific gravity (sg), is the ratio of the mass of one substance to another for equal volumes and standard conditions of temperature and pressure.
Relative densities are usually expressed in the form RD 15/4 °C, where the first number refers to the temperature at which the density of a substance is measured, and the second to the temperature of water against the density of which it is compared; water is usually taken as the standard for solids and liquids. Since 1 litre of water has a mass of 1 kilogram at approximately 4 °C, there is a direct relationship between relative density and density for water at that temperature:
relative density of 1.0 = 1 kilogram per litre (kg/l)
 = 1 000 kilograms (1 tonne) per cubic metre (t/m³)
 = 1 gram per millilitre (g/ml)
 = 1 gram per cubic centimetre (g/cm³ or g/cc)
 = 62.428 pounds per cubic foot
For gases, relative density is usually compared to dry air of normal carbon dioxide content at the same temperature and pressure.

Chemicals

Variation with temperature

The maximum density of water is at 4°C (more accurately at 3.98°C or 277.13 K). The change in the density of water with temperature is as follows:

°C	density: kg/l	°C	density: kg/l	°C	density: kg/l
0	0.99987	4	1.00000	10	0.99972
1	0.99993	5	0.99999	15	0.99913
2	0.99997	6	0.99997	20	0.99822
3	0.99999				

The relative densities of various substances are indicated below, together with the density in pounds per cubic foot; density in kilograms per litre is approximately the same as the relative density. In this table approximate average values are given at 4 °C and relative to water at 4 °C and under normal atmospheric temperature and pressure. By definition, a substance with relative density less than 1 will float on water (when it does not mix), and one with relative density greater than 1 will not float.

For any substance, density at t_1 °C = mass/volume at t_1 °C,

and relative density t_1/t_2 °C $= \dfrac{\text{density of the substance at } t_1 \text{ °C}}{\text{density of water at } t_2 \text{ °C}}$

Since the density of water at 4 °C is unity, relative densities compared to water at 4 °C are equal to density whatever the temperature; that is, for example, RD 15/4 °C of a substance is the same as density at 15 °C.

	Relative density	Pounds per cubic foot
Acid: acetic	1.05	66
muriatic (40%)	1.20	75
nitric (91%)	1.50	94
sulphuric: 90%	1.81	113
100%	1.83	114
Alcohol: ethyl	0.79	49
methyl	0.80	50
Aluminium	2.7	168
Antimony	6.7	417
Asbestos	2.4	150
Ashes	0.7	44
Asphalt	1.4	87
Bismuth	9.8	600
Bone	1.8	112
Brass (60 Cu/40 Zn)	8.4	520
Brick: building	2.5	156
medium	1.8	112
Bromine	3.1	194
Bronze (90 Cu/10 Sn)	8.8	550
Butter	0.9	57
Carbon, graphite	2.3	144
Cellulose	1.3	79
Cement, Portland	3.1	194
Chalk	2.3	143
Charcoal	0.4	25
Chloroform	1.5	95
Chromium	7.1	445
Clay	2.2	137
Coal: anthracite	1.6	100
bituminous	1.4	87
lignite	2.2	137
Cobalt	8.9	555
Concrete: general	2.3	145
lightweight	1.6	100
Copper	8.9	556
Cork	0.24	15
Cotton	1.5	94
Diamonds	3.5	218
Ether	0.74	46
German silver	8.6	536
Glass: crown	2.6	160
crystal	3.0	187
flint	4.0	250
Glass wool	0.5	31
Gold	19.3	1 205
Gold coin	17.2	1 070
Granite	2.7	170
Ice	0.92	57

	Relative density	Pounds per cubic foot
Iron: ingot	7.9	490
cast grey	7.2	446
malleable	7.3	457
Lard	0.9	57
Lead	11.34	708
Leather	0.95	59
Lime	0.9	56
Limestone	2.5	155
Magnesium	1.7	109
Manganese	7.4	475
Marble	2.7	169
Mercury	13.6	850
Monel (70 Ni/30 Cu)	8.9	555
Milk	1.03	64
Nickel	8.9	555
Nylon	1.15	72
Oils, vegetable	0.95	59
Olive oil	0.92	57
Paper	0.9	57
Paraffin (kerosene)	0.81	51
Petrol (gasoline)	0.74	46
Petroleum	0.87	54
Platinum	21.4	1 340
Plutonium	19.7	1 230
Resin, epoxy	1.1	70
Rubber	0.94	59
Rubber goods	1.5	94
Salt	0.77	48
Sand, loose	2.5	157
Shale	1.5	94
Silicon	2.4	150
Silver	10.5	655
Slag	2.0	125
Slate	2.8	175
Sodium	0.97	61
Soil, dry, loose	1.2	75
Solder	8.3	520
Sulphur	2.1	130
Tar	1.0	62
Timber: ash	0.75	47
balsa wood	0.15	9
oak	0.75	47
pine	0.55	34
teak	0.85	53
Tin	7.3	455
Titanium	4.5	283
Turpentine	0.87	54
Tungsten	19.3	1 200
Uranium	19.0	1 185
Water: distilled	1.0	62
sea	1.03	64
Wool	1.3	81
Zinc	7.1	440

Two measures sometimes used when considering measurement of relative density (specific gravity) are degrees Baumé (°Bé) and degrees Twaddell (°Tw); these are similar to degrees API (for which see page 134). The basic original formulae are:

degrees Baumé $= \dfrac{140}{RD} - 130$ (for a substance lighter than water)

or $= 145 - \dfrac{145}{RD}$ (for a substance heavier than water)

degrees Twaddell $= \dfrac{RD - 1}{0.005}$

where RD = relative density (specific gravity) in kg/l at 60/60 °F

Chemicals

Main values are:

Relative densities less than 1

RD (kg/l)	°Bé	RD (kg/l)	°Bé	RD (kg/l)	°Bé	RD (kg/l)	°Bé	RD (kg/l)	°Bé
0.60	103.3	0.68	75.9	0.76	54.2	0.84	36.7	0.92	22.2
0.61	99.5	0.69	72.9	0.77	51.8	0.85	34.7	0.93	20.5
0.62	95.8	0.70	70.0	0.78	49.5	0.86	32.8	0.94	18.9
0.63	92.2	0.71	67.2	0.79	47.2	0.87	30.9	0.95	17.4
0.64	88.7	0.72	64.4	0.80	45.0	0.88	29.1	0.96	15.8
0.65	85.4	0.73	61.8	0.81	42.8	0.89	27.3	0.97	14.3
0.66	82.1	0.74	59.2	0.82	40.7	0.90	25.6	0.98	12.9
0.67	79.0	0.75	56.7	0.83	38.7	0.91	23.8	0.99	11.4
								1.00	10.0

Relative densities greater than 1

RD (kg/l)	°Bé	°Tw	RD (kg/l)	°Bé	°Tw	RD (kg/l)	°Bé	°Tw
1.00	0.0	0	1.35	37.6	70	1.70	59.7	140
1.05	6.9	10	1.40	41.4	80	1.75	62.1	150
1.10	13.2	20	1.45	45.0	90	1.80	64.4	160
1.15	18.9	30	1.50	48.3	100	1.85	66.6	170
1.20	24.2	40	1.55	51.5	110	1.90	68.7	180
1.25	29.0	50	1.60	54.4	120	1.95	70.6	190
1.30	33.5	60	1.65	57.1	130	2.00	72.5	200

Measures in general

The UK chemical industries began a change over to the metric system beginning in 1971 and mainly complete by 1973. Measures of special interest are included in the following main sections (for paint, see Construction, page 127).

Fertilisers

Primary nutrients

There are three main nutrients in fertiliser:

Nitrogen (N), taken up by plants in nitrate (NO_3) or ammonium (NH_4) form.

Phosphorus (P), usually in the form of P_2O_5 (phosphate), where P is converted to P_2O_5 by multiplying by 2.29, and P_2O_5 is converted to P by multiplying by 0.44.

Potassium (K), usually in the form of K_2O (potash), where K is converted to K_2O by multiplying by 1.2, and K_2O is converted to K by multiplying by 0.83.

Soil

Classification of soils, in terms of the diameter of solid particles, is:

gravel and stones	above 2 mm
sand	0.05 to 2 mm
silt	0.002 to 0.05 mm
clay	below 0.002 mm

Classification in terms of nutrient content is made by means of soil analysis indexes, which classify in terms of milligrams of each element per litre of air dried, ground soil. These indexes are:

Index	Phosphorus (P) mg/l	Potassium (K) mg/l	Magnesium (Mg) mg/l	Nitrate (N) mg/l
0	0– 9	0– 60	0– 25	0– 25
1	10– 15	61– 120	26– 50	26– 50
2	16– 25	121– 240	51– 100	51–100
3	26– 45	241– 400	101– 175	101–150
4	46– 70	401– 600	176– 250	151–250
5	71–100	601– 900	251– 350	251–350
6	101–140	901–1500	351– 600	over 350
7	141–200	1501–2400	601–1000	
8	201–280	2401–3600	1001–1500	
9	over 280	over 3600	over 1500	

Analysis of the soil by various methods gives a measure of the index for each element, and recommendations as to amounts of fertiliser are usually made in relation to the index level of any soil. For example, at soil P or K index 2 or above, economic responses in the United Kingdom of cereals, grasses and legumes to additional P or K are rare, and it is only necessary to maintain existing nutrient levels for those crops.

It is not possible in general to determine the N index by testing, and the estimate of the N index is usually based on past crops; for example, a last crop of peas or potatoes will have left an N index of 1.

An index is also used to express the concentration of soluble salts in the soil; this is the measure of conductivity, expressed in units of microsiemens; the index is:

Index	Conductivity (microsiemens)	Index	Conductivity (microsiemens)	Index	Conductivity (microsiemens)
0	1900–2200	4	2710–2800	8	3710–4000
1	2210–2400	5	2810–3000	9	4010 and over
2	2410–2600	6	3010–3300		
3	2610–2700	7	3310–3700		

Additional amounts of fertiliser required are usually expressed in the metric system as kilograms per hectare, litres per hectare, or grams per litre; for example, UK recommendations for barley grown on light soils at index 0 would be 125 kg/ha N, 75 kg/ha P_2O_5 and 75 kg/ha K_2O.

Relationships between metric and other units are as follows:

1 kilogram per hectare (kg/ha) = 14.274 9 ounces per acre (oz/acre)
= 0.892 179 pound per acre (lb/acre)
= 0.007 966 hundredweight per acre (cwt/acre)
1 ounce per acre (oz/acre) = 0.070 053 kilogram per hectare (kg/ha)
1 pound per acre (lb/acre) = 1.120 85 kilograms per hectare (kg/ha)
1 hundredweight per acre (cwt/acre) = 125.535 kilograms per hectare (kg/ha)
1 litre per hectare (l/ha) = 14.242 9 fluid ounces per acre (fl oz/acre)
= 0.712 147 pint per acre (pt/acre)
= 0.106 907 US gallon per acre (US gal/acre)
= 0.089 018 UK gallon per acre (UK gal/acre)
1 fluid ounce per acre (fl oz/acre) = 0.070 210 litre per hectare (l/ha)
1 pint per acre (pt/acre) = 1.404 20 litres per hectare (l/ha)
1 US gallon per acre (US gal/acre) = 9.353 96 litres per hectare (l/ha)
1 UK gallon per acre (UK gal/acre) = 11.233 6 litres per hectare (l/ha)

Soil reaction

This is measured by pH ('potential hydrogen'), which denotes the acidity and alkalinity of a substance. A pH of 7 means a neutral substance, 0–7 means it is acidic, and 7–14 that it is alkaline.

Normal UK agricultural soil has a value for pH of 4–8. Adding lime reduces acidity (increases pH).

The following table indicates for some crops the soil pH levels for the United Kingdom below which crop growth is affected on mineral soils, and so the danger level at which lime must be applied:

	pH		pH		pH
Arable crops		Lettuce	6.1	*Flowers*	
Barley	5.9	Mint	6.6	Begonia	5.3
Beet, sugar	5.9	Onions	5.7	Carnations	6.0
Maize	5.5	Parsnips	5.4	Daffodils	6.1
Oats	5.3	Peas	5.9	Hydrangeas (pink)	5.9
Potatoes	4.9	Rhubarb	5.4	Hydrangeas (blue)	4.1
Swedes	5.4	Spinach	5.8	Lavender	6.1
Wheat	5.5	Tomatoes (outdoor)	5.1	Roses, hybrid tea	5.6
Vegetable crops		Turnips	5.4	Tulips	5.9
Asparagus	5.9	*Grasses and clovers*		*Fruit*	
Cabbages	5.4	Clover, red	5.9	Apples	5.0
Carrots	5.7	Clover, wild white	4.7	Pears	5.3
Cauliflowers	5.6	Lucerne	6.2	Plums	5.6
Cucumbers	5.5	Vetches	5.9	Strawberries	5.1

Response to fertilisers

1 unit of plant nutrients (N–P–K) produces very roughly 10 units of basic food.
1 tonne of basic food provides approximately 5 000 calories (21 kilojoules) per day for 1 year.

Lubricating oil

Viscosity, the most important property of lubricating oil, is a measure of its ability to flow. Dynamic or absolute viscosity is force by time per area; since viscosity is affected by the mass of a liquid, kinematic viscosity is also used as a measure, being dynamic viscosity divided by density.

Chemicals

Conversions

In addition to the main SI units of the pascal second for dynamic viscosity, and square metre per second for kinematic viscosity, the centipoise is used as a measure of dynamic viscosity, and the centistoke as a measure of kinematic viscosity:

Dynamic or absolute

1 poundal second per square foot (pdl s/ft²)
= 1.488 16 pascal seconds (Pa s) or newton seconds per square metre (N s/m²)
= 1 488.16 millipascal seconds (mPa s) or centipoises (cP)
1 pound-force second per square foot (lbf s/ft²)
= 47.880 3 pascal seconds or newton seconds per square metre
= 47 880.3 millipascal seconds or centipoises
1 pound-force second per square inch (lbf s/in²), also called a reyn
= 6 894.76 pascal seconds or newton seconds per square metre
1 pascal second or newton second per square metre, also called a poiseuille (Pl)
= 1000 centipoises
= 0.671 969 poundal second per square foot
= 0.020 885 4 pound-force second per square foot
= 0.000 145 038 pound-force second per square inch
1 millipascal second or centipoise
= 0.000 671 969 poundal second per square foot
= 0.000 020 885 4 pound-force second per square foot

Kinematic

1 square inch per second (in²/s)
= 645.16 square millimetres per second (mm²/s) or centistokes (cSt)
1 square foot per hour (ft²/h)
= 25.806 4 square millimetres per second or centistokes
1 square millimetre per second or centistoke
= 0.001 550 00 square inch per second
= 0.038 750 1 square foot per hour

Viscosity values

Lubricating oils have viscosities ranging from 10 to 1 000 centistokes at 100°F (37.8°C); by comparison water has a viscosity of about 1 centistoke.
Centipoises = centistokes × density (at the relevant temperature).

Viscosity varies with temperature; this is indicated as follows for water:
at 0°C viscosity is 1.79 centipoises
at 20°C viscosity is 1.0 centipoise
at 100°C viscosity is 0.28 centipoise
That is, viscosity falls as temperature rises. Conversely fluidity rises with temperature; this is measured by the rhe: 1 rhe = 1/poise or 'reciprocal' poise.

Density

Density of lubricating oil is, in general:
at   0°F (−18 °C) 0.9 kg/l
   210°F (99 °C) 0.825 kg/l

Other measures

There are a range of other measures for viscosity, which are not directly related to the SI units.

SAE

The Society of Automotive Engineers (SAE) in America developed a system which grades oils. Multi-grade oils combine low viscosity of 10W grades for easy low-temperature starting (fluidity is comparatively high), with the high viscosity of the 30 to 50 grades for better load capacity in bearings (viscosity remains relatively high) at normal engine running temperature. The effect of temperature can be seen from the following table, giving approximate values for the SAE grades in centistokes:

SAE grade	Centistokes: at 0°F (−17.8°C)	at 100°F (37.8°C)	at 210°F (98.9°C)
10W	1 950	41	6.0
20W	6 550	71	8.5
30		114	11.3
40		173	14.8
50		270	19.7
10W–30		76	12.7
20W–40		93	13.7

Saybolt

This system is based on the time taken for the flow of liquid from one vessel to another. The Saybolt Universal Second (SUS) is the time in seconds for 60ml of oil to flow out of the cup in a Saybolt viscometer through a carefully specified opening. This measure is only very roughly related to centistokes; approximately, for the values in the SAE table, SUS is equal to cSt multiplied by 4½ to 7½. Saybolt Furol Seconds are used for viscous oils; very roughly: 1 Saybolt Furol Second = 10 Saybolt Universal Seconds.

Redwood

This is a UK system based on the time for a flow as in the case of Saybolt. Relatively mobile oils are measured in a number of seconds Redwood I, and more viscous oils in seconds Redwood II; a larger orifice speeds up the time of flow by about 10 — very roughly, 1 second Redwood II = 10 seconds Redwood I. This measure is again only roughly related to centistokes: approximately, for the values in the SAE table, sec Red I is equal to cSt multiplied by 4 to 7; very roughly sec Red I is 87.5–90% of SUS.

Engler

This system, used in Germany, Italy and some other European countries, is based on the ratio of the time for flow of oil to the time for an equal volume of distilled water at the same temperature. Results are given in terms of the Engler degree (°E). Very approximately, for the values in the SAE table, °E is equal to 13–18% of cSt; very roughly, °E is 2.8–3.2% of SUS and 3.0–3.7% of sec Red I.

Petrochemicals

Crude petroleum is predominantly a complex mixture of chemical compounds, called hydrocarbons because they are composed largely of the two elements hydrogen and carbon.
Since crude oil is a mixture it has no fixed boiling point, but has a boiling or distillation range which may start as low as 20°C and end above 400°C; generally a low boiling point is associated with a low number of carbon atoms in the molecule. Distillation makes use of the difference in volatility or boiling point of different components or fractions in the mixture. The main fractions into which crude oil can be separated by distillation are as follows:

	Boiling-point range °C	Carbon atoms in the molecule
Light distillates		
petroleum gases	below 0	1–4
gasoline (petrols)	0–65	5–6
naphtha	65–170	6–10
kerosene (paraffin)	170–250	10–14
Middle distillates		
gas oil	250–340	14–19
Residue		
lubricating oil and wax feedstocks	340–500	19–35
bitumen feedstocks	over 500	over 35

Simplest of the structures is one where four hydrogen atoms are joined to a single carbon atom; this is the gas methane (CH_4). Other basic structures are ethylene (C_2H_4) and benzene (C_6H_6).

Plastics and resins

UN production estimates refer to the production of plastic materials and artificial resins (excluding synthetic rubber, man-made fibres etc) obtained by chemical transformation of natural organic substances or by chemical synthesis, and are classified in three groups:
A. *Condensation:* including polycondensation and polyaddition products, formed by reaction between several molecules of the same or different chemical constitution, in which the structural units are normally linked together by functional groups (eg, aminoplasts, alkyd resins, epoxy resins, silicones)
B. *Polymerisation:* including copolymerisation, obtained by the union of monomers with multiple carbon-carbon bonds or molecules of different chemical constitution (eg, polyethylene, polystyrene, polyvinyl derivatives)
C. *Other processes,* including regenerated cellulose, hardened proteins, natural resins modified by fusion, artificial resins, chemical derivatives of natural rubber, and other high polymers, artificial resins and artificial plastic materials (including alginic acid and linoxyn).

Chemicals

Synthetic fibres

Main types are polyamides (eg nylon), polyesters (eg Terylene), polyacrylics (eg Acrilan) and polypropylene.

Pesticides and fertilisers

DDT is a chlorinated hydrocarbon (dichloro-diphenyl-trichloroethane). Ammonia and sulphur are derived from oil and natural gas; ammonia is a basic source of nitrogen for fertilisers.

Detergents

These are synthetic soaps made from organic chemicals largely derived from petroleum.

Solvents for paints, cosmetics and pharmaceuticals

Chemical solvents usually contain oxygen and chlorine as well as hydrogen and carbon. Ethylene oxide and ethyl alcohol (C_2H_5OH) are among basic materials used.

Boiling points of the main alcohols are:

	°C
Methyl alcohol (or methanol)	65 (low boiling)
Ethyl alcohol (or ethanol)	78 (low boiling)
Isopropyl alcohol	82 (low boiling)
Secondary butyl alcohol	100 (low boiling)
Isobutyl alcohol	107 (medium boiling)
Normal butyl alcohol	118 (medium boiling)
Methyl isobutyl carbinol	132 (medium boiling)

Industrial chemicals

These include anti-knock compound (tetra-ethyl lead) and anti-freeze (ethylene glycol).

Rubber

For natural rubber see page 108.
Synthetic rubber means unsaturated synthetic substances which can be transformed by 'vulcanising' with sulphur, solenium or tellerium into non-thermoplastic substances; such substances having an elasticity such that, at 15–20 °C, they will not break on being extended to 3 times their original length and will return after being extended to 2 times their original length, within a period of 2 hours, to a length not greater than $1\frac{1}{2}$ times the original length.

Rubber hardness

Hardness of a rubber is its resistance to deformation, usually measured by penetration of a rigid indenter applied with force. Measurement is usually made in terms of:
Shore durometer A, which has a pointer pressed under certain conditions of pressure into a rubber sample; the scale measures from 0° for soft to 100° for absolutely hard (maximum indentation = 0°, and zero indentation = 100°).
Shore durometer D, which has a truncated cone indentor, measuring also on a scale from 0° to 100°.
Wallace hardness meter, which reads in terms of International Rubber Hardness Degrees (IRHD).

International Rubber Hardness Degrees measure hardness, as with the Shore scales, from 0° to 100°. The scale is based on a logarithmic progression, with conditions that $\log_{10}M$ at the midpoint of the curve of the progression is 0.364, and the maximum slope is equal to 57 IRHD per 1 increase in $\log_{10}M$, where M = meganewtons per square metre (MN/m^2).
Different methods of testing are related through the amount of differential indentation (usually in 0.01 mm) to IRHD. Shore A readings are usually within ±1° of IRHD, except below about 30° where they are rather lower; for synthetic rubber, correspondence may be less close.

Examples of rubber hardness

	Shore A (approx IRHD)
Natural rubber	20–100
Styrene	35–90
Butyl	40–70
Hard rubber	65–95

Rubber plasticity

Plasticity or 'viscosity' is usually measured in terms of Mooney viscosity. This measures the drag ('torque') when a rotor is revolved at 2 rpm within a rubber sample under specified conditions; a specific temperature is maintained, usually 100°C. The scale runs from 0 to 200, with 0 meaning maximum viscosity (zero force applied) and 200 zero viscosity (maximum force applied); the basic torque applied is 8.31 N m when forces of 100 N are applied to the rotor.

Sulphuric and other acids

Sulphuric acid production, as reported in UN figures, is included without adjustment where the original estimates are given in terms of 66° Baumé (that is, 93–100% H_2SO_4). Conversion for production from other countries, reporting at less than 100%, is made for sulphuric and other acids as follows:
showing the conversion from degrees Baumé (°Bé) (also see pages 122–123)

Sulphuric acid		Hydrochloric acid		Nitric acid	
°Bé	% H_2SO_4	°Bé	% HCl	°Bé	% HNO_3
50.3	63	18.8	30	34.3	50
53.0	67	19.9	32	38.9	60
55.0	70	21	34	42.4	70
60.5	79	22	36	45.1	80
65.1	90	23	38	47.2	90
65.5	92	24	40	49.2	100

The relative densities (kg/l) implied for sulphuric acid at the varying percentages of strength are, as at 20°C:

%		%	
63	1.531	79	1.716
67	1.576	90	1.814
70	1.611	92	1.824

with 100% H_2SO_4 having a relative density (kg/l) of 1.831.

Computers

Digital computer

A digital computer is a machine which performs operations on data represented in digital, discrete or number form. In electronic computers the number system used is that of binary notation. Data are recorded in the form of bits (binary digits) 0 or 1. Bits are grouped into bytes (8 bits) or words (24–32 bits).

Units
1 hartley = $\log_2 10$ bits = 3.321 928 bits (b). For data transmission,
1 segment = 64 bytes (b), 1 000 segments = 1 kilosegment.
K or k = 1 024 (2^{10}) or one thousand (10^3); in reference to processor size, and, by extension, to program size, it is usually taken as the higher value (based on 2^n).
1 kilobit or kilobyte (kb or Kb) = 1 024 or 1 000 bits or bytes
1 megabit or megabyte (Mb) = 1 048 576 or 1 000 000 bits or bytes

Analog computer

An analog computer is a machine which performs functions upon numbers in other than digital form, that is, on data presented in a continuous form. In mechanical analog computers the numbers are often represented by the physical dimensions of the components. In electrical analog computers numbers may be represented by voltages.

Binary system

A system for representing numbers by two digits, 0 and 1.
In the usual decimal system, each addition of a numerical character means multiplication by 10 (also see page 15); in the binary system addition of an extra character means multiplication by 2 as shown in the following table:

	Binary system		Decimal system	
		powers of 2		powers of 10
One	1	2^0	1	10^0
Two	10	2^1	2	
Three	11		3	
Four	100	2^2	4	
Five	101		5	
Six	110		6	
Seven	111		7	
Eight	1000	2^3	8	
Nine	1001		9	
Ten	1010		10	10^1

Computers

A table of powers of 2 in terms of numbers of the decimal system follows:

2^n	n	2^{-n}
2	1	0.5
4	2	0.25
8	3	0.125
16	4	0.062 5
32	5	0.031 25
64	6	0.015 625
128	7	0.007 812 5
256	8	0.003 906 25
512	9	0.001 953 125
1 024	10	0.000 976 562 5
2 048	11	0.000 488 281 25
4 096	12	0.000 244 140 625
8 192	13	0.000 122 070 312 5
16 384	14	0.000 061 035 156 25
32 768	15	0.000 030 517 578 125
65 536	16	0.000 015 258 789 062 5
131 072	17	0.000 007 629 394 531 25
262 144	18	0.000 003 814 697 265 625
524 288	19	0.000 001 907 348 632 812 5
1 048 576	20	0.000 000 953 674 316 406 25
2 097 152	21	0.000 000 476 837 158 203 125
4 194 304	22	0.000 000 238 418 579 101 562 5
8 388 608	23	0.000 000 119 209 289 550 781 25
16 777 216	24	0.000 000 059 604 644 775 390 625
33 554 432	25	0.000 000 029 802 322 387 695 313
67 108 864	26	0.000 000 014 901 161 193 847 656
134 217 728	27	0.000 000 007 450 580 596 923 828
268 435 456	28	0.000 000 003 725 290 298 461 914
536 870 912	29	0.000 000 001 862 645 149 230 957
1 073 741 824	30	0.000 000 000 931 322 574 615 479
2 147 483 648	31	0.000 000 000 465 661 287 307 739
4 294 967 296	32	0.000 000 000 232 830 643 653 870
8 589 934 592	33	0.000 000 000 116 415 321 826 935
17 179 869 184	34	0.000 000 000 058 207 660 913 467
34 359 738 368	35	0.000 000 000 029 103 830 456 734
68 719 476 736	36	0.000 000 000 014 551 915 228 367
137 438 953 472	37	0.000 000 000 007 275 957 614 183
274 877 906 944	38	0.000 000 000 003 637 978 807 092
549 755 813 888	39	0.000 000 000 001 818 989 403 546
1 099 511 627 776	40	0.000 000 000 000 909 494 701 773

Hardware and software

Hardware is the term used to describe the electronic machinery making up a computer system. Software refers to the programs which give instructions to the computer.

Program and language

A program gives instructions to the computer to carry out various operations. Programs can be written in a number of different languages; for example Algol, Basic, Cobol, Fortran etc. Software programs called compilers enable the computer to translate the languages used by the programmer.

Data

This term means the information given to the computer on which it is to perform the operations detailed in a program. Data can be 'input' from punched cards, paper tape, magnetic tape or disc.

Real time

This is a method of operation where data is absorbed by the computer at the actual time of its occurrence.

Input and output

Punched cards

This is a card which uses 12 positions in each of a number of different columns to represent instructions or numbers by use of a code. Cards are usually from 21–90 columns, 80 columns being the most widely used; columns are numbered from left to right.

Paper tape

This is normally 5, 6, 7 or 8 track tape; that is, there is space for that number of data holes across the tape. Each row of holes and/or spaces represents a character or number specified by the code used. The ISO recommendation is for a standard 8-track tape.

Magnetic tape

Magnetic tape is the commonest form of additional store used for computers; it can store programs or data. It is usually in the form of a continuous strip of $\frac{1}{2}''$ (12.7 mm) wide plastic material wound on reels, usually of $10\frac{1}{2}''$ (267 mm) diameter.

Magnetic disc

This is a storage device consisting of a number of flat circular plates, with tracks on the surface to store the data.

Output devices

These are the various means of presenting the results obtained by executing the operations detailed in the program instructions on the data. Results can be given on a line-printer, allowing for up to 160 characters per line, and with speeds from about 300 to 2000 lines per minute; they can also be given in the form of charts or graphs, on paper tape, punched cards or magnetic tape in code, or on a visual display unit.

Abbreviations

mip = million instructions per second
ram = random-access memory

Construction

Aggregates

Bulk materials that are used in the construction industry. They are used either with binders (for example, cement bitumen, tar) in composite materials such as concrete, mortar or bituminous mixtures for roads, or on their own as road sub-bases, railway ballast or special fill. They are usually sold in bulk by the tonne. Relative density is about 2.1.

Bricks

Measures

1 rod of brickwork = 272 ft² (25.3 m²), and requires approximately 4 500 bricks. Bricks are sold by 1 000 for building contracts, but are also available in smaller quantities.
1 load (generally obsolete) = 500 bricks.
Brickwork is measured by m².

Sizes

UK standard 'work size' of bricks is
215 mm × 102.5 mm × 65 mm (8.5 in × 4.0 in × 2.6 in).
Other sizes are in general available.

Weight

Bricks weigh 2–3 kg ($4\frac{1}{2}$–7 lb) each; that is, 2–3 tonnes per 1000.
Brickwork weighs between 1 400 to 2 400 kg/m³.

Quantities of bricks and mortar

Wall thickness (mm)	Quantities per square metre	
	Bricks (number)	Mortar (m³)
102.5 ($\frac{1}{2}$ brick)	60	0.028–0.03
215 (1 brick)	120	0.05–0.06
327.5 ($1\frac{1}{2}$ brick)	180	0.07–0.10

When measuring quantities of bricks required per square metre of brickwork, a cutting and wastage factor should be added to the above figures.

Haulage

Lorries can carry about 10 000 bricks.

Cement

Ordinary portland cement is produced by heating together chalk or limestone and clay or shale.
Rapid-hardening portland cement is similar to ordinary, but more finely ground; there is a higher rate of gain of strength, leading to rapid-hardening.
Sulphate-resisting cement has its composition adjusted to resist attack by sulphates, occurring in some types of soil.
Aluminous cement has an alumina content over 30% (portland cement has an alumina content of about 5%).

Measures

United Kingdom
Cement is sold in bulk by the tonne, and in 50 kg (110 lb) bags; the bag was formerly 112 lb (50.8 kg) before the change to the metric system.

United States
Bushel = 80 or 100 lb (36 or 45 kg)
Barrel (net): masonry = 280 lb (127 kg)
              portland = 376 lb (170 kg)
Bag = 94 lb (43 kg)

Canada
Barrel = 350 lb (159 kg)

Density

Relative density of portland cement is 3.0–3.2; 'bulk density' of cement powder (allowing for air in between particles) is about 1.4 (85 lb per cubic foot).

Concrete

Composition

Concrete is made from cement, aggregates and water; chemical and admixtures or fillers are also used, to alter handling and placing characteristics and long-term durability. The proportions of the ingredients are varied to suit the required performance.

Ready mixed concrete

Supplied by volume of full compacted concrete in cubic metres. Specification by compressive strength in Newtons per square millimetre (N/mm²) measured from standard cube specimens, or by prescribed proportions of the basic ingredients.

Density

	kg/m³	lb/ft³
normal concrete[a]	2 300	140
lightweight concrete[b]	650–2 000	40–125

[a]With natural aggregates. [b]Made by incorporating air bubbles in the mix or using synthetic lightweight aggregates.

Target mean strength is the least strength for which a concrete may be designed making allowance for variability in materials, etc. Strength is usually measured in terms of newtons per square millimetre; average strength is about 27 N/mm² (roughly 4 000 lbf/in²).

Glass

Following a change to the metric system, UK standard thicknesses are as follows (showing also the old equivalent); the tolerance range and mass is also shown:

	Nominal thickness mm	Tolerance range mm	Mass kg/m²
Sheet glass (clear)	2 (18 oz)	1.8–2.2	5.0
	3 (24 oz)	2.8–3.2	7.5
	4 (32 oz)	3.7–4.3	10.0
	5 (3/16 in)	4.7–5.3	12.5
	6 (1/4 in)	5.7–6.3	15.0
Float glass (clear)	3	2.8–3.2	7.5
	4	3.8–4.2	10.0
	5	4.8–5.2	12.5
	6	5.8–6.2	15.0
	10	9.7–10.3	25.0
	12	11.7–12.3	30.0
	15	14.5–15.5	37.5
	19	18.0–20.0	47.5
	25	24.0–26.0	63.5
Rough cast	5 (3/16 in)	4.5–5.5	12.5
	6 (1/3 in)	5.5–6.5	15.0
	10 (3/8 in)	9.7–10.8	25.0

Properties

average values are:
Density 2 560 kg/m³
Refractive index (see page 158) 1.52

Heating and ventilating

General heat conversions are included on page 67, with temperature conversions on pages 82 and 83; some special conversion factors are:

Thermal capacity: per unit mass (specific heat capacity)
1 Btu per pound degree Fahrenheit (Btu/lb °F)
= 4.186 8 kilojoules per kilogram kelvin (kJ/kg K)
per unit volume
1 Btu per cubic foot degree Fahrenheit (Btu/ft³ °F)
= 67.066 1 kilojoules per cubic metre kelvin (kJ/m³ K)
Intensity of heat-flow rate
1 Btu per square foot hour (Btu/ft² h)
= 3.154 59 watts per square metre (W/m²)
Thermal conductance (coefficient of thermal transmittance)
1 Btu per square foot hour degree Fahrenheit (Btu/ft² h °F)
= 5.678 26 watts per square metre kelvin (W/m² K)
Thermal conductivity
1 Btu inch per square foot hour degree Fahrenheit (Btu in/ft² h °F)
= 0.144 228 watt per metre kelvin (W/m K)
Thermal resistivity
1 square foot hour degree Fahrenheit per Btu inch (ft² h °F/Btu in)
= 6.933 47 metres kelvin per watt (m K/W)
Thermal resistivity is the reciprocal of thermal conductivity.

The kelvin is generally used instead of the degree Celsius: K = °C + 273.15; the interval of 1 kelvin equals 1 degree Celsius.

Old units

1 clo   = 0.200 371 2 kelvin square metre per watt (K m²/W)
1 langley = 41.84 kilojoules per square metre (kJ/m²)

Paint

The following table shows the main standard range of containers for paint, following the UK change to the metric system. Also indicated is the approximate spreading capacity on non-porous surfaces:

Metric	Imperial	Spreading capacity: in square metres			in square yards		
		Primer	Gloss	Emulsion	Primer	Gloss	Emulsion
500 ml	0.88 pint	6	7½	9	7	9	10½
1 litre	0.88 quart	12	15	18	14	18	21
2.5 litre	0.55 gallon	29	37	44	35	44	53
5 litre	1.10 gallons	59	74	88	70	88	105

Construction

Roads

Special conversion factors

Coverage: binder chippings or mixed material (reciprocal conversion for n)
n square yards per UK gallon = 5.437 08/n litres per square metre
n square yards per UK-ton = 1 215.18/n kilograms per square metre

Grass seeding: 1 ounce per square yard = 33.905 7 grams per square metre

Water supply

Density

For distilled water at 4°C (maximum density):
1 millilitre weighs 1 gram
1 litre weighs 1 kilogram
1 cubic metre weighs 1 tonne
1 UK fluid ounce weighs 1.002 2 avoirdupois ounces (28.413 g)
1 UK gallon weighs 10.022 lb (4.546 kg)
1 US gallon weighs 8.345 lb (3.785 kg)
1 cubic foot weighs 62.428 lb (28.317 kg)
1 UK (long) ton contains 223.5 UK gallons (1 016.05 litres)
1 US (short) ton contains 239.7 US gallons (907.18 litres)

For salt water (with relative density of 1.027):
1 cubic metre weighs approximately 1.03 tonnes
1 cubic foot weighs approximately 64 lb (29 kg)
1 UK gallon weighs approximately 10.3 lb (4.7 kg)
1 UK (long) ton contains approximately 217.6 UK gallons (989 litres)

Flow

A cusec represents a volume of water equivalent to the flow of one cubic foot of water for one second.
1 cusec
= 60 cubic feet per minute
= 86 400 cubic feet per day
= 373.730 UK gallons per minute
= 0.538 171 million UK gallons per day (mgd)
= 0.028 316 8 cubic metre per second (cumec)
= 2 446.576 cubic metres per day (m^3/d)
= 2.446 576 thousand cubic metres per day (tcmd or Ml/d)
= 28.316 8 litres per second
1 cubic foot per minute = 0.471 947 litre per second
1 UK gallon per minute = 0.075 768 litre per second
1 US gallon per minute = 0.063 090 litre per second
1 cubic metre per second (cumec) = 35.314 7 cusecs
= 19.005 mn UK gallons per day (mgd)
1 litre per second = 13.198 2 UK gallons per minute = 0.035 314 7 cusec
= 2.118 88 cubic feet per minute

1 cusec will supply a population of 18 000 with 30 UK gallons per head per day.

A *miner's inch* is the flow of water through one in^2; this varies according to the head of water, usually from 1.36–1.73 ft^3/min = 0.64–0.82 litre/second.

Coverage and drainage

An acre foot represents a volume of water sufficient to cover an acre to a depth of 1 foot.
1 acre foot = 43 560 cubic feet = 1 233.48 cubic metres
= 271 328 UK gallons = 325 851 US gallons
1 acre foot per day = 0.504 cusec
1 cusec = 1.983 acre feet per day

Flowing continuously for one day, 1 cusec will cover 5 acres to a depth of $4\frac{3}{4}$ inches.

1 hectare metre = 10 000 cubic metres = 353 147 cubic feet = 8.107 14 acre feet
1 acre foot = 0.123 348 hectare metre
1 cubic foot per 1 000 acres = 6.997 2 litres per square kilometre
= 0.069 972 litre per hectare
= 0.006 997 cubic metre per square kilometre

A *million acre* is equivalent to 43 560 million cubic feet, and is sufficient to cover an area of 10 square miles to a depth of $156\frac{1}{4}$ feet.

Flow per unit area
1 cubic foot per second per square mile (ft^3/s mile²)
= 1 cusec per square mile
= 10.933 litres per second per square kilometre (l/s km²)
1 cubic foot per second per 1 thousand acres (ft^3/s 1 000 acre)
= 1 cusec per 1 thousand acres
= 6.997 2 litres per second per square kilometre (l/s km²)
1 litre per second per square kilometre
= 0.091 46 cubic foot per second per square mile (ft^3/s mile²)
= 0.142 9 cubic foot per second per 1 thousand acres (ft^3/s 1 000 acre)

Transmissivity
1 UK gallon per day per foot (gal/d ft)
= 0.014 9 cubic metre per day per metre (m^3/d m)
1 cubic metre per day per metre (m^3/d m)
= 67.047 UK gallons per day per foot (gal/d ft)

Hydraulic conductivity
1 UK gallon per day per square foot (gal/d ft²)
= 0.048 9 cubic metre per day per square metre (m^3/d m²)
1 cubic metre per day per square metre (m^3/d m²)
= 20.436 UK gallons per day per square foot (gal/d ft²)

Precipitation

1 inch of rainfall on 1 acre = 101.2 UK tons = 102.8 tonnes
1 millimetre of rainfall on 1 square metre = 1 kilogram
1 millimetre of rainfall on 1 hectare = 10 tonnes = 9.8 UK tons

Water meters

Water meters intended for metering of cold water, should, under OIML recommendations, be capable of withstanding a pressure of 1.5 MPa (15 bar).

Hardness of water

The hardness of water is usually measured by the amount of Calcium Carbonate in the water; this is expressed as parts per million (ppm) or in UK degrees, which are grains per 1 UK gallon of water (1 part in 70 000 of water is one degree).

The usual classification is:

	ppm	UK degrees
soft	0– 5	0– 70
slightly hard	5–10	70–140
moderately hard	10–15	140–210
very hard	over 15	over 210

Electronics

Electromagnetic measures

Electromagnetic spectrum

The following is a broad outline of the main divisions:

Frequency (hertz)	Wavelength (metres)	Description
3×10^3 to 3×10^{12}	1×10^5 to 1×10^{-4}	radio waves
3×10^{11} to 4×10^{14}	1×10^{-3} to 8×10^{-7}	infrared
4×10^{14} to 1×10^{15}	8×10^{-7} to 3×10^{-7}	visible light
1×10^{15} to 6×10^{16}	3×10^{-7} to 5 $\times 10^{-9}$	ultraviolet
6×10^{16} to 3×10^{20}	5×10^{-9} to 1×10^{-12}	X-rays
3×10^{18} to 3×10^{24}	1×10^{-10} to 1×10^{-16}	gamma rays

The relationship between frequency and wavelength is defined as follows:
wave velocity = frequency × wavelength. Wave velocity of the electromagnetic spectrum is constant for a given medium, and for the speed of light in a vacuum is approximately 3×10^8 metres per second (more exactly 2.997 924 58 $\times 10^8$ m/s). Hence, approximately:
Frequency in Hz = 3×10^8/Wavelength in metres
Frequency in kHz = 3×10^5/Wavelength in metres
Frequency in MHz = 3×10^2/Wavelength in metres

Electronics

Old units

Ångström (Å) = 10^{-10} metre = approximately 3×10^{18} Hz.
Wave number = reciprocal of wavelength = 1/m or 1 m^{-1}
1 kayser (or rydberg) = 1/cm
1 X unit (or X-ray unit or Siegbahn unit) = $1.002\,02 \times 10^{-4}$ nm

Electromagnetic units summary

For definitions of the main SI units, see pages 14 and 17; a summary of the relationships follows:
Rate of flow of electric current: ampere (A) = watt (W)/volt (V)
Quantity of electricity or electric charge: coulomb (C) = A s
Power rate: watt (W) = J/s
Electric potential: volt (V) = W/A
Electric resistance: ohm (Ω) = V/A
Electric conductance: siemens (S) = 1/ohm = A/V
Electric capacitance: farad (F) = A s /V = C/V
Electric field strength: volt per metre (V/m)
Magnetic flux: weber (Wb) = V s
Inductance: henry (H) = V s/A
Magnetic flux density: tesla (T) = Wb/m^2
Magnetic field strength: ampere per metre (A/m)

Old International units (as replaced 1948)

UK and West Germany	United States
1 A (int 1948) = 0.999 85 A	1 A (int 1948) = 0.999 835 A
1 C (int 1948) = 0.999 85 C	1 C (int 1948) = 0.999 835 C
1 W (int 1948) = 1.000 19 W	1 W (int 1948) = 1.000 165 W
1 V (int 1948) = 1.000 34 V	1 V (int 1948) = 1.000 330 V
1 Ω (int 1948) = 1.000 49 Ω	1 Ω (int 1948) = 1.000 495 Ω
1 F (int 1948) = 0.999 51 F	1 F (int 1948) = 0.999 505 F
1 H (int 1948) = 1.000 49 H	1 H (int 1948) = 1.000 495 H

Electromagnetic and electrostatic units

Electromagnetic units (EMU)

1 EMU of current	= 10 A	= 1 abampere
1 EMU of charge	= 10 C	= 1 abcoulomb
1 EMU of potential	= 10 nV	= 1 abvolt
1 EMU of resistance	= 1 nΩ	= 1 abohm
1 EMU of conductance	= 1 GS	= 1 abmho
1 EMU of capacitance	= 1 GF	= 1 abfarad
1 EMU of inductance	= 1 nH	= 1 abhenry

Electrostatic units (ESU)
(where c = velocity of light in free space = 299 792 458 m/s)

1 ESU of current	= 1/10 c A	= 333.564 095 pA	= 1 statampere
1 ESU of charge	= 1/10 c C	= 333.564 095 pC	= 1 statcoulomb
1 ESU of potential	= 10^{-6} c V	= 299.792 458 V	= 1 statvolt
1 ESU of resistance	= 10^{-5} c^2 Ω	= 898.755 179 GΩ	= 1 statohm
1 ESU of conductance	= $10^{5}/c^2$ S	= 1.112 650 pS	= 1 statmho
1 ESU of capacitance	= $10^{5}/c^2$ F	= 1.112 650 pF	= 1 statfarad
1 ESU of inductance	= 10^{-5} c^2 H	= 898.755 179 GH	= 1 stathenry

Other old units

biot (Bi)	= 10 amperes = 1 abampere
faraday (based on carbon-12)	= 96 487 coulombs
faraday (chemical)	= 96 495.7 coulombs
faraday (physical)	= 96 521.9 coulombs
franklin (Fr)	= (0.1/c) 10^{-9} coulomb
(where c = speed of light)	= $\frac{1}{3}$ 10^{-9} coulomb (approx)
debye (D)	= 10^{-18} franklin centimetre
gamma	= 10^{-9} tesla
gauss (Gs)	= 10^{-4} tesla
gilbert (Gb)	= $10/4\pi$ ampere
maxwell (Mx)	= 10^{-8} weber
mho	= 1/ohm = 1 siemens
oersted (Oe)	= $1000/4\pi$ amperes per metre
unit pole	= 125.663 7 nanowebers

Electromagnetic constants

Where c = speed of light in a vacuum (or in free space)
= $2.997\,924\,58 \times 10^8$ m/s
and μ_o = magnetic constant (permeability of a vacuum or of free space)
= $4\pi\,10^{-7}$ H/m = $12.566\,371 \times 10^{-7}$ H/m
then ε_o = electric constant (permittivity of a vacuum or of free space)
= $1/\mu_o c^2$ = $8.854\,187\,82 \times 10^{-12}$ F/m

Diamagnetic substances have magnetic permeability less than μ_o.
Paramagnetic substances have magnetic permeability slightly above μ_o.
Ferromagnetic substances have magnetic permeability well above μ_o.

Radio wave frequencies

Radio regulations were in general revised in 1979 by the International Telecommunication Union (ITU), revisions to come into effect in general from January 1, 1982.

For purposes of allocation, the ITU divides the world into three main regions:
Region 1: Europe, Soviet Union, Mongolia, Middle East (excl Iran) and Africa
Region 2: America, Greenland and East Pacific
Region 3: Asia (including Iran, excluding Soviet Union and Mongolia) and West Pacific
The ITU controls allocations within the frequency range from 9 kHz (9×10^3 Hz) to 400 GHz (4×10^{11} Hz). Within this range, the range from 9–148.5 kHz is mainly for telecommunications and radionavigation, and other frequencies are divided between the many different kinds of use, which include: public broadcasting, fixed or mobile telecommunications (including maritime), radionavigation (including aeronautical and maritime), amateur, space research, radio astronomy, satellites (including meteorological, radionavigation, etc). Standard frequencies and time signals are at (central frequency) 2500 kHz, 5000 kHz, 10000 kHz, 15000 kHz, 20000 kHz, 25000 kHz, and (for satellites) 400.1 MHz; distress and calling frequencies are at 495–505 kHz (centred on 500 kHz) and 2173.5–2190.5 kHz (centred on 2182 kHz). It may be noted, in connection with the above frequencies, that the ITU uses the multiple kilohertz up to 27500 kHz (27.5 MHz), the multiple megahertz from 27.5 MHz up to 10000 MHz (10 GHz), and the multiple gigahertz from 10 GHz up to the recognised end of 'radio waves' or 'hertzian waves' at 3000 GHz.

Broadcasting frequencies are in general as follows (where kHz = 10^3 Hz, MHz = 10^6 Hz, GHz = 10^9 Hz; allocations as fixed in 1979, not all of which are exclusive to broadcasting):

Region 1	Region 2	Region 3
148.5–283.5 kHz		
526.5–1606.5 kHz	525–1705 kHz	526.5–1606.5 kHz
2300–2498 kHz	2300–2495 kHz	2300–2495 kHz
3200–3400 kHz	3200–3400 kHz	3200–3400 kHz
3950–4000 kHz		3900–4000 kHz
4750–4995 kHz	4750–4995 kHz	4750–4995 kHz
5005–5060 kHz	5005–5060 kHz	5005–5060 kHz
5950–6200 kHz	5950–6200 kHz	5950–6200 kHz
7100–7300 kHz		7100–7300 kHz
9500–9900 kHz	9500–9900 kHz	9500–9900 kHz
11650–12050 kHz	11650–12050 kHz	11650–12050 kHz
13600–13800 kHz	13600–13800 kHz	13600–13800 kHz
15100–15600 kHz	15100–15600 kHz	15100–15600 kHz
17550–17900 kHz	17550–17900 kHz	17550–17900 kHz
21450–21850 kHz	21450–21850 kHz	21450–21850 kHz
25670–26100 kHz	25670–26100 kHz	25670–26100 kHz
47–68 MHz	54–72 MHz	47–50 MHz, 54–68 MHz
87.5–108 MHz	76–108 MHz	87–108 MHz
174–230 MHz	174–216 MHz	174–230 MHz
470–960 MHz	470–608 MHz, 614–890 MHz	470–960 MHz
2500–2690 MHz[a]	2500 MHz–2690 MHz[a]	2500–2690 MHz[a]
11.7–12.5 GHz[b]	12.1–12.7 GHz[b]	11.7–12.2 GHz[b]
		12.2–12.5 GHz
		12.5–12.75 GHz[a]
	22.5–23 GHz[a]	22.5–23 GHz[a]
40.5–42.5 GHz[b]	40.5–42.5 GHz[b]	40.5–42.5 GHz[b]
84–86 GHz[b]	84–86 GHz[b]	84–86 GHz[b]

[a]Broadcasting via satellite.   [b]Also includes broadcasting via satellite.

Electronics

The general BBC classification of frequencies is:

Low frequency (LF)	30 kHz − 300 kHz
Medium frequency (MF)	300 kHz − 3 MHz
High frequency (HF)	3 MHz − 30 MHz
Very high frequency (VHF)	30 MHz − 300 MHz
Ultra high frequency (UHF)	300 MHz − 3 GHz
Super high frequency (SHF)	3 GHz − 30 GHz
Extra high frequency (EHF)	30 GHz − 300 GHz

Sound broadcasting

The main sound frequency ranges are (also see above):
Low frequency (LF) band: 148.5–283.5 kHz
Medium frequency (MF) band: 525–1705 kHz
High frequency (HF) band: 2300–26100 kHz (not all sections)
Very high frequency (VHF) band: 47–108 MHz (not all sections)

The following table gives conversions between frequency and wavelength
(metres) for main general sound ranges, using the customary approximation for
wave velocity equal to 3×10^8 m/s. Since this is a 'reciprocal' type of
relationship, the kilohertz tables also apply for converting from metres to
kilohertz; for example, 200 kHz = 1500 m and 1500 kHz = 200 m. A full range
of conversions is shown, including some for frequencies not allocated to
broadcasting.

Low frequency (long wave)

kHz	m	kHz	m	kHz	m	kHz	m	kHz	m
150	2000	180	1667	210	1429	240	1250	270	1111
155	1935	185	1622	215	1395	245	1224	275	1091
160	1875	190	1579	220	1364	250	1200	280	1071
165	1818	195	1538	225	1333	255	1176		
170	1765	200	1500	230	1304	260	1154		
175	1714	205	1463	235	1277	265	1132		

Medium frequency (medium wave)

kHz	m	kHz	m	kHz	m	kHz	m	kHz	m
525	571	770	389	1020	294	1270	236	1520	197
530	566	780	385	1030	291	1280	234	1530	196
540	556	790	380	1040	288	1290	233	1540	195
550	545	800	375	1050	286	1300	231	1550	194
560	536	810	370	1060	283	1310	229	1560	192
570	526	820	366	1070	280	1320	227	1570	191
580	517	830	361	1080	278	1330	226	1580	190
590	508	840	357	1090	275	1340	224	1590	189
600	500	850	353	1100	273	1350	222	1600	188
610	492	860	349	1110	270	1360	221	1610	186
620	484	870	345	1120	268	1370	219	1620	185
630	476	880	341	1130	265	1380	217	1630	184
640	469	890	337	1140	263	1390	216	1640	183
650	462	900	333	1150	261	1400	214	1650	182
660	455	910	330	1160	259	1410	213	1660	181
670	448	920	326	1170	256	1420	211	1670	180
680	441	930	323	1180	254	1430	210	1680	179
690	435	940	319	1190	252	1440	208	1690	178
700	429	950	316	1200	250	1450	207	1700	176
710	423	960	313	1210	248	1460	205	1705	176
720	417	970	309	1220	246	1470	204		
730	411	980	306	1230	244	1480	203		
740	405	990	303	1240	242	1490	201		
750	400	1000	300	1250	240	1500	200		
760	395	1010	297	1260	238	1510	199		

High frequency (short wave)

kHz	m	kHz	m	kHz	m	kHz	m	kHz	m
2300	130.4	7300	41.1	12300	24.4	17300	17.3	22300	13.5
2400	125.0	7400	40.5	12400	24.2	17400	17.2	22400	13.4
2500	120.0	7500	40.0	12500	24.0	17500	17.1	22500	13.3
2600	115.4	7600	39.5	12600	23.8	17600	17.0	22600	13.3
2700	111.1	7700	39.0	12700	23.6	17700	16.9	22700	13.2
2800	107.1	7800	38.5	12800	23.4	17800	16.9	22800	13.2
2900	103.4	7900	38.0	12900	23.3	17900	16.8	22900	13.1
3000	100.0	8000	37.5	13000	23.1	18000	16.7	23000	13.0
3100	96.8	8100	37.0	13100	22.9	18100	16.6	23100	13.0
3200	93.7	8200	36.6	13200	22.7	18200	16.5	23200	12.9
3300	90.9	8300	36.1	13300	22.6	18300	16.4	23300	12.9
3400	88.2	8400	35.7	13400	22.4	18400	16.3	23400	12.8
3500	85.7	8500	35.3	13500	22.2	18500	16.2	23500	12.8
3600	83.3	8600	34.9	13600	22.1	18600	16.1	23600	12.7
3700	81.1	8700	34.5	13700	21.9	18700	16.0	23700	12.7
3800	78.9	8800	34.1	13800	21.7	18800	16.0	23800	12.6
3900	76.9	8900	33.7	13900	21.6	18900	15.9	23900	12.6
4000	75.0	9000	33.3	14000	21.4	19000	15.8	24000	12.5
4100	73.2	9100	33.0	14100	21.3	19100	15.7	24100	12.4
4200	71.4	9200	32.6	14200	21.1	19200	15.6	24200	12.4
4300	69.8	9300	32.3	14300	21.0	19300	15.5	24300	12.3
4400	68.2	9400	31.9	14400	20.8	19400	15.5	24400	12.3
4500	66.7	9500	31.6	14500	20.7	19500	15.4	24500	12.2
4600	65.2	9600	31.2	14600	20.5	19600	15.3	24600	12.2
4700	63.8	9700	30.9	14700	20.4	19700	15.2	24700	12.1
4800	62.5	9800	30.6	14800	20.3	19800	15.2	24800	12.1
4900	61.2	9900	30.3	14900	20.1	19900	15.1	24900	12.0
5000	60.0	10000	30.0	15000	20.0	20000	15.0	25000	12.0
5100	58.8	10100	29.7	15100	19.9	20100	14.9	25100	12.0
5200	57.7	10200	29.4	15200	19.7	20200	14.9	25200	11.9
5300	56.6	10300	29.1	15300	19.6	20300	14.8	25300	11.9
5400	55.6	10400	28.8	15400	19.5	20400	14.7	25400	11.8
5500	54.5	10500	28.6	15500	19.4	20500	14.6	25500	11.8
5600	53.6	10600	28.3	15600	19.2	20600	14.6	25600	11.7
5700	52.6	10700	28.0	15700	19.1	20700	14.5	25700	11.7
5800	51.7	10800	27.8	15800	19.0	20800	14.4	25800	11.6
5900	50.8	10900	27.5	15900	18.9	20900	14.4	25900	11.6
6000	50.0	11000	27.3	16000	18.7	21000	14.3	26000	11.5
6100	49.2	11100	27.0	16100	18.6	21100	14.2	26100	11.5
6200	48.4	11200	26.8	16200	18.5	21200	14.2		
6300	47.6	11300	26.5	16300	18.4	21300	14.1		
6400	46.9	11400	26.3	16400	18.3	21400	14.0		
6500	46.2	11500	26.1	16500	18.2	21500	14.0		
6600	45.5	11600	25.9	16600	18.1	21600	13.9		
6700	44.8	11700	25.6	16700	18.0	21700	13.8		
6800	44.1	11800	25.4	16800	17.9	21800	13.8		
6900	43.5	11900	25.2	16900	17.8	21900	13.7		
7000	42.9	12000	25.0	17000	17.6	22000	13.6		
7100	42.3	12100	24.8	17100	17.5	22100	13.6		
7200	41.7	12200	24.6	17200	17.4	22200	13.5		

Electronics

Very high frequency (ultra short-wave)

MHz	m	MHz	m	MHz	m	MHz	m	MHz	m
47	6.38	60	5.00	73	4.11	86	3.49	99	3.03
48	6.25	61	4.92	74	4.05	87	3.45	100	3.00
49	6.12	62	4.84	75	4.00	88	3.41	101	2.97
50	6.00	63	4.76	76	3.95	89	3.37	102	2.94
51	5.88	64	4.69	77	3.90	90	3.33	103	2.91
52	5.77	65	4.62	78	3.85	91	3.30	104	2.88
53	5.66	66	4.55	79	3.80	92	3.26	105	2.86
54	5.56	67	4.48	80	3.75	93	3.23	106	2.83
55	5.45	68	4.41	81	3.70	94	3.19	107	2.80
56	5.36	69	4.35	82	3.66	95	3.16	108	2.78
57	5.26	70	4.29	83	3.61	96	3.13		
58	5.17	71	4.23	84	3.57	97	3.09		
59	5.08	72	4.17	85	3.53	98	3.06		

Television broadcasting

For UK television, channels on the 405 line system have a width of 5 MHz, and those on the 625 line system a width of 8 MHz.
The UK frequencies are:
405 line system (vhf):
Channel 1   45.00–41.50 MHz
Channel 2   51.75–48.25 MHz
Channel 3   56.75–53.25 MHz
Channel 4   61.75–58.25 MHz
Channel 5   66.75–63.25 MHz
Channel 6   179.75–176.25 MHz
increasing by 5 MHz per channel to:
Channel 13   214.75–211.25 MHz
For any channel between 6 and 13, the MHz value
is (channel number − 6) × 5 added to the number for channel 6.
625 line system (uhf):
Channel 21   471.25–477.25 MHz
increasing by 8 MHz per channel to:
Channel 68   847.25–853.25 MHz
For any channel between 21 and 68, the MHz value
is (channel number − 21) × 8 added to the number for channel 21.
In the above ranges, the nominal carrier frequency is shown in each case, with the first frequency for vision and the second for sound; the vision signal requires a band of frequencies arranged assymetrically around the vision carrier frequency quoted above and the sound signal occupies a narrower band centred on the sound carrier frequency.

Satellite broadcasting

The main frequencies used are within the ranges:
2.50–2.69 GHz
11.7–12.5 GHz
40.5–42.5 GHz
84–86 GHz

Microelectronics

Materials

A *semiconductor* is a material in which the electrical conductivity lies between that of conductors and insulators.
A *chip* (or die) is a small piece of silicon on which there is a completely unpackaged semiconductor device, such as a transistor or integrated circuit.

Devices

A *discrete device* is a single-function packaged component; for example, a transistor, resistor or diode, used as switches, amplifiers etc.
An *integrated circuit* is a device containing a combination of electronic components and devices, all on a single piece of solid material, and which are indivisibly connected to perform a function, such as the provision of a memory.

Purpose

Various kinds of memory are:
Read-only memory (Rom) is a memory into which information is written during the manufacturing process and which thereafter cannot be altered.
Programmable read-only memory (Prom) is a memory into which information can be written after the device is manufactured, but thereafter cannot be altered.
Random access memory (Ram) is a memory in which information can be entered or retrieved from any storage position.

Size

The size of integrated circuits is classified as follows, using as a base unit the number of memory bits or logic gates (also see computer, page 125):

	Memory bits (number)	Logic gates (number)
Small-scale integration (SSI)		1–20
Medium-scale integration (MSI)	under 1 000	20–100
Large-scale integration (LSI)	1 000–16 000	100–5 000
Very-large-scale integration (VLSI)	over 16 000	over 5 000

Number of memory cells per single silicon chip:
1970   1 000   (1k)
1976   16 000 (16 k)
1979   64 000 (64 k)

Energy

Measures

The main SI unit for measuring energy of all forms is the joule (J); the SI joule replaced the 'international' joule which had become obsolete in 1948; the 1948 joule was approximately equal to 1.000 19 SI joules (UK and West German value) or 1.000 165 SI joules (United States).
The other main energy unit used in conjunction with the joule, in the field of electricity, is the kilowatt hour, where 3.6 megajoules (MJ) = 3 600 000 joules = 1 kilowatt hour (kW h) = 1 000 watt hours (W h).
Other measures of energy, which are being replaced in varying degrees by the SI unit, are as follows:

British thermal unit and therm: see page 19 for current definitions. The Btu used by the UK gas industry is related to the 15°C calorie (see below) rather than the international table calorie; hence Btu_{15} = Btu × 4.185 5/4.186 8 = 1.054 73 kJ. Where not qualified, Btu here means the international table Btu. Obsolescent types of British thermal unit are: the 60°F Btu which was the heat needed to raise the temperature of one pound of water through one degree Fahrenheit from 60° to 61°; symbolically $Btu_{60/61}$ = 1.054 5 kJ; the mean Btu which was 1/180 of the heat needed to raise the temperature of one pound of liquid water from 32°F to 212°F; symbolically Btu_{mean} = 1.055 8 kJ.

Centigrade heat unit (Chu) = one-hundredth part of the heat needed to raise 1 pound of water from 0°C to 100°C; also called the 'celsius heat unit' or 'pound calorie'. Approximately, 1 Chu = 1.8 Btu = 1.900 4 kJ.

Calories. The calorie was originally defined as the quantity of heat needed to raise one gram of water through one degree celsius. There are three main types:
thermochemical or 'defined' calorie (cal_{th}) = 4.184 J;
15°C calorie (cal_{15}) = the heat needed to raise the temperature of one gram of water through one degree celsius from 14.5°C to 15.5°C = approx. 4.185 5 J;
International Table calorie (cal_{IT}) = 4.186 8 J.
In the energy field, the International Table and 15°C calories are the main measures in use; the UK gas industry uses the 15°C calorie.
Other multiples of the calorie in use are:
kilocalorie 15°C $(kcal_{15})$ = 1 000 cal_{15} = 4.185 5 kJ
kilocalorie, international table $(kcal_{IT})$ = 1 000 cal_{IT} = 4.186 8 kJ
thermie 15°C (th_{15}) = 1 000 $kcal_{15}$ = 1 000 000 cal_{15} = 4.185 5 MJ
thermie, international table (th_{IT}) = 1 000 $kcal_{IT}$ = 1 000 000 cal_{IT} = 4.186 8 MJ.
The international kilocalorie is called a frigorie (fg) when used in a negative sense for the extraction of heat.
The calorie is sometimes called a 'small' or 'gram' calorie, the kilocalorie a 'large' or 'kilogram' calorie, and the thermie a 'tonne' calorie; these terms are mainly used with reference to the 15°C calorie.

Litre atmosphere. 1 litre atmosphere (1 atm) = 101.325 J.

Energy

Conversions

The following table gives conversions for the main energy units:

to From	Btu	kcal$_{IT}$	kJ	W h
	multiply by			
Btu	1	0.251 996	1.055 06	0.293 071
Btu$_{15}$	0.999 689 5	0.251 917	1.054 73	0.292 980
kcal$_{IT}$	3.968 32	1	4.186 8	1.163
kcal$_{15}$	3.967 09	0.999 689 5	4.185 5	1.162 64
kJ	0.947 817	0.238 846	1	0.277 778
W h	3.412 14	0.859 845	3.6	1

The above table can also be used for the following multiples:
therms/100 = 1 000 Btu (therm = 100 000 Btu);
1 megacalorie (Mcal$_{IT}$) or thermie (th$_{IT}$) = 1 000 kcal$_{IT}$;
1 megacalorie (Mcal$_{15}$) or thermie (th$_{15}$) = 1 000 kcal$_{15}$;
1 megajoule (MJ) = 1 000 kJ;
1 kilowatt hour (kW h) = 1 000 W h.

For heat energy content ('calorific value'), weight (mass) basis:

to From	therm/tonne	Btu/lb	kcal$_{IT}$/kg (= cal$_{IT}$/g)	kJ/g (= MJ/kg) (= GJ/tonne)
	multiply by			
Therm/tonne	1	45.359 2	25.199 6	0.105 506
Btu/lb	0.022 046	1	0.555 556	0.002 326
kcal$_{IT}$/kg	0.039 683	1.8	1	0.004 186 8
kcal$_{15}$/kg	0.039 671	1.799 44	0.999 689 5	0.004 185 5
kJ/g	9.478 17	429.923	238.846	1

For heat energy content ('calorific value'), volume basis (for gases, assuming the same conditions of temperature, pressure and humidity):

to From	Btu/UK gal	Btu/ft³	kcal$_{IT}$/m³	MJ/m³ (= kJ/l)
	multiply by			
Btu/UK gal	1	6.228 83	55.431 3	0.232 080
Btu/ft³	0.160 544	1	8.899 15	0.037 258 9
kcal$_{IT}$/m³	0.018 040 4	0.112 370	1	0.004 186 8
kcal$_{15}$/m³	0.018 034 7	0.112 335	0.999 689 5	0.004 185 5
MJ/m³	4.308 86	26.839 2	238.846	1

Note that 100 000 Btu = 1 therm; for converting therm/UK gal to other measures use Btu/UK gal and divide by 100 000.

Standards of temperature, pressure and humidity vary; the UK gas industry standard is usually 60°F, 30 in Hg and saturated with water vapour, while the metric standard is usually 1.013 25 bar and dry, with either 0°C or 15°C (also see the section on gas). UN comparisons are given with 15°C, the international standard.
Main conversion factors are as follows: UK measures are at 60°F, 30 in Hg under a gravity corresponding to 53°N (equivalent to 1.013 740 5 bar) and saturated, metric measures at 1.013 25 bar (approx. 760 mm Hg) dry, and for the temperature specified:

to From	Btu/ft³	kcal$_{IT}$/m³ at 0°C	MJ/m³ at 0°C	MJ/m³ at 15°C
	multiply by			
Btu/ft³	1	9.547	0.039 97	0.037 89[a]
Btu$_{15}$/ft³	0.999 7	9.544	0.039 96	0.037 88[a]
kcal$_{IT}$/m³ at 0°C	0.104 74	1	0.004 187	0.003 969
kcal$_{15}$/m³ at 0°C	0.104 71	0.999 69	0.004 186	0.003 968
MJ/m³ at 0°C	25.018	238.85	1	0.947 9
MJ/m³ at 15°C	26.392	252.0	1.055	1

[a] These are based on a conversion from 30 in Hg at standard conditions including standard gravity. The conversion factors used by the UK gas industry are usually based on gravity at 53°N, with 30 in Hg = 1.013 740 5 bar instead of the standard conversion 1.015 92 bar. Conversions from Btu/ft³ are then approximately 0.215% higher, with 0.037 97 instead of the 0.037 89 shown here for the conversion to MJ/m³ at 15°C, and 0.037 96 instead of 0.037 88.

For gases, a heat input factor is used for calculating the interchangeability of gases from different sources; this is:
Wobbe number = H (heating value) / $\sqrt{\text{relative density}}$
Conversion from UK to metric units is as shown in the above table; for example, from Btu/ft³ to MJ/m³ at 15°C:
Wobbe number (UK units) × 0.037 88 gives Wobbe number (metric units).

Energy value comparisons

The following are approximate energy values, showing 'gross' values which assume 100% efficiency in utilisation.

	Therms/tonne	Btu/lb	kcal$_{IT}$/kg	kJ/g
Cowdung (50% moisture)	83	3 700	2 060	8.6
Wood: green	97	4 400	2 400	10
dry	161	7 310	4 060	17
Peat: mild	106	4 790	2 660	11
sod	137	6 200	3 400	14
Lignite	200	9 000	5 000	21
Coke	280	12 500	6 900	29
Coal: bituminous	290	13 000	7 200	30
anthracite	320	14 500	8 100	34
Oil: heavy fuel	406	18 400	10 200	43
fuel	420	19 000	10 600	44
gas	433	19 200	10 700	45

Some average conversion factors, as estimated from those used officially are:

	Therms/tonne	Btu/lb	kcal$_{IT}$/kg	kJ/g
Coal: UN (and EEC)	282	12 600	7 000	29.3
UK	243	11 000	6 120	25.6
Petroleum: UN	408	18 500	10 300	43.1
UK	427	19 400	10 800	45.1

	Btu/ft³	kcal$_{IT}$/m³	kJ/m³	MJ/m³ (= kJ/l)
Natural gas: UN	1 050	9 320	39 000	39.0
UK	1 030	9 160	38 400	38.4
Manufactured gas: UN	470	4 200	17 600	17.6

It may be noted, when using the SI measure of kilojoules per litre (megajoules per cubic metre), that the average estimate for energy value from breathing oxygen is 20 kJ/l.

Energy

Further detail follows for average gross energy values of certain fuels, as used in the United Kingdom (1979 averages):

	Therms/tonne	Btu/lb	kcal$_{IT}$/kg (= cal$_{IT}$/g)	kJ/g
Coal, as used for:				
All consumers (average)	243	11 000	6 120	25.6
Power stations	224	10 200	5 640	23.6
Gas works	295	13 400	7 430	31.1
Coke ovens	285	12 900	7 180	30.1
Collieries	256	11 600	6 450	27.0
Agriculture	285	12 900	7 180	30.1
Iron and steel industry	276	12 500	6 960	29.1
Other industry	261	11 800	6 580	27.5
Railways	295	13 400	7 430	31.1
Water transport	276	12 500	6 960	29.1
Domestic households etc:				
house coal	285	12 900	7 180	30.1
anthracite and dry steam coal	316	14 300	7 960	33.3
Other uses	261	11 800	6 580	27.5
Coke:				
General, incl. low temperature	266	12 100	6 700	28.1
Coke breeze (coke screened below ¾")	231	10 500	5 820	24.4
Other solid fuel	262	11 900	6 600	27.6
Petroleum:				
Crude oil (average)	427	19 400	10 800	45.1
Liquefied petroleum gas	470	21 300	11 800	49.6
Other gases	496	22 500	12 500	52.3
Light distillate feedstock for gasworks	453	20 500	11 400	47.8
Aviation spirit and wide-cut gasoline	447	20 300	11 300	47.2
Aviation turbine fuel	440	20 000	11 100	46.4
Motor spirit	445	20 200	11 200	46.9
Burning oil	441	20 000	11 100	46.5
Vaporising oil	435	19 700	11 000	45.9
Gas/diesel oil (incl. derv)	431	19 500	10 900	45.5
Fuel oil	406	18 400	10 200	42.8
Creosote/pitch mixtures	370	16 800	9 300	39.0

Coal equivalents

For comparisons of different forms of energy, the United Nations estimates are usually converted to 'tonnes of coal equivalent' (tce), where the net calorific value of coal is taken as 7 000 kcal/kg. The UN defines brown coal and lignite as coal with a gross calorific value under 5 700 kcal/kg (24 kJ/g) or tce of 0.81. Following are coal equivalents for:

1 tonne of:	tce
Coal, anthracite and bituminous	1.0
Coal, low grade:	
New Zealand	0.84
Pakistan	0.7
Soviet Union	0.81–0.84
Recovered slurries:	
France, Spain, United Kingdom	0.7
Czechoslovakia	0.6
Hungary	0.515
Turkey	0.5
Coal briquettes	1.0
Cokes of anthracite or bituminous coal	0.9
Cokes of brown coal or lignite	0.67
Lignite briquettes	0.67

	tce
Lignite and brown coal:	
Czechoslovakia, France, North Korea	0.6
Chile	0.59
United States	0.57
Canada	0.52
Albania, Austria, Bulgaria, Jugoslavia, New Zealand, Portugal, Soviet Union, Spain	0.5
Hungary	0.4
Italy	0.36
Australia, Denmark, Greece, India, Japan, South Korea, Mongolia, Rumania, Thailand, Turkey	0.33
Germany, East and West, Poland	0.3
Peat briquettes	0.5
Peat for fuel:	
Finland	0.3–0.43
Burundi, Ireland	0.5
Soviet Union	0.31–0.34
Crude petroleum	1.47
Natural gas liquids	1.67
Liquefield petroleum gases	1.68
Natural gasoline	1.66
Motor spirit	1.61
Kerosene and jet fuels	1.59
Fuel oils	1.5

1 000 cubic metres (at 15°C and 760 mm Hg) of:

Manufactured gas	0.6
Refinery gas	1.75
Natural gas	1.33

1 000 kilowatt hours of electricity (hydro, nuclear & geothermal)	0.123[a]

[a]Approximately, 1 kW h/8 = 1 kg coal equivalent.

Details of the calorific value for natural gas in various countries is as follows (as used by the UN):

	kcal$_{IT}$/m³	MJ/m³		kcal$_{IT}$/m³	MJ/m³
Algeria	9 450	39.6	Italy	9 150	38.3
Argentina	8 300	34.8	Japan	9 600	40.2
Australia	8 900	37.3	Jugoslavia	9 900	41.4
Austria	9 770	40.9	Kuwait	9 320	39.0
Bangladesh	8 675	36.3	Malaysia	9 320	39.0
Barbados	9 320	39.0	Mexico	8 572	35.9
Belgium	8 400	35.2	Morocco	9 320	39.0
Bolivia	8 300	34.8	Netherlands	8 465	35.4
Brazil	9 200	38.5	New Zealand	10 160	42.5
Canada	8 900	37.3	Nigeria	9 320	39.0
Chile	8 900	37.3	Pakistan	8 675	36.3
Congo	9 320	39.0	Poland	8 280	34.7
Czechoslovakia	8 000	33.5	Rumania	10 270	43.0
France	9 100	38.1	Saudi Arabia	9 320	39.0
Gabon	9 320	39.0	Soviet Union	8 330	34.9
Germany, West	8 400	35.2	Trinidad & Tobago	9 300	38.9
Hungary	9 020	37.8	Tunisia	11 000	46.1
India	9 216	38.6	United Kingdom	9 485	39.7
Indonesia	9 320	39.0	United States	9 065	38.0
Iran	9 400	39.4	Venezuela	10 145	42.5
Israel	9 250	38.7			

Energy

A table showing main equivalents follows (where volumes are at 15°C and 760 mm Hg):

equals (units of) 1 unit of	Coal tonnes	Petroleum fuel oil tonnes	Natural gas '000 m³	Manu- factured gas '000 m³	Elec- tricity '000 kW h = MW h
Coal (tonne)	1	0.67	0.75	1.7	8.1
Petroleum: fuel oil (tonne)	1.5	1	1.13	2.5	12.2
Natural gas ('000 m³)	1.33	0.89	1	2.2	10.8
Manufactured gas ('000 m³)	0.6	0.4	0.45	1	4.9
Electricity ('000 kW h)	0.123	0.082	0.092	0.21	1

The above are gross equivalents. Net production of electricity from 1 tonne of fuel oil is about 4.0 MW h; that is, thermal efficiency (energy value sent out as a percentage of energy consumed) is about 33% – two-thirds is lost through transformation to electricity. For the United Kingdom, the equivalent of electricity sent out from 1 tonne of coal is 2.27 MW h; thermal efficiency of UK steam power stations is about 28%. The loss of energy in use of hydro-electricity and natural gas is about one-half of that from the use of solid and liquid fuels.

UK conversions usually take an equivalent for petroleum of 1.7 tce.
EEC conversions for coal depend on the proportion of inert matter (ash and water) in different coals; coals with an inert content of less than 20% are converted tonne for tonne, and those with 20% to 67–76% are converted depending on the relative contents of ash and water. Those with inert contents above the upper limits are not taken into account.
For atomic energy (page 141),1 tce is obtained from about 40 grams of natural uranium in a thermal reactor, or from about $\frac{1}{2}$ gram in a fast reactor.

Further information follows on each of the main forms of energy supply.

Coal

Coal is formed by the decomposition of vegetable matter. It has generally passed through the following stages: 1 peat; 2 lignite or brown coal; 3 ordinary soft or bituminous coal; and 4 anthracite or hard coal. Energy value increases for each stage: as noted above from about 10 kJ/g for peat to 20 for lignite, 30 for bituminous coal and 34 for anthracite coal.

United Kingdom measures

Following a change to the metric system, a 50 kg (110.2 lb) sack of coal has replaced the former 1 hundredweight sack (112 lb). Domestic deliveries are usually 5–10 sacks (250–500 kg).

Other old units
1 chaldron of coal = 12 sacks = 36 heaped bushels
= 4½ quarters (approximately 57 kg)

Temperature adjustment

For the United Kingdom, an average of 2.1% increase in consumption is estimated for each fall of 1 degree Celsius below the average 1941–1970, and temperature adjusted fuel consumption allows for this.

Petroleum

Crude petroleum, though used frequently to mean crude oil, can also include natural gas, shale oil, bitumen, asphalt, etc. Main products used for energy are:

Propane: hydrocarbon containing three carbon atoms, gaseous at normal temperature but generally stored and transported under pressure as a liquid. Used for domestic heating and cooking and for industrial purposes.

Butane: hydrocarbon containing four carbon atoms, otherwise as for propane. Additional uses are as a constituent of motor spirit to improve volatility and as a chemical feedstock.

Aviation spirit: specially blended light hydrocarbons intended for use in aviation piston-engined power units.

Wide-cut gasoline: light hydrocarbons intended for use in aviation gas-turbine power units.

Motor spirit: blended light petroleum distillates used as a fuel for spark-ignition internal combustion engines other than aircraft engines. Usual grades are (showing octane number for finished motor spirit):
5 star: 100 and over   3 star: 94 and under 97
4 star: 97 and under 100   2 star: under 94

The octane number is a measure of the anti-knock property of petrol (gasoline), necessary because increasing the compression ratio of a piston-engine causes knocking (detonation). The base for this measure is iso-octane; any petrol with equal anti-knocking value to iso-octane has the number 100, and the number for any other petrol is determined by the percentage of iso-octane in a mixture of iso-octane and normal heptane which has equal anti-knocking properties to that petrol. There are two main types of number:
Research octane number is a better guide to anti-knock quality for mild conditions and low speeds.
Motor octane number is a better guide for heavy load conditions or high speeds. Typically the Research number is higher than the Motor by about 10: 100 Research = 90 Motor. The difference, usually from 8 to 12%, is a measure of the 'sensitivity' of the fuel. A difference of 12 means greater sensitivity – the fuel is more affected by the severity of operating conditions.

Aviation turbine fuel: specially refined kerosene intended for use in aviation gas turbine power units.

Burning oil: (kerosene or paraffin): refined petroleum distillate intermediate in volatility between motor spirit and gas oil, used for lighting and heating.

Vaporising oil: blended kerosene type petroleum distillate used in certain types of spark-ignition engines such as those used for agricultural purposes, stationary engines and boats (sometimes referred to as TVO, or tractor vaporising oil).

Gas/diesel oil:
(a) Derv (Diesel engined road vehicle) fuel: gas/diesel oil suitable for use in high-speed, compression-ignition engines.
(b) Gas oil: petroleum distillate having a distillation range intermediate between kerosene and light lubricating oil. Used as a burner fuel in heating installations, for carburetting water gas, as a wash oil in the extraction of benzole from coal gas and for industrial gas-turbines.

Marine diesel oil: heavier type of gas oil suitable for heavy industrial and marine compression-ignition engines.

Fuel oil: heavy petroleum distillates or petroleum residues or blends of these used in furnaces for the production of heat or power.

Measures

Crude petroleum, and the refined products made from crude oil, are normally measured either by volume in gallons and US barrels, or by weight in tons or tonnes.

UK gallon =	US gallon =	US barrel =
277.42 cubic inches	231 cubic inches	42 US gallons
0.0045 cubic metre	0.0038 cubic metre	0.1590 cubic metre
4.54609 litres	3.785 litres	158.99 litres
1.201 US gallons	0.8327 UK gallons	34.97 UK gallons
0.0286 barrel	0.0238 barrel	

UK (imperial) gallons per UK ton = 4.474 291 litres per tonne
Litres per tonne = 0.223 499 UK (imperial) gallons per UK ton
= 0.006 289 8 US barrels per tonne
US barrels per tonne = 158.987 3 litres per tonne

The relationship between volume and weight is usually measured by density in the United Kingdom (the alternative measure is relative density or specific gravity). The petroleum industry also uses a special measure called the API (American Petroleum Institute) degree:

$$\text{API degrees gravity} = \frac{141.5}{\text{relative density at } 60/60\,°F} - 131.5$$

American oilmen usually reckon quantities of oil produced, moved or processed in barrels per day (bpd or b/d); some European companies and many European consumers reckon in tonnes per year. The loose but simple rule of thumb for conversion is that a barrel a day is roughly 50 tonnes a year, but the relationship varies according to density and so according to product.

Energy

Some rough average multiplying factors are:

	Barrels to tonnes	Tonnes to barrels	Barrels per day to tonnes per year	Tonnes per year to barrels per day
Crude oil	0.136	7.33	49.8	0.0201
Motor spirit	0.118	8.45	43.2	0.0232
Kerosene (paraffin)	0.128	7.80	46.8	0.0214
Gas/diesel oil	0.133	7.50	48.7	0.0205
Fuel oil	0.149	6.70	54.5	0.0184

On the following two pages, tables of conversions are given for densities varying from 0.80 to 1.00 (kg/l, which is equal to t/m³, g/cm³ or g/cc).
For barrels to tonnes the numbers range from 10 to 600 and for barrels per day (b/d) to tonnes per year (t/yr) from 0.1 to 6.0; most figures encountered in these ranges will be in millions, so, for example, 2.0 mn b/d = 92.8 mn t/yr at a density of 0.80.
These tables apply for conversions where densities and volumes are expressed at the same temperature; the standard reference temperature for oil measurement in the United Kingdom, following a change to the metric system, is 15 °C.

The relationship between volume and weight (mass) for UK products has been as follows:

	Litres per tonne		US barrels per tonne	
	1960	1979	1960	1979
Crude oil: indigenous	1160	1190	7.3	7.5
imported	na	1165	na	7.3
Propane	1991	1969	12.5	12.4
Butane	1736	1732	10.9	10.9
Naphtha/LDF	na	1445	na	9.1
Aviation spirit	1409	1390	8.9	8.7
Aviation turbine fuel—wide cut	1320	1315	8.3	8.3
Motor spirit	1369	1345	8.6	8.5
Industrial spirit	1374	1387	8.6	8.7
White spirit	1289	1280	8.1	8.1
Kerosene: aviation turbine fuel	1266	1260	8.0	7.9
Burning oil	1271	1266	8.0	8.0
Vaporising oil	1230	1215	7.7	7.6
Derv fuel	1195	1190	7.5	7.5
Gas/diesel oil: gas oil	1195	1190	7.5	7.5
marine diesel oil	1177	1177	7.4	7.4
Lubricating oils	na	1120	na	7.0
Fuel oil: all grades	1043	1040	6.6	6.5
light	1075	1075	6.8	6.8
medium	1051	1055	6.6	6.6
heavy	1030	1040	6.5	6.5
Bitumen	970	970	6.1	6.1

The relationship between volume and mass (the density) changes over time and by product, as indicated in the previous table, and also according to the temperature. Once the density is established, relationships between various measures can be determined, and these are shown in the table on page 138; this applies for temperature of 15 °C.
The relationships apply for the pressure at which the densities are defined for any oil and are expressed in terms of mass; since this is the weight in a vacuum, the actual weight-in-air will be very slightly less than the mass. The amount by which weight-in-air is less than mass is approximately 0.1%, so the relationships are approximately correct for volume to weight conversions.

Average densities for various products are approximately as follows:

Energy petroleum products	Density	Non-energy petroleum products	Density
Liquefied petroleum gas	0.54	Naphthas[a]	0.72
Aviation spirit (gasoline)	0.73	White spirit	0.81
Motor spirit (gasoline)	0.74	Paraffin wax	0.80
Kerosene	0.81	Lubricating oils	0.90
Jet fuel	0.81	Road oil	0.97
Distillate fuel oil	0.87	Bitumen	1.04
Residual fuel oil	0.95	Petroleum coke	1.14
Fuel oils (undifferentiated)	0.91		

[a]One of the most important feedstocks for petrochemicals.

Average densities (approximate) for petroleum from producer countries are estimated as follows by the United Nations:

	Density		Density		Density
Algeria	0.81	Germany, West	0.87	Peru	0.85
Angola	0.85	Hungary	0.94	Poland	0.85
Argentina	0.86	India	0.83	Qatar	0.83
Australia	0.82	Indonesia	0.85	Rumania	0.84
Austria	0.90	Iran	0.86	Saudi Arabia	0.85
Bahrain	0.86	Iraq	0.85	Soviet Union	0.86
Bolivia	0.80	Israel	0.87	Spain	0.84
Brazil	0.84	Italy	0.92	Syria	0.91
Bulgaria	0.86	Japan	0.86	Trinidad & Tobago	0.89
Burma	0.89	Jugoslavia	0.85	Tunisia	0.82
Canada	0.85	Kuwait	0.86	Turkey	0.88
Chile	0.84	Libya	0.83	United Arab Emirates:	
Colombia	0.89	Malaysia	0.82	Abu Dhabi	0.84
Congo	0.84	Mexico	0.89	Dubai	0.86
Czechoslovakia	0.93	Morocco	0.83	United Kingdom	0.86
Denmark	0.82	Netherlands	0.92	United States	0.85
Ecuador	0.87	Nigeria	0.87	Venezuela	0.90
Egypt	0.87	Norway	0.84	Zaire	0.86
France	0.86	Oman	0.86		
Gabon	0.88	Pakistan	0.86		

Using the above densities, approximate conversions from barrels to tonnes, and barrels per day to tonnes per year, can be obtained for any country from the tables on the following two pages. Other relationships can be obtained from the table on page 138. For example, petroleum from Kuwait has an average density of 0.86 (the same as the average for all petroleum products). From the table it can be found that, for example, the number of barrels per tonne is 7.31. Hence 100 tonnes is 100 × 7.31 = 731 barrels. To obtain the weight of a number of barrels in terms of tonnes, the number of barrels can be divided by 7.31.
It may be noted that for the density table, kg/l = t/m³.

Opec oil prices are in general based on a Saudi Arabian 'marker' light crude oil of 34° API (relative density 0.855).

Energy

Petroleum: barrels to tonnes, for varying densities

Density (kg/l) →	0.80	0.81	0.82	0.83	0.84	0.85	0.86	0.87	0.88	0.89	0.90	0.92	0.94	0.96	0.98	1.00	Density ← (kg/l)
Barrels ↓	t	t	t	t	t	t	t	t	t	t	t	t	t	t	t	t	Barrels ↓
10	1.3	1.3	1.3	1.3	1.3	1.4	1.4	1.4	1.4	1.4	1.4	1.5	1.5	1.5	1.6	1.6	10
20	2.5	2.6	2.6	2.6	2.7	2.7	2.7	2.8	2.8	2.8	2.9	2.9	3.0	3.1	3.1	3.2	20
30	3.8	3.9	3.9	4.0	4.0	4.1	4.1	4.1	4.2	4.2	4.3	4.4	4.5	4.6	4.7	4.8	30
40	5.1	5.2	5.2	5.3	5.3	5.4	5.5	5.5	5.6	5.7	5.7	5.9	6.0	6.1	6.2	6.4	40
50	6.4	6.4	6.5	6.6	6.7	6.8	6.8	6.9	7.0	7.1	7.2	7.3	7.5	7.6	7.8	7.9	50
60	7.6	7.7	7.8	7.9	8.0	8.1	8.2	8.3	8.4	8.5	8.6	8.8	9.0	9.2	9.3	9.5	60
70	8.9	9.0	9.1	9.2	9.3	9.5	9.6	9.7	9.8	9.9	10.0	10.2	10.5	10.7	10.9	11.1	70
80	10.2	10.3	10.4	10.6	10.7	10.8	10.9	11.1	11.2	11.3	11.4	11.7	12.0	12.2	12.5	12.7	80
90	11.4	11.6	11.7	11.9	12.0	12.2	12.3	12.4	12.6	12.7	12.9	13.2	13.5	13.7	14.0	14.3	90
100	12.7	12.9	13.0	13.2	13.4	13.5	13.7	13.8	14.0	14.1	14.3	14.6	14.9	15.3	15.6	15.9	100
110	14.0	14.2	14.3	14.5	14.7	14.9	15.0	15.2	15.4	15.6	15.7	16.1	16.4	16.8	17.1	17.5	110
120	15.3	15.5	15.6	15.8	16.0	16.2	16.4	16.6	16.8	17.0	17.2	17.6	17.9	18.3	18.7	19.1	120
130	16.5	16.7	16.9	17.2	17.4	17.6	17.8	18.0	18.2	18.4	18.6	19.0	19.4	19.8	20.3	20.7	130
140	17.8	18.0	18.3	18.5	18.7	18.9	19.1	19.4	19.6	19.8	20.0	20.5	20.9	21.4	21.8	22.3	140
150	19.1	19.3	19.6	19.8	20.0	20.3	20.5	20.7	21.0	21.2	21.5	21.9	22.4	22.9	23.4	23.8	150
160	20.4	20.6	20.9	21.1	21.4	21.1	21.9	22.1	22.4	22.6	22.9	23.4	23.9	24.4	24.9	25.4	160
170	21.6	21.9	22.2	22.4	22.7	23.0	23.2	23.5	23.8	24.1	24.3	24.9	25.4	25.9	26.5	27.0	170
180	22.9	23.2	23.5	23.8	24.0	24.3	24.6	24.9	25.2	25.5	25.8	26.3	26.9	27.5	28.0	28.6	180
190	24.2	24.5	24.8	25.1	25.4	25.7	26.0	26.3	26.6	26.9	27.2	27.8	28.4	29.0	29.6	30.2	190
200	25.4	25.8	26.1	26.4	26.7	27.0	27.3	27.7	28.0	28.3	28.6	29.3	29.9	30.5	31.2	31.8	200
210	26.7	27.0	27.4	27.7	28.0	28.4	28.7	29.0	29.4	29.7	30.0	30.7	31.4	32.1	32.7	33.4	210
220	28.0	28.3	28.7	29.0	29.4	29.7	30.1	30.4	30.8	31.1	31.5	32.2	32.9	33.6	34.3	35.0	220
230	29.3	29.6	30.0	30.4	30.7	31.1	31.4	31.8	32.2	32.5	32.9	33.6	34.4	35.1	35.8	36.6	230
240	30.5	30.9	31.3	31.7	32.1	32.4	32.8	33.2	33.6	34.0	34.3	35.1	35.9	36.6	37.4	38.2	240
250	31.8	32.2	32.6	33.0	33.4	33.8	34.2	34.6	35.0	35.4	35.8	36.6	37.4	38.2	39.0	39.7	250
260	33.1	33.5	33.9	34.3	34.7	35.1	35.5	36.0	36.4	36.8	37.2	38.0	38.9	39.7	40.5	41.3	260
270	34.3	34.8	35.2	35.6	36.1	36.5	36.9	37.3	37.8	38.2	38.6	39.5	40.4	41.2	42.1	42.9	270
280	35.6	36.1	36.5	36.9	37.4	37.8	38.3	38.7	39.2	39.6	40.1	41.0	41.8	42.7	43.6	44.5	280
290	36.9	37.3	37.8	38.3	38.7	39.2	39.7	40.1	40.6	41.0	41.5	42.4	43.3	44.3	45.2	46.1	290
300	38.2	38.6	39.1	39.6	40.1	40.5	41.0	41.5	42.0	42.4	42.9	43.9	44.8	45.8	46.7	47.7	300
310	39.4	39.9	40.4	40.9	41.4	41.9	42.4	42.9	43.4	43.9	44.4	45.3	46.3	47.3	48.3	49.3	310
320	40.7	41.2	41.7	42.2	42.7	43.2	43.8	44.3	44.8	45.3	45.8	46.8	47.8	48.8	49.9	50.9	320
330	42.0	42.5	43.0	43.5	44.1	44.6	45.1	45.6	46.2	46.7	47.2	48.3	49.3	50.4	51.4	52.5	330
340	43.2	43.8	44.3	44.9	45.4	45.9	46.5	47.0	47.6	48.1	48.7	49.7	50.8	51.9	53.0	54.1	340
350	44.5	45.1	45.6	46.2	46.7	47.3	47.9	48.4	49.0	49.5	50.1	51.2	52.3	53.4	54.5	55.6	350
360	45.8	46.4	46.9	47.5	48.1	48.7	49.2	49.8	50.4	50.9	51.5	52.7	53.8	54.9	56.1	57.2	360
370	47.1	47.6	48.2	48.8	49.4	50.0	50.6	51.2	51.8	52.4	52.9	54.1	55.3	56.5	57.6	58.8	370
380	48.3	48.9	49.5	50.1	50.7	51.4	52.0	52.6	53.2	53.8	54.4	55.6	56.8	58.0	59.2	60.4	380
390	49.6	50.2	50.8	51.5	52.1	52.7	53.3	53.9	54.6	55.2	55.8	57.0	58.3	59.5	60.8	62.0	390
400	50.9	51.5	52.1	52.8	53.4	54.1	54.7	55.3	56.0	56.6	57.2	58.5	59.8	61.1	62.3	63.6	400
410	52.1	52.8	53.5	54.1	54.8	55.4	56.1	56.7	57.4	58.0	58.7	60.0	61.3	62.6	63.9	65.2	410
420	53.4	54.1	54.8	55.4	56.1	56.8	57.4	58.1	58.8	59.4	60.1	61.4	62.8	64.1	65.4	66.8	420
430	54.7	55.4	56.1	56.7	57.4	58.1	58.8	59.5	60.2	60.8	61.5	62.9	64.3	65.6	67.0	68.4	430
440	56.0	56.7	57.4	58.1	58.8	59.5	60.2	60.9	61.6	62.3	63.0	64.4	65.8	67.2	68.6	70.0	440
450	57.2	58.0	58.7	59.4	60.1	60.8	61.5	62.2	63.0	63.7	64.4	65.8	67.3	68.7	70.1	71.5	450
460	58.5	59.2	60.0	60.7	61.4	62.2	62.9	63.6	64.4	65.1	65.8	67.3	68.7	70.2	71.7	73.1	460
470	59.8	60.5	61.3	62.0	62.8	63.5	64.3	65.0	65.8	66.5	67.3	68.7	70.2	71.7	73.2	74.7	470
480	61.1	61.8	62.6	63.3	64.1	64.9	65.6	66.4	67.2	67.9	68.7	70.2	71.7	73.3	74.8	76.3	480
490	62.3	63.1	63.9	64.7	65.4	66.2	67.0	67.8	68.6	69.3	70.1	71.7	73.2	74.8	76.3	77.9	490
500	63.6	64.4	65.2	66.0	66.8	67.6	68.4	69.2	70.0	70.7	71.5	73.1	74.7	76.3	77.9	79.5	500
510	64.9	65.7	66.5	67.3	68.1	68.9	69.7	70.5	71.4	72.2	73.0	74.6	76.2	77.8	79.5	81.1	510
520	66.1	67.0	67.8	68.6	69.4	70.3	71.1	71.9	72.8	73.6	74.4	76.1	77.7	79.4	81.0	82.7	520
530	67.4	68.3	69.1	69.9	70.8	71.6	72.5	73.3	74.2	75.0	75.8	77.5	79.2	80.9	82.6	84.3	530
540	68.7	69.5	70.4	71.3	72.1	73.0	73.8	74.7	75.6	76.4	77.3	79.0	80.7	82.4	84.1	85.9	540
550	70.0	70.8	71.7	72.6	73.5	74.3	75.2	76.1	76.9	77.8	78.7	80.4	82.2	83.9	85.7	87.4	550
560	71.2	72.1	73.0	73.9	74.8	75.7	76.6	77.5	78.3	79.2	80.1	81.9	83.7	85.5	87.3	89.0	560
570	72.5	73.4	74.3	75.2	76.1	77.0	77.9	78.8	79.7	80.7	81.6	83.4	85.2	87.0	88.8	90.6	570
580	73.8	74.7	75.6	76.5	77.5	78.4	79.3	80.2	81.1	82.1	83.0	84.8	86.7	88.5	90.4	92.2	580
590	75.0	76.0	76.9	77.9	78.8	79.7	80.7	81.6	82.5	83.5	84.4	86.3	88.2	90.1	91.9	93.8	590
600	76.3	77.3	78.2	79.2	80.1	81.1	82.0	83.0	83.9	84.9	85.9	87.8	89.7	91.6	93.5	95.4	600

Petroleum: barrels per day (b/d) to tonnes per year (t/yr), for varying densities

Density kg/l →	0.80	0.81	0.82	0.83	0.84	0.85	0.86	0.87	0.88	0.89	0.90	0.92	0.94	0.96	0.98	1.00	Density ← (kg/l)
b/d ↓	t/yr	t/yr	t/yr	t/yr	t/yr	t/yr	t/yr	t/yr	t/yr	t/yr	t/yr	t/yr	t/yr	t/yr	t/yr	t/yr	b/d ↓
0.1	4.6	4.7	4.8	4.8	4.9	4.9	5.0	5.0	5.1	5.2	5.2	5.3	5.5	5.6	5.7	5.8	0.1
0.2	9.3	9.4	9.5	9.6	9.7	9.9	10.0	10.1	10.2	10.3	10.4	10.7	10.9	11.1	11.4	11.6	0.2
0.3	13.9	14.1	14.3	14.4	14.6	14.8	15.0	15.1	15.3	15.5	15.7	16.0	16.4	16.7	17.1	17.4	0.3
0.4	18.6	18.8	19.0	19.3	19.5	19.7	20.0	20.2	20.4	20.7	20.9	21.4	21.8	22.3	22.7	23.2	0.4
0.5	23.2	23.5	23.8	24.1	24.4	24.7	25.0	25.2	25.5	25.8	26.1	26.7	27.3	27.9	28.4	29.0	0.5
0.6	27.9	28.2	28.6	28.9	29.2	29.6	29.9	30.3	30.6	31.0	31.3	32.0	32.7	33.4	34.1	34.8	0.6
0.7	32.5	32.9	33.3	33.7	34.1	34.5	34.9	35.3	35.7	36.2	36.6	37.4	38.2	39.0	39.8	40.6	0.7
0.8	37.1	37.6	38.1	38.5	39.0	39.5	39.9	40.4	40.9	41.3	41.8	42.7	43.6	44.6	45.5	46.4	0.8
0.9	41.8	42.3	42.8	43.3	43.9	44.4	44.9	45.4	46.0	46.5	47.0	48.0	49.1	50.1	51.2	52.2	0.9
1.0	46.4	47.0	47.6	48.2	48.7	49.3	49.9	50.5	51.1	51.6	52.2	53.4	54.5	55.7	56.9	58.0	1.0
1.1	51.1	51.7	52.3	53.0	53.6	54.3	54.9	55.5	56.2	56.8	57.5	58.7	60.0	61.3	62.6	63.8	1.1
1.2	55.7	56.4	57.1	57.8	58.5	59.2	59.9	60.6	61.3	62.0	62.7	64.1	65.5	66.9	68.2	69.6	1.2
1.3	60.4	61.1	61.9	62.6	63.4	64.1	64.9	65.6	66.4	67.1	67.9	69.4	70.9	72.4	73.9	75.4	1.3
1.4	65.0	65.8	66.6	67.4	68.2	69.1	69.9	70.7	71.5	72.3	73.1	74.7	76.4	78.0	79.6	81.2	1.4
1.5	69.6	70.5	71.4	72.2	73.1	74.0	74.9	75.7	76.6	77.5	78.3	80.1	81.8	83.6	85.3	87.0	1.5
1.6	74.3	75.2	76.1	77.1	78.0	78.9	79.8	80.8	81.7	82.6	83.6	85.4	87.3	89.1	91.0	92.8	1.6
1.7	78.9	79.9	80.9	81.9	82.9	83.9	84.8	85.8	86.8	87.8	88.8	90.8	92.7	94.7	96.7	98.7	1.7
1.8	83.6	84.6	85.7	86.7	87.7	88.8	89.8	90.9	91.9	93.0	94.0	96.1	98.2	100.3	102.4	104.5	1.8
1.9	88.2	89.3	90.4	91.5	92.6	93.7	94.8	95.9	97.0	98.1	99.2	101.4	103.6	105.8	108.1	110.3	1.9
2.0	92.8	94.0	95.2	96.3	97.5	98.7	99.8	101.0	102.1	103.3	104.5	106.8	109.1	111.4	113.7	116.1	2.0
2.1	97.5	98.7	99.9	101.1	102.4	103.6	104.8	106.0	107.2	108.5	109.7	112.1	114.6	117.0	119.4	121.9	2.1
2.2	102.1	103.4	104.7	106.0	107.2	108.5	109.8	111.1	112.3	113.6	114.9	117.5	120.0	122.6	125.1	127.7	2.2
2.3	106.8	108.1	109.4	110.8	112.1	113.4	114.8	116.1	117.5	118.8	120.1	122.8	125.5	128.1	130.8	133.5	2.3
2.4	111.4	112.8	114.2	115.6	117.0	118.4	119.8	121.2	122.6	124.0	125.3	128.1	130.9	133.7	136.5	139.3	2.4
2.5	116.1	117.5	119.0	120.4	121.9	123.3	124.8	126.2	127.7	129.1	130.6	133.5	136.4	139.3	142.2	145.1	2.5
2.6	120.7	122.2	123.7	125.2	126.7	128.2	129.8	131.3	132.8	134.3	135.8	138.8	141.8	144.8	147.9	150.9	2.6
2.7	125.3	126.9	128.5	130.0	131.6	133.2	134.7	136.3	137.9	139.4	141.0	144.1	147.3	150.4	153.5	156.7	2.7
2.8	130.0	131.6	133.2	134.9	136.5	138.1	139.7	141.4	143.0	144.6	146.2	149.5	152.7	156.0	159.2	162.5	2.8
2.9	134.6	136.3	138.0	139.7	141.4	143.0	144.7	146.4	148.1	149.8	151.5	154.8	158.2	161.6	164.9	168.3	2.9
3.0	139.3	141.0	142.8	144.5	146.2	148.0	149.7	151.5	153.2	154.9	156.7	160.2	163.6	167.1	170.6	174.1	3.0
3.1	143.9	145.7	147.5	149.3	151.1	152.9	154.7	156.5	158.3	160.1	161.9	165.5	169.1	172.7	176.3	179.9	3.1
3.2	148.6	150.4	152.3	154.1	156.0	157.8	159.7	161.6	163.4	165.3	167.1	170.8	174.6	178.3	182.0	185.7	3.2
3.3	153.2	155.1	157.0	158.9	160.9	162.8	164.7	166.6	168.5	170.4	172.4	176.2	180.0	183.8	187.7	191.5	3.3
3.4	157.8	159.8	161.8	163.8	165.7	167.7	169.7	171.7	173.6	175.6	177.6	181.5	185.5	189.4	193.4	197.3	3.4
3.5	162.5	164.5	166.5	168.6	170.6	172.6	174.7	176.7	178.7	180.8	182.8	186.9	190.9	195.0	199.0	203.1	3.5
3.6	167.1	169.2	171.3	173.4	175.5	177.6	179.7	181.8	183.8	185.9	188.0	192.2	196.4	200.6	204.7	208.9	3.6
3.7	171.8	173.9	176.1	178.2	180.4	182.5	184.7	186.8	188.9	191.1	193.2	197.5	201.8	206.1	210.4	214.7	3.7
3.8	176.4	178.6	180.8	183.0	185.2	187.4	189.6	191.8	194.1	196.3	198.5	202.9	207.3	211.7	216.1	220.5	3.8
3.9	181.1	183.3	185.6	187.8	190.1	192.4	194.6	196.9	199.2	201.4	203.7	208.2	212.7	217.3	221.8	226.3	3.9
4.0	185.7	188.0	190.3	192.7	195.0	197.3	199.6	201.9	204.3	206.6	208.9	213.6	218.2	222.8	227.5	232.1	4.0
4.1	190.3	192.7	195.1	197.5	199.9	202.2	204.6	207.0	209.4	211.8	214.1	218.9	223.6	228.4	233.2	237.9	4.1
4.2	195.0	197.4	199.9	202.3	204.7	207.2	209.6	212.0	214.5	216.9	219.4	224.2	229.1	234.0	238.9	243.7	4.2
4.3	199.6	202.1	204.6	207.1	209.6	212.1	214.6	217.1	219.6	222.1	224.6	229.6	234.6	239.5	244.5	249.5	4.3
4.4	204.3	206.8	209.4	211.9	214.5	217.0	219.6	222.1	224.7	227.2	229.8	234.9	240.0	245.1	250.2	255.3	4.4
4.5	208.9	211.5	214.1	216.7	219.4	222.0	224.6	227.2	229.8	223.4	235.0	240.2	245.5	250.7	255.9	261.1	4.5
4.6	213.6	216.2	218.9	221.6	224.2	226.9	229.6	232.2	234.9	237.6	240.2	245.6	250.9	256.3	261.6	266.9	4.6
4.7	218.2	220.9	223.6	226.4	229.1	231.8	234.6	237.3	240.0	242.7	245.5	250.9	256.4	261.8	267.3	272.7	4.7
4.8	222.8	225.6	228.4	231.2	234.0	236.8	239.5	242.3	245.1	247.9	250.7	256.3	261.8	267.4	273.0	278.5	4.8
4.9	227.5	230.3	233.2	236.0	238.9	241.7	244.5	247.4	250.2	253.1	255.9	261.6	267.3	273.0	278.7	284.3	4.9
5.0	232.1	235.0	237.9	240.8	243.7	246.6	249.5	252.4	255.3	258.2	261.1	266.9	272.7	278.5	284.3	290.2	5.0
5.1	236.8	239.7	242.7	245.6	248.6	251.6	254.5	257.5	260.4	263.4	266.4	272.3	278.2	284.1	290.0	296.0	5.1
5.2	241.4	244.4	247.4	250.5	253.5	256.5	259.5	262.5	265.5	268.6	271.6	277.6	283.7	289.7	295.7	301.8	5.2
5.3	246.0	249.1	252.2	255.3	258.4	261.4	264.5	267.6	270.7	273.7	276.8	283.0	289.1	295.3	301.4	307.6	5.3
5.4	250.7	253.8	257.0	260.1	263.2	266.4	269.5	272.6	275.8	278.9	282.0	288.3	294.6	300.8	307.1	313.4	5.4
5.5	255.3	258.5	261.7	264.9	268.1	271.3	274.5	277.7	280.9	284.1	287.3	293.6	300.0	306.4	312.8	319.2	5.5
5.6	260.0	263.2	266.5	269.7	273.0	276.2	279.5	282.7	286.0	289.2	292.5	299.0	305.5	312.0	318.5	325.0	5.6
5.7	264.6	267.9	271.2	274.5	277.8	281.2	284.5	287.8	291.1	294.4	297.7	304.3	310.9	317.5	324.2	330.8	5.7
5.8	269.3	272.6	276.0	279.4	282.7	286.1	289.5	292.8	296.2	299.6	302.9	309.7	316.4	323.1	329.8	336.6	5.8
5.9	273.9	277.3	280.8	284.2	287.6	291.0	294.4	297.9	301.3	304.7	308.1	315.0	321.8	328.7	335.5	342.4	5.9
6.0	278.5	282.0	285.5	289.0	292.5	296.0	299.4	302.9	306.4	309.9	313.4	320.3	327.3	334.3	341.2	348.2	6.0

Energy

A table of main relationships for varying densities is provided below;
information is adapted from 'Petroleum Measurement Tables' of the American
Society for Testing Materials (ASTM) and the Institute of Petroleum (IP).

Petroleum: relation between volume and mass   Density (kg/l) at 15°C (59°F)

Density (kg/l) at 15°C	API degrees	UK tons per kilolitre (m³)	lb: per UK gal	per US gal	per barrel	UK gal per UK ton	US barrels: per US ton	per tonne	per UK ton	US barrels per day to: US tons per year	tonnes per year	UK tons per year	Density (kg/l) at 15°C
0.50		0.492	5.01	4.17	175	447	11.41	12.58	12.78	32.0	29.0	28.6	0.50
0.52		0.512	5.21	4.34	182	430	10.97	12.10	12.29	33.3	30.2	29.7	0.52
0.54		0.531	5.41	4.51	189	414	10.57	11.65	11.83	34.5	31.3	30.8	0.54
0.56		0.551	5.61	4.67	196	399	10.19	11.23	11.41	35.8	32.5	32.0	0.56
0.58		0.571	5.81	4.84	203	385	9.84	10.84	11.02	37.1	33.7	33.1	0.58
0.60		0.591	6.01	5.01	210	372	9.51	10.48	10.65	38.4	34.8	34.3	0.60
0.61		0.600	6.11	5.09	214	366	9.35	10.31	10.48	39.0	35.4	34.8	0.61
0.62	96.5	0.610	6.21	5.17	217	360	9.20	10.14	10.31	39.7	36.0	35.4	0.62
0.63	92.9	0.620	6.31	5.26	221	355	9.06	9.98	10.14	40.3	36.6	36.0	0.63
0.64	89.4	0.630	6.41	5.34	224	349	8.92	9.83	9.99	40.9	37.1	36.6	0.64
0.65	86.0	0.640	6.51	5.42	228	344	8.78	9.68	9.83	41.6	37.7	37.1	0.65
0.66	82.7	0.650	6.61	5.51	231	339	8.65	9.53	9.68	42.2	38.3	37.7	0.66
0.67	79.5	0.659	6.72	5.59	235	334	8.52	9.39	9.54	42.9	38.9	38.3	0.67
0.68	76.4	0.669	6.82	5.67	238	329	8.39	9.25	9.40	43.5	39.5	38.8	0.68
0.69	73.4	0.679	6.92	5.76	242	324	8.27	9.12	9.26	44.1	40.0	39.4	0.69
0.70	70.4	0.689	7.02	5.84	245	319	8.15	8.99	9.13	44.8	40.6	40.0	0.70
0.71	67.6	0.699	7.12	5.93	249	315	8.04	8.86	9.00	45.4	41.2	40.6	0.71
0.72	64.8	0.709	7.22	6.01	252	310	7.93	8.74	8.88	46.1	41.8	41.1	0.72
0.73	62.1	0.718	7.32	6.09	256	306	7.82	8.62	8.75	46.7	42.4	41.7	0.73
0.74	59.5	0.728	7.42	6.18	259	302	7.71	8.50	8.64	47.3	42.9	42.3	0.74
0.75	57.0	0.738	7.52	6.26	263	298	7.61	8.39	8.52	48.0	43.5	42.8	0.75
0.76	54.5	0.748	7.62	6.34	266	294	7.51	8.28	8.41	48.6	44.1	43.4	0.76
0.77	52.1	0.758	7.72	6.43	270	290	7.41	8.17	8.30	49.3	44.7	44.0	0.77
0.78	49.7	0.768	7.82	6.51	273	287	7.32	8.06	8.19	49.9	45.3	44.5	0.78
0.79	47.4	0.778	7.92	6.59	277	283	7.22	7.96	8.09	50.5	45.8	45.1	0.79
0.80	45.2	0.787	8.02	6.68	280	279	7.13	7.86	7.99	51.2	46.4	45.7	0.80
0.81	43.0	0.797	8.12	6.76	284	276	7.04	7.77	7.89	51.8	47.0	46.3	0.81
0.82	40.9	0.807	8.22	6.84	287	273	6.96	7.67	7.79	52.5	47.6	46.8	0.82
0.83	38.8	0.817	8.32	6.93	291	269	6.87	7.58	7.70	53.1	48.2	47.4	0.83
0.84	36.8	0.827	8.42	7.01	294	266	6.79	7.49	7.61	53.7	48.7	48.0	0.84
0.85	34.8	0.837	8.52	7.09	298	263	6.71	7.40	7.52	54.4	49.3	48.5	0.85
0.86	32.9	0.846	8.62	7.18	301	260	6.63	7.31	7.43	55.0	49.9	49.1	0.86
0.87	31.0	0.856	8.72	7.26	305	257	6.56	7.23	7.35	55.7	50.5	49.7	0.87
0.88	29.1	0.866	8.82	7.34	308	254	6.48	7.15	7.26	56.3	51.1	50.3	0.88
0.89	27.3	0.876	8.92	7.43	312	251	6.41	7.07	7.18	56.9	51.6	50.8	0.89
0.90	25.6	0.886	9.02	7.51	315	248	6.34	6.99	7.10	57.6	52.2	51.4	0.90
0.91	23.8	0.896	9.12	7.59	319	246	6.27	6.91	7.02	58.2	52.8	52.0	0.91
0.92	22.1	0.905	9.22	7.68	322	243	6.20	6.84	6.95	58.9	53.4	52.5	0.92
0.93	20.5	0.915	9.32	7.76	326	240	6.14	6.76	6.87	59.5	54.0	53.1	0.93
0.94	18.9	0.925	9.42	7.84	329	238	6.07	6.69	6.80	60.1	54.5	53.7	0.94
0.95	17.3	0.935	9.52	7.93	333	235	6.01	6.62	6.73	60.8	55.1	54.3	0.95
0.96	15.7	0.945	9.62	8.01	336	233	5.94	6.55	6.66	61.4	55.7	54.8	0.96
0.97	14.2	0.955	9.72	8.10	340	230	5.88	6.48	6.59	62.0	56.3	55.4	0.97
0.98	12.7	0.965	9.82	8.18	343	228	5.82	6.42	6.52	62.7	56.9	56.0	0.98
0.99	11.3	0.974	9.92	8.26	347	226	5.76	6.35	6.46	63.3	57.5	56.5	0.99
1.00	9.9	0.984	10.02	8.35	351	223	5.71	6.29	6.39	64.0	58.0	57.1	1.00
1.01	8.5	0.994	10.12	8.43	354	221	5.65	6.23	6.33	64.6	58.6	57.7	1.01
1.02	7.1	1.004	10.22	8.51	358	219	5.59	6.17	6.27	65.2	59.2	58.3	1.02
1.03	5.7	1.014	10.32	8.60	361	217	5.54	6.11	6.20	65.9	59.8	58.8	1.03
1.04	4.4	1.024	10.42	8.68	365	215	5.49	6.05	6.14	66.5	60.4	59.4	1.04
1.05	3.1	1.033	10.52	8.76	368	213	5.43	5.99	6.09	67.2	60.9	60.0	1.05
1.06	1.8	1.043	10.62	8.85	372	211	5.38	5.93	6.03	67.8	61.5	60.5	1.06
1.07	0.6	1.053	10.72	8.93	375	209	5.33	5.88	5.97	68.4	62.1	61.1	1.07
1.08		1.063	10.82	9.01	379	207	5.28	5.82	5.92	69.1	62.7	61.7	1.08
1.09		1.073	10.92	9.10	382	205	5.23	5.77	5.86	69.7	63.3	62.3	1.09
1.10		1.083	11.02	9.18	386	203	5.19	5.72	5.81	70.4	63.8	62.8	1.10

Energy

Gas

Gas is usually classified as either primary (natural or liquefied petroleum gas) or derived (manufactured).

Natural gas

The term 'natural gas' is applied to gas produced at the surface from underground accumulations of widely varying composition which may or may not be directly associated with accumulation of oil.

Methane, ethane, propane, and the butanes are gases at ordinary atmospheric temperatures and pressures while pentane, hexane, heptane and octane are liquids. Natural gas may contain amounts of these liquid hydrocarbons and it is then known as 'wet gas' as distinct from 'dry gas' containing none or only a small proportion of liquid hydrocarbons. Methane, the main constituent, cannot be liquefied under pressure at atmospheric temperature but propane and the butanes can be liquefied under relatively low pressure at atmospheric temperature, and are then known as 'liquefied petroleum gas' (LPG). Natural gas can be liquefied at atmospheric pressure by cooling to about $-160°C$ ($-256°F$) and is then known as 'liquefied natural gas' (LNG).

The following table outlines the main constituents:

Paraffin hydrocarbons in natural gas

Name	Chemical formula	Boiling point at atmospheric pressure °C	
Methane	CH_4	-161.5	
Ethane	C_2H_6	-88.5	gaseous at ordinary
Propane	C_3H_8	-42.2	atmospheric temperature
Isobutane	C_4H_{10}	-12.1	and pressure
Normal butane	C_4H_{10}	-0.5	
Isopentane	C_5H_{12}	27.9	
Normal pentane	C_5H_{12}	36.1	liquid at ordinary
Normal hexane	C_6H_{14}	69.0	atmospheric temperature
Normal heptane	C_7H_{16}	98.4	and pressure
Normal octane	C_8H_{18}	125.6	

Manufactured gas

This includes:

Gasworks gas: produced by manufacturing plants, including gas produced by carbonisation at gasworks and municipal gas plants and by cracking of natural gas.

Coke-oven gas: obtained as a by-product of solid fuel carbonisation and gasification operations carried out by establishments not dependent on gasworks and municipal gas plants.

Blast-furnace gas: obtained as a by-product in blast furnaces.

Refinery gas: non-condensable gas collected in petroleum refineries.

Liquefied petroleum gas (other than obtained from natural sources): hydrocarbons produced both inside and outside refineries in the course of processing crude petroleum or its derivatives.

Measures

Gas is usually measured either in cubic feet or cubic metres, production and sales volumes being quoted in terms of thousand million (milliard or 10^9) cubic metres annually or million cubic feet daily, depending on the country concerned. Some utilities distribute a gas saturated with water vapour (and may humidify natural gas used); others distribute a dry gas. Gas saturated with water vapour at 60 °F contains 1.74% of water vapour by volume.

In the United Kingdom gas is charged on the basis of calorific value, measured in therms (also see pages 131–132).

The international standard reference conditions for gas (st) are 15°C, 1.013 25 bar (approximately 760 mm Hg), dry. Usual standards used (with different symbols) in different countries are as follows:

Volume standards

	Standard unit	Conditions
United Kingdom United States	Standard cubic foot (Scf)	60°F, 30 in (762 mm) Hg, wet[a] 60°F, 30 in (762 mm) Hg, wet[b]
Netherlands	Normal cubic metre (m_n^3)	15°C, 760 mm Hg, dry
Metric, other than Netherlands	Normal cubic metre (Nm^3)	0°C, 760 mm Hg, dry

[a]With the mercury column measured at 60 °F, under gravity at 53 °N, corresponding to 1 013.740 5 mbar.   [b]With the mercury column measured at 32 °F, under standard gravity of 32.174 ft/s² (9.806 65 m/s²), corresponding to 1 015.9166 mbar.

Due to expansion, the energy value for a cubic metre is lower at higher temperature. Approximate equivalent in terms of energy are:
Normal cubic metre at 0°C (Nm^3) = 1.055 Normal cubic metre at 15°C (m_n^3). Also see page 132 for other relationships.

The special symbol Nm^3, using N for 'normal', is not an SI unit and has no connection with the SI symbol N for newton. Other special symbols used in this and the petroleum industry generally are:
M or T = thousand; MM = million; mrd = milliard; cf = cubic feet.
Hence the following approximate conversion:
1 mrd m³ per year = approximately 100 MM cf/d (approximately 100 million cubic feet per day).
These special symbols are being gradually phased out of use.

Conversions

Liquefied gases weight to volume:

1 tonne of liquid methane (LNG) = 15 US barrels
                                = 1 400 m³ pipeline gas
                                = 53 000 ft³ pipeline gas
1 tonne of liquid propane (LPG) at 60°F = 12.5 US barrels
                                = 500 m³ pipeline gas
                                = 19 000 ft³ pipeline gas

For energy values see pages 132–134.

Electricity

Measures

Electricity as energy is usually measured in terms of the kilowatt hour and related multiples.

1 000 watt hour (W h)	=	1 kilowatt hour (kW h)
1 000 kilowatt hours	=	1 megawatt hour (MW h)
1 000 megawatt hours	=	1 gigawatt hour (GW h)
24 kilowatt hours	=	1 kilowatt day (kW d)
24 000 kilowatt hours	=	1 megawatt day (MW d)

Energy equivalents
1 kilowatt hour = 3.6 megajoules (MJ)
1 megawatt day = 86.4 gigajoules (GJ)

Old unit
Before 1948 the former 'international watt' was in use:
1 watt (international of 1948) = 1.000 19 W (UK and West Germany)
                                or 1.000 165 W (United States)

For other units relating to electricity see electronics.

Energy

Hydro-electricity

Electricity of 10 kW is produced by water falling through a height of 150 feet at the rate of 1 cusec (see page 128 for definition of a cusec).
The energy produced from hydro-electricity is evaluated by the United Nations on the basis of the energy consumed by pumping, applying a theoretical efficiency rate of 70% where no other is available; that is, 30% of energy is lost through the transformation of energy.

Coal and oil power stations

A conventional power station has a capacity of about 600 MW. For energy equivalents see page 134.

Solar power

The sun's radiation provides power through space at about 1400 watts per square metre of cross section of space. This is about 330 calories per second per square metre in old unit terms, where 1 watt = 1 joule per second = 0.239 cal per second. The old measure of calories per square centimetre is related to other units as follows:

$$1 \text{ cal/cm}^2 = 1 \text{ langley} = 4.184 \times 10^4 \text{ J/m}^2$$
$$1 \text{ cal/cm}^2 \text{ min} = 1 \text{ pyron}^a = 697.3 \text{ W/m}^2$$
$$1 \text{ cal/cm}^2 \text{ day}^b = 0.484 \text{ W/m}^2$$
$$1 \text{ W/m}^2 = 2.07 \text{ cal/cm}^2 \text{ day}$$

[a] Formerly called a langley. [b] Also shown as cal/cm²/day.

Of the solar power directed at the earth, nearly one half is reflected back into space or absorbed in the atmosphere etc, leaving about 700 W/m² received at a surface facing the sun. The amount received over a period in a particular area depends on the number of hours of direct sunshine. A general average over the year, for regions between about 45 °N and 45 °S is 200 W/m² (400 cal/cm² day). For a south facing installation, the average for the United Kingdom is about 110 W/m².
The efficiency with which this amount is turned into usable energy varies, but generally operation of solar cells will provide about 35% of the maximum possible, or about 40 W/m² for the United Kingdom.

Solar power systems can be classified as follows:
0.1 kW–2 kW   small scale[a] (individual houses, farms etc)
20 kW–100 kW   medium scale (village power supply)
200 kW–1 MW & over   large scale (small town power supply)

[a] Typically 0.1 kW for domestic water supply, and 1 kW for irrigation.

Units for small scale use solar cells giving about 5–8 W each; for large scale users a collector area of 1 km² is estimated to be capable of producing about 80 MW.

Wind power

Power output increases as the cube of the wind velocity, as indicated by the following general formula for available wind power:
$$P = 0.0137 \times A \times v^3$$
where P = power in watts
     A = cross-sectional area of the windstream (in m²)
     v = velocity of wind (in km/h)
A wind rotor can theoretically extract 0.5926 per unit of available power; where E is general efficiency in using available wind power, the formula becomes:
$$P = 0.0137 A v^3 \times 0.5926 E$$

Typical wind electric-generators start to give power at about 15 km/h (4 m/s or Beaufort force 3) with full output at about 40 km/h (10 m/s or Beaufort force 5–6). Typical output ranges for a wind electric-generator are from 300–6000 watts. Large experimental windmills for producing electricity have a capacity of about 3 megawatts (3 million watts).

Consumption of electricity

The loading factor for some domestic electrical appliances is as follows:

	watts		watts
Lighting	25–150	Hair dryers	350–800
Can openers	60	Polishers	400
Blankets (under or over)	60–100	Hair rollers	450–700
Extractor fans	75	Tea-makers	500
Record players	75	Trolleys (heated)	560
Tape recorders	75	Coffee percolators	750
Coffee grinders	100	Hot trays	750
Refrigerators	100	Toasters	1 050–1 360
Television: mono	100–150	Irons	1 250
colour	150–350	Ironing machines	1 500
Food mixers	100–450	Infrared grills	2 000
Vacuum cleaners (hand)	150	Kettles	2 500–3 000
Blenders	200	Dishwashers	3 000
Waste disposers	250	Tumble dryers	3 000
Power drills	250–500	Washing machines	3 000
Food freezers	300	Central heating	6 000
Spin dryers	300	Cookers, oven, grill	
Vacuum cleaners	300–1 000	and hob	12 000–
Heaters: oil-filled			15 000
radiators	300–2 500		
radiant	500–3 000		
infrared	750–1 500		
convector	1 000–2 500		
fan	2 000–3 000		
immersion	3 000		

In terms of annual consumption, the main unit is the kilowatt hour; following are estimates of the annual consumption of electricity by some main domestic items (equals watts × hours per year used/1 000):

	kW h		kW h
Toaster	20	Television	250–320
Vacuum cleaner	30	Refrigerator	330
Washing machine		Dishwasher	340
single/twin tub	60	Freezer	840
Iron	70	Cooker	1 190
Electric overblanket	100	Water, heater, immersion:	
Washing machine, automatic	200	night only (white meter)	1 200
Kettle	220	night and day	2 060

Atomic energy

Atomic (or nuclear) energy is released by the fission of atoms – the splitting of a heavy nucleus into two (or very rarely more) approximately equal fragments, which is accompanied by the emission of neutrons and the release of energy. Fission is usually caused by the impact of a neutron on the nucleus, sometimes by a charged particle or photon or (occasionally) spontaneously.

A *nuclear reactor* is the plant in which the process of neutron-induced fission is carried on as a controlled chain reaction. The core of the reactor contains fissile fuel (uranium or plutonium), coolant (water, carbon dioxide, liquid sodium or helium) and (in thermal reactors) a moderator of water, deuterium oxide ('heavy water') or graphite, to slow down the fast neutrons emitted in fission. Fast reactors have no moderator and rely on fast-moving neutrons and much more concentrated fuel.
Neutron absorbing control rods control the fission chain reaction. To prevent the escape of radiation there is usually a concrete biological shield and a metal thermal shield (to protect the biological shield from heat). A primary containment (sealed structure) helps to prevent the escape of radioactive materials.

Main types of power reactor are (alphabetically):
AGR   Advanced gas-cooled reactor
BWR   Boiling water reactor
Candu Canadian deuterium reactor
FBR   Fast (breeder) reactor
HTR   High temperature reactor
LWR   Light water reactor (includes BWR and PWR)
Magnox Gas-cooled reactor
PWR   Pressurised water reactor
SGHWR Steam-generating heavy water reactor

Energy

Some special terms are:

Breeding: the process of generating additional supplies of nuclear fuel; eg fissile plutonium from fertile uranium-238 by absorption of neutrons produced in the fissioning of primary plutonium fuel.

Chain reaction: a process whereby one nuclear reaction can cause a similar one; for example, when fission occurs in uranium atoms, neutrons are released which go on to produce fission in neighbouring uranium atoms.

Critical: the term used to describe a chain reaction which is just being maintained at a constant rate; that is, it is just self-sustaining.

Cross section: this is the apparent area presented by a target nucleus to an oncoming neutron; it is a measure of the probability that a specified nuclear reaction will occur.

Reactor core: the central part of a reactor containing the nuclear fuel (such as uranium) the moderator (if any), the coolant and the control rods.

Measures

Special measures concerned with atomic energy are:

Old units
Fermi (femtometre or fm) = 10^{-15} m
Stigma = 10^{-12} m
Barn (b) = 100 fm² = 10^{-28} m², being a unit of area used in measuring nuclear cross sections.
Shed = 10^{-24} barn = 10^{-52} m².

Other
Electron volt (eV) = the kinetic energy acquired by an electron in falling freely through a potential difference of 1 volt in vacuum = $1.602 \times 19 \times 10^{-19}$ J approximately.
1 000 000 electron volts = 1 mega electron volt (MeV)
1 000 000 000 electron volts = 1 giga electron volt (GeV; BeV in the United States where B is 1 billion)
Where MW is 1 million watts, MW(E) stands for electrical and MW(Th) for thermal power or heat output.

For radiation units, see the section on health (pages 150–151), and for units relating to atomic explosions see weapons (page 173).

Energy yield in general

The amount of energy related to mass in general is quantitatively expressed in Einstein's mass-energy equation:

$$E = mc^2$$

where E is the energy obtained from mass m; c is the velocity of light = approx. 3.0×10^8 metres per second. Hence, 1 kilogram of matter totally annihilated is approximately equal to $(3 \times 10^8)^2$ J = 9×10^{16} J.

1 gram = 9×10^{13} J
= 2.5×10^7 kW h
= 5.6×10^{32} eV
= 8.5×10^{10} Btu
and 1 pound = 3.87×10^{13} Btu

Energy from uranium

The energy extracted depends on the fuel and the nuclear reactor performance; the table below outlines a typical efficiency in terms of 1 pound or kilogram of uranium.

Natural uranium consists mainly of U-238 which is fertile but not fissile, and U-235 which is fissile, but only 0.7% by weight; U-235 is lighter, with 3 fewer neutrons. Magnox and CANDU reactors use natural uranium but other thermal reactors need uranium enriched in U-235 up to a level of 2–3%. The table following shows first the energy theoretically available from the complete fissioning of 1 pound or 1 kilogram of natural uranium, and secondly the energy actually achievable from 1 pound or 1 kilogram of natural uranium as used as fuel in a typical AGR or PWR.

	pound	kilogram
Complete fissioning of natural uranium (**maximum theoretically possible if all atoms could be fissioned**)	1.03×10^7 kW h = 430 megawatt days = 3.72×10^7 MJ = 3.3×10^6 lb of coal (at 11 000 Btu/lb equivalent) = 1 500 tce	2.3×10^7 kW h = 950 megawatt days = 8.2×10^7 MJ = 3.3×10^6 kg of coal (at 25.6 MJ/kg equivalent) = 3 200 tce
Achievable fissioning of natural uranium in an AGR or PWR	7.7×10^4 kW h = 3.2 megawatt days = 2.7×10^5 MJ = 2.3×10^4 lb of coal = 10 tce	1.7×10^5 kW h = 7.0 megawatt days = 6.0×10^5 MJ = 2.3×10^4 kg of coal = 23 tce

The 'burn-up' value for reactor fuel is usually expressed in terms of megawatt days (MW d) per tonne of fuel used up in the reactor. The value of 7.0 MW d per kilogram of natural uranium (7 000 MW d/tonne) in the table above refers to the larger quantity of natural uranium from which the enriched fuel was produced.

Fast (breeder) reactor

The achievable fission value shown in the above table takes account of the plutonium bred from U-238 within the fuel and fissioned in situ. By separating unconsumed plutonium from the spent fuel and using it in a fast reactor, the energy extracted from 1 kilogram of natural uranium can be increased to 1 500–2 000 tonnes coal equivalent (tce). A fast reactor is designed to convert U-238 to plutonium by the absorption of neutrons, as well as to produce energy. A plutonium-fuelled core is surrounded by a U-238 blanket, and the neutron economy is such that, on average, more than 1 atom of plutonium is produced in the blanket for each atom fissioned in the core. Hence there is an accumulation of plutonium in the blanket which may be used in other fast reactors. Such a reactor is called a 'breeder' reactor.

Nuclear fusion

Commercially controlled fusion or merging of nuclei, as compared to fission (splitting), requires a temperature of about 200 mn °C, and is not currently a practical means of obtaining controlled energy. The United States has a target date of 1995 for the construction of its first commercial fusion reactor.

Engineering

Measures

Engineering industries in the United Kingdom have in general changed over to the SI metric system, with an estimated one-half having moved from imperial to metric by 1980.
Measures used are as outlined in the general sections on pages 14–19, with conversions on pages 64–83. Measures of special interest are as follows:

Power

The basic SI unit of power is the watt; the most frequently used unit is the kilowatt (= 1 000 watts). The following table gives a summary of conversions for the different types of 'horsepower' (also see pages 17 and 19). The UK measure of horsepower, at 550 ft lbf/s, is also 33 000 ft lbf/min; this is approximately equal to the original estimate of the power of 1 horse in pulling a load. Also, donkey power = 250 watts = approximately $\frac{1}{3}$ horsepower.
Main conversions are:

1 unit of:	equals (units of) ft lbf/s	kgf m/s	kW (kJ/s)
UK horsepower	550	76.040 2	0.745 7
Metric horsepower	542.476	75	0.735 499
Electric horsepower [a]	550.221	76.071	0.746

[a] This is one of the special units based on UK horsepower, taking the approximate value of 0.746 kilowatt.

Metric horsepower is referred to as 'cheval vapeur' (ch or CV) in France, and 'Pferdestärke' (PS) in Germany; other names for metric horsepower are cavallo vapore (cv) and Paardekracht (pk). In France a 'poncelet' is 100 kgf m/s.

Engineering

A table of conversions between kilowatts and UK and metric horsepowers is included on the facing page.

Brake horsepower (bhp), or brake power, is the horsepower generated by an engine which does useful work; this is usually measured at the crankshaft or flywheel. The main European standard is the German DIN (Deutsche Industrie Normal) rating, which measures the power available at the flywheel of an engine when it is in an installed condition (with all ancillaries fitted). The term brake is used, as the force can be measured by the braking power necessary to stop the engine.

Mechanical efficiency = (brake power/ihp × 100) per cent, where ihp = indicated horsepower of the engine.

Torque (moment of force)

Torque is force applied at a right angle at a distance, measured in the UK system by the pound-force foot (lbf ft). The product force by length used as a torque unit is the same as the product length by force used as an energy unit. In the United Kingdom the convention is to express the torque unit as lbf ft and the energy unit as ft lbf; there is not a similar convention in the metric system, but there is a corresponding general usage of N m (force by distance) for torque units and J (which equals N m) for energy. Because torque and energy units are equal in this way, conversions are numerically equal; for example, the torque conversion from lbf ft to N m on page 66 is the same as the energy conversion from ft lbf to J on page 67.

Summary of torque conversions:

From	to	pdl ft	lbf ft	kgf m	N m
		multiply by			
pdl ft		1	0.031 081 0	0.004 297 10	0.042 140 1
lbf ft		32.174 0	1	0.138 255	1.355 82
kgf m		232.715	7.233 01	1	9.806 65
N m		23.730 4	0.737 562	0.101 972	1

Pressure

The main SI unit for pressure is the pascal, but there is some usage of the bar (= 100 kPa) in parts of the engineering industry (for example, machine tools and hydraulics), the bar being approximately equal to normal atmospheric pressure. Details of the various units of pressure are included on page 16, with summary conversions on pages 66–67. Pounds-force per square inch is usually abbreviated to 'psi'.

Rotational frequency

The revolution per second is the main SI unit, but revolutions per minute (rev/min or 'rpm') is also a standard unit; 60 rev/min = 1/s = 1 Hz.

Friction

The 'coefficient of friction' measures the relationship between a force and the load it can move using specified bearings or grease lubrication: coefficient of friction = lbf/lbf = kgf/kgf = N/N. Ordinary greases have friction coefficients of about 0.1; bearings can have lower friction coefficients, down to about 0.001.

Some other items of special interest are included in the following sections of the industry.

Bolts, screws and studs

Threads

Pitch is the distance between the crest of 1 thread and that of the next, parallel to the axis. Threads per inch is the reciprocal of pitch measured in inches. The usual angle of thread with reference to the pitch line is 55° or 60°.

The main British threads are British Standard Whitworth (BSW) and Unified (also used in Canada and the United States). The ISO recommendation for international use is as follows (showing a selected list of the 'first choice' only); the international standard is based on an angle of 60°. All measures in the following table are in millimetres:

Nominal diameter	Pitches	Nominal diameter	Pitches	Nominal diameter	Pitches
1	0.2, 0.25	16	1, 1.5, 2	90	2, 3, 4, 6
1.2	0.2, 0.25	20	1, 1.5, 2, 3.5	100	2, 3, 4, 6
1.6	0.2, 0.35	24	1, 1.5, 2, 3	110	2, 3, 4, 6
2	0.25, 0.4	30	1, 1.5, 2, 3.5	125	2, 3, 4, 6
2.5	0.35, 0.45	36	1.5, 2, 3, 4	140	2, 3, 4, 6
3	0.35, 0.5	42	1.5, 2, 3, 4, 4.5	160	3, 4, 6
4	0.5, 0.7	48	1.5, 2, 3, 4, 5	180	3, 4, 6
5	0.5, 0.8	56	1.5, 2, 3, 4, 5.5	200	3, 4, 6
6	0.75, 1	64	1.5, 2, 3, 4, 6	220	3, 4, 6
8	0.75, 1, 1.25	72	1.5, 2, 3, 4, 6	250	3, 4, 6
10	0.75, 1, 1.25, 1.5	80	1.5, 2, 3, 4, 6	280	4, 6
12	1, 1.25, 1.5, 1.75				

Up to a nominal diameter of 64 mm, the largest pitch is referred to as a 'coarse' pitch, the others being 'fine'. Where a thread is required with a pitch larger than 6 mm, in the diameter range 150–300 mm, a pitch of 8 mm is preferred.

A screw thread in conformity with the International Standard is designated with the letter M, followed by the values of the nominal diameter and the pitch, expressed in millimetres and separated by the sign ×; for example, M6 × 0.75. No indication for pitch means that a coarse pitch is specified.

Pitch of threads for British Standard Whitworth is as follows, showing the exact metric equivalent for fine and coarse threads; diameter is nominal or 'major' diameter (at the outside of the thread):

Nominal diameter		British Standard Whitworth					
		Threads per inch		Pitch of thread			
in	mm			inches		millimetres	
		fine	coarse	fine	coarse	fine	coarse
1/8	3.18		40		0.025		0.64
5/32	3.97		32		0.031		0.79
3/16	4.76	32	24	0.031	0.042	0.79	1.06
1/4	6.35	26	20	0.038	0.05	0.98	1.27
5/16	7.94	22	18	0.045	0.056	1.15	1.41
3/8	9.52	20	16	0.05	0.062	1.27	1.59
7/16	11.11	18	14	0.056	0.071	1.41	1.81
1/2	12.7	16	12	0.062	0.083	1.59	2.12
9/16	14.29	16	12	0.062	0.083	1.59	2.12
5/8	15.88	14	11	0.071	0.091	1.81	2.31
3/4	19.05	12	10	0.083	0.1	2.12	2.54
7/8	22.22	11	9	0.091	0.111	2.31	2.82
1	25.4	10	8	0.1	0.125	2.54	3.18
1 1/8	28.58	9	7	0.111	0.143	2.82	3.63
1 1/4	31.75	9	7	0.111	0.143	2.82	3.63
1 1/2	38.1	8	6	0.125	0.167	3.18	4.23
1 3/4	44.45	7	5	0.143	0.2	3.63	5.08
2	50.8	7	4½	0.143	0.222	3.63	5.64
3	76.2	5	3½	0.2	0.286	5.08	7.26
4	101.6	4½	3	0.222	0.333	5.64	8.47
5	127.0	4	2¾	0.25	0.364	6.35	9.24
6	152.4	4	2½	0.25	0.4	6.35	10.16

The BSW sizes relate only approximately to the ISO sizes; for example M8 is roughly the same as 5/16 BSW (= 7.94 mm) with a coarse pitch of 1.41 mm (18 to the inch), compared with 1.25 mm for the M8 coarse pitch.

Unified screw threads are basically the same as the above BSW threads in the coarse range, except for the 1/2 diameter which has 13 threads per inch (pitch = 0.077 in = 1.95 mm); in the fine range they are as follows, indicating threads per inch for various diameters: 1/4, 28; 5/16 and 3/8, 24; 7/16 and 1/2, 20; 9/16 and 5/8, 18; 3/4, 16; 7/8, 14; 1 to 1 1/2, 12. Equivalents pitches can be obtained from the BSW table, except for 28 threads per inch (pitch = 0.036 in = 0.91 mm).

gineering

K horsepower to kilowatts   1 UK hp = 0.745 700 kW

K hp →	0	1	2	3	4	5	6	7	8	9	← UK hp
	kW	kW	kW	kW	kW	kW	kW	kW	kW	kW	↓
	0.000	0.746	1.491	2.237	2.983	3.728	4.474	5.220	5.966	6.711	0
	7.457	8.203	8.948	9.694	10.440	11.185	11.931	12.677	13.423	14.168	10
	14.914	15.660	16.405	17.151	17.897	18.642	19.388	20.134	20.880	21.625	20
	22.371	23.117	23.862	24.608	25.354	26.099	26.845	27.591	28.337	29.082	30
	29.828	30.574	31.319	32.065	32.811	33.556	34.302	35.048	35.794	36.539	40
	37.285	38.031	38.776	39.522	40.268	41.013	41.759	42.505	43.251	43.996	50
	44.742	45.488	46.233	46.979	47.725	48.470	49.216	49.962	50.708	51.453	60
	52.199	52.945	53.690	54.436	55.182	55.927	56.673	57.419	58.165	58.910	70
	59.656	60.402	61.147	61.893	62.639	63.384	64.130	64.876	65.622	66.367	80
	67.113	67.859	68.604	69.350	70.096	70.841	71.587	72.333	73.079	73.824	90
	74.570										100

ilowatts to UK horsepower   1 kW = 1.341 02 UK hp

W →	0	1	2	3	4	5	6	7	8	9	← kW
↓	UK hp	UK hp	UK hp	UK hp	UK hp	UK hp	UK hp	UK hp	UK hp	UK hp	↓
0	0.000	1.341	2.682	4.023	5.364	6.705	8.046	9.387	10.728	12.069	0
10	13.410	14.751	16.092	17.433	18.774	20.115	21.456	22.797	24.138	25.479	10
20	26.820	28.161	29.502	30.844	32.185	33.526	34.867	36.208	37.549	38.890	20
30	40.231	41.572	42.913	44.254	45.595	46.936	48.277	49.618	50.959	52.300	30
40	53.641	54.982	56.323	57.664	59.005	60.346	61.687	63.028	64.369	65.710	40
50	67.051	68.392	69.733	71.074	72.415	73.756	75.097	76.438	77.779	79.120	50
60	80.461	81.802	83.143	84.484	85.825	87.166	88.507	89.848	91.190	92.531	60
70	93.872	95.213	96.554	97.895	99.236	100.577	101.918	103.259	104.600	105.941	70
80	107.282	108.623	109.964	111.305	112.646	113.987	115.328	116.669	118.010	119.351	80
90	120.692	122.033	123.374	124.715	126.056	127.397	128.738	130.079	131.420	132.761	90
100	134.102										100

etric horsepower to Kilowatts   1 ch or PS = 0.735 499 kW

or PS →	0	1	2	3	4	5	6	7	8	9	← ch or PS
↓	kW	kW	kW	kW	kW	kW	kW	kW	kW	kW	↓
0	0.000	0.735	1.471	2.206	2.942	3.677	4.413	5.148	5.884	6.619	0
10	7.355	8.090	8.826	9.561	10.297	11.032	11.768	12.503	13.239	13.974	10
20	14.710	15.445	16.181	16.916	17.652	18.387	19.123	19.858	20.594	21.329	20
30	22.065	22.800	23.536	24.271	25.007	25.742	26.478	27.213	27.949	28.684	30
40	29.420	30.155	30.891	31.626	32.362	33.097	33.833	34.568	35.304	36.039	40
50	36.775	37.510	38.246	38.981	39.717	40.452	41.188	41.923	42.659	43.394	50
60	44.130	44.865	45.601	46.336	47.072	47.807	48.543	49.278	50.014	50.749	60
70	51.485	52.220	52.956	53.691	54.427	55.162	55.898	56.633	57.369	58.104	70
80	58.840	59.575	60.311	61.046	61.782	62.517	63.253	63.988	64.724	65.459	80
90	66.195	66.930	67.666	68.401	69.137	69.872	70.608	71.343	72.079	72.814	90
100	73.550										100

ilowatts to Metric horsepower   1 kW = 1.359 62 ch or PS

W →	0	1	2	3	4	5	6	7	8	9	← kW
↓	ch or PS	ch or PS	ch or PS	ch or PS	ch or PS	ch or PS	ch or PS	ch or PS	ch or PS	ch or PS	↓
0	0.000	1.360	2.719	4.079	5.438	6.798	8.158	9.517	10.877	12.237	0
10	13.596	14.956	16.315	17.675	19.035	20.394	21.754	23.114	24.473	25.833	10
20	27.192	28.552	29.912	31.271	32.631	33.991	35.350	36.710	38.069	39.429	20
30	40.789	42.148	43.508	44.868	46.227	47.587	48.946	50.306	51.666	53.025	30
40	54.385	55.744	57.104	58.464	59.823	61.183	62.543	63.902	65.262	66.621	40
50	67.981	69.341	70.700	72.060	73.420	74.779	76.139	77.498	78.858	80.218	50
60	81.577	82.937	84.297	85.656	87.106	88.375	89.735	91.095	92.454	93.814	60
70	95.174	96.533	97.893	99.252	100.612	101.972	103.331	104.691	106.050	107.410	70
80	108.770	110.129	111.489	112.849	114.208	115.568	116.927	118.287	119.647	121.006	80
90	122.366	123.726	125.085	126.445	127.804	129.164	130.524	131.883	133.243	134.603	90
100	135.962										100

Engineering

Compressed air

Special usage is as follows:

Pressure. On metrication, gauges are in general calibrated in bar or mbar, in place of pounds-force per square inch.

'Absolute' and 'gauge' pressure· Absolute pressure is expressed with zero pressure as the datum, and gauge pressure with atmospheric pressure as the datum. For clarity absolute and gauge pressure are specified; for example, at a gauge pressure of 1 bar. Symbols used in the United Kingdom and United States are a for absolute and g for gauge, so that pounds-force per square inch absolute is psia, and gauge psig. In German practice, the technical atmosphere symbol (at) becomes ata for absolute and atü (for über meaning gauge) for gauge.

Most compressed air equipment operates at about 6 or 7 bar gauge.

Flow. Air or gas flow under the metric system use cubic capacity per second as follows:

large compressors	m^3/s
pneumatic controls, tools, up to medium sized compressors	dm^3/s (= l/s)
fluidics	cm^3/s (= ml/s)

The usual imperial measure, cubic feet per minute relates to the metric system by:
1 ft³/min (cfm) = 0.47 dm³/s
1 dm³/s   = 2.1 ft³/min

Usual size ranges of compressors are:
Small   under 40 l/s
Medium   40–300 l/s
Large   above 300 l/s

Kinematic viscosity. In the pneumatic field, centistokes is the metric replacement for Redwood seconds, Saybolt seconds and Engler degrees (see pages 123–124 for definitions); quotation at 20 °C has the advantage that it is close to atmospheric temperature, and at the equivalent 68 °F is close to a standard Redwood viscosity temperature of 70 °F.

Specific power consumption. The shaft power input per unit of compressor capacity is measured by:
kW s/m³ = 1 000 J/m³ = J/dm³ = J/litre
A high degree of efficiency gives a low specific power consumption. Required power decreases with altitude, as shown in the following table:

Power consumption by altitude
(joules per litre or cubic decimetre)

Altitude (metres)	Pressure 4 bar (gauge)		7 bar (gauge)	
	single stage[a] J/l	two stage[b] J/l	single stage[a] J/l	two stage[b] J/l
0	258	232	349	302
300	254	229	342	296
600	251	226	336	290
900	248	221	330	284
1 200	243	218	325	280
1 500	237	214	320	273
1 800	232	210	316	268
2 100	229	205	309	262
2 400	226	200	304	256
2 700	222	197	298	251
3 000	206	186	283	237

[a]Compression from initial to final pressure is in a single step or stage.
[b]Compression from initial to final pressure is in two stages or steps with cooling between the stages.

Gears

Circular pitch = circumference/number of teeth
              = $\pi D/N$ where D is diameter and N number of teeth
Diametral pitch = N/D = π × reciprocal of circular pitch (see page 118 for a table of π).
Module = D/N where D is diameter in millimetres.

Some equivalents are:

Circular pitch in	Diametral pitch in	Module mm
0.25	12.566	2.021
0.50	6.283	4.042
0.75	4.188	6.063
1.00	3.142 (π)	8.084
1.25	2.513	10.106
1.50	2.094	12.127
1.75	1.795	14.148
2.00	1.570	16.169

Pressure angle = angle at the pitch line made by the surface of teeth with the radius passing through the same point on the pitch line. This is usually $14\frac{1}{2}°$ (with sine = 0.250 38 or approximately 0.25) or 20°.
Angle de pression = 90° − pressure angle (usually 75° or 70°).

Hydraulics

Recommended practical metric units include:
Pressure: bar
Stress: MPa or N/mm²
Rotational frequency: rev/min (SI unit is 1/s)
Volumetric flow: dm³/min = l/min (SI unit is m³/s)

Motor vehicles

Engine capacity = cylinder capacity × number of cylinders (for cars usually 4 or 6). In Europe, capacity is mainly expressed in terms of litres or cc (cubic centimetres or SI unit symbol cm³):
1 litre = 1 000 millilitres = 1 000 cubic centimetres (cc or cm³)
In the United States engine capacity is also quoted in cubic inches; for conversion from cubic inches to cubic centimetres (cm³ or cc) see page 73.

Cylinder capacity (for 1 cylinder) = swept volume
= area of cylinder bore × piston stroke (length of sweep) = $R^2 \times S$,
where R is radius of the cylinder (= $\frac{1}{2}$ bore) and S is the piston stroke (for area from radius see pages 196–199); also = $\pi \times D^2 \times S/4$, where D is the diameter or bore.

$$Compression\ ratio = \frac{V + v}{v} = \frac{\text{Maximum volume}}{\text{Minimum volume}}$$

where V is the swept volume, and v = volume of space above the piston at the top of the stroke (combustion chamber). The compression ratio is the amount by which the fuel is compressed before combustion.
The usual compression ratio for cars is between 8 and $9\frac{1}{2}$, but ratios can be higher for use with special fuels (see also octane number, page 134).

Engine power. There is no direct relationship between swept volume or compression ratio and output, since this is affected by engine duty and endurance. However, for a normal road-going engine which is tractable, durable and economical as well as giving good performance, a power output of between 40 and 60 bhp per litre is normal (tuning can give outputs up to 100 bhp or more per litre but at the expense of other features, and requiring high-octane fuels).

A turbo-charger, recycling engine exhaust gas flow, can give a power output up to about 90 bhp per litre. A typical variation is 50 bhp per litre with carburettors, 60 bhp/l with fuel injection and 90 bhp/l with turbo-charging.

Engineering

Sieves

The recommended ISO main sizes, based on rounded preferred numbers, are as follows:

micrometre series (μm)

20[a]	90	250	710
45	125	355	
63	180	500	

[a] Lowest supplementary size.

millimetre series (mm)

1.00	2.80	8.0	22.4	63.0
1.40	4.00	11.2	31.5	90.0
2.00	5.60	16.0	45.0	125

Recommended nominal sizes for woven metal wire cloth (with square apertures) are 20 μm–125 mm, and for perforated plate (square or circular apertures) are 4 mm–125 mm for square apertures and 1 mm–125 mm for round apertures.

Tubes

Nominal and outside diameter

In specifying size of tubes, nominal diameter is used as a convenient round number; this is normally only roughly related to the manufacturing size. ISO recommendations for sizes are largely based originally on imperial dimensions as these have been important internationally. In the following table a selection of size recommendations are given for nominal and corresponding outside diameter. The dimensions in millimetres and inches are 'corresponding' values, and are not necessarily exactly equivalent.

Nominal size		Outside diameter		Nominal size		Outside diameter	
mm	in	mm	in	mm	in	mm	in
6	1/8	10.2	0.402	350	14	355.6	14.000
8	1/4	13.5	0.531	400	16	406.4	16.000
10	3/8	17.2	0.677	450	18	457	18·0
15	1/2	21.3	0.840	500	20	508	20.0
20	3/4	26.9	1.059	550	22	559	22·0
25	1	33.7	1.327	600	24	610	24.0
32	1¼	42.4	1.669	650	26	660	26.0
40	1½	48.3	1.900	700	28	711	28·0
50	2	60.3	2.375	750	30	762	30.0
65	2½	76.1	3.000	800	32	813	32.0
80	3	88.9	3.500	850	34	864	34.0
90	3½	101.6	4.000	900	36	914	36.0
100	4	114.3	4.500	1000	40	1016	40.0
125	5	139.7	5.500	1200	48	1220	48.0
150	6	168.3	6.625	1400	56	1420	55.9
175[a]	7[a]	193.7[a]	7.625[a]	1600	64	1620	63.8
200	8	219.1	8.625	1800	72	1820	71.7
225[a]	9[a]	244.5[a]	9.625[a]	2000	80	2020	79.5
250	10	273	10.750	2200	88	2220	87.4
300	12	323.9	12.750				

[a] Sizes to be avoided if possible.

Thickness

The range of thicknesses of wall for general UK use is from 1.2 mm (0.048 in) to 32.0 mm (1.26 in).

Vacuum systems

Old units for the measurement of the rate of leak were:

clusec = 1 centilitre per second at a pressure of 1 millitorr (mtorr cl/s)
lusec = 1 litre per second at a pressure of 1 millitorr (mtorr l/s)
100 clusec = 1 lusec
1000 lusec = 1 torr litre per second (torr l/s)

Metric equivalents:

clusec = 1.333 22 μN m/s
lusec = 133.322 μN m/s
torr l/s = 0.133 322 N m/s

Wire

Special measure: the circular mil (see page 18) is used for wire. For weight of steel wire, see page 154.

Wire gauges (also for sheet metal and wall thickness of tubes)
BG = Birmingham Sheet and Hoop Iron Gauge (former legal system in the United Kingdom)
BWG = Birmingham Wire Gauge (also called Stubs Iron Wire Gauge)
SWG = British Standard Wire Gauge (former legal system in the United Kingdom)
USG = US standard gauge for sheet and plate
AWG = American Wire Gauge (also called B & S = Brown & Sharpe), for electric wire
Stubs' SW = Stubs' Steel Wire Gauge, for soft wire.

International standards do not recognise gauge systems, and gauges have in general been replaced in the United Kingdom by the internationally agreed metric series based on preferred numbers. This is the legal standard in the United Kingdom, the two previously legalised gauges, BG and SWG, having been replaced legally from 1964 (following the Weights and Measures Act 1963). The following table shows the international range for wire diameters, based on the series of R40 preferred numbers; an approximate equivalent in the BG and SWG systems is shown for purpose of comparison.

Metric standard R 40		BG			SWG		
mm	in	gauge no	in	mm	gauge no	in	mm
0.0200	0.00079						
0.0212	0.00083						
0.0224	0.00088						
0.0236	0.00093	52	0.00095	0.0241			
0.0250	0.00098				50	0.0010	0.0254
0.0265	0.00104	51	0.00107	0.0272			
0.0280	0.00110						
0.0300	0.00118	50	0.00120	0.0305	49	0.0012	0.0305
0.0315	0.00124						
0.0335	0.00132	49	0.00135	0.0343			
0.0355	0.00140						
0.0375	0.00148	48	0.00152	0.0386	48	0.0016	0.0406
0.0400	0.00157						
0.0425	0.00167	47	0.00170	0.0432			
0.0450	0.00177						
0.0475	0.00187	46	0.00192	0.049	47	0.0020	0.051
0.050	0.00197						
0.053	0.00209	45	0.00215	0.055			
0.056	0.00220						
0.060	0.00236	44	0.00242	0.061	46	0.0024	0.061
0.063	0.00248						
0.067	0.00264	43	0.00272	0.069	45	0.0028	0.071
0.071	0.00280						
0.075	0.00295	42	0.00306	0.078	44	0.0032	0.081
0.080	0.00315						
0.085	0.00335	41	0.00343	0.087	43	0.0036	0.091
0.090	0.00354						
0.095	0.00374	40	0.00386	0.098	42	0.0040	0.102
0.100	0.0039						
0.106	0.0042	39	0.0043	0.109	41	0.0044	0.112
0.112	0.0044						
0.118	0.0046	38	0.0048	0.122	40	0.0048	0.122
0.125	0.0049						
0.132	0.0052	37	0.0054	0.137	39	0.0052	0.132
0.140	0.0055						
0.150	0.0059	36	0.0061	0.155	38	0.0060	0.152
0.160	0.0063						
0.170	0.0067	35	0.0069	0.175	37	0.0068	0.173
0.180	0.0071						
0.190	0.0075	34	0.0077	0.196	36	0.0076	0.193
0.200	0.0079						
0.212	0.0083				35	0.0084	0.213
0.224	0.0088	33	0.0087	0.221			
0.236	0.0093				34	0.0092	0.237
0.250	0.0098	32	0.0098	0.249			
0.265	0.0104				33	0.0100	0.254
0.280	0.0110	31	0.0110	0.279	32	0.0108	0.274

Engineering

Wire diameter (cont)

Metric standard R 40 mm	in	BG gauge no	in	mm	SWG gauge no	in	mm
0.300	0.0118				31	0.0116	0.295
0.315	0.0124	30	0.0123	0.312	30	0.0124	0.315
0.335	0.0132						
0.355	0.0140	29	0.0139	0.353	29	0.0136	0.345
0.375	0.0148				28	0.0148	0.376
0.400	0.0157	28	0.0156	0.397			
0.425	0.0167				27	0.0164	0.417
0.450	0.0177	27	0.0174	0.443			
0.475	0.0187				26	0.018	0.457
0.50	0.0197	26	0.0196	0.498	25	0.020	0.508
0.53	0.0209						
0.56	0.0220	25	0.0220	0.560	24	0.022	0.559
0.60	0.0236						
0.63	0.0248	24	0.0248	0.629	23	0.024	0.610
0.67	0.0264						
0.71	0.0280	23	0.0278	0.707	22	0.028	0.711
0.75	0.0295						
0.80	0.0315	22	0.0312	0.794	21	0.032	0.813
0.85	0.0335						
0.90	0.0354	21	0.0349	0.886	20	0.036	0.914
0.95	0.0374						
1.00	0.0394	20	0.0392	0.996			
1.06	0.0417				19	0.040	1.016
1.12	0.0441	19	0.0440	1.118			
1.18	0.0465				18	0.048	1.219
1.25	0.0492	18	0.0495	1.257			
1.32	0.0520						
1.40	0.0551	17	0.0556	1.412	17	0.056	1.422
1.50	0.0591						
1.60	0.0630	16	0.0625	1.588	16	0.064	1.626
1.70	0.0669						
1.80	0.0709	15	0.0699	1.775	15	0.072	1.829
1.90	0.0748						
2.00	0.0787	14	0.0785	1.994			
2.12	0.0835				14	0.080	2.032
2.24	0.0882	13	0.0882	2.240			
2.36	0.0929				13	0.092	2.337
2.50	0.0984	12	0.0991	2.517			
2.65	0.1043				12	0.104	2.642
2.80	0.1102	11	0.1113	2.827			
3.00	0.1181				11	0.116	2.946
3.15	0.1240	10	0.1250	3.175			
3.35	0.1319				10	0.128	3.251
3.55	0.1398	9	0.1398	3.551			
3.75	0.1476				9	0.144	3.658
4.00	0.1575	8	0.1570	3.988	8	0.160	4.064
4.25	0.1673						
4.50	0.1772	7	0.1764	4.481	7	0.176	4.470
4.75	0.1870						
5.00	0.1969	6	0.1981	5.032	6	0.192	4.877
5.30	0.2087				5	0.212	5.385
5.60	0.2205	5	0.2225	5.652			
6.00	0.2362				4	0.232	5.893
6.30	0.2480	4	0.2500	6.350			
6.70	0.2638				3	0.252	6.401
7.10	0.2795	3	0.2804	7.122	2	0.276	7.010
7.50	0.2953				1	0.300	7.620
8.00	0.3150	2	0.3147	7.993	0	0.324	8.230
8.50	0.3346				2/0	0.348	8.839
9.00	0.3543	1	0.3532	8.971			
9.50	0.3740				3/0	0.372	9.449
10.00	0.3937	0	0.3964	10.07	4/0	0.4	10.16

Food

Measures

Size of packages

Trade sizes for solid foodstuffs in the United Kingdom are based on imperial and metric sizes with gradual conversion to the metric units. Recommended sizes for the metric system, as agreed by the Tripartite Committee for Standardisation (France, West Germany and the United Kingdom) in 1970 are (with very rough equivalents in lb for some units):

25 g	125 g (replacing ¼ lb)	1 kg (replacing 2 lb)
50 g	250 g (replacing ½ lb)	1.5 kg[a]
75 g[a]	375 g[a]	2 kg (replacing 4 lb)
	500 g (replacing 1 lb)	3 kg (replacing 6 lb)
	750 g[a]	4 kg (replacing 9 lb)
		5 kg (replacing 11 lb)

[a] Recommended only for transitional period.

Metric sizes in the United Kingdom

Following are some of the main changes in foodstuffs which have taken place in the United Kingdom.

Butter and margarine sold prepacked was changed to metric quantities from August 27, 1979, and lard and other cooking fats from December 30, 1979. The new pack sizes are:
125 g replacing 4 oz (113 g)
250 g replacing 8 oz (227 g)
500 g replacing 1 lb (454 g)

Tea prepacked for retail sale could only be made up in metric form from December 31, 1979, with the last day for retail sale in imperial sizes being June 29, 1980. The main new sizes are:
125 g replacing 4 oz (113 g)
250 g replacing 8 oz (227 g)
The full metric range permitted for tea is: 50 g, 125 g, 250 g, 500 g, 750 g, 1 kg, 1.5 kg, 2 kg, 2.5 kg, 3 kg, 4 kg and 5 kg; there is no restriction up to 25 g and over 5 kg.

Instant coffee was allowed to be sold in metric form from July 1, 1979. The main new sizes are:
50 g replacing 2 oz (56 g)
100 g replacing 4 oz (113 g)
200 g replacing 8 oz (227 g)
500 g replacing 1 lb (454 g)
750 g replacing 1½ lb (680 g)

Metric sizes for *sugar* used in the United Kingdom from October 1, 1975, include those in the Tripartite list from 125 g, excluding 375 g, and with the addition of a 2.5 kg size (approximately 5 lb).

For *chocolate* in the form of bars weighing between 85 g and 500 g, the EEC has agreed the following marketing sizes, effective for the United Kingdom from August 1, 1976:

100 g	200 g	400 g
125 g	250 g	500 g
150 g	300 g	

In the weighing out of confectionery, it is possible that the ¼ lb will be replaced in due course, as recommended above, by 125 g.

For *bread*, the authorised UK weights for standard loaves are 400 g (14.1 oz) for small loaves and 800 g (28.2 oz) for large loaves (previously authorised imperial weights were 14 oz and 28 oz).

Unit pricing is a method of pricing which gives, in addition to or in place of the usual price per package, the price per unit of weight or capacity; for example, packages would be marked, under unit pricing, with a figure such as the price in pence per ¼ lb or 100 g, etc.

Food

Size of equipment

The range of metric sizes for general use is:

Cups ('measures')	Spoons
50 ml (1/6)	1.25 ml
75 ml ($\frac{1}{4}$)	2.5 ml
100 ml ($\frac{1}{3}$)	5 ml
150 ml ($\frac{1}{2}$)	10 ml
300 ml (full)	15 ml
	20 ml

The 150 ml size is roughly the UK 'teacup' size of 5 fl oz. and the 300 ml size the 'tumbler' size of 10 fl oz. Also, roughly, the 5 ml spoon (used in pharmaceutical measures) is the 'teaspoon' of $\frac{1}{8}$ fl oz, and the 15 ml spoon the 'tablespoon' of $\frac{1}{2}$ fl oz.
The 150 ml cup holds roughly 150 g of sugar and 100 g of flour.

United States sizes

1 cup	= $\frac{1}{2}$ US liq pt (237 ml)
1 teaspoon	= $1\frac{1}{3}$ US liq drams (4.9 ml)
1 tablespoon	= 4 US liq drams (14.8 ml)

Energy and nutrient requirement

The dieticians' 'calorie' (Cal) is the kilocalorie ('large' calorie or kcal), based on 15°C; this is the heat energy required to raise the temperature of 1 kilogram of water through one degree celsius from 14.5°C to 15.5°C (also see page 131). For SI units, 1 Cal = 4.185 5 kJ, 1 000 Cal = 4.185 5 MJ.

Energy sources

Average approximate estimates for the energy values ('calorific' value) of different foods are as follows:

	Cal/oz	Cal/g	kJ/g
Protein	113	4.0	17
Fat	250	9.0	37
Carbohydrate	106	3.7	16
Ethyl alcohol	200	7.0	29

Energy expenditure

Average rates of energy expenditure are as follows (for the FAO reference man and woman as described below, mean annual temperature 10°C):

	Men Cal	kJ	Women Cal	kJ
Working activities	2.5	10.5	1.8	7.7
Non-occupational:				
rest in bed (basal metabolic rate)	1.0	4.2	0.9	3.7
sitting	1.5	6.4	1.4	5.9
washing, dressing, etc.	3.0	12.6	2.5	10.5
active recreation and/or domestic work	5.2	21.8	3.5	14.6
walking	5.3	22.2	3.6	15.1
swimming, jogging	10	42	9	37

Recommended daily intakes

The *'FAO reference man'* weighs 65 kg, is aged 25 years and is moderately active; he is estimated to require on average per day 3 200 Cal (13.4 MJ). The *'FAO reference woman'* is also 25 and weighs 55 kg; she is estimated to require 2 300 Cal (9.6 MJ) daily.

The energy requirement varies according to temperature; for the FAO reference adults this is as follows, where the reference adult is taken to live in an average annual temperature of 10°C:

Average temperature (annual external) Celsius (degrees)	Energy requirement per day			
	Men Cal	MJ	Women Cal	MJ
−5	3 344	14.0	2 404	10.1
0	3 296	13.8	2 369	9.9
5	3 248	13.6	2 335	9.8
10	3 200	13.4	2 300	9.6
15	3 120	13.1	2 243	9.4
20	3 040	12.7	2 185	9.1
25	2 960	12.4	2 128	8.9

The following table gives the usual recommended average intakes per day of energy ('calories') and protein, based on UK requirements. For energy, the figures are shown in calories and in MJ (= 1 000 kJ).

Age range (years)	Occupation type	Body weight kg	Energy: Cal (= $kcal_{15}$)	MJ	Protein g
Boys					
Under 1		8	800	3.3	20
1		11	1 200	5.0	30
2		13	1 400	5.8	35
3–4		16	1 550	6.5	39
5–6		20	1 730	7.2	43
7–8		25	1 980	8.3	49
9–11		32	2 300	9.5	57
12–14		45	2 600	11.0	66
15–17		61	2 900	12.0	72
Girls					
Under 1		7	720	3.0	18
1		10	1 100	4.5	27
2		13	1 300	5.5	32
3–4		16	1 500	6.3	37
5–6		20	1 670	7.0	42
7–8		25	1 900	8.0	47
9–11		33	2 050	8.5	51
12–14		49	2 150	9.0	53
15–17		55	2 150	9.0	53
Men					
18–34	Sedentary	65	2 500	10.5	63
	Moderately active		2 900	12.0	72
	Very active		3 400	14.0	84
35–64	Sedentary	65	2 400	10.0	60
	Moderately active		2 750	11.5	69
	Very active		3 350	14.0	84
65–74	Sedentary	63	2 400	10.0	60
75 and over	Sedentary	63	2 150	9.0	54
Women					
18–54	Most occupations	55	2 150	9.0	54
	Very active		2 500	10.5	62
55–74	Sedentary	53	1 900	8.0	47
75 and over	Sedentary	53	1 670	7.0	42

Food

An individual's total daily energy requirement is not closely related to body weight, although, for example, the energy cost of walking is directly proportional to body weight. Some variations of metabolic (resting) rate requirement by weight are: at 64 kg, 7.1 MJ; 70 kg, 7.5 MJ; 84 kg, 8.4 MJ. To obtain body weight in kilograms from pounds see page 77.

Generally, an average long-term level of 1 800 calories (7.5 MJ) per day is considered an absolute minimum ration. This is slightly above the normal values for resting metabolism, which are roughly as follows per day for the United Kingdom:

Age range (years)	Cal	MJ	Age range (years)	Cal	MJ
Boys and girls			*Men*		
Under 1	400	1.7	18–34	1 600	6.7
1	600	2.5	35–64	1 500	6.3
2	700	2.9	65–74	1 450	6.1
3–4	800	3.3	75 and over	1 350	5.7
5–6	900	3.8	*Women*		
7–8	1 000	4.2	18–54	1 300	5.4
Boys			55–74 years	1 200	5.0
9–11	1 200	5.0	75 and over	1 100	4.6
12–14	1 400	5.9			
15–17	1 700	7.1			
Girls					
9–11	1 150	4.8			
12–14	1 400	5.9			
15–17	1 400	5.9			

For vitamin requirements see the section on health (page 152).

Food content

The general permitted level of lead in food is 1 milligram per kilogram (1 mg/kg) for the United Kingdom (new level reduced from 2 mg/kg from April 12, 1980). For fish the permitted level is 2 mg/kg and for shellfish 10 mg/kg.

Footwear

Heavy leather is measured in irons in the United Kingdom, footwear and clothing leathers in millimetres, and light flexible leathers in ounces; where iron = 1/48 in, ounce = 1/64 in.

A summary of the relationships is shown in the following table; also see page 68 for a detailed table showing the conversion from fractions of an inch to millimetres.

Fractions of an inch	Millimetres	Irons	Ounces
1/64	0.4	$\frac{3}{4}$	1
1/32	0.8	$1\frac{1}{2}$	2
3/64	1.2	$2\frac{1}{4}$	3
1/16	1.6	3	4
5/64	2.0	$3\frac{3}{4}$	5
3/32	2.4	$4\frac{1}{2}$	6
7/64	2.8	$5\frac{1}{4}$	7
1/8	3.2	6	8
9/64	3.6	$6\frac{3}{4}$	9
5/32	4.0	$7\frac{1}{2}$	10
11/64	4.4	$8\frac{1}{4}$	11
3/16	4.8	9	12
13/64	5.2	$9\frac{3}{4}$	13
7/32	5.6	$10\frac{1}{2}$	14
15/64	6.0	$11\frac{1}{4}$	15
1/4	6.4	12	16
17/64	6.7	$12\frac{3}{4}$	17
9/32	7.1	$13\frac{1}{2}$	18

Use of leather: see hides and skins, page 113.

Shoe sizes

European continental sizes are usually measured by the Paris-point (PP):
3 Paris-points = 20 millimetres;
1 Paris-point = 6.7 millimetres = approximately 4/15 inch.

A broad comparison of UK and European continental sizes follows:

UK sizes	European continental sizes	Millimetres length
Infants		
$\frac{1}{2}$	15.87	106
1	16.51	110
$1\frac{1}{2}$	17.14	114
2	17.78	118
$2\frac{1}{2}$	18.41	123
3	19.05	127
$3\frac{1}{2}$	19.68	131
4	20.32	136
$4\frac{1}{2}$	20.95	140
5	21.59	144
$5\frac{1}{2}$	22.22	148
6	22.86	152
Children		
$6\frac{1}{2}$	23.49	157
7	24.13	161
$7\frac{1}{2}$	24.76	165
8	25.40	169
$8\frac{1}{2}$	26.03	174
9	26.67	178
$9\frac{1}{2}$	27.30	182
10	27.94	186
Boys or girls		
$10\frac{1}{2}$	28.57	190
11	29.21	195
$11\frac{1}{2}$	29.84	199
12	30.48	203
$12\frac{1}{2}$	31.11	207
13	31.75	212
$13\frac{1}{2}$	32.38	216
1	33.02	220
Youths or maids		
$1\frac{1}{2}$	33.65	224
2	34.29	229
$2\frac{1}{2}$	34.92	233
3	35.56	237
$3\frac{1}{2}$	36.19	241
Men or ladies		
4	36.83	246
$4\frac{1}{2}$	37.46	250
5	38.10	254
$5\frac{1}{2}$	38.73	258
6	39.37	262
$6\frac{1}{2}$	40.00	267
7	40.64	271
$7\frac{1}{2}$	41.27	275
8	41.91	279
$8\frac{1}{2}$	42.54	284
9	43.18	288
$9\frac{1}{2}$	43.81	292
10	44.45	296
$10\frac{1}{2}$	45.08	301
11	45.72	305
$11\frac{1}{2}$	46.35	309
12	46.99	313
$12\frac{1}{2}$	47.62	318
13	48.26	322
$13\frac{1}{2}$	48.89	326
14	49.53	330

American women's sizes are approximately $1\frac{1}{2}$ up on the UK sizes, so that, for example, 5 UK equals $6\frac{1}{2}$ American. American men's sizes are approximately $\frac{1}{2}$ higher than the UK equivalent.

Footwear

Mondopoint shoe sizes

The Mondopoint shoe sizing system is an internationally agreed standard, providing length and width of the foot in millimetres.
Length is defined as the distance between the end of the most prominent toe and the most prominent part of the heel, measured with the person standing (with weight equally distributed) and wearing appropriate hose.
Width is defined as the horizontal distance between the outside of the foot at the first and fifth metatarsophalangeal joints, which is generally the broadest part of the foot.
Length markings are expressed in whole numbers, in millimetres; these are in multiples of 5 mm or of 7.5 mm (0.5 being rounded down). The origin of the scale is zero, and the main 5 mm series runs from 105 by 5 mm to 300 mm. The main part of the series of 7.5 mm intervals is as follows:

20	150	180	210	240	270	300
27	157	187	217	247	277	
35	165	195	225	255	285	
42	172	202	232	262	292	

Width markings are also expressed in whole numbers, in millimetres.
Measurements are expressed with the length first; for example 215/82.

Health

Blood

Properties (human blood)

Relative density (at 25°C) = 1.05–1.06
Relative viscosity (at 38°C) = 5–6 (times that of water)
Average temperature = 37°C
Acidity = 7.35–7.45 pH (where 7 is neutral, 0–7 means acidic, 7–14 alkaline)
Coagulation time = $5\frac{1}{2}$–$12\frac{1}{2}$ min
Red blood cell count = 4.0 to 6.0 million per mm³ (average of $4\frac{1}{2}$ mn for women and 5 mn for men per mm³)
White blood cell count = 4 000 to 10 000 per mm³ (increases up to 20 000 with violent physical exertion)
Diameter (red blood cell) = 7 micrometres (μm)

Volume and content

Volume: blood makes up 70 ml per 1 kg of human body weight. For the average man of 65 kg (about 10 stones) this amounts to about 4 litres.
Content: under the UK Road Traffic Act 1972, the prescribed limit of alcohol over which it is not permissible to drive is 80 mg of alcohol per 100 ml of blood. A single whisky or half-pint beer produces about 15–20 mg per 100 ml, a bottle of whisky about 600 mg per 100 ml. The body can eliminate about 15–20 mg of alcohol per 100 ml of blood in 1 hour.
Groups: the main blood groups are determined by the presence or absence of inherited substances ('antigens') A and B. The main groups are:

Group	Antigens present	Possible donors	Incidence (approximate %) UK	USA
A	A	A and O	45	41
B	B	B and O	9	10
AB	A and B	any	3	4
O	neither	O	43	45

Concentration

With the change to SI units, substance concentration, traditionally measured in grams or submultiples of grams per litre or submultiples of litres, is to be measured in moles or submultiples of moles per litre, where the relative molecular or atomic mass is known.
Examples of the main types of units used, in traditional and new form, are as follows:
g/dl will usually be expressed in terms of pmol/l
mg/dl will usually be expressed in terms of μmol/l
mg/dl will usually be expressed in terms of μmol/l or mmol/l
μg/dl will usually be expressed in terms of μmol/l or mmol/l
g/l will usually be expressed in terms of mmol/l

The actual conversion rate depends on the substance concerned, and its atomic or molecular mass. Some examples of conversion rates are as follows:

Substance	Conversion rates		Atomic or molecular mass[a]
Cholesterol	1 g/l	= 2.586 mmol/l,	386.660
	1 mmol/l	= 0.386 7 g/l	
Glucose	1 mg/dl	= 0.055 51 mmol/l,	180.157
	1 mmol/l	= 18.02 mg/dl	
Iron	1 μg/dl	= 0.1791 μmol/l,	55.847
	1 μmol/l	= 5.585 μg/dl	
Lead	1 μg/l	= 0.004 826 μmol/l	207.2
	1 μmol/l	= 207.2 μg/l	

[a] Or 'atomic weight'; see pages 120–121 for a list of atomic weights for all elements.

It may be noted that, for the same multiples of grams and moles, the conversion between moles and grams is the atomic mass or weight, and the conversion between grams and moles its reciprocal (see above, for example, for the lead conversions).

Genetics

Chromosome
A chromosome is a structure in the nucleus of animal cells, containing the thread of DNA (Deoxyribonucleic acid) which transmits genetic information. Number of chromosomes normally in humans: 46 (in 23 pairs).

Coefficient of inbreeding
This is the probability that an individual will have inherited identical genetic traits.
Examples are, for a brother and sister 1 in 4 (coefficient of 0.25), for first cousins 1 in 16 (coefficient of 0.0625).
For a whole population of a large country, the coefficient is virtually zero.

Heart

Properties

Normal heart beat = 70–72 beats per min (can vary from 50–90)
Blood propelled = 60–100 ml per beat
Oxygen consumption of the body = 250 ml per minute for an average man at rest

Blood pressure

Average human blood pressures are:

	mm Hg	kPa
Diastolic[a]	70–90	9–12
Systolic[b]: children	100	13
young adults	100–140	13–19
adults over 40 years	100 + age	13 + (age/7) approx

[a] When the heart is relaxed. [b] When the heart is contracted at each heart beat, forcing blood through the arteries. The systolic blood pressure is taken normally when the human concerned is resting, and values are given here on this basis; strenuous activity can increase systolic blood pressure above this 'normal' level by 60–80 mm Hg (8–11 kPa).

Blood pressures are usually written with the systolic over the diastolic; for example, as 140/90. Traditionally blood pressures have been measured in millimetres of mercury (using a sphygmomanometer); the SI unit recommended as a replacement is the kilopascal (kPa). A table of conversions is shown on the following page.

Vascular resistance, previously measured by dyn second per cubic centimetre (dyn s/cm³) or millimetre of mercury minute per litre (mm Hg min/l), is to be replaced with the SI unit of kilopascal second per litre (kPa s/l), where:
1 dyn s/cm³ = 0.1 kPa s/l
1 mm Hg min/l = 8 kPa s/l

Millimetres of mercury to Kilopascals   1 mm Hg = 0.133 322 kPa

mm Hg →	0	1	2	3	4	5	6	7	8	9	← mm Hg
↓	kPa	kPa	kPa	kPa	kPa	kPa	kPa	kPa	kPa	kPa	↓
0	0.000	0.133	0.267	0.400	0.533	0.667	0.800	0.933	1.067	1.200	0
10	1.33	1.47	1.60	1.73	1.87	2.00	2.13	2.27	2.40	2.53	10
20	2.67	2.80	2.93	3.07	3.20	3.33	3.47	3.60	3.73	3.87	20
30	4.00	4.13	4.27	4.40	4.53	4.67	4.80	4.93	5.07	5.20	30
40	5.33	5.47	5.60	5.73	5.87	6.00	6.13	6.27	6.40	6.53	40
50	6.67	6.80	6.93	7.07	7.20	7.33	7.47	7.60	7.73	7.87	50
60	8.00	8.13	8.27	8.40	8.53	8.67	8.80	8.93	9.07	9.20	60
70	9.33	9.47	9.60	9.73	9.87	10.00	10.13	10.27	10.40	10.53	70
80	10.7	10.8	10.9	11.1	11.2	11.3	11.5	11.6	11.7	11.9	80
90	12.0	12.1	12.3	12.4	12.5	12.7	12.8	12.9	13.1	13.2	90
100	13.3	13.5	13.6	13.7	13.9	14.0	14.1	14.3	14.4	14.5	100
110	14.7	14.8	14.9	15.1	15.2	15.3	15.5	15.6	15.7	15.9	110
120	16.0	16.1	16.3	16.4	16.5	16.7	16.8	16.9	17.1	17.2	120
130	17.3	17.5	17.6	17.7	17.9	18.0	18.1	18.3	18.4	18.5	130
140	18.7	18.8	18.9	19.1	19.2	19.3	19.5	19.6	19.7	19.9	140
150	20.0	20.1	20.3	20.4	20.5	20.7	20.8	20.9	21.1	21.2	150
160	21.3	21.5	21.6	21.7	21.9	22.0	22.1	22.3	22.4	22.5	160
170	22.7	22.8	22.9	23.1	23.2	23.3	23.5	23.6	23.7	23.9	170
180	24.0	24.1	24.3	24.4	24.5	24.7	24.8	24.9	25.1	25.2	180
190	25.3	25.5	25.6	25.7	25.9	26.0	26.1	26.3	26.4	26.5	190
200	26.7	26.8	26.9	27.1	27.2	27.3	27.5	27.6	27.7	27.9	200
210	28.0	28.1	28.3	28.4	28.5	28.7	28.8	28.9	29.1	29.2	210
220	29.3	29.5	29.6	29.7	29.9	30.0	30.1	30.3	30.4	30.5	220
230	30.7	30.8	30.9	31.1	31.2	31.3	31.5	31.6	31.7	31.9	230
240	32.0	32.1	32.3	32.4	32.5	32.7	32.8	32.9	33.1	33.2	240
250	33.3	33.5	33.6	33.7	33.9	34.0	34.1	34.3	34.4	34.5	250
260	34.7	34.8	34.9	35.1	35.2	35.3	35.5	35.6	35.7	35.9	260
270	36.0	36.1	36.3	36.4	36.5	36.7	36.8	36.9	37.1	37.2	270
280	37.3	37.5	37.6	37.7	37.9	38.0	38.1	38.3	38.4	38.5	280
290	38.7	38.8	38.9	39.1	39.2	39.3	39.5	39.6	39.7	39.9	290
300	40.0	40.1	40.3	40.4	40.5	40.7	40.8	40.9	41.1	41.2	300

Kilopascals to Millimetres of mercury   1 kPa = 7.500 616 mm Hg

kPa →	0	1	2	3	4	5	6	7	8	9	← kPa
↓	mm Hg	mm Hg	mm Hg	mm Hg	mm Hg	mm Hg	mm Hg	mm Hg	mm Hg	mm Hg	↓
0	0.0	7.5	15.0	22.5	30.0	37.5	45.0	52.5	60.0	67.5	0
10	75.0	82.5	90.0	97.5	105.0	112.5	120.0	127.5	135.0	142.5	10
20	150	158	165	173	180	188	195	203	210	218	20
30	225	233	240	248	255	263	270	278	285	293	30
40	300	308	315	323	330	338	345	353	360	368	40

Radiation

Radiation is a general term used to describe all waves or rays in the electromagnetic spectrum and also some types of atomic particles; there are two main types of radiation, depending on whether the radiation is ionising or not:
Non-ionising radiation, such as radio and light radiation, is only harmful in high intensities: for example from radio transmitters or lasers (highly concentrated light) or intense rays from nuclear blasts; this may cause burning or charring, etc.
Ionising radiation is radiation which can knock an orbital electron out of an atom to leave a positive ion (charged atom or molecule). Since the orbital electrons are involved in bonding atoms into molecules, ionising radiation can lead to the disruption of the molecule; in living tissue this can interfere with normal cell biochemistry (and in other materials changes in colour or shape, etc can occur).

The two main kinds of ionising radiation are:
directly ionising radiation, such as charged particles (alpha and beta particles, fission fragments, protons, etc); and indirectly ionising radiation, which carries no electric charge, such as neutrons and electromagnetic radiation. Electromagnetic radiation exists in discreet packets called photons.

Whether electromagnetic radiation is ionising or not depends on whether it has sufficient energy to remove an outer orbital electron; the energy required for this is about 30 eV. For electromagnetic radiation, the relationship between frequency and the energy of the photon is given by the equation $E = hy$, where E is the energy of the photon, y is the frequency of the electromagnetic radiation, and h is the Planck constant:
$h = 6.626\,176 \times 10^{-34}$ J Hz^{-1} = $4.135\,7 \times 10^{-15}$ eV Hz^{-1}.
The ionising minimum level of 30 eV corresponds to a frequency of about 7×10^{15} Hz, that is, just after the end of the visible light range and beginning of the ultraviolet range; lower frequency radiations (light, infrared and radio waves) have too little energy to cause ionisation (although they may affect special photoelectric materials). Energy per photon for the ionising levels of radiation is shown in the following table:

	Frequency (hertz)		Energy per photon		
Ultraviolet	1×10^{15} to	6×10^{16}	4 eV	to	250 eV
X-rays	6×10^{16} to	3×10^{20}	250 eV	to	1 200 000 eV
Gamma rays	3×10^{18} to	3×10^{24}	12 000 eV	to	12 000 MeV

Health

Measures

Radioactivity

Radioactive substances are those in which the nuclei of atoms are disintegrating spontaneously, emitting ionising radiation. Radioactivity occurs naturally (eg in uranium and thorium, potassium, potassium-40 and carbon-14) or can be induced artificially by bombardment with radiation (eg by neutrons in a reactor, or by electrons in an X-ray or TV tube). Each radioactive nucleus (radioisotope) has a characteristic half-life, the time taken for any amount of radioactivity to be reduced to half that amount by radioactive disintegration. Hence in 2 half-lives the radioactivity is reduced to one-quarter of the original level, and so on. There are many different radioisotopes and their half-lives vary from fractions of a second to millions of years; for example, radium-216 has a half-life of 0.18 microseconds and another isotope of the same element, radium-226 has a half-life of 1 600 years (also see page 120).

The main unit of measurement for radioactivity has been the Curie (Ci), originally defined as the disintegration rate of the quantity of radon gas in equilibrium with one gram of radium; later a precise disintegration rate was fixed at a level close to that of the earlier definition:

1 Ci = 3.7×10^{10} disintegrations per second.

Another old unit was the rutherford (rd or Rd) = 1×10^6 disintegrations per second.

In 1975 a new unit was recommended for use as an SI unit in this field: the becquerel (Bq) = 1 disintegration per second.
Relationships are:

1 Ci = 3.7×10^{10} Bq = 3.7×10^4 MBq
1 Bq = 2.7×10^{-11} Ci = 0.027 nCi
1 rutherford = 10^6 Bq = 1 MBq
1 Bq = 10^{-6} rutherford.

Concentration of radioactivity in SI terms is usually expressed in MBq/mm³.

Exposure

Radiation exposure is measured by the amount of ionisation in air. The unit is the röntgen (R or sometimes r) = the quantity of X or gamma radiation such that the associated corpuscular emission per 0.001 293 gram of air, produces, in air, ions carrying 1 electrostatic unit of quantity of electricity of either sign.

In 1975 the SI recommended unit became the coulomb per kilogram (C/kg), where:

1 R = 2.58×10^{-4} C/kg = 0.258 mC/kg
1 C/kg = 3.876×10^3 R.

The exposure rate is expressed as röntgen per unit time, usually per second or hour (R/s or R/h or sometimes rps or rph); the SI unit for exposure rate is coulomb per kilogram per second, that is, C/(kg s).

Dose

Radiation exposure, as measured by röntgen in terms of the amount of ionisation in air, is not directly related to the amounts absorbed by different materials. The *unit of absorbed dose* is the measure of the amount of energy absorbed by material exposed to radiation. The main unit has been the rad (rad or rd), or radiation absorbed dose = 10 millijoules per kilogram (10 mJ/kg) or 100 ergs per gram.

In 1975 the SI recommended unit became the gray (Gy) = 1 joule per kilogram (J/kg), where

1 rad = 0.01 Gy, 1 Gy = 100 rad.

The amount of absorbed dose in rads is very approximately the same as the exposure in röntgen, one röntgen giving an absorbed dose of approximately 0.93 rad in soft human tissue.

The absorbed dose rate is expressed as rad or gray per unit time; for example, rad/s or Gy/s.

The rad or gray are suitable units for measuring the amount of biological damage caused by electromagnetic radiation and beta particles, as the damage from those radiations is roughly proportional to the amount of energy deposited. However, other more heavily ionised particles have a proportionately greater effect and a further unit is used to measure biological damage where such particles are present. This is the *unit of dose equivalent*, the rem (rad equivalent man), which is equal to the rad, as weighted by quality factors (Q) which give for each type of radiation a weighting proportional to the risk of causing malignancies: 1 rem = 1 rad × Q

where Q = 1 for electromagnetic radiation and beta particles
Q = 10 for fission neutrons and protons
Q = 20 for alpha particles, heavy recoil particles and fission fragments

Further, where only part of the body is exposed to radiation, or different parts are exposed differently, the International Commission for Radiological Protection (ICRP) recommend weighting factors to apply to different parts of the body to obtain an 'effective whole body dose equivalent'. Where W_T is the weighting factor of the organ or tissue T, then:

effective whole body dose equivalent = Σ dose equivalent of T (in rem) × W_T

The recommended weights are:

Organ or tissue	W_T
Reproductive organs	0.25
Breast	0.15
Red bone marrow	0.12
Lung	0.12
Thyroid	0.03
Bone surfaces	0.03
Other tissues (each)[a]	0.06

[a]Applied to the next five organs or tissues receiving the highest doses, where the stomach, small intestine, upper large intestine and lower large intestine are treated as four separate organs.

A new unit for measuring dose equivalent which is being considered for recommendation as an SI unit is the sievert (Sv), which is the amount of radiation of any kind estimated to produce the same effect in man as 1 gray of X rays or gamma rays:

1 Sv = 1 J/kg
1 Sv = 100 rem
1 rem = 0.01 Sv = 10 mSv.

The weighting factors shown above would apply to the sievert as to the rem. The dose equivalent rate is expressed as rem or sievert per unit time:

3 600 rem per hour = 1 rem per second
1 rem per hour = 10 mSv per hour

Amounts of radiation

Radioactivity

Examples of large amounts of radioactivity are as follows:
A nuclear accident may produce radiation of about
30 000 curies (3×10^4 Ci) = 1 petabecquerel (1×10^{15} Bq).
A nuclear submarine produces waste which could release about
100 000 curies (1×10^5 Ci) = 4 petabecquerel (4×10^{15} Bq).
A nuclear weapon can produce in a nuclear fission detonation, per kiloton of bomb power (also see weapons, pages 173–174):
300 million curies (3×10^8 Ci) = 10 exabecquerel (1×10^{19} Bq)

Exposure

The exposure rate from a nuclear fission detonation varies according to the nature of the surface, and is from 7–12 R per hour per square metre for every curie of activity (6–10 R per hour per square yard).

Dose

For general purposes, the röntgen produces an absorbed dose of about 1 rad, which is roughly equal to 1 rem when considering nuclear explosions.

For a dose of radiation received quickly, the lethal level is roughly 350–550 rem ($3\frac{1}{2}$–$5\frac{1}{2}$ sievert) with an average level of 450 rem ($4\frac{1}{2}$ sievert). A War Emergency Dose (WED) has been set for the United Kingdom at 75 rem ($\frac{3}{4}$ sievert), being the level to which persons could be exposed in carrying out essential tasks; in some circumstances, a level of 150 rem ($1\frac{1}{2}$ sievert) could be absorbed over a period of 7 days.

The recovery rate for a human being is about 10 rem (0.1 sievert) per day.

The average dose to the UK population is about 160 millirem per year ($1\frac{1}{2}$ millisievert per year); some details are shown in the following table:

	Whole body dose equivalent	
	millirem per year (mrem/yr)	millisievert per year (mSv/yr)
Background	106[a]	1.06[a]
of which, cosmic radiation	31	0.31
Man-made	53	0.53
of which, medical (X-rays, etc)	50	0.50
weapon test fallout	1	0.01
nuclear power	0.14	0.0014
Total	159	1.59

[a]Varies geographically with, for example: London 90 mrem/yr (0.9 mSv/yr), Aberdeen 170 mrem/yr (1.7 mSv/yr).

For radiological protection, the ICRP recommend the following limits for safety:

Type of tissue	millirem per year	millisievert per year
Malignancy liable tissue	500[a]	5[a]
Lens of the eye	15 000	150
Other tissue	50 000	500

[a]5 000 millirem (5 rem) per year (50 millisievert per year) for radiation workers.

Health

Respiration

Respiratory pressure, traditionally measured in centimetres of water (using a manometer), is recommended to change to measurement by the SI unit kilopascal. A table of conversions follows:

Resistance to flow (in airways), traditionally measured by centimetres of water second per litre, is to be replaced by the SI unit kilopascal second per litre.

Centimetres of water to Kilopascals $1 \text{ cm H}_2\text{O} = 0.098\,066\,5 \text{ kPa}$

cm $H_2O \rightarrow$	0	1	2	3	4	5	6	7	8	9	$\leftarrow$ cm H_2O
$\downarrow$	kPa	kPa	kPa	kPa	kPa	kPa	kPa	kPa	kPa	kPa	$\downarrow$
0	0.000	0.098	0.196	0.294	0.392	0.490	0.588	0.686	0.785	0.883	0
10	0.981	1.079	1.177	1.275	1.373	1.471	1.569	1.667	1.765	1.863	10
20	1.96	2.06	2.16	2.26	2.35	2.45	2.55	2.65	2.75	2.84	20
30	2.94	3.04	3.14	3.24	3.33	3.43	3.53	3.63	3.73	3.82	30
40	3.92	4.02	4.12	4.22	4.31	4.41	4.51	4.61	4.71	4.81	40
50	4.90	5.00	5.10	5.20	5.30	5.39	5.49	5.59	5.69	5.79	50

Viruses

Size of viruses, compared with blood cell and bacteria sizes, are as follows:

	Diameter in micrometres (μm) or 'microns'
Red blood cell	7
Bacteria: average rod-shaped	2
smallest spherical	0.4
Viruses: flu	0.08
yellow fever	0.02

Vitamins

The generally recommended intakes of vitamins and other nutrients are as follows, for the United Kingdom, per day:

	Men	Women	Boys (9–11 yrs)	Girls (9–11 yrs)
	Amounts in micrograms (μg) (for amounts in milligrams divide by 1000)			
Vitamin A (as retinol)[a]	750	750	575	575
Vitamin B$_1$ (thiamine)[b]	1 200	900	900	800
Vitamin C (ascorbic acid)	30 000	30 000	25 000	25 000
Vitamin D[c]	10	10	10	10
Riboflavin[d]	1 600	1 300	1 200	1 200
Nicotinic acid[e]	18 000	15 000	14 000	14 000
Folate[f]	300	300	300	300
Calcium	500 000	500 000	700 000	700 000
Iron	10 000	12 000	12 000	12 000

[a]In terms of retinol equivalent, where 1 retinol equivalent equals 1 μg retinol of 6 μgβ-carotene or 12 μg of other biologically active carotenoids. In terms of international units (iu), where 1 μg retinol = 3.33 iu retinol or retinol equivalent, the amount of retinol requirement for an adult is 2 500 iu and for a child 1 920 iu.
[b]Thiamin requirements are closely related to carbohydrate intake; usual recommendation is 96 μg thiamin per MJ. [c]The main source of Vitamin D is from the action of ultra-violet light on the skin; the amounts shown are for people with little exposure to sunlight. In terms of international units (iu), where 1 μg Vitamin D = 40 iu Vitamin D, the requirement for people not exposed to sunlight is 400 iu. [d]In relation to energy intake, based on 240 μg/MJ of resting metabolism. [e]In terms of nicotinic acid equivalents; in relation to energy intake, based on 2 700 μg nicotinic acid equivalent per MJ of resting metabolism. 1 nicotinic acid equivalent equals 1 unit of available nicotinic acid or 60 units tryptophan. [f]Human milk provides 5 μg folate/100 ml.

Vitamin E is necessary for normal metabolism; it is found in small amounts in many foods, and larger amounts are found in vegetable oils, some margarines, wheat germ and eggs. Most diets provide 10 mg/day; recommended intake has not been established.

Vitamin K is essential for the clotting of blood; it is found in green vegetables (cabbage, spinach, etc), cauliflower, peas and cereals, and can also be synthesised by bacteria in the intestine. Deficiency of this vitamin is unlikely in a healthy person; a recommended intake has not been established.

Also see page 147 (food) for recommended intakes of energy and protein.

Iron and steel

Steelmaking

Coke oven: this converts coking coal to coke by heating it to about 1 300 °C. 100 units of coal yields about 70 units of coke, and also coke oven gas and other by-products.

Blast furnace: iron ore is smelted with coke to produce pig iron.

Steel furnace: vessel in which pig iron and/or scrap are converted to steel by melting and refining. Main types are —
Basic oxygen: this is generally a top blown process where the gas used is 99.4% minimum purity oxygen, which can also be used as a means of introducing into the bath such slag-making materials etc as may be considered desirable.
Electric: steel furnace in which the melting is done by electricity.
Open hearth: steel furnace heated by flame from openings, using gas or liquid fuel. This process is being phased out in the United Kingdom.
Bessemer converter: air is blown through molten pig iron to remove carbon, manganese, silicon, etc. This process was discontinued in the United Kingdom in 1974.
Main categories (depending on type of ore) are —
Acid: steel furnace with an acid lining for use with materials containing little sulphur or phosphorus.
Basic: steel furnace with an alkali lining, in which sulphur and phosphorus are removed from the materials used.

Rolling mill: mill which forms steel into plates, slabs, rounds, etc.

Crude steel: steel ingots and continuously cast semi-finished products, and liquid steel for castings.

Ingot: a mass of steel, usually between 2 and 20 tonnes, formed by pouring the molten metal into a mould, intended for subsequent hot working.

Ingot tonne: either 1 tonne of ingot steel, or the unit of crude steel weight equivalent to a given quantity of semi-finished and/or finished steel. On average 100 tonnes of finished steel require 132 tonnes of crude steel, that is, an average yield of 76%.

Continuous casting: a casting technique in which liquid steel is continuously solidified while it is being poured, and the length is not determined by the mould dimensions. The resulting solid product is of similar shape to a semi-finished product and, according to its dimensions, is classified as a continuously cast bloom, billet or slab.

Types of steel

Steel is predominantly iron, with less than 2% carbon and other elements in controlled amounts:
Wrought iron: soft ductile metal with very low carbon content, almost pure iron.

on and steel

Pig iron: about 93% iron, 4—4½% carbon, and some silicon, manganese, sulphur nd phosphorus.

Mild steel: soft non-alloy steel (that is, with a low carbon content, about .12—0.25%).

Tinplate: low carbon mild steel sheet, usually under $\frac{1}{16}$ inch (1.5 mm) thick, oated with tin applied either by dipping in molten tin or by electro-deposition.

High carbon steel: steel containing, by weight, not less than 0.60% of carbon and nd having a content, by weight, less than 0.04% of phosphorus and sulphur aken separately and less than 0.07% of these elements taken together (UK efinition).

Alloy steel: any steel containing, by weight, at least: .6% of molybdenum, or 0.5% of silicon, or 0.3% of chromium or nickel, or 0.1% f tungsten or vanadium, or 0.08% of molybdenum. The above is the main UK definition for alloy steel.

Stainless and heat resisting steel: alloy steel containing, by weight, 11.5% or nore of chromium and less than 1.1% of carbon (main UK definition).

High speed steel: alloy steels containing, either with or without other alloying lements, at least two of the following three elements: tungsten, molybdenum nd vanadium, with a total content of these elements taken together of not less han 7% by weight and containing more than 0.6% of carbon by weight (UK efinition).

Iron ore

he following are averages of iron content in ore; they are in general as indicated y the UN, and are approximate:

World producers of iron ore

	% iron		% iron
Algeria	53—55	Korea, South	56
Argentina	51	Liberia	68
Australia	64	Luxembourg	29
Austria	31	Malaysia	56
Belgium	30	Mauritania	65
Brazil	68[a]	Mexico	100
Bulgaria	33	Morocco	55—60
Canada	61	Norway	65
Chile	61	Peru	60
Czechoslovakia	26	Poland	30
Egypt	50	Portugal	50
Finland	66	Rumania	26
France	30	South Africa	60—65
Germany, East	39	Soviet Union	60
Germany, West	32	Spain	50
Greece	43	Sweden	60—65
Hungary	24	Thailand	58
India	63	Tunisia	53
Indonesia	56—58	Turkey	55—60
Italy	44	United Kingdom	26[b]
Japan	54	United States	61
Yugoslavia	35	Venezuela	64

[a]For exports. [b]45% for Cumberland and Glamorgan, 21—29% for Lincs, Leics nd Northants.

Finished steel products

ngots are rolled into semi-finished products (billets, blooms, and slabs) and hese in turn are rolled into finished products (bars, plates, sheets, etc.). These rocesses involve the scrapping of part of the material, so that the weight of the nished product is considerably less than that of the ingot from which it was lled; that loss varies according to the product.

n the seventies the increasing use of the continuous casting process (which by 978 accounted for some 15% of crude steel production) significantly reduced rocessing losses at works with such plant installed. The following table, ublished by the Iron and Steel Statistics Bureau gives conversion factors for rincipal classes of steel products (1978 average). The factor for any one roduct may vary considerably between works, between countries and over me.

	Crude steel to product	Product to crude steel
Non-alloy		
Blooms, billets and slabs — rolled	0.88	1.13
Rounds and squares for tubes	0.84	1.19
Rods and bars for reinforcement	0.82	1.22
Wire rods and other rods and bars in coil	0.82	1.22
Arches, light rails and accessories	0.77	1.30
Other light rolled sections and hot rolled bars	0.80	1.25
Bright steel bars	0.72	1.39
Heavy rails and accessories	0.77	1.30
Other heavy rolled products	0.82	1.22
Plates, 3 mm thick and over	0.73	1.37
Sheets, under 3 mm thick	0.75	1.33
Hot rolled strip	0.73	1.37
Cold rolled strip	0.72	1.39
Tinplate and blackplate	0.74	1.35
Tubes and pipes	0.67	1.49
Tyres, wheels, axles and rolled rings	0.57	1.75
Forgings (other than drop forgings)	0.46	2.17
Castings	0.53	1.89
Average non-alloy	*0.76*	*1.32*
Alloy	*0.71*	*1.41*
Average all non-alloy and alloy products	*0.76*	*1.32*

The average all-items conversion multiplier from product to crude steel, as used by the UN, is 1.337.

Weight (mass) of steel

The density of steel is based internationally on a standard weight (mass) of 7 850 kilograms per cubic metre. Tables on the following pages indicate the weight (mass) for wire, plate, sheet and strip based on this density (for the wire table see page 5 for a general description of the use of the type of table).

For wire, figures are shown in terms of kilograms per 100 metre length, for varying diameters of wire. For plate, sheet and strip, figures are shown in terms of kilograms per cubic metre for varying thickness and width, but a standard one metre length.

As the weight (mass) of different types of steel will vary, the tables shown can be used for different densities to the standard by using multipliers — that is by multiplying by the actual density divided by 7 850. A table of multipliers for densities from 7 500 to 8 690 is given on the following page. Further, since products other than steel will usually have a lower density (water has a density of 1 000 kg/m³ at 4 °C), a table of multipliers is also included for densities in the range from 500 to 2 500 so that the steel tables can also be used for other products. For example, with a density for timber of 700 kg/m³ (page 117) the weight (mass) for planks of timber can be obtained by multiplying the figures in the steel tables by 700/7 850 or 0.089. Also see page 162 for multipliers of main non-ferrous metals.

The tables shown include a selection of various sizes, not all of which are standard recommended sizes for steel. Standard thicknesses of sheet and strip available from the UK steel industry are, in millimetres: 0.6, 0.7, 0.8, 0.9, 1.0, 1.2, 1.6, 2.0, 2.5, 3.0, 4.0, 5.0, 6.0, 8.0, 10.0, 12.5. In the tables of plate, sheet and strip any sizes for which weights are shown, but which are outside the thickness/ wide range available from the UK steel industry, are marked with an asterisk (*). For use of the tables with centimetres, note that 1 cm = 10 mm, and divide millimetres by 10 (delete the last zero or move the decimal point 1 place to the left).

Multipliers for use with tables on steel density

showing multipliers for different levels of density (kg/m³)

Products other than steel

kg/m³		kg/m³		kg/m³	
500	0.064	1200	0.153	1900	0.242
600	0.076	1300	0.166	2000	0.255
700	0.089	1400	0.178	2100	0.268
800	0.102	1500	0.191	2200	0.280
900	0.115	1600	0.204	2300	0.293
1000	0.127	1700	0.217	2400	0.306
1100	0.140	1800	0.229	2500	0.318

Iron and steel

Steel products showing multipliers for different levels of density (kg/m³)

kg/m³		kg/m³		kg/m³		kg/m³		kg/m³		kg/m³		kg/m³		kg/m³	
7500	0.955	7650	0.975	7800	0.994	7950	1.013	8100	1.032	8250	1.051	8400	1.070	8550	1.089
7510	0.957	7660	0.976	7810	0.995	7960	1.014	8110	1.033	8260	1.052	8410	1.071	8560	1.090
7520	0.958	7670	0.977	7820	0.996	7970	1.015	8120	1.034	8270	1.054	8420	1.073	8570	1.092
7530	0.959	7680	0.978	7830	0.997	7980	1.017	8130	1.036	8280	1.055	8430	1.074	8580	1.093
7540	0.961	7690	0.980	7840	0.999	7990	1.018	8140	1.037	8290	1.056	8440	1.075	8590	1.094
7550	0.962	7700	0.981	7850	1.000	8000	1.019	8150	1.038	8300	1.057	8450	1.076	8600	1.096
7560	0.963	7710	0.982	7860	1.001	8010	1.020	8160	1.039	8310	1.059	8460	1.078	8610	1.097
7570	0.964	7720	0.983	7870	1.003	8020	1.022	8170	1.041	8320	1.060	8470	1.079	8620	1.098
7580	0.966	7730	0.985	7880	1.004	8030	1.023	8180	1.042	8330	1.061	8480	1.080	8630	1.099
7590	0.967	7740	0.986	7890	1.005	8040	1.024	8190	1.043	8340	1.062	8490	1.082	8640	1.101
7600	0.968	7750	0.987	7900	1.006	8050	1.025	8200	1.045	8350	1.064	8500	1.083	8650	1.102
7610	0.969	7760	0.989	7910	1.008	8060	1.027	8210	1.046	8360	1.065	8510	1.084	8660	1.103
7620	0.971	7770	0.990	7920	1.009	8070	1.028	8220	1.047	8370	1.066	8520	1.085	8670	1.104
7630	0.972	7780	0.991	7930	1.010	8080	1.029	8230	1.048	8380	1.068	8530	1.087	8680	1.106
7640	0.973	7790	0.992	7940	1.011	8090	1.031	8240	1.050	8390	1.069	8540	1.088	8690	1.107

Weight (mass) of steel: wire with standard density of 7 850 kg/m³

Kilograms per 100 metre length

Diameter → in mm ↓	0.00	0.01	0.02	0.03	0.04	0.05	0.06	0.07	0.08	0.09	← Diameter in mm
	kg/100m	kg/100m	kg/100m	kg/100m	kg/100m	kg/100m	kg/100m	kg/100m	kg/100m	kg/100m	
0.0	0.0000000	0.0000617	0.0002466	0.0005549	0.0009865	0.0015413	0.0022195	0.0030210	0.0039458	0.0049940,	0.
0.1	0.0061654	0.0074601	0.0088781	0.0104195	0.0120841	0.0138721	0.0157834	0.0178179	0.0199758	0.0222570	0.
0.2	0.0246615	0.0271893	0.0298404	0.0326148	0.0355126	0.0385336	0.0416779	0.0449456	0.0483365	0.0518508	0.
0.3	0.0554884	0.0592493	0.0631334	0.0671409	0.0712717	0.0755259	0.0799033	0.0844040	0.0890280	0.0937754	0.
0.4	0.0986460	0.1036400	0.1087572	0.1139978	0.1193617	0.1248489	0.1304593	0.1361931	0.1420503	0.1480307	0.
0.5	0.1541344	0.1603614	0.1667118	0.1731854	0.1797824	0.1865026	0.1933462	0.2003131	0.2074032	0.2146167	0.
0.6	0.2219535	0.2294136	0.2369970	0.2447038	0.2525338	0.2604871	0.2685638	0.2767637	0.2850870	0.2935335	0.
0.7	0.3021034	0.3107966	0.3196131	0.3285529	0.3376160	0.3468024	0.3561121	0.3655451	0.3751015	0.3847811	0.
0.8	0.3945840	0.4045103	0.4145599	0.4247327	0.4350289	0.4454484	0.4559912	0.4666573	0.4774467	0.4883594	0.
0.9	0.4993954	0.5105548	0.5218374	0.5332433	0.5447726	0.5564251	0.5682010	0.5801002	0.5921227	0.6042685	0.
1.0	0.6165376	0.6289300	0.6414457	0.6540847	0.6668470	0.6797327	0.6927416	0.7058739	0.7191294	0.7325083	1.
1.1	0.7460104	0.7596359	0.7733847	0.7872568	0.8012522	0.8153709	0.8296129	0.8439783	0.8584669	0.8730788	1.
1.2	0.8878141	0.9026726	0.9176545	0.9327597	0.9479881	0.9633399	0.9788150	0.9944134	1.0101351	1.0259802	1.
1.3	1.0419485	1.0580401	1.0742550	1.0905933	1.1070548	1.1236397	1.1403479	1.1571793	1.1741341	1.1912122	1.
1.4	1.2084136	1.2257383	1.2431863	1.2607577	1.2784523	1.2962702	1.3142115	1.3322760	1.3504639	1.3687750	1.
1.5	1.3872095	1.4057673	1.4244484	1.4432528	1.4621805	1.4812315	1.5004058	1.5197034	1.5391244	1.5586686	1.
1.6	1.5783361	1.5981270	1.6180412	1.6380786	1.6582394	1.6785235	1.6989309	1.7194616	1.7401156	1.7608929	1.
1.7	1.7817935	1.8028175	1.8239647	1.8452353	1.8666291	1.8881463	1.9097867	1.9315505	1.9534376	1.9754480	1.
1.8	1.9975817	2.0198387	2.0422190	2.0647226	2.0873496	2.1100998	2.1329733	2.1559702	2.1790903	2.2023338	1.
1.9	2.2257006	2.2491907	2.2728041	2.2965408	2.3204008	2.3443841	2.3684907	2.3927206	2.4170738	2.4415504	1.

Diameter → in mm ↓	0.0	0.1	0.2	0.3	0.4	0.5	0.6	0.7	0.8	0.9	← Diameter in mm
	kg/100m	kg/100m	kg/100m	kg/100m	kg/100m	kg/100m	kg/100m	kg/100m	kg/100m	kg/100m	
2	2.4662	2.7189	2.9840	3.2615	3.5513	3.8534	4.1678	4.4946	4.8337	5.1851	
3	5.5488	5.9249	6.3133	6.7141	7.1272	7.5526	7.9903	8.4404	8.9028	9.3775	
4	9.8646	10.3640	10.8757	11.3998	11.9362	12.4849	13.0459	13.6193	14.2050	14.8031	
5	15.4134	16.0361	16.6712	17.3185	17.9782	18.6503	19.3346	20.0313	20.7403	21.4617	
6	22.1954	22.9414	23.6997	24.4704	25.2534	26.0487	26.8564	27.6764	28.5087	29.3534	
7	30.2103	31.0797	31.9613	32.8553	33.7616	34.6802	35.6112	36.5545	37.5101	38.4781	
8	39.4584	40.4510	41.4560	42.4733	43.5029	44.5448	45.5991	46.6657	47.7447	48.8359	
9	49.9395	51.0555	52.1837	53.3243	54.4773	55.6425	56.8201	58.0100	59.2123	60.4268	
10	61.6538	62.8930	64.1446	65.4085	66.6847	67.9733	69.2742	70.5874	71.9129	73.2508	1
11	74.6010	75.9636	77.3385	78.7257	80.1252	81.5371	82.9613	84.3978	85.8467	87.3079	1
12	88.7814	90.2673	91.7655	93.2760	94.7988	96.3340	97.8815	99.4413	101.0135	102.5980	1
13	104.1948	105.8040	107.4255	109.0593	110.7055	112.3640	114.0348	115.7179	117.4134	119.1212	1
14	120.8414	122.5738	124.3186	126.0758	127.8452	129.6270	131.4211	133.2276	135.0464	136.8775	1
15	138.7210	140.5767	142.4448	144.3253	146.2180	148.1231	150.0406	151.9703	153.9124	155.8669	1
16	157.8336	159.8127	161.8041	163.8079	165.8239	167.8524	169.8931	171.9462	174.0116	176.0893	1

Iron and steel

Weight (mass) of steel: sheet and strip with standard density of 7 850 kg/m³

Kilograms per metre length

Thickness → in mm	0.2	0.3	0.4	0.5	0.6	0.7	0.8	0.9	1.0	2.0	3.0 ← Thickness in mm
Width in mm ↓	kg/m	kg/m	kg/m	kg/m	kg/m	kg/m	kg/m	kg/m	kg/m	kg/m	kg/m Width in mm ↓
20	0.03140	0.04710	0.06280	0.07850	0.09420	0.10990	0.12560	0.14130	0.15700	0.31400	0.47100 20
25	0.03925	0.05888	0.07850	0.09812	0.11775	0.13737	0.15700	0.17662	0.19625	0.39250	0.58875 25
30	0.04710	0.07065	0.09420	0.11775	0.14130	0.16485	0.18840	0.21195	0.23550	0.47100	0.70650 30
35	0.05495	0.08243	0.10990	0.13737	0.16485	0.19232	0.21980	0.24727	0.27475	0.54950	0.82425 35
40	0.06280	0.09420	0.12560	0.15700	0.18840	0.21980	0.25120	0.28260	0.31400	0.62800	0.94200 40
45	0.07065	0.10597	0.14130	0.17662	0.21195	0.24727	0.28260	0.31792	0.35325	0.70650	1.05975 45
50	0.07850	0.11775	0.15700	0.19625	0.23550	0.27475	0.31400	0.35325	0.39250	0.78500	1.17750 50
55	0.08635	0.12953	0.17270	0.21587	0.25905	0.30222	0.34540	0.38857	0.43175	0.86350	1.29525 55
60	0.09420	0.14130	0.18840	0.23550	0.28260	0.32970	0.37680	0.42390	0.47100	0.94200	1.41300 60
70	0.10990	0.16485	0.21980	0.27475	0.32970	0.38465	0.43960	0.49455	0.54950	1.09900	1.64850 70
80	0.12560	0.18840	0.25120	0.31400	0.37680	0.43960	0.50240	0.56520	0.62800	1.25600	1.88400 80
90	0.14130	0.21195	0.28260	0.35325	0.42390	0.49455	0.56520	0.63585	0.70650	1.41300	2.11950 90
100	0.15700	0.23550	0.31400	0.39250	0.47100	0.54950	0.62800	0.70650	0.78500	1.57000	2.35500 100
150	0.23550	0.35325	0.47100	0.58875	0.70650	0.82425	0.94200	1.05975	1.17750	2.35500	3.53250 150
200	0.31400	0.47100	0.62800	0.78500	0.94200	1.09900	1.25600	1.41300	1.57000	3.14000	4.71000 200
250	0.39250	0.58875	0.78500	0.98125	1.17750	1.37375	1.57000	1.76625	1.96250	3.92500	5.88750 250
500	0.78500	1.17750	1.57000	1.96250	2.35500	2.74750	3.14000	3.53250	3.92500	7.85000	11.77500 500
750	1.17750*	1.76625	2.35500	2.94375	3.53250	4.12125	4.71000	5.29875	5.88750	11.77500	17.66250 750
1000	1.57000*	2.35500	3.14000	3.92500	4.71000	5.49500	6.28000	7.06500	7.85000	15.70000	23.55000 1000
1250	1.96250*	2.94375*	3.92500*	4.90625	5.88750	6.86875	7.85000	8.83125	9.81250	19.62500	29.43750 1250
1500	2.35500*	3.53250*	4.71000*	5.88750*	7.06500*	8.24250	9.42000	10.59750	11.77500	23.55000	35.32500 1500
1750	2.74750*	4.12125*	5.49500*	6.86875*	8.24250*	9.61625*	10.99000*	12.36375	13.73750	27.47500	41.21250 1750
2000	3.14000*	4.71000*	6.28000*	7.85000*	9.42000*	10.99000*	12.56000*	14.13000*	15.70000*	31.40000*	47.10000* 2000
2250	3.53250*	5.29875*	7.06500*	8.83125*	10.59750*	12.36375*	14.13000*	15.89625*	17.66250*	35.32500*	52.98750* 2250
2500	3.92500*	5.88750*	7.85000*	9.81250*	11.77500*	13.73750*	15.70000*	17.66250*	19.62500*	39.25000*	58.87500* 2500

Thickness → in mm	4	6	8	10	12	14	16	18	20	25	30 ← Thickness in mm
Width in mm ↓	kg/m	kg/m	kg/m	kg/m	kg/m	kg/m	kg/m	kg/m	kg/m	kg/m	kg/m Width in mm ↓
20	0.6280	0.9420	1.2560	1.5700	1.8840	2.1980	2.5120	2.8260	3.1400	3.9250	4.7100 20
25	0.7850	1.1775	1.5700	1.9625	2.3550	2.7475	3.1400	3.5325	3.9250	4.9062	5.8875 25
30	0.9420	1.4130	1.8840	2.3550	2.8260	3.2970	3.7680	4.2390	4.7100	5.8875	7.0650 30
35	1.0990	1.6485	2.1980	2.7475	3.2970	3.8465	4.3960	4.9455	5.4950	6.8687	8.2425 35
40	1.2560	1.8840	2.5120	3.1400	3.7680	4.3960	5.0240	5.6520	6.2800	7.8500	9.4200 40
45	1.4130	2.1195	2.8260	3.5325	4.2390	4.9455	5.6520	6.3585	7.0650	8.8312	10.5975 45
50	1.5700	2.3550	3.1400	3.9250	4.7100	5.4950	6.2800	7.0650	7.8500	9.8125	11.7750 50
55	1.7270	2.5905	3.4540	4.3175	5.1810	6.0445	6.9080	7.7715	8.6350	10.7938	12.9525 55
60	1.8840	2.8260	3.7680	4.7100	5.6520	6.5940	7.5360	8.4780	9.4200	11.7750	14.1300 60
70	2.1980	3.2970	4.3960	5.4950	6.5940	7.6930	8.7920	9.8910	10.9900	13.7375	16.4850 70
80	2.5120	3.7680	5.0240	6.2800	7.5360	8.7920	10.0480	11.3040	12.5600	15.7000	18.8400 80
90	2.8260	4.2390	5.6520	7.0650	8.4780	9.8910	11.3040	12.7170	14.1300	17.6625	21.1950 90
100	3.1400	4.7100	6.2800	7.8500	9.4200	10.9900	12.5600	14.1300	15.7000	19.6250	23.5500 100
150	4.7100	7.0650	9.4200	11.7750	14.1300	16.4850	18.8400	21.1950	23.5500	29.4375	35.3250 150
200	6.2800	9.4200	12.5600	15.7000	18.8400	21.9800	25.1200	28.2600	31.4000	39.2500	47.1000 200
250	7.8500	11.7750	15.7000	19.6250	23.5500	27.4750	31.4000	35.3250	39.2500	49.0625	58.8750 250
500	15.7000	23.5500	31.4000	39.2500	47.1000	54.9500	62.8000	70.6500	78.5000	98.1250	117.7500 500
750	23.5500	35.3250	47.1000	58.8750	70.6500	82.4250	94.2000	105.9750	117.7500	147.1875	176.6250 750
1000	31.4000	47.1000	62.8000	78.5000	94.2000	109.9000	125.6000	141.3000	157.0000	196.2500	235.5000 1000
1250	39.2500	58.8750	78.5000	98.1250	117.7500	137.3750	157.0000	176.6250	196.2500	245.3125	294.3750 1250
1500	47.1000	70.6500	94.2000	117.7500	141.3000	164.8500	188.4000	211.9500	235.5000	294.3750	353.2500 1500
1750	54.9500	82.4250	109.9000	137.3750	164.8500	192.3250	219.8000	247.2750	274.7500	343.4375	412.1250 1750
2000	62.8000*	94.2000	125.6000	157.0000	188.4000	219.8000	251.2000	282.6000	314.0000	392.5000	471.0000 2000
2250	70.6500*	105.9750	141.3000	176.6250	211.9500	247.2750	282.6000	317.9250	353.2500	441.5625	529.8750 2250
2500	78.5000*	117.7500	157.0000	196.2500	235.5000	274.7500	314.0000	353.2500	392.5000	490.6250	588.7500 2500

Iron and steel

Weight (mass) of steel: plate, sheet and strip with standard density of 7 850 kg/m³

Kilograms per metre length

Thickness → in mm	35	40	45	50	55	60	65	70	75	80	85 ←Thickness in mm
Width in mm ↓	kg/m	kg/m	kg/m	kg/m	kg/m	kg/m	kg/m	kg/m	kg/m	kg/m	kg/m Width in mm
300	82.425	94.200	105.975	117.750	129.525	141.300	153.075	164.850	176.625	188.400	200.175
350	96.163	109.900	123.637	137.375	151.112	164.850	178.587	192.325	206.062	219.800	233.538
400	109.900	125.600	141.300	157.000	172.700	188.400	204.100	219.800	235.500	251.200	266.900
450	123.637	141.300	158.962	176.625	194.288	211.950	229.612	247.275	264.937	282.600	300.263
500	137.375	157.000	176.625	196.250	215.875	235.500	255.125	274.750	294.375	314.000	333.625
550	151.112	172.700	194.288	215.875	237.462	259.050	280.638	302.225	323.812	345.400	366.987
600	164.850	188.400	211.950	235.500	259.050	282.600	306.150	329.700	353.250	376.800	400.350
700	192.325	219.800	247.275	274.750	302.225	329.700	357.175	384.650	412.125	439.600	467.075
800	219.800	251.200	282.600	314.000	345.400	376.800	408.200	439.600	471.000	502.400	533.800
900	247.275	282.600	317.925	353.250	388.575	423.900	459.225	494.550	529.875	565.200	600.525
1000	274.750	314.000	353.250	392.500	431.750	471.000	510.250	549.500	588.750	628.000	667.250
1250	343.437	392.500	441.562	490.625	539.687	588.750	637.812	686.875	735.937	785.000	834.062
1500	412.125	471.000	529.875	588.750	647.625	706.500	765.375	824.250	883.125	942.000	1000.875
1750	480.812	549.500	618.187	686.875	755.562	824.250	892.937	961.625	1030.312	1099.000	1167.687
2000	549.500	628.000	706.500	785.000	863.500	942.000	1020.500	1099.000	1177.500	1256.000	1334.500
2250	618.187	706.500	794.812	883.125	971.437	1059.750	1148.062	1236.375	1324.687	1413.000	1501.312
2500	686.875	785.000	883.125	981.250	1079.375	1177.500	1275.625	1373.750	1471.875	1570.000	1668.125
2750	755.562	863.500	971.437	1079.375	1187.312	1295.250	1403.187	1511.125	1619.062	1727.000	1834.937
3000	824.250	942.000	1059.750	1177.500	1295.250	1413.000	1530.750	1648.500	1766.250	1884.000	2001.750
3250	892.937	1020.500	1148.062	1275.625	1403.187	1530.750	1658.312	1785.875	1913.437	2041.000	2168.562
3500	961.625	1099.000	1236.375	1373.750	1511.125	1648.500	1785.875	1923.250	2060.625	2198.000	2335.375
3750	1030.312	1177.500	1324.687	1471.875	1619.062	1766.250	1913.437	2060.625	2207.812	2355.000	2502.187
4000	1099.000*	1256.000*	1413.000*	1570.000*	1727.000*	1884.000*	2041.000*	2198.000*	2355.000*	2512.000*	2669.000*
4500	1236.375*	1413.000*	1589.625*	1766.250*	1942.875*	2119.500*	2296.125*	2472.750*	2649.375*	2826.000*	3002.625*
5000	1373.750*	1570.000*	1766.250*	1962.500*	2158.750*	2355.000*	2551.250*	2747.500*	2943.750*	3140.000*	3336.250*

Thickness → in mm	90	95	100	105	110	115	120	125	130	135	140	150 ←Thickness in mm
Width in mm ↓	kg/m	kg/m	kg/m	kg/m	kg/m	kg/m	kg/m	kg/m	kg/m	kg/m	kg/m	kg/m Width in mm
300	211.95	223.73	235.50	247.27	259.05	270.83	282.60	294.37	306.15	317.92	329.70	353.25
350	247.27	261.01	274.75	288.49	302.22	315.96	329.70	343.44	357.17	370.91	384.65	412.12
400	282.60	298.30	314.00	329.70	345.40	361.10	376.80	392.50	408.20	423.90	439.60	471.00
450	317.92	335.59	353.25	370.91	388.58	406.24	423.90	441.56	459.22	476.89	494.55	529.87
500	353.25	372.87	392.50	412.12	431.75	451.37	471.00	490.62	510.25	529.87	549.50	588.75
550	388.58	410.16	431.75	453.34	474.92	496.51	518.10	539.69	561.28	582.86	604.45	647.62
600	423.90	447.45	471.00	494.55	518.10	541.65	565.20	588.75	612.30	635.85	659.40	706.50
700	494.55	522.03	549.50	576.97	604.45	631.93	659.40	686.87	714.35	741.82	769.30	824.25
800	565.20	596.60	628.00	659.40	690.80	722.20	753.60	785.00	816.40	847.80	879.20	942.00
900	635.85	671.18	706.50	741.82	777.15	812.47	847.80	883.12	918.45	953.78	989.10	1059.75
1000	706.50	745.75	785.00	824.25	863.50	902.75	942.00	981.25	1020.50	1059.75	1099.00	1177.50
1250	883.12	932.19	981.25	1030.31	1079.37	1128.44	1177.50	1226.56	1275.62	1324.69	1373.75	1471.87
1500	1059.75	1118.62	1177.50	1236.37	1295.25	1354.12	1413.00	1471.87	1530.75	1589.62	1648.50	1766.25
1750	1236.37	1305.06	1373.75	1442.44	1511.12	1579.81	1648.50	1717.19	1785.87	1854.56	1923.25	2060.62
2000	1413.00	1491.50	1570.00	1648.50	1727.00	1805.50	1884.00	1962.50	2041.00	2119.50	2198.00	2355.00
2250	1589.62	1677.94	1766.25	1854.56	1942.87	2031.19	2119.50	2207.81	2296.12	2384.44	2472.75	2649.37
2500	1766.25	1864.37	1962.50	2060.62	2158.75	2256.87	2355.00	2453.12	2551.25	2649.37	2747.50	2943.75
2750	1942.87	2050.81	2158.75	2266.69	2374.62	2482.56	2590.50	2698.44	2806.37	2914.31	3022.25	3238.12
3000	2119.50	2237.25	2355.00	2472.75	2590.50	2708.25	2826.00	2943.75	3061.50	3179.25	3297.00	3532.50
3250	2296.12	2423.69	2551.25	2678.81	2806.37	2933.94	3061.50	3189.06	3316.62	3444.19	3571.75	3826.87
3500	2472.75	2610.12	2747.50	2884.87	3022.25	3159.62	3297.00	3434.37	3571.75	3709.12	3846.50	4121.25
3750	2649.37	2796.56	2943.75	3090.94	3238.12	3385.31	3532.50	3679.69	3826.87	3974.06	4121.25	4415.62
4000	2826.00*	2983.00*	3140.00*	3297.00*	3454.00*	3611.00*	3768.00*	3925.00*	4082.00*	4239.00*	4396.00*	4710.00*
4500	3179.25*	3355.87*	3532.50*	3709.12*	3885.75*	4062.37*	4239.00*	4415.62*	4592.25*	4768.87*	4945.50*	5298.75*
5000	3532.50*	3728.75*	3925.00*	4121.25*	4317.50*	4513.75*	4710.00*	4906.25*	5102.50*	5298.75*	5495.00*	5887.50*

Light, optics and photography

Light

Range

Light is the part of the electromagnetic spectrum which can be distinguished by human vision; the range is approximately from 300 to 760 nm (1 000 to 400 THz), and is divided approximately as shown in the following table. The table shows wavelength in the old unit of the Ångström and the modern unit of the nanometre, and also shows frequency in terahertz, that being the unit used in the 1979 definition of the candela.

The exact relationship between wavelength and frequency is:
frequency in hertz = speed of light (in m/s)/wavelength in metres (also see page 128 for further details and for the full electromagnetic spectrum).

That is, frequency in hertz = $2.997\,925 \times 10^8$/wavelength in metres

$$\text{frequency in terahertz} = 2.997\,925 \times 10^{-4}/\text{wavelength in metres}$$
$$= 2.997\,925 \times 10^5/\text{wavelength in nanometres}$$
$$= 299\,792.5/\text{wavelength in nanometres}$$

Colour	Wavelength in: Ångström (10^{-10} m or Å)	nanometres (10^{-9} m or nm)	Frequency: terahertz (10^{12} Hz or THz)
(Infrared[a])	(over 7 600[b])	(over 760[b])	(under 400[b])
Red	6 300–7 600	630–760	480–400
Yellow	5 800–6 300	580–630	520–480
Green	4 800–5 800	480–580	620–520
Blue	4 000–4 800	400–480	750–620
Violet	3 000–4 000	300–400	1 000–750
(Ultraviolet)	(under 3 000[c])	(under 300[c])	(over 1 000[c])

[a]Wavelengths in this range can give a sensation of light up to about 1 050 nm (10 500 Å) or down to about 300 THz. [b]The full infrared range extends to about 1 000 000 nm (10 000 000 Å) or 0.3 THz. [c]The effective visible limit is usually about 360 nm (3 600 Å) or 830 THz; the full ultra violet range extends to about 5 nanometres (50 Å) or 60 000 THz.

Relative visibility changes according to wavelength, with a peak near the centre of the range, and a gradually falling away to either end of the visual range. The brightest colour, as indicated by a light-meter, is at 555 nm (540 THz).
The range which can be distinguished by the eye varies from about 1 nm or 1 THz in the central yellow-green-blue area to about 10 nm or 10 THz at the deep red and violet edges of the visible spectrum.
White is the colour of sunlight and of a substance which reflects sunlight with no absorption of any of the visible rays. Black is the absence of any visible rays and the colour of a substance which absorbs all visible rays.
Measurement of electromagnetic radiation in general is called radiometry; measurement of the portion which can be distinguished by human vision is called photometry.

Doppler effect
Where the source of light is approaching, the wavelength appears lower, and the light becomes more blue; where the source of light is moving away, the wavelength appears higher and the light becomes more red. The latter phenomenon is known as the 'red shift'. The amount of change is:
wavelength observed = $w \times V/(V - v)$
where w = wavelength of the light
V = velocity of light
v = velocity at which the source of the light is moving away from the observer
See also page 128 concerning the velocity of light, and page 165 concerning the Doppler effect as related to sound.

Measures

Luminous intensity
The candela (cd) is the SI unit for measuring luminous intensity (I). The candela was first defined internationally in 1946 and was at that time called the 'new candle'. It replaced the former various candle measures in use at the following approximate rates:
1 candela = 0.98 former international candle
= 0.95 former British standard candle
= 1.107 Hefner-Kerze or HK (former 'Hefner candle')
The former British candle was defined as light from a candle burning under certain conditions.

Up to 1979, the candela was defined as 'the luminous intensity, in the perpendicular direction, of a surface of 1/600 000 square metre of a black body at the temperature of freezing platinum under a pressure of 101 325 newtons per square metre.' (1967 definition). In 1979 the candela was redefined as 'the luminous intensity, in a given direction, of a source which emits monochromatic radiation of frequency 540×10^{12} hertz and which has a radiant intensity in that direction of 1/683 watt per steradian'.
A multiple frequency used is the kilocandela (kcd) = 1 000 cd. Examples of the amount of luminous intensity are: a 100 watt tungsten-filament bulb has an intensity of about 130 cd, and the sun a luminous intensity of about 2×10^{27} cd.

Luminous flux
Luminous flux (Φ) is the rate of flow of light from a source or received by a surface, and indicates the intensity of a source (which is measured in candela). Luminous flux is measured in SI terms by the lumen (lm), which is 'the luminous flux emitted within unit solid angle of 1 steradian by a point source having a uniform luminous intensity of 1 candela.'
That is, 1 lm = 1 cd sr = $\dfrac{1}{4\pi}$ cd; also 1 cd = 4π lm and 1 cd = 1 lm/sr.

The steradian (sr) is an SI unit which is the solid angle at the centre of a sphere arising from an area on the surface of the sphere equal to a square with sides equal to the radius of the sphere (also see page 14). That is, the surface area giving a solid angle of 1 steradian is r^2 where r is the radius of the sphere. Since the total surface area of a sphere is $4\pi r^2$ (see page 190), the total area arising from the solid total angle at the centre is equal to 4π steradians or approximately 12.566 sr. The solid angle of 1 steradian is the following fraction of the total angle at the centre of the sphere and of the surface area:
$r^2/4\pi r^2 = 1/4\pi = 1/12.566 = 0.0796 = 8\%$ of total surface area (approx.). The total luminous flux emitted by a source emitting uniformly in all directions is equal to luminous intensity $\times 4\pi = 12.566$ lumens. If 92% of the area of a sphere is blacked out, the amount of light remaining from a 1 candela source at the centre is 1 lumen. Examples of amounts of luminous flux are: ordinary light bulb = 1 500 lm, flashlight bulb = 1–3 million lm.

The 'quantity of light' emitted by a source is the amount of luminous flux over time, and is measured in SI terms by lumen seconds or lumen hours.

Luminous efficacy (efficiency)
The flow of light from a source of light obtained from a known flow of power will vary according to the efficiency with which the power is turned into light. This is measured in terms of lumen per watt of power consumed. For an average 100 watt bulb with an intensity of 130 candela, the luminous flux for a complete sphere of light would be 1 630 lm (130 × 4π); the average actual flux in a downwards direction is usually about 1 200 lm giving a luminous efficacy of 12 lm/W. That is, for an average bulb, 1 watt of power gives (in a downward direction) about 12 lumen. Fluorescent lights may attain an efficacy of up to about 80 lm/W.
The maximum flow of monochromatic light from a given power source occurs in the brightest colour range at 540 THz (555 nm); this amount is 683 lm/W. For light which is a mixture of colours, the weighted average for that mixture must be determined by multiplying the value of 683 lm/W by the estimated relative visibility for each wavelength in the mixture. For example, daylight has a maximum flow of about 240 lm/W when the differing wavelengths are allowed for (assuming all power goes into the light wavelengths and not other radiations).

Illuminance
The illuminance or illumination (E) of a surface receiving light is measured by the amount of light reaching it per unit area. In SI terms this is measured by the special unit called the lux (lx), which is an illuminance of 1 lumen per square metre.
The illuminance of a room is normally about 200–500 lux; general minimum recommendations are:

	lx
working space continuously occupied	200
casual work	300
other (including reading)	500
critical colour matching	1 000

Light, optics and photography

The relationship between the SI unit and old units is as follows:
1 lux = 1 lm/m²
$\quad\quad$ = 0.092 903 lm/ft²
$\quad\quad$ = 0.092 903 foot-candle (ft-cd or fc)
$\quad\quad$ = 1 000 nox (nx)
$\quad\quad$ = 10^{-4} phot (ph) or fot
$\quad\quad$ = 0.1 milliphot
1 lm/ft² = 1 foot-candle = 10.763 9 lx
1 nox = 0.001 lx
1 phot (ph) = 10^4 lx = 10 klx = 10 000 lx
1 milliphot (mph) = 10 lx

The 'quantity of light' received by a surface, or light exposure (also formerly called quantity of illumination) is measured in SI terms by lux seconds or lux hours.

Luminance
Luminance (*L* or *Lv*) or surface brightness of a source or of reflected light is measured in SI terms by candela per unit of apparent area as viewed from a given direction, the SI unit being candela per square metre (cd/m²).

If all the light falling on a surface were perfectly reflected by the surface, then the amount of luminance would be the same as the amount of illuminance of the light reaching the surface. The reflection factor or reflectance measures the degree to which a surface is not a perfect reflector; it is the ratio reflected light/incident light. Examples of approximate reflectances for different building finishes are:

white emulsion paint on plain plaster surface	0.8
concrete (light grey)	0.4
bricks (fletton)	0.3
timber panelling: medium oak	0.2

For SI units, where unit illuminance is that of a flat uniform diffuser emitting π lumens per square metre, luminance (cd/m²) = (illuminance × reflectance)/π, illuminance being measured in lux.
Luminance of a reflecting surface is sometimes called luminous exitance, and the SI unit for measurement is lumen per square metre.
The luminance of the sun is about 2 000 million cd/m², of a lighted electric bulb about 5 million cd/m², and of a lighted candle about 5 000 cd/m².

The relationship between the SI unit and old units is as follows:
1 cd/m² = 1 nit (nt)
$\quad\quad$ = 0.092 903 cd/ft²
$\quad\quad$ = 0.000 645 cd/in²
$\quad\quad$ = π × 0.092 903 (0.291 864) foot-lambert (ft-L or fL)
$\quad\quad$ = π × 10^{-4} lambert = 0.000 314 lambert (L)
$\quad\quad\quad\quad\quad\quad\quad$ = 0.314 millilambert (mL)
$\quad\quad$ = 1 000π skots
$\quad\quad$ = π apostilb (asb)[a]
$\quad\quad$ = 0.000 1 stilb (sb)
1 nit = 1 cd/m²
1 cd/ft² = 10.763 9 cd/m² (= π ft-L)
1 cd/in² = 1 550.00 cd/m²
1 lambert = 1 lm/cm² = ($10^4/\pi$) cd/m² = 3 183.1 cd/m²
1 foot-lambert = 3.426 26 cd/m²
1 skot = 0.001 apostilb = 0.318 3 mcd/m²
1 apostilb[a] = 1 lm/m² = (1/π) cd/m² = 0.318 3 cd/m²
1 stilb = 1 cd/cm² = 10 000 cd/m² = 10^4 cd/m² = 10 kcd/m²

[a]Sometimes called a meter-lambert or blondel.

Optics

Measures

Power
The unit of refractive power is called the diopter or dioptre (di or dpt or D), where 1 di = 1 m^{-1} = 1/m. This unit is acceptable with SI units.

Wavelength
A special unit used in measuring optical surfaces is the fringe, where 1 fringe = 273 nm = $\frac{1}{2}$ mercury green wavelength of 546 nm (more exactly 546.227 1 nm).

Refractive index

Where light passes through two different materials, the direction of light changes according to the nature of the materials. The angle of change is dependent on the index of refraction = velocity of light in a vacuum/velocity of light in the material.
Where light passes from medium 1 to medium 2, the index of refraction is given by:

$$n_{1,2} = \frac{\sin A_i}{\sin A_r} = \frac{b_1}{b_2}$$

where $n_{1,2}$ is the index of refraction between medium 1 and 2,
A_i is the angle of incidence (in the 1st medium)
A_r is the angle of refraction (in the 2nd medium)
b_1 is the phase velocity of the 1st medium
b_2 is the phase velocity of the 2nd medium

Examples of refractive indexes are: water = 1.33
$\quad\quad\quad\quad\quad\quad\quad\quad\quad\quad\quad\quad$ human eye (cornea) = 1.3376
$\quad\quad\quad\quad\quad\quad\quad\quad\quad\quad\quad\quad$ crown glass = 1.52

Radii of curvature

The radii of curvature of a lens, as related to the distance of the lens from the image and from the object focussed on is:

$$1/r_1 - 1/r_2 = (1/i - 1/d)/(n - 1)$$

where r_1 and r_2 are the radii of curvature of the lens,
i = distance of the lens from the image
d = distance of the object observed from the lens
n = index of refraction of the lens

Polarised light

Light is a transverse wave motion; that is, the vibrations are at right angles to the direction of propagation. Polarised light is light which has been changed from natural (or unpolarised) light to waves where the vibrations are restricted to one plane only. This change occurs when light is reflected twice.
When natural light waves are first reflected from a flat surface, such as glass or water, the intensity of the reflected beam varies with the angle of incidence of the light; if the reflected light is reflected again from another surface, the light coming from the second surface varies in intensity according to the relative angle which the second surface bears to the first, the intensity being greatest when the surfaces are parallel and least when they are at right angles. The light wave vibrations are in one phase only. Such light reflected from a second surface is called 'polarised' light.
Polarised light can be measured by a polariser or polariscope, in which a beam of light enters at one end and is reflected twice to emerge as polarised light at the other end. The polariscope can be used to determine, for example, the concentration of a dissolved substance, when the substance dissolved has 'optical activity' – it causes a rotation of the direction of vibration of polarised light traversing the medium. The amount of optical rotation is proportional to the degree of concentration, so that the polariscope can be used to estimate, for example, the concentration of sugar in a solution. The quality of sugar for international comparisons is usually based on a test of 96 sugar degrees by a polariscope. To convert one unit of refined or unrefined sugar to a basis of 96° polarisation the formula used is [(2 × *P*) − 100]/92, where *P* equals degrees of polarisation as tested by the polariscope.

Laser and maser

When it has the energy to do so, an atom emits a photon of light in about 1 microsecond, and at random. If a photon of the same wavelength passes at the same time as emission is occurring, the atom emits its photon in phase with the other photon – there is stimulated emission.
A laser is a device for arranging the stimulated emission so that there is a high intensity of light. There is '*l*ight *a*mplification by *s*timulated *e*mission of *r*adiation'. Similarly, a maser is a device used to amplify other forms of electromagnetic radiation, especially microwaves. There is '*m*icrowave *a*mplification by *s*timulated *e*mission of *r*adiation'.
The concentration of light intensity by lasers can produce very short pulses of light (10^{-11} s or 100 nanoseconds) with very intense peak power of 10^{14} W or 100 US billion kilowatts.

ght, optics and photography

Photography

Film

Size

The nominal size of a camera is usually that of the film taken by the camera; the image area is usually smaller than the size of the film. Examples of some usual sizes are as follows:

Film size designation	Image size
Still cameras:	
110	13 × 17 mm
135 (35 mm half-frame)	18 × 24 mm
135 (35 mm full-frame)	24 × 36 mm
126	28 × 28 mm
128	28 × 40 mm
127	1 13/16 × 1 9/16 in
127	$1\frac{5}{8} \times 1\frac{5}{8}$ in
127	$1\frac{5}{8} \times 2\frac{1}{2}$ in
120, 620	$1\frac{5}{8} \times 2\frac{1}{4}$ in
120, 220, 70 mm	$2\frac{1}{4} \times 1\frac{3}{4}$ in
120, 620, 220, 70 mm	$2\frac{1}{4} \times 2\frac{1}{4}$ in
120, 220, 70 mm	$2\frac{1}{4} \times 2\frac{3}{4}$ in
120, 620, 220, 70 mm	$2\frac{1}{4} \times 3\frac{1}{4}$ in

Motion-picture cameras:	height	width
8 mm	3.68 × 4.88 mm	
16 mm	7.49 × 10.26 mm	
35 mm	16.03 × 22.05 mm	
35 mm	18.67 × 24.89 mm	
65 mm	23.01 × 52.63 mm	

Film speed

Film speed is the measure of response of photographic material to radiant energy under specified conditions. Exposure (usually designated by H) is the quantity of radiant energy, measured in lux seconds. It is often expressed in $\log_{10} H$ units. The formulae for determining speed are $S = 0.8/H_m$ or $S° = 1 + 10 \log_{10} (0.8/H_m)$ where S or $S°$ = speed, and H_m = exposure in lux seconds. The designation of film speeds has been standardised by the International Standards Organisation. The ISO speed scales are as follows:

ISO speed

Arithmetic	Logarithmic	Arithmetic	Logarithmic
3200	36°	100	21°
2500	35°	80	20°
2000	34°	64	19°
1600	33°	50	18°
1250	32°	40	17°
1000	31°	32	16°
800	30°	25	15°
640	29°	20	14°
500	28°	16	13°
400	27°	12	12°
320	26°	10	11°
250	25°	8	10°
200	24°	6	9°
160	23°	5	8°
125	22°	4	7°

The designation is, for example, ISO 125, ISO 22° or ISO 125/22° (where both types of number are shown). In terms of the numbers the standard replaces, the first (arithmetic) number is equivalent to an ASA value (standard of the American National Standards Institute), and the second (logarithmic) is equivalent to a DIN value (standard of Deutsche Industrie Norm).

Camera stops: in the arithmetic scale, doubling or halving of the film speed is given by equivalent doubling or halving of the numbers; for the logarithmic scale, doubling or halving of speed is given by adding or subtracting 3 (a change of 0.30 or $\log_{10} 2$ in $\log_{10}$ units). The scales coincide at 12.

Lens

Angle of view

A normal camera lens gives an angle of view of 45–55°; extremes can be as low as 15° for a tele-photo long distance view and as high as 100° for wide-ranging views such as those for architectural purposes.

Focal length

The focal length is the distance between the centre of a lens and the plane of the image when the lens is focused on infinity.

Where F = focal length
$\quad\quad v$ = lens to image distance
$\quad\quad u$ = lens to object distance

$$\frac{1}{F} = \frac{1}{v} + \frac{1}{u}$$

This general formula gives the value of F for other than small values of v and u, when the F value may be inaccurate.
Where u = infinity, $F = v$.
The focal length is also defined in the formula $F = h/\tan A$, where h = image size and A = the angle subtended by the object at the lens.

f-number

The f-number (or f-stop) is the ratio of the focal length of the lens and the effective diameter of the lens opening or aperture: f-number $= F/d$, where F is the focal length and d the aperture diameter. Hence for a given focal length, the f-number is larger for a smaller aperture, and smaller for a larger aperture. The f-number is usually expressed in the form $f/2$, meaning $f = 2$. The usual f-numbers are: $f/1$, $f/1.4$, $f/2$, $f/2.8$, $f/4$, $f/5.6$, $f/8$, $f/11$, $f/16$, $f/22$, $f/32$ and $f/45$. Each lens in this series transmits one-half as much light as the preceding lens opening; that is, the f-number series is a series of the square root of a number series where each number is doubled:

area of lens (amount of light)	square root	area of lens (amount of light)	square root
1	1	64	8
2	1.41	128	11.3
4	2	256	16
8	2.83	512	22.6
16	4	1 024	32
32	5.66	2 048	45.3

Sometimes f-numbers are used which are not full 'f-stops' derived from a doubling of the lens area, for example $f/3.5$ and $f/4.5$. For most cameras, where the focal length is fixed, the f-number effectively measures the aperture size.

Colour-temperature

Colours of light, especially in photographic use, are sometimes expressed in terms of colour temperatures, rated in kelvin (K). Colour temperatures are based on the variation in radiations emitted when the temperature of a substance with a high melting point is raised: the radiations emitted begin with those in the infrared range, then the frequency increases with temperature (wavelength falls) and the colour moves through the visible spectrum from red to blue and into ultraviolet. The temperature, for a given substance, provides a measure of the colour, with lower temperatures (colder) relating to the higher wavelength or red end of the spectrum, and higher temperatures (hotter) relating to the lower wavelength or blue end of the spectrum.

Examples of colour temperature are:

warm white lamp (for hotels, restaurants and homes)	2 700 K
photographic daylight	5 500 K
northlight fluorescent lamp (emphasising blues)	6 500 K

Flashlight bulbs are sometimes rated in kelvin to indicate whether they are suitable for use with daylight film or film balanced for a lower colour temperature light source.
Filters, used, for example, to change the balance of a colour source from daylight (5 500 K) towards a different colour such as 3 200 K, are sometimes given a 'shift' value in terms of the 'mired' (microreciprocal degree), where the number of mireds = 1 000 000/K (10^6/K).
Also, 1 decamired = 10 mireds.
The daylight value is 182 mireds, and a shift to 3 200 K (313 mireds) is a shift of 131 mireds (313 − 182).

Minerals

Measures

Gold and silver are usually measured in troy weights (see page 19).
Also: 1 metric carat = 200 milligrams. Symbol in the United Kingdom for metric carat is CM. 100 points = 1 metric carat (1 point = 2 mg).
Assay ton: the number of milligrams in a UK or US assay ton
= the corresponding number of ounces troy in the UK (long) or US (short) ton.
That is: 1 UK assay ton = 32 666⅔ mg; 1 US assay ton = 29 166⅔ mg.

Hardness scales

Scratch hardness (based on the ability to scratch another substance)

Moh's scale
(the basis of Moh's scale is that each substance can be scratched by those higher in the series)

substance	hardness	substance	hardness
Talc	1	Feldspar	6
Gypsum	2	Quartz	7
Calcite	3	Topaz	8
Fluorite	4	Corundum	9
Apatite	5	Diamond	10

Generally, 1–3 is soft, 4–7 is intermediate, and 8–10 is hard.

Some levels for other substances are:

thumb nail	2½	copper	2½–3	glass	4½–6½
aluminium	2–3	mild steel	4–5	knife-blade	6

There is a modified scale, which is the same up to scale 6, but extends the scale so that diamond = 15. The modified scale is:

substance	hardness	substance	hardness
Vitreous fused silica	7	Fused alumina	12
Quartz (7 in basic scale)	8	Silicon carbide	13
Garnet	9	Boron carbide	14
Topaz (8 in basic scale)	10	Diamond (10 in basic scale)	15
Fused zirconia	11		

Indentation hardness

This is based on the size of the indentation from a given load, or on the load to make a certain sized indentation; there are a number of different scales, including the following:

	Based on an indenter of: shape	material
Brinell	sphere	hardened steel or tungsten carbide
Rockwell	sphere	hardened steel
	cone	diamond
Knoop	rhombic-based pyramid	diamond
Monotron	hemisphere	diamond
Vickers	square-based pyramid	diamond

Details on some main systems are:

Brinell hardness (HB) = $F/\pi Dh$
where F = force applied (measured in kilograms-force)
D = diameter (in mm) of the sphere acting as indenter
h = depth of indentation

Rockwell hardness (HR) = $E - e$
where E = 100 or 130 according to the Rockwell system used
$e = h_1 - h_2$, h_1 being the indentation when increasing from an initial force to a total force, and h_2 the indentation left when the force is removed.

Forces applied for some Rockwell systems are (force in newtons and kilograms-force):

System	E	Initial force N	kgf	Force applied N	kgf	Total force N	kgf
C	100	98	10	1 372	140	1 470	150
A	100	98	10	490	50	588	60
B	130	98	10	882	90	980	100
F	100	98	10	490	50	588	60
15 N	100	29.4	3	117.6	12	147	15
15 T	100	29.4	3	117.6	12	147	15
30 N	100	29.4	3	264.6	27	294	30
30 T	100	29.4	3	264.6	27	294	30
45 N	100	29.4	3	411.6	42	441	45
45 T	100	29.4	3	411.6	42	441	45

Vickers hardness (HV) = $2 F \sin \theta / d^2$
where F = force applied to the indenter (in kgf, chosen as 1, 2½, 5, 10, 20, 30, 50 or 100)
$\theta = \frac{1}{2}$ angle of the taper of the indenter (2θ = standard value of 136°)
d = arithmetic mean diagonal diameter of indentation (in mm)

Minerals and alloys

The alloy percentages included in the following list of minerals are intended as rough guides; the exact proportions will vary according to the nature of the finished product and the purpose for which it is intended.

Aluminium: is derived mainly from bauxite. Typical composition of bauxite is Al_2O_3 (alumina) 40–60%; Fe_2O_3 5–30%; water 12–30%; with small amounts of SiO_2 and TiO_2. Aluminium can be alloyed so that it is as strong as steel and only one-third the weight. A simple alloy would be 4% copper, less than 1% each of magnesium and manganese, and the rest aluminium.
Duralumin alloys (average) = 94–95% aluminium, 4% copper, 0.5% manganese, 0.5% magnesium, 0.4% silicon, and not more than 0.5% iron.

Anhydrite: see gypsum.

Antimony: is used to impart hardness and stiffness to lead alloys.
Antimonial lead (hard lead) = 1–12% antimony.
Babbitt metal:
soft = 91% tin, 4½% antimony, 4½% copper.
hard = 89% tin, 7½% antimony, 3½% copper.
lead based = 82½% lead, 15% antimony, 1% tin, 1% arsenic, ½% copper.
Britannia metal = 74–91% tin, 6–24% antimony, ¼–3½% copper, with usually a small amount of lead.
Pewter: see tin.
Type metal = 55–95% lead, 2–28% antimony, 2–20% tin.

Arsenic: up to 0.5% added to lead or copper imparts hardness.

Asbestos: fibrous varieties of some silicate minerals; main variety is chrysotile. The fibre can be very fine; as small diameter as 0.000 000 7 in (compared with wool 0.001 in, cotton 0.000 4 in and nylon 0.000 3 in). Tensile strength of asbestos fabrics is about 100 000 lbf/in² (7 000 kgf/cm²).

Barium: main form is barytes (chiefly barium sulphate); used as a pigment in white paint, and in paper and textile industries and oil-well drilling muds.
Lithopone (white paint pigment) = 67–73% barium sulphate, 26–32% zinc sulphide.

Beryllium: can be commercial beryl or gem variety (emeralds or aquamarines); it is very light with a relative density of 1.85. Is used in nuclear reactors as a moderator and as canning material for fuel elements, because it reflects neutrons.
Beryllium aluminium = 72% beryllium, 28% aluminium; for high strength with relative density of 2.0.
Beryllium copper alloys (beryllium bronzes) = copper base with about 2½% beryllium; this increases strength about 6 times.

Bismuth: as an alloy has a low melting point; bismuth amalgam (with mercury in varying proportions) is used for silvering globes, etc.
Wood's metal = 50% bismuth, 25% lead, 12½% tin, 12½% cadmium, and melts at 70°C.

Borates: in the glass industry 15–50 parts of borax (sodium tetraborate) may be mixed with 1 000 parts of quartz sand to brighten and strengthen the glass.
Boron is used for control rods in nuclear reactors, often alloyed with steel.
Pyrex = borax-silicate glass.

Minerals

Cadmium: used as an alloy it gives strength, enables the withstanding of higher temperatures, and gives a high electrical resistance; used in electro-plating of iron and steel, in bearing metals, and for some types of nuclear reactor control rods, etc.
Cadmium-nickel alloy = $98\frac{1}{2}$% cadmium, $1-1\frac{1}{2}$% nickel.
Cadmium-silver alloy = $96\frac{1}{4}$% cadmium, 3% silver, $\frac{3}{4}$% copper.
Cadmium-copper alloy = copper alloy with 1% cadmium.

China clay (kaolin): is 46% silica (SiO_2), 40% alumina (Al_2O_3) and 14% water. Used in paper manufacture, pottery, paint, etc.

Chromium: as an alloy increases the hardness, tenacity, ductility, resistance to wear and corrosion of steel, and gives a high electrical resistance. Alloys of less than 3% chromium are used in the automobile industry and for rails. Alloys of more than 12% produce stainless and rustless steels.
Chromium iron = 65–70% iron, 25–30% chromium, 5% nickel.

Cobalt: is used for heat-resisting and rustless alloys and steel.
Stellite alloys = 35–80% cobalt, 10–40% chromium, $\frac{1}{4}$% tungsten, 0.1% molybdenum.

Copper: composition of copper alloys can vary widely.
Bronzes:
ancient = 88% copper, 12% tin.
modern (average) = 88% copper, 10% tin, 0.1–2% zinc; usual range is 5–15% tin.
aluminium = copper with $8\frac{1}{2}$–$10\frac{1}{2}$% aluminium, $1\frac{1}{2}$–$3\frac{1}{2}$% iron.
bearing = 70–96% copper, 5–20% tin, 1–2% nickel.
phosphor = 80–95% copper, 5–15% tin, 0.1–$2\frac{1}{2}$% phosphorus.
statuary = 65–85% copper, 10–30% zinc, $2\frac{1}{2}$–5% tin.
Gunmetal = 88–90% copper, 8–10% tin, 2–6% zinc.
Brass = 60–80% copper, 15–20% zinc, 0.1–5% lead. See also zinc.
Cartridge brass = 70% copper, 30% zinc.
UK coinage:
'coppers' = 97% copper, $2\frac{1}{2}$% zinc, $\frac{1}{2}$% tin.
threepenny bit (pre 1971) = 79% copper, 20% zinc, 1% nickel.
'silver' (cupro-nickel) coins = 75% copper, 25% nickel; for silver coins before 1947 see silver.

Diamonds: almost pure carbon; relative density is 3.5 and is hardest mineral (10 on Moh's basic scale). Unit of weight is metric carat; a brilliant cut diamond weighing 1 carat has diameter about 6 mm ($\frac{1}{4}$ in). The 'carat count' is the number of near equal size diamonds per carat, and is a measure of diamond size. Industrial diamonds range in size from about 120 per carat (120-count) to 4 or more carats per stone.

Fluorspar: is used mainly as a flux for open hearth steel; 5–8 lb ($2\frac{1}{4}$–$3\frac{1}{2}$ kg) are needed for every ton (or tonne) of steel. For electric steel smelting 14–40 lb (6–18 kg) are used per ton (or tonne).

Fuller's earth: clay-like minerals, mainly hydrated silicates of aluminium; typical composition is 60% silica (SiO_2) and 20% alumina (Al_2O_3). Absorbs grease and is used for detergents.

Gold: the purity of gold is expressed as parts of 1 000, so that a fineness of 800 is 80% gold. Pure gold is defined as 24 carats (1 000 fine), but usually the highest degree of fineness in use is 22 carats. Dental gold is usually 16 or 20 carat ($62\frac{1}{2}$% or $83\frac{1}{3}$%); gold in jewellery usually ranges from 9 to 22 carat ($37\frac{1}{2}$–$91\frac{2}{3}$%). A golden sovereign is 22 carat ($91\frac{2}{3}$% gold, $8\frac{1}{3}$% copper).
White gold = 12% palladium, 15% nickel or 20–25% platinum.
A standard international bar of gold is 400 troy ounces; bars of 250 troy ounces are also used.

Graphite ('black lead'): the 'lead' in pencils is about 50% graphite, 50% fine clay. Graphite is used as a moderator in nuclear reactors.
Graphite bronze = 89% copper, 10% tin, 1% graphite; for use in bearings.

Gypsum and anhydrite: are calcium sulphates: used for plaster of paris and hard finish plasters; also in pigments, cement, etc.

Iron: see separate iron and steel section.

Lead: used with 1–4% antimony for sheet and foil; see also, under antimony, lead-based babbitt and type metal. Lead sheet is specified by its thickness in millimetres. Before metrication, lead sheet was described in the United Kingdom by its substance in lb/ft²; hence 3 lb lead was 3 lb weight per square foot.

Limestone: mainly calcium carbonate; usually has 22–56% lime (CaO), 0–21% magnesia (MgO). Those with 5–20% MgO are called 'magnesian' limestones, and those with over 20% MgO 'dolomites'. Is used for aggregates, cement, building lime, glass, paper industries, etc.

Magnesium: is the lightest of all metals, two-thirds of the weight of aluminium; when alloyed combines mechanical strength with lightness.
Incendiary bomb = 93% magnesium, 7% aluminium.

Manganese: is a deoxydiser and a desulphuriser for steel. If a fraction of 1% of manganese is added to the steel melt the elastic limit and tenacity is increased; 12% in steel gives high tensile strength and abrasion resistance.
Ferro-manganese = 80% manganese, 20% iron and 0.1–7% carbon.
Spiegeleisen = 15–30% manganese, 80% low-grade iron ore, $4\frac{1}{2}$–$6\frac{1}{2}$% carbon.

Mercury ('quicksilver'): is sold in wrought iron flasks; the standard flask contains 76 lb (34.473 kg) of mercury and is the market unit of quantity. Mercury is used in production of chemicals and drugs, scientific instruments and ammunition, and in extraction of gold and silver. In combination with other substances is called an amalgam.

Mica: this is usually a silicate of aluminium. The value of mica lies in its perfect cleavage – it can be separated easily into sheets 1/1 000 inch thick (1 'mil'). It is used for electrical insulation and, when ground, as a dusting powder for rubber and in paint.

Molybdenum: is principally used for special steels, such as high speed cutting steels; it has a similar effect to chromium or tungsten. 1% or less in steel increases the hardness.
1 ton of molybdenum (Mo) = 1.67 tons of molybdenite (MoS_2).

Nickel: when alloyed to steel increases strength with less reduction in ductility than caused when carbon is used. Steel alloys usually have 0.2–9% nickel; high nickel ('stainless') steels have 7–35%, while up to 50% is used for very high resistance to corrosion. With 13% nickel steel is so strong it can hardly be cut or drilled; with 25% it has a high electrical resistance and is used for resistance wire. Nickel steel or 'invar' = 36% nickel, and does not expand or contract appreciably with temperature variations. Added to iron, 10–15% of nickel increases the strength, hardness and corrosion resistance, and makes it non-magnetic. 48–80% of nickel with iron is highly magnetic.
Monel metal = $\frac{2}{3}$ nickel, $\frac{1}{4}$ copper, with manganese and iron.
Nickel silver ('German silver') = 45–77% copper, 5–30% nickel, 5–45% zinc. For nickel in coinage see copper and silver. For white gold: see gold.

Platinum: the metal and alloys are very resistant to corrosion and are unaffected by normal atmospheric exposure; uses are for instruments, crucibles, electrical contacts, etc. For white gold: see gold.
Platinum–iridium alloy = 65–95% platinum, 5–35% iridium.
Platinum–nickel alloy = 80–95% platinum, 5–20% nickel.
Platinum–tungsten alloy = 92–99% platinum, 1–8% tungsten.

Silicon: useful in alloys as it is fluid when molten and not brittle after casting.
Silicon-aluminium alloy = 10–13% silicon, 86–89% aluminium, 0.5% manganese, 0.5% iron, 0.1% zinc.

Silver: next to gold, the most malleable and ductile of metals; 1 gram of pure silver can be drawn into a wire more than $1\frac{1}{2}$ kilometres long, and silver leaf can be 1/4 000 inch (6 micrometres) thick. Is used for electrical contacts, etc. Electrum metal is a natural gold/silver alloy with 55–88% gold.
UK coinage: silver coins before 1947 = 50% silver, 40% copper, 5% zinc, 5% nickel (before 1920, $92\frac{1}{2}$% silver).
UK standard for plate and jewellery = fineness of 925 silver, 75 copper.

Sulphur: pyrites contains 53% sulphur, 47% iron; in the paper industry 110–300 lb (50–150 kg) of sulphur is used in the manufacture of 1 ton (tonne) of sulphur pulp.

Talc: is hydrated silicate of magnesium with 63.5% SiO_2, 31.7% MgO and 4.8% water. Prepared talc is sometimes called 'French chalk'. Has extreme softness and smoothness (number 1 on Moh's scale).

Tantalum and niobium (columbium): may be alloyed with iron, nickel, tungsten, molybdenum and chromium to give tenacity, ductility, tensile strength, hardness and resistance to corrosion by most acids.
0.5–0.8% of niobium in steel makes it resistant to high temperatures; it is useful as a material in nuclear reactors.
'Tantaloy' = 92% tantalum, $7\frac{1}{2}$% tungsten.

Minerals

Thorium and cerium ('rare earths'): are obtained mainly from monazite (thoria 0–30%, cerium group oxides 39–74%). Thorium is used in magnesium alloys, and in production of nuclear energy fuel. Cerium and other 'rare earth' oxides are called 'lanthanons'; they are used for lighter flints and in electric arc carbons (for cinema projectors, etc).

Tin: main ore is cassiterite; the principal use is in tinplating – tinplate is mild steel up to 0.49 mm thick, coated very thinly with tin metal:
tin can = $1\frac{1}{2}$% tin, $98\frac{1}{2}$% steel.
Babbitt metal: see antimony.
Bronze: see copper
Gunmetal: see copper
Bell metal = 15–25% tin, 75–85% copper.
Pewter = 90–95% tin, 3–8% antimony, 2% copper.
Solder:
soft tin = 63% tin, 37% lead
other = 25–50% tin, 50–75% lead

Titanium: rutile is titanium dioxide; used mainly in pigments. Titanium paints have twice the opacity of zinc, and three times the opacity of white lead paints. Sometimes used as a mixture; for example 30% TiO_2 with 70% $CaSO_4$ (calcium sulphate).

Tungsten ('wolfram'): strengthens steel at ordinary and high temperatures. Less than 2 tons of tungsten supply filaments for 100 million electric bulbs.
1 tonne tungsten (W) = 1.261 tonnes tungsten trioxide (WO_3).
Ferro-tungsten = 75–80% tungsten with iron (and small amounts of silicon, manganese, etc.)
Tungsten steel = 18% tungsten, 4% chromium, 1% vanadium.
Tungsten nickel = 73% tungsten, 23% nickel.

Vanadium: mainly found as vanadium pentoxide (V_2O_5); 1 ton of vanadium (V) = 1.785 tons vanadium pentoxide. Usually less than 1% vanadium is added to steel to increase the toughness and high temperature resistance.
Ferro-vanadium alloy = 35–60% vanadium, balance iron.

Zinc: is used in paint (also see barium). Resists corrosion: rolled zinc alloy (for roofing, etc) contains 1% copper; galvanizing is depositing a thin coat of zinc on iron and steel to prevent rusting. Copper-zinc alloy is used in the electrical industry.
Brass: see copper; for wire, 'alpha' brasses contain 30–37% zinc, while 'beta' brasses for castings, etc., contain 40–49% zinc.
Coinage: see copper.
Zinc amalgam = 89% zinc, 11% mercury.

Zirconium: imparts hardness when alloyed with iron, copper, aluminium and magnesium, etc.; used in production of nuclear power reactor cores.
Cooperite = nickel-zirconium alloy, acid resisting and very hard.

Relation between volume and weight (mass) of various metals

	To obtain lb multiply number of cubic inches by	To obtain kg multiply number of cubic decimetres (litres) by[a]	Weight relative to steel = 1[b]
Cast iron	0.260	7.20	0.917
Steel	0.284	7.85	1.000
Aluminium	0.098	2.70	0.344
Zinc	0.257	7.10	0.904
Tin (white)	0.264	7.31	0.931
Manganese	0.267	7.40	0.943
Brass	0.303	8.40	1.070
Nickel	0.322	8.90	1.134
Copper	0.322	8.92	1.136
Lead	0.410	11.34	1.445
Mercury	0.490	13.55	1.726
Uranium	0.676	18.7	2.382
Tungsten	0.697	19.3	2.459

[a] Equals relative density; for kilograms per cubic metre also multiply by 1 000.
[b] Weights for various sizes can be obtained from the tables for steel on pages 154–156 by applying the weight relative to steel as a multiplier.

Music

Pitch

The normal range of sound which can be heard is from 20 Hz (although some can hear at 15 Hz) to 20 000 Hz. Of this the practical musical range is usually regarded as from 40 to 4 000 Hz.
The international standard musical pitch is 440 Hz for A in the treble stave. The former French, continental or Vienna standard was 435 Hz, and the 1896 Philharmonic standard was 439 Hz.
A subjective measure of the frequency Hertz is the mel, where the mel equals the Hertz at an intensity level of 60 decibels (sometimes 40 dB). Also see sound, pages 165–166 for other sound measures.

Scales

The range of frequencies can be divided into a number of types of scale, the most frequently used being the pentatonic (5-tone), seven-tone, twelve and thirteen tone scales.

Full (tempered) chromatic scale
This is the most widely used western scale, with 13 tones and 12 intervals. It is based on the interval of the octave which is a doubling of frequency.
The full possible range of octaves, based on the standard pitch of 440 Hz for A, can be outlined as follows (in Hertz):

	C	A
C_0	16.35	$27\frac{1}{2}$
C_1	32.70	55
C_2	65.41	110
C_3	130.81	220
C_4	261.63	440[a]
C_5	523.25	880
C_6	1 046.50	1 760
C_7	2 093.00	3 520
C_8	4 186.01	7 040
C_9	8 372.02	14 080
C_{10}	16 744.04	(28 160)[b]

[a] International standard musical pitch.　[b] Inaudible.

Intervals greater than an octave are called compound intervals.

The relationship between A and C in the above table is determined by the division of the octave into twelve intervals, such that the intervals are equal on the logarithmic scale between 1 and 2 which ratio determines the octave interval. (This type of division is the same as that used in measuring the decibel; also see page 166.)
A number of different names are given to the same basic intervals. The table on the facing page sets out various scales for the octave from C_4 to C_5.

The interval between different tones or semi-tones is described by the following names, where the interval can range from any one note to any other.

Name	Fraction of $\log_{10} 2$ (0.301 03)	$\log_{10}$	Ratio (anti-log)
minor second[a]	1/12	0.025 09	1.059 46
major second	2/12 = $\frac{1}{6}$	0.050 17	1.122 46
minor third	3/12 = $\frac{1}{4}$	0.075 26	1.189 21
major third	4/12 = $\frac{1}{3}$	0.100 34	1.259 92
perfect fourth	5/12	0.125 43	1.334 84
augmented fourth[b]	6/12 = $\frac{1}{2}$	0.150 51	1.414 21
perfect fifth	7/12	0.175 60	1.498 31
minor sixth	8/12 = $\frac{2}{3}$	0.200 69	1.587 40
major sixth	9/12 = $\frac{3}{4}$	0.225 77	1.681 79
minor seventh	10/12 = $\frac{5}{6}$	0.250 86	1.781 80
major seventh	11/12	0.275 94	1.887 75
octave	12/12 = 1	0.301 03	2

[a] Or semi-tone.　[b] Or diminished fifth.

For example, the range A to C = minor third = 523.25/440 Hz = 1.189 2
the range D to F = minor third = 349.23/293.66 Hz = 1.189 2

Music

Interval	Log$_{10}$	Savart scale[a] simple[b]	modified[c]	Ratio[f]	Ratio in cents	Millioctaves	Tone number	Symbol[d]	Frequency in Hertz
0	0.0	0	0	1.0	0	0	1	C	261.63
1	0.025 09	25	25	1.059	100	83		{C+ / D−}	277.18
2	0.050 17	50	50	1.122	200	167	2	D	293.66
3	0.075 26	75	75	1.189	300	250		{D+ / E−}	311.13
4	0.100 34	100	100	1.260	400	333	3	E	329.63
5	0.125 43	125	125	1.335	500	417	4	F	349.23
6	0.150 51	151	150	1.414	600	500		{F+ / F−}	369.99
7	0.175 60	176	175	1.498	700	583	5	G	392.00
8	0.200 69	201	200	1.587	800	667		{G+ / A−}	415.30
9	0.225 77	226	225	1.682	900	750	6	A	440[e]
10	0.250 86	251	250	1.782	1 000	833		{A+ / B−}	466.16
11	0.275 94	276	275	1.888	1 100	917	7	B	493.88
12	0.301 03	301	300	2.0	1 200	1 000	8	C	523.25

[a]A savart is regarded as the smallest pitch interval that a human ear can distinguish.   [b]The log rounded to three places and multiplied by 1 000.   [c]The simple savart number rounded to the nearest multiple of 25.   [d]For simplicity, a sharp or augmented semi-tone is shown with the symbol +, and a flat or dimished semi-tone with the symbol −.   [e]International standard musical pitch.   [f]Anti-log.

Harmonics

The frequency of vibration of a string (the fundamental note) is determined by
$f_a = T/(2 \times m \times h)$
where f_a = frequency, T = tension of the string, m = mass per unit length, and h = length of the string.
Hence, if a string is dampened at a point $1/f$ of its length from a fixed end, the note emitted has a frequency f times that of the fundamental note; this is called the $(f-1)$ th overtone or harmonic of the fundamental note.
For example, where $f = 2$, the length of string is halved, and the frequency doubled.

Packaging

Average and minimum systems

Under the *minimum* system, applicable under law in the United Kingdom to all packages before 1980, a container marked with a statement as to the quantity of goods contained had to contain at least that quantity.
Under the *average* system, applicable in law for certain packages within the United Kingdom (and the EEC) from January 1, 1980, the average contents of packages must not be less than the stated quantity (where a package is the combination of a container and the goods it contains, and the nominal quantity is the weight or volume of the contents); a certain proportion of the packages can contain less (up to a point) than the nominal quantity.

Packing rules

Three rules have been established to help the packer conform to the average standards laid down; these are:
1. The actual contents of the packages shall not be less, on average, than the nominal quantity.
2. Not more than 2½% of the packages may be non-standard, ie have negative errors larger than the tolerable negative error (TNE) specified for the nominal quantity.
3. No package may be inadequate, ie have a negative error larger than twice the specified TNE.

The tolerable negative errors (TNE) are as follows:

Nominal quantity of package in grams or millilitres	Tolerable negative error (TNE) as a percentage of nominal quantity	g or ml
5– 50	9	—
50– 100	—	4½
100– 200	4½	—
200– 300	—	9
300– 500	3	—
500– 1 000	—	15
1 000–10 000	1½	—
10 000–15 000	—	150
above 15 000	1	—

In calculating the error as a percentage of nominal quantity, in units of weight or volume, the amount of a tolerable error in the cases shown in the above table shall be rounded up to the nearest one-tenth of a gram or millilitre as the case may be.
A non-standard package is one where the quantity of the goods it contains is less by more than the prescribed amount than the nominal quantity on the package.
An inadequate package is one where the quantity of the goods it contains is less by more than twice the prescribed amount than the nominal quantity on the package.

Packaging ranges

The ranges established by the EEC for nominal quantities of contents of prepackages are shown below for some main items (also see food concerning the change over to metric packages in the United Kingdom):

Product *sold by weight*	Range of nominal quantities *quantity in grams*
Butter	125, 250, 500, 1 000, 1 500, 2 000, 2 500, 5 000
Cereals (ready-to-serve)	250, 375, 500, 750, 1 000, 1 500, 2 000
Rice	125, 250, 500, 1 000, 2 000, 2 500, 5 000
Frozen fruit & vegetables	150, 300, 450, 600, 750, 1 000, 1 500, 2 000, 2 500
Solid toilet and household soaps	25, 50, 75, 100, 150, 200, 250, 300, 400, 500, 1 000

sold by volume	*quantity in millilitres*
Ice cream (for quantities larger than 250 ml)	300, 500, 750, 1 000, 1 500, 2 000, 2 500, 3 000, 4 000, 5 000
Paints and varnishes	25, 50, 125, 250, 375, 500, 750, 1 000, 2 000, 2 500, 4 000, 5 000, 10 000
Lubricating oils	125, 250, 500, 1 000, 2 000, 2 500, 3 000, 4 000, 5 000, 10 000
Toothpaste	25, 50, 75, 100, 125, 150, 200, 250, 300

Paper and printing

Paper

Sizes of printing paper

The UK paper industry in general converted to the use of international paper units during the seventies. Following are the main size classifications, including the former British units.

International paper sizes (ISO)

International paper sizes are trimmed sizes based on an AO sheet which is 1 m² in area, and with sides such that when the larger side is halved the relationship is retained; the relationships between the sides is then in the ratio of $\sqrt{2}:1$.
The ISO-A series of trimmed sizes is as follows:

A series	mm	in
4AO	1682 × 2378	66.22 × 93.62
2AO	1189 × 1682	46.81 × 66.22
A0	841 × 1189	33.11 × 46.81
A1	594 × 841	23.39 × 33.11
A2	420 × 594	16.54 × 23.39
A3	297 × 420	11.69 × 16.54
A4	210 × 297	8.27 × 11.69
A5	148 × 210	5.83 × 8.27
A6	105 × 148	4.13 × 5.83
A7	74 × 105	2.91 × 4.13
A8	52 × 74	2.05 × 2.91
A9	37 × 52	1.46 × 2.05
A10	26 × 37	1.02 × 1.46

There is also an ISO B series (trimmed sizes), little used, which has as a starting point a sheet with 1 metre on one side and $\sqrt{2}$ metre (1.414 m) on the other:

B series	mm	in
B0	1000 × 1414	39.37 × 55.67
B1	707 × 1000	27.83 × 39.37
B2	500 × 707	19.68 × 27.83
B3	353 × 500	13.90 × 19.68
B4	250 × 353	9.84 × 13.90
B5	176 × 250	6.93 × 9.84
B6	125 × 176	4.92 × 6.93
B7	88 × 125	3.46 × 4.92
B8	62 × 88	2.44 × 3.46
B9	44 × 62	1.73 × 2.44
B10	31 × 44	1.22 × 1.73

There is also a special series for envelopes; some main sizes are:

	mm	in
C4	229 × 324	9.02 × 12.76
C5	162 × 229	6.38 × 9.02
C6	114 × 162	4.49 × 6.38
DL	101 × 220	4.33 × 8.66

The above are trimmed sizes; the series for untrimmed stock sizes are the RA series for normal trims, and the SRA series for extra trims. These are as follows:

RA series	mm	in
RA0	860 × 1220	33.86 × 48.03
RA1	610 × 860	24.02 × 33.86
RA2	430 × 610	16.93 × 24.02
SRA series		
SRA0	900 × 1280	35.43 × 50.39
SRA1	640 × 900	25.20 × 35.43
SRA2	450 × 640	17.72 × 25.20

Books

Untrimmed metric equivalents for book papers have been established, based on multiples of 24 mm; these are:

	mm	in
Metric quad crown	768 × 1008	30.24 × 39.68
Metric large quad crown	816 × 1056	32.13 × 41.57
Metric quad demy	888 × 1128	34.96 × 44.41
Metric small quad royal	960 × 1272	37.80 × 50.08

Trimmed book sizes normally allow for trims from head, tail and fore-edge of a page; for the metric sizes above a trim of 3 mm is standard (compared with $\frac{1}{8}$ inch for traditional British sizes):

	Untrimmed size mm	Trimmed size mm
Metric crown 8vo	126 × 192	123 × 186
Metric large crown 8vo	132 × 204	129 × 198
Metric demy 8vo	141 × 222	138 × 216
Metric royal 8vo	159 × 240	156 × 234

Old British sizes

Old British sizes have in general been replaced in the United Kingdom. Some main sizes were:

Trimmed sizes	in	mm
Octavo	8 × 5	203 × 127
Quarto	8 × 10	203 × 254
Foolscap	8 × 13	203 × 330

Untrimmed sizes (full sheet)

	in	mm
Crown	15 × 20	381 × 508
Large post	16½ × 21	419 × 533
Double foolscap	17 × 27	432 × 686
Demy	17½ × 22½	445 × 572
Medium	18 × 23	457 × 584
Royal	20 × 25	508 × 635
Double crown	20 × 30	508 × 762
Imperial	22 × 30	559 × 762
Double demy	22½ × 35	572 × 890
Quad crown	30 × 40	762 × 1016
Large crown	32 × 42	813 × 1067
Quad demy	35 × 45	890 × 1144

Subdivisions of the above full sheets for British and metric sizes are described as follows:
Folio means a full sheet folded or cut in half
Quarto (or 4to) means a full sheet folded or cut into four
Octavo (or 8vo) means a full sheet folded or cut into eight
16mo means a full sheet folded or cut into sixteen

Paper substances

With the change to the metric system, paper substance ('grammage') in the United Kingdom is expressed in terms of grams per square metre. Stock weights are expressed in terms of kg per 1000 sheets (formerly in terms of lb per ream). Grammage was at first expressed in a range based on the R 20 and R 40 series of preferred numbers, but this range has been changed to a range based on a series rounded to 5 g/m². Some paper substances are shown in the table below:

Grammage g/m²	Kilograms per 1000 sheets (kg/1000)				
	SRA1	SRA2	RA1	RA2	A4
25	14.4	7.2	13.1	6.6	1.56
30	17.3	8.6	15.7	7.9	1.87
45	25.9	13.0	23.6	11.8	2.81
60	34.6	17.3	31.5	15.7	3.74
70	40.3	20.2	36.7	18.4	4.37
80	46.1	23.0	42.0	21.0	4.99
85	49.0	24.5	44.6	22.3	5.30
90	51.8	25.9	47.2	23.6	5.61
100	57.6	28.8	52.5	26.2	6.24
105	60.5	30.2	55.1	27.5	6.55
115	66.2	33.1	60.3	30.2	7.17
135	77.8	38.9	70.8	35.4	8.42
155	89.3	44.6	81.3	40.7	9.67
160	92.2	46.1	83.9	42.0	9.98
170	97.9	49.0	89.2	44.6	10.60

Paper measures

1 ream = 500 sheets
2 reams = 1 bundle = 1 000 sheets
5 reams = 1 bale = 2 500 sheets
(for old measures: 1 ream = 480 sheets for writing and 516 sheets for printing; 1 ream = 20 quires).

Paper and printing

Typography

Sizes of type

The basis of the Anglo-American system is the 12-point (pica) em, which measures 0.166 044 of an inch (4.217 518 mm). The point, one twelfth of the em, is 0.013 837 of an inch (0.351 459 8 mm); there are approximately 72 points to an inch (a closer approximation is $72\frac{1}{4}$ points to the inch).

The Didot point, used in continental Europe, is generally defined as 0.376 mm, equal to 0.014 8 in approximately (for West Germany it is defined as 1.000 333/2 660) m = 0.376 065 mm approx). Other points are: Fournier 0.3488 mm (0.0137 in), Casion 0.3516 mm (0.0138 in), German 0.3765 (0.0148 in). 1 cicéro = 12 Didot points = 4.512 mm (0.178 in).

Some comparisons follow:

Anglo-American points	in	mm	Didot points
1	0.014	0.351	0.935
2	0.028	0.703	1.869
3	0.042	1.054	2.804
4	0.055	1.406	3.739
5	0.069	1.757	4.674
6	0.083	2.109	5.608
7	0.097	2.460	6.543
8	0.111	2.812	7.478
9	0.125	3.163	8.413
10	0.138	3.515	9.347
11	0.152	3.866	10.282
12	0.166	4.218	11.217
14	0.194	4.920	13.086
16	0.221	5.623	14.956
18	0.249	6.326	16.825
20	0.277	7.029	18.695
24	0.332	8.435	22.434
30	0.415	10.544	28.042
36	0.498	12.653	33.650
42	0.581	14.761	39.259
48	0.664	16.870	44.867
60	0.830	21.088	56.084
72	0.996	25.305	67.301

Old British sizes of type bore individual names; the equivalents in point sizes of these names are:

Brilliant	$3\frac{1}{2}$	Emerald	$6\frac{1}{2}$	Small pica	11
Diamond	$4\frac{1}{2}$	Minion	7	Pica	12
Pearl or agate	5	Brevier	8	English	14
Ruby	$5\frac{1}{2}$	Bourgeois	9	Great primer	18
Nonpareil	6	Long primer	10	Double pica	22

A metric system is not internationally agreed, but some use is made of a system with 0.025 mm as basic unit for width, and 0.25 mm as a basic unit for character depth.

Pulp

Woodpulp

Woodpulp is paper-making wood (pulpwood) after it has been made into a fibrous mass by mechanical or chemical means.

Pulping yield

The wood input in cubic metres per tonne of air-dry pulp is as follows, varying according to the chemical composition of the wood and the nature of the pulping process:

Type of pulp	Coniferous	Non-coniferous
Mechanical	1.7 to 3.3	
Semi-chemical		1.7 to 4.0
Sulphite, unbleached	3.4 to 6.5	2.6 to 5.3
bleached	3.7 to 7.1	2.7 to 5.7
Sulphate, unbleached	3.6 to 7.0	2.6 to 5.4
bleached	3.9 to 7.5	2.9 to 5.9
Dissolving	4.8 to 10.1	4.0 to 9.0

In terms of tonnes of oven-dry pulp per tonne of oven-dry wood:

	Coniferous	Non-coniferous
Mechanical	0.90 to 0.95	
Semi-chemical		0.70 to 0.83
Sulphite, unbleached	0.48 to 0.51	0.52 to 0.55
bleached	0.44 to 0.47	0.49 to 0.52
Sulphate, unbleached	0.45 to 0.48	0.51 to 0.54
bleached	0.42 to 0.45	0.47 to 0.50
Dissolving	0.31 to 0.36	0.31 to 0.36

While mechanical pulp yields are generally over 90%, those of dissolving pulp are about 34%.

Other pulps

Pulp yields from other materials are approximately as follows:
Straw 46–53%   Waste paper: bond 90%
Esparto grass 40–45%   coated 50%
Rags (cotton, linen) 60–75%

Products

Paper
Consumption of pulp per tonne of finished product in manufacture of paper:
Newsprint   0.19 tonne chemical pulp and 0.83 tonne mechanical pulp
Kraft paper   1.03 tonne chemical pulp
Other paper
and board   0.40 tonne chemical pulp and 0.10 tonne mechanical pulp

Other
Dissolving pulp is used in manufacture of: rayon and acetate fibres, cellophane and cellulose film and other cellulose derivatives.
100 units of dissolving pulp produces 95 units of rayon and acetate fibres, or 100 units of cellophane.

Sound

Range

The limits of human audibility are for frequency of vibrations from about 15 Hz to 20 000 Hz.
Below 15 Hz (sometimes 20 Hz) frequencies are described as infrasonic.
Above 20 000 Hz frequencies are described as ultrasonic. An example of an ultrasonic frequency is that used by a bat as a type of sound radar: the frequency is about 50 000 Hz.

Velocity

The velocity of sound in air at sea level, and at 0°C = 1 087.4 feet per second
= 331.5 metres per second
At 15°C (ICAO standard atmosphere) = 1 116.45 ft/s = 340.294 m/s.
The velocity of sound waves in air is proportional to the square root of absolute temperature; where T is temperature in kelvins (°C + 273.15), speed of sound equals: $S \times \sqrt{1 + (T/273.15)}$,
where S is 1 087.4 for feet per second and 331.5 for metres per second.
The velocity of sound in water is approximately 1 450 m/s at 10°C and 1 480 m/s at 20°C; actual velocity varies with the salinity of the water.
The term supersonic usually means above the speed of sound.
In terms of Mach numbers, Mach 1 = the speed of sound,
Mach 2 = twice the speed of sound, etc.
A sonic 'boom', created when a plane passes the speed of sound, has a pressure of about 3–4 kPa at ground level (30–40 millibars).

Doppler effect
Where the source of a sound is moving relative to the listener, the frequency observed by the listener is different to that created by the source; this is the Doppler effect (which also applies to light frequencies).
Where f = frequency of the sound (in Hz)
S = velocity of sound
v = velocity at which source of sound is moving towards the observer
then, frequency observed (in Hz) = $f \times S/(S - v)$
Where the sound source is approaching, the frequency (or pitch) is higher, and where the sound source is moving away, the frequency (or pitch) is lower than the source frequency (pitch).
For further information on pitch, see Music (page 162).

Sound

Intensity

Physical intensity of sound is measured by the amplitude of a vibration creating sound; loudness is sound intensity as heard by the human ear.

Physical intensity
This can be measured objectively either as: a pressure measurement, in terms of newtons per square metre (pascal), or as a power measurement, in terms of the power creating the sound, in terms of watts per square metre.
The threshold of hearing or audibility is the sound level which is just audible for an average listener. For an average note of frequency taken at 1 000 Hz, the usually accepted level of audibility is taken as 0.000 2 microbar (2×10^{-5} Pa or 0.000 02 Pa); in other words, that is the minimum effective sound pressure which can be heard. In power terms, the threshold is 1 pW/m² (10^{-12} W/m²).
newtons per square metre (pascal), or as a power measurements, in terms of the
Sound is measured above the threshold in terms of ratios relative to the threshold.
The basic unit of interval is the bel:
bel = $\log_{10}(W_1/W_0)$ where W_1 and W_0 are two power levels.
In practice the decibel (dB), equal to one-tenth of a bel, is used:
decibel = $10 \log_{10}(W_1/W_0)$

Since the apparent loudness of a sound also depends on the frequency (pitch) of a sound, sound levels are sometimes weighted to standardise in terms of frequency. Standard frequency responses have been established, the most usual being designated as the 'A' response; this discriminates against low and high frequencies in favour of average frequencies. A sound level weighted according to this system is shown usually as dB(A).

Typical sound levels are, in decibels:

Quiet whisper	30
Conversation	60
Typical machine shop	65
Motor-car horn	100
Heavy lorry at 1 metre	105
Jet taking off	120
UK ship maximum limit[a]	135

[a]For parts of a ship other than sleeping quarters (maximum of 60 dB) and living quarters (maximum of 65 dB).

In general damaging noise is considered to begin at the 80–90 dB level; a hearing impediment may occur above 90 dB(A) for an 8 hour day. For the United Kingdom, permissible noise levels for cars are planned to be reduced, after April 1, 1983, from 84 dB to 80 dB; for lorries from 85–92 dB to 81–88 dB and for buses from 84–92 dB to 81–85 dB.

Loudness
Loudness, as a subjective measure for the listener, is sometimes expressed in measures other than the decibel.

Measures of loudness are:
the phon (p), the subjective equivalent of the decibel, produced by a 1 000 Hz tone (1 phon = 1 dB);
the sone, which has a loudness level of 40 phons (physical intensity of 40 phons). Loudness, N, in sones of any sound is given by $N = 2^{0.1(p-40)}$ where p is the loudness level expressed in phons. Some equivalents are:

phons	sones	phons	sones
40	1.00	80	16.0
50	2.00	90	32.0
60	4.00	100	64.0
65	5.66	105	90.5
70	8.00		

The above formulae for decibels show ratios using common logarithms (base of 10); natural logarithms (base e) are also used, with a basic unit called a neper or napier, with symbol Np or Nep:
neper = $\log_e \sqrt{(W_1/W_0)} = \frac{1}{2}\log_e(W_1/W_0)$

Following are main conversions from power ratios to decibels and nepers, where:
1 decibel = 0.115 1 neper = 1.26 ratio;   1 neper = 8.686 decibels = 7.39 ratio.
The numbers shown for decibels in the table are the common logarithms of the numbers shown in the power ratio column, multiplied by 10.

The table can also be used for determining the number of decibels equivalent to various voltage or current ratios, by multiplying the number of decibels indicated by 2; since, for voltage or current ratios: decibel = $20 \log_{10}(V_1/V_0)$. The reference level for voltage or current ratios, where dB = 0, is the picowatt (dBp), the milliwatt (dBm), watt (dBW), kilowatt (dBk), etc.

Power ratio	dB	neper	Power ratio	dB	neper
1.0	0.000	0.0000	5.5	7.404	0.8524
1.1	0.414	0.0477	5.6	7.482	0.8614
1.2	0.792	0.0912	5.7	7.559	0.8702
1.3	1.139	0.1312	5.8	7.634	0.8789
1.4	1.461	0.1682	5.9	7.709	0.8875
1.5	1.761	0.2027	6.0	7.782	0.8959
1.6	2.041	0.2350	6.1	7.853	0.9041
1.7	2.304	0.2653	6.2	7.924	0.9123
1.8	2.553	0.2939	6.3	7.993	0.9203
1.9	2.788	0.3209	6.4	8.062	0.9281
2.0	3.010	0.3466	6.5	8.129	0.9359
2.1	3.222	0.3710	6.6	8.195	0.9435
2.2	3.424	0.3942	6.7	8.261	0.9511
2.3	3.617	0.4165	6.8	8.325	0.9585
2.4	3.802	0.4377	6.9	8.388	0.9658
2.5	3.979	0.4581	7.0	8.451	0.9730
2.6	4.150	0.4778	7.1	8.513	0.9800
2.7	4.314	0.4966	7.2	8.573	0.9870
2.8	4.472	0.5148	7.3	8.633	0.9939
2.9	4.624	0.5324	7.4	8.692	1.0007
3.0	4.771	0.5493	7.5	8.751	1.0075
3.1	4.914	0.5657	7.6	8.808	1.0141
3.2	5.051	0.5816	7.7	8.865	1.0206
3.3	5.185	0.5970	7.8	8.921	1.0271
3.4	5.315	0.6119	7.9	8.976	1.0334
3.5	5.441	0.6264	8.0	9.031	1.0397
3.6	5.563	0.6405	8.1	9.085	1.0459
3.7	5.682	0.6542	8.2	9.138	1.0521
3.8	5.798	0.6675	8.3	9.191	1.0581
3.9	5.911	0.6805	8.4	9.243	1.0641
4.0	6.021	0.6931	8.5	9.294	1.0700
4.1	6.128	0.7055	8.6	9.345	1.0759
4.2	6.232	0.7175	8.7	9.395	1.0817
4.3	6.335	0.7293	8.8	9.445	1.0874
4.4	6.435	0.7408	8.9	9.494	1.0930
4.5	6.532	0.7520	9.0	9.542	1.0986
4.6	6.628	0.7630	9.1	9.590	1.1041
4.7	6.721	0.7738	9.2	9.638	1.1096
4.8	6.812	0.7843	9.3	9.685	1.1150
4.9	6.902	0.7946	9.4	9.731	1.1204
5.0	6.990	0.8047	9.5	9.777	1.1256
5.1	7.076	0.8146	9.6	9.823	1.1309
5.2	7.160	0.8243	9.7	9.868	1.1361
5.3	7.243	0.8339	9.8	9.912	1.1412
5.4	7.324	0.8432	9.9	9.956	1.1463

Power ratio		dB	neper
10^1	10	10	1.1513
10^2	100	20	2.3026
10^3	1 000	30	3.4539
10^4	10 000	40	4.6052
10^5	100 000	50	5.7565
10^6	1 000 000	60	6.9078
10^7	10 000 000	70	8.0590
10^8	100 000 000	80	9.2103
10^9	1 000 000 000	90	10.3616
10^{10}	10 000 000 000	100	11.5129

Textiles

Some main definitions are as follows:

Man-made fibres = all fibres manufactured by man as distinct from those occurring naturally (for natural textile fibres see pages 110–112). Man-made fibres include: non-cellulosic fibres (such as nylon, Terylene, etc) made from synthetic polymers (called synthetic fibres – also see page 125), natural polymers based on groundnuts, etc) or inorganic materials (glass, etc.); cellulosic fibres made from regenerated cellulose (cuprammonium rayon, viscose) or cellulose esters (acetates and triacetates). Regenerated cellulose fibres were formerly known by the name 'rayon' but the use of this term is not allowed under EEC law.

Continuous filament yarn = a yarn composed of one or more filaments that run the whole length of the yarn (yarn of one filament is called monofilament); in filament yarn the filaments do not necessarily run the whole length.

Discontinuous fibres = short or staple length fibres; man-made staple fibre is usually prepared by cutting or breaking filaments into suitable lengths, generally 1–18 in (2–46 cm).

Tow = a large number of parallel continuous fibres (filaments) without twist.
Twist = the spiral disposition of the component(s) of a yarn, which is usually the result of relative rotation of the extremities of the yarn.
Warp or chain = threads lengthways in a fabric as woven.
Weft, woof or filling = threads widthways in a fabric as woven.
Wale = a column of loops along the length of knitted fabric.
Course = a row of loops across the width of knitted fabric.

Yarn count systems

These measure the thickness of thread. There are two main systems, one measuring weight (mass) per unit length of the fibre, and the other length per unit weight (mass). The first system gives the linear density of the fibre, and this system is now the internationally agreed standard system, using as a unit the tex which measures in grams per kilometre (10^{-6} kg/m).

100 millitex (mtex) = 1 decitex (dtex)
1 000 millitex = 1 tex (tex)
10 decitex = 1 tex
1 000 tex = 1 kilotex (ktex)

The term 'drex' or 'grex' is sometimes used, being equivalent to decitex.

The symbol for linear density expressed in the tex system is Tt.
In the tex and other weight per length systems the count is higher for thicker yarns, while in length per weight systems the count is higher for finer yarns and lower for thicker yarns.
Tables setting out the definitions of main count systems are included below. In the first table, for linear density systems, conversion from numbers or titres to tex values can be made by multiplying by the factor given; in the second table, for length per unit weight systems, conversion to tex is made by dividing the constant shown by the count to be converted.
For example, the equivalent of 800 denier is:
$800 \times 0.111\,1 = 88.9$ tex = 889 decitex
and the equivalent of a worsted yarn count of 20 is:
$885.8/20 = 44.3$ tex
An old unit of linear density not included below is the poumar = 1 lb/1 million yd.

A range of equivalent yarn counts is included on the following page, showing values for each of the main count systems corresponding to a range of tex values.
For decitex ('drex' or 'grex'), multiply the number in the tex column by 10.

Measures

Special measures

Wales or courses per unit length are measured in terms of the number per inch or centimetre.
Gauge = the number of needles per $1\frac{1}{2}$ inches for hosiery, and per unit of width (across the wales) for knitted fabrics; a measure of the closeness of the knit (fineness).
Threads in cloth are measured in terms of the number of picks (for length) or ends (for width) per inch or centimetre; for coarse fabrics, such as jute, threads per 10 centimetres is the main unit.

Twist is measured as the number of turns per inch or metre (for some sectors turns per centimetre). The twist factor or multiplier, when multiplied by the square root of the yarn number, gives the twist; this depends on the material, strength, etc.
Cover factor is the fraction of the surface area which is covered by yarns assuming round yarn shape; this indicates the compactness of weaving.
Poundage utility = the capacity of 1 unit of a fibre to satisfy a particular end-use; it is used because some fibres can wear longer than others. For example, 1 unit of non-cellulosic staple fibre equals 1.37 units of cotton (US rate).

Linear density or direct systems (weight per unit length)

	Symbol	Unit of weight (mass)	Unit of length	Unit of yarn number	Multiplying factor for conversion to tex values
Tex	Tt	gram	kilometre	g/km	1
Denier	Td	gram	9 000 metres	g/9 000 m	0.111 1
Linen (dry spun), hemp and jute	Tj	pound	14 400 yards (spyndle)	lb/14 400 yd	34.45
Woollen (Aberdeen)	Ta	pound	14 400 yards	lb/14 400 yd	34.45

Indirect systems (length per unit weight)

	Symbol	Unit of length	Unit of weight (mass)	Unit of yarn count	Constant for conversion to tex values
Cotton bump yarn	N_B	yard	ounce	yd/oz	31 003
Cotton (English)	Ne_C	840 yards (hank)	pound	840 yd/lb	590.5
Linen (wet or dry spun)	Ne_L	300 yards (lea)	pound	300 yd/lb	1 654
Metric	Nm	kilometre	kilogram	km/kg	1 000
Spun silk	N_S	840 yards (hank)	pound	840 yd/lb	590.5
Typp (thousands of yards per pound)	Nt	1 000 yards	pound	1 000 yd/lb	496.1
Woollen (Alloa)	Nal	11 520 yards (spyndle)	24 pounds	11 520 yd/24 lb	1 033
Woollen (American cut)	Nac	300 yards (cut)	pound	330 yd/lb	1 654
Woollen (American run)	Nar	100 yards	ounce	100 yd/oz	310.0
Woollen (Dewsbury)	Nd	yard	ounce	yd/oz	31 003
Woollen (Galashiels)	Ng	300 yards (cut)	24 ounces	300 yd/24 oz	2 480
Woollen (Hawick)	Nh	300 yards (cut)	26 ounces	300 yd/26 oz	2 687
Woollen (Irish)	Ni_W	yard	0.25 ounce	yd/0.25 oz	7 751
Woollen (West of England)	Nwe	320 yards (snap)	pound	320 yd/lb	1 550
Woollen (Yorkshire)	Ny	256 yards (skein) or yard	pound dram	256 yd/lb or yd/dram	1 938
Worsted	New	560 yards (hank)	pound	560 yd/lb	885.8

Textiles

Tex to other count systems

Tex	Cotton (English) also Spun silk	Denier	Linen dry spun, hemp, jute also Woollen: Aberdeen	Metric	Typp	Woollen: American cut also Linen, wet or dry spun	American run	Dewsbury also Cotton, bump yarn	Galashiels	Hawick	West of England	York-shire	Worsted	Te
1	590.5	9	0.03	1000.0	496.1	1653.5	310.0	31003	2480	2687	1550	1938	885.8	
2	295.3	18	0.06	500.0	248.0	826.8	155.0	15502	1240	1343	775	969	442·9	
3	196.8	27	0.09	333.3	165.4	551.2	103.3	10334	827	896	517	646	295.3	
4	147.6	36	0.12	250.0	124.0	413.4	77.5	7751	620	672	388	484	221.5	
5	118.1	45	0.15	200.0	99.2	330.7	62.0	6201	496	537	310	388	177.2	
6	98.4	54	0.17	166.7	82.7	275.6	51.7	5167	413	448	258	323	147.6	
7	84.4	63	0.20	142.9	70.9	236.2	44.3	4429	354	384	221	277	126.5	
8	73.8	72	0.23	125.0	62.0	206.7	38.8	3875	310	336	194	242	110.7	8
9	65.6	81	0.26	111.1	55.1	183.7	34.4	3445	276	299	172	215	98.4	9
10	59.1	90	0.29	100.0	49.6	165.4	31.0	3100	248	269	155	194	88.6	10
11	53.7	99	0.32	90.9	45.1	150.3	28.2	2818	225	244	141	176	80.5	11
12	49.2	108	0.35	83.3	41.3	137.8	25.8	2584	207	224	129	161	73.8	12
13	45.4	117	0.38	76.9	38.2	127.2	23.8	2385	191	207	119	149	68.1	13
14	42.2	126	0.41	71.4	35.4	118.1	22.1	2215	177	192	111	138	63.3	14
15	39.4	135	0.44	66.7	33.1	110.2	20.7	2067	165	179	103	129	59.1	15
16	36.9	144	0.46	62.5	31.0	103.3	19.4	1938	155	168	97	121	55.4	16
18	32.8	162	0.52	55.6	27.6	91.9	17.2	1722	138	149	86	108	49.2	18
20	29.5	180	0.58	50.0	24.8	82.7	15.5	1550	124	134	78	97	44.3	20
22	26.8	198	0.64	45.5	22.5	75.2	14.1	1409	113	122	70	88	40.3	22
24	24.6	216	0.70	41.7	20.7	68.9	12.9	1292	103	112	65	81	36.9	24
26	22.7	234	0.75	38.5	19.1	63.6	11.9	1192	95	103	60	75	34.1	26
28	21.1	252	0.81	35.7	17.7	59.1	11.1	1107	89	96	55	69	31.6	28
30	19.7	270	0.87	33.3	16.5	55.1	10.3	1033	83	90	52	65	29.5	30
32	18.5	288	0.93	31.3	15.5	51.7	9.7	969	78	84	48	61	27.7	32
34	17.4	306	0.99	29.4	14.6	48.6	9.1	912	73	79	46	57	26.1	34
36	16.4	324	1.05	27.8	13.8	45.9	8.6	861	69	75	43	54	24.6	36
38	15.5	342	1.10	26.3	13.1	43.5	8.2	816	65	71	41	51	23.3	38
40	14.8	360	1.16	25.0	12.4	41.3	7.8	775	62	67	39	48	22.1	40
42	14.1	378	1.22	23.8	11.8	39.4	7.4	738	59	64	37	46	21.1	42
44	13.4	396	1.28	22.7	11.3	37.6	7.0	705	56	61	35	44	20.1	44
46	12.8	414	1.34	21.7	10.8	35.9	6.7	674	54	58	34	42	19.3	46
48	12.3	432	1.39	20.8	10.3	34.4	6.5	646	52	56	32	40	18.5	48
50	11.8	450	1.45	20.0	9.9	33.1	6.2	620	50	54	31	39	17.7	50
52	11.4	468	1.51	19.2	9.5	31.8	6.0	596	48	52	30	37	17.0	52
54	10.9	486	1.57	18.5	9.2	30.6	5.7	574	46	50	29	36	16 4	54
56	10.5	504	1.63	17.9	8.9	29.5	5.5	554	44	48	28	35	15.8	56
60	9.8	540	1.74	16.7	8.3	27.6	5.2	517	41	45	26	32	14.8	60
64	9.2	576	1.86	15.6	7.8	25.8	4.8	484	39	42	24	30	13.8	64
68	8.7	612	1.97	14.7	7.3	24.3	4.6	456	36	40	23	28	13.0	68
72	8.2	648	2.09	13.9	6.9	23.0	4.3	431	34	37	22	27	12.3	72
76	7.8	684	2.21	13.2	6.5	21.8	4.1	408	33	35	20	25	11.7	76
80	7.4	720	2.32	12.5	6.2	20.7	3.9	388	31	34	19	24	11.1	80
84	7.0	756	2.44	11.9	5.9	19.7	3.7	369	30	32	18	23	10.5	84
88	6.7	792	2.55	11.4	5.6	18.8	3.5	352	28	31	18	22	10.1	88
92	6.4	828	2.67	10.9	5.4	18.0	3.4	337	27	29	17	31	9.6	92
100	5.9	900	2.90	10.0	5.0	16.5	3.1	310	25	27	16	19	8.9	100
200	3.0	1800	5.81	5.0	2.5	8.3	1.6	155	12	13	8	10	4.4	200
300	2.0	2700	8.71	3.3	1.7	5.5	1.0	103	8	9	5	6	3.0	300
400	1.5	3600	11.61	2.5	1.2	4.1	0.8	78	6	7	4	5	2.2	400
500	1.2	4500	14.51	2.0	1.0	3.3	0.6	62	5	5	3	4	1.8	500
600	1.0	5400	17.42	1.7	0.8	2.8	0.5	52	4	4	3	3	1.5	600
700	0.8	6300	20.32	1.4	0.7	2.4	0.4	44	4	4	2	3	1.3	700
800	0.7	7200	23.22	1.3	0.6	2.1	0.4	39	3	3	2	2	1.1	800
900	0.7	8100	26.13	1.1	0.6	1.8	0.3	34	3	3	2	2	1.0	900
1000	0.6	9000	29.03	1.0	0.5	1.7	0.3	31	2	3	2	2	0.9	1000

Textiles

United Kingdom (old units)

Cotton yarn			Woollen yarn		
$\frac{1}{2}$ yards	= 1 thread		256 yards	= 1 skein	
20 yards	= 1 skein		300 yards	= 1 cut	
840 yards	= 1 hank		320 yards	= 1 snap	
spyndle	= 18 hanks		45 skeins	= 1 spyndle	
	= 15 120 yards			= 11 520 yards	

Linen yarn			Worsted yarn		
300 yards	= 1 lea (or cut)		80 yards	= 1 wrap	
leas	= 1 hear (or heer)		560 yards	= 1 hank	
hears	= 1 hasp (or hank)				
hasps	= 1 spyndle		*Fabric*		
8 leas	= 1 spyndle		$2\frac{1}{4}$ inches	= 1 nail	
	= 14 400 yards		4 nails	= 1 quarter	
				= 1 span	
				= 9 inches	
Spun silk yarn			4 quarters	= 1 yard	
840 yards	= 1 hank		$1\frac{1}{4}$ yards	= 45 inches	
				= 1 ell	

Other (old units)

Flemish ell = 27 inches = $\frac{3}{4}$ yard
French ell = 54 inches = $1\frac{1}{2}$ yards

Fabric and clothing

Size

Wool blankets
full size blanket = 4.5 square metres (5.40 square yards)
cot blanket = 1.2 square metres (1.40 square yards)

Clothing (United Kingdom)
Following are approximate equivalents of a range of sizes:

Increasing by intervals of:

inch		$1\frac{1}{2}$ inches		2 inches		4 centimetres	
in	cm	in	cm	in	cm	cm	in
29	74	29	74	28	71	72	$28\frac{1}{2}$
30	76	$30\frac{1}{2}$	77	30	76	76	30
31	79	32	81	32	81	80	$31\frac{1}{2}$
32	81	$33\frac{1}{2}$	85	34	86	84	33
33	84	35	89	36	91	88	$34\frac{1}{2}$
34	86	$36\frac{1}{2}$	93	38	97	92	36
35	89	38	97	40	102	96	38
36	91	$39\frac{1}{2}$	100	42	107	100	$39\frac{1}{2}$
37	94	41	104	44	112	104	41
38	97	$42\frac{1}{2}$	108	46	117	108	$42\frac{1}{2}$
39	99	44	112	48	122	112	44
40	102	$45\frac{1}{2}$	116			116	$45\frac{1}{2}$
41	104	47	119			120	47
42	107	$48\frac{1}{2}$	123			124	49
43	109						
44	112						
45	114						
46	117						
47	119						
48	122						
49	124						
50	127						

Collar sizes

in	cm	in	cm		Brassiere sizes[a]			
					in	cm	in	cm
$14\frac{1}{2}$	37	$16\frac{1}{2}$	42		32	70	38	85
15	38	17	43		34	75	40	90
$15\frac{1}{2}$	39–40	$17\frac{1}{2}$	44–45		36	80	42	95
16	41							

[a] European continental measurement is of underbust size (with separate specification of cup size), while UK measurement is across the bust; hence the continental size indicated is smaller than the standard conversion which, for example, is 92 cm for a 36 in brassiere.

Knitting needles and pins

Following are the equivalents for UK and metric sizes for knitting needles and pins:

UK	metric (mm)	UK	metric (mm)	UK	metric (mm)
14	2	8	4	2	7
13	$2\frac{1}{4}$	7	$4\frac{1}{2}$	1	$7\frac{1}{2}$
12	$2\frac{3}{4}$	6	5	0	8
11	3	5	$5\frac{1}{2}$	00	9
10	$3\frac{1}{4}$	4	6	000	10
9	$3\frac{3}{4}$	3	$6\frac{1}{2}$		

Conversions: area

Conversion from linear yards to square yards can be made approximately by multiplying by the following factors (allowing for average width):

material	factor	material	factor
100% cotton	1.13	Man-made fibre mixtures	1.19
100% spun man-made fibre	1.14	Other filament fabrics	1.18

Conversions: area to weight

Conversion factors
1 ounce per square yard (oz/yd²) = 33.905 7 grams per square metre (g/m²)
1 gram per square metre = 0.029 493 5 ounce per square yard
1 pound per square yard (lb/yd²) = 0.542 49 kilogram per square metre (kg/m²)
1 square yard per pound (yd²/lb) = 1843.3 square metres per tonne (m²/t)
1 square metre per tonne = 0.000 542 5 square yard per pound

Relationships for cotton cloth

	Yards per pound	Yards per tonne	Square metres per tonne
General	4.1	9 000	8 500
Hongkong	4.5	9 921	9 370
India	4	8 800	8 300
Soviet Union	3.12	6 900	6 500
United Kingdom	3.1	6 835	6 460
United States	2.84	6 260	5 900

Conversions: number to area

Average conversions are:

	Square metres per item	Square metres per dozen items
Men's coats	3.51	42.14
Men's suits	2.58	30.96
Men's shirts	1.48	17.80
Men's trousers	0.98	11.73
Women's coats	2.26	27.09
Women's dresses	2.09	25.08
Women's skirts	1.25	15.05
Women's blouses	1.00	12.04

Transport

Road, air and railway

Passengers and freight carried by distance

1 passenger-mile = 1.609 344 passenger-kilometres
1 passenger-kilometre = 0.621 371 passenger-mile.
The table on page 69 for conversion of miles to kilometres, and kilometres to miles can also be used for passenger-distance conversions.

1 UK (long) ton-mile = 1.635 17 tonne-kilometres
1 tonne-kilometre = 0.611 558 UK (long) ton-mile
1 US (short) ton-mile = 1.459 97 tonne-kilometres
1 tonne-kilometre = 0.684 944 US (short) ton-mile
1 UK (long) ton-mile/UK gallon = 0.359 687 tonne-kilometre/litre
1 tonne-kilometre/litre = 2.780 20 UK (long) ton-miles/UK gallon
1 US (short) ton-mile/US gallon = 0.385 684 tonne-kilometre/litre
1 tonne-kilometre/litre = 2.592 80 US (short) ton-miles/US gallon

Transport

Fuel consumption

There has been a proposal to convert the retail sale of petrol in the United Kingdom from gallons to litres, taking place mainly from autumn 1981; excise duty on petrol was charged in litres from January 1, 1978.

For general conversion factors between miles per gallon and kilometres per litre, etc., see page 65. In the tables on the following pages conversions are given between miles per UK (and US) gallons and litres per 100 kilometres.

Since this is a 'reciprocal' type of relationship, whereby miles per UK gallon × litres per 100 kilometres = 282.481 for all values, the table applies for converting from either to the other.

For example, 20 miles per UK gallon equals 14.1 litres per 100 kilometres, and 20 litres per 100 kilometres equals 14.1 miles per UK gallon.

Gradients

Angle (°)	Gradient as %[a]	as 1 unit in[b]	Angle (°)	Gradient as %[a]	as 1 unit in[b]
5	8.75	11.43	30	57.74	1.73
10	17.63	5.67	35	70.02	1.43
15	26.79	3.73	40	83.91	1.19
20	36.40	2.75	45	100.00	1.00
25	46.63	2.14			

[a]Equals tangent of angle × 100.　[b]Equals contangent of angle.

Noise

Maximum sound levels allowed in the United Kingdom for motor vehicles range from 77 decibels (A weighting) for motor cycles not over 50 cm³ to 92 dB(A) for most goods vehicles (also see sound, page 166).

Shipping

1 shipping cubic inch = 1/12 cubic foot
12 shipping cubic inches = 1 cubic foot
144 cubic inches = 1 shipping cubic inch

Conversion to cubic metres

shipping cubic inches	cubic metres	shipping cubic inches	cubic metres
1	0.002 360	7	0.016 518
2	0.004 719	8	0.018 878
3	0.007 079	9	0.021 238
4	0.009 439	10	0.023 597
5	0.011 799	11	0.025 957
6	0.014 158	12	0.028 317

Tonnages: ships

Register ton (or Moorsom ton) = 100 cubic feet = 2.832 cubic metres
1 cubic metre = 0.353 register ton.

Gross registered tonnage (grt) is the capacity of the spaces within the hull, and of the enclosed spaces above the deck available for cargo, stores, passengers and crew; measured in cubic feet, with 1 registered ton (as above) equal to 100 cubic feet.

Net registered tonnage (nrt) is the gross tonnage less certain deductions for accommodation of the master, officers and crew, navigation, propelling machines and fuel. On average net tonnage is about 60% of gross tonnage.

Panama and Suez Canal tonnage is calculated in a manner similar to registered tonnage, but there are different rules for determining gross and net tonnage. The gross tonnage is very nearly equal to the British or Moorsom gross tonnage, but the net tonnage can be substantially higher.

A general comparison for a typical cargo liner is:

	British	Panama	Suez
Gross	9913	9900	9906
Net	5900	6958	7370

Deadweight tonnage (dwt or dw) is the weight (mass) of cargo, stores, fuel, passengers and crew carried by the ship when loaded to her maximum summer loadline; it is the difference between a vessel's displacement when light and when loaded. Usually measured in terms of tons of 2 240 lb (long tons in the United States), but also in tonnes. For conversions between UK (long) tons and tonnes see page 66. TPI means tons per inch immersion, usually for tankers. Deadweight tons are used in the United States, and for tankers and bulk carriers.

There is no direct relationship between registered and deadweight tonnage, for the former is a measure of capacity and the latter a measure of weight; the relationship varies widely, but on average 100 gross registered tons is equivalent to 150 deadweight tons. The approximate guide is:
nrt: grt: dwt = 60: 100: 150 or 100: 165: 250

Displacement tonnage is the weight of the ship as represented by the weight (mass) of the water displaced: as built and equipped it is the 'lightweight' displacement; for naval vessels ('naval standard') it includes fuel, water, stores and crew; for merchant ships it usually also includes the deadweight tonnage (that is, displacement tonnage = weight of the ship as built and equipped + deadweight tonnage). 1 displacement ton = 35 cubic feet (35 cubic feet of salt water weighs about 1 UK ton).

Tonnage classification
VLCC = very large crude carrier = 'supertanker' of 200 000 dwt and over, but under 325 000 dwt
ULCC = ultra large crude carrier = 'supertanker' of 325 000 dwt or over

Tonnages: cargo (mercantile or freight)

There are two bases for charging the carriage of cargo: weight and capacity (measurement). If 1 ton (20 cwt) of a cargo occupies more than 40 cubic feet then capacity is usually the basis. Cargoes are selected to give the best combination of payable tons by weight or measurement.

US shipping ton = 40 cubic feet = 1.133 cubic metres
UK shipping ton = 40, 42 or 50 cubic feet = 1.133, 1.189 or 1.416 cubic metres
1 cubic metre = 0.883 US shipping ton
= 0.883, 0.841 or 0.706 UK shipping ton.
1 cubic foot per UK ton = 0.027 870 cubic metre per tonne
1 cubic metre per tonne = 35.881 4 cubic feet per UK ton.

Stowage rates

	ft³/UK ton	m³/t		ft³/UK ton	m³/t
Alcohol	72	2.1	Lead	10	0.3
Apples	80–90	2.2–2.5	Mercury	8	0.2
Bauxite	32	0.9	Oranges (boxes)	85	2.4
Butter (cases)	60	1.7	Rubber (bales)	75	2.1
Cigarettes	100	2.8	Sugar	45	1.3
Coffee	55	1.5	Tea (chests)	70–140	2.0–4.0
Flour	60	1.7	Wool, greasy	90–200	2.5–5.5
Iron ore	16–25	0.4–0.7	Wheat: bulk	45	1.3

For stowage rates of fish, see page 114.

Containers

Standard European sizes of containers are:
20 foot = 20 ft × 8 ft × 8 ft
40 foot = 40 ft × 8 ft × 8½ ft
Containers are sometimes measured in terms of twenty-foot equivalents (TEU or TEQ), being total length of containers in feet divided by 20. Further, a ship may be described in terms of container equivalents, for example as 1500 TEQ, meaning that it is built to take 1500 20 ft containers.

Freight rates

Worldscale is an index used to express freight charges for oil tankers, so that different voyages and ships can be compared. Rates are expressed in terms of Worldscale 100 as the standard for any voyage or ship; Worldscale 100 is the reference for the cost per ton of cargo carried by a standard Worldscale ship with a summer dwt of 19500 and under certain conditions.

Rates are varied every year, so that each Worldscale index must be referred to the specified annual basis; for example, if rates were increased by 20% for one year, Worldscale 100 for the second year would equal Worldscale 120 for the previous year.

Transport

Miles per UK gallon to SI litres per 100 kilometres   Miles per UK gal = 282.481/l per 100 km

Miles/UK gal →	0.0	0.1	0.2	0.3	0.4	0.5	0.6	0.7	0.8	0.9	← Miles/UK gal
↓	l/100 km	l/100 km	l/100 km	l/100 km	l/100 km	l/100 km	l/100 km	l/100 km	l/100 km	l/100 km	↓
1	282.5	256.8	235.4	217.3	201.8	188.3	176.6	166.2	156.9	148.7	1
2	141.2	134.5	128.4	122.8	117.7	113.0	108.6	104.6	100.9	97.4	2
3	94.2	91.1	88.3	85.6	83.1	80.7	78.5	76.3	74.3	72.4	3
4	70.6	68.9	67.3	65.7	64.2	62.8	61.4	60.1	58.9	57.6	4
5	56.5	55.4	54.3	53.3	52.3	51.4	50.4	49.6	48.7	47.9	5
6	47.1	46.3	45.6	44.8	44.1	43.5	42.8	42.2	41.5	40.9	6
7	40.4	39.8	39.2	38.7	38.2	37.7	37.2	36.7	36.2	35.8	7
8	35.3	34.9	34.4	34.0	33.6	33.2	32.8	32.5	32.1	31.7	8
9	31.4	31.0	30.7	30.4	30.1	29.7	29.4	29.1	28.8	28.5	9
10	28.2	28.0	27.7	27.4	27.2	26.9	26.6	26.4	26.2	25.9	10
11	25.7	25.4	25.2	25.0	24.8	24.6	24.4	24.1	23.9	23.7	11
12	23.5	23.3	23.2	23.0	22.8	22.6	22.4	22.2	22.1	21.9	12
13	21.7	21.6	21.4	21.2	21.1	20.9	20.8	20.6	20.5	20.3	13
14	20.2	20.0	19.9	19.8	19.6	19.5	19.3	19.2	19.1	19.0	14
15	18.8	18.7	18.6	18.5	18.3	18.2	18.1	18.0	17.9	17.8	15
16	17.7	17.5	17.4	17.3	17.2	17.1	17.0	16.9	16.8	16.7	16
17	16.6	16.5	16.4	16.3	16.2	16.1	16.1	16.0	15.9	15.8	17
18	15.7	15.6	15.5	15.4	15.4	15.3	15.2	15.1	15.0	14.9	18
19	14.9	14.8	14.7	14.6	14.6	14.5	14.4	14.3	14.3	14.2	19
20	14.1	14.1	14.0	13.9	13.8	13.8	13.7	13.6	13.6	13.5	20
21	13.5	13.4	13.3	13.3	13.2	13.1	13.1	13.0	13.0	12.9	21
22	12.8	12.8	12.7	12.7	12.6	12.6	12.5	12.4	12.4	12.3	22
23	12.3	12.2	12.2	12.1	12.1	12.0	12.0	11.9	11.9	11.8	23
24	11.8	11.7	11.7	11.6	11.6	11.5	11.5	11.4	11.4	11.3	24
25	11.3	11.3	11.2	11.2	11.1	11.1	11.0	11.0	10.9	10.9	25
26	10.9	10.8	10.8	10.7	10.7	10.7	10.6	10.6	10.5	10.5	26
27	10.5	10.4	10.4	10.3	10.3	10.3	10.2	10.2	10.2	10.1	27
28	10.1	10.1	10.0	10.0	9.9	9.9	9.9	9.8	9.8	9.8	28
29	9.7	9.7	9.7	9.6	9.6	9.6	9.5	9.5	9.5	9.4	29
30	9.4	9.4	9.4	9.3	9.3	9.3	9.2	9.2	9.2	9.1	30
31	9.1	9.1	9.1	9.0	9.0	9.0	8.9	8.9	8.9	8.9	31
32	8.8	8.8	8.8	8.7	8.7	8.7	8.7	8.6	8.6	8.6	32
33	8.6	8.5	8.5	8.5	8.5	8.4	8.4	8.4	8.4	8.3	33
34	8.3	8.3	8.3	8.2	8.2	8.2	8.2	8.1	8.1	8.1	34
35	8.1	8.0	8.0	8.0	8.0	8.0	7.9	7.9	7.9	7.9	35
36	7.8	7.8	7.8	7.8	7.8	7.7	7.7	7.7	7.7	7.7	36
37	7.6	7.6	7.6	7.6	7.6	7.5	7.5	7.5	7.5	7.5	37
38	7.4	7.4	7.4	7.4	7.4	7.3	7.3	7.3	7.3	7.3	38
39	7.2	7.2	7.2	7.2	7.2	7.2	7.1	7.1	7.1	7.1	39
40	7.1	7.0	7.0	7.0	7.0	7.0	7.0	6.9	6.9	6.9	40
41	6.9	6.9	6.9	6.8	6.8	6.8	6.8	6.8	6.8	6.7	41
42	6.7	6.7	6.7	6.7	6.7	6.6	6.6	6.6	6.6	6.6	42
43	6.6	6.6	6.5	6.5	6.5	6.5	6.5	6.5	6.4	6.4	43
44	6.4	6.4	6.4	6.4	6.4	6.3	6.3	6.3	6.3	6.3	44
45	6.3	6.3	6.2	6.2	6.2	6.2	6.2	6.2	6.2	6.2	45
46	6.1	6.1	6.1	6.1	6.1	6.1	6.1	6.0	6.0	6.0	46
47	6.0	6.0	6.0	6.0	6.0	5.9	5.9	5.9	5.9	5.9	47
48	5.9	5.9	5.9	5.8	5.8	5.8	5.8	5.8	5.8	5.8	48
49	5.8	5.8	5.7	5.7	5.7	5.7	5.7	5.7	5.7	5.7	49
50	5.6	5.6	5.6	5.6	5.6	5.6	5.6	5.6	5.6	5.5	50
51	5.5	5.5	5.5	5.5	5.5	5.5	5.5	5.5	5.5	5.4	51
52	5.4	5.4	5.4	5.4	5.4	5.4	5.4	5.4	5.4	5.3	52
53	5.3	5.3	5.3	5.3	5.3	5.3	5.3	5.3	5.3	5.2	53
54	5.2	5.2	5.2	5.2	5.2	5.2	5.2	5.2	5.2	5.1	54
55	5.1	5.1	5.1	5.1	5.1	5.1	5.1	5.1	5.1	5.1	55

Miles per US gallon to SI litres per 100 kilometres   Miles per US gal = 235.215/l per 100 km

Miles/US gal →	0.0	0.1	0.2	0.3	0.4	0.5	0.6	0.7	0.8	0.9	← Miles/US gal
↓	l/100 km	l/100 km	l/100 km	l/100 km	l/100 km	l/100 km	l/100 km	l/100 km	l/100 km	l/100 km	↓
1	235.2	213.8	196.0	180.9	168.0	156.8	147.0	138.4	130.7	123.8	1
2	117.6	112.0	106.9	102.3	98.0	94.1	90.5	87.1	84.0	81.1	2
3	78.4	75.9	73.5	71.3	69.2	67.2	65.3	63.6	61.9	60.3	3
4	58.8	57.4	56.0	54.7	53.5	52.3	51.1	50.0	49.0	48.0	4
5	47.0	46.1	45.2	44.4	43.6	42.8	42.0	41.3	40.6	39.9	5
6	39.2	38.6	37.9	37.3	36.8	36.2	35.6	35.1	34.6	34.1	6
7	33.6	33.1	32.7	32.2	31.8	31.4	30.9	30.5	30.2	29.8	7
8	29.4	29.0	28.7	28.3	28.0	27.7	27.4	27.0	26.7	26.4	8
9	26.1	25.8	25.6	25.3	25.0	24.8	24.5	24.2	24.0	23.8	9
10	23.5	23.3	23.1	22.8	22.6	22.4	22.2	22.0	21.8	21.6	10
11	21.4	21.2	21.0	20.8	20.6	20.5	20.3	20.1	19.9	19.8	11
12	19.6	19.4	19.3	19.1	19.0	18.8	18.7	18.5	18.4	18.2	12
13	18.1	18.0	17.8	17.7	17.6	17.4	17.3	17.2	17.0	16.9	13
14	16.8	16.7	16.6	16.4	16.3	16.2	16.1	16.0	15.9	15.8	14
15	15.7	15.6	15.5	15.4	15.3	15.2	15.1	15.0	14.9	14.8	15
16	14.7	14.6	14.5	14.4	14.3	14.3	14.2	14.1	14.0	13.9	16
17	13.8	13.8	13.7	13.6	13.5	13.4	13.4	13.3	13.2	13.1	17
18	13.1	13.0	12.9	12.9	12.8	12.7	12.6	12.6	12.5	12.4	18
19	12.4	12.3	12.3	12.2	12.1	12.1	12.0	11.9	11.9	11.8	19
20	11.8	11.7	11.6	11.6	11.5	11.5	11.4	11.4	11.3	11.3	20
21	11.2	11.1	11.1	11.0	11.0	10.9	10.9	10.8	10.8	10.7	21
22	10.7	10.6	10.6	10.5	10.5	10.5	10.4	10.4	10.3	10.3	22
23	10.2	10.2	10.1	10.1	10.1	10.0	10.0	9.9	9.9	9.8	23
24	9.8	9.8	9.7	9.7	9.6	9.6	9.6	9.5	9.5	9.4	24
25	9.4	9.4	9.3	9.3	9.3	9.2	9.2	9.2	9.1	9.1	25
26	9.0	9.0	9.0	8.9	8.9	8.9	8.8	8.8	8.8	8.7	26
27	8.7	8.7	8.6	8.6	8.6	8.6	8.5	8.5	8.5	8.4	27
28	8.4	8.4	8.3	8.3	8.3	8.3	8.2	8.2	8.2	8.1	28
29	8.1	8.1	8.1	8.0	8.0	8.0	7.9	7.9	7.9	7.9	29
30	7.8	7.8	7.8	7.8	7.7	7.7	7.7	7.7	7.6	7.6	30
31	7.6	7.6	7.5	7.5	7.5	7.5	7.4	7.4	7.4	7.4	31
32	7.4	7.3	7.3	7.3	7.3	7.2	7.2	7.2	7.2	7.1	32
33	7.1	7.1	7.1	7.1	7.0	7.0	7.0	7.0	7.0	6.9	33
34	6.9	6.9	6.9	6.9	6.8	6.8	6.8	6.8	6.8	6.7	34
35	6.7	6.7	6.7	6.7	6.6	6.6	6.6	6.6	6.6	6.6	35
36	6.5	6.5	6.5	6.5	6.5	6.4	6.4	6.4	6.4	6.4	36
37	6.4	6.3	6.3	6.3	6.3	6.3	6.3	6.2	6.2	6.2	37
38	6.2	6.2	6.2	6.1	6.1	6.1	6.1	6.1	6.1	6.0	38
39	6.0	6.0	6.0	6.0	6.0	6.0	5.9	5.9	5.9	5.9	39
40	5.9	5.9	5.9	5.8	5.8	5.8	5.8	5.8	5.8	5.8	40
41	5.7	5.7	5.7	5.7	5.7	5.7	5.7	5.6	5.6	5.6	41
42	5.6	5.6	5.6	5.6	5.5	5.5	5.5	5.5	5.5	5.5	42
43	5.5	5.5	5.4	5.4	5.4	5.4	5.4	5.4	5.4	5.4	43
44	5.3	5.3	5.3	5.3	5.3	5.3	5.3	5.3	5.3	5.2	44
45	5.2	5.2	5.2	5.2	5.2	5.2	5.2	5.1	5.1	5.1	45
46	5.1	5.1	5.1	5.1	5.1	5.1	5.0	5.0	5.0	5.0	46
47	5.0	5.0	5.0	5.0	5.0	5.0	4.9	4.9	4.9	4.9	47
48	4.9	4.9	4.9	4.9	4.9	4.8	4.8	4.8	4.8	4.8	48
49	4.8	4.8	4.8	4.8	4.8	4.8	4.7	4.7	4.7	4.7	49
50	4.7	4.7	4.7	4.7	4.7	4.7	4.6	4.6	4.6	4.6	50
51	4.6	4.6	4.6	4.6	4.6	4.6	4.6	4.5	4.5	4.5	51
52	4.5	4.5	4.5	4.5	4.5	4.5	4.5	4.5	4.5	4.4	52
53	4.4	4.4	4.4	4.4	4.4	4.4	4.4	4.4	4.4	4.4	53
54	4.4	4.3	4.3	4.3	4.3	4.3	4.3	4.3	4.3	4.3	54
55	4.3	4.3	4.3	4.3	4.2	4.2	4.2	4.2	4.2	4.2	55

Transport

The actual rate can be obtained by relating the Worldscale figure for any voyage to the relevant rate; for example, for a voyage Curacao/Rotterdam, Worldscale 125 (1979 basis) or W 125 (1979) would mean that the actual rate was the W 100 rate (per ton) for 1979 multiplied by 125/100 or 1.25.

The *average freight rate assessment* (AFRA) is an independent assessment, carried out monthly, of rates of the average freighting level of all ocean going tankers on commercial charter during the previous month; all types of oil freight charter, whether voyage or time, short or long term, are included in the assessment and the average level in each case is weighted according to the percentage that each represents of the total carrying capacity. This assessment provides a more stable basis than current market levels for invoicing etc.

Load lines

The load line is the line to which the ship may be loaded (generally referred to as 'Plimsoll' line). General markings (there are special markings for timber) are:

TF = tropical fresh water
F = fresh water
T = tropical sea water
S = summer, sea water
W = winter, sea water
WNA = winter, North Atlantic. for vessels under 330 ft in length
LR = registration society (here, for example, Lloyd's Register).

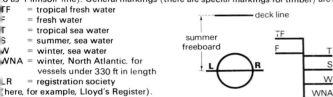

Weapons

Small arms

Bore diameter usually means the diameter from land to land of a rifled barrel (minimum diameter), but sometimes means groove diameter which is measured from groove to groove of a rifled barrel (maximum diameter).
Nominal or designated calibre does not usually correspond exactly to actual bore diameter, although it may do so; the following gives some illustrative values:

| Calibre (nominal) | | Actual bore diameter | |
mm	other[a]	mm	inch
	22	5.5	0.216
6.35		6.35	0.25
7.5		7.823	0.308
7.62	30	7.823	0.308
	303	7.925	0.312
7.92		8.204	0.323
8		8.204	0.323
	38	8.89	0.35
9		9.02	0.355
	45	11.3	0.445
	455	11.6	0.455
	50	12.7	0.50

[a] Nominal inch calibre, measured in hundredths or thousandths, but frequently referred to as the number of hundredths or thousandths; for example, 22 and 303.

Shotguns

The bore or gauge number for shotguns was originally the number of solid round lead balls, of a bore diameter size which could be taken by the gun, required to make a pound (avoirdupois). The smallest bore is now described by the actual size (0.410). Following are some usual sizes:

| Bore or gauge (nominal) | Actual bore diameter | |
	mm	inch
410	10.4	0.410
28	14.0	0.550
20	15.6	0.615
16	16.8	0.662
12	18.5	0.729
10	19.7	0.775
8	21.2	0.835
4	26.7	1.052

Guns

Following are some examples of the range of sizes:

| United Kingdom | | United States | | Soviet Union | |
mm	inch	mm	inch	mm	inch
35	(1.4)	20	(0.8)	(76)	3
40	(1.6)	40	(1.6)	82	(3.2)
(77)	3.0	(76)	3	85[a]	(3.3)
84	(3.3)	90[a]	(3.5)	100[a]	(3.9)
105[a]	(4.1)	105[a]	(4.1)	120[a]	(4.7)
120[a]	(4.7)	120[a]	(4.7)	122[a]	(4.8)
(140)	5½	(152)	6	130	(5.1)
155	(6.1)	155	(6.1)	(140)	5½
175	(6.9)	175	(6.9)	(152)	6
(203)	8	(203)	8	160	(6.3)
				180	(7.1)
				(203)	8
				240	(9.4)

[a] Typical tank main guns.

Bombs and warheads

Tri-nitro-toluene (TNT)

The energy released by TNT is used as the basis of measures of explosions. The standard used here is that 1 kilogram of TNT produces 4.5×10^6 J (1 ton or 'tonne' produces 4.5×10^9 J); the relationship 1 kg TNT = 4.2×10^6 J is also in use.

Atomic (fission) weapons

Energy released by nuclear explosion – fission of all atoms of the fuel within a fraction of a second – is close to the maximum possible for fission (the splitting of each atom into two not quite equal parts). That is, for 1 kilogram of U-235 it is about 8×10^7 MJ or 8×10^{13} J (for further details, see the energy section, page 141).
The magnitude of atomic explosion is usually expressed in terms of the ton of TNT; hence for 1 kilogram of U-235, the magnitude in tons of TNT is:
$(8.2 \times 10^{13}$ J$)/(4.5 \times 10^9$ J$) = 2 \times 10^4$ tons approximately = 20 000 tons.
Larger multiples used in this connection are:
1 kiloton (kT or kt) = 1 000 tons = 4.5×10^{12} J
1 megaton (MT or Mt) = 1 000 kilotons = 1 000 000 tons = 4.5×10^{15} J.
Hence 1 kilogram of U-235 produces an explosion of 20 kilotons.
Uranium and plutonium are the main nuclear fuels; thorium-233 is a possible future fuel for atomic explosions.
Atomic bombs normally use enriched uranium with over 40% and up to 97% of U-235, or plutonium with over 90% Pu-239.

Hydrogen or thermo-nuclear (fusion) weapons

A hydrogen or thermo-nuclear bomb ('H-bomb') is produced by a process of nuclear fusion—the merging of nuclei as compared to the splitting (fission) of atoms in the 'atomic' bomb. Extreme heat – of the order of 100 million °C – is required, and so fusion weapons need a small atomic (fission) charge as an initiator.
Energy released by a thermo-nuclear bomb is of the order of 20 megatons.
Main fuels for the thermo-nuclear bomb are certain kinds of hydrogen atoms: hydrogen-deuterium and hydrogen-tritium.

Neutron bombs or warheads

A neutron bomb is an atomic bomb which releases more of its energy in the form of immediate radiation (a high-intensity blast of neutrons and gamma rays) than the 'conventional' nuclear weapon. An approximate comparison of the type of damage follows:

| | Use of energy released (per cent) | | | |
	Blast	Heat	'Prompt' radiation	Other radiation
H-bomb	45	35	5	15
Neutron warhead	34	24	40	2

Weapons

Nuclear delivery

Missiles

	Range (km)
MRBM = Medium-range ballistic missile	1 100–2 750
IRBM = Intermediate-range ballistic missile	2 750–5 500
ICBM = Intercontinental ballistic missile	over 5 500

Submarines

A Polaris submarine carries 16 missiles, each with 3 thermonuclear warheads.

Satellites

The period of a satellite is the time taken for it to circle the earth in orbit once. The lower the orbit, the shorter the rotation period; examples are:

	Orbit		Rotation period
	km	mi	hours
low orbit	150–500	100–300	$1\frac{1}{2}$
medium altitude	10 000–20 000	6 000–12 000	5–12

Also see page 86 for general satellite information.

Nuclear damage

The effects of nuclear explosions depend on the nature of the weapon and its power. The following tables show the effects for three levels of power, using ground burst weapons:
20 kilotons = atomic bomb dropped on Hiroshima
1 megaton = modern atomic bomb
20 megatons = hydrogen bomb

Persons

The following table shows the effect on people exposed to initial radiation and heat blast in the open. The table takes into account the 'inverse square' law, whereby the intensity of radiation and heat decreases by a factor which is proportional to the square of the distance from the source of the explosion; for example, if distance is trebled, intensity falls to a ninth ($1/3^2$). The distances shown are those beyond which the person will in general not suffer the effects indicated.

Initial effects	Weapon power (ground burst)					
	20 kilotons		1 megaton		20 megatons	
	km	mi	km	mi	km	mi
Death (50–50 chance)[a]	$1\frac{1}{4}$	$\frac{3}{4}$	$2\frac{1}{2}$	$1\frac{1}{2}$	$3\frac{3}{4}$	$2\frac{1}{4}$
Radiation sickness[b]	$1\frac{1}{2}$	1	$2\frac{3}{4}$	$1\frac{3}{4}$	4	$2\frac{1}{2}$
Charring of skin[c]	$1\frac{1}{2}$	1	8	5	26	16

[a]That is, there is a 50–50 chance of death or survival; this is called an LD 50, signifying that there is a lethal dose for 50% of people. This level is taken as 450 rem (4.5 sievert); for nuclear weapon purposes, the röntgen is regarded as about equal to the rad and to the rem.   [b]Taken at the UK 'War Emergency Dose' (WED) level of 75 rem ($\frac{3}{4}$ sievert).   [c]The effect of thermal radiation or heat flash which consists almost entirely, beyond the immediate dangerous blast area, of intense visible light and infrared rays. The distance is shown (for a clear atmosphere) for serious charring of the full thickness of the skin, extending to underlying tissue; reddening of the skin, similar to sunburn, can be suffered up to nearly double the distance shown for charring.

The distances are shown for a ground burst nuclear weapon; for an air burst weapon the distances are about the same for death and radiation sickness effects, and about 50% greater for the effect of heat blast.

For further information concerning radiation and radiation measures see the section on health (pages 150–151).

Shielding for defence against radiation is usually measured in terms of the 'half-value' thickness; this is the thickness of the shield needed to reduce the dose rate in a beam of gamma rays by one half, so that, in general, defence against radiation is given for twice the weapon power indicated in the above table where there is shielding at half-value thickness. Approximate values are:

Shielding material	Half-value thickness (against initial gamma radiation)	
	cm	in
Steel	4	$1\frac{1}{2}$
Concrete	15	6
Earth	20	$7\frac{1}{2}$
Water	33	13

The foregoing table refers to initial effects on people. The effect of downwind fallout depends on atmospheric conditions (especially cloud dimensions and height) and speed of wind, in relation to the time after the explosion occurs; a standard reference time is defined in the United Kingdom to be either $H + 1$ or $H + 7$, meaning one hour or seven hours after detonation. Since the amount of radiation decays over time, the dose-rate is defined on the same time scale as, for example, DR1 and DR7, meaning the dose-rate after 1 hour and after 7 hours. The general 'decay law' is that radiation falls by a factor of 10 as time lengthens by a factor of 7; more exactly, $R_t = R_1 t^{-1.2}$, where R_1 is the nominal dose rate at 1 hour after burst, and R_t is the dose rate at time t (in hours). The following table gives approximate dose-rates for various times after burst, starting from a nominal rate of 100 (rem per hour or, say, sievert per second, since the rate of decay does not depend on the unit used):

Time after burst	Dose rate
1 hour	100
$1\frac{3}{4}$ hours	50
7 hours	10
2 days	1
2 weeks	0.1
14 weeks	0.01

The area of downwind fallout depends on wind conditions; approximate areas which will be contaminated downwind, under average conditions, are given in the following table:

Dose rate at edge of the area specified at DR1		Downwind contamination area (by weapon power)					
		20 kilotons		1 megaton		20 megatons	
rem per hour	sievert per hour	km²	mi²	km²	mi²	km²	mi²
1 000	10	3.4	1.3	230	90	5 000	1 900
100	1	41	16	2 300	900	47 000	18 000
10	0.1	500	200	12 000	4 500	240 000	93 000

Houses

Pressure from the shock wave is likely to cause slight damage to average UK houses at about $\frac{3}{4}$ pounds per square inch (5 kPa), reparable damage (houses remaining habitable) at about $1\frac{1}{2}$ lbf/in² (10 kPa), and irreparable damage at about 6 lbf/in² (40 kPa).

Average range of estimated blast damage to average UK houses is shown in the following table, giving very approximate limits in kilometres and miles:

Type of damage up to range specified	Range of blast damage (by weapon power)					
	20 kilotons		1 megaton		20 megatons	
	km	mi	km	mi	km	mi
Total destruction	0.6	0.4	2.4	1.5	7.2	4.5
Irreparable damage	1.0	0.6	3.6	2.2	10	6
Severe to moderate damage	2.5	1.5	9.0	5.5	25	15
Light damage	4.0	2.5	14.5	9.0	40	25

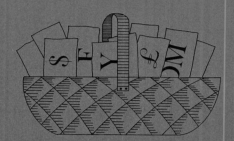

The creation of 'international money' (SDRs)

'The Managing Director's proposal to allocate special drawing rights for the first basic period, adopted as Resolution no. 24-12 by the Board of Governors of the (International Monetary) Fund on October 3, 1969, provided for the creation of approximately SDR 9.5 billion[a] over the three years 1970–72. By December 31, 1969, 105 members with total quotas of $20,872 million (97.8 per cent of total Fund quotas) had deposited instruments of participation. The first allocation of special drawing rights was made on January 1, 1970 to 104 participants at a rate equal to 16.8 per cent of their quotas. The total allocation amounted to SDR 3,414 million.

[a] The unit of value of special drawing rights is equivalent to 0.888671 gram of fine gold. This is equivalent to one U.S. dollar of the weight and fineness in effect on July 1, 1944.'

(Annual Report of the Executive Directors for the Fiscal Year ended April 30, 1970; International Monetary Fund)

Note: this refers to the beginning (1970) value and position; valuation was changed to a basket of 16 currencies from July 1, 1974, and the basket weights were revised in July 1, 1978. The number of currencies in the basket is reduced from 16 to 5, with effect from January 1, 1981.

Useful definitions and formulae

Accountancy

Ratios

Working capital

Working capital ratio = current assets/current liabilities,
where current assets = stock + debtors + cash at bank and in hand + quoted investments, etc.,
current liabilities = creditors + overdraft at bank + taxation + dividends, etc.
The ratio varies according to type of trade and conditions; a ratio from 1 to 3 is usual with a ratio above 2 being generally good.

Liquidity ratio = liquid ('quick') assets/current liabilities, where liquid assets = debtors + cash at bank and in hand + quoted investments (that is assets which can be realised within a month or so, which may not apply to all investments); current liabilities are those which may need to be repaid within the same short period, which may not necessarily include a bank overdraft where it is likely to be renewed. The liquidity ratio is sometimes referred to as the 'acid test'; a ratio under 1 suggests a possibly difficult situation, while too high a ratio may mean that assets are not being usefully employed.

Turnover of working capital = sales/average working capital. The ratio varies according to type of trade; generally a low ratio can mean poor use of resources, while too high a ratio can mean over-trading.

Turnover of stock = sales/average stock,
or (where cost of sales is known) = cost of sales/average stock.
The cost of sales turnover figure is to be preferred as both figures are then on the same valuation basis. This ratio can be expressed as number of times per year, or time taken for stock to be turned over once = (52/number of times) weeks. A low turnover of stock can be a sign of stocks which are difficult to move, and is usually a sign of adverse conditions.

Turnover of debtors = credit sales/average debtors. This indicates efficiency in collecting accounts. An average 'credit period' of about 1 month is usual, but varies according to credit stringency conditions in the economy.

Turnover of creditors = purchases/average creditors. Average payment period is best maintained in line with turnover of debtors.

Sales

Export ratio = exports as a percentage of sales.

Sales per employee = sales/average number of employees.

Assets

Ratios of assets can vary according to the measure of assets used:

Total assets = current assets + fixed assets + other assets,
where fixed assets = property + plant and machinery + motor vehicles, etc,
and other assets = long-term investments + goodwill, etc.

Net assets ('net worth') = total assets − total liabilities
= share capital + reserves

Turnover of net assets = sales/average net assets. As for turnover of working capital, a low ratio can mean poor use of resources.

Assets per employee = assets/average number of employees. Indicates the amount of investment backing for employees.

Profits

Profit margin = (profit/sales) × 100 = profits as a percentage of sales; usually profits before tax.

Profitability = (profit/total assets) × 100 = profits as a percentage of total assets.

Return on capital = (profit/net assets) × 100 = profits as a percentage of net assets ('net worth' or 'capital employed').

All ratios are best compared with those for companies in similar industries, and also compared over time. In addition growth rates for each item (for example sales, profits, etc.) can be obtained by calculating the percentage change over various periods and using the tables on pages 206–213 to obtain the growth rate per annum. Growth rates then provide comparability as between periods of varying lengths.

Investment appraisal

Appraisal for investment usually means considering the rates of return for various projects and selecting the one with the 'best' return. Methods of appraisal for investment depend first on the estimation of the net cash flow from an investment, where all taxes, subsidies, grants, etc., have been allowed for in estimating the cash flow. Methods differ according to the way in which the flows of cash over time are related to the initial investment:

Rate of return = the total of the estimated cash flows over the life of the investment, divided by the number of years life, and expressed as a percentage of the investment. Where a unit of 100 is invested to give the following net cash flows over 10 years: 1, 10.0; 2, 11.0; 3, 12.1; 4, 13.3; 5, 14.6; 6, 16.1; 7, 17.7 8, 19.5; 9, 21.4; 10, 23.6; then:
the crude rate of return is the total of those flows = 159.3, divided by 10 = 15.93, which is 15.93% as a percentage of the 100 units originally invested.

Pay back = the number of years after which the original investment would have been recouped. In the above example, this would be after year 8, when a cumulative amount of 114.3 would have been received net.

Discounted cash flow

The above two methods make no allowance for the time factor in the cash flows; as any sum could be earning interest in an alternative investment, it is more realistic to 'discount' the cash flows to be received in future years by an expected rate of interest. Tables for the amount accumulated by 1 unit at different rates of interest and for different periods are included on pages 214–217. The 'discount factor', giving the present value of any future amount allowing for the rate of interest concerned, is the reciprocal of the figure in the accumulation tables.

The following table shows the effect of 'discounting' the cash flows in the above example at interest rates of 5% and 10%; this follows the convention of regarding the first year as not subject to discounting, so that year 2 is discounted at the rate for 1 year as shown in the discount factor table. Further, the convention of regarding all receipts and payments as taking place on one day of each year is adopted.

Period	Net cash flow	Interest at 5%		Interest at 10%	
		Discount factor	Present value	Discount factor	Present value
1	10.0	1.0000	10.0	1.0000	10.0
2	11.0	0.9524	10.5	0.9091	10.0
3	12.1	0.9070	11.0	0.8264	10.0
4	13.3	0.8638	11.5	0.7513	10.0
5	14.6	0.8227	12.0	0.6830	10.0
6	16.1	0.7835	12.6	0.6209	10.0
7	17.7	0.7462	13.2	0.5645	10.0
8	19.5	0.7107	13.9	0.5132	10.0
9	21.4	0.6768	14.5	0.4665	10.0
10	23.6	0.6446	15.2	0.4241	10.0

The total cash flow at present value is 124.4 discounted at 5%, and 100 discounted at 10%, compared with the crude total flow of 159.3. Assuming an interest rate of 5% the investment of 100 units will give a 'profit' of 24.4, and assuming an interest rate of 10%, the investment of 100 gives a return of exactly 100, so it yields no profit at that rate of interest (this is because the net cash flows used in the example are the same as the amount accumulated from 10 at 10% p.a., as indicated in the table on page 216).

Where the present value of the flow of cash, discounted at a certain rate, exactly equals the initial amount of investment, that rate is sometimes called the DCF 'solution' rate, since it is the rate of return given by the investment made. In the above example, 10% is the DCF solution rate. DCF solution rates are usually calculated by interpolation from rates which are approximately known.

Accountancy

Where the investment is also spread over more than one period, allowance is also made for discounting the investment payments. In the following example the effect of spreading a 100 unit investment over 3 periods is illustrated, discounting taking place at the DCF solution rate which differs accordingly.

Period	Investment in 1 period		Investment in 3 periods	
	Net cash flow	Present value	Net cash flow	Present value
Investment				
1	100	100	25	25.0
2			50	37.8
3			25	14.3
Returns				
1	20	20.0	20	20.0
2	20	16.6	20	15.1
3	20	13.8	20	11.5
4	20	11.5	20	8.7
5	20	9.6	20	6.6
6	20	8.0	20	5.0
7	20	6.6	20	3.8
8	20	5.5	20	2.8
9	20	4.6	20	2.2
0	20	3.8	20	1.6

The total discounted amount or present value is 100 for the 1 period investment example, with a DCF solution rate of 20.3%; for the example with investment over 3 periods, the total discounted amount is 77.2 units (since investment flows are also discounted) with a DCF solution rate of 32.2%. The higher rate is obtained because the investment does not need to be made immediately, but the returns are nevertheless the same.

Economics

National accounts

Definitions of basic items

The following definitions are based on the present 'System of National Accounts' (SNA) as formulated by the United Nations in 1968 (this replaced the former system which was formulated in 1952). Main differences in definitions as used in the United Kingdom national accounts are also indicated.

Factor cost and market value
The basis of valuation for the different items is usually either at factor values ('factor cost') or at market prices (or purchasers' values, which is the cost at the point of delivery). Market price value is the factor cost plus taxes on expenditure net of subsidies falling on each item of expenditure.

Private final consumption expenditure = the outlays of resident households on new durable and non-durable goods and services, less their net sales of second-hand goods, scraps and wastes. The equivalent UK item, 'consumers' expenditure', also includes the expenditure of private non-profit-making institutions serving persons. For valuations at market prices certain taxes (eg motor vehicle licence duty) are classified in the UK system as taxes on expenditure whereas they are classified in the UN system as 'direct taxes'.

Consumer durables = goods acquired by households which have an expected life-time of considerably more than one year and a relatively high value, such as motor cars, refrigerators and washing machines. Dwellings are excluded since they are classed as fixed assets.

Government final consumption expenditure = net current expenditure by both central government and local authorities; this excludes expenditure on (a) grants, subsidies, interest payments and all other transfers (b) stocks and fixed capital. The equivalent UK item, 'general government final consumption' uses a different basis of valuation to the UN system for imputed rent on buildings owned and occupied by public authorities.

Increase in stocks (inventories) = the market value of the physical change during the year in stocks of materials, supplies, work-in-progress, finished products, etc., held by trading enterprises or by government.

Gross fixed capital formation = net expenditure on fixed assets (buildings, vehicles, plant and machinery, etc.) either for replacing or adding to the stock of existing fixed assets.

Exports of goods and services = all transfers of ownership of goods to non-residents, and services provided by resident producers to non-residents. Valued fob.

Imports of goods and services = all transfers of the ownership of goods from non-residents to residents, and services provided by non-resident producers to residents. Valued fob.

Net property income from other countries = property and entrepreneurial income (including dividends, etc.) from other countries, less property and entrepreneurial income paid to other countries.

Consumption of fixed capital = the value, at current replacement cost, of the fixed capital used up during the year as a result of normal wear and tear, foreseen obsolescence and the normal rate of accidental damage.

Stock appreciation or depreciation = that increase or fall in the value of stocks which has been due to the change in prices during the year. This item, used in the UK system, is not quantified in the UN system in which all items are measured net of any stock appreciation.

Compensation of employees = all payments by resident producers of wages and salaries to their employees, in kind and in cash, and of contributions, paid or imputed, in respect of their employees to social security schemes and to private pension, family allowance, casualty insurance, life insurance and similar schemes. The equivalent UK item, 'income from employment', excludes payments to non-resident employees of UK resident employers, but includes receipts by UK resident employees working for non-resident employers. Net receipts by resident employees from non-resident employers are shown in the UN system as 'compensation of employees receivable from the rest of the world'.

Operating surplus = the excess of the value added of resident industries over the sum of their costs of employee compensation, consumption of fixed capital and indirect taxes reduced by subsidies; imputations are included in respect of rent, etc. In the UK system, the operating surplus is equivalent to the sum of income from self-employment, gross trading profits of companies, gross trading surplus of public corporations and general government enterprises and rents of properties, less consumption of fixed capital and stock appreciation.

Indirect taxes = taxes and import duties assessed on producers in respect of the production, sale, purchase or use of goods and services, which they charge to the expenses of production. The equivalent UK item 'taxes on expenditure' includes certain taxes which are classified as direct in the UN system.

Subsidies = all grants on current account made by government to private industries and public corporations.

Formulae

Final expenditure
= private final consumption expenditure ('consumers' expenditure')
+ government final consumption expenditure
+ increase in stocks
+ gross fixed capital formation
+ exports of goods and services

Gross domestic product at market prices
= final expenditure
− imports of goods and services

Gross national product at market prices
= gross domestic product at market prices
+ net property income from other countries

Gross domestic product at factor cost
= gross domestic product at market prices
− indirect taxes
+ subsidies

Economics

National income at market prices

= gross domestic product at market prices
+ net property income from other countries
− consumption of fixed capital

also
= gross national product at market prices
− consumption of fixed capital

also
= compensation of employees
+ compensation of employees receivable from the rest of the world
+ operating surplus
+ net property income from other countries
+ indirect taxes
− subsidies

National income at factor cost

= national income at market prices
− indirect taxes
+ subsidies

also (in the UK system)
= income from employment
+ income from self-employment
+ gross trading profits of companies
+ gross trading surplus of public corporations
+ gross trading surplus of general government enterprises
+ rents of property
+ imputed charge for consumption of non-trading capital
+ net property income from other countries
− stock appreciation (or + stock depreciation)
− consumption of fixed capital

Financial accounts

Saving = current income less current expenditure for each sector, before providing for depreciation and stock appreciation.

Increase in the value of stocks = value of the physical change in stocks, plus stock appreciation or less stock depreciation.

Net acquisition of financial assets = saving, plus capital transfers, less gross domestic fixed capital formation, less the increase in the value of stocks.

External (or 'international') transactions accounts

These are accounts setting out the current and capital transactions of a country with the rest of the world; they are associated with the national accounts, and are also referred to as the 'balance of payments'.

Current external transactions account, or current balance of payments account

Current balance
= exports of goods and services
− imports of goods and services
+ net property income from other countries
− net current transfers to other countries,

where exports, imports and net property income are as defined above for the national accounts, and net current transfers to other countries = current transfers of goods, services and financial assets to other countries, less transfers from other countries, such transfers being made without charge or right to compensation. The balance of exports and imports of goods only is referred to as the visible balance, and the balance of other current items (services, income and transfers) as the invisible balance.

Investment and financing account (investment or lending abroad)

The balance on current account shows whether a country has added to or consumed its net external assets in any period. These net external assets represent the net increase in physical assets, financial assets and gold and foreign currency reserves.

These assets are presented in the UK balance of payments in two groups: *Investment and other capital transactions* which include official long-term capital transactions, investment flows, changes in the balances of other countries held in the United Kingdom, trade credit and other capital flows. *Official financing* which covers changes in the official reserves, net borrowing from the International Monetary Fund and net transactions with other overseas monetary authorities.

The currency flow is the net movement (allowing for a balancing item) of the current balance and investment and other capital flows. The relationships are:

Financing of currency flow
= official financing (= change in official reserves plus net transactions with overseas monetary authorities)
+ allocation of special drawing rights by the IMF
− gold subscription to the IMF

Currency flow less balancing item
= current balance
+ investment and other capital flows

Investment and other capital transactions include flows which are regarded as investment flows when of a long-term and other capital flows when of a short-term nature.

Investment and other capital transactions
= official long-term capital flows (including inter-government loans)
+ private investment flows (including direct and portfolio investment)
+ other capital flows (including changes in net borrowing or lending by UK banks in overseas currencies; changes in overseas holdings of sterling securities, bank deposits, etc.; trade credit; and other official and private short-term flows).

Prices

Constant prices

Estimates of items in the national accounts are first calculated in terms of current prices—actual prices for each period. Estimates at constant prices are obtained by revaluing each item included at the prices of a base date; this provides an indication of changes in volume when different years are compared.
Implicit price deflator is the term used to describe the price index implied by the difference between current and constant price estimates. For example, where the base date is 1975, the implicit price deflator or price index for national income is given by:

$$\frac{\text{National income at current prices}}{\text{National income at 1975 prices}} \times 100$$

This provides the price index for national income with base 1975 = 100.

Retail price index

The general index of retail prices in the United Kingdom measures the changes month by month in the average level of prices of the commodities and services purchased by the great majority of households in the United Kingdom, including practically all wage earners and most small and medium salary earners. Weights for the index are based on information from the annual Family Expenditure Surveys. This index is less widely based than the price index given by the implicit price deflator for all consumers' expenditure.

Purchasing power of money

Changes in the purchasing power of money between any two times can be defined as the inverse of changes in consumer prices between those two times. For example, taking the purchasing power of the pound to be 100p in 1975, its current value is given by:

$$\frac{\text{Index of consumer prices in 1975}}{\text{Current index of consumer prices}} \times 100p$$

The index used for this purpose may vary; the official UK measure of the purchasing power of the pound has been based as follows: from 1914 to 1938 on the Ministry of Labour's cost of living index; from 1938 to 1962 on the implicit price deflator for total consumers' expenditure; from 1962 on the general index of retail prices.

Economics

Index numbers

Index numbers are statistical constructions designed to provide comparisons or numbers or aggregates over a period of years. Where the item being measured is aggregated from a number of individual components, these are weighted to provide an estimate of the average.

The main types of weighted index are:

Laspeyres index, which uses base year weights to multiply against each of the items in the base year and in the year for which the index is being constructed. Where

p_o = the base year price
p_t = the current year price
q_o = the base year quantity (weight)

The Laspeyres index is $\dfrac{\Sigma\, p_t\, q_o}{\Sigma\, p_o\, q_o} \times 100$

That is, the sum of the base year quantities multiplied by the current year prices, divided by the sum of the base year quantities multiplied by the base year prices, multiplied by 100, gives the price index for the current year.

Paasche index, which uses current year weights to multiply against each of the items in the base year and in the year for which the index is being constructed. Where, in addition to the above, q_t = the current year quantity (weight)

The Paasche index is $\dfrac{\Sigma\, p_t\, q_t}{\Sigma\, p_o\, q_t} \times 100$

That is, the sum of the current year quantities multiplied by the current year prices, divided by the sum of the current year quantities multiplied by the base year prices, multiplied by 100, gives the price index for the current year. The implicit price deflator is a Paasche type index number, while the retail price index is a Laspeyres type.

The *Irving Fisher 'Ideal' index* is the geometric mean of the Laspeyres and Paasche indices; using the above symbols, the ideal price index is:

$$\sqrt{\dfrac{\Sigma\, p_t\, q_o}{\Sigma\, p_o\, q_o} \times \dfrac{\Sigma\, p_t\, q_t}{\Sigma\, p_o\, q_t}} \times 100$$

Rates of increase or growth

Growth rates

The rate at which an amount is changing over time is usually expressed as a percentage change from year to year. Where the change is measured over more than one year, the rate of increase or compound growth rate per annum is given by the following formula: where n is the number of years over which the increase is measured, and A is the percentage increase over the period

$$\text{growth rate in \% p.a.} = \left[\left(\dfrac{100 + A}{100}\right)^{-n} \times 100\right] - 100$$

A table for obtaining growth rates from percentage increases is provided on pages 206–213.

Acceleration of growth

Where a rate of increase or growth is increasing through time, it is said to be accelerating and where it is decreasing it is said to be decelerating. For example, a rate of inflation is the percentage change from year to year, but an increase in this rate is an acceleration, and a fall in the rate a deceleration.

Over the period of a business cycle, the rate of growth is positive during expansion, and accelerating during the early stages of recovery; then the rate of growth falls and is small or negative during recession. In terms of calculus (see also page 192): where dy/dt is the first differential ('rate of change') and d^2y/dt^2 is the second differential ('rate of acceleration'), the changes in these rates are indicated in the following diagram (of a sine curve):

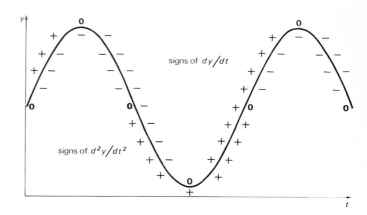

That is, the first differential is positive (there is positive growth) during recovery from a trough; the second differential is at first positive (the rate of growth is increasing), then as recovery continues a 'point of inflexion' is reached at which the second differential becomes zero (the rate of growth, while still positive, begins to slacken); at a peak the first differential becomes zero (the rate of growth changes from positive to negative), while the second differential is still negative; the rate of fall then increases until another point of inflexion is reached (when the second differential is zero), when the rate of fall begins to slow down, becoming zero at the bottom of the trough.

Money

There is no single universally accepted definition of money. Any definition must therefore to some extent be arbitrary and different monetary aggregates will be useful for different purposes.

The main UK definitions of money stock are M_1, M_3 and M_3 sterling. The narrower definition (M_1) comprises holdings of notes and coin outside the banks plus all sight deposit accounts of UK private sector residents denominated in sterling, less 60 per cent of the net value of transit items. This definition can be thought of as representing more closely the functions of money as a medium of exchange, and as including the generally acceptable means of payment in the system.

The wider definition (M_3) covers holding of notes and coin outside the banks plus all deposits of UK residents (other than banks) with the United Kingdom banking sector, including sight and time deposit accounts in sterling or foreign currency and estimated holdings of sterling certificates of deposit by UK residents (other than banks), less 60 per cent of the net value of transit items. Hence M_3 includes M_1 plus other items, the main one of which is bank deposit accounts.
M_3 sterling is defined as M_3 less UK residents' deposits in other currencies.

International money

Definitions used in connection with the International Monetary Fund are as follows:

Quotas. Each member of the Fund has a quota which determines the voting power and subscription of that member, the member's share in an allocation of SDRs and the normal quantitative limitations on the member's use of Fund resources.

Subscriptions are equal to quotas; they are payable partly in reserve assets and partly in the member's currency, or they can be fully paid in a member's currency.

International liquidity is obtained by members as follows:

Reserve positions in the fund are unconditional drawing rights as a result of the payment of reserve assets and of the Fund's net use of their currencies including borrowing.

Credit tranche positions are conditional liquidity rights which can be drawn on if justification is sufficient. The liquidity of credit tranche positions can be enhanced through a stand-by arrangement which indicates the policies of the member on the basis of which the Fund allows the member to purchase a specific amount in a specified period; specific policies may be indicated, for example, in the fields of exchange, monetary and fiscal matters.

Economics

Special drawing rights (SDRs) are unconditional reserve assets created by the Fund to influence the total level of world reserves; member countries that are also participants in the special drawing account receive supplements of SDRs in proportion to their Fund quota. Provision for allocation of SDRs was first made on July 28, 1969.

The value of the SDR from its introduction until end June 1974 was 0.888 671 gram of fine gold. This was also the par value of the US dollar from the formation of the Fund until November 1971. The value of the SDR was fixed by dividing the gold content of 1 troy ounce, namely 31.103 476 8 grams, by 35 and rounding the resulting number to six significant figures (it being established Fund practice to round values to six significant figures).

From July 1974 the SDR was defined as a weighted index ('basket') of 16 currencies. The value of the SDR is determined daily from the market exchange rate for each of the 16 currencies in terms of the US dollar, duly weighted. The rates for the SDR in terms of other currencies is determined by the market exchange rate for those currencies against the US dollar, and the US dollar rate against the SDR.

The relative weights for each of the 16 countries were based on relative exports, but also took account of the importance of a currency internationally. Initial weightings, used from July 1974 to end June 1978, were determined for those countries whose share in the world exports of goods and services averaged more than one per cent in the period 1968–72.
The initial weightings are shown in column (a) in the table below; column (b) lists the currency components, as calculated on June 28, 1974, which are estimated in such a way that the value of an SDR is the sum of each currency component multiplied by the actual number of US dollars per corresponding unit for any day. For June 28, 1974 the value as calculated was equal to US $1.20635, identical with the value on the old method of valuing the SDR

	(a)	(b)		(a)	(b)
United States dollar	33	0.4000	Belgian franc	3½	1.6000
West Germany D'mark	12½	0.3800	Swedish krona	2½	0.1300
United Kingdom pound	9	0.0450	Australian dollar	1½	0.0120
French franc	7½	0.4400	Danish krone	1½	0.1100
Japanese yen	7½	26.0000	Norwegian krone	1½	0.0990
Canadian dollar	6	0.0710	Spanish peseta	1½	1.1000
Italian lira	6	47.0000	Austrian schilling	1	0.2200
Netherlands guilder	4½	0.1400	South African rand	1	0.0082

Beginning July 1, 1978 there was a revised basket of 16 currencies based on statistics for the period 1972–76; the currencies of Iran and Saudi Arabia replaced those of Denmark and South Africa, and weights of some countries were changed. The revised weights were designed in such a way that the value of the SDR for June 30, 1978 was the same using both the old weightings and the new.
It was agreed in September 1980 that the number of currencies in the basket be reduced to those of five countries: United States, West Germany, United Kingdom, France and Japan, with effect from January 1, 1981.

EEC units

Unit of account (ua)
The first EEC unit of account (gold-based) was defined in 1962 as equal in gold value to the US dollar, equal to 0.888 670 88 grams. The relationship between each member's currency and the unit of account was then equal to the relationship between the currency and the US dollar; these were (value at November 1, 1962):

	Member's units per ua	ua per member's unit
original six members		
Belgium/Luxembourg: francs	50	0.02
France: francs	4.937 06	0.202 549
Germany, West: D'marks	4	0.25
Italy: lire	625	0.001 6
Netherlands: guilders	3.62	0.276 243
new members (from Jan 1, 1973)		
Denmark: kroner	7.5	0.133 333
Ireland: punts	0.416 667	2.40
United Kingdom: pounds	0.416 667	2.40

The gold-based unit of account was in use for most EEC purposes until replaced in general by the European unit of account (EUA); it was in use for customs purposes up to December 31, 1978. Up to 1977 the EEC Statistical Office used the 'Eur' unit as a unit of common value in its publications; this was equal to the ua. In 1977 the Eur was replaced by the EUA.

European unit of account (EUA)
In December 1974 the EEC Commission introduced the EUA as a unit to replace progressively other EEC units. A different unit to the ua had become necessary because member's exchange rates fluctuated away from the original gold-based parities. From January 1, 1978 the EUA was introduced for general budgetary purposes.
The value of the EUA is determined from a basket of currencies of EEC members. The weighting of currencies in the basket is based on gross national product and intra-community trade importance. At the outset, the EUA was fixed so that 1 EUA was equal to 1 SDR equal to US $1.20635 at June 28, 1974. At that date the weighting and corresponding quantity of each currency in the basket were as follows:

	Weight (%)	No of units
Belgium: francs	7.9	3.66
Denmark: kroner	3.0	0.217
France: francs	19.5	1.15
Germany, West: D'marks	27.3	0.828
Ireland: punts	1.5	0.007 59
Italy: lire	14.0	109
Luxembourg: francs	0.3	0.14
Netherlands: guilders	9.0	0.286
United Kingdom: pounds	17.5	0.088 5

European currency unit (ecu)
Introduced from March 13, 1979 as a basket of currencies of EEC members, this unit was designed for use within the European Monetary System (EMS). Currency rates for members of the system have a fixed central rate in terms of the ecu, and also upper and lower intervention limits. The various rates and the weights for each currency in the ecu vary when a change in the basic central rate agreed within the system. At the beginning of the system, the composition and value of the ecu was the same as for the EUA. Central rates of EMS members at the beginning of the system were:

	Member's units per ecu
Belgium/Luxembourg: francs	39.458 2
Denmark: kroner	7.085 92
France: francs	5.798 31
Germany, West: D'marks	2.510 64
Ireland: punts	0.662 638
Italy: lire	1 148.15
Netherlands: guilders	2.720 77

Agricultural representative ('green') rates
For agricultural purposes of the Common Agricultural Policy (CAP) EEC farm trade is conducted in terms of common prices expressed in EEC units of value; for those purposes the unit of value was the unit of account (ua) before April 9, 1979 and the ecu from that date.
The conversion rates from the EEC agricultural common prices to national currencies were, at the beginning of the EEC, equal to the fixed parity rates (as shown above for the unit of account). In general from 1969, the agricultural representative ('green') rates have been fixed by Council decisions, and have varied from the fixed rates against the ua or ecu. The general green rates per ecu at April 9, 1979 (on the change from a ua base to an ecu base) were:

	Member's units per ecu	ecu per member's unit
Belgium/Luxembourg: francs	40.819 3	0.024 498 2
Denmark: kroner	7.085 92	0.141 125
France: francs	5.712 59	0.175 052
Germany, West: D'marks	2.814 32	0.355 326
Ireland: punts	0.652 84	1.531 77
Italy: lire	1 005.00	0.000 995 023
Netherlands: guilders	2.814 59	0.355 292
United Kingdom: pounds	0.552 20	1.810 94

Definitions of other forms of international money are as follows:

Eurodollars are dollar deposits held through banks outside the United States. The Eurodollar market is the market through which such dollars are borrowed and on-lent. The term is sometimes used loosely to refer to Eurocurrency markets in general; these include the Eurodollar market and markets in other currencies, such as the Deutsche mark, Swiss franc or sterling, which are similarly defined in terms of the borrowing and lending of the currency in question by banks situated outside the country whose currency is being used.

The Eurobond market is the market through which medium and long-term bonds in eurocurrencies are issued and traded.

For currencies, see pages 226–229

Economics

External trade

Systems of trade

The main systems for recording trade are called general trade and special trade:
General trade. Imports are goods entering for domestic consumption and goods entered into customs storage.
Exports are:
a. 'domestic' or national goods, wholly or partly produced in the country,
b. foreign goods, neither transformed nor declared for domestic consumption in the country, which move out of the country from customs storage;
c. 'domesticised' goods, that is, foreign goods declared for domestic consumption and having paid duty, which move outward without having been transformed.

Where 're-exports' are distinguished, these are the total of foreign and domesticised goods.

Special trade. Imports are goods entering for domestic consumption both direct from other countries, and from customs storage. This is equal to general trade imports, less the items which move outwards from customs storage without entering for domestic consumption (equal to the amount under exports (b) above, but not necessarily the same amount for any one period, due to the time interval between entering and leaving customs.) Exports are categories (a) and (c) above, that is domestic and domesticised goods.

Semi-special trade is also sometimes distinguished, being general trade less all re-exports.

Direct transit trade, consisting of goods entering or leaving for transport purposes only, is generally excluded from both import and export statistics.

The special trade system is in use in most European countries, the main exceptions being the United Kingdom, Ireland, and the Nordic countries.

Value of trade

External trade may be valued at different stages in its transportation from the seller to the buyer. The terms in common use are listed below. UK imports are recorded cif, exports fob. US imports and exports are both recorded fob.

Cost, insurance and freight (cif)
The seller has agreed for the named price to bear all risks of the goods and all expenses up to and including their delivery upon an overseas vessel (or other means of international transport), and also to provide at his own risk and expense for transportation of the goods to the named destination and for insurance covering such transportation.

Free alongside ship (fas)
The seller has agreed for the named price to bear all risks of the goods and all expenses up to and including their delivery upon an overseas vessel (or other vessel).

Free on board (fob)
The seller has agreed for the named price to bear all risks of the goods and all expenses up to and including delivery of the goods upon an overseas vessel.

Cost and freight (c & f)
The seller has agreed for the named price to bear all risk of the goods and all expenses up to and including their delivery upon an overseas vessel and also to provide at his own risk and expense for transportation of the goods to the named destination.

Imports fob and cif
Most countries' exports are recorded fob and imports cif, except the countries listed below whose imports are recorded fob or have been so recorded in past years. The percentage to be added to imports fob to convert them to imports cif is shown in the following table, which estimates are those used by the International Monetary Fund:

Percentage addition to fob to obtain cif

	1950	1960	1965	1970	1975
Australia[a]	15	12	11	11	12
Bolivia	15	17	18	18	13
Canada[a]	4	5	4	3	3
Dominican Republic[a]	14	15	12	14	17
Ecuador	20	14	15	15	17
Guatemala	10	10	9	9	9
Honduras	15	10	10	11	10
New Zealand	13	12	8	7	9
Nicaragua	10	10	9	11	11
Panama	18	10	10	9	9
Paraguay[a]	14	18	17	19	15
Philippines[a]	11	10	11	11	9
South Africa[a]	10	5	4	8	10
United States[a]	7	9	8	6	8
Venezuela[a]	12	12	12	10	13

[a]Countries whose imports were recorded fob at 1975.

The FAO adds an average 12% to convert from fob to cif.

Balance of payments basis
Values of imports (cif) are converted to an fob basis for use in calculating the current balance of payments. The visible trade balance is then the difference between exports and imports of goods both valued on an fob basis, insurance and freight for both exports and imports being included as services.

Volume and unit value index numbers

Volume of imports and exports
Volume index numbers are designed to show movements in imports and exports after eliminating variations due to price changes. For the United Kingdom they are prepared by estimating what the value of the goods imported (or exported) in the current period would have been if their prices had been those of a base period. This estimate is then divided by the value of goods actually imported or exported in the base year, to provide an index (with base year = 100) of the changes in the value of imports and exports at constant prices. The volume index is a Laspeyres type, with base year prices as weights.

Unit values of imports and exports
Index numbers of unit values are intended as guides to changes in the prices of imports and exports and are sometimes referred to as import or export price indices. The unit values are obtained by dividing the value of trade recorded in the month for each selected heading by the corresponding quantity (numbers, tonnes, etc.). As far as possible only those headings are used which cover a sufficiently homogeneous group of commodities, such that their unit values move in much the same way as true prices.

In the UK the indices are constructed by combining the unit values with the quantities recorded in the base year as weights (Laspeyres type), but unit value indices can also be constructed using current weights (Paasche type).

Balance of payments basis
The import and export volume and unit value index numbers are calculated from trade statistics; index numbers comparable with the value of trade on a balance of payments basis are also constructed for the United Kingdom. Weights for commodity groups are altered to allow for the effects of balance of payments adjustments in the base year.

Terms of trade
An index of the terms of trade is derived by dividing the total export unit value index by the total import unit value index, both being on a balance of payments basis. This index rises when the terms of trade become more favourable; that is, when export prices rise more quickly than import prices. Conversely it falls when the terms of trade move against a country because import prices rise faster than export prices.

Economics

Classification of commodities

The Standard International Trade Classification, revision 2 (SITC, rev 2) has in general replaced the former SITC revision; for the United Kingdom the new classification was introduced from January 1, 1978. A list of the main items follows:

Standard International Trade Classification (SITC, rev 2)

Outline of sections, divisions and main groups.

There are 9 sections, given single digits 1 to 9; divisions within these sections have 2-digit numbers and groups within each division have 3-digit numbers. In the list below all sections and divisions are shown, together with selected groups. There are also 4-digit subgroups in the full SITC list, with, for example, 072.3 for 'cocoa butter and cocoa paste' as a subgroup of 072 ('cocoa'), and further breakdowns for some items into a 5-digit level, with, for example, 072.32 for 'cocoa butter (fat or oil)'.

0	**Food and live animals**
00	Live animals
01	Meat and meat preparations
02	Dairy products and birds' eggs
022	Milk and cream
023	Butter
024	Cheese and curd
03	Fish, crustaceans and molluscs, and preparations thereof
04	Cereals and cereal preparations
041	Wheat (including spelt) and meslin, unmilled
042	Rice
043	Barley, unmilled
044	Maize (corn) unmilled
05	Vegetables and fruit
06	Sugar, sugar preparations and honey
07	Coffee, tea, cocoa, spices and manufactures thereof
071	Coffee and coffee substitutes
072	Cocoa
074	Tea and maté
08	Feeding stuff for animals (not including unmilled cereals)
09	Miscellaneous edible products and preparations

1	**Beverages and tobacco**
11	Beverages
112	Alcoholic beverages
12	Tobacco and tobacco manufactures

2	**Crude materials, inedible, except fuels**
21	Hides, skins and furskins, raw
22	Oil seeds and oleaginous fruit
23	Crude rubber (including synthetic and reclaimed)
24	Cork and wood
25	Pulp and waste paper
26	Textile fibres (other than wool tops), and their wastes (not manufactured into yarn or fabric)
263	Cotton
266	Synthetic fibres suitable for spinning
267	Other man-made fibres suitable for spinning and waste of man-made fibres
268	Wool and other animal hair (excluding wool tops)
27	Crude fertilisers and crude minerals (excluding coal, petroleum and precious stones)
28	Metalliferous ores and metal scrap
281	Iron ore and concentrates
29	Crude animal and vegetable materials, nes

3	**Mineral fuels, lubricants and related materials**
32	Coal, coke, and briquettes
33	Petroleum, petroleum products and related materials
333	Petroleum oils, crude, and crude oils obtained from bituminous materials
334	Petroleum products, refined
34	Gas, natural and manufactured
35	Electric current

4	**Animal and vegetable oils, fats and waxes**
41	Animal oils and fats
42	Fixed vegetable oils and fats

43	Animal and vegetable oils and fats, processed, and waxes of animal or vegetable origin
5	**Chemical and related products, nes**
51	Organic chemicals
52	Inorganic chemicals
53	Dyeing, tanning and colouring materials
54	Medicinal and pharmaceutical products
55	Essential oils and perfume materials; toilet, polishing and cleansing preparations
56	Fertilisers, manufactured
57	Explosives and pyrotechnic products
58	Artificial resins and plastic materials, and cellulose esters and ethers
59	Chemical materials and products, nes

6	**Manufactured goods, classified chiefly by material**
61	Leather, leather manufactures, nes and dressed furskins
62	Rubber manufactures, nes
63	Cork and wood manufactures (excluding furniture)
64	Paper, paperboard and articles of paper pulp, of paper or of paperboard
65	Textile yarn, fabrics, made-up articles, nes, and related products
66	Non-metallic mineral manufactures, nes
67	Iron and steel
68	Non-ferrous metals
681	Silver, platinum and other metals of the platinum group
682	Copper
683	Nickel
684	Aluminium
687	Tin
69	Manufactures of metal, nes

7	**Machinery and transport equipment**
71	Power generating machinery and equipment
713	Internal combustion piston engines, and parts thereof, nes
72	Machinery specialised for particular industries
721	Agricultural machinery (excluding tractors) and parts thereof, nes
724	Textile and leather machinery, and parts thereof, nes
73	Metalworking machinery
74	General industrial machinery and equipment, nes, and machine parts, nes
75	Office machines and automatic data processing equipment
76	Telecommunications and sound recording and reproducing apparatus and equipment
761	Television receivers (including receivers incorporating radio-broadcast receivers or sound recorders or reproducers)
77	Electrical machinery, apparatus and appliances, nes, and electrical parts thereof (including non-electrical counterparts, nes of electrical household type equipment)
78	Road vehicles (including air-cushion vehicles)
781	Passenger motor cars (other than public-service type vehicles), including vehicles designed for the transport of both passengers and goods
782	Motor vehicles for the transport of goods or materials and special purpose motor vehicles
79	Other transport equipment
791	Railway vehicles (including hovertrains) and associated equipment
792	Aircraft and associated equipment, and parts thereof, nes
793	Ships, boats (including hovercraft) and floating structures

8	**Miscellaneous manufactured articles**
81	Sanitary, plumbing, heating and lighting fixtures and fittings, nes
82	Furniture and parts thereof
83	Travel goods, handbags and similar containers
84	Articles of apparel and clothing accessories
85	Footwear
87	Professional, scientific and controlling instruments and apparatus, nes
88	Photographic apparatus, equipment and supplies and optical goods, nes watches and clocks
881	Photographic apparatus and equipment, nes
885	Watches and clocks
89	Miscellaneous manufactured articles, nes

9	**Commodities and transactions not classified elsewhere in the SITC**
911.0	Postal packages not classified according to kind
931.0	Special transactions and commodities not classified according to kind
941.0	Animals, live, nes (including zoo animals, dogs, cats, insects, etc)
951.0	Armoured fighting vehicles, arms of war and ammunition therefor, and parts of arms, nes
961.0	Coin (other than gold coin), not being legal tender
971.0	Gold, non-monetary (excluding gold ores and concentrates)

Finance

Money market

Bank of England's minimum lending rate

This is the minimum rate at which members of the discount market have a right to discount British government Treasury bills or other approved bills at the Bank of England. In practice bills are usually discounted at market rates, but the Bank, acting as a lender of last resort, lends at the official discount rate to the discount market against security of such bills or of short-term British government stocks with five years or less to final maturity. Before October 13, 1972 known as Bank Rate. The minimum lending rate was, from that date until May 25, 1978, normally $\frac{1}{2}$ per cent higher than the average rate of discount for Treasury bills established at the weekly tender, rounded to the nearest $\frac{1}{4}$ per cent above. From May 25, 1978 it has been fixed by administrative decision.

Treasury and commercial bills

Bills bear no interest, but are payable at a fixed sum after a certain period, usually 30, 60, 91, 120 or 181 days.

Bills are traded on a discount per year basis, where a year is counted as 365 days in general, but as 360 days for bills expressed in US dollars and other foreign currencies. Where:

F is the final or principal amount of the bill
D is the discount amount
r is the per cent rate of discount
d is the number of days

$$D = F \times \frac{r}{100} \times \frac{d}{365} \text{ (or 360)}$$

The true yield, y, is higher than the discount rate, and is given by:

$y = r \times \dfrac{F}{P}$, where P is the net proceeds $= F - D$.

Also, $P \times 100/F$ is the price per 100 of the bill.
For example, where £100 000 is discounted at 15% for 91 days,

$$D = 100\,000 \times \frac{15}{100} \times \frac{91}{365} = 3\,739.73$$

$P = 100\,000 - 3\,739.73 = 96\,260.27$
price $= 96.260$

$$y = 15 \times \frac{100\,000}{96\,260.27} = 15.5828$$

Certificates of deposit

Certificates of deposit have a fixed interest rate, and are payable after a fixed period.

Short term

Certificates of deposit for up to 1 year are short term certificates. Where:
F is the final amount or principal
P is the proceeds from sale within the period during which the certificate runs
r is the rate at which the certificate was issued
r_x is the rate at which the certificate is quoted for sale
d is the number of days at which the certificate was issued
d_x is the number of days to run until maturity

$$P = F \times \frac{1 + \left(\dfrac{r}{100} \times \dfrac{d}{365^a} \right)}{1 + \left(\dfrac{r_x}{100} \times \dfrac{d_x}{365^a} \right)}$$

Or 360 for US dollar certificates

Medium term

Certificates of deposit for periods of 1 to 5 years are medium term certificates. Proceeds are determined by successive discounting of the final amount at maturity year by year, with addition of annual interest payments.

Letters of credit

The following terms are sometimes used:
'beginning of month' = 1st to 10th inclusive
'middle of month' = 11th to 20th inclusive
'end of month' = 21st to last day

Consumer credit

Rates of interest quoted and charged for consumer credit in the United Kingdom must be accompanied by the annual equivalent percentage rate (APR). Where:
x is the rate of interest quoted for a period less than a year
y is the number of such periods in a year

$$APR = 100 \times \left[\left(1 + \frac{x}{100} \right)^y - 1 \right]$$

For example, a rate of $2\frac{1}{4}$% per month, with $x = 2\frac{1}{4}$, $y = 12$, gives
$APR = 100 \times (1.0225^{12} - 1) = 100 \times (1.306 - 1) = 30.6$.

A table of main rates is included on page 204 for conversion from rates quoted monthly to annual percentage rates.

When a sum is borrowed and repayable in a lump sum after a specified period, the annual percentage rate equivalent is determined as follows. Where:
P is the amount borrowed and repayable
C is the additional amount repayable for credit
n is the period from borrowing to repayment expressed in years

$$APR = 100 \times \left[\left(1 + \frac{C}{P} \right)^{1/n} - 1 \right]$$

For example, an amount of £100, to be repaid after 6 months ($n = 0.5$) by £200 ($C = 100$) gives an APR $= 100 \times (2^2 - 1) = 100 \times (4 - 1) = 300$.

A table of annual percentage rates for fixed sum repayments for monthly periods up to 1 year is included on page 205.

Mortgages

Mortgage repayments are usually repayments of a total fixed sum by regular fixed sum instalments which include both repayment of capital and interest. For general estimation of the amount required to pay off a mortgage at different rates of interest, see the section on interest rates (page 187) and the tables on pages 218–221. Examples of the way in which the fixed instalment is divided between payment of capital and interest are included on the following pages for various rates of interest. Interest payment is high in the early years and capital repayment low with interest amounts gradually falling and capital repayments rising. These tables assume that interest is paid at the end of the year on the balance at the beginning; the monthly rate makes no allowance for any interest within the year, but assumes that the monthly payments are only applied at the end of the year as an annual payment.

Such mortgage repayments result in a variable amount of capital being repaid each year. An alternative method provides for repayment of a fixed capital sum each year, the amount of interest varying according to the balance outstanding. Examples of the payments when fixed capital repayments are made are included on page 186 following.

For fixed capital repayments, it can be seen that interest payments are lower in total, the total instalment paid being higher in the earlier years.

Finance

Mortgage repayments with capital instalment variable (fixed total sum repayable annually)
based on a loan of £10000

	Rate of interest											
	7½%				10%				12½%			
	Payments			Capital balance owing (end-year)	Payments			Capital balance owing (end-year)	Payments			Capital balance owing (end-year)
	Total	Capital	Interest		Total	Capital	Interest		Total	Capital	Interest	
20-year mortgage Years to pay												
20	980.92	230.92	750.00	9769.08	1174.60	174.60	1000.00	9825.40	1380.96	130.96	1250.00	9869.0
19	980.92	248.24	732.68	9520.84	1174.60	192.06	982.54	9633.35	1380.96	147.33	1233.63	9721.7
18	980.92	266.86	714.06	9253.98	1174.60	211.26	963.33	9422.09	1380.96	165.74	1215.21	9555.9
17	980.92	286.87	694.05	8967.10	1174.60	232.39	942.21	9189.70	1380.96	186.46	1194.50	9369.5
16	980.92	308.39	672.53	8658.72	1174.60	255.63	918.97	8934.07	1380.96	209.77	1171.19	9159.7
15	980.92	331.52	649.40	8327.20	1174.60	281.19	893.41	8652.88	1380.96	235.99	1144.97	8923.7
14	980.92	356.38	624.54	7970.81	1174.60	309.31	865.29	8343.58	1380.96	265.49	1115.47	8658.2
13	980.92	383.11	597.81	7587.70	1174.60	340.24	834.36	8003.34	1380.96	298.67	1082.28	8359.5
12	980.92	411.84	569.08	7175.86	1174.60	374.26	800.33	7629.07	1380.96	336.01	1044.95	8023.5
11	980.92	442.73	538.19	6733.13	1174.60	411.69	762.91	7217.39	1380.96	378.01	1002.95	7645.5
10	980.92	475.94	504.98	6257.19	1174.60	452.86	721.74	6764.53	1380.96	425.26	955.70	7220.3
9	980.92	511.63	469.29	5745.56	1174.60	498.14	676.45	6266.38	1380.96	478.42	902.54	6741.9
8	980.92	550.01	430.92	5195.55	1174.60	547.96	626.64	5718.43	1380.96	538.22	842.74	6203.6
7	980.92	591.26	389.67	4604.30	1174.60	602.75	571.84	5115.67	1380.96	605.50	775.46	5598.1
6	980.92	635.60	345.32	3968.70	1174.60	663.03	511.57	4452.64	1380.96	681.19	699.77	4916.9
5	980.92	683.27	297.65	3285.43	1174.60	729.33	445.26	3723.31	1380.96	766.33	614.62	4150.6
4	980.92	734.51	246.41	2550.91	1174.60	802.27	372.33	2921.05	1380.96	862.12	518.83	3288.5
3	980.92	789.60	191.32	1761.31	1174.60	882.49	292.10	2038.56	1380.96	969.89	411.07	2318.6
2	980.92	848.82	132.10	912.49	1174.60	970.74	203.86	1067.81	1380.96	1091.13	289.83	1227.5
1	980.92	912.49	68.44	0.00	1174.60	1067.81	106.78	0.00	1380.96	1227.52	153.44	0.0
Total paid	19618.44	10000.00	9618.44		23491.92	10000.00	13491.92		27619.15	10000.00	17619.15	
Monthly rate	81.74	41.67	40.08		97.88	41.67	56.22		115.08	41.67	73.41	
25-year mortgage Years to pay												
25	897.11	147.11	750.00	9852.89	1101.68	101.68	1000.00	9898.32	1319.43	69.43	1250.00	9930.5
24	897.11	158.14	738.97	9694.75	1101.68	111.85	989.83	9786.47	1319.43	78.11	1241.32	9852.4
23	897.11	170.00	727.11	9524.75	1101.68	123.03	978.65	9663.44	1319.43	87.88	1231.56	9764.5
22	897.11	182.75	714.36	9342.00	1101.68	135.34	966.34	9528.10	1319.43	98.86	1220.57	9665.7
21	897.11	196.46	700.65	9145.55	1101.68	148.87	952.81	9379.23	1319.43	111.22	1208.21	9554.4
20	897.11	211.19	685.92	8934.36	1101.68	163.76	937.92	9215.47	1319.43	125.12	1194.31	9429.3
19	897.11	227.03	670.08	8707.33	1101.68	180.13	921.55	9035.34	1319.43	140.76	1178.67	9288.6
18	897.11	244.06	653.05	8463.27	1101.68	198.15	903.53	8837.19	1319.43	158.36	1161.08	9130.2
17	897.11	262.36	634.75	8200.91	1101.68	217.96	883.72	8619.23	1319.43	178.15	1141.28	8952.0
16	897.11	282.04	615.07	7918.87	1101.68	239.76	861.92	8379.47	1319.43	200.42	1119.01	8751.6
15	897.11	303.19	593.92	7615.68	1101.68	263.73	837.95	8115.74	1319.43	225.48	1093.96	8526.1
14	897.11	325.93	571.18	7289.75	1101.68	290.11	811.57	7825.63	1319.43	253.66	1065.77	8272.5
13	897.11	350.38	546.73	6939.37	1101.68	319.12	782.56	7506.51	1319.43	285.37	1034.07	7987.1
12	897.11	376.65	520.45	6562.72	1101.68	351.03	750.65	7155.48	1319.43	321.04	998.40	7666.1
11	897.11	404.90	492.20	6157.81	1101.68	386.13	715.55	6769.35	1319.43	361.17	958.27	7304.9
10	897.11	435.27	461.84	5722.54	1101.68	424.75	676.94	6344.61	1319.43	406.31	913.12	6898.6
9	897.11	467.92	429.19	5254.63	1101.68	467.22	634.46	5877.39	1319.43	457.10	862.33	6441.5
8	897.11	503.01	394.10	4751.62	1101.68	513.94	587.74	5363.44	1319.43	514.24	805.19	5927.3
7	897.11	540.74	356.37	4210.88	1101.68	565.34	536.34	4798.11	1319.43	578.52	740.91	5348.7
6	897.11	581.29	315.82	3629.59	1101.68	621.87	479.81	4176.24	1319.43	650.84	668.60	4697.9
5	897.11	624.89	272.22	3004.70	1101.68	684.06	417.62	3492.18	1319.43	732.19	587.24	3965.7
4	897.11	671.75	225.35	2332.95	1101.68	752.46	349.22	2739.72	1319.43	823.72	495.72	3142.0
3	897.11	722.14	174.97	1610.81	1101.68	827.71	273.97	1912.01	1319.43	926.68	392.75	2215.3
2	897.11	776.30	120.81	834.52	1101.68	910.48	191.20	1001.53	1319.43	1042.52	276.92	1172.8
1	897.11	834.52	62.59	0.00	1101.68	1001.53	100.15	0.00	1319.43	1172.83	146.60	0.0
Total paid	22427.67	10000.00	12427.67		27542.02	10000.00	17542.02		32985.86	10000.00	22985.86	
Monthly rate	74.76	33.33	41.43		91.81	33.33	58.47		109.95	33.33	76.62	

Finance

Mortgage repayments with capital instalment variable (fixed total sum repayable annually)
based on a loan of £10000

	Rate of interest 15% Payments			Capital balance owing (end-year)	17½% Payments			Capital balance owing (end-year)	20% Payments			Capital balance owing (end-year)
	Total	Capital	Interest		Total	Capital	Interest		Total	Capital	Interest	
20-year mortgage Years to pay												
20	1597.61	97.61	1500.00	9902.39	1822.43	72.43	1750.00	9927.57	2053.57	53.57	2000.00	9946.43
19	1597.61	112.26	1485.36	9790.13	1822.43	85.10	1737.33	9842.47	2053.57	64.28	1989.29	9882.16
18	1597.61	129.10	1468.52	9661.03	1822.43	99.99	1722.43	9742.48	2053.57	77.13	1976.43	9805.02
17	1597.61	148.46	1449.15	9512.57	1822.43	117.49	1704.93	9624.99	2053.57	92.56	1961.00	9712.46
16	1597.61	170.73	1426.89	9341.84	1822.43	138.05	1684.37	9486.94	2053.57	111.07	1942.49	9601.39
15	1597.61	196.34	1401.28	9145.51	1822.43	162.21	1660.21	9324.73	2053.57	133.29	1920.28	9468.10
14	1597.61	225.79	1371.83	8919.72	1822.43	190.60	1631.83	9134.13	2053.57	159.95	1893.62	9308.16
13	1597.61	259.66	1337.96	8660.06	1822.43	223.95	1598.47	8910.17	2053.57	191.93	1861.63	9116.22
12	1597.61	298.61	1299.01	8361.46	1822.43	263.15	1559.28	8647.03	2053.57	230.32	1823.24	8885.90
11	1597.61	343.40	1254.22	8018.06	1822.43	309.20	1513.23	8337.83	2053.57	276.39	1777.18	8609.52
10	1597.61	394.91	1202.71	7623.15	1822.43	363.30	1459.12	7974.53	2053.57	331.66	1721.90	8277.85
9	1597.61	454.14	1143.47	7169.01	1822.43	426.88	1395.54	7547.65	2053.57	397.99	1655.57	7879.86
8	1597.61	522.26	1075.35	6646.75	1822.43	501.59	1320.84	7046.06	2053.57	477.59	1575.97	7402.26
7	1597.61	600.60	997.01	6046.15	1822.43	589.37	1233.06	6456.69	2053.57	573.11	1480.45	6829.15
6	1597.61	690.69	906.92	5355.45	1822.43	692.50	1129.92	5764.19	2053.57	687.73	1365.83	6141.42
5	1597.61	794.30	803.32	4561.16	1822.43	813.69	1008.73	4950.49	2053.57	825.28	1228.28	5316.14
4	1597.61	913.44	684.17	3647.71	1822.43	956.09	866.34	3994.41	2053.57	990.34	1063.23	4325.80
3	1597.61	1050.46	547.16	2597.26	1822.43	1123.40	699.02	2871.00	2053.57	1188.41	865.16	3137.39
2	1597.61	1208.03	389.59	1389.23	1822.43	1320.00	502.43	1551.00	2053.57	1426.09	627.48	1711.30
1	1597.61	1389.23	208.38	0.00	1822.43	1551.00	271.43	0.00	2053.57	1711.30	342.26	0.00
Total paid	31952.29	10000.00	21952.29		36448.51	10000.00	26448.51		41071.31	10000.00	31071.31	
Monthly rate	133.13	41.67	91.47		151.87	41.67	110.20		171.13	41.67	129.46	
25-year mortgage Years to pay												
25	1546.99	46.99	1500.00	9953.01	1781.61	31.61	1750.00	9968.39	2021.19	21.19	2000.00	9978.81
24	1546.99	54.04	1492.95	9898.96	1781.61	37.15	1744.47	9931.24	2021.19	25.42	1995.76	9953.39
23	1546.99	62.15	1484.84	9836.81	1781.61	43.65	1737.97	9887.60	2021.19	30.51	1990.68	9922.88
22	1546.99	71.47	1475.52	9765.34	1781.61	51.28	1730.33	9836.31	2021.19	36.61	1984.58	9886.27
21	1546.99	82.19	1464.80	9683.15	1781.61	60.26	1721.35	9776.05	2021.19	43.93	1977.25	9842.33
20	1546.99	94.52	1452.47	9588.63	1781.61	70.80	1710.81	9705.25	2021.19	52.72	1968.47	9789.61
19	1546.99	108.70	1438.29	9479.93	1781.61	83.19	1698.42	9622.06	2021.19	63.26	1957.92	9726.35
18	1546.99	125.01	1421.99	9354.92	1781.61	97.75	1683.86	9524.30	2021.19	75.92	1945.27	9650.43
17	1546.99	143.76	1403.24	9211.17	1781.61	114.86	1666.75	9409.44	2021.19	91.10	1930.09	9559.33
16	1546.99	165.32	1381.67	9045.85	1781.61	134.96	1646.65	9274.48	2021.19	109.32	1911.87	9450.01
15	1546.99	190.12	1356.88	8855.73	1781.61	158.58	1623.03	9115.90	2021.19	131.19	1890.00	9318.82
14	1546.99	218.63	1328.36	8637.09	1781.61	186.33	1595.28	8929.57	2021.19	157.42	1863.76	9161.40
13	1546.99	251.43	1295.56	8385.67	1781.61	218.94	1562.68	8710.63	2021.19	188.91	1832.28	8972.49
12	1546.99	289.14	1257.85	8096.52	1781.61	257.25	1524.36	8453.38	2021.19	226.69	1794.50	8745.80
11	1546.99	332.52	1214.48	7764.01	1781.61	302.27	1479.34	8151.11	2021.19	272.20	1749.16	8473.77
10	1546.99	382.39	1164.60	7381.61	1781.61	355.17	1426.44	7795.94	2021.19	326.43	1694.75	8147.34
9	1546.99	439.75	1107.24	6941.86	1781.61	417.32	1364.29	7378.62	2021.19	391.72	1629.47	7755.62
8	1546.99	505.72	1041.28	6436.14	1781.61	490.35	1291.26	6888.26	2021.19	470.06	1551.12	7285.56
7	1546.99	581.57	965.42	5854.57	1781.61	576.17	1205.45	6312.10	2021.19	564.08	1457.11	6721.48
6	1546.99	668.81	878.19	5185.76	1781.61	677.00	1104.62	5635.10	2021.19	676.89	1344.30	6044.59
5	1546.99	769.13	777.86	4416.63	1781.61	795.47	986.14	4839.63	2021.19	812.27	1208.92	5232.32
4	1546.99	884.50	662.50	3532.14	1781.61	934.68	846.94	3904.95	2021.19	974.72	1046.46	4257.59
3	1546.99	1017.17	529.82	2514.96	1781.61	1098.25	683.37	2806.71	2021.19	1169.67	851.52	3087.93
2	1546.99	1169.75	377.24	1345.21	1781.61	1290.44	491.17	1516.27	2021.19	1403.60	617.59	1684.32
1	1546.99	1345.21	201.78	0.00	1781.61	1516.27	265.35	0.00	2021.19	1684.32	336.86	0.00
Total paid	38674.85	10000.00	28674.85		44540.33	10000.00	34540.33		50529.68	10000.00	40529.68	
Monthly rate	128.92	33.33	95.58		148.47	33.33	115.13		168.43	33.33	135.10	

Finance

Mortgage repayments with capital instalment fixed (variable total sum repayable annually)
based on a loan of £10000

	Rate of interest											
	10%				15%				20%			
	Payment			Capital balance owing (end-year)	Payments			Capital balance owing (end-year)	Payments			Capital balance owing (end-year)
	Total	Capital	Interest		Total	Capital	Interest		Total	Capital	Interest	
20-year mortgage												
Years to pay												
20	1500.00	500.00	1000.00	9500.00	2000.00	500.00	1500.00	9500.00	2500.00	500.00	2000.00	9500.00
19	1450.00	500.00	950.00	9000.00	1925.00	500.00	1425.00	9000.00	2400.00	500.00	1900.00	9000.00
18	1400.00	500.00	900.00	8500.00	1850.00	500.00	1350.00	8500.00	2300.00	500.00	1800.00	8500.00
17	1350.00	500.00	850.00	8000.00	1775.00	500.00	1275.00	8000.00	2200.00	500.00	1700.00	8000.00
16	1300.00	500.00	800.00	7500.00	1700.00	500.00	1200.00	7500.00	2100.00	500.00	1600.00	7500.00
15	1250.00	500.00	750.00	7000.00	1625.00	500.00	1125.00	7000.00	2000.00	500.00	1500.00	7000.00
14	1200.00	500.00	700.00	6500.00	1550.00	500.00	1050.00	6500.00	1900.00	500.00	1400.00	6500.00
13	1150.00	500.00	650.00	6000.00	1475.00	500.00	975.00	6000.00	1800.00	500.00	1300.00	6000.00
12	1100.00	500.00	600.00	5500.00	1400.00	500.00	900.00	5500.00	1700.00	500.00	1200.00	5500.00
11	1050.00	500.00	550.00	5000.00	1325.00	500.00	825.00	5000.00	1 600.00	500.00	1100.00	5000.00
10	1000.00	500.00	500.00	4500.00	1250.00	500.00	750.00	4500.00	1500.00	500.00	1000.00	4500.00
9	950.00	500.00	450.00	4000.00	1175.00	500.00	675.00	4000.00	1400.00	500.00	900.00	4000.00
8	900.00	500.00	400.00	3500.00	1100.00	500.00	600.00	3500.00	1300.00	500.00	800.00	3500.00
7	850.00	500.00	350.00	3000.00	1025.00	500.00	525.00	3000.00	1200.00	500.00	700.00	3000.00
6	800.00	500.00	300.00	2500.00	950.00	500.00	450.00	2500.00	1100.00	500.00	600.00	2500.00
5	750.00	500.00	250.00	2000.00	875.00	500.00	375.00	2000.00	1000.00	500.00	500.00	2000.00
4	700.00	500.00	200.00	1500.00	800.00	500.00	300.00	1500.00	900.00	500.00	400.00	1500.00
3	650.00	500.00	150.00	1000.00	725.00	500.00	225.00	1000.00	800.00	500.00	300.00	1000.00
2	600.00	500.00	100.00	500.00	650.00	500.00	150.00	500.00	700.00	500.00	200.00	500.00
1	550.00	500.00	50.00	0.00	575.00	500.00	75.00	0.00	600.00	500.00	100.00	0.00
Total paid	20500.00	10000.00	10500.00		25750.00	10000.00	15750.00		31000.00	10000.00	21000.00	
Monthly rate	85.42	41.67	43.75		107.29	41.67	65.62		129.17	41.67	87.50	
25-year mortgage												
Years to pay												
25	1400.00	400.00	1000.00	9600.00	1900.00	400.00	1500.00	9600.00	2400.00	400.00	2000.00	9600.00
24	1360.00	400.00	960.00	9200.00	1840.00	400.00	1440.00	9200.00	2320.00	400.00	1920.00	9200.00
23	1320.00	400.00	920.00	8800.00	1780.00	400.00	1380.00	8800.00	2240.00	400.00	1840.00	8800.00
22	1280.00	400.00	880.00	8400.00	1720.00	400.00	1320.00	8400.00	2160.00	400.00	1760.00	8400.00
21	1240.00	400.00	840.00	8000.00	1660.00	400.00	1260.00	8000.00	2080.00	400.00	1680.00	8000.00
20	1200.00	400.00	800.00	7600.00	1600.00	400.00	1200.00	7600.00	2000.00	400.00	1600.00	7600.00
19	1160.00	400.00	760.00	7200.00	1540.00	400.00	1140.00	7200.00	1920.00	400.00	1520.00	7200.00
18	1120.00	400.00	720.00	6800.00	1480.00	400.00	1080.00	6800.00	1840.00	400.00	1440.00	6800.00
17	1080.00	400.00	680.00	6400.00	1420.00	400.00	1020.00	6400.00	1760.00	400.00	1360.00	6400.00
16	1040.00	400.00	640.00	6000.00	1360.00	400.00	960.00	6000.00	1680.00	400.00	1280.00	6000.00
15	1000.00	400.00	600.00	5600.00	1300.00	400.00	900.00	5600.00	1600.00	400.00	1200.00	5600.00
14	960.00	400.00	560.00	5200.00	1240.00	400.00	840.00	5200.00	1520.00	400.00	1120.00	5200.00
13	920.00	400.00	520.00	4800.00	1180.00	400.00	780.00	4800.00	1440.00	400.00	1040.00	4800.00
12	880.00	400.00	480.00	4400.00	1120.00	400.00	720.00	4400.00	1360.00	400.00	960.00	4400.00
11	840.00	400.00	440.00	4000.00	1060.00	400.00	660.00	4000.00	1280.00	400.00	880.00	4000.00
10	800.00	400.00	400.00	3600.00	1000.00	400.00	600.00	3600.00	1200.00	400.00	800.00	3600.00
9	760.00	400.00	360.00	3200.00	940.00	400.00	540.00	3200.00	1120.00	400.00	720.00	3200.00
8	720.00	400.00	320.00	2800.00	880.00	400.00	480.00	2800.00	1040.00	400.00	640.00	2800.00
7	680.00	400.00	280.00	2400.00	820.00	400.00	420.00	2400.00	960.00	400.00	560.00	2400.00
6	640.00	400.00	240.00	2000.00	760.00	400.00	360.00	2000.00	880.00	400.00	480.00	2000.00
5	600.00	400.00	200.00	1600.00	700.00	400.00	300.00	1600.00	800.00	400.00	400.00	1600.00
4	560.00	400.00	160.00	1200.00	640.00	400.00	240.00	1200.00	720.00	400.00	320.00	1200.00
3	520.00	400.00	120.00	800.00	580.00	400.00	180.00	800.00	640.00	400.00	240.00	800.00
2	480.00	400.00	80.00	400.00	520.00	400.00	120.00	400.00	560.00	400.00	160.00	400.00
1	440.00	400.00	40.00	0.00	460.00	400.00	60.00	0.00	480.00	400.00	80.00	0.00
Total paid	23000.00	10000.00	13000.00		29500.00	10000.00	19500.00		36000.00	10000.00	26000.00	
Monthly rate	76.67	33.33	43.33		98.33	33.33	65.00		120.00	33.33	86.67	

Insurance

For risk, also see probability (pages 193–194); for shipping terms, also see transport (pages 170 and 173)

Adjustment: a settlement of a loss incurred by an insured person.

Average: in marine insurance, the apportionment of loss incurred in transactions between the person suffering the loss and other persons concerned or interested; in other insurance, if the sum insured does not represent the full value of the property at risk, the insurers' liability is limited to the proportion of loss which the sum insured bears to the full value. 'Special condition of average' allows 25% under-insurance before average applies.

Average, general: liability for contributions to cover loss of property (ship and cargo) and any expenditure incurred.

Average, particular: partial loss due to accident, Act of God, or stress of weather; not general average and not shared generally.

Average adjuster: a person who officially calculates the contribution due from each beneficiary as a consequence of a General Average act.

Expectation of life

The following table gives the average number of years persons, at any age level specified, can expect to live in the United Kingdom (1975–77 tables):

Age (years)	Males	Females	Age (years)	Males	Females
0 (birth)	69.6	75.2	45	27.8	33.2
5	66.0	72.0	50	23.4	28.7
10	61.1	67.1	55	19.4	24.4
15	56.2	62.2	60	15.7	20.3
20	51.4	57.3	65	12.4	16.4
25	46.7	52.4	70	9.6	12.9
30	41.9	47.5	75	7.4	9.8
35	37.1	42.7	80	5.6	7.2
40	32.4	37.9	85	4.4	5.4

Simple and compound interest

Simple interest

Definition. If interest is computed on the original principal during the whole life of a transaction, the interest due at the end of the time is called 'simple interest.'
Where:
P is the principal
n is the number of years the sum P is invested
r is the per cent rate of interest
I is the total interest after n years
F is the final amount

$$I = \frac{Prn}{100}$$

$$F = P + I$$

$$F = P \left[1 + \frac{rn}{100} \right]$$

$$P = \frac{100I}{rn}$$

Compound interest

Definition. If at stated intervals during the term of an investment, the interest due is added to the principal and therefore earns interest, the sum by which the original principal has increased by the end of the term of the investment is called 'compound interest'. Where:
P is the principal
n is the number of years the sum P is invested
r is the per cent rate of interest (paid once a year)
I is the total interest after n years
F is the final amount

$$F = P \left[1 + \frac{r}{100} \right]^{n}$$

For estimation of r from F and n (with $P = 1$) see the tables on pages 206–213. For estimation of F from r and n (with $P = 1$) see the tables on pages 214–217.

$$I = F - P = P \left[\left(1 + \frac{r}{100} \right)^{n} - 1 \right]$$

$$P = F \left[1 + \frac{r}{100} \right]^{-n}$$

For estimation of the principal or present value P from r and n (with $F = 1$), the reciprocal of the figure from the tables on pages 214–217 can be used.

$$n = \frac{\log F - \log P}{\log \left[1 + \frac{r}{100} \right]}$$

To find the amount x to pay off 1 unit in equal instalments of principal and interest (paid once a year)

$$x = \frac{\frac{r}{100}}{1 - \left[1 + \frac{r}{100} \right]^{-n}}$$

For estimation of x from r and n see the tables on pages 218–221. The effect on the number of years payment of changing the interest rate r can be seen from these tables; for example, where the interest rate is 9.5%, repayment (say, of a mortgage) of 1 unit over 11 years is 0.15044 per year. Raising the interest rate to 12% means that the repayment period is extended to 14 years for approximately the same amount (in the table 0.15087); an interest rate of 14% raises the period to 20 years (0.15099 in the table) and a rate of 15% raises the period to 36 years for 0.15099, and to 42 years for 0.15042.

To find the final amount (F) after n years, if 1 unit is invested at r per cent compound interest and 1 unit is added every year

$$F = \frac{\left[1 + \frac{r}{100} \right]^{n} - 1}{\frac{r}{100}}$$

To find present value (P) to yield 1 unit per year over n years

$$P = \frac{1 - \left[1 + \frac{r}{100} \right]^{-n}}{\frac{r}{100}}$$

To find the number (n_2) of years it takes a sum to double itself

$$n_2 = \frac{\log 2}{\log \left[1 + \frac{r}{100} \right]}$$

Very approximately $n_2 = 70/r$.

To find the number (n_3) of years it takes a sum to treble itself replace the 2 in the above formula with 3, and so on for quadrupling, etc.

The table on the following page gives number of years to double, etc., for various rates of interest.

Insurance

Rate of compound interest %	Number of years it takes a sum to:				
	double	treble	quadruple	quintuple	sextuple
0.25	277.6	440.0	555.2	644.6	717.6
0.50	139.0	220.3	278.0	322.7	359.2
0.75	92.8	147.0	185.5	215.4	239.8
1.00	69.7	110.4	139.3	161.7	180.1
1.50	46.6	73.8	93.1	108.1	120.3
2.00	35.0	55.5	70·0	81.3	90.5
2.50	28.1	44.5	56.1	65.2	72.6
3.00	23.4	37.2	46.9	54.4	60.6
3.50	20.1	31.9	40.3	46.8	52.1
4.00	17.7	28.0	35.3	41.0	45.7
4.50	15.7	25.0	31.5	36.6	40.7
5.00	14.2	22.5	28.4	33.0	36.7
5.50	12.9	20.5	25.9	30.1	33.5
6.00	11.9	18.9	23.8	27.6	30.7
6.50	11.0	17.4	22.0	25.6	28.5
7.00	10.2	16.2	20.5	23.8	26.5
7.50	9.6	15.2	19.2	22.3	24.8
8.00	9.0	14.3	18.0	20.9	23.3
8.50	8.5	13.5	17.0	19.7	22.0
9.00	8.0	12.7	16.1	18.7	20.8
9.50	7.6	12.1	15.3	17.7	19.7
10.00	7.3	11.5	14.5	16.9	18.8
11.00	6.6	10.5	13.3	15.4	17.2
12.00	6.1	9.7	12.2	14.2	15.8
13.00	5.7	9.0	11.3	13.2	14.7
14.00	5.3	8.4	10.6	12.3	13.7
15.00	5.0	7.9	9.9	11.5	12.8
16.00	4.7	7.4	9.3	10.8	12.1
17.00	4.4	7.0	8.8	10.3	11.4
18.00	4.2	6.6	8.4	9.7	10.8
19.00	4.0	6.3	8.0	9.3	10.3
20.00	3.8	6.0	7.6	8.8	9.8
21.00	3.6	5.8	7.3	8.4	9.4
22.00	3.5	5.5	7.0	8.1	9.0
23.00	3.3	5.3	6.7	7.8	8.7
24.00	3.2	5.1	6.4	7.5	8.3
25.00	3.1	4.9	6.2	7.2	8.0
26.00	3.0	4.8	6.0	7.0	7.8
27.00	2.9	4.6	5.8	6.7	7.5
28.00	2.8	4.5	5.6	6.5	7.3
29.00	2.7	4.3	5.4	6.3	7.0
30.00	2.6	4.2	5.3	6.1	6.8

Investment

Fixed interest securities

The gross flat yield on a security is the annual amount receivable as interest expressed as a percentage of the purchase price. The net flat yield is the gross flat yield less income tax at the standard rate (for the United Kingdom). These yields are used mainly for irredeemable or undated stocks, where the absence of a fixed redemption date does not permit the calculation of any certain capital gain or loss; they are comparable with rates of interest obtainable on deposits, mortgages and other investments that offer no capital gain or loss.

For a description of formulae concerning accumulation from interest rates, etc., see page 187, and for tables see pages 206–221. Also see the section on finance.

The gross redemption yield comprises the gross flat yield together with an apportionment of the calculated capital gain or loss on dated securities held to redemption; more precisely it is the rate of interest which if used to discount future dividends and the sum due at redemption will make their present value equal to the present price of the stock. This is the same rate of interest as the 'DCF solution rate' (see pages 176–177).

Ordinary shares

Nominal share capital = the value of the capital with which the company is registered. The nominal value of a share is the par rate at which it is valued for registration. For other than UK shares, shares may be 'npv' = no par value.

Issued share capital = the value of the capital actually issued.

The asset value of an ordinary share is the total net assets of a company (see page 176), divided by the number of ordinary shares in issue.

Where there is more than one class of share in issue, the net assets belonging to shareholders must be allocated according to the class of preference of capital.

Preference capital is the main type of share capital other than ordinary shares, and usually has preference as to capital on winding up. Hence the value of preference capital, where it occurs, is deducted from net assets to determine the value belonging to ordinary shareholders:

$$\text{Asset value per ordinary share} = \frac{\text{Net assets} - \text{Preference shares (value)}}{\text{Number of ordinary shares}}$$

Gearing is the amount of leverage exerted by the existence of fixed interest capital; where there is a fixed interest payment any increase in profits accrues to the shareholders and any fall in profits reduces the amount attributable to them by the total amount of the fall.

Earnings are profits for shareholders, after payment of interest, etc., and in the case of ordinary shareholders, after payment of any preference dividends. Following the introduction of a changed system of corporation tax in the United Kingdom from April 1973, there are two main methods of assessing earnings for shareholders. This follows because tax paid overseas, while it can be set off against corporation tax on companies, cannot be set off against the tax paid on dividends; the latter can, however, be set off against UK corporation tax paid. Tax paid on dividends is at the standard income tax rate, and a part of this is paid in advance of payment of corporation tax and is called advance corporation tax (ACT). For example:

	No overseas tax paid	All tax paid is overseas
Profits before tax	100	100
less tax (at 52%)	52	52
Profit after tax	48[a]	48[a]
less unrelieved ACT	0	10
Profit after tax and ACT	48[b]	38[b]
Dividend paid gross:	30	30
less tax (at 33%)	10	10
	20	20
Retentions	28	18

Profits after corporation tax (marked [a]) are referred to as earnings on a 'nil' distribution basis, that is, where no dividends are paid and allowed for. Profits after corporation tax and any unrelieved ACT (marked [b]) are referred to as earnings on a 'net' distribution basis, that is, after allowing for the deduction of the ACT which cannot be set off because there are insufficient taxes paid in the United Kingdom against which to offset.

Earnings per share is the total of earnings (on either a nil or net distribution basis) divided by the number of ordinary shares to which those earnings are attributable. Earnings is also sometimes expressed as a percentage of the nominal value of the share.

$$\text{Hence: earnings per share} = \frac{\text{earnings for ordinary shareholders}}{\text{number of ordinary shares}}$$

$$\text{\% earnings rate} = \frac{\text{earnings per share}}{\text{nominal value per share}} \times 100$$

Dividends, like earnings, are usually expressed either as a value per share or as a % rate per nominal value of the share.

Investment

Dividend cover = earnings per share/dividend per share, where earnings per share is usually taken as the value for a full distribution of dividends – 'full' distribution basis. This is usually the same as the 'net' distribution basis, the main exception being the case where payment of additional dividends may involve the company in the payment of further taxation either in the United Kingdom or overseas; cover is then the theoretical maximum dividend which could be paid, after allowing for such additional taxation, divided by the actual dividend.

Price/earnings ratio (P/E ratio) is the number of years earnings in the share price of an ordinary share:

$$\text{P/E ratio} = \frac{\text{price per share}}{\text{earnings per share}}$$

$$\text{Earnings yield \%} = \frac{\text{earnings per share}}{\text{price per share}} \times 100$$

$$= \text{\% earnings rate} \times \frac{\text{nominal value per share}}{\text{market price per share}}$$

$$\text{Dividend yield} = \frac{\text{gross dividend per share}}{\text{price per share}} \times 100$$

$$= \text{\% rate of gross dividend} \times \frac{\text{nominal value per share}}{\text{market price per share}}$$

Scrip issue = 'bonus' issue = shares issued to shareholders for which no payment is required. The price is adjusted in proportion: where the scrip issue is *a* for *b*, the new price = old price × *b*/(*a* + *b*). For example, with a 1 for 3 scrip issue, and a price of 100p before the issue is made ex scrip, the new price = 100p × 3/4 = 75p.

Rights issue = shares issued to shareholders for which payment is made. The price adjustment makes allowance for the amount of the payment made to the company by the shareholders. Where the issue is *a* for *b* at *x* pence per share,

$$\text{the new price} = \frac{(\text{old price} \times b) + (\text{payment} \times a)}{a + b}$$

For example, with an issue of 1 share at 20p for each 3, and price of 100p, the new price = (300 + 20)p/4 = 80p.

Adjustment of previous dividend and earnings rates to the new basis can be made by using the ratio as calculated for the price, taking the estimate of new price/old price as the multiplier to apply to previous earnings and dividends. For example, in the 1 for 3 scrip, the multiplier is 75/100 = 0.75, and a previous dividend of 10p per share would be equivalent after the scrip issue to 10p × 0.75 = 7.5p per share.

Rates of growth. Where dividend and earnings rates have been fully adjusted for all share issues, growth rates can be obtained by using the tables on pages 206–213. For example, where a dividend has gone up from 1.00p to 1.33p per share over 6 years the table on page 206 indicates the growth rate for the dividend as 4.87% p.a. (column for 6 years, 1.33 at the side of the line).

Mathematics

Length, area and volume

In this section *h* = height (vertical), *r* = radius, *d* = diameter

2-dimensional

Circle

Length of circumference = $2\pi r = \pi d$
Area = $\pi r^2 = \pi d^2/4$
Radius = $r = \sqrt{\text{Area}/\pi}$

π = circumference/diameter = 3.141 592 653 589 793... = approx. $3\frac{1}{7}$
$1/\pi$ = diameter/circumference = 0.318 309 886 183 791...

Tables of π and $1/\pi$ are included on page 118, giving conversions between diameter and circumference in connection with the girth of timber. Tables for obtaining areas from radii and radii from areas are included on pages 196–203.

A complete revolution of a line in a clockwise direction back to its original position gives a plane angle of 360°; hence the complete angle at the centre of a circle is 360 degrees, where:
60 seconds (″) = 1 minute (′)
60 minutes = 1 degree
90 degrees = 1 quadrant = 1 right angle
4 quadrants = 360 degrees = 1 circle

In France grade (^{g} or gr) = 1/100 right angle, and 100 grades = 1 right angle.
1 grade = $(\pi/200)$ rad.
Centigrade, in this connection, means 1/10 000 right angle.
The same system is also used in Germany, where the grade is called the 'gon' or 'new grade'. 1 gon = $(\pi/200)$ rad; 100 gon = 1 Rechter.
Also, 'new minute' (^{c}) = 1/100 gon = 10^{-2} gon
  'new second' (^{cc}) = 1/10 000 gon = 10^{-4} gon
The grade or gon = $(\pi/200)$ rad is recognised for use in the United Kingdom from September 1, 1980.
In Belgium, 1 gon = 1/400 circumference.

The radian (rad) is defined as an SI unit (page 14):
1 rad = angle at centre of circle × (radius/circumference)
   = $360°/2\pi$
   = $180°/\pi$
   = 57.295 779 513 082° approx. = 57° 17′ 44.8″ approx.

1° = $\pi/180$ rad
  = 0.017 453 292 520 rad approx.

Radians to degrees				Degrees to radians			
rad	°			°	rad	°	rad
1	= 57.295 8	=	57° 17′ 45″	1	0.017 453 3	10	0.174 532 9
2	= 114.591 6	=	114° 35′ 30″	2	0.034 906 6	20	0.349 065 9
3	= 171.887 3	=	171° 53′ 14″	3	0.052 359 9	30	0.523 598 8
4	= 229.183 1	=	229° 10′ 59″	4	0.069 813 2	40	0.698 131 7
5	= 286.478 9	=	286° 28′ 44″	5	0.087 266 5	50	0.872 664 6
6	= 343.775 7	=	343° 46′ 28″	6	0.104 719 8	60	1.047 197 6
7	= 401.070 5	=	401° 4′ 14″	7	0.122 173 0	70	1.221 730 5
8	= 458.366 2	=	458° 21′ 58″	8	0.139 626 3	80	1.396 263 4
9	= 515.662 0	=	515° 39′ 43″	9	0.157 079 6	90	1.570 796 3

Ellipse

Area = πab where *a* and *b* are the lengths of semi-major and semi-minor axes respectively (2*a* and 2*b* are the lengths of the full axes).

Triangle

Area = $\frac{1}{2}$ base × *h*

Pythagoras' theorem: in a right-angled triangle the square of the hypotenuse (longest side) equals the sum of the squares of the other two sides.

Two triangles are 'similar' if the angles of one are equal to the angles of the other.

Relationship between sides and angles (basic trigonometry):
where *A* is an angle of a right-angled triangle,
tangent of *A* (tan *A*) = opposite side/adjacent side
sine of *A* (sin *A*) = opposite side/hypotenuse
cosine of *A* (cos *A*) = adjacent side/hypotenuse
cotangent of *A* (cot *A*) = 1/tan *A*
cosecant of *A* (cosec *A*) = 1/sin *A*
secant of *A* (sec *A*) = 1/cos *A*

Cosec *A* is sometimes written csc *A*.

Mathematics

Where $\sin A = y$, A is the angle whose sine is y, and this is written as $\sin^{-1} y$. Other functions can be expressed in the same way, and these are referred to as 'inverse' forms.

Where a, b and c denote the lengths of the sides opposite the angles A, B and C respectively (and when dealing with a triangle $A + B + C = 180°$), then:

cosine rule is $\quad \cos A = \dfrac{b^2 + c^2 - a^2}{2bc} \quad$ and similarly for $\cos B$ and $\cos C$

sine rule is $\quad \dfrac{a}{\sin A} = \dfrac{b}{\sin B} = \dfrac{c}{\sin C}$

area $= \frac{1}{2}bc \sin A = \frac{1}{2} ac \sin B = \frac{1}{2}ab \sin C$
$\quad = \sqrt{s(s-a)(s-b)(s-c)}$
where $s = \frac{1}{2}(a + b + c) =$ semi-perimeter of the triangle

Trapezium

Area $= h \times \dfrac{\text{sum of the parallel sides}}{2}$

Regular polygons

Where n is the number of sides of a regular polygon, and a the length of a side, then

Area $= \frac{1}{4}na^2 \cot \dfrac{180°}{n} = \frac{1}{4}n \cot \dfrac{180°}{n} \times$ the square of the length of one of the

sides (a^2). The multiplier, $\frac{1}{4}n \cot 180°/n$, to apply to a^2, is as follows for various polygons:

name of polygon	no. of sides	multiplier	name of polygon	no. of sides	multiplier
Square	4	1.0	Nonagon	9	6.182
Pentagon	5	1.720	Decagon	10	7.694
Hexagon	6	2.598	Undecagon	11	9.366
Heptagon	7	3.634	Duodecagon	12	11.196
Octagon	8	4.828			

Also area $= \frac{1}{2}$ perimeter of sides $\times$ radius of the inscribed circle. The inscribed circle is the circle within the sides, and

radius $= \dfrac{a}{2} \cot \dfrac{180°}{n}$

The circumscribed circle is the circle passing through the points of the polygon, and

radius of circumscribed circle $= \dfrac{a}{2} \csc \dfrac{180°}{n}$

3-dimensional

Sphere

Surface area $= 4\pi r^2 = \pi d^2$

The steradian (sr) is defined as an SI unit (page 14). A complete sphere subtends a solid angle of 4π sr (approx. 12.566 371 sr) at its centre.

1 spat (sp) $= 4\pi =$ unit of solid angle.

Volume $= \frac{4}{3}\pi r^3 = \frac{1}{6}\pi d^3$

Cube

Where a is the length of a side and b is the length of a diagonal
Surface area $= 6a^2 \quad$ Volume $= a^3 \quad b = a\sqrt{3}$

Cylinder

Surface area: of curved surface $=$ perimeter of base $\times$ height $= 2\pi rh$;
$\qquad\qquad$ plus one end $= \pi r(r + 2h)$;
$\qquad\qquad$ plus both ends $= 2\pi r(r + h)$.
Volume $=$ area of base $\times$ height $= \pi r^2 h$

Tables for volumes of timber as shown on page 119 can be used for volumes of cylinders.

Barrel or cask: where the edges are straight, the formula for a cylinder applies. For curved edges, taking d as the internal diameter at the ends and D as the internal diameter at the widest part, the following apply:

measured in inches, volume $= \dfrac{\pi}{12}(2D^2 + d^2)h$ cubic inches
$\qquad\qquad\qquad = 0.261\ 8\ (2D^2 + d^2)h$ cubic inches
$\qquad\qquad\qquad = 0.000\ 943\ 7\ (2D^2 + d^2)h$ UK gallons
$\qquad\qquad\qquad = 0.001\ 133\ (2D^2 + d^2)h$ US gallons
$\qquad\qquad\qquad = 0.004\ 290\ (2D^2 + d^2)h$ litres

measured in metres, volume $= 0.261\ 8\ (2D^2 + d^2)h$ cubic metres
$\qquad\qquad\qquad = 261.8\ (2D^2 + d^2)h$ litres

Cone or pyramid

Surface area: of curved surface $= \frac{1}{2}$ perimeter of base $\times$ slant height;
$\qquad\qquad$ plus base $= (\frac{1}{2}$ perimeter of base $\times$ slant height) $+$ area of base.
Volume $= \frac{1}{3}$ area of base $\times$ height

Trigonometric functions

Basic functions related to triangles are defined in the previous section.

Where a general angle greater than $90°$ is concerned, the following relationships apply:

Quadrant between $90°$ and $180°$
$\tan A = -\tan (180° - A)$
$\sin A = \sin (180° - A)$
$\cos A = -\cos (180° - A)$

Quadrant between $270°$ and $360°$
$\tan A = -\tan (360° - A)$
$\sin A = -\sin (360° - A)$
$\cos A = \cos (360° - A)$

Quadrant between $180°$ and $270°$
$\tan A = \tan (A - 180°)$
$\sin A = -\sin (A - 180°)$
$\cos A = -\cos (A - 180°)$

Values for special angles are:

	0°	30°	45°	60°	90°	180°	270°	360°
tan	0	$\sqrt{3}/3$	1	$\sqrt{3}$	∞	0	∞	0
sin	0	1/2	$\sqrt{2}/2$	$\sqrt{3}/2$	1	0	-1	0
cos	1	$\sqrt{3}/2$	$\sqrt{2}/2$	1/2	0	-1	0	1
cot	∞	$\sqrt{3}$	1	$\sqrt{3}/3$	0	∞	0	∞
cosec	∞	2	$\sqrt{2}$	$2\sqrt{3}/3$	1	∞	-1	∞
sec	1	$2\sqrt{3}/3$	$\sqrt{2}$	2	∞	-1	∞	1

Fundamental identities

$\tan A = \sin A/\cos A$
$\cot A = \cos A/\sin A$
$\sin^2 A + \cos^2 A = 1$,
where $\sin^2 A$ means the square of $\sin A$ and $\cos^2 A$ the square of $\cos A$
$1 + \tan^2 A = \sec^2 A$
$1 + \cot^2 A = \csc^2 A$
$\sin^2 A = \frac{1}{2}(1 - \cos 2A)$
$\cos^2 A = \frac{1}{2}(1 + \cos 2A)$
$\tan^2 A = \dfrac{1 - \cos 2A}{1 + \cos 2A}$
$\sin 2A = 2 \sin A \cos A$
$\cos 2A = \cos^2 A - \sin^2 A$
$\tan 2A = \dfrac{2 \tan A}{1 - \tan^2 A}$

Mathematics

$\sin \frac{1}{2}A = \pm \sqrt{\frac{1}{2}(1 - \cos A)}$, positive for $\frac{1}{2}A$ between $0°$ and $180°$

$\cos \frac{1}{2}A = \pm \sqrt{\frac{1}{2}(1 + \cos A)}$, positive for $\frac{1}{2}A$ between $0°$ and $90°$, $270°$ and $360°$

$\tan \frac{1}{2}A = \pm \sqrt{\dfrac{1 - \cos A}{1 + \cos A}}$, positive for $\frac{1}{2}A$ between $0°$ and $90°$, $180°$ and $270°$

More than one angle:

$\sin (A \pm B) = \sin A \cos B \pm \cos A \sin B$
$\cos (A \pm B) = \cos A \cos B \pm \sin A \sin B$

$\tan (A \pm B) = \dfrac{\tan A \pm \tan B}{1 \pm \tan A \tan B}$

$\sin A + \sin B = 2 \sin \frac{1}{2}(A + B) \cos \frac{1}{2}(A - B)$
$\sin A - \sin B = 2 \cos \frac{1}{2}(A + B) \sin \frac{1}{2}(A - B)$
$\cos A + \cos B = 2 \cos \frac{1}{2}(A + B) \cos \frac{1}{2}(A - B)$
$\cos A - \cos B = -2 \sin \frac{1}{2}(A + B) \sin \frac{1}{2}(A - B)$
$\sin A \sin B = \frac{1}{2} \cos (A - B) - \frac{1}{2} \cos (A + B)$
$\cos A \cos B = \frac{1}{2} \cos (A - B) + \frac{1}{2} \cos (A + B)$
$\sin A \cos B = \frac{1}{2} \sin (A + B) + \frac{1}{2} \sin (A - B)$

Indices

$x^m \times x^n = x^{m+n}$
$x^m / x^n = x^{m-n}$
$x^{-m} = 1/x^m$
$x^{1/n} = \sqrt[n]{x}$
$x^° = 1$

Logarithms

The logarithm y of a number x is the power to which a base a must be raised to equal x; this can be written: $y = \log_a x \quad x = a^y$

Where there are two different bases, $\log_b x = \log_a x / \log_a b$

For any system: $\log_a XY = \log_a X + \log_a Y$
$\log_a X/Y = \log_a X - \log_a Y$

The two main systems of logarithms in use are:
Common (or Briggsian) which uses 10 as a base
Natural (or Napierian) which uses 'e' as a base, where $e = 2.718\,281\,828\,459 \ldots$
$\log_{10}$ is usually described symbolically as log
$\log_e$ is usually described symbolically as ln

To convert from one system to the other, multiply by:
from common to natural: $2.302\,585\,092\,994$ ($\log_e 10$)
from natural to common: $0.434\,294\,481\,903$ ($\log_{10} e$)

Powers of 2 are included in a table on page 126, $\log_{10} 2 = 0.301\,029\,995\,664$

Napierian logarithms form the basis of the neper sound scale (see page 166).

Actual logarithms to base e from 1 to 10 are:

1	0.0000	4	1.3863	7	1.9459	10	2.3026
2	0.6931	5	1.6094	8	2.0794		
3	1.0986	6	1.7918	9	2.1972		

Logarithms to base 10 from 1 to 10 are:

1	0.0000	4	0.6021	7	0.8451	10	1.0000
2	0.3010	5	0.6990	8	0.9031		
3	0.4771	6	0.7782	9	0.9542		

Ratios

If $\dfrac{a}{b} = \dfrac{x}{y}$

then $\dfrac{a}{b} = \dfrac{ma + nx}{mb + ny} = \dfrac{ma - nx}{mb - ny}$, where m and n are real quantities

Equations and curves

$(a \pm b)^2 = a^2 \pm 2ab + b^2$
$(a + b + c)^2 = a^2 + b^2 + c^2 + 2ab + 2ac + 2bc$
$a^2 - b^2 = (a - b)(a + b)$

Straight line

$y = mx + c$, where $m = $ slope of the line, and c is the intercept on the y-axis (where the x-axis is horizontal in a graph and the y-axis vertical)

also, $\dfrac{x}{a} + \dfrac{y}{b} = 1$, where a and b are the intercepts on the x and y axes respectively

and $\dfrac{y - y_1}{x - x_1} = \dfrac{y_2 - y_1}{x_2 - x_1}$, where x_1, y_1 and x_2, y_2 are two points defining the line, measured with respect to the x and y axes.

Quadratic

Where $ax^2 + bx + c = 0$, then $x = \dfrac{-b \pm \sqrt{b^2 - 4ac}}{2a}$, being the 'roots' of the equation.

Logarithmic and exponential

$y = \log_a x$ for logarithmic ($x = a^y$); $x = \log_a y$ for exponential ($y = a^x$).

Sine curve

$y = a \sin (bx + c)$, where $a = $ amplitude = the height of the sine wave, $2\pi/b = $ wavelength = distance from the peak of one wave to the next (also = 'pitch' of thread: see page 142).
Also see economics (page 179) for chart of a sine curve.

Motion

For uniformly accelerated motion:
$v = u + at$, where v is the velocity at time t, a is the acceleration, and u is the initial velocity. This is the velocity-time relationship which adds to initial velocity the acceleration increase through time.

Where s is the distance travelled,
$s = ut + \frac{1}{2}at^2$
and $v^2 = u^2 + 2as$
The SI unit for velocity is metres per second; for standard gravitational acceleration, see page 16.

Combinations and permutations

The number of **combinations** is the number of ways in which r objects can be selected from n objects without account of the order in which the r objects are selected.

The number of **permutations** is the number of different ways in which r objects can be selected from n objects when account is taken of the order of selection of the r objects.

For example, there are four combinations of three letters out of A, B, C and D:
ABC   BCD   CDA   DAB

But twenty-four permutations:

ABC	BCD	CDA	DAB
ACB	BDC	CAD	DBA
BAC	CDB	ACD	ABD
BCA	CBD	ADC	ADB
CAB	DBC	DAC	BAD
CBA	DCB	DCA	BDA

Where $n!$ (factorial n) $= 1 \times 2 \times 3 \times \ldots (n-1) \times n$
eg $7! = 1 \times 2 \times 3 \times 4 \times 5 \times 6 \times 7$
$= 5\,040$

Combination $= C_r^n = \dfrac{n!}{r!\,(n-r)!}$

Mathematics

Permutation $= P_r^n = \dfrac{n!}{(n-r)!}$

Notes. $C_r^n = C_{n-r}^n$

0! may be taken as equal to 1.

Factorial n may also be written as $\underline{|n}$

C_r^n may be written as $_nC_r$ and P_r^n as $_nP_r$

When n is large the Stirling approximation is useful:

$n! = $ approximately $\sqrt{2\pi n}\ \ n^n e^{-n}$

Differentiation and integration (calculus)

The slope of a straight line, as noted above, is m in the equation $y = mx + c$. The slope or gradient of a straight line is also the angle made with the horizontal axis. The gradient of a curve is the gradient of the tangent to the curve at any point.

The gradient is generalised as the differentiation of the line or curve: where $y = f(x)$, (that is, y is a function of x),

differentiation $= \dfrac{dy}{dx} = \dfrac{d(f(x))}{dx} = f'(x)$, where $f'(x)$ is a symbol for $\dfrac{dy}{dx}$

For a straight line, $\dfrac{d(mx+c)}{dx} = m = $ the slope of the line.

dx and dy are called differentials, and $\dfrac{dy}{dx}$ also written as dy/dx,

the differential coefficient.

The derivative of dy/dx is called the second differential coefficient of $f(x)$ and denoted by d^2y/dx^2 or $f''(x)$, and so on with the nth differential coefficient d^ny/dx^n or $f^n(x)$.

Where a function is increasing, the slope is positive and the first differential coefficient positive; where it is decreasing the first differential coefficient is negative. For signs of the first and second differentials see page 179.

Integral of a function $f(x)$ from a to b is the area under the curve between $x = a$ and $x = b$; the symbol is $\int_a^b f(x)\ dx$. For a general integration the symbol is $\int f(x)\ dx$. Integration is the reverse process of differentiation; since the differential of any constant is zero, integration of any function includes an unknown constant amount.

Summary of differentials and integrals

y	$\dfrac{dy}{dx}$	$\int y\ dx = $ integral (with C a constant, unknown)
x^n	nx^{n-1}	$\dfrac{x^{n+1}}{n+1} + C$ except for $n = -1$
x^{-1}		$\log_e x + C$
e^x	e^x	$e^x + C$
e^{ax}	ae^{ax}	$\dfrac{e^{ax}}{a} + C$
a^x	$a^x \log_e a$	$\dfrac{a^x}{\log_e a} + C$ except for $a \leqslant 0,\ a = 1$
$\log_e x$	$1/x$	$x(\log_e x - 1) + C$
$\sin ax$	$a \cos ax$	$-\cos \dfrac{ax}{a} + C$
$\cos ax$	$-a \sin ax$	$\sin \dfrac{ax}{a} + C$
$\tan ax$	$a \sec^2 ax$	$-\log \cos \dfrac{ax}{a} + C$

Series

Arithmetic progression = a series of numbers such that the difference between one number and the next is constant.

Where a is the first term
$\quad d$ is the common difference
$\quad l$ is the last term

The series is: $a,\ a + d,\ a + 2d,\ a + 3d,\ \ldots$

Sum of n terms $= \dfrac{n}{2}[2a + (n-1)d]$

$\qquad\qquad\qquad = \dfrac{n}{2}(a + l)$

Last term $l \qquad = a + (n-1)d$

Geometric progression = a series of numbers such that the ratio between one number and the next is constant; the constant ratio is called the common ratio.

Where a is the first term
$\quad r$ is the common ratio

The series is: $a,\ ar,\ ar^2,\ ar^3,\ \ldots$

Sum of n terms:

when r is less than 1 $\qquad = \dfrac{a(1 - r^n)}{1 - r}$

when r is greater than 1 $\quad = \dfrac{a(r^n - 1)}{r - 1}$

Last term $\qquad\qquad\qquad = ar^{n-1}$

The series of preferred numbers (see page 224) is an example of geometric progression; the common ratios are:

$\sqrt[5]{10},\ \sqrt[10]{10},\ \sqrt[20]{10},\ \sqrt[40]{10},\ \sqrt[80]{10}$

which are approximately 1.58 for R 5 (the series with the fifth root of 10 as the common ratio), 1.26 for R 10, 1.12 for R 20, 1.06 for R 40 and 1.03 for R 80. Thus successive terms in the preferred series increase by the constant amount of approximately 58%, 26%, 12%, 6% and 3% respectively.

Harmonic progression = a series of numbers whose reciprocals form an arithmetic progression:

The series is $\dfrac{1}{a},\ \dfrac{1}{a+d},\ \dfrac{1}{a+2d},\ \ldots$

Power series

$e^x = 1 + x + \dfrac{x^2}{2!} + \dfrac{x^3}{3!} + \ldots$

$e = e^1 = 1 + 1 + \dfrac{1}{2!} + \dfrac{1}{3!} + \ldots$

$\log_e(1 + x) = x - \dfrac{x^2}{2} + \dfrac{x^3}{3} - \dfrac{x^4}{4} + \ldots$ for x between -1 and $+1$

$\sin x = x - \dfrac{x^3}{3!} + \dfrac{x^5}{5!} - \dfrac{x^7}{7!} + \ldots$

$\cos x = 1 - \dfrac{x^2}{2!} + \dfrac{x^4}{4!} - \dfrac{x^6}{6!} + \ldots$

Mathematics

Binomial (Bernoulli)

Where n is a positive integer, then

$$(x + a)^n = x^n + C_1^n x^{n-1} a + C_2^n x^{n-2} a^2 + C_3^n x^{n-3} a^3 + \ldots + C_{n-1}^n x a^{n-1} + a^n$$

where, as noted above, $C_1^n = \dfrac{n!}{1!(n-1)!} = n$, $C_2^n = \dfrac{n!}{2!(n-2)!} = \dfrac{n(n-1)}{2!}$, etc.

For the cases where $a = 1$, and $n = 1$ to 10, binomial coefficients are as follows:

coefficients

1	1	1								
2	1	2	1							
3	1	3	3	1						
4	1	4	6	4	1					
5	1	5	10	10	5	1				
6	1	6	15	20	15	6	1			
7	1	7	21	35	35	21	7	1		
8	1	8	28	56	70	56	28	8	1	
9	1	9	36	84	126	126	84	36	9	1
10	1	10	45	120	210	252	210	120	45	10	1

Expansion in differentials

Taylor's expansion: $f(a + x) = f(a) + x f'(a) + \dfrac{x^2}{2!} f''(a) + \dfrac{x^3}{3!} f'''(a) + \ldots$

Maclaurin's expansion is the special case where $a = 0$.

Statistics

Summation notation

Where there is a series of n values, denoted by $x_1, x_2, x_3, \ldots x_n$ the symbol Σ (sigma) is used to denote their sum; in full the notation is:

$\sum\limits_{i=1}^{n} x_i = x_1 + x_2 + x_3 + \ldots x_n$, where $\sum\limits_{i=1}^{n} x_i$ means the sum of all the x_i

for i increasing from 1 to n. Where the meaning is clear it is usually abbreviated to Σx_i or Σx.

Measures of central tendency

Arithmetic mean, also called the *average*, of a series of quantities, is obtained by finding the sum of the quantities (Σx) and dividing it by the number of quantities (n).
Mean = $\Sigma x/n$, also written as $\bar{x}$ (x bar). Where not otherwise qualified, mean usually means the arithmetic mean, and is here referred to in that way.
eg: in the series 1, 3, 5, 18, 19, 20, 25, the mean is 13, ie $91 \div 7$.
A 'weighted' average is used for index numbers (see page 179).

Geometric mean is the nth root of the product of the n items in the group
$\sqrt[n]{x_1 x_2 x_3 \ldots x_n}$
eg in the series 3, 4, 15 the geometric mean is 5.65, ie $\sqrt[3]{180}$.

Harmonic mean is the reciprocal of the arithmetic mean of the reciprocals of the numbers = $n/(\Sigma 1/x)$.
eg: in the series 1, 3, 5 the harmonic mean is 1.96, ie $3/(1 + 1/3 + 1/5) = 3/1.533$.

Median of a series is that point which so divides it that half the quantities are on one side, half on the other.
eg: in the series 1, 3, 6, 18, 19, 20, 25, the median is 18.
If there are an even number of items in the series, the median is the point midway between the two central items.
eg: in the series 1, 3, 6, 18, 19, 20, the median is 12.

Mode is the most frequently recurring item in any distribution.
eg: in a series of letters where there are 2 *A*s, 3 *B*s, 4 *C*s, 8 *D*s, 6 *E*s and 1 *F*, *D* would be the mode.
For unimodal frequency curves which are fairly symmetrical:
mean − mode = 3 (mean − median) approximately.

Marginal and average

A marginal increase is the increment to a sum of quantities; hence for n quantities $x_1, x_2 \ldots x_n$, where $\Sigma x = x_1 + x_2 + \ldots x_n$ an increment of x_{n+1} gives:

marginal increase, expressed as a percentage = $\dfrac{x_{n+1}}{\Sigma x}$

while average = $\dfrac{\Sigma x + x_{n+1}}{n + 1}$

Measures of dispersion

Range of a set of numbers is the smallest number subtracted from the largest.

Mean absolute deviation is the mean of the sum of the deviations of a series of quantities from the arithmetic mean of those quantities, without regard to the sign of the deviation.

eg: in the series 1, 3, 5 the arithmetic mean is 3 and the deviations are −2, 0, 2; the mean absolute deviation is $2 + 0 + 2 = 4$ divided by 3 = 1.3.

Standard deviation is the square root of the mean of the sum of the *squares* of the deviations of a series from the arithmetic mean of those quantities; that is, as for the mean absolute deviation, but using the squares of the deviations, and the square root of the result.
eg: in the series 1, 3, 5 above, the sum of the squares of the deviations from the arithmetic mean is $4 + 0 + 4 = 8$, and the standard deviation is the square root of

2.67 (8/3), which is 1.6. Symbolically, $s = \sqrt{\sum\limits_{i=1}^{n} (x_i - \bar{x})^2/n}$.

The variance is the sum $\sum\limits_{i=1}^{n} (x_i - \bar{x})^2/n$, so standard deviation = $\sqrt{\text{variance}}$.

The symbol σ (sigma) is often used for standard deviation of a total population, s being then used as the symbol for the standard deviation of a sample.

Coefficient of variation (V) is a measure of relative variation; it equals the standard deviation divided by the mean and multiplied by 100.
eg: in the above series, V = $(1.6/3) \times 100 = 53$

Skewness is said to occur in a frequency distribution when it is not symmetrical about the mean (arithmetic); skewness is positive (to the right) if the mean exceeds the median and negative (to the left) if the median exceeds the mean. There are several measures of skewness:
Pearson's first coefficient = (mean − mode)/standard deviation;
Pearson's second coefficient = 3 (mean − median)/standard deviation.
Coefficient of skewness is the mean of the sum of the *cubes* of the deviations of a series from the mean, divided by the cube of the standard deviation;

symbolically, equals $\sum\limits_{i=1}^{n} (x_i - \bar{x})^3/ns^3$.

A skewed curve is sometimes referred to as a J-shaped curve.

Kurtosis or peakedness is said to occur in a frequency distribution when it is markedly flat (platykurtic) or markedly peaked (leptokurtic), compared to a 'normal' distribution. Coefficient of kurtosis is the mean of the sum of the *fourth powers* of the deviations of a series from the mean, divided by the fourth

power of the standard deviation; symbolically equals $\sum\limits_{i=1}^{n} (x_i - \bar{x})^4/ns^4$.

Probability

Where E is an event which can happen in r ways out of a total of n equally likely ways, then the probability of the event (its success), $p = r/n$. For example, the probability of throwing a 2 or 3 from a dice (which has 6 equally likely ways to fall) is 2 ways/6 ways = 1/3. The probability of the event not occurring (its failure) is $q = 1 - p = 2/3$ in the example.

If p is the probability that an event will occur, then the odds in favour of it happening are $p : q$ (p to q) and the odds against it happening are $q : p$.

Probability distributions

Discrete

If p is the probability that an event will occur in a single trial, and q the probability that it will fail, the probability of r successes in n independent trials is equal to the number of combinations of n items selected r at a time, multiplied by the probability of a success raised to the power of r and by the probability of a failure raised to the power $(n - r)$.

Statistics

That is, the probability that the event will happen r times in n trials is $C_r^n p^r q^{n-r}$ where $r = 0, 1, 2, 3, \ldots . n$. This is the binomial distribution for $(q + p)^n$, which is outlined on the previous page for $x = q$, $a = p$.

In the binomial probability distribution, the mean number of favourable events is np, of unfavourable events nq and the standard deviation $= \sqrt{npq}$ (variance $= npq$).

The Poisson distribution is defined by $p(x) = \dfrac{g^x}{x!} e^{-g}$

where g = mean rate of occurrence of an event = variance; standard deviation $= \sqrt{g}$

If $n > 50$, $np < 5$, the binomial distribution is approximated by a Poisson distribution with $g = np$.

Continuous

The normal distribution (Gaussian distribution) is defined by

$$\frac{1}{s\sqrt{2\pi}} e^{-\frac{1}{2}(x - \bar{x})^2/s^2}$$ where $\bar{x}$ is the mean and s the standard deviation.

For the normal distribution the coefficient of skewness is 0, the coefficient of kurtosis is 3, and the area bounded by the curve and the x axis (the integral) is 1. The probability that x will lie between x_1 and x_2 is the integral from x_1 to x_2 of the above function; that is, the area under the curve between the ordinates x_1 and x_2.

The standard form of the normal distribution has mean $x = 0$ and variance = standard deviation = 1; the formula is

$$\frac{1}{\sqrt{2\pi}} e^{-\frac{1}{2}z^2}$$ where $z = (x - \bar{x})/s$.

For the standard normal curve, 68.27% lies in the area within z equal to plus or minus 1, 95.45% between $z = \pm 2$, and 99.73% between $z = \pm 3$.

For a sampling distribution of a statistic S which is approximately normal, it is to be expected that the mean of the sampling distribution will lie in the intervals $S \pm s$, $S \pm 2s$, and $S \pm 3s$ about 68.27%, 95.45% and 99.73% of the time respectively, where s is the standard deviation (or standard error) of the sampling distribution.

The intervals are called confidence intervals, and the points confidence limits or levels; following is a table of the main confidence levels used:

level %	$s\,(=z)$	level %	$s\,(=z)$	level %	$s\,(=z)$
50	0.6745	95	1.96	98	2.33
68.27	1.00	95.45	2.00	99	2.58
80	1.28	96	2.05	99.73	3.00
90	1.645				

If $np > 5$ and $nq > 5$, the binomial distribution is approximated by a normal distribution with mean np and standard deviation $\sqrt{npq}$ (variance $= npq$).

Curve fitting

Also see equations and curves, page 191.

Modified exponential: $y = ba^x + C$

Gompertz: $y = ba^{dx}$

Modified Gompertz: $y = ba^{dx} + C$

Logistic: $y = 1/(ba^x + C)$

Method of least squares is the method by which, in curve-fitting, the sum of the squares of the deviations of the actual from the curve value is a minimum; the 'best fit' is given by the curve with a least squares minimum.

Interpolation

If a function $f(x)$ is approximately linear, then interpolation for an unknown x_a between 2 known values x_0 and x_1 is given by

$$f(x_a) \approx \frac{1}{x_1 - x_0} [(x_1 - x_a) f(x_0) - (x_0 - x_a) f(x_1)]$$

For example, where $f(x)$ is sin x in radians, interpolation of sin 0.53 (x_a) between sin 0.5 (x_0) with value 0.479 426 and sin 0.6 (x_1) with value 0.564 642, is given by: $\frac{1}{0.10} [(0.07) (0.479\,426) - (-0.03) (0.564\,642)] = 0.504\,991$. Since actual sin 0.53 = 0.505 533, the error $= -0.107\%$.

Correlation

For the two series, $x_1, x_2, \ldots x_n$, and $y_1, y_2, \ldots y_n$, the

$$\text{correlation coefficient} = r = \frac{\sum\limits_{i=1}^{n} (x_i - \bar{x})(y_i - \bar{y})}{ns_x s_y}$$

where $\bar{x}$ and $\bar{y}$ are the means and s_x, s_y the standard deviations of the two series.

The sum $\sum\limits_{i=1}^{n} (x_i - \bar{x})(y_i - \bar{y})$ divided by n is called the covariance and can be written cov (x, y).

The least square 'regression' lines for the two series are:

$$y - \bar{y} = \frac{rs_y}{s_x}(x - \bar{x}) \qquad \text{and} \qquad x - \bar{x} = \frac{rs_x}{s_y}(y - \bar{y})$$

r varies between -1 and $+1$, $r = +1$ meaning completely positive correlation, $r = -1$ completely negative correlation, and $r = 0$ no correlation.

Taxation

Income tax

Under the unified income tax system in the United Kingdom, the amount of tax due is based on various rates applying to each band of income, after deducting the various allowances. The main rate of tax is called the 'standard' or 'basic' rate.

The total of tax due, where the income after allowances is greater than the top limit set for the standard rate, is the sum of the amounts applying to each band of income below that income (the cumulative amount), plus the proportion of the income in the band in which the income falls. For example, for the rates indicated, the tax due for each band of net income and the cumulative amount is

Income (net) £	Tax rate %	Tax due (£): for the band	cumulative
0–11 250	30	3 375	3 375
11 251–13 250	40	800	4 175
13 251–16 750	45	1 575	5 750
16 751–22 250	50	2 750	8 500
22 251–27 750	55	3 025	11 525
over 27 750	60	n	11 525 + n

where $n = (\text{salary} - 27\,750) \times 60/100$.

Hence, for example, total of tax due at £16 750 is £5 750, and at £20 000 it is £5 750 + (3 250 × 50/100) = £5 750 + £1 625 = £7 375.

Value added tax (VAT)

Where a rate of value added tax is expressed as a rate on cost price, the equivalent rate on the total sales price (including the tax) can be obtained from the 'percentage reversals' table on page 222. For example, with a rate of 15% an amount of £100 becomes £115 including tax; the percentage rate to be subtracted from £115 to estimate £100 is 100 × 15/(100 + 15) = 13.0% (as also indicated in the table on page 222). 13.0% of 115 is 15, and is the value added tax included in the amount of 115.

General tables

$$100 \left[\left(1 + \frac{x}{100} \right)^y - 1 \right]$$

Consumer interest rates receive exact definitions for fair trading

'The annual percentage rate of charge is given by the following formula -

$$100 \left[\left(1 + \frac{x}{100} \right)^y - 1 \right]$$

where x is the period rate of charge expressed as a percentage; and y is the number of periods in a year in relation to which the period rate of charge is charged.'

(Consumer Credit (Total Charge for Credit) Regulations 1980, under powers from section 20 of Consumer Credit Act 1974)

Areas of circles from radii

Use of the table: the unit at the side of a line added to
the unit at the head of a column makes up the radius of a circle
for which the area is shown in the position where line and column meet.
For example, 0.1 + 0.01 = 0.11; the area of a circle with radius 0.11 is 0.038

	0.00	0.01	0.02	0.03	0.04	0.05	0.06	0.07	0.08	0.09	
0.0	0.000	0.000	0.001	0.003	0.005	0.008	0.011	0.015	0.020	0.025	0.0
0.1	0.031	0.038	0.045	0.053	0.062	0.071	0.080	0.091	0.102	0.113	0.1
0.2	0.126	0.139	0.152	0.166	0.181	0.196	0.212	0.229	0.246	0.264	0.2
0.3	0.283	0.302	0.322	0.342	0.363	0.385	0.407	0.430	0.454	0.478	0.3
0.4	0.503	0.528	0.554	0.581	0.608	0.636	0.665	0.694	0.724	0.754	0.4
0.5	0.785	0.817	0.849	0.882	0.916	0.950	0.985	1.021	1.057	1.094	0.5
0.6	1.131	1.169	1.208	1.247	1.287	1.327	1.368	1.410	1.453	1.496	0.6
0.7	1.539	1.584	1.629	1.674	1.720	1.767	1.815	1.863	1.911	1.961	0.7
0.8	2.011	2.061	2.112	2.164	2.217	2.270	2.324	2.378	2.433	2.488	0.8
0.9	2.545	2.602	2.659	2.717	2.776	2.835	2.895	2.956	3.017	3.079	0.9
1.0	3.142	3.205	3.269	3.333	3.398	3.464	3.530	3.597	3.664	3.733	1.0
1.1	3.801	3.871	3.941	4.011	4.083	4.155	4.227	4.301	4.374	4.449	1.1
1.2	4.524	4.600	4.676	4.753	4.831	4.909	4.988	5.067	5.147	5.228	1.2
1.3	5.309	5.391	5.474	5.557	5.641	5.726	5.811	5.896	5.983	6.070	1.3
1.4	6.158	6.246	6.335	6.424	6.514	6.605	6.697	6.789	6.881	6.975	1.4
1.5	7.069	7.163	7.258	7.354	7.451	7.548	7.645	7.744	7.843	7.942	1.5
1.6	8.042	8.143	8.245	8.347	8.450	8.553	8.657	8.762	8.867	8.973	1.6
1.7	9.079	9.186	9.294	9.402	9.511	9.621	9.731	9.842	9.954	10.066	1.7
1.8	10.179	10.292	10.406	10.521	10.636	10.752	10.869	10.986	11.104	11.222	1.8
1.9	11.341	11.461	11.581	11.702	11.824	11.946	12.069	12.192	12.316	12.441	1.9
2.0	12.566	12.692	12.819	12.946	13.074	13.203	13.332	13.461	13.592	13.723	2.0
2.1	13.854	13.987	14.120	14.253	14.387	14.522	14.657	14.793	14.930	15.067	2.1
2.2	15.205	15.344	15.483	15.623	15.763	15.904	16.046	16.188	16.331	16.475	2.2
2.3	16.619	16.764	16.909	17.055	17.202	17.349	17.497	17.646	17.795	17.945	2.3
2.4	18.096	18.247	18.398	18.551	18.704	18.857	19.012	19.167	19.322	19.478	2.4
2.5	19.635	19.792	19.950	20.109	20.268	20.428	20.589	20.750	20.912	21.074	2.5
2.6	21.237	21.401	21.565	21.730	21.896	22.062	22.229	22.396	22.564	22.733	2.6
2.7	22.902	23.072	23.243	23.414	23.586	23.758	23.931	24.105	24.279	24.454	2.7
2.8	24.630	24.806	24.983	25.161	25.339	25.518	25.697	25.877	26.058	26.239	2.8
2.9	26.421	26.603	26.786	26.970	27.155	27.340	27.525	27.712	27.899	28.086	2.9
3.0	28.274	28.463	28.653	28.843	29.033	29.225	29.417	29.609	29.802	29.996	3.0
3.1	30.191	30.386	30.582	30.778	30.975	31.172	31.371	31.570	31.769	31.969	3.1
3.2	32.170	32.371	32.573	32.776	32.979	33.183	33.388	33.593	33.799	34.005	3.2
3.3	34.212	34.420	34.628	34.837	35.046	35.257	35.467	35.679	35.891	36.103	3.3
3.4	36.317	36.531	36.745	36.961	37.176	37.393	37.610	37.828	38.046	38.265	3.4
3.5	38.485	38.705	38.926	39.147	39.369	39.592	39.815	40.039	40.264	40.489	3.5
3.6	40.715	40.942	41.169	41.396	41.625	41.854	42.084	42.314	42.545	42.776	3.6
3.7	43.008	43.241	43.475	43.709	43.943	44.179	44.415	44.651	44.888	45.126	3.7
3.8	45.365	45.604	45.843	46.084	46.325	46.566	46.808	47.051	47.295	47.539	3.8
3.9	47.784	48.029	48.275	48.522	48.769	49.017	49.265	49.514	49.764	50.014	3.9
4.0	50.265	50.517	50.769	51.022	51.276	51.530	51.785	52.040	52.296	52.553	4.0
4.1	52.810	53.068	53.327	53.586	53.846	54.106	54.367	54.629	54.891	55.154	4.1
4.2	55.418	55.682	55.947	56.212	56.478	56.745	57.012	57.280	57.549	57.818	4.2
4.3	58.088	58.359	58.630	58.901	59.174	59.447	59.720	59.995	60.270	60.545	4.3
4.4	60.821	61.098	61.375	61.653	61.932	62.211	62.491	62.772	63.053	63.335	4.4
4.5	63.617	63.900	64.184	64.468	64.753	65.039	65.325	65.612	65.899	66.187	4.5
4.6	66.476	66.765	67.055	67.346	67.637	67.929	68.222	68.515	68.808	69.103	4.6
4.7	69.398	69.693	69.990	70.287	70.584	70.882	71.181	71.480	71.780	72.081	4.7
4.8	72.382	72.684	72.987	73.290	73.594	73.898	74.203	74.509	74.815	75.122	4.8
4.9	75.430	75.738	76.047	76.356	76.666	76.977	77.288	77.600	77.913	78.226	4.9

Use of the table: the unit at the side of a line added to
the unit at the head of a column makes up the radius of a circle
for which the area is shown in the position where line and column meet.
For example, 5.1 + 0.01 = 5.11; the area of a circle with radius 5.11 is 82.034

	0.00	0.01	0.02	0.03	0.04	0.05	0.06	0.07	0.08	0.09	
5.0	78.540	78.854	79.169	79.485	79.801	80.118	80.436	80.754	81.073	81.393	5.0
5.1	81.713	82.034	82.355	82.677	83.000	83.323	83.647	83.971	84.296	84.622	5.1
5.2	84.949	85.276	85.603	85.932	86.261	86.590	86.920	87.251	87.583	87.915	5.2
5.3	88.247	88.581	88.915	89.249	89.584	89.920	90.257	90.594	90.932	91.270	5.3
5.4	91.609	91.948	92.289	92.630	92.971	93.313	93.656	93.999	94.343	94.688	5.4
5.5	95.033	95.379	95.726	96.073	96.421	96.769	97.118	97.468	97.818	98.169	5.5
5.6	98.520	98.873	99.225	99.579	99.933	100.287	100.643	100.999	101.355	101.713	5.6
5.7	102.070	102.429	102.788	103.148	103.508	103.869	104.231	104.593	104.956	105.319	5.7
5.8	105.683	106.048	106.413	106.779	107.146	107.513	107.881	108.250	108.619	108.988	5.8
5.9	109.359	109.730	110.102	110.474	110.847	111.220	111.594	111.969	112.345	112.721	5.9
6.0	113.097	113.475	113.853	114.231	114.610	114.990	115.371	115.752	116.133	116.516	6.0
6.1	116.899	117.282	117.666	118.051	118.437	118.823	119.210	119.597	119.985	120.374	6.1
6.2	120.763	121.153	121.543	121.934	122.326	122.718	123.111	123.505	123.899	124.294	6.2
6.3	124.690	125.086	125.483	125.880	126.278	126.677	127.076	127.476	127.877	128.278	6.3
6.4	128.680	129.082	129.485	129.889	130.293	130.698	131.104	131.510	131.917	132.324	6.4
6.5	132.732	133.141	133.550	133.960	134.371	134.782	135.194	135.607	136.020	136.433	6.5
6.6	136.848	137.263	137.678	138.095	138.512	138.929	139.347	139.766	140.185	140.605	6.6
6.7	141.026	141.447	141.869	142.292	142.715	143.139	143.563	143.988	144.414	144.840	6.7
6.8	145.267	145.695	146.123	146.552	146.981	147.411	147.842	148.273	148.705	149.138	6.8
6.9	149.571	150.005	150.440	150.875	151.310	151.747	152.184	152.621	153.060	153.499	6.9
7.0	153.938	154.378	154.819	155.260	155.702	156.145	156.588	157.032	157.477	157.922	7.0
7.1	158.368	158.814	159.261	159.709	160.157	160.606	161.056	161.506	161.957	162.408	7.1
7.2	162.860	163.313	163.766	164.220	164.675	165.130	165.586	166.042	166.499	166.957	7.2
7.3	167.415	167.874	168.334	168.794	169.255	169.717	170.179	170.642	171.105	171.569	7.3
7.4	172.034	172.499	172.965	173.431	173.898	174.366	174.835	175.304	175.773	176.244	7.4
7.5	176.715	177.186	177.658	178.131	178.605	179.079	179.553	180.029	180.505	180.981	7.5
7.6	181.458	181.936	182.415	182.894	183.374	183.854	184.335	184.816	185.299	185.782	7.6
7.7	186.265	186.749	187.234	187.719	188.205	188.692	189.179	189.667	190.156	190.645	7.7
7.8	191.134	191.625	192.116	192.608	193.100	193.593	194.086	194.581	195.075	195.571	7.8
7.9	196.067	196.563	197.061	197.559	198.057	198.557	199.056	199.557	200.058	200.560	7.9
8.0	201.062	201.565	202.068	202.573	203.078	203.583	204.089	204.596	205.103	205.611	8.0
8.1	206.120	206.629	207.139	207.650	208.161	208.672	209.185	209.698	210.212	210.726	8.1
8.2	211.241	211.756	212.272	212.789	213.307	213.825	214.343	214.863	215.383	215.903	8.2
8.3	216.424	216.946	217.469	217.992	218.515	219.040	219.565	220.090	220.616	221.143	8.3
8.4	221.671	222.199	222.728	223.257	223.787	224.318	224.849	225.381	225.913	226.446	8.4
8.5	226.980	227.514	228.049	228.585	229.121	229.658	230.196	230.734	231.273	231.812	8.5
8.6	232.352	232.893	233.434	233.976	234.519	235.062	235.606	236.150	236.695	237.241	8.6
8.7	237.787	238.334	238.882	239.430	239.979	240.528	241.078	241.629	242.180	242.732	8.7
8.8	243.285	243.838	244.392	244.947	245.502	246.057	246.614	247.171	247.728	248.287	8.8
8.9	248.846	249.405	249.965	250.526	251.087	251.649	252.212	252.775	253.339	253.904	8.9
9.0	254.469	255.035	255.601	256.168	256.736	257.304	257.873	258.443	259.013	259.584	9.0
9.1	260.155	260.727	261.300	261.873	262.447	263.022	263.597	264.173	264.750	265.327	9.1
9.2	265.904	266.483	267.062	267.641	268.222	268.803	269.384	269.966	270.549	271.132	9.2
9.3	271.716	272.301	272.886	273.472	274.059	274.646	275.234	275.822	276.411	277.001	9.3
9.4	277.591	278.182	278.774	279.366	279.959	280.552	281.146	281.741	282.336	282.932	9.4
9.5	283.529	284.126	284.724	285.322	285.921	286.521	287.121	287.722	288.324	288.926	9.5
9.6	289.529	290.133	290.737	291.342	291.947	292.553	293.160	293.767	294.375	294.983	9.6
9.7	295.592	296.202	296.813	297.424	298.035	298.648	299.261	299.874	300.488	301.103	9.7
9.8	301.719	302.335	302.951	303.569	304.187	304.805	305.424	306.044	306.665	307.286	9.8
9.9	307.907	308.530	309.153	309.776	310.401	311.026	311.651	312.277	312.904	313.531	9.9

Areas of circles from radii

Use of the table: the unit at the side of a line added to
the unit at the head of a column makes up the radius of a circle
for which the area is shown in the position where line and column meet.
For example, 11 + 0.1 = 11.1; the area of a circle with radius 11.1 is 387.076

	0.0	0.1	0.2	0.3	0.4	0.5	0.6	0.7	0.8	0.9	
10	314.159	320.474	326.851	333.292	339.795	346.361	352.989	359.681	366.435	373.253	10
11	380.133	387.076	394.081	401.150	408.281	415.476	422.733	430.053	437.435	444.881	11
12	452.389	459.961	467.595	475.292	483.051	490.874	498.759	506.707	514.719	522.792	12
13	530.929	539.129	547.391	555.716	564.104	572.555	581.069	589.646	598.285	606.987	13
14	615.752	624.580	633.471	642.424	651.441	660.520	669.662	678.867	688.134	697.465	14
15	706.858	716.315	725.834	735.415	745.060	754.768	764.538	774.371	784.267	794.226	15
16	804.248	814.332	824.480	834.690	844.963	855.299	865.697	876.159	886.683	897.270	16
17	907.920	918.633	929.409	940.247	951.149	962.113	973.140	984.230	995.382	1006.598	17
18	1017.876	1029.217	1040.621	1052.088	1063.618	1075.210	1086.865	1098.584	1110.365	1122.208	18
19	1134.115	1146.084	1158.117	1170.212	1182.370	1194.591	1206.874	1219.221	1231.630	1244.102	19
20	1256.637	1269.235	1281.895	1294.619	1307.405	1320.254	1333.166	1346.141	1359.179	1372.279	20
21	1385.442	1398.668	1411.957	1425.309	1438.724	1452.201	1465.741	1479.345	1493.010	1506.739	21
22	1520.531	1534.385	1548.303	1562.283	1576.326	1590.431	1604.600	1618.831	1633.126	1647.483	22
23	1661.903	1676.385	1690.931	1705.539	1720.210	1734.945	1749.741	1764.601	1779.524	1794.509	23
24	1809.557	1824.668	1839.842	1855.079	1870.379	1885.741	1901.166	1916.654	1932.205	1947.819	24
25	1963.495	1979.235	1995.037	2010.902	2026.830	2042.821	2058.874	2074.991	2091.170	2107.412	25
26	2123.717	2140.084	2156.515	2173.008	2189.564	2206.183	2222.865	2239.610	2256.418	2273.288	26
27	2290.221	2307.217	2324.276	2341.398	2358.582	2375.829	2393.140	2410.513	2427.948	2445.447	27
28	2463.009	2480.633	2498.320	2516.070	2533.883	2551.759	2569.697	2587.698	2605.763	2623.890	28
29	2642.079	2660.332	2678.648	2697.026	2715.467	2733.971	2752.538	2771.167	2789.860	2808.615	29
30	2827.433	2846.314	2865.258	2884.265	2903.334	2922.467	2941.662	2960.920	2980.240	2999.624	30
31	3019.071	3038.580	3058.152	3077.787	3097.485	3117.245	3137.069	3156.955	3176.904	3196.916	31
32	3216.991	3237.128	3257.329	3277.592	3297.918	3318.307	3338.759	3359.274	3379.851	3400.491	32
33	3421.194	3441.960	3462.789	3483.681	3504.635	3525.652	3546.732	3567.875	3589.081	3610.350	33
34	3631.681	3653.075	3674.532	3696.052	3717.635	3739.281	3760.989	3782.760	3804.594	3826.491	34
35	3848.451	3870.474	3892.559	3914.707	3936.918	3959.192	3981.529	4003.928	4026.381	4048.916	35
36	4071.504	4094.155	4116.869	4139.645	4162.485	4185.387	4208.352	4231.380	4254.470	4277.624	36
37	4300.840	4324.120	4347.462	4370.866	4394.334	4417.865	4441.458	4465.114	4488.833	4512.615	37
38	4536.460	4560.367	4584.338	4608.371	4632.467	4656.626	4680.847	4705.132	4729.479	4753.889	38
39	4778.362	4802.898	4827.497	4852.158	4876.883	4901.670	4926.520	4951.433	4976.408	5001.447	39
40	5026.548	5051.712	5076.939	5102.229	5127.582	5152.997	5178.476	5204.017	5229.621	5255.288	40
41	5281.017	5306.810	5332.665	5358.583	5384.564	5410.608	5436.715	5462.884	5489.116	5515.411	41
42	5541.769	5568.190	5594.674	5621.220	5647.830	5674.502	5701.237	5728.034	5754.895	5781.819	42
43	5808.805	5835.854	5862.966	5890.141	5917.378	5944.679	5972.042	5999.468	6026.957	6054.509	43
44	6082.123	6109.801	6137.541	6165.344	6193.210	6221.139	6249.130	6277.185	6305.302	6333.482	44
45	6361.725	6390.031	6418.399	6446.831	6475.325	6503.882	6532.502	6561.185	6589.930	6618.739	45
46	6647.610	6676.544	6705.541	6734.601	6763.723	6792.909	6822.157	6851.468	6880.842	6910.279	46
47	6939.778	6969.341	6998.966	7028.654	7058.405	7088.218	7118.095	7148.034	7178.037	7208.102	47
48	7238.229	7268.420	7298.674	7328.990	7359.369	7389.811	7420.316	7450.884	7481.514	7512.208	48
49	7542.964	7573.783	7604.665	7635.610	7666.617	7697.687	7728.821	7760.017	7791.275	7822.597	49
50	7853.982	7885.429	7916.939	7948.512	7980.148	8011.847	8043.608	8075.433	8107.320	8139.270	50
51	8171.282	8203.358	8235.497	8267.698	8299.962	8332.289	8364.679	8397.132	8429.647	8462.225	51
52	8494.867	8527.571	8560.337	8593.167	8626.059	8659.015	8692.033	8725.114	8758.258	8791.464	52
53	8824.734	8858.066	8891.461	8924.919	8958.440	8992.024	9025.670	9059.379	9093.151	9126.986	53
54	9160.884	9194.845	9228.868	9262.955	9297.104	9331.316	9365.590	9399.928	9434.328	9468.792	54
55	9503.318	9537.907	9572.558	9607.273	9642.051	9676.891	9711.794	9746.760	9781.789	9816.880	55
56	9852.035	9887.252	9922.532	9957.875	9993.281	10028.749	10064.281	10099.875	10135.532	10171.252	56
57	10207.035	10242.880	10278.789	10314.760	10350.794	10386.891	10423.050	10459.273	10495.558	10531.907	57
58	10568.318	10604.792	10641.328	10677.928	10714.590	10751.315	10788.104	10824.954	10861.868	10898.845	58
59	10935.884	10972.986	11010.151	11047.379	11084.670	11122.023	11159.440	11196.919	11234.461	11272.066	59

Use of the table: the unit at the side of a line added to
the unit at the head of a column makes up the radius of a circle
for which the area is shown in the position where line and column meet.
For example, 61 + 0.1 = 61.1; the area of a circle with radius 61.1 is 11728.225

	0.0	0.1	0.2	0.3	0.4	0.5	0.6	0.7	0.8	0.9	
60	11309.734	11347.464	11385.257	11423.114	11461.033	11499.015	11537.059	11575.167	11613.337	11651.570	60
61	11689.866	11728.225	11766.647	11805.131	11843.679	11882.289	11920.962	11959.698	11998.496	12037.358	61
62	12076.282	12115.269	12154.319	12193.432	12232.608	12271.846	12311.148	12350.512	12389.939	12429.429	62
63	12468.981	12508.597	12548.275	12588.016	12627.820	12667.687	12707.617	12747.609	12787.664	12827.783	63
64	12867.964	12908.207	12948.514	12988.883	13029.316	13069.811	13110.369	13150.990	13191.673	13232.420	64
65	13273.229	13314.101	13355.036	13396.034	13437.094	13478.218	13519.404	13560.653	13601.965	13643.340	65
66	13684.778	13726.278	13767.841	13809.467	13851.156	13892.908	13934.723	13976.600	14018.540	14060.543	66
67	14102.609	14144.738	14186.930	14229.184	14271.501	14313.882	14356.324	14398.830	14441.399	14484.030	67
68	14526.724	14569.482	14612.301	14655.184	14698.130	14741.138	14784.209	14827.343	14870.540	14913.800	68
69	14957.123	15000.508	15043.956	15087.467	15131.041	15174.678	15218.377	15262.140	15305.965	15349.853	69
70	15393.804	15437.818	15481.894	15526.034	15570.236	15614.501	15658.829	15703.219	15747.673	15792.189	70
71	15836.769	15881.411	15926.115	15970.883	16015.714	16060.607	16105.563	16150.582	16195.664	16240.809	71
72	16286.016	16331.287	16376.620	16422.016	16467.475	16512.996	16558.581	16604.228	16649.938	16695.711	72
73	16741.547	16787.446	16833.407	16879.432	16925.519	16971.669	17017.882	17064.157	17110.496	17156.897	73
74	17203.361	17249.888	17296.478	17343.131	17389.846	17436.625	17483.466	17530.370	17577.337	17624.366	74
75	17671.459	17718.614	17765.832	17813.113	17860.457	17907.864	17955.333	18002.865	18050.460	18098.118	75
76	18145.839	18193.623	18241.469	18289.379	18337.351	18385.386	18433.483	18481.644	18529.867	18578.154	76
77	18626.503	18674.915	18723.390	18771.927	18820.528	18869.191	18917.917	18966.706	19015.558	19064.472	77
78	19113.450	19162.490	19211.593	19260.759	19309.988	19359.279	19408.634	19458.051	19507.531	19557.074	78
79	19606.680	19656.348	19706.080	19755.874	19805.731	19855.651	19905.634	19955.679	20005.788	20055.959	79
80	20106.193	20156.490	20206.850	20257.272	20307.758	20358.306	20408.917	20459.591	20510.327	20561.127	80
81	20611.989	20662.915	20713.903	20764.954	20816.067	20867.244	20918.483	20969.785	21021.150	21072.578	81
82	21124.069	21175.623	21227.239	21278.918	21330.660	21382.465	21434.333	21486.263	21538.257	21590.313	82
83	21642.432	21694.614	21746.858	21799.166	21851.536	21903.969	21956.465	22009.024	22061.646	22114.330	83
84	22167.078	22219.888	22272.761	22325.697	22378.695	22431.757	22484.881	22538.068	22591.318	22644.631	84
85	22698.007	22751.445	22804.947	22858.511	22912.138	22965.828	23019.580	23073.396	23127.274	23181.215	85
86	23235.219	23289.286	23343.416	23397.608	23451.863	23506.182	23560.563	23615.006	23669.513	23724.082	86
87	23778.715	23833.410	23888.168	23942.989	23997.872	24052.819	24107.828	24162.900	24218.035	24273.233	87
88	24328.494	24383.817	24439.203	24494.652	24550.164	24605.739	24661.377	24717.077	24772.840	24828.666	88
89	24884.555	24940.507	24996.522	25052.599	25108.739	25164.943	25221.208	25277.537	25333.929	25390.383	89
90	25446.900	25503.481	25560.123	25616.829	25673.598	25730.429	25787.323	25844.281	25901.300	25958.383	90
91	26015.529	26072.737	26130.008	26187.342	26244.739	26302.199	26359.722	26417.307	26474.955	26532.666	91
92	26590.440	26648.277	26706.176	26764.139	26822.164	26880.252	26938.403	26996.617	27054.893	27113.233	92
93	27171.635	27230.100	27288.628	27347.218	27405.872	27464.588	27523.368	27582.210	27641.114	27700.082	93
94	27759.113	27818.206	27877.362	27936.581	27995.863	28055.208	28114.615	28174.086	28233.619	28293.215	94
95	28352.874	28412.595	28472.380	28532.227	28592.137	28652.110	28712.146	28772.245	28832.406	28892.631	95
96	28952.918	29013.268	29073.681	29134.156	29194.695	29255.296	29315.960	29376.687	29437.477	29498.330	96
97	29559.245	29620.224	29681.265	29742.369	29803.536	29864.765	29926.058	29987.413	30048.831	30110.312	97
98	30171.856	30233.462	30295.132	30356.864	30418.659	30480.517	30542.438	30604.422	30666.468	30728.577	98
99	30790.750	30852.985	30915.282	30977.643	31040.066	31102.553	31165.102	31227.714	31290.388	31353.126	99
00	31415.927	31478.790	31541.716	31604.705	31667.757	31730.871	31794.049	31857.289	31920.592	31983.958	100

Radii of circles from areas

Use of the table: the unit at the side of a line added to
the unit at the head of a column makes up the area of a circle
for which the radius is shown in the position where line and column meet.
For example, 0.1 + 0.01 = 0.11; the radius of a circle with area 0.11 is 0.187

	0.00	0.01	0.02	0.03	0.04	0.05	0.06	0.07	0.08	0.09	
0.0	0.0000	0.0564	0.0798	0.0977	0.1128	0.1262	0.1382	0.1493	0.1596	0.1693	0
0.1	0.1784	0.1871	0.1954	0.2034	0.2111	0.2185	0.2257	0.2326	0.2394	0.2459	0.
0.2	0.2523	0.2585	0.2646	0.2706	0.2764	0.2821	0.2877	0.2932	0.2985	0.3038	0.
0.3	0.3090	0.3141	0.3192	0.3241	0.3290	0.3338	0.3385	0.3432	0.3478	0.3523	0.
0.4	0.3568	0.3613	0.3656	0.3700	0.3742	0.3785	0.3827	0.3868	0.3909	0.3949	0.
0.5	0.3989	0.4029	0.4068	0.4107	0.4146	0.4184	0.4222	0.4260	0.4297	0.4334	0.
0.6	0.4370	0.4406	0.4442	0.4478	0.4514	0.4549	0.4583	0.4618	0.4652	0.4687	0.
0.7	0.4720	0.4754	0.4787	0.4820	0.4853	0.4886	0.4918	0.4951	0.4983	0.5015	0.
0.8	0.5046	0.5078	0.5109	0.5140	0.5171	0.5202	0.5232	0.5262	0.5293	0.5323	0
0.9	0.5352	0.5382	0.5412	0.5441	0.5470	0.5499	0.5528	0.5557	0.5585	0.5614	0.
1.0	0.5642	0.5670	0.5698	0.5726	0.5754	0.5781	0.5809	0.5836	0.5863	0.5890	1
1.1	0.5917	0.5944	0.5971	0.5997	0.6024	0.6050	0.6077	0.6103	0.6129	0.6155	1.
1.2	0.6180	0.6206	0.6232	0.6257	0.6283	0.6308	0.6333	0.6358	0.6383	0.6408	1.
1.3	0.6433	0.6457	0.6482	0.6507	0.6531	0.6555	0.6580	0.6604	0.6628	0.6652	1.
1.4	0.6676	0.6699	0.6723	0.6747	0.6770	0.6794	0.6817	0.6840	0.6864	0.6887	1.
1.5	0.6910	0.6933	0.6956	0.6979	0.7001	0.7024	0.7047	0.7069	0.7092	0.7114	1.
1.6	0.7136	0.7159	0.7181	0.7203	0.7225	0.7247	0.7269	0.7291	0.7313	0.7334	1.
1.7	0.7356	0.7378	0.7399	0.7421	0.7442	0.7464	0.7485	0.7506	0.7527	0.7548	1.
1.8	0.7569	0.7590	0.7611	0.7632	0.7653	0.7674	0.7695	0.7715	0.7736	0.7756	1.
1.9	0.7777	0.7797	0.7818	0.7838	0.7858	0.7878	0.7899	0.7919	0.7939	0.7959	1.
2.0	0.7979	0.7999	0.8019	0.8038	0.8058	0.8078	0.8098	0.8117	0.8137	0.8156	2.
2.1	0.8176	0.8195	0.8215	0.8234	0.8253	0.8273	0.8292	0.8311	0.8330	0.8349	2.
2.2	0.8368	0.8387	0.8406	0.8425	0.8444	0.8463	0.8482	0.8500	0.8519	0.8538	2.
2.3	0.8556	0.8575	0.8593	0.8612	0.8630	0.8649	0.8667	0.8686	0.8704	0.8722	2.
2.4	0.8740	0.8759	0.8777	0.8795	0.8813	0.8831	0.8849	0.8867	0.8885	0.8903	2.
2.5	0.8921	0.8938	0.8956	0.8974	0.8992	0.9009	0.9027	0.9045	0.9062	0.9080	2.
2.6	0.9097	0.9115	0.9132	0.9150	0.9167	0.9184	0.9202	0.9219	0.9236	0.9253	2.
2.7	0.9271	0.9288	0.9305	0.9322	0.9339	0.9356	0.9373	0.9390	0.9407	0.9424	2.
2.8	0.9441	0.9458	0.9474	0.9491	0.9508	0.9525	0.9541	0.9558	0.9575	0.9591	2.
2.9	0.9608	0.9624	0.9641	0.9657	0.9674	0.9690	0.9707	0.9723	0.9739	0.9756	2.
3.0	0.9772	0.9788	0.9805	0.9821	0.9837	0.9853	0.9869	0.9885	0.9901	0.9918	3.
3.1	0.9934	0.9950	0.9966	0.9982	0.9997	1.0013	1.0029	1.0045	1.0061	1.0077	3.
3.2	1.0093	1.0108	1.0124	1.0140	1.0155	1.0171	1.0187	1.0202	1.0218	1.0233	3.
3.3	1.0249	1.0265	1.0280	1.0295	1.0311	1.0326	1.0342	1.0357	1.0372	1.0388	3.
3.4	1.0403	1.0418	1.0434	1.0449	1.0464	1.0479	1.0495	1.0510	1.0525	1.0540	3.
3.5	1.0555	1.0570	1.0585	1.0600	1.0615	1.0630	1.0645	1.0660	1.0675	1.0690	3.
3.6	1.0705	1.0720	1.0734	1.0749	1.0764	1.0779	1.0794	1.0808	1.0823	1.0838	3.
3.7	1.0852	1.0867	1.0882	1.0896	1.0911	1.0925	1.0940	1.0955	1.0969	1.0984	3.
3.8	1.0998	1.1013	1.1027	1.1041	1.1056	1.1070	1.1085	1.1099	1.1113	1.1128	3
3.9	1.1142	1.1156	1.1170	1.1185	1.1199	1.1213	1.1227	1.1241	1.1256	1.1270	3.
4.0	1.1284	1.1298	1.1312	1.1326	1.1340	1.1354	1.1368	1.1382	1.1396	1.1410	4
4.1	1.1424	1.1438	1.1452	1.1466	1.1480	1.1493	1.1507	1.1521	1.1535	1.1549	4.
4.2	1.1562	1.1576	1.1590	1.1604	1.1617	1.1631	1.1645	1.1658	1.1672	1.1686	4.
4.3	1.1699	1.1713	1.1726	1.1740	1.1754	1.1767	1.1781	1.1794	1.1808	1.1821	4.
4.4	1.1835	1.1848	1.1861	1.1875	1.1888	1.1902	1.1915	1.1928	1.1942	1.1955	4.
4.5	1.1968	1.1982	1.1995	1.2008	1.2021	1.2035	1.2048	1.2061	1.2074	1.2087	4.
4.6	1.2101	1.2114	1.2127	1.2140	1.2153	1.2166	1.2179	1.2192	1.2205	1.2218	4.
4.7	1.2231	1.2244	1.2257	1.2270	1.2283	1.2296	1.2309	1.2322	1.2335	1.2348	4.
4.8	1.2361	1.2374	1.2386	1.2399	1.2412	1.2425	1.2438	1.2451	1.2463	1.2476	4.
4.9	1.2489	1.2502	1.2514	1.2527	1.2540	1.2552	1.2565	1.2578	1.2590	1.2603	4.

Use of the table: the unit at the side of a line added to
the unit at the head of a column makes up the area of a circle
for which the radius is shown in the position where line and column meet.
For example, 5.1 + 0.01 = 5.11; the radius of a circle with area 5.11 is 1.2754

	0.00	0.01	0.02	0.03	0.04	0.05	0.06	0.07	0.08	0.09	
5.0	1.2616	1.2628	1.2641	1.2653	1.2666	1.2679	1.2691	1.2704	1.2716	1.2729	5.0
5.1	1.2741	1.2754	1.2766	1.2779	1.2791	1.2803	1.2816	1.2828	1.2841	1.2853	5.1
5.2	1.2866	1.2878	1.2890	1.2903	1.2915	1.2927	1.2940	1.2952	1.2964	1.2976	5.2
5.3	1.2989	1.3001	1.3013	1.3025	1.3038	1.3050	1.3062	1.3074	1.3086	1.3098	5.3
5.4	1.3111	1.3123	1.3135	1.3147	1.3159	1.3171	1.3183	1.3195	1.3207	1.3219	5.4
5.5	1.3231	1.3243	1.3255	1.3267	1.3279	1.3291	1.3303	1.3315	1.3327	1.3339	5.5
5.6	1.3351	1.3363	1.3375	1.3387	1.3399	1.3411	1.3422	1.3434	1.3446	1.3458	5.6
5.7	1.3470	1.3482	1.3493	1.3505	1.3517	1.3529	1.3541	1.3552	1.3564	1.3576	5.7
5.8	1.3587	1.3599	1.3611	1.3623	1.3634	1.3646	1.3658	1.3669	1.3681	1.3692	5.8
5.9	1.3704	1.3716	1.3727	1.3739	1.3750	1.3762	1.3774	1.3785	1.3797	1.3808	5.9
6.0	1.3820	1.3831	1.3843	1.3854	1.3866	1.3877	1.3889	1.3900	1.3912	1.3923	6.0
6.1	1.3934	1.3946	1.3957	1.3969	1.3980	1.3991	1.4003	1.4014	1.4026	1.4037	6.1
6.2	1.4048	1.4060	1.4071	1.4082	1.4093	1.4105	1.4116	1.4127	1.4139	1.4150	6.2
6.3	1.4161	1.4172	1.4184	1.4195	1.4206	1.4217	1.4228	1.4240	1.4251	1.4262	6.3
6.4	1.4273	1.4284	1.4295	1.4306	1.4318	1.4329	1.4340	1.4351	1.4362	1.4373	6.4
6.5	1.4384	1.4395	1.4406	1.4417	1.4428	1.4439	1.4450	1.4461	1.4472	1.4483	6.5
6.6	1.4494	1.4505	1.4516	1.4527	1.4538	1.4549	1.4560	1.4571	1.4582	1.4593	6.6
6.7	1.4604	1.4615	1.4625	1.4636	1.4647	1.4658	1.4669	1.4680	1.4691	1.4701	6.7
6.8	1.4712	1.4723	1.4734	1.4745	1.4755	1.4766	1.4777	1.4788	1.4799	1.4809	6.8
6.9	1.4820	1.4831	1.4842	1.4852	1.4863	1.4874	1.4884	1.4895	1.4906	1.4916	6.9
7.0	1.4927	1.4938	1.4948	1.4959	1.4970	1.4980	1.4991	1.5002	1.5012	1.5023	7.0
7.1	1.5033	1.5044	1.5054	1.5065	1.5076	1.5086	1.5097	1.5107	1.5118	1.5128	7.1
7.2	1.5139	1.5149	1.5160	1.5170	1.5181	1.5191	1.5202	1.5212	1.5223	1.5233	7.2
7.3	1.5244	1.5254	1.5264	1.5275	1.5285	1.5296	1.5306	1.5316	1.5327	1.5337	7.3
7.4	1.5348	1.5358	1.5368	1.5379	1.5389	1.5399	1.5410	1.5420	1.5430	1.5441	7.4
7.5	1.5451	1.5461	1.5472	1.5482	1.5492	1.5502	1.5513	1.5523	1.5533	1.5543	7.5
7.6	1.5554	1.5564	1.5574	1.5584	1.5595	1.5605	1.5615	1.5625	1.5635	1.5645	7.6
7.7	1.5656	1.5666	1.5676	1.5686	1.5696	1.5706	1.5717	1.5727	1.5737	1.5747	7.7
7.8	1.5757	1.5767	1.5777	1.5787	1.5797	1.5807	1.5817	1.5828	1.5838	1.5848	7.8
7.9	1.5858	1.5868	1.5878	1.5888	1.5898	1.5908	1.5918	1.5928	1.5938	1.5948	7.9
8.0	1.5958	1.5968	1.5978	1.5988	1.5998	1.6007	1.6017	1.6027	1.6037	1.6047	8.0
8.1	1.6057	1.6067	1.6077	1.6087	1.6097	1.6107	1.6116	1.6126	1.6136	1.6146	8.1
8.2	1.6156	1.6166	1.6176	1.6185	1.6195	1.6205	1.6215	1.6225	1.6235	1.6244	8.2
8.3	1.6254	1.6264	1.6274	1.6283	1.6293	1.6303	1.6313	1.6323	1.6332	1.6342	8.3
8.4	1.6352	1.6361	1.6371	1.6381	1.6391	1.6400	1.6410	1.6420	1.6429	1.6439	8.4
8.5	1.6449	1.6458	1.6468	1.6478	1.6487	1.6497	1.6507	1.6516	1.6526	1.6536	8.5
8.6	1.6545	1.6555	1.6565	1.6574	1.6584	1.6593	1.6603	1.6612	1.6622	1.6632	8.6
8.7	1.6641	1.6651	1.6660	1.6670	1.6679	1.6689	1.6698	1.6708	1.6718	1.6727	8.7
8.8	1.6737	1.6746	1.6756	1.6765	1.6775	1.6784	1.6794	1.6803	1.6812	1.6822	8.8
8.9	1.6831	1.6841	1.6850	1.6860	1.6869	1.6879	1.6888	1.6897	1.6907	1.6916	8.9
9.0	1.6926	1.6935	1.6944	1.6954	1.6963	1.6973	1.6982	1.6991	1.7001	1.7010	9.0
9.1	1.7019	1.7029	1.7038	1.7047	1.7057	1.7066	1.7075	1.7085	1.7094	1.7103	9.1
9.2	1.7113	1.7122	1.7131	1.7141	1.7150	1.7159	1.7168	1.7178	1.7187	1.7196	9.2
9.3	1.7205	1.7215	1.7224	1.7233	1.7242	1.7252	1.7261	1.7270	1.7279	1.7289	9.3
9.4	1.7298	1.7307	1.7316	1.7325	1.7334	1.7344	1.7353	1.7362	1.7371	1.7380	9.4
9.5	1.7389	1.7399	1.7408	1.7417	1.7426	1.7435	1.7444	1.7453	1.7463	1.7472	9.5
9.6	1.7481	1.7490	1.7499	1.7508	1.7517	1.7526	1.7535	1.7544	1.7553	1.7563	9.6
9.7	1.7572	1.7581	1.7590	1.7599	1.7608	1.7617	1.7626	1.7635	1.7644	1.7653	9.7
9.8	1.7662	1.7671	1.7680	1.7689	1.7698	1.7707	1.7716	1.7725	1.7734	1.7743	9.8
9.9	1.7752	1.7761	1.7770	1.7779	1.7788	1.7797	1.7806	1.7814	1.7823	1.7832	9.9

Use of the table: The unit at the side of a line added to
the unit at the head of a column makes up the area of a circle
for which the radius is shown in the position where line and column meet.
For example, 11 + 0.1 = 11.1; the radius of a circle with area 11.1 is 1.8797

	0.0	0.1	0.2	0.3	0.4	0.5	0.6	0.7	0.8	0.9	
10	1.7841	1.7930	1.8019	1.8107	1.8195	1.8282	1.8369	1.8455	1.8541	1.8627	10
11	1.8712	1.8797	1.8881	1.8965	1.9049	1.9133	1.9216	1.9298	1.9381	1.9462	11
12	1.9544	1.9625	1.9706	1.9787	1.9867	1.9947	2.0027	2.0106	2.0185	2.0264	12
13	2.0342	2.0420	2.0498	2.0576	2.0653	2.0730	2.0806	2.0883	2.0959	2.1035	13
14	2.1110	2.1185	2.1260	2.1335	2.1409	2.1484	2.1558	2.1631	2.1705	2.1778	14
15	2.1851	2.1924	2.1996	2.2068	2.2140	2.2212	2.2284	2.2355	2.2426	2.2497	15
16	2.2568	2.2638	2.2708	2.2778	2.2848	2.2917	2.2987	2.3056	2.3125	2.3194	16
17	2.3262	2.3330	2.3399	2.3466	2.3534	2.3602	2.3669	2.3736	2.3803	2.3870	17
18	2.3937	2.4003	2.4069	2.4135	2.4201	2.4267	2.4332	2.4398	2.4463	2.4528	18
19	2.4592	2.4657	2.4722	2.4786	2.4850	2.4914	2.4978	2.5041	2.5105	2.5168	19
20	2.5231	2.5294	2.5357	2.5420	2.5482	2.5545	2.5607	2.5669	2.5731	2.5793	20
21	2.5854	2.5916	2.5977	2.6038	2.6099	2.6160	2.6221	2.6282	2.6342	2.6403	21
22	2.6463	2.6523	2.6583	2.6643	2.6702	2.6762	2.6821	2.6881	2.6940	2.6999	22
23	2.7058	2.7116	2.7175	2.7233	2.7292	2.7350	2.7408	2.7466	2.7524	2.7582	23
24	2.7640	2.7697	2.7754	2.7812	2.7869	2.7926	2.7983	2.8040	2.8096	2.8153	24
25	2.8209	2.8266	2.8322	2.8378	2.8434	2.8490	2.8546	2.8602	2.8657	2.8713	25
26	2.8768	2.8823	2.8879	2.8934	2.8989	2.9043	2.9098	2.9153	2.9207	2.9262	26
27	2.9316	2.9370	2.9425	2.9479	2.9533	2.9586	2.9640	2.9694	2.9747	2.9801	27
28	2.9854	2.9907	2.9961	3.0014	3.0067	3.0119	3.0172	3.0225	3.0278	3.0330	28
29	3.0383	3.0435	3.0487	3.0539	3.0591	3.0643	3.0695	3.0747	3.0799	3.0850	29
30	3.0902	3.0953	3.1005	3.1056	3.1107	3.1158	3.1209	3.1260	3.1311	3.1362	30
31	3.1413	3.1463	3.1514	3.1564	3.1615	3.1665	3.1715	3.1765	3.1815	3.1865	31
32	3.1915	3.1965	3.2015	3.2065	3.2114	3.2164	3.2213	3.2263	3.2312	3.2361	32
33	3.2410	3.2459	3.2508	3.2557	3.2606	3.2655	3.2704	3.2752	3.2801	3.2849	33
34	3.2898	3.2946	3.2994	3.3042	3.3091	3.3139	3.3187	3.3235	3.3282	3.3330	34
35	3.3378	3.3426	3.3473	3.3521	3.3568	3.3615	3.3663	3.3710	3.3757	3.3804	35
36	3.3851	3.3898	3.3945	3.3992	3.4039	3.4086	3.4132	3.4179	3.4225	3.4272	36
37	3.4318	3.4365	3.4411	3.4457	3.4503	3.4549	3.4595	3.4641	3.4687	3.4733	37
38	3.4779	3.4825	3.4870	3.4916	3.4962	3.5007	3.5052	3.5098	3.5143	3.5188	38
39	3.5234	3.5279	3.5324	3.5369	3.5414	3.5459	3.5504	3.5548	3.5593	3.5638	39
40	3.5682	3.5727	3.5772	3.5816	3.5860	3.5905	3.5949	3.5993	3.6038	3.6082	40
41	3.6126	3.6170	3.6214	3.6258	3.6302	3.6345	3.6389	3.6433	3.6477	3.6520	41
42	3.6564	3.6607	3.6651	3.6694	3.6737	3.6781	3.6824	3.6867	3.6910	3.6953	42
43	3.6996	3.7039	3.7082	3.7125	3.7168	3.7211	3.7254	3.7296	3.7339	3.7382	43
44	3.7424	3.7467	3.7509	3.7551	3.7594	3.7636	3.7678	3.7721	3.7763	3.7805	44
45	3.7847	3.7889	3.7931	3.7973	3.8015	3.8057	3.8098	3.8140	3.8182	3.8224	45
46	3.8265	3.8307	3.8348	3.8390	3.8431	3.8473	3.8514	3.8555	3.8597	3.8638	46
47	3.8679	3.8720	3.8761	3.8802	3.8843	3.8884	3.8925	3.8966	3.9007	3.9047	47
48	3.9088	3.9129	3.9170	3.9210	3.9251	3.9291	3.9332	3.9372	3.9413	3.9453	48
49	3.9493	3.9534	3.9574	3.9614	3.9654	3.9694	3.9734	3.9774	3.9814	3.9854	49
50	3.9894	3.9934	3.9974	4.0014	4.0053	4.0093	4.0133	4.0173	4.0212	4.0252	50
51	4.0291	4.0331	4.0370	4.0410	4.0449	4.0488	4.0528	4.0567	4.0606	4.0645	51
52	4.0684	4.0723	4.0762	4.0801	4.0840	4.0879	4.0918	4.0957	4.0996	4.1035	52
53	4.1074	4.1112	4.1151	4.1190	4.1228	4.1267	4.1305	4.1344	4.1382	4.1421	53
54	4.1459	4.1498	4.1536	4.1574	4.1613	4.1651	4.1689	4.1727	4.1765	4.1803	54
55	4.1841	4.1879	4.1917	4.1955	4.1993	4.2031	4.2069	4.2107	4.2145	4.2182	55
56	4.2220	4.2258	4.2295	4.2333	4.2371	4.2408	4.2446	4.2483	4.2521	4.2558	56
57	4.2595	4.2633	4.2670	4.2707	4.2745	4.2782	4.2819	4.2856	4.2893	4.2930	57
58	4.2967	4.3004	4.3041	4.3078	4.3115	4.3152	4.3189	4.3226	4.3263	4.3299	58
59	4.3336	4.3373	4.3410	4.3446	4.3483	4.3519	4.3556	4.3593	4.3629	4.3666	59

Use of the table: the unit at the side of a line added to
the unit at the head of a column makes up the area of a circle
for which the radius is shown in the position where line and column meet.
For example, 61 + 0.1 = 61.1; the radius of a circle with area 61.1 is 4.4101

	0.0	0.1	0.2	0.3	0.4	0.5	0.6	0.7	0.8	0.9	
60	4.3702	4.3738	4.3775	4.3811	4.3847	4.3884	4.3920	4.3956	4.3992	4.4028	60
61	4.4065	4.4101	4.4137	4.4173	4.4209	4.4245	4.4281	4.4317	4.4353	4.4388	61
62	4.4424	4.4460	4.4496	4.4532	4.4567	4.4603	4.4639	4.4674	4.4710	4.4746	62
63	4.4781	4.4817	4.4852	4.4888	4.4923	4.4959	4.4994	4.5029	4.5065	4.5100	63
64	4.5135	4.5170	4.5206	4.5241	4.5276	4.5311	4.5346	4.5381	4.5416	4.5451	64
65	4.5486	4.5521	4.5556	4.5591	4.5626	4.5661	4.5696	4.5731	4.5765	4.5800	65
66	4.5835	4.5870	4.5904	4.5939	4.5974	4.6008	4.6043	4.6077	4.6112	4.6146	66
67	4.6181	4.6215	4.6250	4.6284	4.6319	4.6353	4.6387	4.6422	4.6456	4.6490	67
68	4.6524	4.6558	4.6593	4.6627	4.6661	4.6695	4.6729	4.6763	4.6797	4.6831	68
69	4.6865	4.6899	4.6933	4.6967	4.7001	4.7035	4.7068	4.7102	4.7136	4.7170	69
70	4.7203	4.7237	4.7271	4.7305	4.7338	4.7372	4.7405	4.7439	4.7472	4.7506	70
71	4.7539	4.7573	4.7606	4.7640	4.7673	4.7707	4.7740	4.7773	4.7807	4.7840	71
72	4.7873	4.7906	4.7940	4.7973	4.8006	4.8039	4.8072	4.8105	4.8138	4.8171	72
73	4.8204	4.8237	4.8270	4.8303	4.8336	4.8369	4.8402	4.8435	4.8468	4.8501	73
74	4.8533	4.8566	4.8599	4.8632	4.8664	4.8697	4.8730	4.8762	4.8795	4.8828	74
75	4.8860	4.8893	4.8925	4.8958	4.8990	4.9023	4.9055	4.9088	4.9120	4.9153	75
76	4.9185	4.9217	4.9250	4.9282	4.9314	4.9346	4.9379	4.9411	4.9443	4.9475	76
77	4.9507	4.9540	4.9572	4.9604	4.9636	4.9668	4.9700	4.9732	4.9764	4.9796	77
78	4.9828	4.9860	4.9892	4.9924	4.9955	4.9987	5.0019	5.0051	5.0083	5.0115	78
79	5.0146	5.0178	5.0210	5.0241	5.0273	5.0305	5.0336	5.0368	5.0400	5.0431	79
80	5.0463	5.0494	5.0526	5.0557	5.0589	5.0620	5.0652	5.0683	5.0714	5.0746	80
81	5.0777	5.0808	5.0840	5.0871	5.0902	5.0934	5.0965	5.0996	5.1027	5.1058	81
82	5.1090	5.1121	5.1152	5.1183	5.1214	5.1245	5.1276	5.1307	5.1338	5.1369	82
83	5.1400	5.1431	5.1462	5.1493	5.1524	5.1555	5.1586	5.1616	5.1647	5.1678	83
84	5.1709	5.1740	5.1770	5.1801	5.1832	5.1862	5.1893	5.1924	5.1954	5.1985	84
85	5.2016	5.2046	5.2077	5.2107	5.2138	5.2168	5.2199	5.2229	5.2260	5.2290	85
86	5.2321	5.2351	5.2382	5.2412	5.2442	5.2473	5.2503	5.2533	5.2564	5.2594	86
87	5.2624	5.2654	5.2685	5.2715	5.2745	5.2775	5.2805	5.2835	5.2865	5.2896	87
88	5.2926	5.2956	5.2986	5.3016	5.3046	5.3076	5.3106	5.3136	5.3166	5.3196	88
89	5.3226	5.3255	5.3285	5.3315	5.3345	5.3375	5.3405	5.3434	5.3464	5.3494	89
90	5.3524	5.3553	5.3583	5.3613	5.3643	5.3672	5.3702	5.3731	5.3761	5.3791	90
91	5.3820	5.3850	5.3879	5.3909	5.3938	5.3968	5.3997	5.4027	5.4056	5.4086	91
92	5.4115	5.4145	5.4174	5.4203	5.4233	5.4262	5.4291	5.4321	5.4350	5.4379	92
93	5.4408	5.4438	5.4467	5.4496	5.4525	5.4555	5.4584	5.4613	5.4642	5.4671	93
94	5.4700	5.4729	5.4758	5.4787	5.4816	5.4845	5.4875	5.4904	5.4932	5.4961	94
95	5.4990	5.5019	5.5048	5.5077	5.5106	5.5135	5.5164	5.5193	5.5221	5.5250	95
96	5.5279	5.5308	5.5337	5.5365	5.5394	5.5423	5.5452	5.5480	5.5509	5.5538	96
97	5.5566	5.5595	5.5623	5.5652	5.5681	5.5709	5.5738	5.5766	5.5795	5.5823	97
98	5.5852	5.5880	5.5909	5.5937	5.5966	5.5994	5.6023	5.6051	5.6079	5.6108	98
99	5.6136	5.6164	5.6193	5.6221	5.6249	5.6278	5.6306	5.6334	5.6363	5.6391	99
100	5.6419	5.6447	5.6475	5.6504	5.6532	5.6560	5.6588	5.6616	5.6644	5.6672	100

Annual percentage rates

Use of the table: the monthly rate, made up by the number at each side of a line and the fraction or decimal unit at the head of a column, is equivalent to the annual percentage rate shown in the position where line and column meet. For example, the APR for a monthly rate of $2\frac{1}{4}$% is 30.6%.

Actual annual percentage rate of interest per year (APR) corresponding to the rate per month indicated

Monthly rates with fractions

	0	$\frac{1}{8}$	$\frac{1}{4}$	$\frac{3}{8}$	$\frac{1}{2}$	$\frac{5}{8}$	$\frac{3}{4}$	$\frac{7}{8}$	
0	0.0	1.5	3.0	4.6	6.2	7.8	9.4	11.0	0
1	12.7	14.4	16.1	17.8	19.6	21.3	23.1	25.0	1
2	26.8	28.7	30.6	32.5	34.5	36.5	38.5	40.5	2
3	42.6	44.7	46.8	48.9	51.1	53.3	55.5	57.8	3
4	60.1	62.4	64.8	67.2	69.6	72.0	74.5	77.0	4
5	79.6	82.2	84.8	87.4	90.1	92.8	95.6	98.4	5
6	101.2	104.1	107.0	109.9	112.9	115.9	119.0	122.1	6
7	125.2	128.4	131.6	134.9	138.2	141.5	144.9	148.3	7
8	151.8	155.3	158.9	162.5	166.2	169.9	173.6	177.4	8
9	181.3	185.2	189.1	193.1	197.1	201.2	205.4	209.6	9
10	213.8	218.1	222.5	226.9	231.4	235.9	240.5	245.1	10
11	249.8	254.6	259.4	264.3	269.2	274.2	279.3	284.4	11
12	289.6	294.8	300.2	305.5	311.0	316.5	322.1	327.7	12
13	333.5	339.2	345.1	351.0	357.0	363.1	369.3	375.5	13
14	381.8	388.2	394.6	401.2	407.8	414.5	421.2	428.1	14
15	435.0	442.0	449.2	456.3	463.6	471.0	478.4	486.0	15
16	493.6	501.3	509.1	517.0	525.0	533.1	541.3	549.6	16
17	558.0	566.5	575.1	583.8	592.6	601.4	610.4	619.5	17
18	628.8	638.1	647.5	657.0	666.7	676.5	686.3	696.3	18
19	706.4	716.6	727.0	737.5	748.0	758.7	769.6	780.5	19
20	791.6	802.8	814.2	825.6	837.2	849.0	860.8	872.8	20
21	885.0	897.3	909.7	922.2	934.9	947.8	960.8	973.9	21
22	987.2	1000.7	1014.3	1028.0	1041.9	1056.0	1070.2	1084.6	22
23	1099.1	1113.8	1128.7	1143.7	1158.9	1174.3	1189.9	1205.6	23
24	1221.5	1237.6	1253.8	1270.2	1286.9	1303.7	1320.6	1337.8	24
25	1355.2	1372.8	1390.5	1408.5	1426.6	1444.9	1463.5	1482.2	25

Monthly rates with decimals

	0.0	0.1	0.2	0.3	0.4	0.5	0.6	0.7	0.8	0.9	
0	0.0	1.2	2.4	3.7	4.9	6.2	7.4	8.7	10.0	11.4	0
1	12.7	14.0	15.4	16.8	18.2	19.6	21.0	22.4	23.9	25.3	1
2	26.8	28.3	29.8	31.4	32.9	34.5	36.1	37.7	39.3	40.9	2
3	42.6	44.2	45.9	47.6	49.4	51.1	52.9	54.6	56.4	58.3	3
4	60.1	62.0	63.8	65.7	67.7	69.6	71.5	73.5	75.5	77.5	4
5	79.6	81.6	83.7	85.8	88.0	90.1	92.3	94.5	96.7	99.0	5
6	101.2	103.5	105.8	108.2	110.5	112.9	115.3	117.8	120.2	122.7	6
7	125.2	127.8	130.3	132.9	135.5	138.2	140.9	143.6	146.3	149.0	7
8	151.8	154.6	157.5	160.3	163.2	166.2	169.1	172.1	175.1	178.2	8
9	181.3	184.4	187.5	190.7	193.9	197.1	200.4	203.7	207.1	210.4	9
10	213.8	217.3	220.8	224.3	227.8	231.4	235.0	238.7	242.4	246.1	10
11	249.8	253.6	257.5	261.4	265.3	269.2	273.2	277.3	281.3	285.4	11
12	289.6	293.8	298.0	302.3	306.6	311.0	315.4	319.8	324.3	328.9	12
13	333.5	338.1	342.7	347.5	352.2	357.0	361.9	366.8	371.7	376.7	13
14	381.8	386.9	392.0	397.2	402.5	407.8	413.1	418.5	424.0	429.5	14
15	435.0	440.6	446.3	452.0	457.8	463.6	469.5	475.4	481.4	487.5	15
16	493.6	499.8	506.0	512.3	518.6	525.0	531.5	538.0	544.6	551.3	16
17	558.0	564.8	571.6	578.5	585.5	592.6	599.7	606.8	614.1	621.4	17
18	628.8	636.2	643.7	651.3	659.0	666.7	674.5	682.4	690.3	698.3	18
19	706.4	714.6	722.8	731.2	739.6	748.0	756.6	765.2	773.9	782.7	19
20	791.6	800.6	809.6	818.7	827.9	837.2	846.6	856.1	865.6	875.2	20
21	885.0	894.8	904.7	914.7	924.8	934.9	945.2	955.6	966.0	976.6	21
22	987.2	998.0	1008.8	1019.7	1030.8	1041.9	1053.1	1064.5	1075.9	1087.5	22
23	1099.1	1110.9	1122.7	1134.7	1146.8	1158.9	1171.2	1183.6	1196.1	1208.7	23
24	1221.5	1234.3	1247.3	1260.4	1273.6	1286.9	1300.3	1313.8	1327.5	1341.3	24
25	1355.2	1369.2	1383.4	1397.7	1412.1	1426.6	1441.3	1456.0	1471.0	1486.0	25

se of the table: the table shows the annual percentage rate of interest actually
aid when 100 units are repaid with the amount of units shown in the column at
ach side of a line after the number of months shown at the top of a column.
or example, the APR when 100 units is repaid with 105 units after 2 months is
4.0%.

Annual percentage rate (APR) corresponding to the amount repaid per 100 units borrowed after the number of months shown

months amount repaid	1	2	3	4	5	6	7	8	9	10	11	12 months	amount repaid
00	0.0	0.0	0.0	0.0	0.0	0.0	0.0	0.0	0.0	0.0	0.0	0.0	100
01	12.7	6.2	4.1	3.0	2.4	2.0	1.7	1.5	1.3	1.2	1.1	1.0	101
02	26.8	12.6	8.2	6.1	4.9	4.0	3.5	3.0	2.7	2.4	2.2	2.0	102
03	42.6	19.4	12.6	9.3	7.4	6.1	5.2	4.5	4.0	3.6	3.3	3.0	103
04	60.1	26.5	17.0	12.5	9.9	8.2	7.0	6.1	5.4	4.8	4.4	4.0	104
05	79.6	34.0	21.6	15.8	12.4	10.2	8.7	7.6	6.7	6.0	5.5	5.0	105
06	101.2	41.9	26.2	19.1	15.0	12.4	10.5	9.1	8.1	7.2	6.6	6.0	106
07	125.2	50.1	31.1	22.5	17.6	14.5	12.3	10.7	9.4	8.5	7.7	7.0	107
08	151.8	58.7	36.0	26.0	20.3	16.6	14.1	12.2	10.8	9.7	8.8	8.0	108
09	181.3	67.7	41.2	29.5	23.0	18.8	15.9	13.8	12.2	10.9	9.9	9.0	109
10	213.8	77.2	46.4	33.1	25.7	21.0	17.7	15.4	13.6	12.1	11.0	10.0	110
11	249.8	87.0	51.8	36.8	28.5	23.2	19.6	16.9	14.9	13.3	12.1	11.0	111
12	289.6	97.4	57.4	40.5	31.3	25.4	21.4	18.5	16.3	14.6	13.2	12.0	112
13	333.5	108.2	63.0	44.3	34.1	27.7	23.3	20.1	17.7	15.8	14.3	13.0	113
14	381.8	119.5	68.9	48.2	37.0	30.0	25.2	21.7	19.1	17.0	15.4	14.0	114
15	435.0	131.3	74.9	52.1	39.9	32.2	27.1	23.3	20.5	18.3	16.5	15.0	115
16	493.6	143.6	81.1	56.1	42.8	34.6	29.0	24.9	21.9	19.5	17.6	16.0	116
17	558.0	156.5	87.4	60.2	45.8	36.9	30.9	26.6	23.3	20.7	18.7	17.0	117
18	628.8	170.0	93.9	64.3	48.8	39.2	32.8	28.2	24.7	22.0	19.8	18.0	118
19	706.4	184.0	100.5	68.5	51.8	41.6	34.7	29.8	26.1	23.2	20.9	19.0	119
20	791.6	198.6	107.4	72.8	54.9	44.0	36.7	31.5	27.5	24.5	22.0	20.0	120
21	885.0	213.8	114.4	77.2	58.0	46.4	38.6	33.1	28.9	25.7	23.1	21.0	121
22	987.2	229.7	121.5	81.6	61.2	48.8	40.6	34.8	30.4	26.9	24.2	22.0	122
23	1099.1	246.3	128.9	86.1	64.4	51.3	42.6	36.4	31.8	28.2	25.3	23.0	123
24	1221.5	263.5	136.4	90.7	67.6	53.8	44.6	38.1	33.2	29.5	26.4	24.0	124
25	1355.2	281.5	144.1	95.3	70.8	56.2	46.6	39.8	34.7	30.7	27.6	25.0	125
26	1501.2	300.2	152.0	100.0	74.1	58.8	48.6	41.4	36.1	32.0	28.7	26.0	126
27	1660.5	319.6	160.1	104.8	77.5	61.3	50.6	43.1	37.5	33.2	29.8	27.0	127
28	1834.3	339.8	168.4	109.7	80.8	63.8	52.7	44.8	39.0	34.5	30.9	28.0	128
29	2023.6	360.8	176.9	114.7	84.3	66.4	54.7	46.5	40.4	35.7	32.0	29.0	129
30	2229.8	382.7	185.6	119.7	87.7	69.0	56.8	48.2	41.9	37.0	33.1	30.0	130
31	2454.2	405.4	194.5	124.8	91.2	71.6	58.9	49.9	43.3	38.3	34.3	31.0	131
32	2698.3	429.0	203.6	130.0	94.7	74.2	61.0	51.7	44.8	39.5	35.4	32.0	132
33	2963.5	453.5	212.9	135.3	98.3	76.9	63.0	53.4	46.3	40.8	36.5	33.0	133
34	3251.6	478.9	222.4	140.6	101.9	79.6	65.2	55.1	47.7	42.1	37.6	34.0	134
35	3564.4	505.3	232.2	146.0	105.5	82.2	67.3	56.9	49.2	43.4	38.7	35.0	135
36	3903.7	532.8	242.1	151.5	109.2	85.0	69.4	58.6	50.7	44.6	39.9	36.0	136
37	4271.7	561.2	252.3	157.1	112.9	87.7	71.5	60.4	52.2	45.9	41.0	37.0	137
38	4670.3	590.7	262.7	162.8	116.6	90.4	73.7	62.1	53.6	47.2	42.1	38.0	138
39	5102.1	621.3	273.3	168.6	120.4	93.2	75.9	63.9	55.1	48.5	43.2	39.0	139
40	5569.4	653.0	284.2	174.4	124.2	96.0	78.0	65.7	56.6	49.7	44.3	40.0	140
41	6074.9	685.8	295.3	180.3	128.1	98.8	80.2	67.4	58.1	51.0	45.5	41.0	141
42	6621.4	719.8	306.6	186.3	132.0	101.6	82.4	69.2	59.6	52.3	46.6	42.0	142
43	7211.9	755.1	318.2	192.4	135.9	104.5	84.6	71.0	61.1	53.6	47.7	43.0	143
44	7849.7	791.6	330.0	198.6	139.9	107.4	86.8	72.8	62.6	54.9	48.9	44.0	144
45	8538.1	829.4	342.1	204.9	143.9	110.2	89.1	74.6	64.1	56.2	50.0	45.0	145
50	12874.6	1039.1	406.2	237.5	164.6	125.0	100.4	83.7	71.7	62.7	55.6	50.0	150
55	19130.0	1286.7	477.2	272.4	186.3	140.2	112.0	93.0	79.4	69.2	61.3	55.0	155
60	28047.5	1577.7	555.4	309.6	208.9	156.0	123.8	102.4	87.1	75.8	67.0	60.0	160
65	40620.0	1917.9	641.2	349.2	232.6	172.2	136.0	111.9	95.0	82.4	72.7	65.0	165
70	58162.2	2313.8	735.2	391.3	257.3	189.0	148.3	121.7	102.9	89.0	78.4	70.0	170
75	82400.5	2772.3	837.9	435.9	283.1	206.2	161.0	131.5	110.9	95.7	84.1	75.0	175
80	115583.1	3301.2	949.8	483.2	309.9	224.0	173.9	141.5	119.0	102.5	89.9	80.0	180
90	221231.5	4604.6	1203.2	585.9	366.7	261.0	200.5	161.9	135.3	116.0	101.4	90.0	190
00	409500.0	6300.0	1500.0	700.0	427.8	300.0	228.1	182.8	152.0	129.7	113.0	100.0	200

Interest rates and growth rates

$$F = 1 \times \left[1 + \frac{r}{100}\right]^n$$

Use of the table: the table shows the annual compound rate per cent of interest or growth ('r' in the formula) which, accumulating over the period shown at the head of a column (n), makes 1 unit increase (or decrease) to the amount shown in the column at each side of a line (F).
For example, an increase from 1 to 1.10 (a 10% increase), if achieved over 5 years will have resulted from an annual compound interest or growth rate of 1.92%

Interest rate or growth rate producing an accumulated amount from 1 unit compounded annually

F	months 3	months 6	months 9	years 1	years 2	years 3	years 4	years 5	years 6	years 7	years 8	years 9	years 10	years 11	years 12	years 13	n
0.90	−34.39	−19.00	−13.11	−10.00	−5.13	−3.45	−2.60	−2.09	−1.74	−1.49	−1.31	−1.16	−1.05	−0.95	−0.87	−0.81	0.90
0.91	−31.43	−17.19	−11.82	−9.00	−4.61	−3.09	−2.33	−1.87	−1.56	−1.34	−1.17	−1.04	−0.94	−0.85	−0.78	−0.72	0.9
0.92	−28.36	−15.36	−10.52	−8.00	−4.08	−2.74	−2.06	−1.65	−1.38	−1.18	−1.04	−0.92	−0.83	−0.76	−0.69	−0.64	0.9
0.93	−25.19	−13.51	−9.22	−7.00	−3.56	−2.39	−1.80	−1.44	−1.20	−1.03	−0.90	−0.80	−0.72	−0.66	−0.60	−0.56	0.9
0.94	−21.93	−11.64	−7.92	−6.00	−3.05	−2.04	−1.53	−1.23	−1.03	−0.88	−0.77	−0.69	−0.62	−0.56	−0.51	−0.47	0.9
0.95	−18.55	−9.75	−6.61	−5.00	−2.53	−1.70	−1.27	−1.02	−0.85	−0.73	−0.64	−0.57	−0.51	−0.47	−0.43	−0.39	0.9
0.96	−15.07	−7.84	−5.30	−4.00	−2.02	−1.35	−1.02	−0.81	−0.68	−0.58	−0.51	−0.45	−0.41	−0.37	−0.34	−0.31	0.9
0.97	−11.47	−5.91	−3.98	−3.00	−1.51	−1.01	−0.76	−0.61	−0.51	−0.43	−0.38	−0.34	−0.30	−0.28	−0.25	−0.23	0.9
0.98	−7.76	−3.96	−2.66	−2.00	−1.01	−0.67	−0.50	−0.40	−0.34	−0.29	−0.25	−0.22	−0.20	−0.18	−0.17	−0.16	0.9
0.99	−3.94	−1.99	−1.33	−1.00	−0.50	−0.33	−0.25	−0.20	−0.17	−0.14	−0.13	−0.11	−0.10	−0.09	−0.08	−0.08	0.9
1.00	0.00	0.00	0.00	0.00	0.00	0.00	0.00	0.00	0.00	0.00	0.00	0.00	0.00	0.00	0.00	0.00	1.0
1.01	4.06	2.01	1.34	1.00	0.50	0.33	0.25	0.20	0.17	0.14	0.12	0.11	0.10	0.09	0.08	0.08	1.0
1.02	8.24	4.04	2.68	2.00	1.00	0.66	0.50	0.40	0.33	0.28	0.25	0.22	0.20	0.18	0.17	0.15	1.0
1.03	12.55	6.09	4.02	3.00	1.49	0.99	0.74	0.59	0.49	0.42	0.37	0.33	0.30	0.27	0.25	0.23	1.0
1.04	16.99	8.16	5.37	4.00	1.98	1.32	0.99	0.79	0.66	0.56	0.49	0.44	0.39	0.36	0.33	0.30	1.0
1.05	21.55	10.25	6.72	5.00	2.47	1.64	1.23	0.98	0.82	0.70	0.61	0.54	0.49	0.44	0.41	0.38	1.0
1.06	26.25	12.36	8.08	6.00	2.96	1.96	1.47	1.17	0.98	0.84	0.73	0.65	0.58	0.53	0.49	0.45	1.0
1.07	31.08	14.49	9.44	7.00	3.44	2.28	1.71	1.36	1.13	0.97	0.85	0.75	0.68	0.62	0.57	0.52	1.0
1.08	36.05	16.64	10.81	8.00	3.92	2.60	1.94	1.55	1.29	1.11	0.97	0.86	0.77	0.70	0.64	0.59	1.0
1.09	41.16	18.81	12.18	9.00	4.40	2.91	2.18	1.74	1.45	1.24	1.08	0.96	0.87	0.79	0.72	0.67	1.0
1.10	46.41	21.00	13.55	10.00	4.88	3.23	2.41	1.92	1.60	1.37	1.20	1.06	0.96	0.87	0.80	0.74	1.1
1.11	51.81	23.21	14.93	11.00	5.36	3.54	2.64	2.11	1.75	1.50	1.31	1.17	1.05	0.95	0.87	0.81	1.1
1.12	57.35	25.44	16.31	12.00	5.83	3.85	2.87	2.29	1.91	1.63	1.43	1.27	1.14	1.04	0.95	0.88	1.1
1.13	63.05	27.69	17.70	13.00	6.30	4.16	3.10	2.47	2.06	1.76	1.54	1.37	1.23	1.12	1.02	0.94	1.1
1.14	68.90	29.96	19.09	14.00	6.77	4.46	3.33	2.66	2.21	1.89	1.65	1.47	1.32	1.20	1.10	1.01	1.1
1.15	74.90	32.25	20.48	15.00	7.24	4.77	3.56	2.83	2.36	2.02	1.76	1.57	1.41	1.28	1.17	1.08	1.1
1.16	81.06	34.56	21.88	16.00	7.70	5.07	3.78	3.01	2.50	2.14	1.87	1.66	1.50	1.36	1.24	1.15	1.1
1.17	87.39	36.89	23.29	17.00	8.17	5.37	4.00	3.19	2.65	2.27	1.98	1.76	1.58	1.44	1.32	1.22	1.1
1.18	93.88	39.24	24.69	18.00	8.63	5.67	4.22	3.37	2.80	2.39	2.09	1.86	1.67	1.52	1.39	1.28	1.1
1.19	100.53	41.61	26.10	19.00	9.09	5.97	4.44	3.54	2.94	2.52	2.20	1.95	1.75	1.59	1.46	1.35	1.1
1.20	107.36	44.00	27.52	20.00	9.54	6.27	4.66	3.71	3.09	2.64	2.31	2.05	1.84	1.67	1.53	1.41	1.2
1.21	114.36	46.41	28.94	21.00	10.00	6.56	4.88	3.89	3.23	2.76	2.41	2.14	1.92	1.75	1.60	1.48	1.2
1.22	121.53	48.84	30.36	22.00	10.45	6.85	5.10	4.06	3.37	2.88	2.52	2.23	2.01	1.82	1.67	1.54	1.2
1.23	128.89	51.29	31.79	23.00	10.91	7.14	5.31	4.23	3.51	3.00	2.62	2.33	2.09	1.90	1.74	1.61	1.2
1.24	136.42	53.76	33.22	24.00	11.36	7.43	5.53	4.40	3.65	3.12	2.73	2.42	2.17	1.97	1.81	1.67	1.2
1.25	144.14	56.25	34.65	25.00	11.80	7.72	5.74	4.56	3.79	3.24	2.83	2.51	2.26	2.05	1.88	1.73	1.2
1.26	152.05	58.76	36.09	26.00	12.25	8.01	5.95	4.73	3.93	3.36	2.93	2.60	2.34	2.12	1.94	1.79	1.2
1.27	160.14	61.29	37.53	27.00	12.69	8.29	6.16	4.90	4.06	3.47	3.03	2.69	2.42	2.20	2.01	1.86	1.2
1.28	168.44	63.84	38.98	28.00	13.14	8.58	6.37	5.06	4.20	3.59	3.13	2.78	2.50	2.27	2.08	1.92	1.2
1.29	176.92	66.41	40.43	29.00	13.58	8.86	6.57	5.22	4.34	3.70	3.23	2.87	2.58	2.34	2.14	1.98	1.2
1.30	185.61	69.00	41.88	30.00	14.02	9.14	6.78	5.39	4.47	3.82	3.33	2.96	2.66	2.41	2.21	2.04	1.3
1.31	194.50	71.61	43.34	31.00	14.46	9.42	6.98	5.55	4.60	3.93	3.43	3.05	2.74	2.49	2.28	2.10	1.3
1.32	203.60	74.24	44.80	32.00	14.89	9.70	7.19	5.71	4.74	4.05	3.53	3.13	2.82	2.56	2.34	2.16	1.3
1.33	212.90	76.89	46.26	33.00	15.33	9.97	7.39	5.87	4.87	4.16	3.63	3.22	2.89	2.63	2.40	2.22	1.3
1.34	222.42	79.56	47.73	34.00	15.76	10.25	7.59	6.03	5.00	4.27	3.73	3.31	2.97	2.70	2.47	2.28	1.3
1.35	232.15	82.25	49.20	35.00	16.19	10.52	7.79	6.19	5.13	4.38	3.82	3.39	3.05	2.77	2.53	2.34	1.3
1.36	242.10	84.96	50.68	36.00	16.62	10.79	7.99	6.34	5.26	4.49	3.92	3.48	3.12	2.83	2.60	2.39	1.3
1.37	252.28	87.69	52.16	37.00	17.05	11.06	8.19	6.50	5.39	4.60	4.01	3.56	3.20	2.90	2.66	2.45	1.3
1.38	262.67	90.44	53.64	38.00	17.47	11.33	8.39	6.65	5.51	4.71	4.11	3.64	3.27	2.97	2.72	2.51	1.3
1.39	273.30	93.21	55.13	39.00	17.90	11.60	8.58	6.81	5.64	4.82	4.20	3.73	3.35	3.04	2.78	2.57	1.3
1.40	284.16	96.00	56.62	40.00	18.32	11.87	8.78	6.96	5.77	4.92	4.30	3.81	3.42	3.11	2.84	2.62	1.4
1.41	295.25	98.81	58.11	41.00	18.74	12.13	8.97	7.11	5.89	5.03	4.39	3.89	3.50	3.17	2.90	2.68	1.4
1.42	306.59	101.64	59.61	42.00	19.16	12.40	9.16	7.26	6.02	5.14	4.48	3.97	3.57	3.24	2.97	2.73	1.4
1.43	318.16	104.49	61.11	43.00	19.58	12.66	9.35	7.42	6.14	5.24	4.57	4.05	3.64	3.31	3.03	2.79	1.4
1.44	329.98	107.36	62.61	44.00	20.00	12.92	9.54	7.57	6.27	5.35	4.66	4.13	3.71	3.37	3.09	2.84	1.4

Use of the table: the table shows the annual compound rate per cent of interest or growth ('r' in the formula) which, accumulating over the period shown at the head of a column (n), makes 1 unit increase to the amount shown in the column at each side of a line (F).
For example, an increase from 1 to 1.50 (a 50% increase), if achieved over 5 years will have resulted from an annual compound interest or growth rate of 8.45%.

$$F = 1 \times \left[1 + \frac{r}{100} \right]^n$$

Interest rate or growth rate producing an accumulated amount from 1 unit compounded annually

F	months 3	months 6	months 9	years 1	years 2	years 3	years 4	years 5	years 6	years 7	years 8	years 9	years 10	years 11	years 12	years 13	F
1.45	342.05	110.25	64.12	45.00	20.42	13.19	9.73	7.71	6.39	5.45	4.75	4.21	3.79	3.44	3.14	2.90	1.45
1.46	354.37	113.16	65.63	46.00	20.83	13.44	9.92	7.86	6.51	5.56	4.84	4.29	3.86	3.50	3.20	2.95	1.46
1.47	366.95	116.09	67.14	47.00	21.24	13.70	10.11	8.01	6.63	5.66	4.93	4.37	3.93	3.56	3.26	3.01	1.47
1.48	379.79	119.04	68.66	48.00	21.66	13.96	10.30	8.16	6.75	5.76	5.02	4.45	4.00	3.63	3.32	3.06	1.48
1.49	392.88	122.01	70.18	49.00	22.07	14.22	10.48	8.30	6.87	5.86	5.11	4.53	4.07	3.69	3.38	3.12	1.49
1.50	406.25	125.00	71.71	50.00	22.47	14.47	10.67	8.45	6.99	5.96	5.20	4.61	4.14	3.75	3.44	3.17	1.50
1.51	419.89	128.01	73.24	51.00	22.88	14.73	10.85	8.59	7.11	6.06	5.29	4.69	4.21	3.82	3.49	3.22	1.51
1.52	433.79	131.04	74.77	52.00	23.29	14.98	11.04	8.73	7.23	6.16	5.37	4.76	4.28	3.88	3.55	3.27	1.52
1.53	447.98	134.09	76.30	53.00	23.69	15.23	11.22	8.88	7.35	6.26	5.46	4.84	4.34	3.94	3.61	3.33	1.53
1.54	462.45	137.16	77.84	54.00	24.10	15.48	11.40	9.02	7.46	6.36	5.55	4.91	4.41	4.00	3.66	3.38	1.54
1.55	477.20	140.25	79.38	55.00	24.50	15.73	11.58	9.16	7.58	6.46	5.63	4.99	4.48	4.06	3.72	3.43	1.55
1.56	492.24	143.36	80.93	56.00	24.90	15.98	11.76	9.30	7.69	6.56	5.72	5.07	4.55	4.13	3.78	3.48	1.56
1.57	507.57	146.49	82.47	57.00	25.30	16.23	11.94	9.44	7.81	6.66	5.80	5.14	4.61	4.19	3.83	3.53	1.57
1.58	523.20	149.64	84.02	58.00	25.70	16.47	12.12	9.58	7.92	6.75	5.88	5.21	4.68	4.25	3.89	3.58	1.58
1.59	539.13	152.81	85.58	59.00	26.10	16.72	12.29	9.72	8.04	6.85	5.97	5.29	4.75	4.31	3.94	3.63	1.59
1.60	555.36	156.00	87.14	60.00	26.49	16.96	12.47	9.86	8.15	6.94	6.05	5.36	4.81	4.37	3.99	3.68	1.60
1.61	571.90	159.21	88.70	61.00	26.89	17.20	12.64	9.99	8.26	7.04	6.13	5.43	4.88	4.42	4.05	3.73	1.61
1.62	588.75	162.44	90.26	62.00	27.28	17.45	12.82	10.13	8.37	7.13	6.22	5.51	4.94	4.48	4.10	3.78	1.62
1.63	605.91	165.69	91.83	63.00	27.67	17.69	12.99	10.26	8.48	7.23	6.30	5.58	5.01	4.54	4.16	3.83	1.63
1.64	623.39	168.96	93.40	64.00	28.06	17.93	13.16	10.40	8.59	7.32	6.38	5.65	5.07	4.60	4.21	3.88	1.64
1.65	641.20	172.25	94.97	65.00	28.45	18.17	13.34	10.53	8.70	7.42	6.46	5.72	5.14	4.66	4.26	3.93	1.65
1.66	659.33	175.56	96.55	66.00	28.84	18.40	13.51	10.67	8.81	7.51	6.54	5.79	5.20	4.72	4.31	3.98	1.66
1.67	677.80	178.89	98.13	67.00	29.23	18.64	13.68	10.80	8.92	7.60	6.62	5.86	5.26	4.77	4.37	4.02	1.67
1.68	696.59	182.24	99.72	68.00	29.61	18.88	13.85	10.93	9.03	7.69	6.70	5.93	5.32	4.83	4.42	4.07	1.68
1.69	715.73	185.61	101.30	69.00	30.00	19.11	14.02	11.07	9.14	7.78	6.78	6.00	5.39	4.89	4.47	4.12	1.69
1.70	735.21	189.00	102.89	70.00	30.38	19.35	14.19	11.20	9.25	7.88	6.86	6.07	5.45	4.94	4.52	4.17	1.70
1.71	755.04	192.41	104.49	71.00	30.77	19.58	14.35	11.33	9.35	7.97	6.94	6.14	5.51	5.00	4.57	4.21	1.71
1.72	775.21	195.84	106.08	72.00	31.15	19.81	14.52	11.46	9.46	8.06	7.01	6.21	5.57	5.05	4.62	4.26	1.72
1.73	795.75	199.29	107.68	73.00	31.53	20.05	14.69	11.59	9.57	8.15	7.09	6.28	5.63	5.11	4.67	4.31	1.73
1.74	816.64	202.76	109.28	74.00	31.91	20.28	14.85	11.71	9.67	8.23	7.17	6.35	5.70	5.16	4.72	4.35	1.74
1.75	837.89	206.25	110.89	75.00	32.29	20.51	15.02	11.84	9.78	8.32	7.25	6.42	5.76	5.22	4.77	4.40	1.75
1.76	859.51	209.76	112.50	76.00	32.66	20.74	15.18	11.97	9.88	8.41	7.32	6.48	5.82	5.27	4.82	4.44	1.76
1.77	881.51	213.29	114.11	77.00	33.04	20.96	15.34	12.10	9.98	8.50	7.40	6.55	5.88	5.33	4.87	4.49	1.77
1.78	903.88	216.84	115.72	78.00	33.42	21.19	15.51	12.22	10.09	8.59	7.47	6.62	5.94	5.38	4.92	4.54	1.78
1.79	926.63	220.41	117.34	79.00	33.79	21.42	15.67	12.35	10.19	8.67	7.55	6.68	5.99	5.44	4.97	4.58	1.79
1.80	949.76	224.00	118.96	80.00	34.16	21.64	15.83	12.47	10.29	8.76	7.62	6.75	6.05	5.49	5.02	4.63	1.80
1.81	973.28	227.61	120.58	81.00	34.54	21.87	15.99	12.60	10.39	8.85	7.70	6.81	6.11	5.54	5.07	4.67	1.81
1.82	997.20	231.24	122.21	82.00	34.91	22.09	16.15	12.72	10.50	8.93	7.77	6.88	6.17	5.59	5.12	4.71	1.82
1.83	1021.51	234.89	123.84	83.00	35.28	22.32	16.31	12.85	10.60	9.02	7.85	6.95	6.23	5.65	5.16	4.76	1.83
1.84	1046.23	238.56	125.47	84.00	35.65	22.54	16.47	12.97	10.70	9.10	7.92	7.01	6.29	5.70	5.21	4.80	1.84
1.85	1071.35	242.25	127.11	85.00	36.01	22.76	16.63	13.09	10.80	9.19	7.99	7.07	6.35	5.75	5.26	4.85	1.85
1.86	1096.88	245.96	128.74	86.00	36.38	22.98	16.78	13.21	10.90	9.27	8.07	7.14	6.40	5.80	5.31	4.89	1.86
1.87	1122.83	249.69	130.39	87.00	36.75	23.20	16.94	13.34	11.00	9.35	8.14	7.20	6.46	5.86	5.35	4.93	1.87
1.88	1149.20	253.44	132.03	88.00	37.11	23.42	17.10	13.46	11.09	9.44	8.21	7.27	6.52	5.91	5.40	4.98	1.88
1.89	1175.99	257.21	133.68	89.00	37.48	23.64	17.25	13.58	11.19	9.52	8.28	7.33	6.57	5.96	5.45	5.02	1.89
1.90	1203.21	261.00	135.33	90.00	37.84	23.86	17.41	13.70	11.29	9.60	8.35	7.39	6.63	6.01	5.49	5.06	1.90
1.91	1230.86	264.81	136.98	91.00	38.20	24.07	17.56	13.82	11.39	9.69	8.42	7.45	6.68	6.06	5.54	5.10	1.91
1.92	1258.95	268.64	138.64	92.00	38.56	24.29	17.71	13.94	11.49	9.77	8.50	7.52	6.74	6.11	5.59	5.15	1.92
1.93	1287.49	272.49	140.29	93.00	38.92	24.50	17.87	14.05	11.58	9.85	8.57	7.58	6.80	6.16	5.63	5.19	1.93
1.94	1316.47	276.36	141.96	94.00	39.28	24.72	18.02	14.17	11.68	9.93	8.64	7.64	6.85	6.21	5.68	5.23	1.94
1.95	1345.90	280.25	143.62	95.00	39.64	24.93	18.17	14.29	11.77	10.01	8.71	7.70	6.91	6.26	5.72	5.27	1.95
1.96	1375.79	284.16	145.29	96.00	40.00	25.15	18.32	14.41	11.87	10.09	8.78	7.76	6.96	6.31	5.77	5.31	1.96
1.97	1406.14	288.09	146.96	97.00	40.36	25.36	18.47	14.52	11.96	10.17	8.84	7.82	7.02	6.36	5.81	5.35	1.97
1.98	1436.95	292.04	148.63	98.00	40.71	25.57	18.62	14.64	12.06	10.25	8.91	7.89	7.07	6.41	5.86	5.40	1.98
1.99	1468.24	296.01	150.31	99.00	41.07	25.78	18.77	14.75	12.15	10.33	8.98	7.95	7.12	6.46	5.90	5.44	1.99

$$F = 1 \times \left[1 + \frac{r}{100} \right]^n$$

Use of the table: the table shows the annual compound rate per cent of interest or growth ('r' in the formula) which, accumulating over the period shown at the head of a column (n), makes 1 unit increase to the amount shown in the column at each side of a line (F)
For example, an increase from 1 to 2.10 (a 110% increase), if achieved over 5 years will have resulted from an annual compound interest or growth rate of 16.00%

Interest rate or growth rate producing an accumulated amount from 1 unit compounded annually

F	months 3	months 6	months 9	years 1	years 2	years 3	years 4	years 5	years 6	years 7	years 8	years 9	years 10	years 11	years 12	years 13	n
2.00	1500.00	300.00	151.98	100.00	41.42	25.99	18.92	14.87	12.25	10.41	9.05	8.01	7.18	6.50	5.95	5.48	2.00
2.01	1532.24	304.01	153.67	101.00	41.77	26.20	19.07	14.98	12.34	10.49	9.12	8.07	7.23	6.55	5.99	5.52	2.01
2.02	1564.97	308.04	155.35	102.00	42.13	26.41	19.22	15.10	12.43	10.57	9.19	8.13	7.28	6.60	6.03	5.56	2.02
2.03	1598.18	312.09	157.04	103.00	42.48	26.62	19.36	15.21	12.53	10.64	9.25	8.18	7.34	6.65	6.08	5.60	2.03
2.04	1631.89	316.16	158.73	104.00	42.83	26.83	19.51	15.33	12.62	10.72	9.32	8.24	7.39	6.70	6.12	5.64	2.04
2.05	1666.10	320.25	160.42	105.00	43.18	27.03	19.66	15.44	12.71	10.80	9.39	8.30	7.44	6.74	6.16	5.68	2.05
2.06	1700.81	324.36	162.11	106.00	43.53	27.24	19.80	15.55	12.80	10.88	9.45	8.36	7.49	6.79	6.21	5.72	2.06
2.07	1736.04	328.49	163.81	107.00	43.87	27.45	19.95	15.66	12.89	10.95	9.52	8.42	7.55	6.84	6.25	5.76	2.07
2.08	1771.77	332.64	165.51	108.00	44.22	27.65	20.09	15.77	12.98	11.03	9.59	8.48	7.60	6.88	6.29	5.80	2.08
2.09	1808.03	336.81	167.22	109.00	44.57	27.85	20.24	15.89	13.07	11.11	9.65	8.54	7.65	6.93	6.34	5.83	2.09
2.10	1844.81	341.00	168.92	110.00	44.91	28.06	20.38	16.00	13.16	11.18	9.72	8.59	7.70	6.98	6.38	5.87	2.10
2.11	1882.12	345.21	170.63	111.00	45.26	28.26	20.52	16.11	13.25	11.26	9.78	8.65	7.75	7.02	6.42	5.91	2.11
2.12	1919.96	349.44	172.34	112.00	45.60	28.46	20.67	16.22	13.34	11.33	9.85	8.71	7.80	7.07	6.46	5.95	2.12
2.13	1958.35	353.69	174.06	113.00	45.95	28.66	20.81	16.33	13.43	11.41	9.91	8.76	7.85	7.12	6.50	5.99	2.13
2.14	1997.27	357.96	175.77	114.00	46.29	28.87	20.95	16.43	13.52	11.48	9.98	8.82	7.90	7.16	6.55	6.03	2.14
2.15	2036.75	362.25	177.49	115.00	46.63	29.07	21.09	16.54	13.61	11.56	10.04	8.88	7.96	7.21	6.59	6.07	2.15
2.16	2076.78	366.56	179.21	116.00	46.97	29.27	21.23	16.65	13.70	11.63	10.10	8.93	8.01	7.25	6.63	6.10	2.16
2.17	2117.37	370.89	180.94	117.00	47.31	29.47	21.37	16.76	13.78	11.70	10.17	8.99	8.06	7.30	6.67	6.14	2.17
2.18	2158.53	375.24	182.67	118.00	47.65	29.66	21.51	16.87	13.87	11.78	10.23	9.05	8.10	7.34	6.71	6.18	2.18
2.19	2200.26	379.61	184.40	119.00	47.99	29.86	21.65	16.97	13.96	11.85	10.29	9.10	8.15	7.39	6.75	6.22	2.19
2.20	2242.56	384.00	186.13	120.00	48.32	30.06	21.79	17.08	14.04	11.92	10.36	9.16	8.20	7.43	6.79	6.25	2.20
2.21	2285.44	388.41	187.87	121.00	48.66	30.26	21.93	17.19	14.13	12.00	10.42	9.21	8.25	7.48	6.83	6.29	2.21
2.22	2328.91	392.84	189.60	122.00	49.00	30.45	22.06	17.29	14.22	12.07	10.48	9.27	8.30	7.52	6.87	6.33	2.22
2.23	2372.97	397.29	191.34	123.00	49.33	30.65	22.20	17.40	14.30	12.14	10.54	9.32	8.35	7.56	6.91	6.36	2.23
2.24	2417.63	401.76	193.09	124.00	49.67	30.84	22.34	17.50	14.39	12.21	10.61	9.37	8.40	7.61	6.95	6.40	2.24
2.25	2462.89	406.25	194.83	125.00	50.00	31.04	22.47	17.61	14.47	12.28	10.67	9.43	8.45	7.65	6.99	6.44	2.25
2.26	2508.76	410.76	196.58	126.00	50.33	31.23	22.61	17.71	14.56	12.35	10.73	9.48	8.50	7.69	7.03	6.47	2.26
2.27	2555.24	415.29	198.33	127.00	50.67	31.42	22.75	17.82	14.64	12.42	10.79	9.54	8.54	7.74	7.07	6.51	2.27
2.28	2602.34	419.84	200.09	128.00	51.00	31.62	22.88	17.92	14.72	12.50	10.85	9.59	8.59	7.78	7.11	6.55	2.28
2.29	2650.06	424.41	201.84	129.00	51.33	31.81	23.02	18.02	14.81	12.57	10.91	9.64	8.64	7.82	7.15	6.58	2.29
2.30	2698.41	429.00	203.60	130.00	51.66	32.00	23.15	18.13	14.89	12.64	10.97	9.70	8.69	7.87	7.19	6.62	2.30
2.31	2747.40	433.61	205.36	131.00	51.99	32.19	23.28	18.23	14.97	12.71	11.03	9.75	8.73	7.91	7.23	6.65	2.31
2.32	2797.02	438.24	207.13	132.00	52.32	32.38	23.42	18.33	15.06	12.77	11.09	9.80	8.78	7.95	7.26	6.69	2.32
2.33	2847.30	442.89	208.89	133.00	52.64	32.57	23.55	18.43	15.14	12.84	11.15	9.85	8.83	7.99	7.30	6.72	2.33
2.34	2898.22	447.56	210.66	134.00	52.97	32.76	23.68	18.53	15.22	12.91	11.21	9.91	8.87	8.04	7.34	6.76	2.34
2.35	2949.80	452.25	212.43	135.00	53.30	32.95	23.81	18.64	15.30	12.98	11.27	9.96	8.92	8.08	7.38	6.79	2.35
2.36	3002.04	456.96	214.21	136.00	53.62	33.14	23.94	18.74	15.39	13.05	11.33	10.01	8.97	8.12	7.42	6.83	2.36
2.37	3054.96	461.69	215.98	137.00	53.95	33.33	24.08	18.84	15.47	13.12	11.39	10.06	9.01	8.16	7.46	6.86	2.37
2.38	3108.54	466.44	217.76	138.00	54.27	33.51	24.21	18.94	15.55	13.19	11.45	10.11	9.06	8.20	7.49	6.90	2.38
2.39	3162.81	471.21	219.54	139.00	54.60	33.70	24.34	19.04	15.63	13.25	11.51	10.17	9.10	8.24	7.53	6.93	2.39
2.40	3217.76	476.00	221.33	140.00	54.92	33.89	24.47	19.14	15.71	13.32	11.56	10.22	9.15	8.28	7.57	6.97	2.40
2.41	3273.40	480.81	223.11	141.00	55.24	34.07	24.60	19.23	15.79	13.39	11.62	10.27	9.19	8.33	7.61	7.00	2.41
2.42	3329.74	485.64	224.90	142.00	55.56	34.26	24.73	19.33	15.87	13.46	11.68	10.32	9.24	8.37	7.64	7.03	2.42
2.43	3386.78	490.49	226.69	143.00	55.88	34.44	24.85	19.43	15.95	13.52	11.74	10.37	9.29	8.41	7.68	7.07	2.43
2.44	3444.54	495.36	228.49	144.00	56.20	34.63	24.98	19.53	16.03	13.59	11.80	10.42	9.33	8.45	7.72	7.10	2.44
2.45	3503.00	500.25	230.28	145.00	56.52	34.81	25.11	19.63	16.11	13.66	11.85	10.47	9.37	8.49	7.75	7.14	2.45
2.46	3562.19	505.16	232.08	146.00	56.84	34.99	25.24	19.73	16.19	13.72	11.91	10.52	9.42	8.53	7.79	7.17	2.46
2.47	3622.10	510.09	233.88	147.00	57.16	35.18	25.36	19.82	16.27	13.79	11.97	10.57	9.46	8.57	7.83	7.20	2.47
2.48	3682.74	515.04	235.69	148.00	57.48	35.36	25.49	19.92	16.34	13.85	12.02	10.62	9.51	8.61	7.86	7.24	2.48
2.49	3744.12	520.01	237.49	149.00	57.80	35.54	25.62	20.02	16.42	13.92	12.08	10.67	9.55	8.65	7.90	7.27	2.49
2.50	3806.25	525.00	239.30	150.00	58.11	35.72	25.74	20.11	16.50	13.99	12.14	10.72	9.60	8.69	7.93	7.30	2.50
2.51	3869.13	530.01	241.11	151.00	58.43	35.90	25.87	20.21	16.58	14.05	12.19	10.77	9.64	8.73	7.97	7.34	2.51
2.52	3932.76	535.04	242.93	152.00	58.75	36.08	25.99	20.30	16.65	14.12	12.25	10.82	9.68	8.77	8.01	7.37	2.52
2.53	3997.15	540.09	244.74	153.00	59.06	36.26	26.12	20.40	16.73	14.18	12.30	10.86	9.73	8.80	8.04	7.40	2.53
2.54	4062.31	545.16	246.56	154.00	59.37	36.44	26.24	20.49	16.81	14.24	12.36	10.91	9.77	8.84	8.08	7.43	2.54

Use of the table: the table shows the annual compound rate per cent of interest or growth ('r' in the formula) which, accumulating over the period shown at the head of a column (n), makes 1 unit increase to the amount shown in the column at each side of a line (F).
For example, an increase from 1 to 2.60 (a 160% increase), if achieved over 5 years will have resulted from an annual compound interest or growth rate of 21.06%

$$F = 1 \times \left[1 + \frac{r}{100} \right]^n$$

Interest rates and growth rates

Interest rate or growth rate producing an accumulated amount from 1 unit compounded annually

F	months 3	months 6	months 9	years 1	years 2	years 3	years 4	years 5	years 6	years 7	years 8	years 9	years 10	years 11	years 12	years 13	n / F
2.55	4128.25	550.25	248.38	155.00	59.69	36.62	26.37	20.59	16.88	14.31	12.41	10.96	9.81	8.88	8.11	7.47	2.55
2.56	4194.97	555.36	250.20	156.00	60.00	36.80	26.49	20.68	16.96	14.37	12.47	11.01	9.86	8.92	8.15	7.50	2.56
2.57	4262.47	560.49	252.03	157.00	60.31	36.98	26.61	20.78	17.04	14.44	12.52	11.06	9.90	8.96	8.18	7.53	2.57
2.58	4330.77	565.64	253.86	158.00	60.62	37.15	26.74	20.87	17.11	14.50	12.58	11.11	9.94	9.00	8.22	7.56	2.58
2.59	4399.86	570.81	255.69	159.00	60.93	37.33	26.86	20.97	17.19	14.56	12.63	11.15	9.98	9.04	8.25	7.60	2.59
2.60	4469.76	576.00	257.52	160.00	61.25	37.51	26.98	21.06	17.26	14.63	12.69	11.20	10.03	9.07	8.29	7.63	2.60
2.61	4540.47	581.21	259.35	161.00	61.55	37.68	27.10	21.15	17.34	14.69	12.74	11.25	10.07	9.11	8.32	7.66	2.61
2.62	4612.00	586.44	261.19	162.00	61.86	37.86	27.23	21.24	17.41	14.75	12.79	11.30	10.11	9.15	8.36	7.69	2.62
2.63	4684.35	591.69	263.03	163.00	62.17	38.03	27.35	21.34	17.49	14.81	12.85	11.34	10.15	9.19	8.39	7.72	2.63
2.64	4757.53	596.96	264.87	164.00	62.48	38.21	27.47	21.43	17.56	14.88	12.90	11.39	10.19	9.23	8.43	7.75	2.64
2.65	4831.55	602.25	266.71	165.00	62.79	38.38	27.59	21.52	17.64	14.94	12.96	11.44	10.24	9.26	8.46	7.78	2.65
2.66	4906.41	607.56	268.56	166.00	63.10	38.56	27.71	21.61	17.71	15.00	13.01	11.48	10.28	9.30	8.49	7.82	2.66
2.67	4982.12	612.89	270.14	167.00	63.40	38.73	27.83	21.70	17.78	15.06	13.06	11.53	10.32	9.34	8.53	7.85	2.67
2.68	5058.69	618.24	272.26	168.00	63.71	38.90	27.95	21.79	17.86	15.12	13.11	11.58	10.36	9.38	8.56	7.88	2.68
2.69	5136.11	623.61	274.11	169.00	64.01	39.08	28.07	21.89	17.93	15.18	13.17	11.62	10.40	9.41	8.60	7.91	2.69
2.70	5214.41	629.00	275.97	170.00	64.32	39.25	28.19	21.98	18.00	15.25	13.22	11.67	10.44	9.45	8.63	7.94	2.70
2.71	5293.58	634.41	277.83	171.00	64.62	39.42	28.30	22.07	18.08	15.31	13.27	11.71	10.48	9.49	8.66	7.97	2.71
2.72	5373.63	639.84	279.69	172.00	64.92	39.59	28.42	22.16	18.15	15.37	13.32	11.76	10.52	9.52	8.70	8.00	2.72
2.73	5454.57	645.29	281.55	173.00	65.23	39.76	28.54	22.25	18.22	15.43	13.38	11.81	10.56	9.56	8.73	8.03	2.73
2.74	5536.41	650.76	283.41	174.00	65.53	39.93	28.66	22.33	18.29	15.49	13.43	11.85	10.61	9.60	8.76	8.06	2.74
2.75	5619.14	656.25	285.28	175.00	65.83	40.10	28.78	22.42	18.36	15.55	13.48	11.90	10.65	9.63	8.80	8.09	2.75
2.76	5702.78	661.76	287.15	176.00	66.13	40.27	28.89	22.51	18.44	15.61	13.53	11.94	10.69	9.67	8.83	8.12	2.76
2.77	5787.34	667.29	289.02	177.00	66.43	40.44	29.01	22.60	18.51	15.67	13.58	11.99	10.73	9.70	8.86	8.15	2.77
2.78	5872.82	672.84	290.89	178.00	66.73	40.61	29.13	22.69	18.58	15.73	13.63	12.03	10.77	9.74	8.89	8.18	2.78
2.79	5959.22	678.41	292.77	179.00	67.03	40.78	29.24	22.78	18.65	15.79	13.68	12.08	10.81	9.78	8.93	8.21	2.79
2.80	6046.56	684.00	294.65	180.00	67.33	40.95	29.36	22.87	18.72	15.85	13.74	12.12	10.84	9.81	8.96	8.24	2.80
2.85	6497.50	712.25	304.07	185.00	68.82	41.78	29.93	23.30	19.07	16.14	13.99	12.34	11.04	9.99	9.12	8.39	2.85
2.90	6972.81	741.00	313.55	190.00	70.29	42.60	30.50	23.73	19.42	16.43	14.24	12.56	11.23	10.16	9.28	8.53	2.90
2.95	7473.35	770.25	323.09	195.00	71.76	43.42	31.06	24.16	19.76	16.71	14.48	12.77	11.42	10.33	9.43	8.68	2.95
3.00	8000.00	800.00	332.67	200.00	73.21	44.22	31.61	24.57	20.09	16.99	14.72	12.98	11.61	10.50	9.59	8.82	3.00
3.05	8553.65	830.25	342.32	205.00	74.64	45.02	32.15	24.99	20.42	17.27	14.96	13.19	11.80	10.67	9.74	8.96	3.05
3.10	9135.21	861.00	352.01	210.00	76.07	45.81	32.69	25.39	20.75	17.54	15.19	13.40	11.98	10.83	9.89	9.09	3.10
3.15	9745.60	892.25	361.76	215.00	77.48	46.59	33.22	25.79	21.07	17.81	15.42	13.60	12.16	10.99	10.03	9.23	3.15
3.20	10385.76	924.00	371.56	220.00	78.89	47.36	33.75	26.19	21.39	18.08	15.65	13.80	12.33	11.15	10.18	9.36	3.20
3.25	11056.64	956.25	381.41	225.00	80.28	48.12	34.27	26.58	21.71	18.34	15.87	13.99	12.51	11.31	10.32	9.49	3.25
3.30	11759.21	989.00	391.31	230.00	81.66	48.88	34.78	26.97	22.02	18.60	16.10	14.19	12.68	11.46	10.46	9.62	3.30
3.35	12494.45	1022.25	401.26	235.00	83.03	49.63	35.29	27.35	22.32	18.85	16.31	14.38	12.85	11.62	10.60	9.75	3.35
3.40	13263.36	1056.00	411.26	240.00	84.39	50.37	35.79	27.73	22.63	19.10	16.53	14.57	13.02	11.77	10.74	9.87	3.40
3.45	14066.95	1090.25	421.31	245.00	85.74	51.10	36.29	28.10	22.92	19.35	16.74	14.75	13.18	11.92	10.87	9.99	3.45
3.50	14906.25	1125.00	431.40	250.00	87.08	51.83	36.78	28.47	23.22	19.60	16.95	14.93	13.35	12.06	11.00	10.12	3.50
3.60	16696.16	1196.00	451.74	260.00	89.74	53.26	37.74	29.20	23.80	20.08	17.36	15.30	13.67	12.35	11.26	10.36	3.60
3.70	18641.61	1269.00	472.27	270.00	92.35	54.67	38.69	29.91	24.37	20.55	17.77	15.65	13.98	12.63	11.52	10.59	3.70
3.80	20751.36	1344.00	492.99	280.00	94.94	56.05	39.62	30.60	24.92	21.01	18.16	15.99	14.28	12.90	11.77	10.82	3.80
3.90	23034.41	1421.00	513.88	290.00	97.48	57.41	40.53	31.28	25.46	21.46	18.54	16.33	14.58	13.17	12.01	11.04	3.90
4.00	25500.00	1500.00	534.96	300.00	100.00	58.74	41.42	31.95	25.99	21.90	18.92	16.65	14.87	13.43	12.25	11.25	4.00
4.10	28157.61	1581.00	556.21	310.00	102.48	60.05	42.30	32.60	26.51	22.33	19.29	16.97	15.15	13.69	12.48	11.46	4.10
4.20	31016.96	1664.00	577.64	320.00	104.94	61.34	43.16	33.24	27.02	22.75	19.65	17.29	15.43	13.94	12.70	11.67	4.20
4.30	34088.01	1749.00	599.24	330.00	107.36	62.61	44.00	33.87	27.52	23.17	20.00	17.59	15.70	14.18	12.92	11.87	4.30
4.40	37380.96	1836.00	621.00	340.00	109.76	63.86	44.83	34.49	28.01	23.57	20.35	17.89	15.97	14.42	13.14	12.07	4.40
4.50	40906.25	1925.00	642.93	350.00	112.13	65.10	45.65	35.10	28.49	23.97	20.68	18.19	16.23	14.65	13.35	12.27	4.50
4.60	44674.56	2016.00	665.03	360.00	114.48	66.31	46.45	35.69	28.96	24.36	21.02	18.48	16.49	14.88	13.56	12.46	4.60
4.70	48696.81	2109.00	687.28	370.00	116.79	67.51	47.24	36.28	29.42	24.74	21.34	18.76	16.74	15.11	13.76	12.64	4.70
4.80	52984.16	2204.00	709.70	380.00	119.09	68.69	48.02	36.85	29.88	25.12	21.66	19.04	16.98	15.33	13.96	12.82	4.80
4.90	57548.01	2301.00	732.26	390.00	121.36	69.85	48.78	37.42	30.33	25.49	21.98	19.31	17.22	15.54	14.16	13.00	4.90
5.00	62400.00	2400.00	754.99	400.00	123.61	71.00	49.53	37.97	30.77	25.85	22.28	19.58	17.46	15.76	14.35	13.18	5.00

$$F = 1 \times \left[1 + \frac{r}{100}\right]^n$$

Use of the table: the table shows the annual compound rate per cent of interest or growth ('r' in the formula) which, accumulating over the period shown at the head of a column (n) makes 1 unit increase (or decrease) to the amount shown in the column at each side of a line (F).
For example, an increase from 1 to 1.10 (a 10% increase), if achieved over 15 years will have resulted from an annual compound interest or growth rate of 0.64%

Interest rate or growth rate producing an accumulated amount from 1 unit compounded annually

F	years 14	years 15	years 16	years 17	years 18	years 19	years 20	years 21	years 22	years 23	years 24	years 25	years 30	years 35	years 40	years 45	years 50	F
0.90	−0.75	−0.70	−0.66	−0.62	−0.58	−0.55	−0.53	−0.50	−0.48	−0.46	−0.44	−0.42	−0.35	−0.30	−0.26	−0.23	−0.21	0.90
0.91	−0.67	−0.63	−0.59	−0.55	−0.52	−0.50	−0.47	−0.45	−0.43	−0.41	−0.39	−0.38	−0.31	−0.27	−0.24	−0.21	−0.19	0.91
0.92	−0.59	−0.55	−0.52	−0.49	−0.46	−0.44	−0.42	−0.40	−0.38	−0.36	−0.35	−0.33	−0.28	−0.24	−0.21	−0.19	−0.17	0.92
0.93	−0.52	−0.48	−0.45	−0.43	−0.40	−0.38	−0.36	−0.34	−0.33	−0.32	−0.30	−0.29	−0.24	−0.21	−0.18	−0.16	−0.15	0.93
0.94	−0.44	−0.41	−0.39	−0.36	−0.34	−0.33	−0.31	−0.29	−0.28	−0.27	−0.26	−0.25	−0.21	−0.18	−0.15	−0.14	−0.12	0.94
0.95	−0.37	−0.34	−0.32	−0.30	−0.28	−0.27	−0.26	−0.24	−0.23	−0.22	−0.21	−0.20	−0.17	−0.15	−0.13	−0.11	−0.10	0.95
0.96	−0.29	−0.27	−0.25	−0.24	−0.23	−0.21	−0.20	−0.19	−0.19	−0.18	−0.17	−0.16	−0.14	−0.12	−0.10	−0.09	−0.08	0.96
0.97	−0.22	−0.20	−0.19	−0.18	−0.17	−0.16	−0.15	−0.14	−0.14	−0.13	−0.13	−0.12	−0.10	−0.09	−0.08	−0.07	−0.06	0.97
0.98	−0.14	−0.13	−0.13	−0.12	−0.11	−0.11	−0.10	−0.10	−0.09	−0.09	−0.08	−0.08	−0.07	−0.06	−0.05	−0.04	−0.04	0.98
0.99	−0.07	−0.07	−0.06	−0.06	−0.06	−0.05	−0.05	−0.05	−0.05	−0.04	−0.04	−0.04	−0.03	−0.03	−0.03	−0.02	−0.02	0.99
1.00	0.00	0.00	0.00	0.00	0.00	0.00	0.00	0.00	0.00	0.00	0.00	0.00	0.00	0.00	0.00	0.00	0.00	1.00
1.01	0.07	0.07	0.06	0.06	0.06	0.05	0.05	0.05	0.05	0.04	0.04	0.04	0.03	0.03	0.02	0.02	0.02	1.01
1.02	0.14	0.13	0.12	0.12	0.11	0.10	0.10	0.09	0.09	0.09	0.08	0.08	0.07	0.06	0.05	0.04	0.04	1.02
1.03	0.21	0.20	0.18	0.17	0.16	0.16	0.15	0.14	0.13	0.13	0.12	0.12	0.10	0.08	0.07	0.07	0.06	1.03
1.04	0.28	0.26	0.25	0.23	0.22	0.21	0.20	0.19	0.18	0.17	0.16	0.16	0.13	0.11	0.10	0.09	0.08	1.04
1.05	0.35	0.33	0.31	0.29	0.27	0.26	0.24	0.23	0.22	0.21	0.20	0.20	0.16	0.14	0.12	0.11	0.10	1.05
1.06	0.42	0.39	0.36	0.34	0.32	0.31	0.29	0.28	0.27	0.25	0.24	0.23	0.19	0.17	0.15	0.13	0.12	1.06
1.07	0.48	0.45	0.42	0.40	0.38	0.36	0.34	0.32	0.31	0.29	0.28	0.27	0.23	0.19	0.17	0.15	0.14	1.07
1.08	0.55	0.51	0.48	0.45	0.43	0.41	0.39	0.37	0.35	0.34	0.32	0.31	0.26	0.22	0.19	0.17	0.15	1.08
1.09	0.62	0.58	0.54	0.51	0.48	0.45	0.43	0.41	0.39	0.38	0.36	0.35	0.29	0.25	0.22	0.19	0.17	1.09
1.10	0.68	0.64	0.60	0.56	0.53	0.50	0.48	0.45	0.43	0.42	0.40	0.38	0.32	0.27	0.24	0.21	0.19	1.10
1.11	0.75	0.70	0.65	0.62	0.58	0.55	0.52	0.50	0.48	0.45	0.44	0.42	0.35	0.30	0.26	0.23	0.21	1.11
1.12	0.81	0.76	0.71	0.67	0.63	0.60	0.57	0.54	0.52	0.49	0.47	0.45	0.38	0.32	0.28	0.25	0.23	1.12
1.13	0.88	0.82	0.77	0.72	0.68	0.65	0.61	0.58	0.56	0.53	0.51	0.49	0.41	0.35	0.31	0.27	0.24	1.13
1.14	0.94	0.88	0.82	0.77	0.73	0.69	0.66	0.63	0.60	0.57	0.55	0.53	0.44	0.38	0.33	0.29	0.26	1.14
1.15	1.00	0.94	0.88	0.83	0.78	0.74	0.70	0.67	0.64	0.61	0.58	0.56	0.47	0.40	0.35	0.31	0.28	1.15
1.16	1.07	0.99	0.93	0.88	0.83	0.78	0.74	0.71	0.68	0.65	0.62	0.60	0.50	0.42	0.37	0.33	0.30	1.16
1.17	1.13	1.05	0.99	0.93	0.88	0.83	0.79	0.75	0.72	0.68	0.66	0.63	0.52	0.45	0.39	0.35	0.31	1.17
1.18	1.19	1.11	1.04	0.98	0.92	0.87	0.83	0.79	0.76	0.72	0.69	0.66	0.55	0.47	0.41	0.37	0.33	1.18
1.19	1.25	1.17	1.09	1.03	0.97	0.92	0.87	0.83	0.79	0.76	0.73	0.70	0.58	0.50	0.44	0.39	0.35	1.19
1.20	1.31	1.22	1.15	1.08	1.02	0.96	0.92	0.87	0.83	0.80	0.76	0.73	0.61	0.52	0.46	0.41	0.37	1.20
1.21	1.37	1.28	1.20	1.13	1.06	1.01	0.96	0.91	0.87	0.83	0.80	0.77	0.64	0.55	0.48	0.42	0.38	1.21
1.22	1.43	1.33	1.25	1.18	1.11	1.05	1.00	0.95	0.91	0.87	0.83	0.80	0.67	0.57	0.50	0.44	0.40	1.22
1.23	1.49	1.39	1.30	1.23	1.16	1.10	1.04	0.99	0.95	0.90	0.87	0.83	0.69	0.59	0.52	0.46	0.41	1.23
1.24	1.55	1.44	1.35	1.27	1.20	1.14	1.08	1.03	0.98	0.94	0.90	0.86	0.72	0.62	0.54	0.48	0.43	1.24
1.25	1.61	1.50	1.40	1.32	1.25	1.18	1.12	1.07	1.02	0.97	0.93	0.90	0.75	0.64	0.56	0.50	0.45	1.25
1.26	1.66	1.55	1.45	1.37	1.29	1.22	1.16	1.11	1.06	1.01	0.97	0.93	0.77	0.66	0.58	0.51	0.46	1.26
1.27	1.72	1.61	1.51	1.42	1.34	1.27	1.20	1.14	1.09	1.04	1.00	0.96	0.80	0.69	0.60	0.53	0.48	1.27
1.28	1.78	1.66	1.55	1.46	1.38	1.31	1.24	1.18	1.13	1.08	1.03	0.99	0.83	0.71	0.62	0.55	0.49	1.28
1.29	1.84	1.71	1.60	1.51	1.42	1.35	1.28	1.22	1.16	1.11	1.07	1.02	0.85	0.73	0.64	0.57	0.51	1.29
1.30	1.89	1.76	1.65	1.56	1.47	1.39	1.32	1.26	1.20	1.15	1.10	1.05	0.88	0.75	0.66	0.58	0.53	1.30
1.31	1.95	1.82	1.70	1.60	1.51	1.43	1.36	1.29	1.23	1.18	1.13	1.09	0.90	0.77	0.68	0.60	0.54	1.31
1.32	2.00	1.87	1.75	1.65	1.55	1.47	1.40	1.33	1.27	1.21	1.16	1.12	0.93	0.80	0.70	0.62	0.56	1.32
1.33	2.06	1.92	1.80	1.69	1.60	1.51	1.44	1.37	1.30	1.25	1.20	1.15	0.96	0.82	0.72	0.64	0.57	1.33
1.34	2.11	1.97	1.85	1.74	1.64	1.55	1.47	1.40	1.34	1.28	1.23	1.18	0.98	0.84	0.73	0.65	0.59	1.34
1.35	2.17	2.02	1.89	1.78	1.68	1.59	1.51	1.44	1.37	1.31	1.26	1.21	1.01	0.86	0.75	0.67	0.60	1.35
1.36	2.22	2.07	1.94	1.83	1.72	1.63	1.55	1.47	1.41	1.35	1.29	1.24	1.03	0.88	0.77	0.69	0.62	1.36
1.37	2.27	2.12	1.99	1.87	1.76	1.67	1.59	1.51	1.44	1.38	1.32	1.27	1.05	0.90	0.79	0.70	0.63	1.37
1.38	2.33	2.17	2.03	1.91	1.81	1.71	1.62	1.55	1.47	1.41	1.35	1.30	1.08	0.92	0.81	0.72	0.65	1.38
1.39	2.38	2.22	2.08	1.96	1.85	1.75	1.66	1.58	1.51	1.44	1.38	1.33	1.10	0.95	0.83	0.73	0.66	1.39
1.40	2.43	2.27	2.13	2.00	1.89	1.79	1.70	1.62	1.54	1.47	1.41	1.35	1.13	0.97	0.84	0.75	0.68	1.40
1.41	2.48	2.32	2.17	2.04	1.93	1.82	1.73	1.65	1.57	1.51	1.44	1.38	1.15	0.99	0.86	0.77	0.69	1.41
1.42	2.54	2.37	2.22	2.08	1.97	1.86	1.77	1.68	1.61	1.54	1.47	1.41	1.18	1.01	0.88	0.78	0.70	1.42
1.43	2.59	2.41	2.26	2.13	2.01	1.90	1.80	1.72	1.64	1.57	1.50	1.44	1.20	1.03	0.90	0.80	0.72	1.43
1.44	2.64	2.46	2.31	2.17	2.05	1.94	1.84	1.75	1.67	1.60	1.53	1.47	1.22	1.05	0.92	0.81	0.73	1.44

Use of the table: the table shows the annual compound rate per cent of interest or growth ('r' in the formula) which, accumulating over the period shown at the head of a column (n), makes 1 unit increase to the amount shown in the column at each side of a line (F).
For example, an increase from 1 to 1.50 (a 50% increase), if achieved over 15 years will have resulted from an annual compound interest or growth rate of 2.74%

$$F = 1 \times \left[1 + \frac{r}{100} \right]^n$$

Interest rates and growth rates

Interest rate or growth rate producing an accumulated amount from 1 unit compounded annually

F	years 14	years 15	years 16	years 17	years 18	years 19	years 20	years 21	years 22	years 23	years 24	years 25	years 30	years 35	years 40	years 45	years 50	n / F
1.45	2.69	2.51	2.35	2.21	2.09	1.97	1.88	1.79	1.70	1.63	1.56	1.50	1.25	1.07	0.93	0.83	0.75	1.45
1.46	2.74	2.56	2.39	2.25	2.12	2.01	1.91	1.82	1.74	1.66	1.59	1.53	1.27	1.09	0.95	0.84	0.76	1.46
1.47	2.79	2.60	2.44	2.29	2.16	2.05	1.94	1.85	1.77	1.69	1.62	1.55	1.29	1.11	0.97	0.86	0.77	1.47
1.48	2.84	2.65	2.48	2.33	2.20	2.08	1.98	1.88	1.80	1.72	1.65	1.58	1.32	1.13	0.98	0.88	0.79	1.48
1.49	2.89	2.69	2.52	2.37	2.24	2.12	2.01	1.92	1.83	1.75	1.68	1.61	1.34	1.15	1.00	0.89	0.80	1.49
1.50	2.94	2.74	2.57	2.41	2.28	2.16	2.05	1.95	1.86	1.78	1.70	1.64	1.36	1.17	1.02	0.91	0.81	1.50
1.51	2.99	2.79	2.61	2.45	2.32	2.19	2.08	1.98	1.89	1.81	1.73	1.66	1.38	1.18	1.04	0.92	0.83	1.51
1.52	3.04	2.83	2.65	2.49	2.35	2.23	2.12	2.01	1.92	1.84	1.76	1.69	1.41	1.20	1.05	0.93	0.84	1.52
1.53	3.08	2.88	2.69	2.53	2.39	2.26	2.15	2.05	1.95	1.87	1.79	1.72	1.43	1.22	1.07	0.95	0.85	1.53
1.54	3.13	2.92	2.74	2.57	2.43	2.30	2.18	2.08	1.98	1.90	1.82	1.74	1.45	1.24	1.09	0.96	0.87	1.54
1.55	3.18	2.96	2.78	2.61	2.46	2.33	2.22	2.11	2.01	1.92	1.84	1.77	1.47	1.26	1.10	0.98	0.88	1.55
1.56	3.23	3.01	2.82	2.65	2.50	2.37	2.25	2.14	2.04	1.95	1.87	1.79	1.49	1.28	1.12	0.99	0.89	1.56
1.57	3.27	3.05	2.86	2.69	2.54	2.40	2.28	2.17	2.07	1.98	1.90	1.82	1.51	1.30	1.13	1.01	0.91	1.57
1.58	3.32	3.10	2.90	2.73	2.57	2.44	2.31	2.20	2.10	2.01	1.92	1.85	1.54	1.32	1.15	1.02	0.92	1.58
1.59	3.37	3.14	2.94	2.77	2.61	2.47	2.35	2.23	2.13	2.04	1.95	1.87	1.56	1.33	1.17	1.04	0.93	1.59
1.60	3.41	3.18	2.98	2.80	2.65	2.50	2.38	2.26	2.16	2.06	1.98	1.90	1.58	1.35	1.18	1.05	0.94	1.60
1.61	3.46	3.23	3.02	2.84	2.68	2.54	2.41	2.29	2.19	2.09	2.00	1.92	1.60	1.37	1.20	1.06	0.96	1.61
1.62	3.51	3.27	3.06	2.88	2.72	2.57	2.44	2.32	2.22	2.12	2.03	1.95	1.62	1.39	1.21	1.08	0.97	1.62
1.63	3.55	3.31	3.10	2.92	2.75	2.60	2.47	2.35	2.25	2.15	2.06	1.97	1.64	1.41	1.23	1.09	0.98	1.63
1.64	3.60	3.35	3.14	2.95	2.79	2.64	2.50	2.38	2.27	2.17	2.08	2.00	1.66	1.42	1.24	1.11	0.99	1.64
1.65	3.64	3.39	3.18	2.99	2.82	2.67	2.54	2.41	2.30	2.20	2.11	2.02	1.68	1.44	1.26	1.12	1.01	1.65
1.66	3.69	3.44	3.22	3.03	2.86	2.70	2.57	2.44	2.33	2.23	2.13	2.05	1.70	1.46	1.28	1.13	1.02	1.66
1.67	3.73	3.48	3.26	3.06	2.89	2.74	2.60	2.47	2.36	2.25	2.16	2.07	1.72	1.48	1.29	1.15	1.03	1.67
1.68	3.78	3.52	3.30	3.10	2.92	2.77	2.63	2.50	2.39	2.28	2.19	2.10	1.74	1.49	1.31	1.16	1.04	1.68
1.69	3.82	3.56	3.33	3.13	2.96	2.80	2.66	2.53	2.41	2.31	2.21	2.12	1.76	1.51	1.32	1.17	1.05	1.69
1.70	3.86	3.60	3.37	3.17	2.99	2.83	2.69	2.56	2.44	2.33	2.24	2.15	1.78	1.53	1.34	1.19	1.07	1.70
1.71	3.91	3.64	3.41	3.21	3.03	2.86	2.72	2.59	2.47	2.36	2.26	2.17	1.80	1.54	1.35	1.20	1.08	1.71
1.72	3.95	3.68	3.45	3.24	3.06	2.90	2.75	2.62	2.50	2.39	2.29	2.19	1.82	1.56	1.37	1.21	1.09	1.72
1.73	3.99	3.72	3.49	3.28	3.09	2.93	2.78	2.64	2.52	2.41	2.31	2.22	1.84	1.58	1.38	1.23	1.10	1.73
1.74	4.04	3.76	3.52	3.31	3.12	2.96	2.81	2.67	2.55	2.44	2.33	2.24	1.86	1.60	1.39	1.24	1.11	1.74
1.75	4.08	3.80	3.56	3.35	3.16	2.99	2.84	2.70	2.58	2.46	2.36	2.26	1.88	1.61	1.41	1.25	1.13	1.75
1.76	4.12	3.84	3.60	3.38	3.19	3.02	2.87	2.73	2.60	2.49	2.38	2.29	1.90	1.63	1.42	1.26	1.14	1.76
1.77	4.16	3.88	3.63	3.42	3.22	3.05	2.90	2.76	2.63	2.51	2.41	2.31	1.92	1.64	1.44	1.28	1.15	1.77
1.78	4.20	3.92	3.67	3.45	3.26	3.08	2.93	2.78	2.66	2.54	2.43	2.33	1.94	1.66	1.45	1.29	1.16	1.78
1.79	4.25	3.96	3.71	3.48	3.29	3.11	2.95	2.81	2.68	2.56	2.46	2.36	1.96	1.68	1.47	1.30	1.17	1.79
1.80	4.29	4.00	3.74	3.52	3.32	3.14	2.98	2.84	2.71	2.59	2.48	2.38	1.98	1.69	1.48	1.31	1.18	1.80
1.81	4.33	4.03	3.78	3.55	3.35	3.17	3.01	2.87	2.73	2.61	2.50	2.40	2.00	1.71	1.49	1.33	1.19	1.81
1.82	4.37	4.07	3.81	3.59	3.38	3.20	3.04	2.89	2.76	2.64	2.53	2.42	2.02	1.73	1.51	1.34	1.20	1.82
1.83	4.41	4.11	3.85	3.62	3.41	3.23	3.07	2.92	2.78	2.66	2.55	2.45	2.03	1.74	1.52	1.35	1.22	1.83
1.84	4.45	4.15	3.88	3.65	3.45	3.26	3.10	2.95	2.81	2.69	2.57	2.47	2.05	1.76	1.54	1.36	1.23	1.84
1.85	4.49	4.19	3.92	3.69	3.48	3.29	3.12	2.97	2.84	2.71	2.60	2.49	2.07	1.77	1.55	1.38	1.24	1.85
1.86	4.53	4.22	3.95	3.72	3.51	3.32	3.15	3.00	2.86	2.73	2.62	2.51	2.09	1.79	1.56	1.39	1.25	1.86
1.87	4.57	4.26	3.99	3.75	3.54	3.35	3.18	3.03	2.89	2.76	2.64	2.54	2.11	1.80	1.58	1.40	1.26	1.87
1.88	4.61	4.30	4.02	3.78	3.57	3.38	3.21	3.05	2.91	2.78	2.67	2.56	2.13	1.82	1.59	1.41	1.27	1.88
1.89	4.65	4.34	4.06	3.82	3.60	3.41	3.23	3.08	2.94	2.81	2.69	2.58	2.14	1.84	1.60	1.42	1.28	1.89
1.90	4.69	4.37	4.09	3.85	3.63	3.44	3.26	3.10	2.96	2.83	2.71	2.60	2.16	1.85	1.62	1.44	1.29	1.90
1.91	4.73	4.41	4.13	3.88	3.66	3.46	3.29	3.13	2.99	2.85	2.73	2.62	2.18	1.87	1.63	1.45	1.30	1.91
1.92	4.77	4.44	4.16	3.91	3.69	3.49	3.32	3.16	3.01	2.88	2.76	2.64	2.20	1.88	1.64	1.46	1.31	1.92
1.93	4.81	4.48	4.20	3.94	3.72	3.52	3.34	3.18	3.03	2.90	2.78	2.66	2.22	1.90	1.66	1.47	1.32	1.93
1.94	4.85	4.52	4.23	3.98	3.75	3.55	3.37	3.21	3.06	2.92	2.80	2.69	2.23	1.91	1.67	1.48	1.33	1.94
1.95	4.89	4.55	4.26	4.01	3.78	3.58	3.40	3.23	3.08	2.95	2.82	2.71	2.25	1.93	1.68	1.50	1.34	1.95
1.96	4.92	4.59	4.30	4.04	3.81	3.61	3.42	3.26	3.11	2.97	2.84	2.73	2.27	1.94	1.70	1.51	1.35	1.96
1.97	4.96	4.62	4.33	4.07	3.84	3.63	3.45	3.28	3.13	2.99	2.87	2.75	2.29	1.96	1.71	1.52	1.37	1.97
1.98	5.00	4.66	4.36	4.10	3.87	3.66	3.47	3.31	3.15	3.01	2.89	2.77	2.30	1.97	1.72	1.53	1.38	1.98
1.99	5.04	4.69	4.39	4.13	3.90	3.69	3.50	3.33	3.18	3.04	2.91	2.79	2.32	1.99	1.74	1.54	1.39	1.99

Interest rates
and growth rates

$$F = 1 \times \left[1 + \frac{r}{100}\right]^n$$

Use of the table: the table shows the annual compound rate per cent of interest or growth ('r' in the formula) which, accumulating over the period shown at the head of a column (n), makes 1 unit increase to the amount shown in the column at each side of a line (F).
For example, an increase from 1 to 2.10 (a 110% increase), if achieved over 15 years will have resulted from an annual compound interest or growth rate of 5.07%

Interest rate or growth rate producing an accumulated amount from 1 unit compounded annually

F	years 14	years 15	years 16	years 17	years 18	years 19	years 20	years 21	years 22	years 23	years 24	years 25	years 30	years 35	years 40	years 45	years 50	F
2.00	5.08	4.73	4.43	4.16	3.93	3.72	3.53	3.36	3.20	3.06	2.93	2.81	2.34	2.00	1.75	1.55	1.40	2.00
2.01	5.11	4.76	4.46	4.19	3.95	3.74	3.55	3.38	3.22	3.08	2.95	2.83	2.35	2.01	1.76	1.56	1.41	2.01
2.02	5.15	4.80	4.49	4.22	3.98	3.77	3.58	3.40	3.25	3.10	2.97	2.85	2.37	2.03	1.77	1.57	1.42	2.02
2.03	5.19	4.83	4.52	4.25	4.01	3.80	3.60	3.43	3.27	3.13	2.99	2.87	2.39	2.04	1.79	1.59	1.43	2.03
2.04	5.22	4.87	4.56	4.28	4.04	3.82	3.63	3.45	3.29	3.15	3.02	2.89	2.40	2.06	1.80	1.60	1.44	2.04
2.05	5.26	4.90	4.59	4.31	4.07	3.85	3.65	3.48	3.32	3.17	3.04	2.91	2.42	2.07	1.81	1.61	1.45	2.05
2.06	5.30	4.94	4.62	4.34	4.10	3.88	3.68	3.50	3.34	3.19	3.06	2.93	2.44	2.09	1.82	1.62	1.46	2.06
2.07	5.33	4.97	4.65	4.37	4.12	3.90	3.70	3.53	3.36	3.21	3.08	2.95	2.45	2.10	1.84	1.63	1.47	2.07
2.08	5.37	5.00	4.68	4.40	4.15	3.93	3.73	3.55	3.38	3.24	3.10	2.97	2.47	2.11	1.85	1.64	1.48	2.08
2.09	5.41	5.04	4.72	4.43	4.18	3.96	3.75	3.57	3.41	3.26	3.12	2.99	2.49	2.13	1.86	1.65	1.49	2.09
2.10	5.44	5.07	4.75	4.46	4.21	3.98	3.78	3.60	3.43	3.28	3.14	3.01	2.50	2.14	1.87	1.66	1.49	2.10
2.11	5.48	5.10	4.78	4.49	4.24	4.01	3.80	3.62	3.45	3.30	3.16	3.03	2.52	2.16	1.88	1.67	1.50	2.11
2.12	5.51	5.14	4.81	4.52	4.26	4.03	3.83	3.64	3.47	3.32	3.18	3.05	2.54	2.17	1.90	1.68	1.51	2.12
2.13	5.55	5.17	4.84	4.55	4.29	4.06	3.85	3.67	3.50	3.34	3.20	3.07	2.55	2.18	1.91	1.69	1.52	2.13
2.14	5.58	5.20	4.87	4.58	4.32	4.09	3.88	3.69	3.52	3.36	3.22	3.09	2.57	2.20	1.92	1.71	1.53	2.14
2.15	5.62	5.24	4.90	4.61	4.34	4.11	3.90	3.71	3.54	3.38	3.24	3.11	2.58	2.21	1.93	1.72	1.54	2.15
2.16	5.65	5.27	4.93	4.63	4.37	4.14	3.93	3.74	3.56	3.40	3.26	3.13	2.60	2.22	1.94	1.73	1.55	2.16
2.17	5.69	5.30	4.96	4.66	4.40	4.16	3.95	3.76	3.58	3.43	3.28	3.15	2.62	2.24	1.96	1.74	1.56	2.17
2.18	5.72	5.33	4.99	4.69	4.42	4.19	3.97	3.78	3.61	3.45	3.30	3.17	2.63	2.25	1.97	1.75	1.57	2.18
2.19	5.76	5.36	5.02	4.72	4.45	4.21	4.00	3.80	3.63	3.47	3.32	3.19	2.65	2.26	1.98	1.76	1.58	2.19
2.20	5.79	5.40	5.05	4.75	4.48	4.24	4.02	3.83	3.65	3.49	3.34	3.20	2.66	2.28	1.99	1.77	1.59	2.20
2.21	5.83	5.43	5.08	4.78	4.50	4.26	4.04	3.85	3.67	3.51	3.36	3.22	2.68	2.29	2.00	1.78	1.60	2.21
2.22	5.86	5.46	5.11	4.80	4.53	4.29	4.07	3.87	3.69	3.53	3.38	3.24	2.69	2.30	2.01	1.79	1.61	2.22
2.23	5.90	5.49	5.14	4.83	4.56	4.31	4.09	3.89	3.71	3.55	3.40	3.26	2.71	2.32	2.03	1.80	1.62	2.23
2.24	5.93	5.52	5.17	4.86	4.58	4.34	4.11	3.92	3.73	3.57	3.42	3.28	2.72	2.33	2.04	1.81	1.63	2.24
2.25	5.96	5.56	5.20	4.89	4.61	4.36	4.14	3.94	3.75	3.59	3.44	3.30	2.74	2.34	2.05	1.82	1.64	2.25
2.26	6.00	5.59	5.23	4.91	4.63	4.38	4.16	3.96	3.78	3.61	3.46	3.32	2.76	2.36	2.06	1.83	1.64	2.26
2.27	6.03	5.62	5.26	4.94	4.66	4.41	4.18	3.98	3.80	3.63	3.47	3.33	2.77	2.37	2.07	1.84	1.65	2.27
2.28	6.06	5.65	5.29	4.97	4.69	4.43	4.21	4.00	3.82	3.65	3.49	3.35	2.79	2.38	2.08	1.85	1.66	2.28
2.29	6.10	5.68	5.31	4.99	4.71	4.46	4.23	4.02	3.84	3.67	3.51	3.37	2.80	2.40	2.09	1.86	1.67	2.29
2.30	6.13	5.71	5.34	5.02	4.74	4.48	4.25	4.05	3.86	3.69	3.53	3.39	2.82	2.41	2.10	1.87	1.68	2.30
2.35	6.29	5.86	5.49	5.15	4.86	4.60	4.36	4.15	3.96	3.78	3.62	3.48	2.89	2.47	2.16	1.92	1.72	2.35
2.40	6.45	6.01	5.62	5.28	4.98	4.72	4.47	4.26	4.06	3.88	3.72	3.56	2.96	2.53	2.21	1.96	1.77	2.40
2.45	6.61	6.16	5.76	5.41	5.10	4.83	4.58	4.36	4.16	3.97	3.80	3.65	3.03	2.59	2.27	2.01	1.81	2.45
2.50	6.76	6.30	5.89	5.54	5.22	4.94	4.69	4.46	4.25	4.06	3.89	3.73	3.10	2.65	2.32	2.06	1.85	2.50
2.60	7.06	6.58	6.15	5.78	5.45	5.16	4.89	4.66	4.44	4.24	4.06	3.90	3.24	2.77	2.42	2.15	1.93	2.60
2.70	7.35	6.85	6.40	6.02	5.67	5.37	5.09	4.84	4.62	4.41	4.23	4.05	3.37	2.88	2.51	2.23	2.01	2.70
2.80	7.63	7.11	6.65	6.24	5.89	5.57	5.28	5.03	4.79	4.58	4.38	4.20	3.49	2.99	2.61	2.31	2.08	2.80
2.90	7.90	7.36	6.88	6.46	6.09	5.76	5.47	5.20	4.96	4.74	4.54	4.35	3.61	3.09	2.70	2.39	2.15	2.90
3.00	8.16	7.60	7.11	6.68	6.29	5.95	5.65	5.37	5.12	4.89	4.68	4.49	3.73	3.19	2.78	2.47	2.22	3.00
3.10	8.42	7.83	7.33	6.88	6.49	6.14	5.82	5.54	5.28	5.04	4.83	4.63	3.84	3.29	2.87	2.55	2.29	3.10
3.20	8.66	8.06	7.54	7.08	6.68	6.31	5.99	5.70	5.43	5.19	4.97	4.76	3.95	3.38	2.95	2.62	2.35	3.20
3.30	8.90	8.28	7.75	7.28	6.86	6.49	6.15	5.85	5.58	5.33	5.10	4.89	4.06	3.47	3.03	2.69	2.42	3.30
3.40	9.13	8.50	7.95	7.46	7.04	6.65	6.31	6.00	5.72	5.46	5.23	5.02	4.16	3.56	3.11	2.76	2.48	3.40
3.50	9.36	8.71	8.14	7.65	7.21	6.82	6.46	6.15	5.86	5.60	5.36	5.14	4.26	3.64	3.18	2.82	2.54	3.50
3.60	9.58	8.91	8.34	7.83	7.38	6.97	6.61	6.29	6.00	5.73	5.48	5.26	4.36	3.73	3.25	2.89	2.59	3.60
3.70	9.80	9.11	8.52	8.00	7.54	7.13	6.76	6.43	6.13	5.85	5.60	5.37	4.46	3.81	3.32	2.95	2.65	3.70
3.80	10.01	9.31	8.70	8.17	7.70	7.28	6.90	6.56	6.26	5.98	5.72	5.49	4.55	3.89	3.39	3.01	2.71	3.80
3.90	10.21	9.50	8.88	8.33	7.85	7.43	7.04	6.70	6.38	6.10	5.83	5.59	4.64	3.97	3.46	3.07	2.76	3.90
4.00	10.41	9.68	9.05	8.50	8.01	7.57	7.18	6.82	6.50	6.21	5.95	5.70	4.73	4.04	3.53	3.13	2.81	4.00
4.10	10.60	9.86	9.22	8.65	8.15	7.71	7.31	6.95	6.62	6.33	6.06	5.81	4.82	4.11	3.59	3.19	2.86	4.10
4.20	10.79	10.04	9.38	8.81	8.30	7.85	7.44	7.07	6.74	6.44	6.16	5.91	4.90	4.19	3.65	3.24	2.91	4.20
4.30	10.98	10.21	9.54	8.96	8.44	7.98	7.57	7.19	6.85	6.55	6.27	6.01	4.98	4.26	3.71	3.29	2.96	4.30
4.40	11.16	10.38	9.70	9.11	8.58	8.11	7.69	7.31	6.97	6.65	6.37	6.11	5.06	4.32	3.77	3.35	3.01	4.40
4.50	11.34	10.55	9.86	9.25	8.72	8.24	7.81	7.42	7.08	6.76	6.47	6.20	5.14	4.39	3.83	3.40	3.05	4.50

Use of the table: the table shows the annual compound rate per cent of interest or growth ('r' in the formula) which, accumulating over the period shown at the head of a column (n), makes 1 unit increase to the amount shown in the column at each side of a line (F).
For example, an increase from 1 to 5.10 (a 410% increase), if achieved over 15 years will have resulted from an annual compound interest or growth rate of 11.47%

$$F = 1 \times \left[1 + \frac{r}{100} \right]^n$$

Interest rates and growth rates

Interest rate or growth rate producing an accumulated amount from 1 unit compounded annually

n	years 14	years 15	years 16	years 17	years 18	years 19	years 20	years 21	years 22	years 23	years 24	years 25	years 30	years 35	years 40	years 45	years 50	n F
4.60	11.52	10.71	10.01	9.39	8.85	8.36	7.93	7.54	7.18	6.86	6.57	6.29	5.22	4.46	3.89	3.45	3.10	4.60
4.70	11.69	10.87	10.16	9.53	8.98	8.49	8.05	7.65	7.29	6.96	6.66	6.39	5.29	4.52	3.94	3.50	3.14	4.70
4.80	11.86	11.02	10.30	9.67	9.11	8.61	8.16	7.76	7.39	7.06	6.75	6.48	5.37	4.58	4.00	3.55	3.19	4.80
4.90	12.02	11.18	10.44	9.80	9.23	8.72	8.27	7.86	7.49	7.15	6.85	6.56	5.44	4.65	4.05	3.59	3.23	4.90
5.00	12.18	11.33	10.58	9.93	9.35	8.84	8.38	7.97	7.59	7.25	6.94	6.65	5.51	4.71	4.11	3.64	3.27	5.00
5.10	12.34	11.47	10.72	10.06	9.47	8.95	8.49	8.07	7.69	7.34	7.02	6.73	5.58	4.77	4.16	3.69	3.31	5.10
5.20	12.50	11.62	10.85	10.18	9.59	9.06	8.59	8.17	7.78	7.43	7.11	6.82	5.65	4.82	4.21	3.73	3.35	5.20
5.30	12.65	11.76	10.99	10.31	9.71	9.17	8.70	8.27	7.88	7.52	7.20	6.90	5.72	4.88	4.26	3.78	3.39	5.30
5.40	12.80	11.90	11.12	10.43	9.82	9.28	8.80	8.36	7.97	7.61	7.28	6.98	5.78	4.94	4.31	3.82	3.43	5.40
5.50	12.95	12.04	11.24	10.55	9.93	9.39	8.90	8.46	8.06	7.69	7.36	7.06	5.85	4.99	4.35	3.86	3.47	5.50
5.60	13.09	12.17	11.37	10.67	10.04	9.49	9.00	8.55	8.15	7.78	7.44	7.13	5.91	5.05	4.40	3.90	3.51	5.60
5.70	13.24	12.30	11.49	10.78	10.15	9.59	9.09	8.64	8.23	7.86	7.52	7.21	5.97	5.10	4.45	3.94	3.54	5.70
5.80	13.38	12.43	11.61	10.89	10.26	9.69	9.19	8.73	8.32	7.94	7.60	7.28	6.03	5.15	4.49	3.98	3.58	5.80
5.90	13.52	12.56	11.73	11.01	10.36	9.79	9.28	8.82	8.40	8.02	7.68	7.36	6.10	5.20	4.54	4.02	3.61	5.90
6.00	13.65	12.69	11.85	11.12	10.47	9.89	9.37	8.91	8.49	8.10	7.75	7.43	6.15	5.25	4.58	4.06	3.65	6.00
6.10	13.79	12.81	11.97	11.22	10.57	9.98	9.46	8.99	8.57	8.18	7.83	7.50	6.21	5.30	4.62	4.10	3.68	6.10
6.20	13.92	12.93	12.08	11.33	10.67	10.08	9.55	9.08	8.65	8.26	7.90	7.57	6.27	5.35	4.67	4.14	3.72	6.20
6.30	14.05	13.05	12.19	11.43	10.77	10.17	9.64	9.16	8.73	8.33	7.97	7.64	6.33	5.40	4.71	4.17	3.75	6.30
6.40	14.18	13.17	12.30	11.54	10.86	10.26	9.73	9.24	8.80	8.41	8.04	7.71	6.38	5.45	4.75	4.21	3.78	6.40
6.50	14.31	13.29	12.41	11.64	10.96	10.35	9.81	9.32	8.88	8.48	8.11	7.77	6.44	5.49	4.79	4.25	3.81	6.50
6.60	14.43	13.41	12.52	11.74	11.05	10.44	9.89	9.40	8.96	8.55	8.18	7.84	6.49	5.54	4.83	4.28	3.85	6.60
6.70	14.55	13.52	12.62	11.84	11.15	10.53	9.98	9.48	9.03	8.62	8.25	7.91	6.55	5.58	4.87	4.32	3.88	6.70
6.80	14.67	13.63	12.73	11.94	11.24	10.62	10.06	9.56	9.10	8.69	8.31	7.97	6.60	5.63	4.91	4.35	3.91	6.80
6.90	14.79	13.74	12.83	12.03	11.33	10.70	10.14	9.63	9.18	8.76	8.38	8.03	6.65	5.67	4.95	4.39	3.94	6.90
7.00	14.91	13.85	12.93	12.13	11.42	10.78	10.22	9.71	9.25	8.83	8.45	8.09	6.70	5.72	4.99	4.42	3.97	7.00
7.10	15.03	13.96	13.03	12.22	11.50	10.87	10.30	9.78	9.32	8.90	8.51	8.16	6.75	5.76	5.02	4.45	4.00	7.10
7.20	15.14	14.07	13.13	12.31	11.59	10.95	10.37	9.86	9.39	8.96	8.57	8.22	6.80	5.80	5.06	4.48	4.03	7.20
7.30	15.26	14.17	13.23	12.40	11.68	11.03	10.45	9.93	9.46	9.03	8.64	8.28	6.85	5.84	5.10	4.52	4.06	7.30
7.40	15.37	14.27	13.33	12.49	11.76	11.11	10.53	10.00	9.52	9.09	8.70	8.34	6.90	5.89	5.13	4.55	4.08	7.40
7.50	15.48	14.38	13.42	12.58	11.84	11.19	10.60	10.07	9.59	9.16	8.76	8.39	6.95	5.93	5.17	4.58	4.11	7.50
7.60	15.59	14.48	13.51	12.67	11.93	11.27	10.67	10.14	9.66	9.22	8.82	8.45	6.99	5.97	5.20	4.61	4.14	7.60
7.70	15.70	14.58	13.61	12.76	12.01	11.34	10.75	10.21	9.72	9.28	8.88	8.51	7.04	6.01	5.24	4.64	4.17	7.70
7.80	15.80	14.68	13.70	12.84	12.09	11.42	10.82	10.28	9.79	9.34	8.94	8.56	7.09	6.04	5.27	4.67	4.19	7.80
7.90	15.91	14.77	13.79	12.93	12.17	11.49	10.89	10.34	9.85	9.40	8.99	8.62	7.13	6.08	5.30	4.70	4.22	7.90
8.00	16.01	14.87	13.88	13.01	12.25	11.57	10.96	10.41	9.91	9.46	9.05	8.67	7.18	6.12	5.34	4.73	4.25	8.00
8.10	16.12	14.97	13.97	13.09	12.32	11.64	11.03	10.47	9.98	9.52	9.11	8.73	7.22	6.16	5.37	4.76	4.27	8.10
8.20	16.22	15.06	14.05	13.18	12.40	11.71	11.09	10.54	10.04	9.58	9.16	8.78	7.27	6.20	5.40	4.79	4.30	8.20
8.30	16.32	15.15	14.14	13.26	12.48	11.78	11.16	10.60	10.10	9.64	9.22	8.83	7.31	6.23	5.43	4.82	4.32	8.30
8.40	16.42	15.24	14.23	13.34	12.55	11.85	11.23	10.67	10.16	9.69	9.27	8.89	7.35	6.27	5.46	4.84	4.35	8.40
8.50	16.52	15.34	14.31	13.42	12.62	11.92	11.29	10.73	10.22	9.75	9.33	8.94	7.39	6.31	5.50	4.87	4.37	8.50
8.60	16.61	15.43	14.39	13.49	12.70	11.99	11.36	10.79	10.28	9.81	9.38	8.99	7.44	6.34	5.53	4.90	4.40	8.60
8.70	16.71	15.51	14.48	13.57	12.77	12.06	11.42	10.85	10.33	9.86	9.43	9.04	7.48	6.38	5.56	4.92	4.42	8.70
8.80	16.81	15.60	14.56	13.65	12.84	12.13	11.49	10.91	10.39	9.92	9.48	9.09	7.52	6.41	5.59	4.95	4.45	8.80
8.90	16.90	15.69	14.64	13.72	12.91	12.19	11.55	10.97	10.45	9.97	9.54	9.14	7.56	6.45	5.62	4.98	4.47	8.90
9.00	16.99	15.78	14.72	13.80	12.98	12.26	11.61	11.03	10.50	10.02	9.59	9.19	7.60	6.48	5.65	5.00	4.49	9.00
9.10	17.09	15.86	14.80	13.87	13.05	12.32	11.67	11.09	10.56	10.08	9.64	9.23	7.64	6.51	5.68	5.03	4.52	9.10
9.20	17.18	15.95	14.88	13.94	13.12	12.39	11.74	11.15	10.61	10.13	9.69	9.28	7.68	6.55	5.70	5.06	4.54	9.20
9.30	17.27	16.03	14.96	14.02	13.19	12.45	11.80	11.20	10.67	10.18	9.74	9.33	7.72	6.58	5.73	5.08	4.56	9.30
9.40	17.36	16.11	15.03	14.09	13.26	12.52	11.86	11.26	10.72	10.23	9.79	9.38	7.76	6.61	5.76	5.11	4.58	9.40
9.50	17.45	16.19	15.11	14.16	13.32	12.58	11.91	11.32	10.78	10.28	9.83	9.42	7.79	6.64	5.79	5.13	4.61	9.50
9.60	17.53	16.27	15.18	14.23	13.39	12.64	11.97	11.37	10.83	10.33	9.88	9.47	7.83	6.68	5.82	5.15	4.63	9.60
9.70	17.62	16.35	15.26	14.30	13.45	12.70	12.03	11.43	10.88	10.38	9.93	9.51	7.87	6.71	5.84	5.18	4.65	9.70
9.80	17.71	16.43	15.33	14.37	13.52	12.76	12.09	11.48	10.93	10.43	9.98	9.56	7.90	6.74	5.87	5.20	4.67	9.80
9.90	17.79	16.51	15.41	14.44	13.58	12.82	12.15	11.54	10.98	10.48	10.02	9.60	7.94	6.77	5.90	5.23	4.69	9.90
0.00	17.88	16.59	15.48	14.50	13.65	12.88	12.20	11.59	11.03	10.53	10.07	9.65	7.98	6.80	5.93	5.25	4.71	10.00

213

Interest rates

$$F = 1 \times \left[1 + \frac{r}{100} \right]^n$$

Use of the table: the table shows the amount ('F' in the formula) accumulated from 1 unit growing at the annual compound interest rate shown at the head of a column (r) over the period shown in the column at each side of a line (n).
For example, where the annual compound interest rate earned is 0.50%, 1 unit accumulates after 5 years to 1.0253

Accumulated amount of 1 unit

n Years	% rate 0.25	% rate 0.50	% rate 0.75	% rate 1.00	% rate 1.25	% rate 1.50	% rate 1.75	% rate 2.00	% rate 2.25	% rate 2.50
1	1.0025	1.0050	1.0075	1.0100	1.0125	1.0150	1.0175	1.0200	1.0225	1.0250
2	1.0050	1.0100	1.0151	1.0201	1.0252	1.0302	1.0353	1.0404	1.0455	1.0506
3	1.0075	1.0151	1.0227	1.0303	1.0380	1.0457	1.0534	1.0612	1.0690	1.0769
4	1.0100	1.0202	1.0303	1.0406	1.0509	1.0614	1.0719	1.0824	1.0931	1.1038
5	1.0126	1.0253	1.0381	1.0510	1.0641	1.0773	1.0906	1.1041	1.1177	1.1314
6	1.0151	1.0304	1.0459	1.0615	1.0774	1.0934	1.1097	1.1262	1.1428	1.1597
7	1.0176	1.0355	1.0537	1.0721	1.0909	1.1098	1.1291	1.1487	1.1685	1.1887
8	1.0202	1.0407	1.0616	1.0829	1.1045	1.1265	1.1489	1.1717	1.1948	1.2184
9	1.0227	1.0459	1.0696	1.0937	1.1183	1.1434	1.1690	1.1951	1.2217	1.2489
10	1.0253	1.0511	1.0776	1.1046	1.1323	1.1605	1.1894	1.2190	1.2492	1.2801
11	1.0278	1.0564	1.0857	1.1157	1.1464	1.1779	1.2103	1.2434	1.2773	1.3121
12	1.0304	1.0617	1.0938	1.1268	1.1608	1.1956	1.2314	1.2682	1.3060	1.3449
13	1.0330	1.0670	1.1020	1.1381	1.1753	1.2136	1.2530	1.2936	1.3354	1.3785
14	1.0356	1.0723	1.1103	1.1495	1.1900	1.2318	1.2749	1.3195	1.3655	1.4130
15	1.0382	1.0777	1.1186	1.1610	1.2048	1.2502	1.2972	1.3459	1.3962	1.4483
16	1.0408	1.0831	1.1270	1.1726	1.2199	1.2690	1.3199	1.3728	1.4276	1.4845
17	1.0434	1.0885	1.1354	1.1843	1.2351	1.2880	1.3430	1.4002	1.4597	1.5216
18	1.0460	1.0939	1.1440	1.1961	1.2506	1.3073	1.3665	1.4282	1.4926	1.5597
19	1.0486	1.0994	1.1525	1.2081	1.2662	1.3270	1.3904	1.4568	1.5262	1.5987
20	1.0512	1.1049	1.1612	1.2202	1.2820	1.3469	1.4148	1.4859	1.5605	1.6386
21	1.0538	1.1104	1.1699	1.2324	1.2981	1.3671	1.4395	1.5157	1.5956	1.6796
22	1.0565	1.1160	1.1787	1.2447	1.3143	1.3876	1.4647	1.5460	1.6315	1.7216
23	1.0591	1.1216	1.1875	1.2572	1.3307	1.4084	1.4904	1.5769	1.6682	1.7646
24	1.0618	1.1272	1.1964	1.2697	1.3474	1.4295	1.5164	1.6084	1.7058	1.8087
25	1.0644	1.1328	1.2054	1.2824	1.3642	1.4509	1.5430	1.6406	1.7441	1.8539
26	1.0671	1.1385	1.2144	1.2953	1.3812	1.4727	1.5700	1.6734	1.7834	1.9003
27	1.0697	1.1442	1.2235	1.3082	1.3985	1.4948	1.5975	1.7069	1.8235	1.9478
28	1.0724	1.1499	1.2327	1.3213	1.4160	1.5172	1.6254	1.7410	1.8645	1.9965
29	1.0751	1.1556	1.2420	1.3345	1.4337	1.5400	1.6539	1.7758	1.9065	2.0464
30	1.0778	1.1614	1.2513	1.3478	1.4516	1.5631	1.6828	1.8114	1.9494	2.0976
31	1.0805	1.1672	1.2607	1.3613	1.4698	1.5865	1.7122	1.8476	1.9933	2.1500
32	1.0832	1.1730	1.2701	1.3749	1.4881	1.6103	1.7422	1.8845	2.0381	2.2038
33	1.0859	1.1789	1.2796	1.3887	1.5067	1.6345	1.7727	1.9222	2.0840	2.2589
34	1.0886	1.1848	1.2892	1.4026	1.5256	1.6590	1.8037	1.9607	2.1308	2.3153
35	1.0913	1.1907	1.2989	1.4166	1.5446	1.6839	1.8353	1.9999	2.1788	2.3732
36	1.0941	1.1967	1.3086	1.4308	1.5639	1.7091	1.8674	2.0399	2.2278	2.4325
37	1.0968	1.2027	1.3185	1.4451	1.5835	1.7348	1.9001	2.0807	2.2779	2.4933
38	1.0995	1.2087	1.3283	1.4595	1.6033	1.7608	1.9333	2.1223	2.3292	2.5557
39	1.1023	1.2147	1.3383	1.4741	1.6233	1.7872	1.9672	2.1647	2.3816	2.6196
40	1.1050	1.2208	1.3483	1.4889	1.6436	1.8140	2.0016	2.2080	2.4352	2.6851
41	1.1078	1.2269	1.3585	1.5038	1.6642	1.8412	2.0366	2.2522	2.4900	2.7522
42	1.1106	1.2330	1.3686	1.5188	1.6850	1.8688	2.0723	2.2972	2.5460	2.8210
43	1.1133	1.2392	1.3789	1.5340	1.7060	1.8969	2.1085	2.3432	2.6033	2.8915
44	1.1161	1.2454	1.3893	1.5493	1.7274	1.9253	2.1454	2.3901	2.6619	2.9638
45	1.1189	1.2516	1.3997	1.5648	1.7489	1.9542	2.1830	2.4379	2.7218	3.0379
46	1.1217	1.2579	1.4102	1.5805	1.7708	1.9835	2.2212	2.4866	2.7830	3.1139
47	1.1245	1.2642	1.4207	1.5963	1.7929	2.0133	2.2600	2.5363	2.8456	3.1917
48	1.1273	1.2705	1.4314	1.6122	1.8154	2.0435	2.2996	2.5871	2.9096	3.2715
49	1.1301	1.2768	1.4421	1.6283	1.8380	2.0741	2.3398	2.6388	2.9751	3.3533
50	1.1330	1.2832	1.4530	1.6446	1.8610	2.1052	2.3808	2.6916	3.0420	3.4371
51	1.1358	1.2896	1.4639	1.6611	1.8843	2.1368	2.4225	2.7454	3.1105	3.5230
52	1.1386	1.2961	1.4748	1.6777	1.9078	2.1689	2.4648	2.8003	3.1805	3.6111
53	1.1415	1.3026	1.4859	1.6945	1.9317	2.2014	2.5080	2.8563	3.2520	3.7014
54	1.1443	1.3091	1.4970	1.7114	1.9558	2.2344	2.5519	2.9135	3.3252	3.7939
55	1.1472	1.3156	1.5083	1.7285	1.9803	2.2679	2.5965	2.9717	3.4000	3.8888

Use of the table: the table shows the amount ('F' in the formula) accumulated from 1 unit growing at the annual compound interest rate shown at the head of a column (r) over the period shown in the column at each side of a line (n). For example, where the annual compound interest rate earned is 3.5%, 1 unit accumulates after 5 years to 1.1877

$$F = 1 \times \left[1 + \frac{r}{100} \right]^{n}$$

Accumulated amount of 1 unit

n Years	% rate 3.0	% rate 3.5	% rate 4.0	% rate 4.5	% rate 5.0	% rate 5.5	% rate 6.0	% rate 6.5	% rate 7.0	% rate 7.5	n Years
1	1.0300	1.0350	1.0400	1.0450	1.0500	1.0550	1.0600	1.0650	1.0700	1.0750	1
2	1.0609	1.0712	1.0816	1.0920	1.1025	1.1130	1.1236	1.1342	1.1449	1.1556	2
3	1.0927	1.1087	1.1249	1.1412	1.1576	1.1742	1.1910	1.2079	1.2250	1.2423	3
4	1.1255	1.1475	1.1699	1.1925	1.2155	1.2388	1.2625	1.2865	1.3108	1.3355	4
5	1.1593	1.1877	1.2167	1.2462	1.2763	1.3070	1.3382	1.3701	1.4026	1.4356	5
6	1.1941	1.2293	1.2653	1.3023	1.3401	1.3788	1.4185	1.4591	1.5007	1.5433	6
7	1.2299	1.2723	1.3159	1.3609	1.4071	1.4547	1.5036	1.5540	1.6058	1.6590	7
8	1.2668	1.3168	1.3686	1.4221	1.4775	1.5347	1.5938	1.6550	1.7182	1.7835	8
9	1.3048	1.3629	1.4233	1.4861	1.5513	1.6191	1.6895	1.7626	1.8385	1.9172	9
10	1.3439	1.4106	1.4802	1.5530	1.6289	1.7081	1.7908	1.8771	1.9672	2.0610	10
11	1.3842	1.4600	1.5395	1.6229	1.7103	1.8021	1.8983	1.9992	2.1049	2.2156	11
12	1.4258	1.5111	1.6010	1.6959	1.7959	1.9012	2.0122	2.1291	2.2522	2.3818	12
13	1.4685	1.5640	1.6651	1.7722	1.8856	2.0058	2.1329	2.2675	2.4098	2.5604	13
14	1.5126	1.6187	1.7317	1.8519	1.9799	2.1161	2.2609	2.4149	2.5785	2.7524	14
15	1.5580	1.6753	1.8009	1.9353	2.0789	2.2325	2.3966	2.5718	2.7590	2.9589	15
16	1.6047	1.7340	1.8730	2.0224	2.1829	2.3553	2.5404	2.7390	2.9522	3.1808	16
17	1.6528	1.7947	1.9479	2.1134	2.2920	2.4848	2.6928	2.9170	3.1588	3.4194	17
18	1.7024	1.8575	2.0258	2.2085	2.4066	2.6215	2.8543	3.1067	3.3799	3.6758	18
19	1.7535	1.9225	2.1068	2.3079	2.5270	2.7656	3.0256	3.3086	3.6165	3.9515	19
20	1.8061	1.9898	2.1911	2.4117	2.6533	2.9178	3.2071	3.5236	3.8697	4.2479	20
21	1.8603	2.0594	2.2788	2.5202	2.7860	3.0782	3.3996	3.7527	4.1406	4.5664	21
22	1.9161	2.1315	2.3699	2.6337	2.9253	3.2475	3.6035	3.9966	4.4304	4.9089	22
23	1.9736	2.2061	2.4647	2.7522	3.0715	3.4262	3.8197	4.2564	4.7405	5.2771	23
24	2.0328	2.2833	2.5633	2.8760	3.2251	3.6146	4.0489	4.5331	5.0724	5.6729	24
25	2.0938	2.3632	2.6658	3.0054	3.3864	3.8134	4.2919	4.8277	5.4274	6.0983	25
26	2.1566	2.4460	2.7725	3.1407	3.5557	4.0231	4.5494	5.1415	5.8074	6.5557	26
27	2.2213	2.5316	2.8834	3.2820	3.7335	4.2444	4.8223	5.4757	6.2139	7.0474	27
28	2.2879	2.6202	2.9987	3.4297	3.9201	4.4778	5.1117	5.8316	6.6488	7.5759	28
29	2.3566	2.7119	3.1187	3.5840	4.1161	4.7241	5.4184	6.2107	7.1143	8.1441	29
30	2.4273	2.8068	3.2434	3.7453	4.3219	4.9840	5.7435	6.6144	7.6123	8.7550	30
31	2.5001	2.9050	3.3731	3.9139	4.5380	5.2581	6.0881	7.0443	8.1451	9.4116	31
32	2.5751	3.0067	3.5081	4.0900	4.7649	5.5473	6.4534	7.5022	8.7153	10.1174	32
33	2.6523	3.1119	3.6484	4.2740	5.0032	5.8524	6.8406	7.9898	9.3253	10.8763	33
34	2.7319	3.2209	3.7943	4.4664	5.2533	6.1742	7.2510	8.5092	9.9781	11.6920	34
35	2.8139	3.3336	3.9461	4.6673	5.5160	6.5138	7.6861	9.0623	10.6766	12.5689	35
36	2.8983	3.4503	4.1039	4.8774	5.7918	6.8721	8.1473	9.6513	11.4239	13.5115	36
37	2.9852	3.5710	4.2681	5.0969	6.0814	7.2501	8.6361	10.2786	12.2236	14.5249	37
38	3.0748	3.6960	4.4388	5.3262	6.3855	7.6488	9.1543	10.9467	13.0793	15.6143	38
39	3.1670	3.8254	4.6164	5.5659	6.7048	8.0695	9.7035	11.6583	13.9948	16.7853	39
40	3.2620	3.9593	4.8010	5.8164	7.0400	8.5133	10.2857	12.4161	14.9745	18.0442	40
41	3.3599	4.0978	4.9931	6.0781	7.3920	8.9815	10.9029	13.2231	16.0227	19.3976	41
42	3.4607	4.2413	5.1928	6.3516	7.7616	9.4755	11.5570	14.0826	17.1443	20.8524	42
43	3.5645	4.3897	5.4005	6.6374	8.1497	9.9967	12.2505	14.9980	18.3444	22.4163	43
44	3.6715	4.5433	5.6165	6.9361	8.5572	10.5465	12.9855	15.9729	19.6285	24.0975	44
45	3.7816	4.7024	5.8412	7.2482	8.9850	11.1266	13.7646	17.0111	21.0025	25.9048	45
46	3.8950	4.8669	6.0748	7.5744	9.4343	11.7385	14.5905	18.1168	22.4726	27.8477	46
47	4.0119	5.0373	6.3178	7.9153	9.9060	12.3841	15.4659	19.2944	24.0457	29.9363	47
48	4.1323	5.2136	6.5705	8.2715	10.4013	13.0653	16.3939	20.5485	25.7289	32.1815	48
49	4.2562	5.3961	6.8333	8.6437	10.9213	13.7838	17.3775	21.8842	27.5299	34.5951	49
50	4.3839	5.5849	7.1067	9.0326	11.4674	14.5420	18.4202	23.3067	29.4570	37.1897	50
51	4.5154	5.7804	7.3910	9.4391	12.0408	15.3418	19.5254	24.8216	31.5190	39.9790	51
52	4.6509	5.9827	7.6866	9.8639	12.6428	16.1856	20.6969	26.4350	33.7253	42.9774	52
53	4.7904	6.1921	7.9941	10.3077	13.2749	17.0758	21.9387	28.1533	36.0861	46.2007	53
54	4.9341	6.4088	8.3138	10.7716	13.9387	18.0149	23.2550	29.9833	38.6122	49.6658	54
55	5.0821	6.6331	8.6464	11.2563	14.6356	19.0058	24.6503	31.9322	41.3150	53.3907	55

$$F = 1 \times \left[1 + \frac{r}{100} \right]^n$$

Use of the table: the table shows the amount ('F' in the formula) accumulated from 1 unit growing at the annual compound interest rate shown at the head of a column (r) over the period shown in the column at each side of a line (n). For example, where the annual compound interest rate earned is 8.5%, 1 unit accumulates after 5 years to 1.504

Accumulated amount of 1 unit

n Years	% rate 8.0	% rate 8.5	% rate 9.0	% rate 9.5	% rate 10.0	% rate 11.0	% rate 12.0	% rate 13.0	% rate 14.0	% rate 15.0	n Years
1	1.080	1.085	1.090	1.095	1.100	1.110	1.120	1.130	1.140	1.150	1
2	1.166	1.177	1.188	1.199	1.210	1.232	1.254	1.277	1.300	1.323	2
3	1.260	1.277	1.295	1.313	1.331	1.368	1.405	1.443	1.482	1.521	3
4	1.360	1.386	1.412	1.438	1.464	1.518	1.574	1.630	1.689	1.749	4
5	1.469	1.504	1.539	1.574	1.611	1.685	1.762	1.842	1.925	2.011	5
6	1.587	1.631	1.677	1.724	1.772	1.870	1.974	2.082	2.195	2.313	6
7	1.714	1.770	1.828	1.888	1.949	2.076	2.211	2.353	2.502	2.660	7
8	1.851	1.921	1.993	2.067	2.144	2.305	2.476	2.658	2.853	3.059	8
9	1.999	2.084	2.172	2.263	2.358	2.558	2.773	3.004	3.252	3.518	9
10	2.159	2.261	2.367	2.478	2.594	2.839	3.106	3.395	3.707	4.046	10
11	2.332	2.453	2.580	2.714	2.853	3.152	3.479	3.836	4.226	4.652	11
12	2.518	2.662	2.813	2.971	3.138	3.498	3.896	4.335	4.818	5.350	12
13	2.720	2.888	3.066	3.254	3.452	3.883	4.363	4.898	5.492	6.153	13
14	2.937	3.133	3.342	3.563	3.797	4.310	4.887	5.535	6.261	7.076	14
15	3.172	3.400	3.642	3.901	4.177	4.785	5.474	6.254	7.138	8.137	15
16	3.426	3.689	3.970	4.272	4.595	5.311	6.130	7.067	8.137	9.358	16
17	3.700	4.002	4.328	4.678	5.054	5.895	6.866	7.986	9.276	10.761	17
18	3.996	4.342	4.717	5.122	5.560	6.544	7.690	9.024	10.575	12.375	18
19	4.316	4.712	5.142	5.609	6.116	7.263	8.613	10.197	12.056	14.232	19
20	4.661	5.112	5.604	6.142	6.727	8.062	9.646	11.523	13.743	16.367	20
21	5.034	5.547	6.109	6.725	7.400	8.949	10.804	13.021	15.668	18.822	21
22	5.437	6.018	6.659	7.364	8.140	9.934	12.100	14.714	17.861	21.645	22
23	5.871	6.530	7.258	8.064	8.954	11.026	13.552	16.627	20.362	24.891	23
24	6.341	7.085	7.911	8.830	9.850	12.239	15.179	18.788	23.212	28.625	24
25	6.848	7.687	8.623	9.668	10.835	13.585	17.000	21.231	26.462	32.919	25
26	7.396	8.340	9.399	10.587	11.918	15.080	19.040	23.991	30.167	37.857	26
27	7.988	9.049	10.245	11.593	13.110	16.739	21.325	27.109	34.390	43.535	27
28	8.627	9.818	11.167	12.694	14.421	18.580	23.884	30.633	39.204	50.066	28
29	9.317	10.653	12.172	13.900	15.863	20.624	26.750	34.616	44.693	57.575	29
30	10.063	11.558	13.268	15.220	17.449	22.892	29.960	39.116	50.950	66.212	30
31	10.868	12.541	14.462	16.666	19.194	25.410	33.555	44.201	58.083	76.144	31
32	11.737	13.607	15.763	18.250	21.114	28.206	37.582	49.947	66.215	87.565	32
33	12.676	14.763	17.182	19.983	23.225	31.308	42.092	56.440	75.485	100.700	33
34	13.690	16.018	18.728	21.882	25.548	34.752	47.143	63.777	86.053	115.805	34
35	14.785	17.380	20.414	23.960	28.102	38.575	52.800	72.069	98.100	133.176	35
36	15.968	18.857	22.251	26.237	30.913	42.818	59.136	81.437	111.834	153.152	36
37	17.246	20.460	24.254	28.729	34.004	47.528	66.232	92.024	127.491	176.125	37
38	18.625	22.199	26.437	31.458	37.404	52.756	74.180	103.987	145.340	202.543	38
39	20.115	24.086	28.816	34.447	41.145	58.559	83.081	117.506	165.687	232.925	39
40	21.725	26.133	31.409	37.719	45.259	65.001	93.051	132.782	188.884	267.864	40
41	23.462	28.354	34.236	41.303	49.785	72.151	104.217	150.043	215.327	308.043	41
42	25.339	30.764	37.318	45.227	54.764	80.088	116.723	169.549	245.473	354.250	42
43	27.367	33.379	40.676	49.523	60.240	88.897	130.730	191.590	279.839	407.387	43
44	29.556	36.217	44.337	54.228	66.264	98.676	146.418	216.497	319.017	468.495	44
45	31.920	39.295	48.327	59.379	72.890	109.530	163.988	244.641	363.679	538.769	45
46	34.474	42.635	52.677	65.020	80.180	121.579	183.666	276.445	414.594	619.585	46
47	37.232	46.259	57.418	71.197	88.197	134.952	205.706	312.383	472.637	712.522	47
48	40.211	50.191	62.585	77.961	97.017	149.797	230.391	352.992	538.807	819.401	48
49	43.427	54.457	68.218	85.367	106.719	166.275	258.038	398.881	614.239	942.311	49
50	46.902	59.086	74.358	93.477	117.391	184.565	289.002	450.736	700.233	1083.657	50
51	50.654	64.109	81.050	102.358	129.130	204.867	323.682	509.332	798.266	1246.206	51
52	54.706	69.558	88.344	112.082	142.043	227.402	362.524	575.545	910.023	1433.137	52
53	59.083	75.470	96.295	122.729	156.247	252.417	406.027	650.366	1037.426	1648.108	53
54	63.809	81.885	104.962	134.389	171.872	280.182	454.751	734.913	1182.666	1895.324	54
55	68.914	88.846	114.408	147.156	189.059	311.002	509.321	830.452	1348.239	2179.622	55

Use of the table: the table shows the amount ('F' in the formula) accumulated from 1 unit growing at the annual compound interest rate shown at the head of a column (r) over the period shown in the column at each side of a line (n). For example, where the annual compound interest rate earned is 17%, 1 unit accumulates after 5 years to 2.192

$$F = 1 \times \left[1 + \frac{r}{100} \right]^n$$

Accumulated amount of 1 unit

n Years	% rate 16	% rate 17	% rate 18	% rate 19	% rate 20	% rate 21	% rate 22	% rate 23	% rate 24	% rate 25	n Years
1	1.160	1.170	1.180	1.190	1.200	1.210	1.220	1.230	1.240	1.250	1
2	1.346	1.369	1.392	1.416	1.440	1.464	1.488	1.513	1.538	1.562	2
3	1.561	1.602	1.643	1.685	1.728	1.772	1.816	1.861	1.907	1.953	3
4	1.811	1.874	1.939	2.005	2.074	2.144	2.215	2.289	2.364	2.441	4
5	2.100	2.192	2.288	2.386	2.488	2.594	2.703	2.815	2.932	3.052	5
6	2.436	2.565	2.700	2.840	2.986	3.138	3.297	3.463	3.635	3.815	6
7	2.826	3.001	3.185	3.379	3.583	3.797	4.023	4.259	4.508	4.768	7
8	3.278	3.511	3.759	4.021	4.300	4.595	4.908	5.239	5.590	5.960	8
9	3.803	4.108	4.435	4.785	5.160	5.560	5.987	6.444	6.931	7.451	9
10	4.411	4.807	5.234	5.695	6.192	6.727	7.305	7.926	8.594	9.313	10
11	5.117	5.624	6.176	6.777	7.430	8.140	8.912	9.749	10.657	11.642	11
12	5.936	6.580	7.288	8.064	8.916	9.850	10.872	11.991	13.215	14.552	12
13	6.886	7.699	8.599	9.596	10.699	11.918	13.264	14.749	16.386	18.190	13
14	7.988	9.007	10.147	11.420	12.839	14.421	16.182	18.141	20.319	22.737	14
15	9.266	10.539	11.974	13.590	15.407	17.449	19.742	22.314	25.196	28.422	15
16	10.748	12.330	14.129	16.172	18.488	21.114	24.086	27.446	31.243	35.527	16
17	12.468	14.426	16.672	19.244	22.186	25.548	29.384	33.759	38.741	44.409	17
18	14.463	16.879	19.673	22.901	26.623	30.913	35.849	41.523	48.039	55.511	18
19	16.777	19.748	23.214	27.252	31.948	37.404	43.736	51.074	59.568	69.389	19
20	19.461	23.106	27.393	32.429	38.338	45.259	53.358	62.821	73.864	86.736	20
21	22.574	27.034	32.324	38.591	46.005	54.764	65.096	77.269	91.592	108.420	21
22	26.186	31.629	38.142	45.923	55.206	66.264	79.418	95.041	113.574	135.525	22
23	30.376	37.006	45.008	54.649	66.247	80.180	96.889	116.901	140.831	169.407	23
24	35.236	43.297	53.109	65.032	79.497	97.017	118.205	143.788	174.631	211.758	24
25	40.874	50.658	62.669	77.388	95.396	117.391	144.210	176.859	216.542	264.698	25
26	47.414	59.270	73.949	92.092	114.475	142.043	175.936	217.537	268.512	330.872	26
27	55.000	69.345	87.260	109.589	137.371	171.872	214.642	267.570	332.955	413.590	27
28	63.800	81.134	102.967	130.411	164.845	207.965	261.864	329.112	412.864	516.988	28
29	74.009	94.927	121.501	155.189	197.814	251.638	319.474	404.807	511.952	646.235	29
30	85.850	111.065	143.371	184.675	237.376	304.482	389.758	497.913	634.820	807.794	30
31	99.586	129.946	169.177	219.764	284.852	368.423	475.505	612.433	787.177	1009.742	31
32	115.520	152.036	199.629	261.519	341.822	445.792	580.116	753.292	976.099	1262.177	32
33	134.003	177.883	235.563	311.207	410.186	539.408	707.741	926.550	1210.363	1577.722	33
34	155.443	208.123	277.964	370.337	492.224	652.683	863.444	1139.656	1500.850	1972.152	34
35	180.314	243.503	327.997	440.701	590.668	789.747	1053.402	1401.777	1861.054	2465.190	35
36	209.164	284.899	387.037	524.434	708.802	955.594	1285.150	1724.186	2307.707	3081.488	36
37	242.631	333.332	456.703	624.076	850.562	1156.269	1567.883	2120.748	2861.557	3851.860	37
38	281.452	389.998	538.910	742.651	1020.675	1399.085	1912.818	2608.520	3548.330	4814.825	38
39	326.484	456.298	635.914	883.754	1224.810	1692.893	2333.638	3208.480	4399.930	6018.531	39
40	378.721	533.869	750.378	1051.668	1469.772	2048.400	2847.038	3946.430	5455.913	7523.164	40
41	439.317	624.626	885.446	1251.484	1763.726	2478.564	3473.386	4854.109	6765.332	9403.955	41
42	509.607	730.813	1044.827	1489.266	2116.471	2999.063	4237.531	5970.555	8389.011	11754.944	42
43	591.144	855.051	1232.896	1772.227	2539.765	3628.866	5169.788	7343.782	10402.374	14693.679	43
44	685.727	1000.410	1454.817	2108.950	3047.718	4390.928	6307.141	9032.852	12898.944	18367.099	44
45	795.444	1170.479	1716.684	2509.651	3657.262	5313.023	7694.712	11110.408	15994.690	22958.874	45
46	922.715	1369.461	2025.687	2986.484	4388.714	6428.757	9387.549	13665.802	19833.416	28698.593	46
47	1070.349	1602.269	2390.311	3553.916	5266.457	7778.796	11452.810	16808.937	24593.436	35873.241	47
48	1241.605	1874.655	2820.567	4229.160	6319.749	9412.344	13972.428	20674.992	30495.860	44841.551	48
49	1440.262	2193.346	3328.269	5032.701	7583.698	11388.936	17046.362	25430.240	37814.867	56051.939	49
50	1670.704	2566.215	3927.357	5988.914	9100.438	13780.612	20796.561	31279.195	46890.435	70064.923	50
51	1938.016	3002.472	4634.281	7126.808	10920.526	16674.541	25371.805	38473.410	58144.139	87581.154	51
52	2248.099	3512.892	5468.452	8480.901	13104.631	20176.195	30953.602	47322.295	72098.732	109476.443	52
53	2607.795	4110.084	6452.773	10092.272	15725.557	24413.195	37763.395	58206.422	89402.428	136845.553	53
54	3025.042	4808.798	7614.272	12009.804	18870.669	29539.966	46071.341	71593.899	110859.011	171056.941	54
55	3509.049	5626.294	8984.841	14291.667	22644.802	35743.359	56207.036	88060.496	137465.173	213821.177	55

Interest rates

$$x = \frac{\dfrac{r}{100}}{1 - \left[1 + \dfrac{r}{100}\right]^{-n}}$$

Use of the table: the table shows the equal annual payment ('x' in the formula) required to pay off a loan of 1 unit where the annual compound interest rate paid is shown at the head of a column (r) and the number of years for which payment is made is shown in the column at each side of a line (n). For example, where the annual compound interest rate paid is 0.5%, 1 unit is paid off after 5 years by an equal annual payment of 0.2030

Equal annual payment to pay off a loan of 1 unit   Mortgage repayments

r / n	% rate 0.25	% rate 0.50	% rate 0.75	% rate 1.00	% rate 1.25	% rate 1.50	% rate 1.75	% rate 2.00	% rate 2.25	% rate 2.50	n
Years											**Years**
1	1.0025	1.0050	1.0075	1.0100	1.0125	1.0150	1.0175	1.0200	1.0225	1.0250	1
2	0.5019	0.5038	0.5056	0.5075	0.5094	0.5113	0.5132	0.5150	0.5169	0.5188	2
3	0.3350	0.3367	0.3383	0.3400	0.3417	0.3434	0.3451	0.3468	0.3484	0.3501	3
4	0.2516	0.2531	0.2547	0.2563	0.2579	0.2594	0.2610	0.2626	0.2642	0.2658	4
5	0.2015	0.2030	0.2045	0.2060	0.2076	0.2091	0.2106	0.2122	0.2137	0.2152	5
6	0.1681	0.1696	0.1711	0.1725	0.1740	0.1755	0.1770	0.1785	0.1800	0.1815	6
7	0.1443	0.1457	0.1472	0.1486	0.1501	0.1516	0.1530	0.1545	0.1560	0.1575	7
8	0.1264	0.1278	0.1293	0.1307	0.1321	0.1336	0.1350	0.1365	0.1380	0.1395	8
9	0.1125	0.1139	0.1153	0.1167	0.1182	0.1196	0.1211	0.1225	0.1240	0.1255	9
10	0.1014	0.1028	0.1042	0.1056	0.1070	0.1084	0.1099	0.1113	0.1128	0.1143	10
11	0.0923	0.0937	0.0951	0.0965	0.0979	0.0993	0.1007	0.1022	0.1036	0.1051	11
12	0.0847	0.0861	0.0875	0.0888	0.0903	0.0917	0.0931	0.0946	0.0960	0.0975	12
13	0.0783	0.0796	0.0810	0.0824	0.0838	0.0852	0.0867	0.0881	0.0896	0.0910	13
14	0.0728	0.0741	0.0755	0.0769	0.0783	0.0797	0.0812	0.0826	0.0841	0.0855	14
15	0.0680	0.0694	0.0707	0.0721	0.0735	0.0749	0.0764	0.0778	0.0793	0.0808	15
16	0.0638	0.0652	0.0666	0.0679	0.0693	0.0708	0.0722	0.0737	0.0751	0.0766	16
17	0.0602	0.0615	0.0629	0.0643	0.0657	0.0671	0.0685	0.0700	0.0714	0.0729	17
18	0.0569	0.0582	0.0596	0.0610	0.0624	0.0638	0.0652	0.0667	0.0682	0.0697	18
19	0.0540	0.0553	0.0567	0.0581	0.0595	0.0609	0.0623	0.0638	0.0653	0.0668	19
20	0.0513	0.0527	0.0540	0.0554	0.0568	0.0582	0.0597	0.0612	0.0626	0.0641	20
21	0.0489	0.0503	0.0516	0.0530	0.0544	0.0559	0.0573	0.0588	0.0603	0.0618	21
22	0.0468	0.0481	0.0495	0.0509	0.0523	0.0537	0.0552	0.0566	0.0581	0.0596	22
23	0.0448	0.0461	0.0475	0.0489	0.0503	0.0517	0.0532	0.0547	0.0562	0.0577	23
24	0.0430	0.0443	0.0457	0.0471	0.0485	0.0499	0.0514	0.0529	0.0544	0.0559	24
25	0.0413	0.0427	0.0440	0.0454	0.0468	0.0483	0.0497	0.0512	0.0527	0.0543	25
26	0.0398	0.0411	0.0425	0.0439	0.0453	0.0467	0.0482	0.0497	0.0512	0.0528	26
27	0.0383	0.0397	0.0411	0.0424	0.0439	0.0453	0.0468	0.0483	0.0498	0.0514	27
28	0.0370	0.0384	0.0397	0.0411	0.0425	0.0440	0.0455	0.0470	0.0485	0.0501	28
29	0.0358	0.0371	0.0385	0.0399	0.0413	0.0428	0.0443	0.0458	0.0473	0.0489	29
30	0.0346	0.0360	0.0373	0.0387	0.0402	0.0416	0.0431	0.0446	0.0462	0.0478	30
31	0.0336	0.0349	0.0363	0.0377	0.0391	0.0406	0.0421	0.0436	0.0452	0.0467	31
32	0.0326	0.0339	0.0353	0.0367	0.0381	0.0396	0.0411	0.0426	0.0442	0.0458	32
33	0.0316	0.0329	0.0343	0.0357	0.0372	0.0386	0.0401	0.0417	0.0433	0.0449	33
34	0.0307	0.0321	0.0334	0.0348	0.0363	0.0378	0.0393	0.0408	0.0424	0.0440	34
35	0.0299	0.0312	0.0326	0.0340	0.0355	0.0369	0.0385	0.0400	0.0416	0.0432	35
36	0.0291	0.0304	0.0318	0.0332	0.0347	0.0362	0.0377	0.0392	0.0408	0.0425	36
37	0.0283	0.0297	0.0311	0.0325	0.0339	0.0354	0.0369	0.0385	0.0401	0.0417	37
38	0.0276	0.0290	0.0303	0.0318	0.0332	0.0347	0.0362	0.0378	0.0394	0.0411	38
39	0.0269	0.0283	0.0297	0.0311	0.0326	0.0341	0.0356	0.0372	0.0388	0.0404	39
40	0.0263	0.0276	0.0290	0.0305	0.0319	0.0334	0.0350	0.0366	0.0382	0.0398	40
41	0.0257	0.0270	0.0284	0.0299	0.0313	0.0328	0.0344	0.0360	0.0376	0.0393	41
42	0.0251	0.0265	0.0278	0.0293	0.0307	0.0323	0.0338	0.0354	0.0371	0.0387	42
43	0.0246	0.0259	0.0273	0.0287	0.0302	0.0317	0.0333	0.0349	0.0365	0.0382	43
44	0.0240	0.0254	0.0268	0.0282	0.0297	0.0312	0.0328	0.0344	0.0360	0.0377	44
45	0.0235	0.0249	0.0263	0.0277	0.0292	0.0307	0.0323	0.0339	0.0356	0.0373	45
46	0.0230	0.0244	0.0258	0.0272	0.0287	0.0303	0.0318	0.0335	0.0351	0.0368	46
47	0.0226	0.0239	0.0253	0.0268	0.0283	0.0298	0.0314	0.0330	0.0347	0.0364	47
48	0.0221	0.0235	0.0249	0.0263	0.0278	0.0294	0.0310	0.0326	0.0343	0.0360	48
49	0.0217	0.0231	0.0245	0.0259	0.0274	0.0290	0.0306	0.0322	0.0339	0.0356	49
50	0.0213	0.0227	0.0241	0.0255	0.0270	0.0286	0.0302	0.0318	0.0335	0.0353	50
51	0.0209	0.0223	0.0237	0.0251	0.0266	0.0282	0.0298	0.0315	0.0332	0.0349	51
52	0.0205	0.0219	0.0233	0.0248	0.0263	0.0278	0.0294	0.0311	0.0328	0.0346	52
53	0.0202	0.0215	0.0229	0.0244	0.0259	0.0275	0.0291	0.0308	0.0325	0.0343	53
54	0.0198	0.0212	0.0226	0.0241	0.0256	0.0272	0.0288	0.0305	0.0322	0.0339	54
55	0.0195	0.0208	0.0223	0.0237	0.0253	0.0268	0.0285	0.0301	0.0319	0.0337	55

Use of the table: the table shows the equal annual payment ('x' in the formula) required to pay off a loan of 1 unit where the annual compound interest rate paid is shown at the head of a column (r) and the number of years for which payment is made is shown in the column at each side of a line (n). For example, where the annual compound interest rate paid is 3.5%, 1 unit is paid off after 5 years by an equal annual payment of 0.2215

$$x = \frac{\dfrac{r}{100}}{1 - \left[1 + \dfrac{r}{100}\right]^{-n}}$$

Equal annual payment to pay off a loan of 1 unit   Mortgage repayments

n Years	r % rate 3.0	% rate 3.5	% rate 4.0	% rate 4.5	% rate 5.0	% rate 5.5	% rate 6.0	% rate 6.5	% rate 7.0	% rate 7.5	r n Years
1	1.0300	1.0350	1.0400	1.0450	1.0500	1.0550	1.0600	1.0650	1.0700	1.0750	1
2	0.5226	0.5264	0.5302	0.5340	0.5378	0.5416	0.5454	0.5493	0.5531	0.5569	2
3	0.3535	0.3569	0.3603	0.3638	0.3672	0.3707	0.3741	0.3776	0.3811	0.3845	3
4	0.2690	0.2723	0.2755	0.2787	0.2820	0.2853	0.2886	0.2919	0.2952	0.2986	4
5	0.2184	0.2215	0.2246	0.2278	0.2310	0.2342	0.2374	0.2406	0.2439	0.2472	5
6	0.1846	0.1877	0.1908	0.1939	0.1970	0.2002	0.2034	0.2066	0.2098	0.2130	6
7	0.1605	0.1635	0.1666	0.1697	0.1728	0.1760	0.1791	0.1823	0.1856	0.1888	7
8	0.1425	0.1455	0.1485	0.1516	0.1547	0.1579	0.1610	0.1642	0.1675	0.1707	8
9	0.1284	0.1314	0.1345	0.1376	0.1407	0.1438	0.1470	0.1502	0.1535	0.1568	9
10	0.1172	0.1202	0.1233	0.1264	0.1295	0.1327	0.1359	0.1391	0.1424	0.1457	10
11	0.1081	0.1111	0.1141	0.1172	0.1204	0.1236	0.1268	0.1301	0.1334	0.1367	11
12	0.1005	0.1035	0.1066	0.1097	0.1128	0.1160	0.1193	0.1226	0.1259	0.1293	12
13	0.0940	0.0971	0.1001	0.1033	0.1065	0.1097	0.1130	0.1163	0.1197	0.1231	13
14	0.0885	0.0916	0.0947	0.0978	0.1010	0.1043	0.1076	0.1109	0.1143	0.1178	14
15	0.0838	0.0868	0.0899	0.0931	0.0963	0.0996	0.1030	0.1064	0.1098	0.1133	15
16	0.0796	0.0827	0.0858	0.0890	0.0923	0.0956	0.0990	0.1024	0.1059	0.1094	16
17	0.0760	0.0790	0.0822	0.0854	0.0887	0.0920	0.0954	0.0989	0.1024	0.1060	17
18	0.0727	0.0758	0.0790	0.0822	0.0855	0.0889	0.0924	0.0959	0.0994	0.1030	18
19	0.0698	0.0729	0.0761	0.0794	0.0827	0.0862	0.0896	0.0932	0.0968	0.1004	19
20	0.0672	0.0704	0.0736	0.0769	0.0802	0.0837	0.0872	0.0908	0.0944	0.0981	20
21	0.0649	0.0680	0.0713	0.0746	0.0780	0.0815	0.0850	0.0886	0.0923	0.0960	21
22	0.0627	0.0659	0.0692	0.0725	0.0760	0.0795	0.0830	0.0867	0.0904	0.0942	22
23	0.0608	0.0640	0.0673	0.0707	0.0741	0.0777	0.0813	0.0850	0.0887	0.0925	23
24	0.0590	0.0623	0.0656	0.0690	0.0725	0.0760	0.0797	0.0834	0.0872	0.0911	24
25	0.0574	0.0607	0.0640	0.0674	0.0710	0.0745	0.0782	0.0820	0.0858	0.0897	25
26	0.0559	0.0592	0.0626	0.0660	0.0696	0.0732	0.0769	0.0807	0.0846	0.0885	26
27	0.0546	0.0579	0.0612	0.0647	0.0683	0.0720	0.0757	0.0795	0.0834	0.0874	27
28	0.0533	0.0566	0.0600	0.0635	0.0671	0.0708	0.0746	0.0785	0.0824	0.0864	28
29	0.0521	0.0554	0.0589	0.0624	0.0660	0.0698	0.0736	0.0775	0.0814	0.0855	29
30	0.0510	0.0544	0.0578	0.0614	0.0651	0.0688	0.0726	0.0766	0.0806	0.0847	30
31	0.0500	0.0534	0.0569	0.0604	0.0641	0.0679	0.0718	0.0758	0.0798	0.0839	31
32	0.0490	0.0524	0.0559	0.0596	0.0633	0.0671	0.0710	0.0750	0.0791	0.0832	32
33	0.0482	0.0516	0.0551	0.0587	0.0625	0.0663	0.0703	0.0743	0.0784	0.0826	33
34	0.0473	0.0508	0.0543	0.0580	0.0618	0.0656	0.0696	0.0737	0.0778	0.0820	34
35	0.0465	0.0500	0.0536	0.0573	0.0611	0.0650	0.0690	0.0731	0.0772	0.0815	35
36	0.0458	0.0493	0.0529	0.0566	0.0604	0.0644	0.0684	0.0725	0.0767	0.0810	36
37	0.0451	0.0486	0.0522	0.0560	0.0598	0.0638	0.0679	0.0720	0.0762	0.0805	37
38	0.0445	0.0480	0.0516	0.0554	0.0593	0.0633	0.0674	0.0715	0.0758	0.0801	38
39	0.0438	0.0474	0.0511	0.0549	0.0588	0.0628	0.0669	0.0711	0.0754	0.0798	39
40	0.0433	0.0468	0.0505	0.0543	0.0583	0.0623	0.0665	0.0707	0.0750	0.0794	40
41	0.0427	0.0463	0.0500	0.0539	0.0578	0.0619	0.0661	0.0703	0.0747	0.0791	41
42	0.0422	0.0458	0.0495	0.0534	0.0574	0.0615	0.0657	0.0700	0.0743	0.0788	42
43	0.0417	0.0453	0.0491	0.0530	0.0570	0.0611	0.0653	0.0696	0.0740	0.0785	43
44	0.0412	0.0449	0.0487	0.0526	0.0566	0.0608	0.0650	0.0693	0.0738	0.0782	44
45	0.0408	0.0445	0.0483	0.0522	0.0563	0.0604	0.0647	0.0691	0.0735	0.0780	45
46	0.0404	0.0441	0.0479	0.0518	0.0559	0.0601	0.0644	0.0688	0.0733	0.0778	46
47	0.0400	0.0437	0.0475	0.0515	0.0556	0.0598	0.0641	0.0686	0.0730	0.0776	47
48	0.0396	0.0433	0.0472	0.0512	0.0553	0.0596	0.0639	0.0683	0.0728	0.0774	48
49	0.0392	0.0430	0.0469	0.0509	0.0550	0.0593	0.0637	0.0681	0.0726	0.0772	49
50	0.0389	0.0426	0.0466	0.0506	0.0548	0.0591	0.0634	0.0679	0.0725	0.0771	50
51	0.0385	0.0423	0.0463	0.0503	0.0545	0.0588	0.0632	0.0677	0.0723	0.0769	51
52	0.0382	0.0420	0.0460	0.0501	0.0543	0.0586	0.0630	0.0676	0.0721	0.0768	52
53	0.0379	0.0417	0.0457	0.0498	0.0541	0.0584	0.0629	0.0674	0.0720	0.0767	53
54	0.0376	0.0415	0.0455	0.0496	0.0539	0.0582	0.0627	0.0672	0.0719	0.0765	54
55	0.0373	0.0412	0.0452	0.0494	0.0537	0.0581	0.0625	0.0671	0.0717	0.0764	55

Interest rates

$$x = \dfrac{\dfrac{r}{100}}{1 - \left[1 + \dfrac{r}{100}\right]^{-n}}$$

Use of the table: the table shows the equal annual payment ('x' in the formula) required to pay off a loan of 1 unit where the annual compound interest rate paid is shown at the head of a column (r) and the number of years for which payment is made is shown in the column at each side of a line (n). For example, where the annual compound interest rate paid is 8.5%, 1 unit is paid off after 5 years by an equal annual payment of 0.25377

Equal annual payment to pay off a loan of 1 unit   Mortgage repayments

n Years	r % rate 8.0	% rate 8.5	% rate 9.0	% rate 9.5	% rate 10.0	% rate 11.0	% rate 12.0	% rate 13.0	% rate 14.0	% rate 15.0	r n Years
1	1.08000	1.08500	1.09000	1.09500	1.10000	1.11000	1.12000	1.13000	1.14000	1.15000	1
2	0.56077	0.56462	0.56847	0.57233	0.57619	0.58393	0.59170	0.59948	0.60729	0.61512	2
3	0.38803	0.39154	0.39505	0.39858	0.40211	0.40921	0.41635	0.42352	0.43073	0.43798	3
4	0.30192	0.30529	0.30867	0.31206	0.31547	0.32233	0.32923	0.33619	0.34320	0.35027	4
5	0.25046	0.25377	0.25709	0.26044	0.26380	0.27057	0.27741	0.28431	0.29128	0.29832	5
6	0.21632	0.21961	0.22292	0.22625	0.22961	0.23638	0.24323	0.25015	0.25716	0.26424	6
7	0.19207	0.19537	0.19869	0.20204	0.20541	0.21222	0.21912	0.22611	0.23319	0.24036	7
8	0.17401	0.17733	0.18067	0.18405	0.18744	0.19432	0.20130	0.20839	0.21557	0.22285	8
9	0.16008	0.16342	0.16680	0.17020	0.17364	0.18060	0.18768	0.19487	0.20217	0.20957	9
10	0.14903	0.15241	0.15582	0.15927	0.16275	0.16980	0.17698	0.18429	0.19171	0.19925	10
11	0.14008	0.14349	0.14695	0.15044	0.15396	0.16112	0.16842	0.17584	0.18339	0.19107	11
12	0.13270	0.13615	0.13965	0.14319	0.14676	0.15403	0.16144	0.16899	0.17667	0.18448	12
13	0.12652	0.13002	0.13357	0.13715	0.14078	0.14815	0.15568	0.16335	0.17116	0.17911	13
14	0.12130	0.12484	0.12843	0.13207	0.13575	0.14323	0.15087	0.15867	0.16661	0.17469	14
15	0.11683	0.12042	0.12406	0.12774	0.13147	0.13907	0.14682	0.15474	0.16281	0.17102	15
16	0.11298	0.11661	0.12030	0.12403	0.12782	0.13552	0.14339	0.15143	0.15962	0.16795	16
17	0.10963	0.11331	0.11705	0.12083	0.12466	0.13247	0.14046	0.14861	0.15692	0.16537	17
18	0.10670	0.11043	0.11421	0.11805	0.12193	0.12984	0.13794	0.14620	0.15462	0.16319	18
19	0.10413	0.10790	0.11173	0.11561	0.11955	0.12756	0.13576	0.14413	0.15266	0.16134	19
20	0.10185	0.10567	0.10955	0.11348	0.11746	0.12558	0.13388	0.14235	0.15099	0.15976	20
21	0.09983	0.10370	0.10762	0.11159	0.11562	0.12384	0.13224	0.14081	0.14954	0.15842	21
22	0.09803	0.10194	0.10590	0.10993	0.11401	0.12231	0.13081	0.13948	0.14830	0.15727	22
23	0.09642	0.10037	0.10438	0.10845	0.11257	0.12097	0.12956	0.13832	0.14723	0.15628	23
24	0.09498	0.09897	0.10302	0.10713	0.11130	0.11979	0.12846	0.13731	0.14630	0.15543	24
25	0.09368	0.09771	0.10181	0.10596	0.11017	0.11874	0.12750	0.13643	0.14550	0.15470	25
26	0.09251	0.09658	0.10072	0.10491	0.10916	0.11781	0.12665	0.13565	0.14480	0.15407	26
27	0.09145	0.09556	0.09973	0.10397	0.10826	0.11699	0.12590	0.13498	0.14419	0.15353	27
28	0.09049	0.09464	0.09885	0.10312	0.10745	0.11626	0.12524	0.13439	0.14366	0.15306	28
29	0.08962	0.09381	0.09806	0.10236	0.10673	0.11561	0.12466	0.13387	0.14320	0.15265	29
30	0.08883	0.09305	0.09734	0.10168	0.10608	0.11502	0.12414	0.13341	0.14280	0.15230	30
31	0.08811	0.09237	0.09669	0.10106	0.10550	0.11451	0.12369	0.13301	0.14245	0.15200	31
32	0.08745	0.09174	0.09610	0.10051	0.10497	0.11404	0.12328	0.13266	0.14215	0.15173	32
33	0.08685	0.09118	0.09556	0.10000	0.10450	0.11363	0.12292	0.13234	0.14188	0.15150	33
34	0.08630	0.09066	0.09508	0.09955	0.10407	0.11326	0.12260	0.13207	0.14165	0.15131	34
35	0.08580	0.09019	0.09464	0.09914	0.10369	0.11293	0.12232	0.13183	0.14144	0.15113	35
36	0.08534	0.08976	0.09424	0.09876	0.10334	0.11263	0.12206	0.13162	0.14126	0.15099	36
37	0.08492	0.08937	0.09387	0.09843	0.10303	0.11236	0.12184	0.13143	0.14111	0.15086	37
38	0.08454	0.08901	0.09354	0.09812	0.10275	0.11213	0.12164	0.13126	0.14097	0.15074	38
39	0.08419	0.08868	0.09324	0.09784	0.10249	0.11191	0.12146	0.13112	0.14085	0.15065	39
40	0.08386	0.08838	0.09296	0.09759	0.10226	0.11172	0.12130	0.13099	0.14075	0.15056	40
41	0.08356	0.08811	0.09271	0.09736	0.10205	0.11155	0.12116	0.13087	0.14065	0.15049	41
42	0.08329	0.08786	0.09248	0.09715	0.10186	0.11139	0.12104	0.13077	0.14057	0.15042	42
43	0.08303	0.08763	0.09227	0.09696	0.10169	0.11125	0.12092	0.13068	0.14050	0.15037	43
44	0.08280	0.08741	0.09208	0.09678	0.10153	0.11113	0.12083	0.13060	0.14044	0.15032	44
45	0.08259	0.08722	0.09190	0.09663	0.10139	0.11101	0.12074	0.13053	0.14039	0.15028	45
46	0.08239	0.08704	0.09174	0.09648	0.10126	0.11091	0.12066	0.13047	0.14034	0.15024	46
47	0.08221	0.08688	0.09160	0.09635	0.10115	0.11082	0.12059	0.13042	0.14030	0.15021	47
48	0.08204	0.08673	0.09146	0.09623	0.10104	0.11074	0.12052	0.13037	0.14026	0.15018	48
49	0.08189	0.08659	0.09134	0.09613	0.10095	0.11067	0.12047	0.13033	0.14023	0.15016	49
50	0.08174	0.08646	0.09123	0.09603	0.10086	0.11060	0.12042	0.13029	0.14020	0.15014	50
51	0.08161	0.08635	0.09112	0.09594	0.10078	0.11054	0.12037	0.13026	0.14018	0.15012	51
52	0.08149	0.08624	0.09103	0.09586	0.10071	0.11049	0.12033	0.13023	0.14015	0.15010	52
53	0.08138	0.08614	0.09094	0.09578	0.10064	0.11044	0.12030	0.13020	0.14014	0.15009	53
54	0.08127	0.08605	0.09087	0.09571	0.10059	0.11039	0.12026	0.13018	0.14012	0.15008	54
55	0.08118	0.08597	0.09079	0.09565	0.10053	0.11035	0.12024	0.13016.	0.14010	0.15007	55

Use of the table: the table shows the equal annual payment ('x' in the formula) required to pay off a loan of 1 unit where the annual compound interest rate paid is shown at the head of a column (r) and the number of years for which payment is made is shown in the column at each side of a line (n). For example, where the annual compound interest rate paid is 17%, 1 unit is paid off after 5 years by an equal annual payment of 0.312564

$$x = \frac{\frac{r}{100}}{1 - \left[1 + \frac{r}{100}\right]^{-n}}$$

Equal annual payment to pay off a loan of 1 unit   Mortgage repayments

n Years	% rate 16	% rate 17	% rate 18	% rate 19	% rate 20	% rate 21	% rate 22	% rate 23	% rate 24	% rate 25	n Years
1	1.160000	1.170000	1.180000	1.190000	1.200000	1.210000	1.220000	1.230000	1.240000	1.250000	1
2	0.622963	0.630829	0.638716	0.646621	0.654545	0.662489	0.670450	0.678430	0.686429	0.694444	2
3	0.445258	0.452574	0.459924	0.467308	0.474725	0.482175	0.489658	0.497173	0.504718	0.512295	3
4	0.357375	0.364533	0.371739	0.378991	0.386289	0.393632	0.401020	0.408451	0.415926	0.423442	4
5	0.305409	0.312564	0.319778	0.327050	0.334380	0.341765	0.349206	0.356700	0.364248	0.371847	5
6	0.271390	0.278615	0.285910	0.293274	0.300706	0.308203	0.315764	0.323389	0.331074	0.338819	6
7	0.247613	0.254947	0.262362	0.269855	0.277424	0.285067	0.292782	0.300568	0.308422	0.316342	7
8	0.230224	0.237690	0.245244	0.252885	0.260609	0.268415	0.276299	0.284259	0.292293	0.300399	8
9	0.217082	0.224691	0.232395	0.240192	0.248079	0.256053	0.264111	0.272249	0.280465	0.288756	9
10	0.206901	0.214657	0.222515	0.230471	0.238523	0.246665	0.254895	0.263208	0.271602	0.280073	10
11	0.198861	0.206765	0.214776	0.222891	0.231104	0.239411	0.247807	0.256289	0.264852	0.273493	11
12	0.192415	0.200466	0.208628	0.216896	0.225265	0.233730	0.242285	0.250926	0.259648	0.268448	12
13	0.187184	0.195378	0.203686	0.212102	0.220620	0.229234	0.237939	0.246728	0.255598	0.264543	13
14	0.182898	0.191230	0.199678	0.208235	0.216893	0.225647	0.234491	0.243418	0.252423	0.261501	14
15	0.179358	0.187822	0.196403	0.205092	0.213882	0.222766	0.231738	0.240791	0.249919	0.259117	15
16	0.176414	0.185004	0.193710	0.202523	0.211436	0.220441	0.229530	0.238697	0.247936	0.257241	16
17	0.173952	0.182662	0.191485	0.200414	0.209440	0.218555	0.227751	0.237021	0.246359	0.255759	17
18	0.171885	0.180706	0.189639	0.198676	0.207805	0.217020	0.226313	0.235676	0.245102	0.254586	18
19	0.170142	0.179067	0.188103	0.197238	0.206462	0.215769	0.225148	0.234593	0.244098	0.253656	19
20	0.168667	0.177690	0.186820	0.196045	0.205357	0.214745	0.224202	0.233720	0.243294	0.252916	20
21	0.167416	0.176530	0.185746	0.195054	0.204444	0.213906	0.223432	0.233016	0.242649	0.252327	21
22	0.166353	0.175550	0.184846	0.194229	0.203690	0.213218	0.222805	0.232446	0.242132	0.251858	22
23	0.165447	0.174721	0.184090	0.193542	0.203065	0.212652	0.222294	0.231984	0.241716	0.251485	23
24	0.164673	0.174019	0.183454	0.192967	0.202548	0.212187	0.221877	0.231611	0.241382	0.251186	24
25	0.164013	0.173423	0.182919	0.192487	0.202119	0.211804	0.221536	0.231308	0.241113	0.250948	25
26	0.163447	0.172917	0.182467	0.192086	0.201762	0.211489	0.221258	0.231062	0.240897	0.250758	26
27	0.162963	0.172487	0.182087	0.191750	0.201467	0.211229	0.221030	0.230863	0.240723	0.250606	27
28	0.162548	0.172121	0.181765	0.191468	0.201221	0.211015	0.220843	0.230701	0.240583	0.250485	28
29	0.162192	0.171810	0.181494	0.191232	0.201016	0.210838	0.220691	0.230570	0.240470	0.250387	29
30	0.161886	0.171545	0.181264	0.191034	0.200846	0.210692	0.220566	0.230463	0.240379	0.250310	30
31	0.161623	0.171318	0.181070	0.190869	0.200705	0.210572	0.220464	0.230376	0.240305	0.250248	31
32	0.161397	0.171126	0.180906	0.190729	0.200587	0.210472	0.220380	0.230306	0.240246	0.250198	32
33	0.161203	0.170961	0.180767	0.190612	0.200489	0.210390	0.220311	0.230249	0.240198	0.250159	33
34	0.161036	0.170821	0.180650	0.190514	0.200407	0.210322	0.220255	0.230202	0.240160	0.250127	34
35	0.160892	0.170701	0.180550	0.190432	0.200339	0.210266	0.220209	0.230164	0.240129	0.250101	35
36	0.160769	0.170599	0.180466	0.190363	0.200283	0.210220	0.220171	0.230133	0.240104	0.250081	36
37	0.160662	0.170512	0.180395	0.190305	0.200235	0.210182	0.220140	0.230109	0.240084	0.250065	37
38	0.160571	0.170437	0.180335	0.190256	0.200196	0.210150	0.220115	0.230088	0.240068	0.250052	38
39	0.160492	0.170373	0.180284	0.190215	0.200163	0.210124	0.220094	0.230072	0.240055	0.250042	39
40	0.160424	0.170319	0.180240	0.190181	0.200136	0.210103	0.220077	0.230058	0.240044	0.250033	40
41	0.160365	0.170273	0.180204	0.190152	0.200113	0.210085	0.220063	0.230047	0.240035	0.250027	41
42	0.160315	0.170233	0.180172	0.190128	0.200095	0.210070	0.220052	0.230039	0.240029	0.250021	42
43	0.160271	0.170199	0.180146	0.190107	0.200079	0.210058	0.220043	0.230031	0.240023	0.250017	43
44	0.160234	0.170170	0.180124	0.190090	0.200066	0.210048	0.220035	0.230025	0.240019	0.250014	44
45	0.160201	0.170145	0.180105	0.190076	0.200055	0.210040	0.220029	0.230021	0.240015	0.250011	45
46	0.160174	0.170124	0.180089	0.190064	0.200046	0.210033	0.220023	0.230017	0.240012	0.250009	46
47	0.160150	0.170106	0.180075	0.190053	0.200038	0.210027	0.220019	0.230014	0.240010	0.250007	47
48	0.160129	0.170091	0.180064	0.190045	0.200032	0.210022	0.220016	0.230011	0.240008	0.250006	48
49	0.160111	0.170078	0.180054	0.190038	0.200026	0.210018	0.220013	0.230009	0.240006	0.250004	49
50	0.160096	0.170066	0.180046	0.190032	0.200022	0.210015	0.220011	0.230007	0.240005	0.250004	50
51	0.160083	0.170057	0.180039	0.190027	0.200018	0.210013	0.220009	0.230006	0.240004	0.250003	51
52	0.160071	0.170048	0.180033	0.190022	0.200015	0.210010	0.220007	0.230005	0.240003	0.250002	52
53	0.160061	0.170041	0.180028	0.190019	0.200013	0.210009	0.220006	0.230004	0.240003	0.250002	53
54	0.160053	0.170035	0.180024	0.190016	0.200011	0.210007	0.220005	0.230003	0.240002	0.250001	54
55	0.160046	0.170030	0.180020	0.190013	0.200009	0.210006	0.220004	0.230003	0.240002	0.250001	55

Percentage reversals

Note. The percentage 'reversal' is the term used here for the value which brings a gross amount, including a percentage, back to the net figure before the percentage was added. For example, 100 + 10% = 110; 110 − 9.1% = 100, where 9.1% is the percentage 'reversal' of 10%

Use of the table: the unit at the side of a line for each section, added to the unit at the head of a column, makes up the number for which the percentage 'reversal' is shown in the position where line and column meet. For example, 10 + 0.1 = 10.1; the percentage 'reversal' of 10.1% is 9.2%

%	% 0.0	% 0.1	% 0.2	% 0.3	% 0.4	% 0.5	% 0.6	% 0.7	% 0.8	% 0.9
0	0.0	0.1	0.2	0.3	0.4	0.5	0.6	0.7	0.8	0.9
1	1.0	1.1	1.2	1.3	1.4	1.5	1.6	1.7	1.8	1.9
2	2.0	2.1	2.2	2.2	2.3	2.4	2.5	2.6	2.7	2.8
3	2.9	3.0	3.1	3.2	3.3	3.4	3.5	3.6	3.7	3.8
4	3.8	3.9	4.0	4.1	4.2	4.3	4.4	4.5	4.6	4.7
5	4.8	4.9	4.9	5.0	5.1	5.2	5.3	5.4	5.5	5.6
6	5.7	5.7	5.8	5.9	6.0	6.1	6.2	6.3	6.4	6.5
7	6.5	6.6	6.7	6.8	6.9	7.0	7.1	7.1	7.2	7.3
8	7.4	7.5	7.6	7.7	7.7	7.8	7.9	8.0	8.1	8.2
9	8.3	8.3	8.4	8.5	8.6	8.7	8.8	8.8	8.9	9.0
10	9.1	9.2	9.3	9.3	9.4	9.5	9.6	9.7	9.7	9.8
11	9.9	10.0	10.1	10.2	10.2	10.3	10.4	10.5	10.6	10.6
12	10.7	10.8	10.9	11.0	11.0	11.1	11.2	11.3	11.3	11.4
13	11.5	11.6	11.7	11.7	11.8	11.9	12.0	12.0	12.1	12.2
14	12.3	12.4	12.4	12.5	12.6	12.7	12.7	12.8	12.9	13.0
15	13.0	13.1	13.2	13.3	13.3	13.4	13.5	13.6	13.6	13.7
16	13.8	13.9	13.9	14.0	14.1	14.2	14.2	14.3	14.4	14.5
17	14.5	14.6	14.7	14.7	14.8	14.9	15.0	15.0	15.1	15.2
18	15.3	15.3	15.4	15.5	15.5	15.6	15.7	15.8	15.8	15.9
19	16.0	16.0	16.1	16.2	16.2	16.3	16.4	16.5	16.5	16.6
20	16.7	16.7	16.8	16.9	16.9	17.0	17.1	17.1	17.2	17.3
21	17.4	17.4	17.5	17.6	17.6	17.7	17.8	17.8	17.9	18.0
22	18.0	18.1	18.2	18.2	18.3	18.4	18.4	18.5	18.6	18.6
23	18.7	18.8	18.8	18.9	19.0	19.0	19.1	19.2	19.2	19.3
24	19.4	19.4	19.5	19.5	19.6	19.7	19.7	19.8	19.9	19.9
25	20.0	20.1	20.1	20.2	20.3	20.3	20.4	20.4	20.5	20.6
26	20.6	20.7	20.8	20.8	20.9	20.9	21.0	21.1	21.1	21.2
27	21.3	21.3	21.4	21.4	21.5	21.6	21.6	21.7	21.8	21.8
28	21.9	21.9	22.0	22.1	22.1	22.2	22.2	22.3	22.4	22.4
29	22.5	22.5	22.6	22.7	22.7	22.8	22.8	22.9	23.0	23.0
30	23.1	23.1	23.2	23.3	23.3	23.4	23.4	23.5	23.5	23.6
31	23.7	23.7	23.8	23.8	23.9	24.0	24.0	24.1	24.1	24.2
32	24.2	24.3	24.4	24.4	24.5	24.5	24.6	24.6	24.7	24.8
33	24.8	24.9	24.9	25.0	25.0	25.1	25.1	25.2	25.3	25.3
34	25.4	25.4	25.5	25.5	25.6	25.7	25.7	25.8	25.8	25.9
35	25.9	26.0	26.0	26.1	26.1	26.2	26.3	26.3	26.4	26.4
36	26.5	26.5	26.6	26.6	26.7	26.7	26.8	26.8	26.9	27.0
37	27.0	27.1	27.1	27.2	27.2	27.3	27.3	27.4	27.4	27.5
38	27.5	27.6	27.6	27.7	27.7	27.8	27.8	27.9	28.0	28.0
39	28.1	28.1	28.2	28.2	28.3	28.3	28.4	28.4	28.5	28.5
40	28.6	28.6	28.7	28.7	28.8	28.8	28.9	28.9	29.0	29.0
41	29.1	29.1	29.2	29.2	29.3	29.3	29.4	29.4	29.5	29.5
42	29.6	29.6	29.7	29.7	29.8	29.8	29.9	29.9	30.0	30.0
43	30.1	30.1	30.2	30.2	30.3	30.3	30.4	30.4	30.5	30.5
44	30.6	30.6	30.7	30.7	30.7	30.8	30.8	30.9	30.9	31.0
45	31.0	31.1	31.1	31.2	31.2	31.3	31.3	31.4	31.4	31.5
46	31.5	31.6	31.6	31.6	31.7	31.7	31.8	31.8	31.9	31.9
47	32.0	32.0	32.1	32.1	32.2	32.2	32.2	32.3	32.3	32.4
48	32.4	32.5	32.5	32.6	32.6	32.7	32.7	32.8	32.8	32.8
49	32.9	32.9	33.0	33.0	33.1	33.1	33.2	33.2	33.2	33.3

%	% 0.0	% 0.1	% 0.2	% 0.3	% 0.4	% 0.5	% 0.6	% 0.7	% 0.8	% 0.9
50	33.3	33.4	33.4	33.5	33.5	33.6	33.6	33.6	33.7	33.7
51	33.8	33.8	33.9	33.9	33.9	34.0	34.0	34.1	34.1	34.2
52	34.2	34.3	34.3	34.3	34.4	34.4	34.5	34.5	34.6	34.6
53	34.6	34.7	34.7	34.8	34.8	34.9	34.9	34.9	35.0	35.0
54	35.1	35.1	35.1	35.2	35.2	35.3	35.3	35.4	35.4	35.4
55	35.5	35.5	35.6	35.6	35.6	35.7	35.7	35.8	35.8	35.9
56	35.9	35.9	36.0	36.0	36.1	36.1	36.1	36.2	36.2	36.3
57	36.3	36.3	36.4	36.4	36.5	36.5	36.5	36.6	36.6	36.7
58	36.7	36.7	36.8	36.8	36.9	36.9	36.9	37.0	37.0	37.1
59	37.1	37.1	37.2	37.2	37.3	37.3	37.3	37.4	37.4	37.5
60	37.5	37.5	37.6	37.6	37.7	37.7	37.7	37.8	37.8	37.8
61	37.9	37.9	38.0	38.0	38.0	38.1	38.1	38.2	38.2	38.2
62	38.3	38.3	38.3	38.4	38.4	38.5	38.5	38.5	38.6	38.6
63	38.7	38.7	38.7	38.8	38.8	38.8	38.9	38.9	38.9	39.0
64	39.0	39.1	39.1	39.1	39.2	39.2	39.2	39.3	39.3	39.4
65	39.4	39.4	39.5	39.5	39.5	39.6	39.6	39.6	39.7	39.7
66	39.8	39.8	39.8	39.9	39.9	39.9	40.0	40.0	40.0	40.1
67	40.1	40.2	40.2	40.2	40.3	40.3	40.3	40.4	40.4	40.4
68	40.5	40.5	40.5	40.6	40.6	40.7	40.7	40.7	40.8	40.8
69	40.8	40.9	40.9	40.9	41.0	41.0	41.0	41.1	41.1	41.1
70	41.2	41.2	41.2	41.3	41.3	41.3	41.4	41.4	41.5	41.5
71	41.5	41.6	41.6	41.6	41.7	41.7	41.7	41.8	41.8	41.8
72	41.9	41.9	41.9	42.0	42.0	42.0	42.1	42.1	42.1	42.2
73	42.2	42.2	42.3	42.3	42.3	42.4	42.4	42.4	42.5	42.5
74	42.5	42.6	42.6	42.6	42.7	42.7	42.7	42.8	42.8	42.8
75	42.9	42.9	42.9	43.0	43.0	43.0	43.1	43.1	43.1	43.1
76	43.2	43.2	43.2	43.3	43.3	43.3	43.4	43.4	43.4	43.5
77	43.5	43.5	43.6	43.6	43.6	43.7	43.7	43.7	43.8	43.8
78	43.8	43.9	43.9	43.9	43.9	44.0	44.0	44.0	44.1	44.1
79	44.1	44.2	44.2	44.2	44.3	44.3	44.3	44.4	44.4	44.4
80	44.4	44.5	44.5	44.5	44.6	44.6	44.6	44.7	44.7	44.7
81	44.8	44.8	44.8	44.8	44.9	44.9	44.9	45.0	45.0	45.0
82	45.1	45.1	45.1	45.1	45.2	45.2	45.2	45.3	45.3	45.3
83	45.4	45.4	45.4	45.4	45.5	45.5	45.5	45.6	45.6	45.6
84	45.7	45.7	45.7	45.7	45.8	45.8	45.8	45.9	45.9	45.9
85	45.9	46.0	46.0	46.0	46.1	46.1	46.1	46.1	46.2	46.2
86	46.2	46.3	46.3	46.3	46.4	46.4	46.4	46.4	46.5	46.5
87	46.5	46.6	46.6	46.6	46.7	46.7	46.7	46.7	46.8	46.8
88	46.8	46.8	46.9	46.9	46.9	46.9	47.0	47.0	47.0	47.1
89	47.1	47.1	47.1	47.2	47.2	47.2	47.3	47.3	47.3	47.3
90	47.4	47.4	47.4	47.5	47.5	47.5	47.5	47.6	47.6	47.6
91	47.6	47.7	47.7	47.7	47.8	47.8	47.8	47.8	47.9	47.9
92	47.9	47.9	48.0	48.0	48.0	48.1	48.1	48.1	48.1	48.2
93	48.2	48.2	48.2	48.3	48.3	48.3	48.3	48.4	48.4	48.4
94	48.5	48.5	48.5	48.5	48.6	48.6	48.6	48.6	48.7	48.7
95	48.7	48.7	48.8	48.8	48.8	48.8	48.9	48.9	48.9	49.0
96	49.0	49.0	49.0	49.1	49.1	49.1	49.1	49.2	49.2	49.2
97	49.2	49.3	49.3	49.3	49.4	49.4	49.4	49.4	49.5	49.5
98	49.5	49.5	49.5	49.6	49.6	49.6	49.6	49.7	49.7	49.7
99	49.7	49.8	49.8	49.8	49.8	49.9	49.9	49.9	49.9	50.0

Glossary and index

Glossary

Numbers

Preferred numbers

The following table gives the series of preferred numbers recommended by ISO for use where a range of sizes is required (see, for example, wire pages 145–146). These are designated R 5, R 10, R 20, R 40 and R 80 in order of preference; the R 80 series is to be used only exceptionally. The R stands for Renard and the number indicates the particular root of 10 on which the series is based; the numbers in the series are not exact theoretical values but are rounded (see also page 192).

Basic series				Serial number
R 5	R 10	R 20	R 40	
1.00	1.00	1.00	1.00	0
			1.06	1
		1.12	1.12	2
			1.18	3
	1.25	1.25	1.25	4
			1.32	5
		1.40	1.40	6
			1.50	7
1.60	1.60	1.60	1.60	8
			1.70	9
		1.80	1.80	10
			1.90	11
	2.00	2.00	2.00	12
			2.12	13
		2.24	2.24	14
			2.36	15
2.50	2.50	2.50	2.50	16
			2.65	17
		2.80	2.80	18
			3.00	19
	3.15	3.15	3.15	20
			3.35	21
		3.55	3.55	22
			3.75	23
4.00	4.00	4.00	4.00	24
			4.25	25
		4.50	4.50	26
			4.75	27
	5.00	5.00	5.00	28
			5.30	29
		5.60	5.60	30
			6.00	31
6.30	6.30	6.30	6.30	32
			6.70	33
		7.10	7.10	34
			7.50	35
	8.00	8.00	8.00	36
			8.50	37
		9.00	9.00	38
			9.50	39
10.00	10.00	10.00	10.00	40

Exceptional R 80 series

1.00	1.40	2.00	2.80	4.00	5.60	8.00
1.03	1.45	2.06	2.90	4.12	5.80	8.25
1.06	1.50	2.12	3.00	4.25	6.00	8.50
1.09	1.55	2.18	3.07	4.37	6.15	8.75
1.12	1.60	2.24	3.15	4.50	6.30	9.00
1.15	1.65	2.30	3.25	4.62	6.50	9.25
1.18	1.70	2.36	3.35	4.75	6.70	9.50
1.22	1.75	2.43	3.45	4.87	6.90	9.75
1.25	1.80	2.50	3.55	5.00	7.10	
1.28	1.85	2.58	3.65	5.15	7.30	
1.32	1.90	2.65	3.75	5.30	7.50	
1.36	1.95	2.72	3.87	5.45	7.75	

Other numbers

Roman numerals

I	1	X	10	C	100	M	1 000
V	5	L	50	D	500		

In making up other numbers, a smaller number placed after a larger is to be added to it, and a smaller number placed before a larger is to be taken from it; for example:

I	1	VI	6	XX	20	LXX	70
II	2	VII	7	XXX	30	LXXX	80
III	3	VIII	8	XL	40	XC	90
IV	4	IX	9	L	50	C	100
V	5	X	10	LX	60	CM	900

Anglo-Asian (Bangladesh, India, Pakistan)

1 lac or lakh = 1,00,000 = 100 000 = one hundred thousand
10 lacs or lakhs = 10,00,000 = 1 000 000 = one million
1 arab[a] = 100 crores = 1,00,00,00,000 = 1 000 000 000 = one thousand million

[a]Or arb.

Portugal

1 conto = 1 000 escudos

General

2 items		= 1 pair
12 items =	6 pairs	= 1 dozen[a]
20 items =	10 pairs	= 1 score[b]
144 items =	12 dozen	= 1 gross
1 728 items =	12 gross	= 1 great gross

[a]1 long or baker's dozen is 13 items.   [b]1 long score is 21 items.

100 items = 1 short hundred
120 items = 1 long hundred

Mathematical symbols

+	plus or positive	$\geqq$	equal to or greater than
−	minus or negative	$\leqq$	equal to or less than
±	plus or minus, positive or negative	$\gg$	much greater than
×	multiplied by	$\ll$	much less than
÷ /	divided by	$r!$ / $\lfloor r$	factorial r
=	equal to	$\sqrt{\ }$	square root
≡	identically equal to	$\sqrt[r]{\ }$	rth root
≠	not equal to	r^n	r to the power of n
≢	not identically equal to	∝	is proportional to or varies with
≃ ≈ ≅	approximately equal to	∞	infinity
		%	per cent
⌣	of the order of or similar to	‰	per mille (thousand)
>	greater than	Σ	sum of
<	less than	Π	product of
≯	not greater than	Δ	difference
≮	not less than	∴	therefore

Also see pages 189 and 190 for trigonometric symbols

Greek alphabet

Α	α	alpha	Ι	ι	iota	Ρ	ρ	rho
Β	β	beta	Κ	κ	kappa	Σ	σ or s	sigma
Γ	γ	gamma	Λ	λ	lambda	Τ	τ	tau
Δ	δ	delta	Μ	μ	mu	Υ	υ	upsilon
Ε	ε	epsilon	Ν	ν	nu	Φ	φ	phi
Ζ	ζ	zeta	Ξ	ξ	xi	Χ	χ	chi
Η	η	eta	Ο	ο	omicron	Ψ	ψ	psi
Θ	θ	theta	Π	π	pi	Ω	ω	omega

Common abbreviations and symbols

Also see atomic table (pages 120–121) for symbols of elements and page 167 for symbols of textile measuring systems. Some of the symbols shown here are not among those recommended under the International System of Units.

a	atto (as prefix) or are
A	ampere
Å	ångström
a/c	account
ac	acre
AC	appellation contrôlée
ACT	advance corporation tax
apoth.	apothecaries
@	at
at	technical atmosphere
AT	atomic time
atm	standard atmosphere
AU	astronomical unit
av.	
avdp	avoirdupois
avoir	
bbl	barrel
b/d	barrels per day
bd ft	board foot
Bé	Baumé
bhp	brake horsepower
bpd	barrels per day
BST	British summer time
BSW	British Standard Whitworth
Btu	British thermal unit
bu	bushel
c	centi (as prefix) or carat
C	coulomb, Celsius or centigrade
cal	calorie
Cal	calorie (dieticians')
cc	cubic centimetre
cd	candela or cord
cf	cubic foot
c & f	cost and freight
cg	centigram
CGS	centimetre, gram and second
ch	chain or metric horsepower or chhatack
ch²	square chain
Chu	centigrade heat unit
Ci	curie
c & i	cost and insurance
cif	cost, insurance and freight
ck	cask
cl	centilitre
cm	centimetre
cm²	square centimetre
cm³	cubic centimetre
CM	metric carat
coa	cash on arrival
cod	cash on delivery
cP	centipoise
cSt	centistokes
ct	metric carat
ctl	cental
cu.	cubic
cwo	cash with order
cwt	hundredweight
d	deci (as prefix) or day
da	deca or deka
dB	decibel
DCE	domestic credit expansion

DCF	discounted cash flow
DIN	Deutsche industrie normal
dk	deka or deca
dl	decilitre
dm	decimetre
dm³	cubic decimetre
doz.	dozen
dr	dram
drm	drachm
dw	deadweight tonnage
dwt	pennyweight
DWT	deadweight tonnage
E	Engler
E & OE	errors and omissions excepted
est.	estimated
ET	ephemeris time
eV	electron volt
f	femto (as prefix)
F	farad or Fahrenheit
fa	free alongside
faa	free of all average
faq	fair average quality
fas	free alongside ship
fbm	foot board measure
ffa	free from alongside
fg	frigorie
fga	foreign general average
fib	free into bunkers
Fifo	first in, first out
fio	free in and out
fios	free in and out stowed
fiot	free in and out trimmed
fl drm	fluid drachm
fl oz	fluid ounce
fob	free on board
foq	free on quay
for	free on rail
fos	free on steamer
fot	free on trucks
ft	foot
ft²	square foot
ft³	cubic foot
fur	furlong
g	gram
G	giga (as prefix)
γ	microgram
g_n	standard gravity value
gal	gallon
Gal	galileo
gm	gram
gn	grain
gr	grain
grt	
GRT	gross registered tonnage
gsm	grams per square metre
GW	gigawatt
h	hecto (as prefix) or hour
H	henry
ha	hectare
hhd	hogshead
hl	hectolitre
hp	horsepower
hw	high water
Hz	hertz
ihp	indicated horsepower
in	inch
ips	inches per second
iu	international unit
J	joule
k	kilo (as prefix)
K	kelvin

kcal	kilocalorie
kg	kilogram
kgf	kilogram-force
kHz	kilohertz
kilo	kilogram
kJ	kilojoule
kl	kilolitre
km	kilometre
km²	square kilometre
kn	international knot
kp	kilopond
ksi	kips per square inch
kW h	kilowatt hour
l or L	litre
lat.	latitude
lb	pound
lbf	pound-force
Lifo	last in, first out
lk	link
lm	lumen
ln	logarithm to base e
LNG	liquefied natural gas
loa	length overall
long.	longitude
LPG	liquefied petroleum gas
lw	low water
lwl	length on the waterline
ly	light year
m	milli (as prefix) or metre
M	mega (as prefix) or money stock
μ	micro (as prefix) or micron
m²	square metre
m³	cubic metre
mb	
mbar	millibar
md	maund
mg	milligram
MHz	megahertz
mi	mile
min	minute or minim
ml	millilitre
mm	millimetre
μm	micrometre
mm²	square millimetre
mm³	cubic millimetre
mn	million
m_n^3	normal cubic metre
mph	miles per hour
mrd	milliard
MW	megawatt
my	myria (as prefix)
n	nano (as prefix)
N	newton
na	not available
ndw	
NDW	net deadweight
nes	not elsewhere shown or specified
net	netto (lowest)
nm	nanometre
Nm³	normal cubic metre
n mile	international nautical mile
nom.	nominal
nop	not otherwise provided
nos	not otherwise shown
npv	no par value
nrt	
NRT	net registered tonnage
Ω	ohm
op	overproof
oz	ounce, avoirdupois
ozf	ounce-force
oz tr	ounce, troy

p	pico (as prefix)
P	poise
Pa	pascal
pc	parsec
pdl	poundal
P/E	price/earnings ratio
pH	potential hydrogen
pk	peck
pm	picometre
ppm	parts per million
psi	pounds per square inch
pt	pint
ptg std	petrograd standard
pz	pièze
q	quintal
qn	quotation
qr	quarter
qt	quart
R	Rankine or röntgen
rad	radian
rd	running days
RD	refer to drawer or relative density
Red	Redwood
rp	return of post
rpm	revolutions per minute
s	second
S	siemens
SAE	Society of Automotive Engineers
Scf	standard cubic foot
SDR	special drawing right
sec	second
sg	specific gravity
SI	International system of units
sk	sack
smd	standard man-day
sn	sthène
sq.	square
sr	steradian
st	stone
St	stokes
std	standard
stp	standard temperature and pressure
SUS	Saybolt universal second
t	tonne or metric ton
T	tera (as prefix) or tesla
tce	tonnes of coal equivalent
TEU	twenty-foot equivalent units
thou	one-thousandth of an inch
TPI	tons per inch immersion
tr	troy
TR	tons registered
u	unified atomic mass unit
ua	unit of account
up	underproof
UT	universal time
UTC	coordinated universal time
V	volt
W	watt
Wb	weber
wpa	with particular average
xc	ex coupon
xd	ex dividend
yd	yard
yd²	square yard
yd³	cubic yard

Country codes and currencies

In the following table, country codes are included for reference; the currency code is that introduced by the International Organisation for Standardisation (ISO), and refers to the main currency unit. The country position refers to mid-1980.

Currencies in use

Rates of exchange between currencies have in general been floating from the early 1970's. The change in the relative equivalent of currencies is referred to as devaluation from the point of view of the currency for which more are being exchanged for another, and revaluation or upvaluation where less are being

offered for another. For example, when the United Kingdom changed its rate of exchange against the United States dollar in 1967, the number of pounds per dollar changed from 0.357 approximately to 0.417 approximately, an increase and so a devaluation − of 16.7%. From the US viewpoint, the number of dollars per pound fell from 2.80 to 2.40, so there was an effective revaluation or upvaluation of the dollar against the pound of 14.3%.

For any devaluation, the corresponding rate of revaluation can be determined from the 'percentage reversals' table on page 222, for example, the percentage reversal of 16.7% is 14.3% (from the above illustration).

Following is a list of currencies and divisions for each country.

Country				Currency	
Country codes			Name	Code ISO	Currency unit and divisions
UN 3-digit	ISO Alpha-2	Alpha-3			
004	AF	AFG	Afghanistan	AFA	Afgháni = 100 puls
008	AL	ALB	Albania	ALL	Lek = 100 quintars
012	DZ	DZA	Algeria	DZD	Dinar = 100 centimes
			American Samoa: see Samoa, American		
020	AD	AND	Andorra	FRF	French franc, and
				ESP	Spanish peseta
024	AO	AGO	Angola	AOK	Kwanza = 100 lwei
028	AG	ATG	Antigua	XCD	East Caribbean dollar = 100 cents
			Antilles, Netherlands: see Netherlands Antilles		
032	AR	ARG	Argentina	ARP	Argentine peso = 100 centavos
036	AU	AUS	Australia	AUD	Australian dollar = 100 cents
040	AT	AUT	Austria	ATS	Schilling = 100 groschen
044	BS	BHS	Bahamas	BSD	Bahamian dollar = 100 cents
048	BH	BHR	Bahrain	BHD	Bahrain dinar = 1 000 fils
050	BD	BGD	Bangladesh	BDT	Taka = 100 poisha
052	BB	BRB	Barbados	BBD	Barbados dollar = 100 cents
056	BE	BEL	Belgium	BEF	Belgian franc = 100 centimes
084	BZ	BLZ	Belize	BZD	Belize dollar = 100 cents
204	BJ	BEN	Benin	XOF	CFA franc = 100 centimes
060	BM	BMU	Bermuda	BMD	Bermuda dollar = 100 cents
064	BT	BTN	Bhutan	INR	Indian rupee; also Ngultrum = 100 chetrum
068	BO	BOL	Bolivia	BOP	Bolivian peso = 100 centavos
072	BW	BWA	Botswana	BWP	Pula = 100 thebes
076	BR	BRA	Brazil	BRC	Cruzeiro = 100 centavos
086	IO	IOT	British Indian Ocean Territory	MUR	Mauritius rupee = 100 cents, and
				SCR	Seychelles rupee = 100 cents
			British Virgin Islands: see Virgin Islands, British		
096	BN	BRN	Brunei	BND	Brunei dollar = 100 cents
100	BG	BGR	Bulgaria	BGL	Lev = 100 stotinki
104	BU	BUR	Burma	BUK	Kyat = 100 pyas
108	BI	BDI	Burundi	BIF	Burundi franc = 100 centimes
116	KH	KHM	Cambodia	KHR	Riel = 100 sen
120	CM	CMR	Cameroon	XAF	CFA franc = 100 centimes
124	CA	CAN	Canada	CAD	Canadian dollar = 100 cents
132	CV	CPV	Cape Verde	CVE	Cape Verde escudo = 100 centavos
136	KY	CYM	Cayman Islands	KYD	Cayman Islands dollar = 100 cents
140	CF	CAF	Central African Republic	XAF	CFA franc = 100 centimes
148	TD	TCD	Chad	XAF	CFA franc = 100 centimes
152	CL	CHL	Chile	CLP	Chilean peso = 100 centavos
156	CN	CHN	China	CNY	Yuan = 10 chiao (jiao) = 100 fen
162	CX	CXR	Christmas Island	AUD	Australian dollar = 100 cents
166	CC	CCK	Cocos Islands	AUD	Australian dollar = 100 cents
170	CO	COL	Colombia	COP	Colombian peso = 100 centavos
174	KM	COM	Comoros	KMF	Comoros franc = 100 centimes
178	CG	COG	Congo	XAF	CFA franc = 100 centimes
184	CK	COK	Cook Islands	NZD	New Zealand dollar = 100 cents
188	CR	CRI	Costa Rica	CRC	Colón = 100 céntimos
192	CU	CUB	Cuba	CUP	Cuban peso = 100 centavos
196	CY	CYP	Cyprus	CYP	Cyprus pound = 1 000 mils
200	CS	CSK	Czechoslovakia	CSK	Koruna (crown) = 100 haler
208	DK	DNK	Denmark	DKK	Danish krone = 100 øre
262	DJ	DJI	Djibouti	DJF	Djibouti franc = 100 centimes
212	DM	DMA	Dominica	XCD	East Caribbean dollar = 100 cents
214	DO	DOM	Dominican Republic	DOP	Dominican peso = 100 centavos

Country codes and currencies

Country				Currency	
Country codes			Name	Code	Currency unit and divisions
UN 3-digit	ISO Alpha-2	Alpha-3		ISO	
218	EC	ECU	Ecuador	ECS	Sucre = 100 centavos
818	EG	EGY	Egypt	EGP	Egyptian pound = 100 piastres = 1 000 millièmes
			Eire: see Ireland, Republic of		
222	SV	SLV	El Salvador	SVC	Colón = 100 centavos
226	GQ	GNQ	Equatorial Guinea	GQE	Ekwele = 100 céntimos
230	ET	ETH	Ethiopia	ETB	Birr = 100 cents
238	FK	FLK	Falkland Islands	FKP	Falkland Island pound = 100 new pence
234	FO	FRO	Faroes	DKK	Danish krone = 100 øre
242	FJ	FJI	Fiji	FJD	Fiji dollar = 100 cents
246	FI	FIN	Finland	FIM	Markka = 100 penni
			Formosa: see Taiwan		
250	FR	FRA	France	FRF	French franc = 100 centimes
			French Polynesia: see Polynesia, French		
266	GA	GAB	Gabon	XAF	CFA franc = 100 centimes
270	GM	GMB	Gambia	GMD	Dalasi = 100 bututs
278	DD	DDR	Germany, East	DDM	Mark (Ostmark) = 100 pfennig
280	DE	DEU	Germany, West	DEM	Deutsche mark = 100 pfennig
288	GH	GHA	Ghana	GHC	Cedi = 100 pesewas
292	GI	GIB	Gibraltar	GIP	Gibraltar pound = 100 new pence
300	GR	GRC	Greece	GRD	Drachma = 100 lepta
304	GL	GRL	Greenland	DKK	Danish krone = 100 øre
308	GD	GRD	Grenada	XCD	East Caribbean dollar = 100 cents
312	GP	GLP	Guadeloupe	FRF	French franc = 100 centimes
316	GU	GUM	Guam	USD	US dollar = 100 cents
320	GT	GTM	Guatemala	GTQ	Quetzal = 100 centavos
254	GF	GUF	Guiana, French	FRF	French franc = 100 centimes
324	GN	GIN	Guinea	GNS	Syli = 100 cauris
624	GW	GNB	Guinea-Bissau	GWP	Guinea peso = 100 centavos
328	GY	GUY	Guyana	GYD	Guyana dollar = 100 cents
332	HT	HTI	Haiti	HTG	Gourde = 100 centimes
			Holland: see Netherlands		
340	HN	HND	Honduras	HNL	Lempira = 100 centavos
344	HK	HKG	Hongkong	HKD	Hongkong dollar = 100 cents
348	HU	HUN	Hungary	HUF	Forint = 100 fillér
352	IS	ISL	Iceland	ISK	Icelandic króna = 100 aurar (øre)
356	IN	IND	India	INR	Indian rupee = 100 paisa
360	ID	IDN	Indonesia	IDR	Rupiah = 100 sen
364	IR	IRN	Iran	IRR	Rial = 100 dinars
368	IQ	IRQ	Iraq	IQD	Iraqi dinar = 20 dirhams = 1 000 fils
372	IE	IRL	Ireland, Republic of	IEP	Punt = 100 pighne
376	IL	ISR	Israel	ILS	Shekel = 100 new agorot
380	IT	ITA	Italy	ITL	Italian lira = 100 centesimi
384	CI	CIV	Ivory Coast	XOF	CFA franc = 100 centimes
388	JM	JAM	Jamaica	JMD	Jamaican dollar = 100 cents
392	JP	JPN	Japan	JPY	Yen = 100 sen
396	JT	JTN	Johnston Island	USD	United States dollar = 100 cents
400	JO	JOR	Jordan	JOD	Jordan dinar = 1 000 fils
890	YU	YUG	Jugoslavia	YUD	Jugoslav dinar = 100 paras
			Kampuchea: see Cambodia		
404	KE	KEN	Kenya	KES	Kenya shilling = 100 cents
296	KI	KIR	Kiribati	AUD	Australian dollar = 100 cents
408	KP	PRK	Korea, North	KPW	North Korean Won = 100 chon (jun)
410	KR	KOR	Korea, South	KRW	South Korean Won = 100 chon (jun)
414	KW	KWT	Kuwait	KWD	Kuwaiti dinar = 10 dirhams = 1 000 fils
418	LA	LAO	Laos	LAK	new Kip = 100 at
422	LB	LBN	Lebanon	LBP	Lebanese pound = 100 piastres
426	LS	LSO	Lesotho	LSM	Loti (maloti for 2 or more) = 100 lisente
430	LR	LBR	Liberia	LRD	Liberian dollar = 100 cents
434	LY	LBY	Libya	LYD	Libyan dinar = 1 000 dirhams
438	LI	LIE	Liechtenstein	CHF	Swiss franc = 100 centimes (rappen)
442	LU	LUX	Luxembourg	LUF	Luxembourg franc = 100 centimes

Country codes and currencies

Country				Currency	
Country codes			Name	Code	Currency unit and divisions
UN 3-digit	ISO Alpha-2	Alpha-3		ISO	
446	MO	MAC	Macao	MOP	Pataca = 100 avos
450	MG	MDG	Madagascar	MGF	Madagascar franc = 100 centimes
454	MW	MWI	Malawi	MWK	Kwacha = 100 tambala
458	MY	MYS	Malaysia	MYR	Ringgit = 100 sen
462	MV	MDV	Maldives	MVR	Maldivian rupee = 100 laris
466	ML	MLI	Mali	MLF	Mali franc = 100 centimes
470	MT	MLT	Malta	MTP	Maltese pound = 100 cents = 1 000 mils
			Marianas, Northern: see Pacific Islands, US		
474	MQ	MTQ	Martinique	FRF	French franc = 100 centimes
478	MR	MRT	Mauritania	MRO	Ouguiya = 5 khoums
480	MU	MUS	Mauritius	MUR	Mauritius rupee = 100 cents
484	MX	MEX	Mexico	MXP	Mexican peso = 100 centavos
488	MI	MID	Midway Islands	USD	US dollar = 100 cents
492	MC	MCO	Monaco	FRF	French franc = 100 centimes
496	MN	MNG	Mongolia	MNT	Tugrik or Tögrög = 100 möngö
500	MS	MSR	Montserrat	XCD	East Caribbean dollar = 100 cents
504	MA	MAR	Morocco	MAD	Dirham = 100 centimes
508	MZ	MOZ	Mozambique	MZM	Metical = 100 centavos
			Namibia: see South-West Africa		
520	NR	NRU	Nauru	AUD	Australian dollar = 100 cents
524	NP	NPL	Nepal	NPR	Nepalese rupee = 2 mohur = 100 paisa (pice)
528	NL	NLD	Netherlands	NLG	Guilder (florin) = 100 cents
532	AN	ANT	Netherlands Antilles	ANG	Netherlands Antillian guilder (florin) = 100 cents
540	NC	NCL	New Caledonia	XPF	CFP franc = 100 centimes
			New Hebrides: see Vanuatu		
554	NZ	NZL	New Zealand	NZD	New Zealand dollar = 100 cents
558	NI	NIC	Nicaragua	NIC	Córdoba = 100 centavos
562	NE	NER	Niger	XOF	CFA franc = 100 centimes
566	NG	NGA	Nigeria	NGN	Naira = 100 kobo
570	NU	NIU	Niue	NZD	New Zealand dollar = 100 cents
574	NF	NFK	Norfolk Island	AUD	Australian dollar = 100 cents
578	NO	NOR	Norway	NOK	Norwegian krone = 100 øre
512	OM	OMN	Oman	OMR	Rial Omani = 1 000 baizas
582	PC	PCI	Pacific Islands, US	USD	US dollar = 100 cents
586	PK	PAK	Pakistan	PKR	Pakistan rupee = 100 paisa
590	PA	PAN	Panama	PAB	Balboa = 100 centésimos
598	PG	PNG	Papua New Guinea	PGK	Kina = 100 toea
600	PY	PRY	Paraguay	PYG	Guaraní = 100 céntimos
604	PE	PER	Peru	PES	Sol = 100 centavos
608	PH	PHL	Philippines	PHP	Philippine peso = 100 centavos
612	PN	PCN	Pitcairn	NZD	New Zealand dollar = 100 cents
616	PL	POL	Poland	PLZ	Zloty = 100 groszy
258	PF	PYF	Polynesia, French	XPF	CFP franc = 100 centimes
620	PT	PRT	Portugal	PTE	Escudo = 100 centavos
630	PR	PRI	Puerto Rico	USD	US dollar = 100 cents
634	QA	QAT	Qatar	QAR	Qatar riyal = 100 dirhams
638	RE	REU	Reunion	FRF	French franc = 100 centimes
			Rhodesia: see Zimbabwe		
642	RO	ROM	Rumania	ROL	Leu = 100 bani
			Russia: see Soviet Union		
646	RW	RWA	Rwanda	RWF	Rwanda franc = 100 centimes
732	EH	ESH	Sahara, Western	MAD	Moroccan dirham = 100 centimes
658	KN	KNA	St Christopher (St Kitts)	XCD	East Caribbean dollar = 100 cents
654	SH	SHN	St Helena	SHP	St Helena pound = 100 new pence
662	LC	LCA	St Lucia	XCD	East Caribbean dollar = 100 cents
666	PM	SPM	St Pierre and Miquelon	FRF	French franc = 100 centimes
670	VC	VCT	St Vincent	XCD	East Caribbean dollar = 100 cents
			Salvador, El: see El Salvador		
016	AS	ASM	Samoa, American	USD	US dollar = 100 cents
882	WS	WSM	Samoa, Western	WST	Tala (dollar) = 100 sene (cents)
674	SM	SMR	San Marino	ITL	Italian lira = 100 centesimi
678	ST	STP	Sao Tome and Principe	STD	Dobra = 100 céntimos

Country codes and currencies

Country				Currency	
Country codes			Name	Code	Currency unit and divisions
UN 3-digit	ISO Alpha-2	Alpha-3		ISO	
682	SA	SAU	Saudi Arabia	SAR	Saudi riyal = 20 quirsh = 100 hallalas
686	SN	SEN	Senegal	XOF	CFA franc = 100 centimes
690	SC	SYC	Seychelles	SCR	Seychelles rupee = 100 cents
			Siam: see Thailand		
694	SL	SLE	Sierra Leone	SLL	Leone = 100 cents
702	SG	SGP	Singapore	SGD	Singapore dollar = 100 cents
090	SB	SLB	Solomon Islands	SBD	Solomon Islands dollar = 100 cents
706	SO	SOM	Somalia	SOS	Somali shilling = 100 centesimi
710	ZA	ZAF	South Africa	ZAR	Rand = 100 cents
616	NA	NAM	South-West Africa	ZAR	South African rand = 100 cents
810	SU	SUN	Soviet Union	SUR	Rouble = 100 kopecks
724	ES	ESP	Spain	ESP	Peseta = 100 céntimos
144	LK	LKA	Sri Lanka	LKR	Sri Lanka rupee = 100 cents
736	SD	SDN	Sudan	SDP	Sudanese pound = 100 piastres = 1 000 millièmes
740	SR	SUR	Surinam	SRG	Surinam guilder (florin) = 100 cents
748	SZ	SWZ	Swaziland	SZL	Lilangeni (Emalangeni for 2 or more) = 100 cents
752	SE	SWE	Sweden	SEK	Swedish krona = 100 öre
756	CH	CHE	Switzerland	CHF	Swiss franc (franken) = 100 centimes (rappen)
760	SY	SYR	Syria	SYP	Syrian pound = 100 piastres
			Tahiti: see Polynesia, French		
101	TW	TWN	Taiwan	TWD	New Taiwan dollar = 100 cents
834	TZ	TZA	Tanzania	TZS	Tanzanian shilling = 100 cents
764	TH	THA	Thailand	THB	Baht = 100 satang
626	TP	TMP	Timor, East	TPE	Timor escudo = 100 centavos, and
				IDR	Indonesian rupiah = 100 sen
768	TG	TGO	Togo	XOF	CFA franc = 100 centimes
772	TK	TKL	Tokelau	NZD	New Zealand dollar = 100 cents
776	TO	TON	Tonga	TOP	Pa'anga = 100 seniti
780	TT	TTO	Trinidad and Tobago	TTD	Trinidad and Tobago dollar = 100 cents
788	TN	TUN	Tunisia	TND	Tunisian dinar = 1 000 millimes
792	TR	TUR	Turkey	TRL	Turkish lira = 100 kurus (piastres)
796	TC	TCA	Turks and Caicos Islands	USD	US dollar = 100 cents
798	TV	TUV	Tuvalu	AUD	Australian dollar
800	UG	UGA	Uganda	UGS	Uganda shilling = 100 cents
784	AE	ARE	United Arab Emirates	AED	UAE dirham = 100 fils
826	GB	GBR	United Kingdom	GBP	Pound = 100 new pence
840	US	USA	United States of America	USD	Dollar = 100 cents
854	HV	HVO	Upper Volta	XOF	CFA franc = 100 centimes
858	UY	URY	Uruguay	UYP	new Uruguayan peso = 100 centésimos
			USSR: see Soviet Union		
548	VU	VUT	Vanuatu	VUF	Vanuatu franc = 100 centimes
336	VA	VAT	Vatican	ITL	Vatican or Italian lira = 100 centesimi
862	VE	VEN	Venezuela	VEB	Bolívar = 100 céntimos
704	VN	VNM	Vietnam	VND	Dong = 10 chao = 100 sau
092	VG	VGB	Virgin Islands, British	USD	US dollar = 100 cents
850	VI	VIR	Virgin Islands, US	USD	US dollar = 100 cents
872	WK	WAK	Wake Island	USD	US dollar = 100 cents
876	WF	WLF	Wallis & Futuna Islands	XPF	CFP franc = 100 centimes
			Western Sahara: see Sahara, Western		
			Western Samoa: see Samoa, Western		
886	YE	YEM	Yemen, North	YER	Yemeni rial = 100 fils
720	YD	YMD	Yemen, South	YDD	Yemeni dinar = 1 000 fils
			Yugoslavia: see Jugoslavia		
180	ZR	ZAR	Zaire	ZRZ	Zaire = 100 makuta = 10 000 sengi
894	ZM	ZMB	Zambia	ZMK	Kwacha = 100 ngwee
			Zanzibar: see Tanzania		
716	ZW	ZWE	Zimbabwe	ZWD	Zimbabwe dollar = 100 cents

Index